EMPIRES OF THE ATLANTIC WORLD

EMPIRES OF THE ATLANTIC WORLD

Britain and Spain in America
1492–1830

J. H. Elliott

Yale University Press
New Haven and London

For information about this and other Yale University Press publications, please contact:
U.S. Office: sales.press@yale.edu   yalebooks.com
Europe Office: sales@yaleup.co.uk   www.yalebooks.co.uk

Set in Sabon by J&L Composition, Filey, North Yorkshire
Printed in the USA

Library of Congress Cataloging-in-Publication Data

Elliott, John Huxtable.
 Empires of the Atlantic world: Britain and Spain in America, 1492–1830/J.H. Elliott.
  p. cm.
 Includes bibliographical references and index.
 ISBN 0–300–11431–1 (cl.: alk. paper)
 1. America—History—To 1810. 2. Great Britain—Colonies—America—History.
 3. Spain—Colonies—America—History. 4. British—Atlantic Ocean Region—History.
 5. Spaniards—Atlantic Ocean Region—History. 6. America—Colonization. 7. United
 States—History—Colonial period, ca. 1600–1775. I. Title.
 E18.82.E44 2006
 970′.02—dc22

                                                                                    2005034842

A catalogue record for this book is available from the British Library

ISBN 978-0-300-12399-9 (pbk)

Published with assistance from the Annie Burr Lewis Fund.

CONTENTS

Illustrations

Maps

Introduction. Worlds Overseas

'Oh, how much better the land seems from the sea than the sea from the land!'[1] The Spanish official who crossed the Atlantic in 1573 can hardly have been alone in his sentiments. After anything up to twelve weeks tossing on the high seas, the European emigrants – more than 1.5 million of them between 1500 and 1780s[2] – who stumbled uncertainly onto American soil must have felt in the first instance an overwhelming sense of relief. 'We were sure', wrote María Díaz from Mexico City in 1577 to her daughter in Seville, 'that we were going to perish at sea, because the storm was so strong that the ship's mast snapped. Yet in spite of all these travails, God was pleased to bring us to port . . .'[3] Some fifty years later Thomas Shepard, a Puritan minister emigrating to New England, wrote after surviving a tempest: 'This deliverance was so great that I then did think if ever the Lord did bring me to shore again I should live like one come and risen from the dead.'[4]

Differences of creed and of national origin paled before the universality of experience that brought emigrants three thousand miles or more from their European homelands to a new and strange world on the farther shores of the Atlantic. Fear and relief, apprehension and hope, were sentiments that knew no cultural boundaries. The motives of emigrants were various – to work (or alternatively not to work), to escape an old society or build a new one, to acquire riches, or, as early colonists in New England expressed it, to secure a 'competencie'[5] – but they all faced the same challenge of moving from the known to the unknown, and of coming to terms with an alien environment that would demand of them numerous adjustments and a range of new responses.

Yet, to a greater or lesser degree, those reponses would be shaped by a home culture whose formative influence could never be entirely escaped, even by those who were most consciously rejecting it for a new life beyond the seas. Emigrants to the New World brought with them too much cultural baggage for it to be lightly discarded in their new American environment. It was, in any event, only by reference to the familiar that they could make some sense of the unfamiliar that lay all around them.[6] They therefore constructed for themselves new societies which, even when different in intent from those they left behind them in Europe, unmistakably replicated many of the most characteristic features of metropolitan societies as they knew – or imagined – them at the time of their departure.

It is not therefore surprising that David Hume, in his essay *Of National Characters*, should have asserted that 'the same set of manners will follow a nation, and adhere to them over the whole globe, as well as the same laws and languages. The Spanish, English, French and Dutch colonies, are all distinguishable even between the tropics.'[7] Nature, as he saw it, could never extinguish nurture. Yet contemporaries with first-hand experience of the new colonial societies in process of formation on the other side of the Atlantic were in no doubt that they deviated in important respects from their mother countries. While eighteenth-century European observers might explain the differences by reference to a process of degeneration that was allegedly inherent in the American environment,[8] for them at least the fact of deviation was not in itself in dispute. Nature as well as nurture had formed the new colonial worlds.

In practice, the colonization of the Americas, like all colonization, consisted of a continuous interplay between imported attitudes and skills, and often intractable local conditions which might well impose themselves to the extent of demanding from the colonists responses that differed markedly from metropolitan norms. The result was the creation of colonial societies which, while 'distinguishable' from each other, to use Hume's formulation, were also distinguishable from the metropolitan communities from which they had sprung. New Spain was clearly not old Spain, nor was New England old England.

Attempts have been made to explain the differences between imperial metropolis and peripheral colony in terms both of the push of the old and the pull of the new. In an influential work published in 1964 Louis Hartz depicted the new overseas societies as 'fragments of the larger whole of Europe struck off in the course of the revolution which brought the west into the modern world'. Having spun off at a given moment from their metropolitan societies of origin, they evinced the 'immobilities of fragmentation', and were programmed for ever not only by the place but also by the time of their origin.[9] Their salient characteristics were those of their home societies at the moment of their conception, and when the home societies moved on to new stages of development, their colonial offshoots were caught in a time-warp from which they were unable to break free.

Hartz's immobile colonial societies were the antithesis of the innovative colonial societies that Frederick Jackson Turner and his followers saw as emerging in response to 'frontier' conditions.[10] A frontier, they argued, stimulated invention and a rugged individualism, and was the most important element in the formation of a distinctively 'American' character. In this hypothesis, both widely accepted and widely criticized,[11] 'American' was synonymous with 'North American'. The universality of frontiers, however, made the hypothesis readily extendable to other parts of the globe. If such a phenomenon as a 'frontier spirit' exists, there seems in principle no good reason why it should not be found in those regions of the New World settled by the Spaniards and the Portuguese as well as by the British.[12] This realization lay behind the famous plea made in 1932 by Herbert Bolton, the historian of the American borderlands, for historians to write an 'epic of Greater America' – an enterprise that would take as fundamental the premise that the Americas shared a common history.[13]

Yet Bolton's plea never evoked the response for which he hoped.[14] The sheer scale of the proposed enterprise was no doubt too daunting, and caution was reinforced by scepticism as over-arching explanations like the frontier hypothesis failed to stand the test of investigation on the ground. Dialogue between historians of the different Americas had never been close, and it was still further reduced as a generation of historians of British North America examined in microscopic detail aspects of the history of individual colonies, or – increasingly – of one or other of the local communities of which these colonies were composed. The growing parochialism, which left the historian of colonial Virginia barely within hailing distance of the historian of New England, and consigned the Middle Colonies (New York, New Jersey, Pennsylvania and Delaware) to a middle that had no outer edges, offered little chance of a serious exchange of ideas between historians of British America and those of other parts of the continent. Simultaneously the historians of Iberian America – the Mexicanists, the Brazilianists and the Andeanists – pursued their separate paths, with all too little reference to each other's findings. Where the history of the Americas was concerned, professionalization and atomization moved in tandem.

An 'epic of Greater America' becomes more elusive with each new monograph and every passing year. In spite of this, there has been a growing realization that certain aspects of local experience in any one part of the Americas can be fully appreciated only if set into a wider context, whether pan-American or Atlantic in its scope. This view has had a strong influence on the study of slavery,[15] and is currently giving a new impetus to discussions of the process of European migration to the New World.[16] Implicitly or explicitly such discussions involve an element of comparison, and comparative history may prove a useful device for helping to reassemble the fragmented history of the Americas into a new and more coherent pattern.

An outsider to American history, the great classical historian Sir Ronald Syme observed in a brief comparative survey of colonial elites that 'the Spanish and English colonies afford obvious contrasts', and he found an 'engaging topic of speculation' in their 'divergent fortunes'.[17] These 'obvious contrasts' inspired a suggestive, if flawed, attempt in the 1970s to pursue them at some length. James Lang, after examining the two empires in turn in his *Conquest and Commerce. Spain and England in the Americas*,[18] defined Spain's empire in America as an 'empire of conquest', and Britain's as an 'empire of commerce', a distinction that can be traced back to the eighteenth century. More recently, Claudio Véliz has sought the cultural origins of the divergence between British and Hispanic America in a comparison between two mythical animals – a Spanish baroque hedgehog and a Gothic fox. The comparison, while ingenious, is not, however, persuasive.[19]

Comparative history is – or should be – concerned with similarities as well as differences,[20] and a comparison of the history and culture of large and complicated political organisms that culminates in a series of sharp dichotomies is unlikely to do justice to the complexities of the past. By the same token, an insistence on similarity at the expense of difference is liable to be equally reductionist, since it tends to conceal diversity beneath a factitious unity. A comparative approach to the history of colonization requires the identification in equal measure of the points of similarity and contrast, and an attempt at explanation and analysis that does justice to both. Given the number of colonizing powers, however, and the multiplicity of the societies they established in the Americas, a sustained comparison embracing the entire New World is likely to defy the efforts of any individual historian. None the less, a more limited undertaking, which is confined, like the present one, to two European empires in the Americas, may suggest at least something of the possibilities, and the problems, inherent in a comparative approach.

In reality, even a comparison reduced to two empires proves to be far from straightforward. 'British America' and, still more, 'Spanish America' were large and diverse entities embracing on the one hand isolated Caribbean islands and, on the other, mainland territories, many of them remote from one another, and sharply differentiated by climate and geography. The climate of Virginia is not that of New England, nor is the topography of Mexico that of Peru. These differing regions, too, had their own distinctive pasts. When the first Europeans arrived, they found an America peopled in different ways, and at very different levels of density. Acts of war and settlement involved European intrusions into the space of existing indigenous societies; and even if Europeans chose to subsume the members of these societies under the convenient name of 'Indian', their peoples differed among themselves at least as much as did the sixteenth-century inhabitants of England and Castile.

[Variables of time existed too, as well as variables of place. As colonies grew and developed, so they changed.]So also did the metropolitan societies that had given birth to them. In so far as the colonies were not isolated and self-contained units, but remained linked in innumerable ways to the imperial metropolis, they were not immune to the changes in values and customs that were occurring at home. Newcomers would continue to arrive from the mother country, bringing with them new attitudes and life-styles that permeated the societies in which they took up residence. Equally, books and luxury items imported from Europe would introduce new ideas and tastes. News, too, circulated with growing speed and frequency around an Atlantic world that was shrinking as communications improved.

Similarly, changing ideas and priorities at the centre of empire were reflected in changes in imperial policy, so that the third or fourth generation of settlers might well find itself operating within an imperial framework in which the assumptions and responses of the founding fathers had lost much of their former relevance. This in turn forced changes. There were obvious continuities between the

America of the first English settlers and the British America of the mid-eighteenth century, but there were important discontinuities as well – discontinuities brought about by external and internal change alike. The 'immobilities of fragmentation' detected by Louis Hartz were therefore relative at best. British and Spanish America, as the two units of comparison, did not remain static but changed over time.

It still remains plausible, however, that the moment of 'fragmentation' – of the founding of a colony – constituted a defining moment for the self-imagining, and consequently for the emerging character, of these overseas societies. Yet, if so, there are obvious difficulties in comparing communities founded at very different historical moments. Spain's first colonies in America were effectively established in the opening decades of the sixteenth century; England's in the opening decades of the seventeenth. The profound changes that occurred in European civilization with the coming of the Reformation inevitably had an impact not only on the metropolitan societies but also on colonizing policies and the colonizing process itself. A British colonization of North America undertaken at the same time as Spain's colonization of Central and South America would have been very different in character from the kind of colonization that occurred after a century that saw the establishment of Protestantism as the official faith in England, a notable reinforcement of the place of parliament in English national life, and changing European ideas about the proper ordering of states and their economies.

The effect of this time-lag is to inject a further complication into any process of comparison which seeks to assess the relative weight of nature and nurture in the development of British and Spanish territories overseas. The Spaniards were the pioneers in the settlement of America, and the English, arriving later, had the Spanish example before their eyes. While they might, or might not, avoid the mistakes made by the Spaniards, they were at least in a position to formulate their policies and procedures in the light of Spanish experience, and adjust them accordingly. The comparison, therefore, is not between two self-contained cultural worlds, but between cultural worlds that were well aware of each other's presence, and were not above borrowing each other's ideas when this suited their needs. If Spanish ideas of empire influenced the English in the sixteenth century, the Spaniards repaid the compliment by attempting to adopt British notions of empire in the eighteenth. Similar processes, too, could occur in the colonial societies themselves. Without the example of the British colonies before them, would the Spanish colonies have thought the previously unthinkable and declared their independence in the early nineteenth century?

When account is taken of all the variables introduced by place, time, and the effects of mutual interaction, any sustained comparison of the colonial worlds of Britain and Spain in America is bound to be imperfect. The movements involved in writing comparative history are not unlike those involved in playing the accordion. The two societies under comparison are pushed together, but only to be pulled apart again. Resemblances prove after all to be not as close as they look at first sight; differences are discovered which at first lay concealed. Comparison is therefore a constantly fluctuating process, which may well seem on closer inspection to offer less than it promises. This should not in itself, however, be sufficient to rule the attempt out of court. Even imperfect comparisons can help to shake historians out of their provincialisms, by provoking new questions and offering new perspectives. It is my hope that this book will do exactly that.

⌈In my view the past is too complex, and too endlessly fascinating in its infinite variety, to be reduced to simple formulae. I have therefore rejected any attempt to squeeze different aspects of the histories of British and Spanish America into neat compartments that would allow their similarities and differences to be listed and offset. Rather, by constantly comparing, juxtaposing and interweaving the two stories, I have sought to reassemble a fragmented history, and display the development of these two great New World civilizations over the course of three centuries, in the hope that a light focused on one of them at a given moment will simultaneously cast a secondary beam over the history of the other.⌉

Inevitably the attempt to write the history of large parts of a hemisphere over such a broad stretch of time means that much has been left out. While well aware that some of the most exciting scholarship in recent years has been devoted to the topic of African slavery in the Atlantic world and to the recovery of the past of the indigenous peoples of America, my principal focus has been the development of the settler societies and their relationship with their mother countries. This, I hope, will give some coherence to the story. I have, however, always tried to bear in mind that the developing colonial societies were shaped by the constant interaction of European and non-European peoples, and hope to have been able to suggest why, at particular times and in particular places, the interaction occurred as it did. Yet even in placing the prime emphasis on the settler communities, I was still forced to paint with a broad brush. The confinement of my story to Spanish, rather than Iberian, America means the almost total exclusion of the Portuguese settlement of Brazil, except for glancing references to the sixty-year period, from 1580 to 1640, when it formed part of Spain's global monarchy. In discussing British North America I have tried to allow some space to the Middle Colonies, the source of so much historical attention in recent years, but plead guilty to what will no doubt be regarded by many as excessive attention to New England and Virginia. I must also plead guilty, in writing of British and Spanish America alike, to devoting far more attention to the mainland colonies than to the Caribbean islands. Hard choices are inevitable in a work that ranges so widely over time and space.

Such a work necessarily depends very largely on the writings of others. There is now an immense literature on the history of the colonial societies of British and Spanish America alike, and I have had to pick my way through the publications of a large number of specialists, summarizing their findings as best I could in the relatively limited space at my disposal, and seeking to find a point of resolution between conflicting interpretations that neither distorts the conclusions of others, nor privileges those that fit most easily into a comparative framework. To all these works, and many others not cited in the notes or bibliography, I am deeply indebted, even when – and perhaps especially when – I disagree with them.

The idea for this book first came to me at the Institute for Advanced Study in Princeton, at a moment when I felt that the time had come to move away from the history of Habsburg Spain and Europe, and take a harder look at Spain's inter-action with its overseas possessions. As I had by then spent almost seventeen years in the United States, there seemed to me a certain logic in looking at colonial Spanish America in a context that would span the Atlantic and allow me to draw parallels between the American experiences of Spaniards and Britons. I am deeply indebted to colleagues and visiting members at the Institute who encouraged and assisted my first steps towards a survey of the two colonial empires, and also to friends and colleagues in the History Department of Princeton University. In particular I owe a debt of gratitude of Professors Stephen Innes and William B. Taylor, both of them former visiting members of the Institute, who invited me to the University of Virginia in 1989 to try out some of my early ideas in a series of seminars.

My return to England in 1990 to the Regius Chair of Modern History in Oxford meant that I largely had to put the project to one side for seven years, but I am grateful for a series of lecture invitations that enabled me to keep the idea alive and to develop some of the themes that have found a place in this book. Among these were the Becker Lectures at Cornell University in 1992, the Stenton Lecture at the University of Reading in 1993, and in 1994 the Radcliffe Lectures at the University of Warwick, a pioneer in the development of Comparative American studies in this country under the expert guidance of Professors Alistair Hennessy and Anthony McFarlane. I have also at various times benefited from careful and perceptive criticisms of individual lectures or articles by colleagues on both sides of the Atlantic, including Timothy Breen, Nicholas Canny, Jack Greene, John Murrin, Mary Beth Norton, Anthony Pagden and Michael Zuckerman. Josep Fradera of the Pompeu Fabra University in Barcelona, and Manuel Lucena Giraldo of the Consejo Superior de Investigaciones Científicas in Madrid have been generous with their suggestions and advice on recent publications.

In Oxford itself, I learnt much from two of my graduate students, Kenneth Mills and Cayetana Alvarez de Toledo, working respectively on the histories of colonial Peru and New Spain. Retirement allowed me at last to settle down to the writing of the book, a task made much easier by the accessibility of the splendid Vere Harmsworth Library in Oxford's new Rothermere American Institute. As the work approached completion the visiting Harmsworth Professor of American History at Oxford for 2003–4, Professor Richard Beeman of the University of Pennsylvania, very generously offered to read through my draft text. I am enormously grateful to him for the close scrutiny he gave it, and for his numerous suggestions for its improvement, which I have done my best to follow.

Edmund Morgan and David Weber commented generously on the text when it had reached its nearly final form, and I have also benefited from the comments of Jonathan Brown and Peter Bakewell on individual sections. At a late stage in the proceedings Philip Morgan devoted much time and thought to preparing a detailed list of suggestions and further references. While it was impossible to follow them all up in the time available to me, his suggestions have enriched the book, and have enabled me to see in a new light some of the questions I have sought to address.

In the final stages of the preparation of the book I am much indebted to Sarah-Jane White, who gave generously of her time to put the bibliography into shape. I am grateful, too, to Bernard Dod and Rosamund Howe for their copy-editing, to Meg Davis for preparing the index and to Julia Ruxton for her indefatigable efforts in tracking down and securing the illustrations I suggested. At Yale University Press Robert Baldock has taken a close personal interest in the progress of the work, and has been consistently supportive, resourceful and encouraging. I am deeply grateful to him and his team, and in particular to Candida Brazil and Stephen Kent, for all they have done to move the book speedily and efficiently through the various stages of production and to ensure its emergence in such a handsome form. Fortunate the author who can count on such support.

Oriel College, Oxford
7 November 2005

Note on the Text

Spelling, punctuation and capitalization of English and Spanish texts of the sixteenth to eighteenth centuries have normally been modernized, except in a number of instances where it seemed desirable to retain them in their original form.

The names of Spanish monarchs have been anglicized, with the exception of Charles II of Spain, who appears as Carlos II in order to avoid confusion with the contemporaneous Charles II of England.

PART 1

Occupation

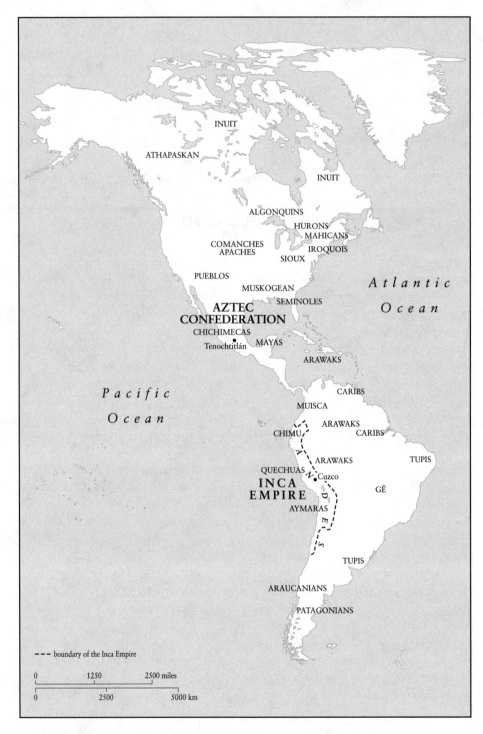

INUIT

ATHAPASKAN

INUIT

ALGONQUINS

HURONS
MAHICANS

COMANCHES   IROQUOIS
APACHES
SIOUX

PUEBLOS

MUSKOGEAN

SEMINOLES

Atlantic

Ocean

**AZTEC
CONFEDERATION**

CHICHIMECAS

Tenochtitlán   MAYAS

ARAWAKS

CARIBS

Pacific

Ocean

MUISCA

ARAWAKS

CHIMU   CARIBS

ARAWAKS   TUPIS

QUECHUAS   Cuzco

**INCA
EMPIRE**   GÊ

AYMARAS

TUPIS

ARAUCANIANS

PATAGONIANS

- - - boundary of the Inca Empire

0   1250   2500 miles

0   2500   5000 km

Map 1. The Peoples of America, 1492.
Based on Pierre Chaunu, *L'Amérique et les Amériques* (Paris 1964), map. 3.

CHAPTER 1

Intrusion and Empire

Hernán Cortés and Christopher Newport

A shrewd notary from Extremadura, turned colonist and adventurer, and a one-armed ex-privateer from Limehouse, in the county of Middlesex. Eighty-seven years separate the expeditions, led by Hernán Cortés and Captain Christopher Newport respectively, that laid the foundations of the empires of Spain and Britain on the mainland of America. The first, consisting of ten ships, set sail from Cuba on 18 February 1519. The second, of only three ships, left London on 29 December 1606, although the sailing date was the 19th for Captain Newport and his men, who still reckoned by the Julian calendar. That the English persisted in using a calendar abandoned by Spain and much of the continent in 1582 was a small but telling indication of the comprehensive character of the change that had overtaken Europe during the course of those eighty-seven years. The Lutheran Reformation, which was already brewing when Cortés made his precipitate departure from Cuba, unleashed the forces that were to divide Christendom into warring religious camps. The decision of the England of Elizabeth to cling to the old reckoning rather than accept the new Gregorian calendar emanating from the seat of the anti-Christ in Rome suggests that – in spite of the assumptions of later historians – Protestantism and modernity were not invariably synonymous.[1]

After reconnoitring the coastline of Yucatán, Cortés, whose ships were lying off the island which the Spaniards called San Juan de Ulúa, set off in his boats on 22 April 1519 for the Mexican mainland with some 200 of his 530 men.[2] Once ashore, the intruders were well received by the local Totonac inhabitants before being formally greeted by a chieftain who explained that he governed the province on behalf of a great emperor, Montezuma, to whom the news of the arrival of these strange bearded white men was hastily sent. During the following weeks, while waiting for a reply from Montezuma, Cortés reconnoitred the coastal region, discovered that there were deep divisions in Montezuma's Mexica empire, and, in a duly notarized ceremony, formally took possession of the country, including the land yet to be explored, in the name of Charles, King of Spain.[3] In this he was following the instructions of his immediate superior, Diego Velázquez, the governor of Cuba, who had ordered that 'in all the islands that are discovered, you should leap on shore in the presence of your scribe and many witnesses, and in the name of their Highnesses take and assume possession of them with all possible solemnity.'[4]

In other respects, however, Cortés, the protégé and one-time secretary of Velázquez, proved considerably less faithful to his instructions. The governor of Cuba had specifically ordered that the expedition was to be an expedition for trade and exploration. He did not authorize Cortés to conquer or to settle.[5] Velázquez's purpose was to keep his own interests alive while seeking formal authorization from Spain to establish a settlement on the mainland under his own jurisdiction, but Cortés and his confidants had other ideas. Cortés's intention from the first had been to *poblar* – to settle any lands that he should discover – and this could be done only by defying his superior and securing his own authorization from the crown. This he now proceeded to do in a series of brilliant manoeuvres. By the laws of medieval Castile the community could, in certain circumstances, take collective action against a 'tyrannical' monarch or minister. Cortés's expeditionary force now reconstituted itself as a formal community, by incorporating itself on 28 June 1519 as a town, to be known as Villa Rica de Vera Cruz, which the Spaniards promptly started to lay out and build. The new municipality, acting in the name of the king in place of his 'tyrannical' governor of Cuba, whose authority it rejected, then appointed Cortés as its mayor (*alcalde mayor*) and captain of the royal army. By this manoeuvre, Cortés was freed from his obligations to the 'tyrant' Velázquez. Thereafter, following the king's best interests, he could lead his men inland to conquer the empire of Montezuma, and transform nominal possession into real possession of the land.[6]

Initially the plan succeeded better than Cortés could have dared to hope, although its final realization was to be attended by terrible trials and tribulations for the Spaniards, and by vast losses of life among the Mesoamerican population. On 8 August he and some three hundred of his men set off on their march into the interior, in a bid to reach Montezuma in his lake-encircled city of Tenochtitlán (fig. 1). As they moved inland, they threw down 'idols' and set up crosses in Indian places of worship, skirmished, fought and manoeuvred their way through difficult, mountainous country, and picked up a host of Mesoamerican allies, who were chafing under the dominion of the Mexica. On 8 November, Cortés and his men began slowly moving down the long causeway that linked the lakeshore to the city, 'marching with great difficulty', according to the account written many years later by his secretary and chaplain, Francisco López de Gómara, 'because of the pressure of the crowds that came out to see them'. As they drew closer, they found '4,000 gentlemen of the court . . . waiting to receive them', until finally, as they approached the wooden drawbridge, the Emperor Montezuma himself came forward to greet them, walking under 'a pallium of gold and green feathers, strung about with silver hangings, and carried by four gentlemen (fig. 2)'.[7]

It was an extraordinary moment, this moment of encounter between the representatives of two civilizations hitherto unknown to each other: Montezuma II, outwardly impassive but inwardly troubled, the 'emperor' of the Nahuatl-speaking Mexica, who had settled on their lake island in the fertile valley of Mexico around 1345, and had emerged after a series of ruthless and bloody campaigns as the head of a confederation, the Triple Alliance, that had come to dominate central Mexico; and the astute and devious Hernán Cortés, the self-appointed champion of a King of Spain who, four months earlier, had been elected Holy Roman Emperor, under the name of Charles V, and was now, at least nominally, the most powerful sovereign in Renaissance Europe.

The problem of mutual comprehension made itself felt immediately. Cortés, in Gómara's words, 'dismounted and approached Montezuma to embrace him in the Spanish fashion, but was prevented by those who were supporting him, for it was a sin to touch him'. Taking off a necklace of pearls and cut glass that he was wearing, Cortés did, however, manage to place it around Montezuma's neck. The gift seems to have given Montezuma pleasure, and was reciprocated with two necklaces, each hung with eight gold shrimps. They were now entering the city, where Montezuma placed at the disposal of the Spaniards the splendid palace that had once belonged to his father.

After Cortés and his men had rested, Montezuma returned with more gifts, and then made a speech of welcome in which, as reported by Cortés, he identified the Spaniards as descendants of a great lord who had been expelled from the land of the Nahuas and were now returning to claim their own. He therefore submitted himself and his people to the King of Spain, as their 'natural lord'. This 'voluntary' surrender of sovereignty, which is likely to have been no more than a Spanish interpretation, or deliberate misinterpretation, of characteristically elaborate Nahuatl expressions of courtesy and welcome, was to be followed by a further, and more formal, act of submission a few days later, after Cortés, with typical boldness, had seized Montezuma and taken him into custody.[8]

Cortés had secured what he wanted: a *translatio imperii*, a transfer of empire, from Montezuma to his own master, the Emperor Charles V. In Spanish eyes this transfer of empire gave Charles legitimate authority over the land and dominions of the Mexica. It thus justified the subsequent actions of the Spaniards, who, after being forced by an uprising in the city to fight their way out of Tenochtitlán under cover of darkness, spent the next fourteen months fighting to recover what they regarded as properly theirs. With the fall of Tenochtitlán in August 1521 after a bitter siege, the Mexica empire was effectively destroyed. Mexico had become, in fact as well as theory, a possession of the Crown of Castile, and in due course was to be transformed into Spain's first American viceroyalty, the viceroyalty of New Spain.

By the time of Christopher Newport's departure from London in December 1606, the story of Cortés and his conquest of Mexico was well known in England. Although Cortés's *Letters of Relation* to Charles V had enjoyed wide circulation on the continent, there is no evidence of any particular interest in him in the

British Isles during the reign of Henry VIII. In 1496 Henry's father, tempted by the lure of gold and spices, and anxious not to be excluded by the Spaniards and Portuguese, had authorized John Cabot to 'conquer and possess' in the name of the King of England any territory he should come across on his North Atlantic voyage not yet in Christian hands.[9] But after the death of Henry VII in 1509, Tudor England, enriched by the discovery of the Newfoundland fisheries but disappointed in the prospects of easy wealth, turned away from transatlantic enterprises, and for half a century left the running to the Spaniards, the Portuguese and the French. In the 1550s, when Mary Tudor's marriage made Charles's son and heir, Philip, for a brief time King of England, Richard Eden used his translation into English of the first three books of Peter Martyr's *Decades of the New World* to urge his compatriots to take lessons from the Spaniards. It was not until around 1580, however, that they began to pay serious attention to his words.[10]

By then, English overseas voyages had significantly increased in both number and daring, and religious hostility, sharpening the collective sense of national consciousness, was making an armed confrontation between England and Spain increasingly probable. In anticipation of the conflict, books and pamphlets became the instruments of war. In 1578 Thomas Nicholas, a merchant who had been imprisoned in Spain, translated into English a much shortened version of López de Gómara's *History of the Indies* under the title of *The Pleasant Historie of the Conquest of the Weast India*. Here English readers could read, although in mutilated form, a vivid account of the conquest of Mexico, based on information derived from Cortés himself.[11] Not only did Nicholas drastically cut Gómara's text, but he also managed to give it a distinctively English colouring. Where Gómara introduced Montezuma's formal surrender of sovereignty to Charles V by saying that he summoned a council and Cortes 'which was attended by all the lords of Mexico and the country round', English readers would no doubt have been gratified to learn that he 'proclaimed a Parliament', after which 'Mutezuma and the burgesses of Parliament in order yielded themselves for vassals of the King of Castile, promising loyalty'.[12]

A few years later, Richard Hakluyt the younger, who had emerged as the principal promoter and propagandist of English overseas empire, reminded the readers of his *Principall Navigations* how 'Hernando Cortés, being also but a private gentleman of Spain . . . took prisoner that mighty Emperor Mutezuma in his most chief and famous city of Mexico, which at that instant had in it above the number of 500,000 Indians at the least, and in short time after obtained not only the quiet possession of the said city, but also of his whole Empire.'[13] The taking of possession had hardly been 'short' or 'quiet', but Hakluyt's message was clear enough.

A few Elizabethans were coming to realize, as Cortés himself had realized after observing the devastation by his compatriots of the islands they had ravaged in the Caribbean, that the acquisition of empire demanded a firm commitment to settle and colonize. The preface to John Florio's 1580 English translation of Jacques Cartier's account of his discovery of Canada (New France) informed

English readers that 'the Spaniards never prospered or prevailed but where they planted';[14] and in his *Discourse of Western Planting* of 1584 Richard Hakluyt cited with approbation Gómara's remarks on the folly of Cortés's predecessor, Juan de Grijalva, who, on reaching the coast of Yucatán, failed to found a settlement.[15] In that same year an English expedition identified Roanoke Island, off the coast of what was later to become North Carolina, as a base for privateering attacks on the Spanish West Indies. But Walter Raleigh, for one, saw its potential as a base not only for privateering but also for colonization, and in the following year Roanoke was to become the setting for England's first serious, although ultimately abortive, attempt at transatlantic settlement (fig. 4).[16]

Although Raleigh's Roanoke colony ended in failure, it would provide valuable lessons for the more sustained Jacobean programme of colonization that was to begin with Christopher Newport's expedition of 1606–7. But the loss of the colony meant that, lacking any base in the Americas, Newport's expedition, unlike that of Cortés, had to be organized and financed from the home country. The Cortés expedition had been funded in part by Diego Velázquez out of his resources as governor of Cuba, and in part by private deals between Cortés and two wealthy islanders who advanced him supplies on credit.[17] The Newport expedition was financed and organized by a London-based joint-stock company, the Virginia Company, which received its charter from James VI and I in April 1606, granting it exclusive rights to settle the Chesapeake Bay area of the American mainland. Under the same charter a Plymouth-based company was given colonizing rights further to the north. Although funding was provided by the investors, many of whom were City merchants, the appointment of a thirteen-man royal council with regulatory powers gave the Company the assurance of state backing for its enterprise.[18]

Where Cortés, therefore, was nominally serving under the orders of the royal governor of Cuba, from whom he broke free at the earliest opportunity, Newport was a company employee. The company chose more wisely than the governor of Cuba. Cortés was too clever, and too ambitious, to be content with playing second string. His father, an Extremaduran *hidalgo*, or minor nobleman, had fought in the campaign against the Moors to reconquer southern Spain. The son, who learnt Latin and seems to have mastered the rudiments of the law while a student in Salamanca, made the Atlantic crossing in 1506, at the age of twenty-two.[19] When Cortés left for the Indies it was hardly his intention to serve out his life as a public notary. Like every impoverished *hidalgo* he aspired to fame and fortune, and is said to have dreamed one night, while working as a notary in the little town of Azúa on the island of Hispaniola, that one day he would be dressed in fine clothes and be waited on by many exotic retainers who would sing his praises and address him with high-sounding titles. After the dream, he told his friends that one day he would dine to the sound of trumpets, or else die on the gallows.[20] But for all his ambitions, he knew how to bide his time, and the years spent in Hispaniola, and then in Cuba, gave him a good understanding of the opportunities, and the dangers, that awaited those who wanted to make their fortunes in the

New World. If he lacked military experience when he set out on the conquest of Mexico, he had developed the qualities of a leader, and had become a shrewd judge of men.

Newport, too, was an adventurer, but of a very different kind.[21] Born in 1561, the son of a Harwich shipmaster, he had the sea in his blood. In 1580, on his first recorded transatlantic voyage, he jumped ship in the Brazilian port of Bahía, but was back in England by 1584, when he made the first of his three marriages. By now he was a shipmaster who had served his apprenticeship, and was gaining the experience that would make him one of the outstanding English seamen of his age. The years that followed saw him engaged in trading and raiding, as England went to war with Spain. He took service with London merchants, and he sailed to Cadiz with Drake in 1587, remaining behind to engage in privateering activities off the Spanish coast. In 1590 he made his first independent voyage to the Caribbean as captain of the *Little John*, and lost his right arm in a sea-fight off the coast of Cuba when attempting to capture two treasure ships coming from Mexico. His third marriage, in 1595, to the daughter of a wealthy London gold-smith, made him a partner in major new commercial and privateering ventures, and provided him with a well-equipped man-of-war. Thereafter he made almost annual voyages to the West Indies, and by the time of the Anglo-Spanish peace settlement of 1604 he knew the Caribbean better than any other Englishman of his times. His long experience of Spanish American waters and his impressive seafaring skills therefore made him a natural choice in 1606 as the man to plant a colony for the Virginia Company on the North American mainland (fig. 3).

Of the 105 'first planters', as the men who composed Newport's expedition were called, thirty-six were classed as gentlemen.[22] There were also a number of craftsmen, including four carpenters, two bricklayers, a mason, a blacksmith, a tailor and a barber, and twelve labourers. The proportion of gentlemen was high, and would become still higher by the time the new colony had twice been rein-forced from England, giving it six times as many gentlemen as in the population of the home country.[23] It was also high in relation to the number in Cortés's band, which was five times as large. Of the so-called 'first conquerors', who were pres-ent with Cortés at the founding of Vera Cruz, only sixteen were clearly regarded as *hidalgos*.[24] But many more had pretensions to gentility, and Bernal Díaz del Castillo goes so far as to claim in his *History of the Conquest of New Spain* that 'all the rest of us were *hidalgos*, although some were not of such clear lineage as others, because it is well known that in this world not all men are born equal, either in nobility or virtue.'[25] The Cortés expedition included some professional soldiers, and many other men who, during their years in the Indies, had partici-pated in raiding parties to various of the Caribbean islands, or joined previous expeditions for reconnaissance, barter and settlement. It also included two clerics (Newport's expedition had on board 'Master Robert Hunt *Preacher*'), and a number of notaries, as well as craftsmen and members of specialist trades. Effectively, Cortés's company was composed of a cross-section of the residents of Cuba, which was deprived of nearly a third of its Spanish population when the expedition set sail.[26] It was therefore well acclimatized to New World conditions, unlike Newport's party, which, within six months of arrival, had lost almost half its number to disease.[27]

The fact that the company on board Newport's ships were styled 'planters' was a clear indication of the purpose of the voyage. For the English in the age of the Tudors and Stuarts, 'plantation' – meaning a planting of people – was synonymous with 'colony'.[28] This was standard usage in Tudor Ireland, where 'colonies' or 'plantations' were the words employed to designate settlements of English in areas not previously subject to English governmental control.[29] Both words evoked the original *coloniae* of the Romans – simultaneously farms or landed estates, and bodies of emigrants, particularly veterans, who had left home to 'plant', or settle and cultivate (*colere*), lands elsewhere.[30] These people were known as 'planters' rather than 'colonists', a term that does not seem to have come into use before the eighteenth century. In 1630, when the British had established a number of New World settlements, an anonymous author would write: 'by a colony we mean a society of men drawn out of one state or people, and transplanted into another country.'[31]

The Spanish equivalent of 'planter' was *poblador*. In 1498, when Luis Roldán rebelled against the government of the Columbus brothers on Hispaniola, he rejected the name of *colonos* for himself and his fellow settlers of the island, and demanded that they should be known as *vecinos* or householders, with all the rights accruing to *vecinos* under Castilian law.[32] A *colón* was, in the first instance, a labourer who worked land for which he paid rent, and Roldán would have none of this. Subsequent usage upheld his stand. During the period of Habsburg rule Spain's American territories, unlike those of the English, were not called 'colonies'. They were kingdoms in the possession of the Crown of Castile, and they were inhabited, not by *colonos*, but by conquerors (*conquistadores*) and their descendants, and by *pobladores*, or settlers, the name given to all later arrivals.

The English, by contrast, were always 'planters', not 'conquerors'. The discrepancy between English and Spanish usage would at first sight suggest fundamentally different approaches to overseas settlement. Sir Thomas Gates and his fellow promoters of the Virginia Company had asked the crown to grant a licence 'to make habitation plantation and to deduce a Colonie of sundry of our people' in 'that part of America commonly called Virginia . . .'[33] There was no mention here of conquest, whereas the agreement between the Castilian crown and Diego Velázquez in 1518 authorized him to 'go to discover and conquer Yucatán and Cozumel'.[34] But the idea of conquest was never far away from the promoters of English colonization in the sixteenth and early seventeenth centuries. The Spaniards had given the lead, and the Spanish example was very much in the elder Richard Hakluyt's mind when he wrote in his *Pamphlet for the Virginia Enterprise* of 1585 that in the face of opposition from the Indians 'we may, if we will proceed with extremity, conquer, fortify, and plant in soils most sweet, most pleasant, most strong, and most fertile, and in the end bring them all in subjection and to civility.'[35] The degree to which 'conquest' entered into the equation would depend on the behaviour and reactions of the indigenous population when Newport and his men set foot on land.

First impressions were hardly encouraging. Approaching Chesapeake Bay, Captain Newport put a party ashore on a cape he christened 'Cape Henry', after the Prince of Wales, only to have them 'assaulted by 5 Salvages, who hurt 2 of the English very dangerously'.[36] Although the English were unaware of the fact, this was not the first encounter of the local inhabitants with European intruders. The Spanish had been seeking to establish fortified posts along the coast, first at Santa Elena, in the future South Carolina, in 1557, and then in Florida, where Pedro Menéndez de Avilés founded St Augustine in 1565 after exterminating a settlement of French Huguenots.[37] Five years later, with Menéndez's blessing, a party of eight Jesuits set out from Santa Elena under the leadership of Father Juan Bautista de Segura, the vice-provincial of the Jesuit Order in Florida. They had as their guide and translator a young Algonquian chief who had been picked up on an earlier expedition, given the baptismal name of Don Luis de Velasco in honour of the viceroy of New Spain, and taken to Spain, where he was presented to Philip II. Presumably in a bid to return to his native land he encouraged the Jesuits to establish their mission at 'Ajacán', whose exact location on the Chesapeake is unknown, but which may have been some five miles from the future Jamestown. In 1571 Velasco, who had made his excuses and returned to live among his own people, led an Indian attack which wiped out the mission. Following a Spanish punitive expedition in 1572 the Ajacán experiment was abandoned. If, as has been suggested, Velasco was none other than Opechancanough, the brother of the local 'emperor' Powhatan, Newport and his men had fixed their sights on a land where the ways of Europeans were already known and not admired.[38]

In search of a safer landing-place, Newport's expedition moved across the bay and up river, finally putting ashore on 13 May 1607 at what was to be the site of Jamestown, the colony's first settlement. The London Company had named a resident council of seven to govern the colony, and ground-clearing and the construction of a fort began immediately under its supervision. Jamestown, with its deep anchorage, was to be the English Vera Cruz, a base for reconnaissance and for obtaining supplies by sea.

Here the Indians, like those of Vera Cruz, seemed favourably disposed: 'the Salvages often visited us kindly (fig. 5).'[39] Newport took a party to explore the higher reaches of the river, and, after passing 'divers small habitations . . . arrived at a town called Powhatan, consisting of some 12 houses pleasantly seated on a hill'. Beyond this were falls, which made the river unnavigable for their boat. On one of the 'little islets at the mouth of the falls', Newport 'set up a cross with this inscription *Jacobus Rex*. 1607, and his own name below. At the erecting hereof we prayed for our king and our own prosperous success in this his action, and proclaimed him king, with a great shout.'[40] The English, like the Spaniards in Mexico, had formally taken possession of the land.

In both instances tender consciences might question their right to do so. 'The first objection', Robert Gray was to observe in *A Good Speed to Virginia* (1609), 'is, by what right or warrant we can enter into the lands of these savages, take away their rightful inheritance from them, and plant ourselves in their places, being unwronged or unprovoked by them.'[41] This was a problem with which the Spaniards had long had to wrestle. Spanish claims to New World dominion were based primarily on the Alexandrine bulls of 1493–4. These, following the precedent set by papal policy towards the Portuguese crown in *Romanus Pontifex* (1455), gave the monarchs of Castile dominion over any islands or mainland discovered or still to be discovered on the westward route to Asia, on condition that they assumed responsibility for protecting and evangelizing the indigenous inhabitants.[42]

Since a favourable reaction of the indigenous population to such a take-over could hardly be taken for granted, their willingness to submit peacefully came to be tested by the formal reading aloud to them of the *requerimiento*, the notorious legal document drawn up in 1512 by the eminent jurist Juan López de Palacios Rubios, and routinely used on all expeditions of discovery and conquest, including that of Hernán Cortés. The document, after briefly outlining Christian doctrine and the history of the human race, explained that Saint Peter and his successors possessed jurisdiction over the whole world, and had granted the newly discovered lands to Ferdinand and Isabella and their heirs, to whom the local population must submit, or face the waging of a just war against them.[43] The right of the papacy to dispose of non-Christian lands and peoples in this way was in due course to be contested by Spanish scholastics like Francisco de Vitoria, but papal concession was to remain fundamental to Spanish claims to possession of the Indies, although it might be reinforced or supplemented, as Cortés tried to supplement it, by other arguments.

Papal authorization was obviously not an option for Protestant England when it found itself faced with identical problems over rights of occupation and possession, although the general tenor of the argument based on papal donation could easily be adapted to English circumstances, as it was by Richard Hakluyt: 'Now the Kings and Queens of England have the name of Defenders of the Faith; by which title I think they are not only charged to maintain and patronize the faith of Christ, but also to enlarge and advance the same.'[44] England, therefore, like Spain, acquired a providential mission in America, a mission conceived, as by Christopher Carleill in 1583, in terms of 'reducing the savage people to Christianity and civility . . .'[45]

At the time of Newport's arrival, the Virginia Company is more likely to have been exercised by prior Spanish claims to the land than by those of its indigenous inhabitants, with whom it was hoped that the colonists could live side by side in peace. A few years later William Strachey dismissed Spanish claims with contempt: 'No prince may lay claim to any amongst these new discoveries . . . than what his people have discovered, took actual possession of, and passed over to right . . .'[46] Physical occupation of the land and putting it to use in conformity with established practice at home was the proper test of ownership in English eyes.

This Roman Law argument of *res nullius* could conveniently be deployed against Spaniards who had failed to establish their nominal claims by actual settlement; but soon it also became the principal justification for seizing land from the Indians,[47] although in the early years of settlement it seemed wise to cover all eventualities. In a sermon preached before the Virginia Company in 1610 William Crashaw advanced a range of arguments to justify the Virginia enterprise. One of these, borrowed from the Spanish theologian Francisco de Vitoria,[48] was based on the universal right conferred by the 'law of nations' (*ius gentium*) to freedom of trade and communication. 'Christians', he asserted, 'may traffic with the heathen.' There were other justifications too. 'We will', he continued, 'take from them only that they may spare us. First, their superfluous land' – the *res nullius* argument. 'Secondly, their superfluous commodities . . .' Finally, there was England's national mission, as formulated by Christopher Carleill and others during the reign of Queen Elizabeth. 'We give to the Savages what they most need. 1. Civility for their bodies. 2. Christianity for their souls.'[49] All possible moral and legal objections to the enterprise were thus conveniently met.

In conducting relations with the Indians, Newport and his colleagues were under firm instructions from the company: 'In all your passages you must have great care not to offend the Naturals if you can eschew it . . .'[50] No doubt inspired by the example of Mexico, where the indigenous population was alleged to have believed that the strange white visitors were immortal, the council in London also told the resident councillors to conceal any deaths among the colonists, and thus prevent 'the Country people' from perceiving 'they are but common men'.[51] But the local tribes seem to have been neither deceived nor overawed. While Newport was still away on his reconnaissance of the James River, a surprise raid on the fort at Jamestown left two English dead, and a dozen or more wounded. The English ships retaliated by bombarding Indian villages along the waterfront.[52] The establishment of a working relationship with the inhabitants was clearly considerably more complicated than the London sponsors of the expedition had envisaged.

The situation facing the settlers looks, at first sight, like a miniature version of that which faced Cortés in Mexico. The territory on which they had established themselves, known as Tsenacommacah, was dominated by an 'emperor', Powhatan, with whom Newport engaged in an exchange of presents when they first met near the Powhatan falls. For the last quarter of a century Powhatan had been building up his power, and through warfare and cunning had established his paramountcy over the numerous Algonquian-speaking tribes of the region. His 'empire' seems to have been the nearest equivalent in North America to the Aztec empire far to the south,[53] although in populousness and wealth it did not begin to rival that of Montezuma. During the sixteenth century the diseases which the Spaniards had brought with them from Europe had spread northwards, ravaging the Indian tribes in the coastal regions, and leaving in their wake a sparsely settled population.[54] Where Montezuma's empire in central America had a population estimated at anything from five to twenty-five millions when Cortés first set foot on Mexican soil, that of Powhatan consisted in 1607 of some thirteen to fifteen thousand.[55] The differences in size and density of the indigenous population would profoundly affect the subsequent character of the two colonial worlds.

Powhatan, however, outwitted the white intruders, as Montezuma did not. Described by Captain John Smith as 'a tall, well proportioned man, with a sour look', he could not compete in grandeur with Montezuma, but none the less lived in a style which impressed the English. 'About his person ordinarily attendeth a guard of 40 or 50 of the tallest men his country doth afford. Every night upon the 4 quarters of his house are 4 sentinels each standing from other a flight shoot, and at every half hour one from the Corps du garde doth hollow, unto whom every sentinel doth answer round from his stand; if any fail, they presently send forth an officer that beateth him extremely.'[56] Powhatan was quick to see possible advantages to himself in the presence of these foreign intruders. He could make use of the goods that the English brought with them, and especially their much coveted copper, to reinforce his own position in the region by increasing the dependence of the lesser chieftains on him. The English, with their muskets, would also be valuable military allies against the enemies of the Powhatan Confederacy, the Monacan and the Chesapeake. Since, if they wanted to stay, they would be dependent on his people for their supplies of food, he was well placed to reduce them to the status of another subject tribe. The exchange of presents with Newport when the two men met at the falls duly ratified a military alliance with the English against his enemies.[57]

The English, for their part, were playing the same game, hoping to turn Powhatan and his people into tributaries who would work for them to keep the infant colony supplied with food. But there were problems about how to achieve this. William Strachey would later quote Sir Thomas Gates to the effect that 'there was never any invasion, conquest, or far off plantation that had success without some party in the place itself or near it. Witness all the conquests made in those parts of the world, and all that the Spaniards have performed in *America*.'[58] Resentment among rival tribes at Powhatan's dominance might in theory have made this possible, but in practice Powhatan was so much in control of the local scene that there proved to be only limited scope for the leaders of the new colony to follow Cortés's example and play off one tribal grouping against another.

In June 1607, when Newport sailed for England to fetch supplies for the hungry and disease-ridden settlement, Captain John Smith, a member of the resident seven-man council, was deputed to lead expeditions into the interior, where he would attempt to negotiate with the Chickahominy tribe, who were settled in the heart of Powhatan's empire but did not form part of it. In December, however, he was taken prisoner by a party headed by Powhatan's brother and eventual successor, Opechancanough, and held for several weeks. Mystery surrounds the rituals to which Smith was subjected in his captivity and his 'rescue' by Powhatan's daughter Pocahontas, but the episode appears to be one element in the process by which Powhatan sought to subordinate the English and bring them within the confines of Tsenacommacah.[59] In conversations with Powhatan, Smith described Newport as 'my father',[60] and Powhatan may have seen Smith as an inferior chieftain, who, once he had spent time among his people and become an adopted Powhatan, could safely be returned to the English settlement and help ensure its obedience. He was released in early January just as Newport arrived back in the starving colony with much-needed supplies.

Following Newport's departure for England in April 1608 for further reinforcements of new settlers and supplies, Smith successfully forced his way into a commanding position in the faction-ridden colony. A professional soldier with long experience of warfare in continental Europe, he was elected in September into the presidency of the settlement, which badly needed the gifts of leadership that he alone seemed capable of providing.

A Powhatan shaman is alleged to have predicted that 'bearded men should come and take away their country'[61] – a prophecy like that which is said to have influenced the behaviour of Montezuma. But in Virginia, as in Mexico, this and other alleged 'prophecies' may have been no more than rationalizations of defeat concocted after the event,[62] and Powhatan at least showed no sign of resigned submission to a predetermined fate. He had the cunning and the skills to play a cat-and-mouse game with the Jamestown settlement, capitalizing on its continuing inability to feed itself. If the English needed an Hernán Cortés to counter his wiles, only Captain Smith, who had gained some knowledge of Indian ways during the time of his captivity, had any hope of filling the part.

The contrast between Powhatan's confident attitude and the hesitations of Montezuma is revealed at its sharpest by the bizarre episode of Powhatan's 'coronation', which has parallels with what had happened in Tenochtitlán eight decades earlier. Just as Cortés was determined to wrap his actions in the mantle of legitimacy by obtaining Montezuma's 'voluntary' submission, so the Virginia Company, possibly attracted by the Mexican precedent, sought a comparable legitimation for its actions.

Newport returned from England in September 1608 with instructions from the company to secure a formal recognition from Powhatan of the overlordship of James I. But Powhatan, unlike Montezuma, was not in custody, and resolutely refused to come to Jamestown for the ceremony. 'If your king have sent me presents,' he informed Newport, 'I also am a king, and this my land . . . Your father is to come to me, not I to him . . .' Newport therefore had no choice but to take the presents in person to Powhatan's capital, Werowacomoco. These consisted of a basin, ewer, bed, furniture, and 'scarlet cloak and apparel', which, 'with much ado', they put on him, according to Captain Smith's scornful account of a ceremony of which he deeply disapproved. 'But a foul trouble there was', wrote Smith, 'to make him kneel to receive his crown, he neither knowing the majesty, nor meaning of a crown, nor bending of the knee . . . At last by leaning hard on his shoulders, he a little stooped, and Newport put the crowne on his head.'

Once he had recovered from his fright at hearing a volley of shots, Powhatan reciprocated by presenting Newport with his 'old shoes and his mantle' (fig. 6).[63]

Powhatan was clearly no Montezuma. Nor, it turned out, did his 'empire' offer anything comparable to those fabulous riches extracted by the Spaniards from that of Montezuma. The letters patent of 1606 authorized the colony's council to 'dig, mine and search for all manner of mines of gold, silver and copper', with one-fifth (the Spanish *quinto real*) of the gold and silver, and one-fifteenth of the copper, to be automatically set aside for the crown.[64] Initially, hopes ran very high. A letter home from one of the colonists, dating from May or June 1607, reported that

> such a bay, a river and a land did never the eye of man behold; and at the head of the river, which is 160 miles long, are rocks and mountains, that promiseth infinite treasure: but our forces be yet too weak, to make further discovery: now is the king's majesty offered the most stately, rich kingdom in the world, never possessed by any Christian prince; be you one means among many to further our seconding, to conquer this land, as well as you were a means to further the discovery of it: And you yet may live to see England more rich, and renowned, than any kingdom, in all Ewroopa [*sic*].[65]

'To conquer this land.' The mentality, at least, was that of Cortés and his men, and the motivation was the same: riches, conceived in terms of gold, silver and tribute. But the high hopes were soon dashed. 'Silver and gold have they none . . .', reported Dudley Carleton in August 1607.[66] Even trading prospects were severely limited. 'The commodities of this country, what they are in Esse, is not much to be regarded, the inhabitants having no commerce with any nation, no respect of profit . . .'[67] Limited local resources; a colony oversupplied with gentlemen unwilling to turn their hands to work; a parent organization at home, the Virginia Company, ill-informed about the local situation and impatient for quick profits; and a dangerous dependence on the Powhatans for supplies of corn – all these brought the colony to the brink of disaster. There was an absence of continuity in the direction of the colony as Newport made his frequent voyages to and from England to keep Jamestown's lifeline open, although Captain Smith did his best to instil some discipline among the settlers. At the same time, rejecting Newport's conciliatory approach to the Indians, he adopted bullying and intimidating tactics that seem to have been inspired by those of Cortés, and brought him some success in securing food supplies.[68]

Looking back many years later on his experiences of a colony that he left in 1609, never to return, Smith remarked on the importance of having the right men in positions of leadership: 'Columbus, Cortez, Pitzara, Soto, Magellanes, and the rest served more than apprenticeship to learn how to begin their most memorable attempts in the West Indies . . .'[69] This indeed was true, but neither the circumstances, nor perhaps his own temperament, allowed Smith to achieve a repeat performance of the conquest of Mexico on North American soil. For many years the survival of the settlement was to hang in the balance, with alternating peace and hostilities between the Powhatans and the English, until the so-called 'Great Massacre' of some 400 of the 1,240 colonists in 1622 precipitated a conflict in which the English gradually gained the upper hand.[70] But the Virginia colony that emerged from these harsh birth-throes differed sharply in many ways from the viceroyalty of New Spain. Unlike New Spain, it was not established on the tribute and services of the indigenous population, whose numbers were rapidly depleted by hunger, war and disease. And salvation, when it came, came not from gold but from tobacco.

Motives and methods

Cortés, outmanoeuvred by royal officials, returned to Spain in 1528 to put his case to the Emperor, who confirmed him as captain-general, but not governor of New Spain. He returned there in 1530, but after costly and exhausting expeditions to the Pacific coast searching for a route to China and the Moluccas, he moved back to Spain in 1540, never again to return to the land he had conquered for Castile. Christopher Newport, for his part, left the service of the Virginia Company in 1611, apparently as a result of his dissatisfaction with its efforts to keep the Jamestown settlement supplied, and died in Java in 1617 on the third of a series of voyages on behalf of the East India Company. Both men had cause to feel disappointment with their treatment, but each, in his own way, had laid the foundations for an empire. Cortés, an inspired leader, beached his boats and led his expedition resolutely into the interior of an unknown land to conquer it for his royal master. Newport, ever the professional sailor, was the great enabler, who explored the waterways of the Chesapeake, and, after establishing a tiny settlement on the edges of a continent, opened the lifeline with the mother country that would allow it to survive.

Their two expeditions, although separated in time and space, possessed enough similarities to suggest certain common characteristics in the process of Spanish and British overseas colonization, as well as significant differences that would become increasingly marked as the years went by. The Spanish and British empires in America have been described respectively as empires of 'conquest' and of 'commerce',[71] but even these two expeditions would seem to indicate that motivations are not easily compartmentalized into neat categories, and that approaches to colonization resist straightforward classification. Was Cortés, with his almost obsessive determination to settle the land, no more than a gold-hungry conqueror? And were the promoters of the Virginia enterprise purely concerned with commercial opportunities, to the exclusion of all else?

There are sufficient references in Tudor and Stuart promotional literature to the activities of the Spaniards in America to make it clear that English attitudes to colonizing ventures were influenced in important ways by Spanish precedents. Yet at the same time, the English, like the Spaniards, had their own priorities and agenda, which themselves were shaped by historical preoccupations, cumulative experience and contemporary concerns. The aspirations and activities of both the planters of Jamestown and the conquerors of Mexico can only be fully appreciated within the context of a national experience of conquest and settlement which, in both instances, stretched back over many centuries. For historically, Castile and England were both proto-colonial powers long before they set out to colonize America.

Medieval England pursued a policy of aggressive expansion into the non-English areas of the British Isles, warring with its Welsh, Scottish and Irish neighbours and establishing communities of English settlers who would advance English interests and promote English values on alien Celtic soil.[72] The English, therefore, were no strangers to colonization, combining it with attempts at conquest which brought mixed results. Failure against Scotland was balanced by eventual success in Wales, which was formally incorporated in 1536 into the Crown of England, itself now held by a Welsh dynasty. Across the sea the English struggled over the centuries with only limited success to subjugate Gaelic Ireland and 'plant' it with settlers from England. Many of the lands seized by the Normans in the twelfth and thirteenth centuries were recovered by the Irish during the fourteenth and fifteenth;[73] and although in 1540 Henry VIII elevated Ireland to the status of a kingdom, English authority remained precarious or non-existent beyond the densely populated and rich agricultural area of the Pale. With the conversion of Henry's England to Protestantism the effective assertion of this authority over a resolutely Catholic Ireland acquired a new urgency in English eyes. The reign of Elizabeth was to see an intensified planting of new colonies on Irish soil, and, in due course, a new war of conquest. The process of the settlement and subjugation of Ireland by the England of Elizabeth, pursued over several decades, absorbed national energies and resources that might otherwise have been directed more intensively, and at an earlier stage, to the founding of settlements on the other side of the Atlantic.

In medieval Spain, the land of the *Reconquista*, the pattern of combined conquest and colonization was equally well established. The Reconquista was a prolonged struggle over many centuries to free the soil of the Iberian peninsula from Moorish domination. At once a military and a religious enterprise, it was a war for booty, land and vassals, and a crusade to recover for the Christians the vast areas of territory that had been lost to Islam. But it also involved a massive migration of people, as the crown allocated large tracts of land to individual nobles, to the military-religious orders engaged in the process of reconquest, and to city councils, which were given jurisdiction over large hinterlands. Attracted by the new opportunities, artisans and peasants moved southwards in large numbers from northern and central Castile to fill the empty spaces. In Spain, as in the British Isles, the process of conquest and settlement helped to establish forms of behaviour, and create habits of mind, easily transportable to distant parts of the world in the dawning age of European overseas expansion.[74]

The conquest and settlement of Al-Andalus and Ireland were still far from complete when fourteenth-century Europeans embarked on the exploration of the hitherto unexplored waters and islands of the African and eastern Atlantic.[75] Here the Portuguese were the pioneers. It was the combined desire of Portuguese merchants for new markets and of nobles for new estates and vassals that provided the impetus for the first sustained drive for overseas empire in the history of Early Modern Europe.[76] Where the Portuguese pointed the way, others followed. The kings of Castile, in particular, could not afford to let their Portuguese cousins steal a march on them. The Castilian conquest and occupation of the Canary Islands between 1478 and 1493 constituted a direct response by the Crown of Castile to the challenge posed by the spectacular expansion of Portuguese power and wealth.[77]

The early participation of Genoese merchants in Portugal's overseas enterprises, and the consequent transfer to an expanding Atlantic world of techniques of colonization first developed in the eastern Mediterranean,[78] gave Portugal's empire from its early stages a marked commercial orientation. This would be reinforced by the nature of the societies with which the Portuguese came into contact. Neither Portuguese resources, nor local conditions, were conducive to the seizure of vast areas of territory in Africa and Asia. Manpower was limited, local societies were resilient, and climate and disease tended to take a heavy toll of newly arrived Europeans. As a result, the overseas empire established by the Portuguese in the fifteenth and sixteenth centuries consisted largely of a string of fortresses and factories (*feitorias*) – trading posts and enclaves – on the margins of the unconquered continents of Africa and Asia. The most obvious exceptions were Madeira and the Azores, and then, from the 1540s, Brazil, as the Portuguese became alarmed by reports of French designs on the territory and took the first steps towards bringing it under more effective control. By contrast, the Spaniards began constructing for themselves, from the very early stages of their movement overseas, something more akin to an empire of conquest and settlement.

The process had begun with the subjugation of the Guanche population of the Canary Islands and continued with Columbus. For all his Genoese origins and long residence in Lisbon, he seems, as he returned from his first voyage in 1492, to have had something more in mind than the establishment of an overseas trading base. 'Be sure', he wrote in his Journal, addressing Ferdinand and Isabella, 'that this island [Hispaniola] and all the others are as much your own as is Castile, for all that is needed here is a seat of government and to command them to do what you wish'; and he went on to say of the inhabitants of Hispaniola, whom he described as 'naked and with no experience of arms and very timid', that 'they are suitable to take orders and be made to work, sow and do anything else that may be needed, and build towns and be taught to wear clothes and adopt our customs.'[79] Here already can be discerned the outlines of a programme which would today be regarded as that of the archetypal colonial regime: the establishment of a seat of government and of rule over the indigenous population; the induction of that population into the working methods of a European-style economy, producing European-style commodities; and the acceptance on behalf of the colonizing power of a civilizing mission, which was to include the wearing of European clothes and the adoption of Christianity. This would in due course become the programme of the Spaniards in America.

There were reasons both metropolitan and local why the Spanish overseas enterprise should have moved in this direction. The Reconquista had firmly established the tradition of territorial conquest and settlement in Castile. Columbus, who watched Ferdinand and Isabella make their triumphal entry into the Moorish city of Granada on its surrender in January 1492, participated in, and turned to his own advantage, the euphoria generated by this climactic moment in the long history of the Reconquista. From the vantage-point of 1492 it was natural to think in terms of the continuing acquisition of territory and of the extension of the Reconquista beyond the shores of Spain. Across the straits lay Morocco; and, as Columbus would soon demonstrate, across the Atlantic lay the Indies.

Alongside the tradition of territorial settlement and expansion, however, late medieval Castile also possessed a strong mercantile tradition, and it could have followed either route when embarking on its overseas ventures.[80] But conditions in the Indies themselves encouraged a territorial approach, as conditions facing the Portuguese in Africa and Asia did not. Disappointingly for Columbus, the Caribbean offered no equivalent of the lucrative trading networks in the Indian Ocean, although the first Spanish settlers in Hispaniola and Cuba would engage in a certain amount of *rescate*, or barter, with the inhabitants of neighbouring islands. While some gold would be found on Hispaniola, precious metals were not a major commodity of local exchange, and if the Spaniards wanted them it soon became clear that they would have to get them for themselves. The exploitation of mineral resources therefore demanded dominion of the land.

The indigenous societies of the New World, too, were very different in character from those of Africa and Asia. In the first place they were vulnerable – vulnerable to European technological superiority and to European diseases – in ways that the societies of Africa and Asia were not. Moreover, it soon transpired that these peoples had apparently never heard the Christian gospel preached. Their conversion, therefore, became a first priority, and would constitute – with papal blessing – the principal justification for a continuing Spanish presence in the newly found Indies. Castile, already uniquely favoured by God in the triumphant reconquest of Granada, now had a recognized mission across the newly navigated 'Ocean Sea' – the mission to convert these benighted peoples and introduce them to the benefits of *policía* (civility), or, in other words, to European norms of behaviour. In accordance with the terms of the Alexandrine bulls, Castile, by way of compensation for its efforts, was granted certain rights. The inhabitants of Hispaniola, and subsequently those of Cuba and other islands seized by the Spaniards, became vassals of the crown, and a potential labour force for crown and colonists – not, technically, as slaves, because vassalage and slavery were incompatible, but as labourers conscripted for public and private works.

The nature of the Indies and its inhabitants therefore favoured an approach based on conquest and subjugation rather than on the establishment of a string of trading enclaves, thus reinforcing the conquering and colonizing, rather than the mercantile, aspects of the medieval Castilian tradition. But, after the first heady moments, the Caribbean began to look distinctly disappointing as a theatre for conquest and colonization. Hispaniola was not, after all, to prove a source of abundant gold; and its Taíno population, which the first Spanish settlers had seen as vassals and as a potential labour force, rapidly succumbed to European diseases and became extinct before their eyes.[81] The same proved true of the other islands which they seized in their frenetic search for gold. For a moment it seemed as if the imperial experiment would be over almost as soon as it had begun: the meagre returns scarcely warranted such a heavy investment of resources. But once the lineaments of a great American landmass were revealed, and Cortés went on to overthrow the empire of the Aztecs, it was clear that Spain's empire of the Indies had come to stay. The discovery and conquest of Peru a decade later served to drive the lesson home. Here were vast sedentary populations, which could be brought under Spanish control with relative ease. Dominion over land brought with it dominion over people, and also – as large deposits of silver were discovered in the Andes and northern Mexico – dominion over resources on an unimagined scale.

The Cortés expedition – an expedition conceived in terms of subjugation and settlement – therefore fitted into a general pattern of behaviour developed in the course of the Iberian Reconquista and transported in the wake of Columbus to the Caribbean. Traditionally, the Reconquista had relied on a combination of state sponsorship and private initiative, the balance between them being determined at any given moment by the relative strength of crown and local forces. The monarch would 'capitulate' with a commander, who in turn would assume responsibility for financing and organizing a military expedition under the conditions outlined in the agreement. The expectation was that the expedition would pay for itself out of the booty of conquest, and the followers of the captain, or *caudillo*, would receive their reward in the form of an allocation of land, booty and tribute-paying vassals.[82] None of this would have been foreign to Cortés, whose father and uncle took part in the final stages of the Granada campaign. Not surprisingly, he pursued his conquest of Mexico as if he were conducting a campaign against the Moors. He tended to refer to Mesoamerican temples as 'mosques',[83] and in making his alliances with local Indian *caciques*, or when inducing Montezuma to accept Castilian overlordship, he resorted to strategies often used against the petty local rulers of Moorish Andalusia. Similarly, in his dealings with the crown, on whose approval he was more than usually dependent because of the ambiguous nature of his relationship with his immediate superior, the governor of Cuba, he was scrupulously careful to follow traditional Reconquista practice, meticulously setting aside the royal fifth before distributing any booty among his men.[84]

But Cortés showed himself to be something more than a *caudillo* in the traditional mould. Unlike Pedrarias Dávila, who as governor of Darien from 1513 murdered and massacred his way through the isthmus of Panama with his marauding band, Cortés, for all the brutality and ruthlessness of his conduct,

[margin, handwritten] Not alot of people originally until they took over the Aztecs.

adopted from the first a more constructive approach to the enterprise of conquest. He had arrived in Hispaniola in the wake of his distant relative and fellow Extremaduran, Nicolás de Ovando, who had been appointed the royal governor of the island in 1501, with instructions to rescue it from the anarchy into which it had descended under the regime of the Columbus brothers, and to establish the colony on solid foundations.[85] By the time Ovando left Hispaniola in 1509, seventeen towns had been established on the island, Indians had been allotted by distribution (*repartimiento*) to settlers who were charged with instructing them in Christian doctrine in return for the use of their labour, and cattle raising and sugar planting had begun to provide alternative sources of wealth to the island's rapidly diminishing supply of gold.

Cortés would have seen for himself something of the transformation of Hispaniola into a well-ordered and economically viable community, while at the same time his Caribbean experiences made him aware of the devastating consequences of uncontrolled rapine by adventurers who possessed no abiding stake in the land. He therefore struggled to prevent a recurrence in Mexico of the mindless style of conquest that had left nothing but devastation in its wake. As expressed by Gómara, his philosophy was that 'without settlement there is no good conquest, and if the land is not conquered, the people will not be converted. Therefore the maxim of the conqueror must be to settle.'[86] It was to encourage settlement that he arranged the *repartimiento* of Indians among his companions, who were to hold them in trust, or *encomienda*, and promoted the founding or refounding of cities in a country which already had large ceremonial complexes and urban concentrations. And it was to encourage conversion that he invited the first Franciscans – the so-called 'twelve apostles' – to come to Mexico. Conquest, conversion and colonization were to be mutually supportive.

Effective colonization would not be possible without a serious attempt to develop the resources of the land, and Cortés himself, with his sugar plantations on his Cuernavaca estates and his promotion of long-distance trading ventures, practised what he preached.[87] But he was only one among the many conquistadores and early settlers who displayed marked entrepreneurial characteristics. As new waves of Spanish immigrants moved across the continent in the aftermath of the conquest of Mexico and Peru, it became clear that the easiest forms of wealth – silver and Indians – were reserved for the fortunate few. Disappointed conquistadores and new immigrants therefore had to fend for themselves as best they could. This meant, as it had meant in the lands recovered by the Christians in medieval Andalusia, applying their skills as artisans in the cities, or exploiting local possibilities to develop new sources of wealth. The sixteenth-century settlers of Guatemala, for instance – a region without silver mines – developed an export trade in indigo, cacao and hides for American and European markets.[88]

Entrepreneurial as well as seigneurial aspirations were therefore to be found in this Spanish American colonial society, and already in the first half of the century that great chronicler of the Indies, Gonzalo Fernández de Oviedo, was expressing pride in Spanish entrepreneurial accomplishments: 'We found no sugar mills when we arrived in these Indies, and all these we have built with our own hands and industry in so short a time.'[89] Similarly, Gómara's praise for the success of the Spaniards in 'improving' Hispaniola and Mexico shows that the language of improvement was being used by the Spaniards a century before English colonists turned to it in order to justify to themselves and to others their presence in the Caribbean and the North American mainland.[90]

Spain's empire of the Indies, then, cannot be summarily categorized as an empire of conquest, reflecting exclusively the military and seigneurial values of the metropolitan society that founded it. As Cortés's vision – and practice – make clear, there were counter-currents at work, which were perfectly capable of flourishing, given the right conditions. But those conditions would in part be set and shaped by the requirements and interests of the crown. The scale of the conquests was simply too large, the potential resources of the continent too vast, for the crown to remain indifferent to the ways in which those resources were exploited and developed. Tradition, obligation and self-interest all worked from the very beginning to ensure close royal involvement in Spanish overseas settlement.

The united Spain created by the dynastic union of Isabella of Castile and Ferdinand of Aragon in 1469 bore the imprint of their unique authority. Their restoration of order in the peninsula after years of civil war and anarchy, and the triumphant completion of the Reconquista under their leadership, had brought the monarchs unparalleled prestige by the time the overseas enterprise was launched. Their investment in Columbus – a rare example of direct financial participation by the crown in overseas expeditions of discovery and conquest[91] – had yielded rich returns. But their 'capitulations' with Columbus proved to have been over-generous. Having asserted their authority with such difficulty at home, they were not inclined to let their subjects get the better of them overseas. The crown would therefore seek to rein in Columbus's excessive powers, and would keep a close watch over subsequent developments in the Indies, making sure that royal officials accompanied, and followed hard on, expeditions of conquest, in order to uphold the crown's interests, impose its authority, and prevent the emergence of over-mighty subjects.

The case for intervention and control by the crown was further strengthened by its obligations under the terms of the Alexandrine bulls to look to the spiritual and material well-being of its newly acquired Indian vassals. It was incumbent on the royal conscience to prevent unrestricted exploitation of the indigenous population by the colonists. With the acquisition of millions of these new vassals as a result of the conquests of Mexico and Peru, the obligation was still further increased. Just as the crown, following Reconquista practice, insisted on retaining ultimate authority over the process of territorial acquisition and settlement, so also it insisted on retaining ultimate authority when it came to the protection of the Indians and the salvation of their souls.

But more than the crown's conscience was at stake. The Indians were a source of tribute and of labour, and the crown was determined to have its share of both.

As it struggled under Charles V to maintain its European commitments – to fight its wars with the French and defend Christendom from the Turk – so its dependence on the assets of empire grew. The discovery in 1545 of the silver mountain of Potosí in the high Andes, followed the next year by that of important silver deposits at Zacatecas, in northern Mexico, vastly enhanced those assets, turning Castile's possessions in the Indies into a great reservoir of riches, which, in the eyes of its European rivals, would be used to promote Charles's aspirations after universal monarchy. As Cortés had told Charles in the second of his letters from Mexico, he might call himself 'the emperor of this kingdom with no less glory than of Germany, which, by the Grace of God, Your Sacred Majesty already possesses'.[92]

Even if Charles and his successors ignored the suggestion, and declined to adopt the title of 'Emperor of the Indies', Cortés's vision of the monarchs of Castile as masters of a New World empire was very soon to be an established fact. Charles and his successors saw this empire as a vast resource for meeting their financial necessities. Their consequent concern for the exploitation of its silver deposits and the safe annual shipment of the bullion to Seville was therefore translated into continuing attention to the affairs of the Indies, and into a set of policies and practices in which fiscal considerations inevitably tended to have the upper hand. In the Europe of the sixteenth century, silver meant power; and Cortés and Pizarro, by unlocking the treasures of the Indies, had shown how the conquest and settlement of overseas empire could add immeasurably to the power of European states.

In the circumstances, it was not surprising that the England of Elizabeth should have expressed its own imperial aspirations, nicely symbolized by the 'Armada portrait' of Queen Elizabeth, with her hand on the globe and an imperial crown at her side.[93] Empire calls forth empire, and although Elizabeth's 'empire' was essentially an empire of 'Great Britain' embracing all the British Isles, the notion of *imperium* was flexible enough to be capable of extension to English plantations not only in Ireland but on the farther shores of the Atlantic.[94] It was important, too, for Hakluyt and other promoters of overseas colonization to refute any Spanish claims to possession of the New World based on papal donation by the Alexandrine bulls. In his *Historie of Travell into Virginia* of 1612, William Strachey roundly asserted that the King of Spain 'hath no more title, nor colour of title, to this place (which our industry and expenses have only made ours . . .), than hath any Christian prince'.[95]

While Spain served as stimulus, exemplar, and sometimes as warning, English empire-builders could equally well look to precedents in their own backyard. Ireland, like the reconquered kingdom of Granada, was both kingdom and colony, and, like Andalusia, constituted a useful testing-ground of empire.[96] For example, the English had for centuries been seeking to enmesh Irish kings and chieftains in a network of allegiance, and the model of Montezuma's submission was hardly a necessary prerequisite for the Virginia Company to come up with the farce of Powhatan's 'coronation'.

It is therefore no accident that the Elizabethans most active in devising the first American projects – Sir Humphrey Gilbert, Sir Walter Raleigh, Ralph Lane, Thomas White – were deeply involved in the schemes for Irish plantation. It was not until he went to Ireland in 1566 as a soldier and planter that Gilbert began to appreciate how colonization could bring to its promoters territorial wealth and power.[97] In the early years of Elizabeth, growing hostility to Spain, and the burning desire of the English to get their hands on the riches of the Spanish Indies, made it natural that strategic and privateering interests should predominate over any enterprise of a less ephemeral character. But in his abortive voyage of 1578 Gilbert seems to have been moving beyond piracy towards some sort of colonizing scheme.[98] The failure of the voyage pushed him still further in the same direction, and in 1582 he devised a project for the settlement of 8.5 million acres of North American mainland in the region known as *Norumbega*.[99]

Sir Humphrey Gilbert belonged to that West Country connection – Raleighs, Carews, Gilberts, Grenvilles – with its trading, privateering and colonizing interests, initially in Ireland, which can be seen as an English counterpart to the Extremadura connection that produced Nicolás de Ovando, Hernán Cortés, Francisco Pizarro, and many other Spanish conquerors and settlers of America.[100] His plans were designed to provide landed estates for that same class of rural gentry and younger sons which had looked to land and vassals in Ireland as a means of realizing its aspirations. The Irish experience was of a kind to encourage gentlemen adventurers – men imbued with similar values and ideals to those to be found among the Spanish conquistadores, for there was nothing exclusively Spanish about the conquistador ideal. It inspired Sir Walter Raleigh with his wild schemes for wealth and glory through the conquest of the 'large, rich, and bewtiful empyre of Guiana', and it filled the heads of the gentlemen adventurers of Jamestown with dreams of gold and Indians.[101]

But if there were some suggestive similarities in English and Castilian plans for overseas expansion – plans which, although carried out under state sponsorship and subject to state control, were heavily dependent on private and collective initiatives for their realization – there were also some important differences. England under Elizabeth was moving, however reluctantly, in the direction of religious pluralism, and this was to be reflected in the new colonizing ventures. It was symptomatic, for instance, that one of the main proponents of Gilbert's colonization scheme was Sir George Peckham, a Roman Catholic, and the colony was at least partially envisaged as offering alternative space to the English Catholic community.[102] In 1620, inspired by comparable urgings for an alternative space, a group of separatists under the leadership of William Bradford would land at Cape Cod and move across Massachusetts Bay to establish themselves in New Plymouth. The willingness of the English crown to sanction projects designed to provide refuge in America for a harassed minority contrasted strikingly with the determination of the Spanish crown to prevent the migration of Jews, Moors and heretics to the Indies.

It was also a reflection of the changing times that England's transatlantic enterprise was sustained by a more coherent economic philosophy than that which attended Spain's first ventures overseas. Commercial considerations had admittedly been present from the beginning of the Spanish enterprise, and had been central to Columbus's presentation of his case at court. The colonization of Venezuela in the early 1530s was actually undertaken by a commercial organization, the Seville branch of the German merchant-banking firm of the Welsers, with results as disappointing as those that would later attend the efforts of the Virginia Company.[103] But the discovery of silver in such vast quantities, and the overwhelming importance of precious metals in the cargoes for Seville, inevitably relegated other American commodities, however valuable, to a subordinate status in Spain's transatlantic trade. Although by the middle years of the sixteenth century some Spaniards were already expressing concern about the economic as well as the moral consequences of the constant influx of American silver into the Iberian peninsula,[104] those who benefited from it – starting with the crown – had little inducement to listen to the theorists.

In the England of Elizabeth, however, the promoters of overseas colonization were still having to look for arguments that would advance their cause. Although the younger Hakluyt's writings were suffused with anti-Spanish and patriotic sentiments, patriotism by itself was not enough. Colonization schemes required merchant capital, and it was essential to present them in terms that would appeal to the mercantile community, with which the Hakluyts themselves had close connections.[105] At a time when the country was anxiously casting around for new export markets, this meant emphasizing the value of colonies as an outlet for domestic manufactures. Again, the example of Spain was uppermost in the younger Hakluyt's mind. Warning his compatriots of the likely consequences of Philip II's acquisition of Portugal and its overseas territories in 1580, he reminded them that '. . . whenever the rule and government of the East and West Indies . . . shall be in one prince, they neither will receive English cloth nor yet any vent of their commodities to us, having then so many places of their own to make vent and interchange of their commodities. For all the West Indies is a sufficient vent of all their wines, and of all their wool indraped . . .'[106]

The case was further strengthened by the growing anxiety in Elizabethan England about the alarming social consequences of overpopulation. Spain and Portugal, wrote Hakluyt somewhat optimistically in his *Discourse of Western Planting*, 'by their discoveries have found such occasion of employment, that these many years we have not heard scarcely of any pirate of those two nations: whereas we and the French are most infamous for our outrageous, common and daily piracies.' In contrast with Spain, 'many thousands of idle persons are within this realm, which having no way to be set on work be either mutinous and seek alteration in the state, or at least very burdensome to the common wealth'.[107] Colonization, therefore, became a remedy for the home country's social and economic problems, as Hakluyt conjured up for the benefit of contemporaries and posterity the vision of a great English commercial empire, which would redound both to the honour of the nation and the profit of its industrious inhabitants.

It was ironical that, at the very time when Hakluyt and his friends were vigorously arguing the case for overseas empire, a number of informed and sophisticated Spaniards were beginning to question its value to Spain. In his great *General History of Spain*, written in the early 1580s, Juan de Mariana summed up the increasingly ambivalent feelings of his generation towards the acquisition of its American possessions: 'From the conquest of the Indies have come advantages and disadvantages. Among the latter, our strength has been weakened by the multitude of people who have emigrated and are scattered abroad; the sustenance we used to get from our soil, which was by no means bad, we now expect in large measure from the winds and waves that bring home our fleets; the prince is in greater necessity than he was before, because he has to go to the defence of so many regions; and the people are made soft by the luxury of their food and dress.'[108]

Mariana's words were a foretaste of things to come. The years around 1600, when the ominous word 'decline' first began to be uttered in Spain, saw the beginnings of an intensive Castilian debate about the problems afflicting Castilian society and the Castilian economy.[109] From the earliest stages of this debate, the alleged benefits to Spain of the silver of the Indies were the subject of particularly critical scrutiny. 'Our Spain', wrote one of the most eloquent and intelligent of the participants, Martín González de Cellorigo, 'has its eyes so fixed on trade with the Indies, from which it gets its gold and silver, that it has given up trading with its neighbours; and if all the gold and silver that the natives of the New World have found, and go on finding, were to come to it, they would not make it as rich or powerful as it would be without them.'[110] In this reading, precious metals were not after all the true yardstick of wealth, and real prosperity was to be measured by national productivity, and not by a fortuitous inflow of bullion.

This was a lesson that still had to be learnt, outside as much as inside Spain itself. The insistence of Hakluyt and his friends on an empire based on the exchange of commodities rather than on the acquisition of precious metals played its part in helping to give merchants and their values a new prominence in the English national consciousness at a moment when in Castile a minority was struggling against heavy odds to promote a similar awareness of the crucial importance of those same values for national salvation.[111] English merchants, too, benefited from a social and political system which offered them more room for manoeuvre than their Castilian counterparts, who found it difficult to protect their interests against the arbitrary financial requirements of the Spanish crown.

The fact that the English were embarking on overseas colonization at a time when their society was acquiring a more commercial orientation in response to internal pressures and to a changing climate of national and international opinion about the relationship of profit and power,[112] inevitably gave a slant to the English colonial enterprise that was not to be found in the opening stages of

Castile's overseas expansion. The founding of the Virginia Company in 1606 under royal charter reflected the new determination of merchants and gentry to combine personal profit and national advantage by means of a corporate organization which owed more to their own energy and enthusiasm than to that of the state.[113] The very fact that the agent of colonization was to be a trading company pointed towards a future English 'empire of commerce'.

Yet the tensions that bedevilled the Company from the outset suggest that an empire of commerce was by no means foreordained. The seigneurial aspirations that nearly wrecked the Jamestown settlement were to recur frequently in English colonizing projects of the seventeenth century. Indigenous labour might be in short supply, but the introduction of a slave labour force would in due course allow for the growth in the British Caribbean of societies characterized by the same kind of attitude to conspicuous consumption as was to be found in the Hispanic-American world.

If large quantities of silver had indeed been found in Virginia, there is little reason to doubt that the development of an extractive economy would have created a high-spending elite which would have more than lived up to the dreams of the gentlemen settlers of Jamestown. But the lack of silver and indigenous labour in these early British settlements forced on the settlers a developmental as against an essentially exploitative rationale; and this in turn gave additional weight to those qualities of self-reliance, hard work and entrepreneurship that were assuming an increasingly prominent place in the national self-imagining and rhetoric of seventeenth-century England.

The presence or absence of silver, and of large native populations that could be domesticated to European purposes, had other implications, too, for the two imperial enterprises. With much less immediate profit to be expected from overseas colonization, the British crown maintained a relatively low profile in the crucial opening stages of colonial development. This contrasted strikingly with the interventionist behaviour of the Spanish crown, which had an obvious and continuing interest in securing for itself a regular share of the mineral wealth that was being extracted in the Indies. Similarly, with fewer Indians to be exploited and converted, the British crown and the Anglican church had much less reason than their Spanish counterparts to display a close interest in the well-being of the indigenous population in the newly settled lands.

As a result of this relatively low level of royal and ecclesiastical interest, there was correspondingly more chance for a transatlantic transfer of minority and libertarian elements from the metropolitan culture to British than to Spanish America. While Massachusetts was a reflection of the growing pluralism of English society, it was also a reflection of the relative lack of concern felt by the British crown in these critical early stages of colonization over the character of the communities that its subjects were establishing on the farther shores of the Atlantic. There was, said Lord Cottington, no point in troubling oneself about the behaviour of settlers who 'plant tobacco and Puritanism only, like fools'.[114] The Spanish crown, acutely aware of its own dependence on American silver and of the vulnerability of its silver resources to foreign attack, could not afford the luxury of so casual an approach to settlement in its overseas possessions.

If, then – as the Cortés and Jamestown expeditions suggest – many of the same aspirations attended the birth of Spain's and Britain's empires in America, accidents both of environment and of timing would do much to ensure that they developed in distinctive ways. But in the early stages of settlement, the creators of these Spanish and British transatlantic communities found themselves confronted by similar problems and challenges. They had to take 'possession' of the land in the fullest sense of the word; they had to work out some kind of relationship with the peoples who already inhabited it; they had to sustain and develop their communities within an institutional framework which was only partly of their own devising; and they had to establish an equilibrium between their own developing needs and aspirations, and those of the metropolitan societies from which they had sprung. At once liberated and constrained by their American environment, their responses would be conditioned both by the Old World from which they came, and by the New World which they now set out to master and make their own.

Spain was more involved due to the resources

CHAPTER 2

Occupying American Space

Europeans engaged in the conquest and settlement of America were confronted by a challenge of almost inconceivable immensity – the mastering of American space. As described by William Burke in his *Account of the European Settlements in America*, first published in 1757, 'America extends from the North pole to the fifty-seventh degree of South latitude; it is upwards of eight thousand miles in length; it sees both hemispheres; it has two summers and a double winter; it enjoys all the variety of climates which the earth affords; it is washed by the two great oceans.'[1]

As Burke indicates, American space varied enormously in its physical and climatic characteristics. There was not one America but many, and these different Americas lent themselves to different styles of settlement and exploitation.[2] Far to the north, Basque or English fishermen attracted from the fifteenth century by the rich fishing grounds off Newfoundland, would be faced by a bleak and inhospitable coastal landscape. Further south, the view of land from the sea was more encouraging. The Reverend Francis Higginson, writing home to his friends in England in 1629, observed the 'fine woods and green trees by land and these yellow flowers painting the sea', which 'made us all desirous to see our new paradise of New England, whence we saw such fore-running signals of fertility afar off'.[3] Inland, however, lay dark forests, and the frightening unknown. To the south again was the Chesapeake Bay and Virginia, described by Captain Smith as 'a country in America that lieth between the degrees of 34 and 44 of the north latitude', where 'the summer is hot as in Spain; the winter cold as in France and England.'[4]

The Spaniards who reached the Caribbean and moved onwards into central and southern America were faced with landscapes and climates of extreme contrasts – tropical islands in the Antilles, barren scrubland in the Yucatán peninsula, the volcanic high plateau or *altiplano* of northern and central Mexico, and the dense tropical vegetation of the central American isthmus. While there was a climatic unity to the tropical world of the Caribbean islands and central America, southern America was a continent of violent extremes, and nowhere more than in Peru, as the great Jesuit writer, José de Acosta, noted in his *Natural and Moral History of the Indies* at the end of the sixteenth century: 'Peru is divided into three long and narrow strips, the plains, the sierras and the Andes. The plains run along the sea-coast; the sierra is all slopes, with some valleys; the Andes are dense mountains ... It is astonishing to see how, in a distance of as little as fifty leagues, equally far from the equator and the pole, there should be such diversity that in one part it is almost always raining, in one it almost never rains, and in the other it rains during one season and not another.'[5]

Distances in this South American world were vast, and were made still vaster by the impossible character of so much of the terrain. In the kingdom of New Granada, for instance, the combination of a hot, damp climate and dramatic changes of level between the Magdalena valley and the Cordillera Oriental of modern Colombia meant that after a sixty-day transatlantic crossing from Seville to the Caribbean port city of Cartagena, it took a minimum of another thirty days to cover the thousand kilometres from Cartagena to Santa Fe de Bogotá.[6]

How were the Spaniards, and those other Europeans who followed them, to take possession of so much space? The mastering of America, as effected by Europeans, involved three related processes: the symbolic taking of possession; physical occupation of the land, which entailed either the subjection or the expulsion of its indigenous inhabitants; and the peopling of the land by settlers and their descendants in sufficient numbers to ensure that its resources could be developed in conformity with European expectations and practices.

Symbolic occupation

The symbolic taking of possession tended to consist in the first instance of a ceremonial act, the nature and extent of which were likely to be as much conditioned by circumstance as by national tradition.[7] The Spanish and the English alike accepted the Roman Law principle of *res nullius*, whereby unoccupied land remained the common property of mankind, until being put to use. The first user then became the owner.[8] According to the thirteenth-century Castilian legal code of the *Siete Partidas*, 'it rarely happens that new islands arise out of the sea. But if this should happen and some new island appears, we say that it should belong to him who first settles it.'[9] A similar principle would govern land titles in Spanish colonial America: possession was conditional on occupation and use.[10] In claiming sovereignty, however, the Spaniards, unlike the English, had little or no need of the doctrine of *res nullius*, since their title was based on the original papal concession to the Spanish crown. Arriving, moreover, in lands for the most part already well settled by indigenous populations, their principal preoccupation would be to justify their lordship over peoples rather than land.[11] In this, the most serious objections faced by the crown would come from within Spain itself, rather than from foreign rivals who lacked the power to enforce their own counter-claims.

Even if claims to sovereignty were entirely valid in the eyes of those who made them, the formal taking of possession by some form of ceremony constituted a useful statement of intent, directed at least as much to other European princes as to the local population. Both in Castile and England, taking possession of a property was traditionally accompanied by symbolic acts, such as beating the bounds, cutting branches, or scooping up earth. When the Castilians seized Tenerife in the Canary Islands in 1464, Diego de Herrera secured the formal submission of the local chiefs. He then had the royal standard raised, and made a circuit of two leagues, 'stamping the ground with his feet as a sign of possession and cutting the branches of trees . . .'[12] Columbus makes no mention of such a ceremony following his landfall at San Salvador, but he raised the standard of Ferdinand and Isabella, and had the solemn declaration of their rights to the island duly notarized. Subsequently, as he noted in his Journal, he did the same in the other islands: 'I did not wish to pass by any island without taking possession of it, although it might be said that once one had been taken, they all were.'[13]

The delimitation of the areas allocated respectively to the crowns of Castile and Portugal by the bull *Inter Caetera* of 4 May 1493 did not preclude ceremonial assertions of possession when captains and commanders set foot on new soil. In his instructions to Pedro Margarit, dated 9 April 1494, Columbus ordered that, wherever he went, 'along all the roads and footpaths' he should have 'high crosses and boundary stones erected, and also crosses on the trees and crosses in any other appropriate place, where they cannot fall down . . . because, praise be to God, the land belongs to Christians, and this will serve as a permanent memorial, and you should also place on some tall and large trees the names of their Royal Highnesses.'[14] Comparable rituals occurred as the Spaniards made their way across mainland America, with Balboa walking into the Pacific in 1513 with raised banner and drawn sword to take possession of the ocean and the surrounding land and islands on behalf of the Crown of Castile. Similarly, Cortés was scrupulous in following the instructions given him by the governor of Cuba to 'assume possession . . . with all possible solemnity', and in Honduras in 1526 tufts of grass would be pulled up and earth scooped up by hand.[15]

The clearest English analogy to these practices occurred on Sir Humphrey Gilbert's Newfoundland voyage in 1583. On landing, he had his commission under the Great Seal 'solemnly read' to an assembled company of his own men, together with a motley band of English and foreign merchants and fishermen. He then 'took possession of the said land in the right of the Crown of England by digging of a turf and receiving the same with an hazel wand, delivered unto him after the manner of the Law and custom of England'. The land in question, known as 'Norumbega' since Verrazano's account of it in 1524, had the advantage of being of unknown dimensions and infinitely expandable boundaries. After the assembled company had affirmed its consent and its obedience to the queen, 'the arms of England engraven in lead' were set up on a wooden pillar.[16]

Without the benefit of a papal donation, the English crown was compelled, as here, to assert its own rights over 'remote, barbarous and heathen lands, countries, and territories not actually possessed of any Christian prince or people',[17] and trust that they would be respected by other European powers. Since Spain in fact regarded the entire Atlantic coastline from the Florida peninsula to Newfoundland as part of its own territory of La Florida,[18] such trust was likely to be misplaced. It is in this context that the principle of *res nullius* became of much greater service to the English than to the Spaniards. It could be used both against other European powers which had made claims to American territory but had done nothing to implement them, and also against an indigenous population which had failed to use the land in accordance with European criteria.[19] The ceremony at St John's harbour was a clear declaration of Gilbert's intention of transforming a land in which at the time of his arrival 'nothing appeared more than Nature itself without art'.[20] Once art was applied to nature, the land was no longer *res nullius* and passed into legitimate and permanent ownership.

It was naturally easier to make use of the principle of *res nullius* where the land was at best thinly populated by indigenous peoples than where they were very obviously present, as they were in the mainland territories seized by the Spaniards, or even in Virginia. When the Jamestown settlement was established in what was clearly Powhatan territory, the Virginia Company obviously felt that the setting up of a cross and the proclamation of James I as king were somehow insufficient to establish English sovereignty, and so resorted to the dubious staging of Powhatan's 'coronation'. In Virginia and elsewhere, as on Captain George Waymouth's New England voyage of 1605, the English followed Spanish practice in setting up crosses,[21] but in general the more elaborate rituals used by Gilbert seem not to have been followed by subsequent generations of English settlers.[22] This may have reflected the lack of any felt need, given the sparseness of the indigenous population and the fact that English suzerainty over vast, if indeterminate, regions had already been asserted.

There were, however, other and additional ways of asserting territorial possession, of which the most widely practised was the renaming of the land. Columbus was lavish in his bestowal of new names on the islands, capes and geographical features that he encountered on his voyages: sacred names, beginning with San Salvador, names of the royal family (Fernandina or Juana), descriptive names appropriate to some striking physical feature, or names that simply conformed with those already inscribed on his own imaginative landscape of the lands he had reached, starting with 'the Indies' themselves.[23] The obsession with names and naming was shared by his monarchs, who told him in a letter of 1494 that they wanted to know 'how many islands have been found up to now. Of those islands you have named, what name has been given to each, because in your letters you give the names of some but not all of these.' They also wanted to know 'the names that the Indians call them'.[24]

While this process of renaming, which extended to all the European powers in the Americas, can reasonably be described as a 'manifestation of power', and an act of 'Christian imperialism',[25] it was by no means a uniquely European habit. When the Mexica incorporated the various states of central Mexico into their empire, they either transliterated their place-names into Nahuatl, or gave them new, Nahuatl names unrelated to those by which their inhabitants knew them.[26] When Cortés, therefore, decided to rename Montezuma's empire *Nueva España* because of 'the similarity between this land and that of Spain, its fertility and great size and the cold and many other things', he was unwittingly following the practice of his indigenous predecessors.[27]

The English followed suit. *Norumbega* is a name of unknown, but allegedly Indian origin.[28] Later, it was sometimes called North Virginia, but in his 'Description' of the territory in 1616, John Smith astutely renamed it *New England*, just as Cortés had renamed the land of the Mexica *New Spain*.[29] Initially, however, 'malicious minds amongst sailors and others, drowned that name with the echo of Nusconcus, Canaday, and Penaquid.'[30] In his dedicatory preface Smith therefore appealed to the Prince of Wales 'to change their Barbarous names, for such English, as posterity may say, Prince Charles was their godfather'. The prince duly obliged, although not in time to prevent the incorporation of many Indian names into Smith's *A Description of New England*. The text therefore had to be preceded by a table of correspondences, like Southampton for Aggawom, and Ipswich for Sowocatuck.[31]

The Spaniards and the English in fact seem to have adopted much the same approach to the renaming of American places, preferring new names to old when they settled, but not necessarily ruling out indigenous names, in so far as they could catch or pronounce them. Tenochtitlán became Mexico City, but Qosqo was easily transformed into Cuzco, and the indigenous Cuba prevailed over the Spanish Juana. Indigenous names, however, were frequently too long and difficult for Europeans, and, not surprisingly, a stream 'called in the Indian tongue Conamabsqunoocant' was 'commonly called the Duck River' by the New England colonists.[32] But there was also prejudice against Indian names. In 1619, for example, the inhabitants of Kiccowtan petitioned Virginia's House of Burgesses to 'change the savage name' to Elizabeth City.[33] The natural tendency, in any event, was for settlers to choose the names of their home towns – Trujillo, Mérida, Dorchester, Boston – and in so doing to bring the unknown within the orbit of the known.

Among Spanish captains and colonists a popular option was to choose the names of saints for whom they felt a particular devotion, or whose day in the liturgical calendar had been the day of discovery or of a town's foundation. The result, as the Spanish chronicler Fernández de Oviedo remarked, was that 'anyone looking at one of our navigational charts for one of these coasts seems to be reading a not very well ordered calendar or catalogue of the saints.'[34] It was a practice that would later be ridiculed by the Bostonian, Cotton Mather.[35] Where English settlers were concerned, the sacred was more likely to be confined to biblical names, like Salem, or to expressions of gratitude for divine guidance and mercy, as with Roger Williams, who 'in a sense

of God's merciful providence unto me in my distress called the place
Providence . . .'[36]

The new names were quick to be recorded on maps, like John Smith's New
England map of 1616. Cartography, too, was a symbolic taking of possession, at
once recording the imposition of European rule by the eradication of indigenous
names, and asserting national rights to American territory against European
rivals. From the very beginnings of overseas discovery and settlement the Spanish
crown had shown a keen interest in obtaining detailed information about the
character and extent of its newly acquired territories. As with so much else in
sixteenth-century Spain, it was the reign of Philip II, a monarch with a
Renaissance thirst for knowledge combined with a passion for detail and for
accurate representation, that first saw a serious attempt to bring method and system to what had previously been a haphazard process.[37] In 1571 a new post of
'principal cosmographer of the Indies' was created. The first holder, Juan López
de Velasco, was charged with producing a definitive chronicle and atlas of the
New World, and Francisco Domínguez, a Portuguese cartographer, was sent out
to New Spain to create survey maps. This first and apparently abortive initiative
was followed in 1573 by the famous project, inspired by the great reforming president of the Council of the Indies, Juan de Ovando, for a massive questionnaire
addressed to local officials throughout Spanish America, requesting the most
detailed information about the character, the history and the resources of their
communities, together with maps. The somewhat sporadic results of this cartographical exercise, which reflected an indigenous as well as a colonial vision of
Spanish New World communities, duly found their way to Spain, where the
crown's obsession with concealing knowledge of its American possessions from
its rivals ensured that the maps remained hidden away in the archives.[38]

It was not for another 150 years that the British imperial authorities displayed
a comparable interest in the acquisition and production of maps. At the end of
the seventeenth century the Board of Trade possessed no more than a few maps,
and it was only after the Peace of Utrecht, under the pressure of intercolonial
rivalries, that changes began to occur. In 1715 the Board began searching for maps
of the colonies, and requested copies of the best maps available in France. In view
of the unsuccessful nature of the search, it noted 'the necessity of sending an able
person from hence to take a survey, and make exact maps of all the several
colonies from north to south, which the French have done for themselves, from
whence they reap great advantages whilst we continue in the dark'.[39]

Yet the lack of official interest did not preclude the making and dissemination
of maps of British America in the seventeenth century, although the quality of
these, in comparison with those produced by the Dutch in the same period, was
poor.[40] Maps of Puritan New England reflected the establishment and growth of
the 'New English Canaan', constituting a sacred geography for the elect.[41] But,
even more important, a map with reassuring English words and names, like that
included in John Smith's depiction of New England, served as a useful instrument
for promoting colonization in a society where the attractions of transatlantic

migration had to be sold to potential emigrants. To keep these matters secret, in the manner of the Spaniards, would simply have imposed an additional obstacle to settlement overseas.

Physical occupation

The various maps of British North America represented a public affirmation of the new ownership of the land. But land that was claimed still had to be physically occupied, and there was a wide gap between cartographical affirmation and what was actually happening on the ground. Technically, in both Spanish and British America, the land was vested in the crown once its sovereignty had been proclaimed. It was then for the crown to arrange for its allocation, in order to attach settlers to the soil. There were various ways in which this could be done. One was to give commanders and colonizers powers to distribute plots of land once possession had been taken. In 1523, for instance, the Spanish crown, in capitulating with Vázquez de Ayllón for the exploration of Florida, authorized him to distribute 'water, lands, and building lots (solares)'.[42] Similarly, on his Newfoundland expedition of 1583, Sir Humphrey Gilbert, in conformity with his letters patent issued by the queen by virtue of her royal authority, 'granted in fee farm divers parcels of land lying by the waterside' at St John's harbour.[43]

An alternative method, to which the British crown several times resorted, was to issue charters to groups of interested individuals who constituted themselves into companies, like the Massachusetts Bay Company of 1629. The nearest to company colonization in Spanish America was the authorization given in 1528 to two Sevillian agents of the German commercial house of the Welser for the discovery, conquest and settlement of Venezuela, but the name of the Welser seems to have been carefully kept out of the agreement, allowing them to disclaim responsibility for the actions of their company agents and representatives.[44] More frequently the British crown, less concerned than the Spanish crown with the retention of close control over its American possessions, would make proprietary grants to chosen patentees, like George Calvert, Lord Baltimore, whose son Cecilius received the seals and charter for the colonization of Maryland in 1632.[45] Proprietors in turn would proceed to allocate land on the terms most likely to prove attractive to settlers, while conserving as many rights to themselves as they could. But the process of land acquisition and settlement remained considerably more haphazard in British than in Spanish America. Some English colonies – Plymouth, Connecticut and Rhode Island – received no royal charters, and this only enhanced the ambiguities surrounding their rights to settle in Indian territory. At least in the initial stages of settlement, these New England colonists sought to resolve their legal and moral dilemmas by negotiating land purchases from the Indians.[46]

There could, however, be no lasting settlement of American land without the establishment and acceptance of some form of civil authority. On landing on the coast of Mexico in June 1519, Cortés's first action was to found the town of Vera

Cruz. His purpose in doing this was to establish a civil authority, which would both legitimize his past and future actions, and lay the foundations for permanent Spanish settlement in Montezuma's realms. 'The new alcaldes [mayors] and officers', writes Gómara, 'accepted their wands of authority and took possession of their offices, and at once met in council, as is customary in the villages and towns of Castile.'[47] A similar process was at work when the *Mayflower* dropped anchor off Provincetown in November 1620. In this instance the Pilgrims before going ashore agreed to 'covenant and combine ourselves together into a civil body politic, for our better ordering and preservation'.[48] They went on to elect John Carver as their Governor, just as the town council of Vera Cruz went on to elect Cortés as Captain and Justicia Mayor.

Spaniards and Englishmen therefore regarded the reconstitution of European civil society in an alien environment as the essential preliminary to their permanent occupation of the land. As participants in the same western tradition, both these colonizing peoples took it for granted that the patriarchal family, ownership of property, and a social ordering that as nearly as possible patterned the divine were the essential elements of any properly constituted civil society. But both were to find that American conditions were not always conducive to their re-creation on the farther shores of the Atlantic in the forms to which they were accustomed. The dissolving effects of space, at work from the outset, gave rise to responses which would eventually produce societies that, although still recognizably European, appeared sufficiently different to justify their being described as 'American'.

These responses were determined by a combination of metropolitan tradition and local circumstance, and would vary by region as well as by nationality. The New England response, for example, was to differ in important ways from that of Virginia. But in so far as the differences between New England and Virginia were conditioned by local topography, these paled into insignificance when set against the enormous geographical and climatic differences between the areas of Spanish and British colonization on the American mainland. The Spaniards were faced with jungles, mountain ranges and deserts which made William Bradford's 'hideous and desolate wilderness' of New England[49] look like a garden of Eden by comparison.

The Spaniards, too, lacked great rivers like the Mississippi, the Missouri, the Ohio and the St Lawrence to take settlers deep into the interior. Yet in spite of the apparently overwhelming geographical disadvantages they encountered, the Spaniards had fanned out through the continent within a generation of the capture of Tenochtitlán. The English, on the other hand, although faced with a more benevolent geography, had a preference for clustering close to the Atlantic seaboard until the eighteenth century; only in the Hudson and Connecticut River valleys, and in parts of the Chesapeake region, did settlement of the interior begin from the outset.[50] It is a striking commentary on English predilections that, for the first twenty years of its existence, the inhabitants of Dedham in Massachusetts, with immense spaces around them, continued to parcel out tiny house lots, and disposed in all of less than 3,000 acres of land.[51] It seems ironical that New England colonists who saw themselves as charged with an 'errand into the wilderness' should so resolutely have turned their backs upon it.

The determination of the Spaniards to range far and wide through American space, in spite of the vast distances and terrible hardships involved, can be attributed partly to their ambitions and expectations, and partly to long-established Iberian traditions. Unlike the English, they soon became aware that just over the horizon were to be found large polities and densely settled lands. There was early evidence, too, of the existence of deposits of gold and silver, for which the settlers of Jamestown were to hunt in vain. Hunger for riches and lordship and a restless ambition for fame lured conquistadores like Hernando de Soto, in his epic journey through the American South between 1539 and 1542, deep into the interior in ways that few Englishmen after Sir Walter Raleigh were willing to emulate. 'Why', asked Captain John Smith, 'should English men despair and not do so much as any? . . . Seeing honour is our lives ambition, and our ambition after death, to have an honourable memory of our life . . .'[52] But appeals to honour seem to have fallen on deaf ears among English settlers who saw all around them apparently vacant land awaiting occupation. In particular, New Englanders, according to William Wood writing in 1634, were 'well contented and look not so much at abundance as at competency'.[53] 'Competency' as an ideal left little room for glory.

'Competency' – the willingness to settle for a life-style that brought sufficiency rather than riches – was an aspiration that was not confined to English, or some English, colonists. Letters exchanged between sixteenth-century Spanish settlers in the Indies and their relatives back home suggest that the relatively modest ambition of *pasar mejor* – becoming better off – was seen by Spaniards as a good enough reason for risking the hazards of a transatlantic crossing, just as it was by their English equivalents. 'This is a good land for those who want to be virtuous, hard-working and well-respected', wrote a settler in Mexico in 1586 about the prospects that awaited a young man thinking of emigrating from Spain.[54] But the presence in Spanish-occupied lands of precious metals and a docile labour force served to perpetuate in the Hispanic world conceptions of wealth in terms of booty and lordship that were instinctive to those nurtured in the traditions created by the prolonged medieval movement of the Reconquista against Islamic Spain.[55] For new arrivals in the Spanish Indies, the ever-present possibility of a sudden bonanza served as a continuing inducement to move on.

The corollary of this was that Spanish settlers, or at least first-generation Spanish settlers, would set much less value on land as a desirable commodity in itself than the settlers of seventeenth-century English America. It was vassals, rather than land, that they wanted, and it would have been neither desirable nor practicable to clear of their indigenous inhabitants such densely settled lands as those of central Mexico.[56] Those Spaniards who commanded the services of tribute-paying Indians could look forward to enjoying a seigneurial income and life-style without the trouble of developing large estates, for which in any event there were few market outlets until the immigrant population became large enough to generate new wants. Consequently, the subjugation of those regions most densely settled by the indigenous population was the immediate priority for the conquistadores and first settlers from Spain, since these were the regions that offered the best hope of lordship over vassals, and hence the easy route to riches.

The Spanish settlement of America was therefore based on the domination of peoples, and this involved taking possession of vast areas of territory. In the nature of things, such areas could only be thinly settled by the colonists, and it was natural that, if only for purposes of self-protection, they should band together in towns. But the early predisposition of Spanish colonial society in the Indies to assume an urban form can also be traced back to established practice and collective attitudes. When Ferdinand and Isabella despatched Nicolás de Ovando to Hispaniola in 1501 to restore order to a colony that had descended into anarchy, they instructed him to establish cities at appropriate locations on the island.[57] This would help to provide rootless colonists with a fixed point and focus. A policy of urbanization in the Indies was consonant, too, with the practices developed during the Reconquista in medieval Spain, where the southward movement of the Castilians was based on cities and towns which were granted jurisdiction by the crown over large areas of hinterland.

Spaniards in any event shared the Mediterranean predisposition towards urban life, and it was not by accident that Cortés's compact for civil government when landing in Mexico, unlike the civil compact of the *Mayflower* Pilgrims, assumed from the outset an urban form. The ideal of the city as a perfect community was deeply rooted in the Hispanic tradition, and for human beings to live far away from society was regarded as contrary to nature. Following the Roman tradition, too, cities were seen as visible evidence of *imperium*, and memories of the Roman Empire were never far away from the minds of Spanish captains and bureaucrats.

In the Antilles, to their amazement, the Spaniards encountered for the first time peoples who did not live in cities,[58] but as soon as they reached mainland America they found themselves on more familiar ground. Here once more was an urban world with some resemblances to their own. The great pre-Columbian cities – Tlaxcala, Tenochtitlán, Cuzco – reminded them initially of Spanish and European cities, like Venice or Granada, and provided further evidence that they were now in a world that boasted a higher level of civilization than that of the Antilles. Cortés wrote of Tenochtitlán: 'The city is as big as Seville or Córdoba . . . There is also one square twice as big as that of Salamanca.'[59] No English settler on the thinly settled North American seaboard would have been able to draw such parallels between Indian centres of population and Norwich or Bristol. No doubt on closer inspection the resemblances between the European city and these Indian cities or ceremonial complexes of Mesoamerica and the Andes proved to be not quite as great as the conquistadores assumed in the first flush of enthusiasm. But the very existence of large Indian population centres on the American mainland confirmed Spanish preconceptions about the relationship between cities and civilized living, and offered an additional inducement to the construction in Spain's new American possessions of an essentially urban civilization.[60]

The town, indeed, was to become the basis for Spanish dominion in America. Occasionally it might be a pre-Columbian town, remodelled to conform to Spanish styles of living, as happened with Cuzco or with the Mexico City that arose from the ruins of Tenochtitlán. Usually it was a new foundation. But either way it offered the Indians clear evidence of the determination of the conquerors to put down roots and stay, just as it also offered clear evidence to the conquerors themselves that the crown wanted them to abandon their restless ways and establish a stable society, in accordance with metropolitan norms. It is enough to look at the ordinances for the 'good government' of New Spain, issued by Hernán Cortés in 1524, to see how the earlier experience of anarchy in the Antilles had etched itself into the consciousness of those responsible for the establishment and preservation of Spanish dominion in the Indies. The ordinances insist that the conversion of the Indians made it essential that the Spaniards should stay put, and not 'every day be thinking of leaving, or returning to Spain, which would destroy these lands and their inhabitants, as experience in the islands settled up to now has shown'. To achieve this, all those who possessed Indians were to promise to stay put for the next eight years; the married men among them were to bring their wives over from Castile within a year and a half, while the remainder were to marry their mistresses within the same period; and Indian-holding inhabitants of all the cities and towns of New Spain were to establish households in the towns to which they belonged.[61]

The town was therefore to provide the setting for the stable family life without which effective long-term colonization was regarded as impossible. It was also to act as the essential agency for the distribution, settlement and control of the land. Cortés himself, on first arriving in Hispaniola from his native Extremadura, was told by Governor Ovando's secretary that he should 'register as a citizen, by which he would acquire a caballería, that is, a building lot and certain lands for cultivation'.[62] This was standard practice – the allocation of a building lot, along with an additional grant of land, with free possession,[63] on the outskirts of the town. Following the system established by Ovando in Hispaniola in 1503, which itself drew on practices developed in metropolitan Spain during the Reconquista, the leading citizens of the towns of mainland America were also assigned Indians in *repartimiento* or *encomienda*.

Over large parts of Spanish America the encomienda became the chosen instrument for satisfying the demand of the conquerors for a share of the spoils, in the form of Indian tribute and services, and at the same time for discouraging them from laying waste the land and moving on in search of more plunder. In arranging for the *depósito* or *repartimiento* of Indians among his restless followers, Cortés took the first steps in mainland America towards the establishment of what was to become the fully fledged encomienda system.[64] He assigned encomiendas to 300 of his men – about 40 per cent of the survivors of the army that captured Tenochtitlán, and about 6 per cent of the total European population of the Indies at that time.[65] Pizarro followed suit in 1532 when he made the first *depósitos* of Peruvian Indians among his companions in San Miguel de

Piura, before leaving for his encounter with Atahualpa in Cajamarca. The accompanying documents, which made it clear that these grants of Indians constituted rewards for services, specified what were to be the essential characteristics of the encomienda in its initial stages – the obligation of the Indians to perform labour services for those who held them in deposit, and the obligation of the depositories to instruct their Indians in the Christian faith, and to treat them well.[66]

The crown subsequently ratified the grants made by Pizarro, as it had previously ratified those made by Cortés, and by the 1540s there were some 600 *encomenderos* in the viceroyalty of New Spain, and 500 in Peru.[67] This suggests that a New World feudal aristocracy was already in the making, but the encomienda would evolve in ways which were to disappoint the high hopes of the conquistadores. Deeply concerned by the maltreatment and brutal exploitation of their Indians by many of the encomenderos, and then by the horrifying decline in the size of the Indian population, the crown sought, with varying degrees of success, to transform the heavy labour services of encomienda Indians into the payment of tribute. In its determination to prevent the rise of a European-style aristocracy, the crown also struggled to prevent the automatic perpetuation of encomiendas through family inheritance. Although rebellion by the settlers in Peru and widespread opposition in New Spain forced it to revoke the notorious clause in the New Laws of 1542 by which all encomiendas were to revert to the crown on the death of the current holder, the transmission of the encomienda from one generation to another was never to become automatic. The crown remained the master.[68]

Above all, the encomienda remained what it had always been – a grant of Indians, not of land. When land was abandoned by the Indians, it reverted to the crown, and not to the encomendero to whom the Indians had been assigned.[69] But although in principle the encomienda had nothing to do with land-ownership, encomenderos and their families were well positioned to take advantage of expanding opportunities as colonial societies developed and the urban population increased. Obliged by law to live in towns and cities, and not in the areas where they held their encomiendas, the encomenderos were precluded from becoming a European territorial aristocracy living on their estates.

In spite of these constraints, their privileged status, their social influence, and the income provided by their encomiendas would enable the shrewder among them to purchase large tracts of land which their heirs would one day develop for stock raising or cereal production to minister to the needs of rapidly expanding towns. In accordance with metropolitan usage, however, there remained strict limitations on land-ownership in Spain's American possessions. The possession of land was conditional on its occupation or use, although, in accordance with Castilian law, the subsoil remained the inalienable possession of the crown;[70] property-owners could set up boundary markers, but were not allowed to fence off their estates – in contrast to British America, where fences were visible symbols that land had been 'improved';[71] shepherds and others were allowed free passage across private estates; and woods and water remained in common ownership.[72]

The outcome of the process by which encomenderos and other privileged and wealthy settlers could acquire landed property would be the emergence of what was to be the classic Spanish American model of a colonial society built on the twin foundations of the city and the rural estate, the *estancia* or *hacienda*, which varied considerably in size and function according to local circumstances. In some areas, like the Oaxaca region of Mexico, there were medium or small-sized rural holdings, although the development of the *mayorazgo* or entail system, transmitting property as an inalienable inheritance to a single heir, gave an impulse to the long-term concentration of smaller holdings into large estates.[73] But the city remained central to the enterprise, with 246, or nearly half, of the encomenderos of New Spain registered as householders, or *vecinos,* of the new Mexico City. The remainder became householders in newly created towns which sprang up in the wake of the conquest.[74] In response to the legal requirement that encomenderos and others should also be *vecinos,* there was a rush to found and build such new towns in the first post-conquest decades in New Spain and Peru. By 1580 there were some 225 towns and cities in the Spanish Indies, with a total Hispanic population of perhaps 150,000, at a low estimate of six to a household.[75] By 1630 the number had increased to 331,[76] and many more were to be founded in the eighteenth century.

Already before Philip II's famous ordinances of 1573 on the situation and layout of New World towns,[77] these towns had acquired the distinctive features which were now belatedly decreed as the norm: a *plaza mayor*, bordered by a church and civic buildings, and a regular pattern of streets on the grid-iron plan, which Ovando had adopted when he rebuilt Santo Domingo after the cyclone of 1502. There were good European precedents for this grid-iron or chequer-board pattern, not least among them the camp city of Santa Fe, from which Ferdinand and Isabella besieged the Moorish stronghold of Granada. Rectilinear town planning had the sanction, too, of the Roman architectural writer Vitruvius and had been made fashionable by Renaissance architectural theory.[78] But the fundamental simplicity of the grid-iron plan, and ease of layout and construction, made it eminently transferable to a Hispanic colonial society that was in a hurry to re-establish the convivial familiarities of the urban existence it had left behind in Spain.

The rectilinear cities of Spanish colonial America, with their monumental civic and religious buildings and spacious streets, extended outwards into indefinite space. With no city walls to block the vistas (other than in coastal cities threatened by foreigners, or in dangerous frontier regions),[79] they proclaimed the reality of Spanish domination over an alien world. They also had the desired effect of anchoring a potentially restless settler population, and giving a much-needed stability to the new colonial society in process of formation.

By the early seventeenth century the English were well aware of the urban pattern of Spanish settlement in the Indies, and perhaps, too, of the Spanish

American model of urban design. In 1605 George Waymouth produced a set of plans, both rectilinear and radial, for a colonial town in North America, although these fanciful designs seem to have owed more to Renaissance theory than to Spanish practice.[80] In 1622, however, the Virginia Company, desperate to save the struggling English colony after the recent Indian onslaught, made a direct reference to the Spanish system of colonization by means of cities in a letter of instructions to the Governor and Council of Virginia. Insisting on the importance of the colonists staying together in order to defend themselves against Indian attacks, the letter continued: '. . . In which regard, as also for their better civil government (which mutual society doth most conduce unto) we think it fit, that the houses and building be so contrived together, as may make if not handsome towns, yet compact and orderly villages; that this is the most proper, and successful manner of proceedings in new plantations, besides those of former ages, the example of the Spaniards in the West Indies doth fully instance . . .'[81]

But the settlers of Virginia proved recalcitrant. It had long since become clear that the local Indian population would produce neither the tribute nor the labour force that could form the basis of a Spanish-style encomienda system, although the Virginia Company initially seems to have envisaged something very similar when it gave instructions in 1609 that tribute should be collected from every tribal chieftain in the form of local commodities, like maize and animal skins, and that a specified number of Indians should perform weekly labour services for the colonists.[82] The Indians, it transpired, were not prepared to co-operate. There remained the land, and once the rich potential of tobacco planting became apparent, the attractions of land occupation and ownership proved irresistible. The Indians remained a threat, and in the wake of their attack in 1622 the settlers embarked on overt anti-Indian policies, forcing them off their land in the lower peninsula. By 1633 a six-mile long pale had been constructed, leaving 300,000 acres cleared of Indian occupation.[83] More forts and blockhouses were built after another Indian attack in 1644, and the frontiers of settlement were pushed inexorably forward into Indian territory. As the Indian threat diminished, so too did the need for the settlers to live together in communities on the Jamestown model. As a result, the colonial society established in Virginia was to be characterized by that very dispersal of the settlers which the council of the Virginia Company had sought to prevent in 1622.

With large river-front plantations spreading west and north along the waterways, the Virginian response to space differed not only from that of the colonists of Spanish America but also from that of the New Englanders who were simultaneously establishing their colonies to the north.[84] There were almost no towns in Virginia and the Chesapeake margins, as London officials observed with annoyance and visitors with surprise.[85] The society of colonial Virginia was to be one of isolated farms and of great estates – but great estates that differed from the haciendas of Spanish America in having resident owners. Where the landowning oligarchy of New Spain and Peru lived in the cities, that of Virginia lived on its estates; and when its members met each other on public occasions, they did so not in towns, but in court houses and churches which stood dispersed through the rural landscape, located at points where residents of the county could enjoy equal access to their facilities.[86]

For a rather more urban landscape it was necessary to look to the more northerly English settlements, where a different pattern of colonization developed during the course of the seventeenth century. Whereas communal living was in effect abandoned in Virginia after the collapse of the Jamestown experiment, the more controlled settlement patterns of Massachusetts led to the development of a landscape of contiguous settlements consisting of small towns and those 'compact and orderly villages' for which the Virginia Company had pleaded in vain.[87] By 1700 there were between 120 and 140 towns in New England,[88] although their character and appearance bore little relation to those of the towns in Spanish America. Essentially the New England township consisted of tracts of land granted to a particular group, with a village sited near the centre. The village church formed a place of assembly, and each village would have its commons. As in Spanish towns, families were allocated a house lot, along with parcels of land for cultivation outside the residential centre. The allocation of land was conditional, as in Spanish America, on its being 'improved' and put to use.[89]

By the end of the seventeenth century, however, British America had also succeeded in generating, along with innumerable villages and townships, several cities along the Atlantic seaboard: in particular Boston, Newport, Philadelphia and Charles Town, along with New York, the city founded by the Dutch as New Amsterdam.[90] Outside New England, where towns tended to follow the local topography, the new cities, too, were often built with a regularity reminiscent of that of Spanish colonial cities, even if the inspiration seems to have come from Renaissance ideals of town planning. The streets of Charles Town (later Charleston), in the new settlement of Carolina, were planned around 1672 to conform to the ideals of regularity and symmetry that inspired Christopher Wren's plans for rebuilding London after the Great Fire of 1666.[91] 'Be sure', ordered William Penn a decade later in founding Philadelphia, 'to settle the figure of the town, so as that the streets hereafter may be uniform down to the water from the country bounds . . . Let the houses built be in a line (fig. 9).'[92] In accordance with his wishes, Philadelphia was laid out on the grid-iron plan, to create what Josiah Quincy would describe in 1773 as 'the most regular, best laid out city in the world'.[93] The geometric regularity of Philadelphia, the largest city yet built by British settlers, proved highly influential, and by the end of the seventeenth century, the grid-iron had become, other than in New England, the predominant form of urban design in British, as in Spanish, America.[94]

Yet in spite of the growth of its towns, British America remained in comparison with Spanish America an overwhelmingly rural society. For all the problems of public order in Hispanic American cities, the urban character of Spanish colonial society provided a continuing element of social control, inhibiting the dispersal of the colonial population through the countryside. British America was eventually to prove a far more geographically mobile society, characterized by a steady westward migration towards the agricultural frontier as the threat of Indian attack diminished.[95] This was true even of New England, where strenuous, and partially successful, efforts were made to achieve a controlled dispersal as new immigrants began to arrive. Where Virginia, in order to meet the colony's chronic need of settlers, had to tilt its land distribution heavily in favour of individual interests through its headright system of land grants for each individual brought into the colony, the so-called 'Great Migration' of the 1630s, with its continuing influx of new arrivals, gave the leaders of New England's colonization sufficient leeway to frame policies which would balance more nearly the aspirations of the individual and the needs of the community.[96] Moreover, where the first immigrants to the Chesapeake region were primarily young single males, at least 60 per cent of travellers to New England were accompanied by family members.[97] The preponderance of families in the immigration to New England, together with a much better generational and gender balance than was to be found among the Chesapeake immigrants, gave the new colony the cohesiveness and potential for stability that would continue to elude Virginia until the final years of the century.

The New England immigrants, too, knew that they were coming to a Puritan commonwealth. It is true that, even in Plymouth Colony, there were from the beginning so-called 'strangers' or 'particulars' alongside the Pilgrims, whose presence proved a source of continuing dissension and strain.[98] But there was a sufficient degree of consensus among the majority of the immigrants to allow the leadership to embark on their great experiment of building a godly community. 'We all came into these parts of America with one and the same end and aim,' began the preamble to the New England Articles of Confederation of 1643, 'namely, to advance the kingdom of our Lord Jesus Christ, and to enjoy the liberties of the gospel in purity with peace.'[99]

Yet the failure of the simultaneous Puritan experiment on Providence Island, off the Nicaraguan coast, shows that, even among 'visible saints', godly discipline was not of itself sufficient to ensure the development of a viable colony.[100] In an effort to secure adequate returns for its shareholders, the Providence Island Company insisted on exercising centralized control from England, including control of land distribution. Lacking security of tenure, and as mere tenants at halves, with half the profits of their labour going to the investors, the Providence Island colonists lacked the inducement to experiment and innovate. Inexperienced in growing tropical products, they persisted with the planting of tobacco, although it proved to be of poor quality. They also seem to have given up too soon on their various attempts at new forms of specialization, which would be the salvation of another island colony, Barbados, as it moved away in the 1640s from tobacco to the production of new crops, and especially sugar.[101] When a Spanish invading force wiped out the Providence Island colony in 1641, they destroyed a failed settlement.

One of the reasons why the Massachusetts Bay colonists escaped the fate of Providence Island was that they took their charter with them, thus establishing from the beginning local control over the regulation of their lives and the distribution of the land. In Massachusetts, as in Virginia, untrammelled private ownership of land was to be crucial to success, in spite of the attempts of contemporary Puritan publicists to suggest that the motivations behind the establishment of the two colonies were fundamentally different. 'This plantation [of Massachusetts]', wrote Emmanuel Downing to Sir John Coke, 'and that of Virginia went not forth upon the same reasons nor for the same end. Those of Virginia went forth for profit . . . Those [of Massachusetts] went upon two other designs, some to satisfy their own curiosity in point of conscience, others to transport the Gospel to those heathen that never heard thereof.'[102]

This distinction, which was to become canonical, between profit-motivated Virginians and pious New Englanders obscures the awkward truth that the profit motive was strongly present in New England from the outset and exercised a powerful influence over the founding of new towns.[103] While the Puritan leadership remained committed to the preservation of a communal spirit, even at the expense of expansion into the wilderness, New England towns were created and controlled by land corporations whose membership was not coterminous with the municipal, let alone the religious, community. To participate, it was necessary to be not simply a resident but an 'inhabitant' – a shareholder or town proprietor, the equivalent of the Spanish American *vecino*.[104] These land corporations of 'inhabitants' were dominated by a handful of entrepreneurs and speculators, who saw the accumulation of land as a major source of profit and were responsible for launching many of the towns of seventeenth-century New England.[105]

Roger Williams, seeing his own colony of Rhode Island falling prey to the designs of Boston speculators, warned that the 'God land will be (as now it is) as great a God with us English as God gold was with the Spaniards.'[106] None the less, the tension between individual profit and collective ideals in the early stages of the colonization of New England proved creative. It endowed the northern colonies with a form of landscape and community distinct from that of other parts of British America. Its township pattern of land distribution inhibited the development in New England of a class of great landlords, like the tobacco planters of Virginia or the patroons of colonial New York, where settlement patterns had been established during the period of Dutch colonization.[107] In 1628, the Dutch West India Company had sought to revive its fortunes by mobilizing private capital and securing immigrants through an offer of generous land grants along the New Netherland coastline and up the Hudson river to entrepreneurs prepared to import European colonists who would farm the allocated land. Although the resulting patroonships failed to produce a significant increase in the colony's population, they offered a model for the future. Following the English seizure of the colony in 1664, the later seventeenth-century governors of what was now New York showed themselves at least as lavish as the Dutch in the generosity of their land grants. Although parts of the colony were to be settled by freehold farmers, other parts, and especially the Hudson Valley region, were characterized as a result by their distinctive manorial system, and a rural society of patrician landowners and their tenant farmers, very different from New England's rural society of independent farmers.

New England's continuing adherence to a set of common ideals gave it a stability and cohesion that another holy experiment towards the end of the seventeenth century – Pennsylvania – would have much greater difficulty in attaining. Starting later than New England and Virginia, Pennsylvania and the Middle Colonies as a whole would need time to develop the elements of cohesion provided in the north-east by the small town, and in the south by the plantation.[108] Penn himself hoped to establish an orderly pattern of development based on contiguous townships, but his hopes of creating a structured society with a sense of community comparable to that to be found in New England were subverted by the emergence of speculative landlords and by the dilution of the original Quaker ideals of the colony as new settlers arrived. Pennsylvania enjoyed the advantage over New England of possessing a rich alluvial soil, while settler occupation was greatly facilitated by the relative thinness of Indian settlement and the abundance of land. In the Middle Colonies much of this land, unlike that of New England, had already been worked by Indians in pre-Columbian times. The cleared land, with its fertile soil, would prove ideal for the development of a rural society of small freeholders, whose conduct and attitudes had been shaped by the European family farm. With family interests tending to take priority over communal ideals, the environment of the Middle Colonies proved highly favourable to the emergence of a competitive market economy, but considerably less favourable to the achievement of social cohesion and political stability.[109]

Stability was in fact slow to come to the Middle Colonies, where the continuous arrival of shiploads of new immigrants kept the region in a state of flux. By the eighteenth century, these immigrants were coming no longer solely from England, but also from Scotland, Ireland and continental Europe, thus creating a volatile mixture of ethnic groups. On arrival in Philadelphia or Baltimore they soon moved out again in search of land, adding to the pressures on the western agricultural frontier produced by the rapid natural growth of a colonial population considerably healthier than that of contemporary Europe. Observers lamented their failure to settle in towns. 'They acquire', complained a British official, 'no attachment to Place; but wandering about Seems engrafted in their Nature . . .'[110]

The refusal to acquire 'attachment to Place' was the nightmare of the official mind in British and Spanish America alike. In Spanish America the grant of Indians in encomienda, the predilection for urban living, and the weight of royal authority in backing up this predilection with legislation and enforcement, did something to tie the colonists to place, but it seemed to successive viceroys of New Spain and Peru that they were fighting a losing battle. Encomiendas were in the hands of a privileged few; new immigrants, even when willing to work, often found it difficult to obtain employment once the new colonial societies had established themselves; and from the middle years of the sixteenth century vagrants of Spanish origin – mostly unmarried young men or those who had left their wives behind in Spain – were joined by growing numbers of mestizos, blacks and mulattoes. The Spanish crown was especially concerned by the danger presented by these vagrants to the integrity of Indian villages and communities, and continued its attempts throughout the colonial period to curb their wanderings, although with very limited success.[111]

In British America, the constraints were weaker from the beginning, and the pressures even more intense. In the absence of a strong royal government to give shape and direction to settlement policies, the prime constraint on movement into the North American interior in the initial years of settlement was the existence of a sparsely settled but none the less ubiquitous Indian population. This set up barriers to expansion which were not only physical but also moral and psychological. In the early stages of colonization the immigrants to Virginia and New England envisaged themselves as settling among Indians with whom they looked forward to trading and other relations to mutual benefit. Nor indeed would the first English settlements have survived without Indian assistance and Indian supplies. But even where friendly relations were established with individual Indian tribes, undercurrents of fear and prejudice added a note of wariness to the relationship. Fears of Indian 'treachery' were never far from the surface, and tended to be reinforced by every incident of mutual misunderstanding. The English, too, were caught up in inter-tribal rivalries of which they had little or no knowledge or understanding, and which made it difficult for them to know whether or not they found themselves among friends. For the settlers of Virginia, the defining moment came with the 'massacre' of 1622; for those of New England with the murder in 1634 by the Pequots of two captains and their crew, and the chain of events which culminated in the brutal Pequot War of 1637.[112]

Yet for tiny settlements of immigrants, neither total isolation nor a permanent state of hostility was a viable option. The settlers needed at least a degree of co-operation from the Indians for the practicalities of everyday life, and, as the settlements grew, they needed Indian land. In the early stages of colonization, considerations of morality and expediency alike led the colonists to negotiate land purchases from the Indians, although, as the balance of numbers tilted in favour of the colonists, the tendency simply to encroach on Indian land became increasingly hard to resist. But it became clear in Virginia as well as in New England that some *modus vivendi* was needed if there were not to be an unending succession of raids and counter-raids arising over territorial disputes. In Virginia a peace treaty in 1646 and a comprehensive statute passed by the assembly in 1662 attempted to provide some safeguard for Indian rights to land;[113] in the New England colonies, statutory limits were placed on the rights of the settlers to purchase Indian land. For their part the Indians, their numbers much diminished by the epidemics of 1616–17 and 1633–4, were generally willing to sell as long as they could retain their right to hunt, fish and gather on the land they had surrendered.[114]

Although the Pequot War left the initiative in New England firmly in the hands of the settlers, and relations were reasonably amicable with the Indian tribes in the three decades preceding the outbreak of King Philip's War in 1675, there were psychological as well as legal and moral barriers to unrestricted movement inland. On the edges of the clusters of villages lay the 'wilderness' – a fraught and emotive word in the New England vocabulary of the seventeenth century. 'What could they see', wrote William Bradford of the safe arrival of the Pilgrims at Cape Cod, 'but a hideous and desolate wilderness, full of wild beasts and wild men?'[115] A few years later John Winthrop, after a longer acquaintance with the land, was still writing in similar terms of the colonists coming together 'into a wilderness, where are nothing but wild beasts and beastlike men . . .'[116] The image of the wilderness, with its biblical connotations, possessed a strong hold over the minds of the settlers, and not only those of New England. Virginia's colonists, too, saw themselves as living in a 'Wildernesse' and surrounded by 'Heathen'.[117] But the image of the wilderness was ambiguous. On the one hand it implied danger and darkness – a land where Satan ruled. But on the other it implied a place of retreat and refuge, in which trials and tribulations would strengthen and refine the faithful as they struggled to tame and improve the wild land.[118]

There were tensions in the thought of the settlers between these competing interpretations of the wilderness – tensions that do not seem to have troubled the Spaniards, for whom biblical imagery was less all-pervasive. The Spanish equivalent of the concept of 'wilderness' would seem to have been either *despoblado*[119] – an isolated and 'uninhabited' area far from the heartlands of empire – or 'desert' (*desierto*). If the desert conjured up images of the early church fathers, to whom the early friars in the New World could reasonably be compared,[120] it was not a place for the ordinary run of mortals, who required a social existence to realize their full potential. The Puritans too were aware of the desocializing effects of the wilderness, and sought to legislate against it, as when Massachusetts passed a law in 1635 ordering that all houses should be built within half a mile of the meeting-house.[121] They sought, too, to ward off its dangers by constructing hedges, walls and fences, all of them frontiers of exclusion. The Spanish settlers, on the other hand, clustered in towns and thinly spread across a continent many of whose peoples they had subdued, sought rather to incorporate those peoples within a world the Spaniards had already claimed as their own. Frontiers would inevitably spring up – in northern Mexico or in Chile – where further Spanish incursion was blocked by powerful tribes, but even these frontiers were to prove highly permeable as the Spaniards sought to continue their advance by other means.[122]

Yet even as the English colonists built their palisades, they sought to push them back. The pressures to do so were in part psychological – the wilderness, for all its dangers, was there to be tamed. But they were also created by demographic facts. As the numbers of settlers grew, so too did their need for space. Against this, even the mechanisms of social control imposed by the Puritan leadership could not prevail indefinitely. The wilderness constituted no permanent barrier against the force of numbers.

Peopling the land

To establish a permanent presence in the New World, the Spaniards and the English were dependent, at least in the first stages of settlement, on a steady stream of immigrants. Mortality rates among the first arrivals were very high. A different climate and environment, different food – or sheer scarcity of food – hardship and deprivation, took a heavier toll than Indian arrows. 'All of us', wrote a Franciscan who arrived in Santo Domingo in 1500, 'became ill, some more, others less.'[123] During the first decade in Hispaniola two-thirds of the Spaniards may have died, while nearly half the Pilgrims perished of disease and exposure during their first New England winter.[124] Until the gender imbalance inherent in the first transatlantic migratory movements was corrected, there was no chance of the white population holding its ground, let alone increasing, without a continuous supply of immigrants from the mother country.

Over the centuries Castilians had been drawn to southern Spain, and the English to Ireland, in their search for land and opportunity. The existence of this migratory tradition suggests that neither people was likely to see the Atlantic as an insuperable barrier to further migration once transatlantic sailings became reasonably well established. But there would need to be good reason to embark on the hazardous ocean crossing, and this was likely to come from severe pressures at home, or the lure of richer rewards and a better life overseas, or some combination of the two.[125]

When Castile launched out on its conquest of the Indies, there was no overwhelming compulsion in terms of population pressure to expand overseas; but the system of land-ownership in some regions – notably Extremadura, which contained no more than 7 per cent of Spain's population but provided 17 per cent of its overseas migrants in the period up to 1580 – was sufficiently inequitable to encourage the more adventurous among the deprived and the disappointed to seek new opportunities elsewhere.[126] Reports of fabulous riches to be found in the Indies provided a strong incentive to these mostly young men to up stakes and go, although probably with the expectation of returning home once they had made their fortunes overseas. By placing themselves in the service of an influential local figure, and drawing on the extensive family networks which soon criss-crossed the Spanish Atlantic, these first migrants – and often involuntary colonists – succeeded in making the crossing, if not necessarily the fortunes which they believed to be awaiting them in the Indies.

Once the crown was committed to establishing a permanent Spanish presence in the Indies, it was naturally concerned to curb the migration of these footloose adventurers, and encourage the transatlantic movement of potentially more reliable elements in the population, who possessed the determination and the skills to help develop the natural resources of the land. It established an appropriate instrument for control in the *Casa de la Contratación* – the House of Trade set up in Seville in 1503, which was made responsible for the regulation of all emigration to the Indies – and nominated Seville as the sole point of departure for the Indies.

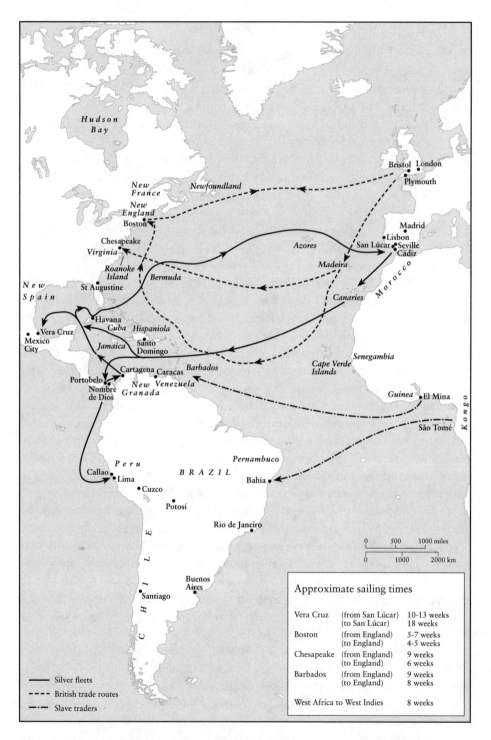

Map 2. The Early Modern Atlantic World.
Based on D. W. Meinig, *The Shaping of America*, vol. 1, *Atlantic America, 1492–1800*
(1986), fig. 8; *The Oxford History of the British Empire* (1998), vol. 1, map 1.1; and
Ian K. Steele, *The English Atlantic, 1675–1740* (1986), figs 2 and 3.

Would-be emigrants had to present the necessary documents relating to their background and place of birth to officials of the Casa in order to receive a royal licence for the transatlantic crossing. From the earliest years, therefore, this was a controlled emigration, and restrictions were added – or sometimes relaxed – in accordance with changing priorities and needs. The passage of foreigners, for instance, was legally prohibited, except for a short period between 1526 and 1538, but the definition of 'foreigner' was far from clear. Technically it even included the inhabitants of the Crown of Aragon, but in practice there seems to have been no impediment to their travelling to the Indies, although their numbers seem to have been small. This was overwhelmingly a migration from the Crown of Castile, with Andalusia providing a third of the emigrants.

While non-Spaniards were officially excluded from Spain's American possessions, individuals with a legitimate reason for going could apply for naturalization or secure a special licence.[127] Jews, Moors, gypsies and heretics were all forbidden entry to the Indies. In the earlier years of colonization it was possible to find ways around these prohibitions, but evasion became more difficult after 1552, when it was decreed that potential emigrants must furnish proof from their home towns and villages of their *limpieza de sangre*, demonstrating the absence of any taint of Jewish or Moorish blood.[128]

In comparison with the elaborate efforts made by the Spanish crown to control and regulate the process of overseas emigration, the efforts of the early Stuarts in the same direction were puny. In 1607 James I renewed the standing restrictions on travel to foreign ports without first securing a licence, and in 1630 Charles I invoked his father's proclamation to ensure that emigrants to New England would be registered at their port of departure. During the course of the 1630s – the decade of the Great Migration – the king and Archbishop Laud became increasingly preoccupied by 'such an universal running to New England' and elsewhere, at a time when settlers were needed for Ireland; but although the clerks at the port of London conscientiously recorded the names and details of emigrants, the Privy Council was unable in practice to control the movement of emigration.[129]

Even the Spanish crown, however, with far stricter regulatory procedures and with emigration to the Indies allowed only from a single port, achieved only a limited success. Documents could be falsified, ships' captains bribed, and there was a high rate of attrition among crew members and soldiers on the transatlantic fleets, who would jump ship on arriving at Vera Cruz, Portobelo or Cartagena de las Indias, and disappear into American space.[130] If the Spanish crown achieved only limited success in preventing clandestine emigration, its efforts in the early stages of colonization to promote the kind of emigration of which it approved were an almost total failure. In 1512, for instance, a royal councillor proposed that poor families should be shipped across the Atlantic at the state's expense. Yet assisted emigration for peasant and artisan families seems to have been of limited effect, and the crown was unwilling to approve the system of free transport in return for a period of enforced labour service on arrival in the Indies which was to have such a future in the Anglo-American world. This would have led to a form of white servitude quite unacceptable in a world so heavily populated by 'free' Indians.[131] As far as official efforts to redress the balance of the sexes were concerned, the constant repetition of royal orders that wives should join their husbands in the Indies suggests that they were widely flouted, and in 1575 Philip II had to suspend preferential measures to facilitate the emigration of unmarried females because of complaints from Peru that the arrival of so many dissolute women from Spain was endangering family stability and public morality.[132]

For all the efforts of the Spanish crown to control and direct the movement of people to the Indies, it remained – as subsequent British migratory movements would remain – firmly subject to the laws of supply and demand. As the population of Castile grew over the course of the sixteenth century – possibly from under 4 million to 6.5 million[133] – the pressures to move became more intense, but much of the movement was internal, into the towns and cities. The restriction of the port of departure to Seville must itself have acted as a deterrent for those who lived far away, especially if they were travelling with their families; and to move on from Seville to the Indies entailed extra commitment and heavy additional expense. The transatlantic crossing, including the cost of provisions for the journey, was not cheap. The 20 or more ducats required by the 1580s for the passage of a single adult, with a further 10–20 for provisions, would suggest that emigrants dependent on their wages would either have to sell up before setting sail, or would need to rely on remittances from relatives who had preceded them to the Indies. In order to meet their costs, many would sign up as the servants of more affluent passengers, or would seek to travel as part of the entourage of a new viceroy or an important royal or clerical official.[134]

The total number of emigrants from Spain to the Indies over the length of the sixteenth century is generally put at 200,000–250,000, or an average of 2,000–2,500 a year.[135] The majority of these gravitated to the two viceroyalties – 36 per cent to Peru and 33 per cent to New Spain – while New Granada received 9 per cent, central America 8 per cent, Cuba 5 per cent and Chile 4 per cent.[136] There was, inevitably, a heavy preponderance of men in the initial stages of emigration, but by the middle years of the century, as conditions in the Indies began to be stabilized, the proportion of women emigrants started to rise, and there was an increase in the emigration of families, often going to join a husband or father who had successfully established himself in America. During the seventeenth century, indeed, just over 60 per cent of Andalusian emigrants went in family units,[137] and family and clientage networks played a crucial part in Spain's settlement of the Indies. But even in the 1560s and 1570s, when the sixteenth-century emigration flow was at its highest, women never reached as many as a third of the total of all registered emigrants.[138]

Although many letters survive from sixteenth-century settlers in Spanish America begging relatives back home to join them,[139] the greatest deterrent to a more massive migratory movement from the Iberian peninsula to the Indies was probably to be found neither in the cost of the journey, nor in the Sevillian monopoly of sailings and the complexity of bureaucratic procedures, but in the relatively limited opportunities once the first stage of colonization had passed. Because of the presence, especially in the viceroyalties of New Spain and Peru, of a large Indian labour force, reinforced where necessary by the importation of slaves from Africa, there was no extensive labour market in the Spanish Indies to provide immigrants with work. Artisans who arrived from Spain would find themselves in competition with Indian craftsmen who had been quick to master European skills, and the unsuccessful would join the ranks of that floating population of vagrants, of which the viceroys were always complaining.[140] There was a significant return movement from America to Spain – perhaps of the order of 10–20 per cent[141] – and while many of those returning were ecclesiastics and officials who had completed their overseas assignment, or settlers paying short-term visits to their homeland for business or family reasons, some at least must have been emigrants whose high hopes of a new life in the Indies had been dashed.

In North America, by contrast, with its more sparsely settled indigenous population, labour prospects for immigrants were far better. England, too, was believed by contemporaries to be suffering from overpopulation. Its total area of 50,333 square miles supported a population of some 4 million in 1600,[142] whereas the population of the Crown of Castile (147,656 square miles) fell from some 6.5 million in the middle decades of the sixteenth century to 6 million at its end as a result of devastating harvest failure and plague in the 1590s.[143] The pressures in England for overseas migration were correspondingly stronger. But the West Indies or the North American mainland were not the only possible destinations for English emigrants. The principal deterrent to New World emigration in the early seventeenth century was not the absence of opportunity but the much easier option of migration to Ireland, which received some two hundred thousand immigrants from England, Wales and Scotland during the first seventy years of the century.[144] If the new transatlantic settlements were to be peopled, therefore, it would be necessary to offer substantial inducements to potential emigrants to make the more expensive and hazardous crossing to America, and to resort to recruitment devices which were hardly needed in Spanish America, with its rich supply of indigenous labour. Projectors and proprietors went to great lengths to promote settlement in their colonies by emphasizing their attractiveness in promotional literature – a genre which did not exist in Spain, where a work like Sir William Alexander's *An Encouragement to Colonies* (1624) would have had little point or purpose.

Promotional tracts like *New England's Plantation* (1630) made much of the opportunities of a land that was represented to the English public as largely empty, and ripe for improvement: 'Here wants as yet the good company of honest Christians to bring with them horses, kine and sheep to make use of this fruitful land: great pity it is to see so much good ground for corn and for grass as any is under the heavens, to lie altogether unoccupied, when so many honest men and their families in old *England* through the populousness thereof, do make very hard shift to live one by the other . . . The Indians are not able to make use of the one fourth part of the land, neither have they any settled places, as towns to dwell in, nor any ground as they challenge for their own possession, but change their habitation from place to place.' Here, then, was space in abundance, together with no more than a thin population of Indians 'who generally profess to like well of our coming and planting here . . .'[145] – a benign picture comparable to that found in the early promotional literature for Virginia, where the image of the Indian was suitably adjusted to refute popular notions of his bestiality.[146]

Mere promotion, however, was unlikely to do much more than bring the possibilities of emigration to America to the attention of people who might not otherwise have considered them; and in any event letters from settlers, comparable to those sent home from Spanish America, and encouraging friends and relatives to join them on the other side of the ocean, are likely to have proved more influential than impersonal publicity. 'Here', wrote the minister Thomas Welde in 1632 to his former parishioners in Tarling, 'I find three great blessings, peace, plenty, and health in a comfortable measure . . .'[147] The message was attractive, and when it could be presented as promoting God's work and God's design, it could be counted upon to receive a particularly attentive and sympathetic hearing from the more godly members of the community.

Religion, which in the Spanish movement to the New World was channelled into the evangelizing activities of members of the religious orders anxious to win new converts for the faith, exercised a broader influence over English transatlantic emigration. It played its part in the settlement of Virginia – which received a significant influx of Puritans[148] – and of Maryland, originally founded to provide a place of refuge for Catholics. But although the prospect of building John Winthrop's 'city upon a hill' was one impelling element in the Great Migration to America in the 1630s, it hardly represents the exclusive and overwhelming force that subsequent generations claimed it to be as they rewrote the history of New England to shape it to their own preconceptions and agenda.[149] Only 21,000 of the 69,000 Britons who crossed the Atlantic in the Great Migration went to New England.[150] Of these some 20–25 per cent were servants, who may or may not have had Puritan inclinations, and there were enough profane and ungodly settlers to prove a source of constant anxiety to the New England ministers.

Among British, as among Spanish, emigrants the motives for emigration were naturally mixed, and the cost of the journey – described in 1630 as 'wondrous dear'[151] – was a deterrent in the British Isles, just as it was in Spain. The basic cost of the eight- to twelve-week transatlantic passage was about the same in the two countries in the early seventeenth century – £5 or 20 ducats (at an exchange rate of 4 ducats to the pound) – and to this had to be added the cost of provisions and of commodities which would be needed on arrival in America. In order to make the crossing, therefore, the majority of emigrants from the British Isles, as from Spain, would either have to sell up their property, or secure some form of assisted passage. But since the need for settlers was greater in British than in Spanish America, more intensive and systematic efforts had to be made to find ways of financing the passage of those emigrants from the British Isles who could not pay for themselves.

Accordingly, from 1618 Virginia developed its headright system, under which a hundred acres of land was offered to each settler, and a further hundred for every person he brought with him.[152] But throughout the Anglo-American world indentured service became the most effective and pervasive instrument for the encouragement of transatlantic emigration.[153] Terms of service varied, but most servants emigrating to the Caribbean and the Chesapeake signed up for four to five years,[154] and legal and institutional constraints were much more binding than the kind of arrangements generally negotiated by Spanish emigrants who secured a free passage by entering the service of some travelling dignitary, and who could usually expect to gain their independence through voluntary agreement within a relatively short time after arrival in the Indies.[155] In British America conditions of service varied widely, according to time and place, and some servants were able, as in Maryland, to make use of their legal rights as contracted labourers to secure redress in the county courts from tyrannical masters.[156] But for many others indentured service was the equivalent of slavery.

Until plantation-owners in the West Indies and the Chesapeake found an alternative, and – as they hoped – more submissive, source of labour in the importation of African slaves, unfree white labour was vital for the peopling and exploitation of British America. Indentured servants constituted 75–85 per cent of the settlers who emigrated to the Chesapeake in the seventeenth century, and perhaps 60 per cent of the emigrants to all British colonies in America during the course of the century came with some form of labour contract.[157] Of the indentured servants, 23.3 per cent were women.[158]

These figures make it clear that in the British world, as in the Spanish, there was a massive superiority of men to women in the first century of colonization, the exception being the emigrants to New England, 40 per cent of whom between 1620 and 1649 were women.[159] The much more favourable sex ratio of women to men in New England than in the other colonies created a white population that by 1650 was nearly able to sustain itself by reproduction alone, whereas the white population of the Chesapeake could only be sustained by a constant supply of new immigrants. With male immigrants to the region outnumbering female by six to one in the 1630s and still by as many as three to one in the 1650s, large numbers of men remained unmarried.[160]

Mortality rates, too, in the tidewater region were appallingly high, with possibly as many as 40 per cent of the new arrivals dying within two years, many of them of the malaria that was endemic in the swampy, low-lying land.[161] The effect of this was to be seen in brief marriages, small families, and children often deprived of one or both of their parents at an early age. At an annual death rate of around 10 per cent, perhaps 40 per cent of all indentured servants arriving in the middle decades of the seventeenth century died before they could complete their term of service. Those who survived to become freedmen married late, or did not marry at all, and tended to become bachelor inmates in the households of others. The combined effect of such high mortality rates in Virginia and Maryland and of the prevailing sexual imbalance was to create volatile societies in which patterns of behaviour were subjected to the disproportionate influence of newly arrived immigrants. It was only in the last years of the century that the population born in the Chesapeake colonies finally outnumbered the new arrivals.[162]

As New England, with the benefit of its healthy climate and an early age for marriage, succeeded in the second half of the seventeenth century in meeting its labour needs largely from natural growth, its supply of immigrants tapered off, with new arrivals choosing the West Indies or the Middle Colonies in preference. Yet the overall level of emigration to the New World remained high. During the first century of the British colonization of America, some 530,000 men and women crossed the Atlantic – between twice and four times the number of Spanish emigrants during the equivalent period a century earlier. But there was more need of their labour in the territories claimed by the British crown, and more readily available land to be 'improved'.

The different rates of migration are at least crudely reflected in the comparative figures for the size of the settler populations of the Caribbean and mainland America. By 1570, three-quarters of a century after the first voyages of discovery, the white population of Spanish America is thought to have been of the order of 150,000. By 1700, some eighty years after the settlement of Jamestown, British America had a white population of some 250,000.[163] It was a population that, if it lived on the mainland, still hugged the Atlantic seaboard, but was increasingly beginning to look westward in the search for more space. This meant, necessarily, more Indian land. By contrast, strung out across the central and southern hemisphere, an urbanized Spanish population of immigrants and their American-born children and grandchildren suffered few of the same spatial constraints. They looked out from the window grills of their town houses over landscapes that had been rapidly emptying themselves of their Indian inhabitants. For their confrontation with American space was also a massive confrontation with its indigenous population – a confrontation that brought demographic catastrophe on an almost unimaginable scale.

Reconnoiter- make a military observation of a region

CHAPTER 3

Confronting American Peoples

A mosaic of peoples

If the America encountered by the Spaniards and the English consisted of a multi-plicity of micro-worlds, each with its own geographical and climatic characteris-tics, the same was no less true of the peoples that inhabited it. Something of this diversity became apparent to Columbus as he reconnoitred the Caribbean islands, although in his effort to make this strange new world comprehensible to himself and his fellow Europeans, he ignored or failed to detect many of the social, polit-ical and linguistic differences among the peoples he encountered, and simply divided them into two contrasting groups, the Taínos or Arawaks, and the fero-cious, man-eating Caribs who preyed upon them.[1] Living in villages and grouped into five major polities under chieftains who left a permanent legacy to western cultures in the word *cacique*,[2] the Taínos of Hispaniola presented a series of puzzles to the Spaniards, that were still far from being resolved when the polities disintegrated and the people died out. Had they ever heard of the Christian gospel, and if not, why not? Why were they naked, and yet apparently unashamed? Were they, as first appearances suggested, innocent beings, prelap-sarian men and women who had somehow escaped the fall? What god, if any, did they worship, and were they ripe for conversion to Christianity, as Columbus assumed? Did they live in stable communities conforming to European notions of *policía* or civility, or were their lives – as many Spaniards increasingly came to believe – more like those of beasts than of men?

These were the kind of questions that the Spaniards asked as they made their first acquaintance with the peoples of America; and in one form or another they repeated themselves as the invaders moved on from the Antilles to mainland America, where they found themselves faced with a multiplicity of new peoples, new cultures and new languages. On the strength of many years of residence in Hispaniola, Gonzalo Fernández de Oviedo decided that what he regarded as the inordinately thick skulls of the Indian inhabitants of his island were indicative of a 'bestial and ill-intentioned mind', and he saw no hope of their being able to absorb Christian doctrine.[3] On the other hand, Cortés had no doubt, on arriving in Mexico, that he had come across peoples of a very different calibre from those of the Antilles, and that this in turn would have important implications for their future prospects as subjects of the Spanish crown: '. . . we believe that had we interpreters and other people to explain to them the error of their ways and the nature of the True Faith, many of them, and perhaps even all, would soon renounce their false beliefs and come to the true knowledge of God; for they live in a more civilized and reasonable manner than any other people we have seen in these parts up to the present.'[4]

Although for taxonomic purposes the Spaniards would indiscriminately lump all the peoples of America together under the name of Indians – a practice that would be continued by the English colonists – they were well aware of their cultural and ethnic diversity. Given the linguistic problems they encountered on their arrival on the mainland, this could hardly be otherwise. On his march into the interior of Mexico, Cortés was exceptionally fortunate to have the linguistic services of a compatriot, Jerónimo de Águilar, whose eight years of captivity in Yucatán had made him fluent in Chontal Maya, and of Doña Marina – the famous Malinche – who had lived much of her life among the Maya, but whose first language was the Nahuatl of the Mexica. Cortés was thus able to make contact with the world of the Mexica through the Mayan language that, by force of circumstance, Malinche and Águilar spoke in common. Even then there were formidable difficulties, since Nahuatl, although increasingly dominant, was only one among the languages of Mexico, and Malinche herself spoke a dialect from the southern part of Montezuma's empire.[5] The English in North America encountered a similar linguistic diversity, as John Smith noted in his *Description of Virginia*: 'Amongst those people are thus many several nations of sundry languages, that environ Powhatan's territories . . . All those not any one understandeth another but by interpreters.'[6] Lacking the benefit of a Jerónimo de Águilar to help them communicate with the Indians, the Jamestown colonists exchanged the thirteen-year-old Thomas Savage for a trusted servant of Powhatan, and the boy soon learnt enough of the Algonquian spoken by the Powhatans to act as an interpreter.[7]

Europeans themselves – least of all the inhabitants of the Iberian peninsula – were no strangers to linguistic and cultural diversity. Cortés acknowledged as much when the captive Montezuma embarrassingly asked him about the identity of the hostile army commanded by Pánfilo de Narváez which had landed on the Mexican coast on the orders of Diego Velázquez to bring Cortés and his men to heel. He explained that 'as our Emperor has many kingdoms and lordships, there is a great diversity of peoples in them, some of them very brave and others even braver. We ourselves come from Old Castile, and are called Castilians, and that captain in Cempoala and the people with him are from another province, called Vizcaya. These are called Vizcayans, and they speak like the Otomís, near Mexico . . .'[8]

Otomís or Basques, Castilians or Mexica – they were all examples of the infinite diversity of the human race. But the Americas presented the Europeans, and in the first instance the Spaniards, with such a broad range of cultural and social differences as to stimulate intense curiosity about the reasons for this diversity and provoke considerable speculation about the stages of development of the peoples of the world.[9] Nothing in his years in the Antilles had prepared Cortés for the sophistication of the civilization he found on reaching Mexico. Here were great cities and ordered polities, which bore comparison with those of Christendom: '. . . these people live almost like those in Spain, and in as much harmony and order as there, and considering that they are barbarous and so far from the knowledge of God and cut off from all civilized nations, it is truly remarkable to see what they have achieved in all things.'[10] The empire of the Incas was to evoke similarly admiring responses from sympathetic Spanish observers. 'It is almost incredible', wrote Agustín de Zárate, 'that a barbarous and unlettered people could have been ruled in so orderly a way.'[11]

Although the Spanish discovery of the Aztec and Inca empires brought into question conventional European notions of barbarism by showing that peoples without the benefits of Christianity, or even of writing, could in some respects at least attain to European levels of civility,[12] it gradually became apparent that few if any other parts of the continent contained polities of comparable scale and sophistication. The first Spanish sightings of the Maya world of Yucatán suggested a high level of civilization, but the Spaniards remained baffled by the political and social complexity of a peninsula divided into eighteen or more distinctive polities which warred with each other and displayed very varying degrees of internal unity. This lack of cohesion was to make the Spanish conquest of Yucatán a slow and dispiriting process, spanning two generations and not finally completed until the subjugation of the Itza kingdom of Peten in 1697.[13] A similar lack of cohesion was to be found among the settled agricultural communities of what is now northern Colombia, although the numerous chiefdoms may have been on the way to some form of unification when Jiménez de Quesada and his men advanced up the Magdalena valley in 1536 to establish what would come to be called the kingdom of New Granada. But the Muisca, unlike the Maya, were a pacific people who offered no resistance.[14] In other regions, however, the Spaniards encountered peoples of a very different temper – in particular the Araucanian Indians of Chile, who would fight them to a standstill, and the hunter-gathering Chichimeca tribes of northern Mexico who, as seen by Spaniards, fully conformed to the traditional European image of a barbarous people. The Chichimecs lived, according to the sixteenth-century Spanish doctor Juan de Cárdenas, 'like brute savages'.[15]

North America, like central and southern America, contained a multiplicity of tribal and linguistic groups, perhaps some five hundred in all.[16] Of these, only the stratified society of the Natchez Indians of the Lower Mississippi and the Algonquian-speaking 'empire' of Powhatan could stand any form of comparison with the centrally directed polities ruled by Montezuma and Atahualpa,[17] while the absence from the lands first settled by the English of cities like those which so impressed the Spaniards made it less likely that these North American peoples would break free from the European stereotype of the barbarian and the savage. Captain John Smith, in a fine display of the semantic confusion generated by the European encounter with the inhabitants of the New World, compared the success of Cortés and 'scarce three hundred Spaniards' in conquering Tenochtitlán, 'where thousands of Salvages dwelled in strong houses', with the failure of the English colonists to subdue the tribes of tidewater Virginia. The reasons, he appeared to think, lay partly in the failure of the English to organize a well-disciplined force like that of Cortés, but also in the disparities between the peoples with whom they were confronted. The thousands of Mexican 'Salvages', he noted, 'were a civilized people' with houses and wealth, whereas the indigenous inhabitants of Virginia were 'mere Barbarians as wild as beasts'.[18]

However awkwardly expressed, Smith's contrast between the indigenous peoples encountered by the Spaniards in central Mexico and those upon whose lives the English intruded in the Chesapeake, points to major differences in the character and outcome of the military confrontations that opened the way to imperial rule. The superiority of European military technology, with its weapons of steel and its gunpowder, gave the invaders a critical edge over peoples whose arms were limited to bows and arrows, slings and stones, axes, clubs and wooden swords, even when, as among the Mexica, these were made especially lethal by the addition of razor-sharp obsidian flakes.[19] Firearms may have been slow and cumbersome, and gunpowder easily affected by humid conditions, but the slender steel blades of their Toledo swords gave the Spaniards a powerful advantage in close combat. Initially, too, their superiority was magnified by the psychological impact of the surprise created by guns and horses – 'deer . . . as tall as the roof', as the Mexica described them.[20] But the surprise would wear off, and, as the dogged resistance of Tenochtitlán and Manco Inca's rebellion of 1536 would show, the indigenous opponents of the invaders soon learnt to evolve responses that reduced the impact of a European weaponry not always well adapted to American conditions.

Yet, as Smith hinted, the very fact that the Mexican 'Salvages' were 'a civilized people' was to play into the hands of the Spaniards. The imperial structures organized by the Mexica and the Incas, with their concentration of power at a central point, made them vulnerable to a European take-over in ways that the looser tribal groupings of Yucatán or North America were not. Seize the supreme figure of authority and the mechanisms of imperial power were thrown into disarray, as Cortés and Pizarro demonstrated. Once final victory was secured – thanks in large part to the assistance of peoples who had chafed at Mexica or Inca domination – it was relatively easy to revive the old lines of command and replace one set of masters with another. The Spaniards thus found themselves in a position of authority over vast populations, which were accustomed to paying tribute and to receiving orders from an imperial centre. The conquerors enjoyed the advantage, too, of having been victorious in battle, thus demonstrating the superiority of their own deity in a cosmic order in which the winners dictated the hierarchy of the gods. Faced, therefore, by peoples who either resigned themselves

S. American
N. American- Nomadic

to defeat or regarded the Spanish victory as a liberation from Mexica or Inca repression, the conquerors were well placed to consolidate their domination over the heartlands of the empires they had won.

Nomadic peoples, on the other hand, presented the Europeans with military problems of a very different order. So too did the relatively loose groupings of tribes without permanently fixed points of settlement, like those that faced the Spaniards in other parts of central and southern America and the English to the north. It was not difficult to play off one tribe against another, but the very fluidity of tribal relationships meant that successes were liable to be temporary, as alliances shifted and tribes regrouped. Initial hopes of peaceful coexistence were all too easily blighted by European greed for land or gold, and by mutual misunderstandings between peoples who still had to take each other's measure. After conquering central Mexico, the Spaniards had high hopes of finding new riches far to the north – hopes that would fade with the failure of Coronado's expedition deep into the interior of North America in 1540–2. The passage of Coronado's men, like that of De Soto's expedition of 1539–43 into the North American south-east, was marked by armed clashes with the Zuni and other peoples on whose territories they encroached.[21] Mutual incomprehension clouded attempts at dialogue, even in those regions where reports of the brutality of the Spaniards had not preceded their arrival.

If the North American interior was for a long time expendable for the Spaniards, north-western Mexico was not. Here, in the border areas between the sedentary peoples of central Mexico and the nomadic tribes of the north, Beltrán Nuño de Guzmán had savagely carved out a new kingdom, New Galicia, in the early 1530s. The behaviour of the Spaniards provoked an Indian uprising, the Mixton War of 1541–2, which shook the newly created viceroyalty of New Spain to its foundations. Once the revolt was suppressed, strategies had to be devised for incorporating these border peoples, and for defending the Spanish settlements that were beginning to spring up, as land was distributed to encomenderos and the friars began arriving. Problems of defence were compounded as the discovery of the first silver deposits at Zacatecas in 1546 precipitated a rush of miners and ranchers into lands populated by the nomadic Chichimeca peoples, who had never been subject to Mexica domination. In the following decades the protection of the mining towns and the Camino Real – the silver route which linked the mines of New Galicia to Mexico City – would become a high priority for successive viceroys.

Their attempts during the second half of the sixteenth century to deal with the Chichimeca problem vividly illustrate the difficulties that faced Spaniards and English alike on the fringes of empire.[22] An obvious and immediate response was to build a string of forts – *presidios* as the Spaniards called them. In the same way, the colonists of Virginia would build Forts Royal, Charles and Henry in the aftermath of the 'massacre' of 1644.[23] But the garrisoning of forts had important implications for colonial life. Encomenderos had an obligation to provide for the defence of regions in which they held their encomiendas, and initially in New

Galicia a few powerful encomenderos were responsible for the defence of the borderlands.[24] But once *presidios* were built, they needed permanent garrisons, and this in turn pointed to the need for a professional soldiery. From the 1560s, when bands of Chichimec warriors began intensively raiding Spanish towns, a full-scale frontier war was under way, and this war brought into being the first bodies of paid professional soldiers in New Spain, initially most of them creoles.[25] But payment imposed strains on the royal treasury in the viceroyalty that the crown was unwilling, or unable, to bear in full. This meant that war, wherever possible, had to be made to pay for itself, and the easiest method was to allow the frontier garrisons to sell their Chichimeca captives as slaves – legitimate treatment, under Europe's rules of 'just war', for those who had failed, after due warning, to submit to the authority of the Spanish crown. But, as war was transformed into a lucrative business, so the inducement to bring it to a rapid end diminished. Along the north-western frontier of New Spain, as later on the southern frontiers of Chile in the war against the Araucanian Indians, self-financing warfare guaranteed its own prolongation.[26]

Given the perceived threat from the Indians among whom they had settled, English colonists, like Spanish colonists, promptly set about organizing themselves for defence, adapting to local needs and conditions the militia system they brought with them from England.[27] The establishment of forts and frontier lines in Virginia pointed, as it did in New Spain, to the need to supplement the militia with paid professionals. But this demanded levels of taxation that the planters were reluctant to bear, and during Bacon's rebellion of 1675–6 the rebels sought to adopt the strategy pursued in New Spain and Chile of making war pay for itself by organizing plundering raids into Indian settlements.[28]

Although the militia system in Virginia seems to have been less effective than its counterpart in New England, where the presence of towns and villages made it possible to concentrate defence, the Chesapeake region had less need of it once the now almost centenarian Opechancanough was captured in 1646. The governor, William Berkeley, planned to send him to England, but the decrepit chief, dignified to the end, was shot in the back by a vengeful militiaman while languishing in gaol. With the acceptance by his successor of a treaty bringing the third Anglo-Powhatan War to an end, the English colony of Virginia effectively supplanted the Powhatan polity of Tsenacommacah. The Powhatans, who agreed to pay the English a tribute of twenty beaver skins a year, were excluded from their homeland between the York and James rivers, and allotted a reservation north of the York river instead. In the following decades, as new immigrants arrived, the English settlement expanded irresistibly, encroaching even on the Powhatan reservation. Although the colonists still found themselves frustratingly dependent on Powhatan and non-Powhatan middlemen in their attempts to trade for furs with the Tuscarooras and Cherokees, in general they had less need of the Indians as the colony became increasingly self-supporting. By contrast, the native Americans were growing steadily more dependent on the supply of European goods, and their dependence discouraged them from risking further confrontations.[29]

In New England the crushing defeat of the Pequots in the war of 1636–7 seems at first sight comparable in its impact to the defeat of the Powhatan in Virginia, but here, in contrast to the Chesapeake region, the increasing dominance of the settlers and their continuing encroachments on Indian territory led to major tribal realignments which built up formidable possibilities for future resistance. The consequences were felt throughout New England when the Wampanoag chief Metacom ('King Philip') and his allies launched a fierce assault in 1675, and the region was plunged into more than a year of bitter and bloody conflict, with many English settlements put to the torch.[30]

The variety of Indian responses to the European intrusion – the rapid collapse of the organized empires of the Incas and the Aztecs, the passivity of the Muisca Indians of the kingdom of New Granada, the prolonged resistance of the Chichimeca and the Araucanians, the exasperated bellicosity of the Powhatan and the Wampanoag – makes it clear that tribal traditions and culture were as important in determining the outcome of any confrontation as were the varieties of approach adopted by the Europeans themselves. In the numerous encounters of civilizations on the fringes of European settlement, a pervasive but varied and uneven process of mutual acculturation was under way. All too often in the first instance this involved acculturation to war. The indigenous peoples, at first terrified by European firearms, were soon craving for them, and there was always some settler or trader ready to oblige, like Thomas Morton of Merrymount in the Plymouth Plantation: '. . . first he taught them how to use them . . . And having thus instructed them, he employed some of them to hunt and fowl for him, so as they became far more active in that employment than any of the English, by reason of their swiftness of foot and nimbleness of body . . . And here I may take occasion to bewail the mischief that this wicked man began in these parts . . . So as the Indians are full of pieces all over, both fowling pieces, muskets, pistols etc.'[31]

[margin note: Taught the indians how use firearms.]

Transferring to America the legislation used in Granada against the Moors, the Spaniards from the earliest years of settlement prohibited the sale of weapons to the Indians and their holding of firearms – a policy which seems to have been successfully maintained, at least in the heartlands of empire. Nor were Indians allowed to carry swords or ride on horseback.[32] The English also legislated against Indian ownership of firearms, but exceptions were made, and it proved impossible to prevent settlers like Morton trading in guns, especially in the border regions.[33] Horses, too, were assimilated into the military culture of the indigenous peoples, notably the Araucanians and the Apaches, both of whom chose warfare as a way of life.[34] Besides adjusting to European military technology, peoples who had often fought wars primarily to achieve some form of symbolic ascendancy now learnt to fight for land and possessions, just as they also learnt to fight for the purpose of killing. For their part, Europeans had to learn to adapt their fighting methods to meet native tactics of guerrilla warfare – the sudden ambushes, for instance, and the frightening attacks from out of the forests.[35] Following the methods used with such success in the conquest of the

[margin note: This was to make sure the Spaniards always had the upper hand. The English also tried this, but exceptions were made.]

The Europeans used the indians against one another

Aztec and Inca empires, they also turned to Indians to help them in their wars against Indians, pitting one tribe against another, and building up networks of Indian allies. The Spaniards recruited Indian allies along the Chichimec frontier, winning over recently pacified tribes with gifts and privileges, such as exemptions from tribute and the granting of licences for the possession of horses and guns; the Virginians created a buffer zone of friendly Indians; the New Englanders depended on the Mohegans and other friendly tribes as auxiliaries in King Philip's War.[36] *allies were important ↑*

Disease from Europe & Spain

The most effective of all allies, however, in the imposition of European supremacy was not human but biological – those Old World diseases which the invaders and settlers unwittingly brought with them to the New. Estimates of the total population of the Americas on the eve of the arrival of the first Europeans have varied wildly, from under 20 million to 80 million or more. Of these 20 to 80 million, the North American population constituted between 1 and 2 million in the assessment of minimalist demographic historians, and as many as 18 million in that of the maximalists.[37] While the totals will always be a matter of debate, there is no dispute that the arrival of the Europeans brought demographic catastrophe in its train, with losses of around 90 per cent in the century or so following the first contact.[38]

The degree to which that catastrophe was the result of atrocities committed in the course of conquest and of the subsequent maltreatment and exploitation of the indigenous peoples by the new masters of the land was already a source of fierce discussion among Spanish observers in the age of conquest, and has remained so to this day. Bartolomé de Las Casas's *Brief Account of the Destruction of the Indies*, first published in Seville in 1552, etched itself into the European consciousness as an unsparing record of the barbarous behaviour of his compatriots, and there were others, equally well informed, to second his words. 'The Spaniards', wrote Alonso de Zorita, a judge of the Mexican Audiencia, in his 'Brief Relation of the Lords of New Spain', 'compelled them to give whatever they asked, and inflicted unheard-of cruelties and tortures upon them.'[39] For others, however, the cruelty lay elsewhere. 'It is my opinion and that of many who have had dealings with them', wrote Bernardo Vargas Machuca in a refutation of Las Casas, 'that to paint cruelty in its full colours, there is no need to do more than portray an Indian.'[40]

The crown had laws to protect the Indians

In practice, there was no advantage to the Spaniards in killing off their tribute payers and labour supply, although this did not prevent many of them from flouting the laws introduced by the crown for the protection of the Indians, seizing them on unauthorized (and sometimes authorized) slaving raids which wrenched them out of their own environment, and exploiting them to the limits and beyond. But, as Zorita himself recognized, the Indians were dying out not only because of the 'unheard-of cruelties and tortures' that he catalogued, but also because of the 'plagues that have affected them', although he ascribed the susceptibility to disease of the Mexican Indians to the demoralization caused by hard labour and the disruption of traditional ways of life.[41]

There can be no doubting the psychological impact on the indigenous peoples of America of the trauma induced by the sudden destruction of their world. It was reflected, for instance, in the growth of drunkenness among them, a phenomenon noted in the areas of Spanish and English settlement alike.[42] Their susceptibility to disease, however, was not simply the result, as Zorita believed, of the demoralization caused by conquest and exploitation. It was above all their previous isolation from Eurasian epidemics that made them so vulnerable to the diseases brought from Europe. These diseases afflicted not only peoples who suffered the trauma of conquest and colonization but also those whose contacts with Europeans were no more than sporadic, or else were mediated through several removes.

Forms of sickness that in Europe were not necessarily lethal brought devastating mortality rates to populations that had not built up the immunity that would enable them to resist. In Mesoamerica the smallpox which ravaged the Mexica defenders of Tenochtitlán in 1520–1 and killed Montezuma's successor, Cuitláhuac, after a few weeks of rule, was followed during the succeeding decades by waves of epidemics, many of them still difficult to identify with certainty: 1531–4, measles; 1545, typhus and pulmonary plague, an epidemic that struck on a horrendous scale; 1550, mumps; 1559–63, measles, influenza, mumps and diphtheria; 1576–80, typhus, smallpox, measles, mumps; 1595, measles. Comparable waves struck the peoples of the Andes, who were stricken by smallpox in the 1520s, well before Pizarro embarked on his conquest of Peru.[43] Over the course of a century the decline in the size of the indigenous populations of Mexico and Peru appears to have been of the order of 90 per cent, although there were significant regional and local variations. The highland regions of Peru, for instance, seem to have suffered less than lower-lying areas, and the impact of the epidemics was affected both by the degree of intensity of settlement by Europeans, and by the settlement patterns of indigenous populations, with dispersed settlements being more likely to escape.[44]

Just as the coming of European diseases preceded European settlement in the Andes, so death stalked the Atlantic coast of North America well before the arrival of the English in any large numbers. Already in the sixteenth century sporadic contacts with Europeans had unleashed major epidemics, as when the Spanish ship that was to carry away the young Indian 'Don Luis de Velasco' entered the Chesapeake Bay in 1561.[45] As the contacts multiplied, so did the sicknesses. There is evidence that the indigenous population of Virginia was in decline before the founding of Jamestown in 1607, and major epidemics are reported for 1612–13 and 1616–17 in the region soon to be called New England, where the Patuxets were simply wiped out.[46] As a result, the English found themselves settling in a land that was already partially depopulated. Although this was disappointing in so far as it reduced the chances of their finding an adequate supply of native labour, it also had its advantages, as some of the settlers appreciated. Captain John Smith remarked that 'it is much better to help to plant a country than unplant it and then replant it', as, in his view, the Spaniards had done, killing off their Indians and then finding it necessary to import African slaves to replace them. 'But their Indians', he continued, 'were in such multitudes, the Spaniards had no other remedy; and ours such a few, and so dispersed, it were nothing in a short time to bring them to labour and obedience.'[47]

This was a somewhat optimistic assessment, especially coming from one of the founders of a colony that failed signally to bring its Indians 'to labour and obedience', and would soon be importing large numbers of Africans to make good the deficiency. But the relative sparsity of the Indian presence along the North Atlantic coast did much to smooth the path for the first English settlers, and enabled them to 'plant a country' on new foundations in ways that were impossible for the conquerors of Mexico and Peru. John Winthrop put it succinctly in a letter of 1634 to Sir Nathaniel Rich: '. . . For the natives, they are all near dead of the smallpox, so as the Lord hath cleared our title to what we possess.'[48] In reality the intervention of providence did not solve the 'Indian question' to quite the degree that the earlier English settlers liked to think. But it made it a different kind of question, in character and scale, from that which faced Spanish settlers who found themselves the masters of multitudes – if shrinking multitudes – of vanquished Indians.

Christianity and civility

[handwritten: Reduced means to convince in this context.]

While the Spaniards, unlike the English, had effective dominion over large numbers of Indians, the English saw their mission in America in the same terms as the Spaniards – as one of 'reducing the savage people to Christianity and civility', in Christopher Carleill's words of 1583.[49] In this context to 'reduce' (in Spanish, *reducir*) meant in the vocabulary of the sixteenth and seventeenth centuries not to level down,[50] but to bring back or restore, and in particular to restore by persuasion or argument. 'To be reduced is to be convinced', according to the definition of the word in Sebastián de Covarrubias's Castilian dictionary of 1611.[51] These were peoples who had to be converted to a knowledge and understanding of the true faith, ideally by persuasion, but, as some argued, by compulsion if necessary, for had not Christ commanded: *'compel them to come in'*?[52]

[handwritten: They felt it may be necessary to "compel" the indians into christianity]

If the commitment to conversion was paramount, the reduction to 'civility' was to prove a great deal more problematical. What constituted a 'civilized' being, and in what respects did the peoples of America fail to meet the necessary criteria? Smith's description of the 'savages' of Tenochtitlán as 'a civilized people'[53] suggests something of the confusion in European minds as they came into contact with peoples whose customs were so different from their own. If it soon became apparent that levels of civilization, as defined by Europeans, varied enormously from one Amerindian people to another, it still remained to be decided how far those at the top of the scale, in Mesoamerica and the Andes, conformed to the necessary standards of civility, and how far their new masters should intervene to correct their failings.

Since this was a problem that first confronted the Spaniards, it is not surprising that both Spanish America and Spain itself should have been wracked by a series of highly charged debates about the character and aptitudes of the Indians. The Spaniards, by reason of their priority, were forced to be pioneers, evolving by trial and error a set of policies and practices that would determine the extent to which the peoples under their domination were to be 'reduced' to European norms of behaviour.[54] The novelty of the challenge, and the sheer scale of the obligation imposed on them by the Alexandrine bulls to bring these unknown peoples to the faith, forced the Spanish authorities in church and state to develop what was in effect a programme for conversion – a programme that would slide by sometimes imperceptible stages into widespread hispanicization. In terms both of a programmatic approach and of a systematic effort to implement it, the English colonization of North America would show nothing comparable.

The intensity of the Spanish effort to convert the peoples of the New World to Christianity is only comprehensible in the context of the spiritual preoccupations of late fifteenth- and early sixteenth-century Christendom, and particularly those of the Iberian peninsula. The hunger for spiritual regeneration and renewal among sections of both the church and the laity unleashed a great movement for reform, which already by the end of the fifteenth century had made a profound impact on European civilization. The reform movement often possessed millenarian and apocalyptic overtones, especially in Spain, where the completion of the Reconquista created its own climate of spiritual euphoria. The defeat of Islam, the conquest of Jerusalem, the conversion of the world, which was regarded as a prelude to its ending – all these hopes and expectations were conjoined in the obsessive mentality of Columbus and inspired many of those with whom he came into contact, including Ferdinand and Isabella themselves.[55] In 1492 Columbus in effect launched Spain and its monarchs on a world-wide messianic mission, although the nature of the mission makes it strange that, while the expedition included an interpreter, there was no priest on board. This deficiency was remedied on his 1493 voyage, when he took with him a Benedictine, three Franciscans, and a Catalan Hieronymite, Ramón Pané, whose experiences on Hispaniola led him to write the first in the great series of ethnographical treatises on the indigenous peoples of America produced by members of the religious orders.[56]

The presence of the religious in the Antilles meant that the activities of the settlers, especially in relation to the indigenous population, were now exposed to the scrutiny of those who came to the New World with a very different agenda. The effects of this became apparent with the arrival in Hispaniola in 1510 of four Dominicans, one of whom, Fray Antonio de Montesinos, preached a sermon on the island on the Sunday before Christmas 1511 that was to reverberate across the ocean. His denunciations of the settlers for their barbaric treatment of the Indians was to affect many lives, including that of a priest on Hispaniola, Bartolomé de Las Casas, who had his own repartimiento of Indians, but would later join the Dominican Order, and, as the 'Apostle of the Indians', would become a tireless campaigner on their behalf. Montesinos's sermon made a public issue of the whole question of the legality of the encomienda and the status of the Indians under Spanish rule. At least symbolically, it marked the opening of 'the Spanish struggle for justice in the conquest of America', and forced the crown, which initially reacted adversely to Dominican meddling in such sensitive matters, to address the issue in the light of its own obligations under the papal bulls. The outcome was the convocation by Ferdinand in 1512 of a special junta of theologians and officials in Burgos, and the publication of the Laws of Burgos, the first comprehensive code of legislation for the Spanish Indies.[57]

The Junta, which included among its members partisans of both the Indians and the encomenderos, laid down a series of principles which were to be fundamental to Spain's future government of the Indies. While the Junta did not condemn the encomienda it stipulated that the Indians must be treated as a free people, in conformity with the wishes of Ferdinand and the late Queen Isabella. As a free people, they were entitled to hold property, and – although they could be set to work – they must be remunerated for their labour. In conformity with the bull of Alexander VI they also had to be instructed in the Christian faith.[58]

The encomienda was still allowed but the indians had to be paid. (handwritten margin note)

The reassertion of the need to instruct Indians in the faith underlined the crown's commitment to the process of evangelization – a commitment that was reinforced by the series of concessions granted it by the papacy for the establishment of a church in America under royal control. In 1486 Rome had granted the crown the *Patronato* of the church in the kingdom of Granada, thus conferring on it the right of presentation to all major ecclesiastical benefices in a realm that was still not fully liberated from Moorish control. A series of papal bulls in the following years, starting with Alexander VI's *Inter caetera* of 1493 with its concession to the crown of exclusive rights to evangelization in its transatlantic possessions, cumulatively extended the royal Patronato to the Indies. In 1501 Alexander granted the crown in perpetuity all tithes collected in the Indies, in order to support the work of evangelization, and in a bull of 1508 Julius II gave Ferdinand the right for which he had been patiently working, of presenting to all cathedrals and ecclesiastical benefices in Spain's American territories. Once its Patronato was recognized, the crown began to establish the first dioceses in America, in the Antilles in 1511, and on the mainland in 1513.[59]

While the framework for an institutional church in Spanish America was now in place, it was the religious orders which launched and led the campaign for the conversion of the Indians. Cortés, deeply suspicious of the pomp and corruption of the secular clergy, urged the crown in his fourth letter, of 15 October 1524, to turn to the friars for the evangelization of the conquered peoples of Mexico.[60] In fact they had already made their appearance. Twelve Franciscans under the leadership of Fray Martín de Valencia – the famous 'twelve apostles' – had reached Mexico four months earlier, the precursors of what was to be a vast programme of conversion and indoctrination. They were followed in 1526 by twelve Dominicans, and seven years later by the Augustinians. In Peru a similar process was soon under way, starting with the three Dominicans who embarked with

Pizarro in Panama. One of these was Father Valverde, famous for his confrontation with Atahualpa, who accompanied Pizarro throughout the conquest and became the first Bishop of Cuzco. As numbers increased, so convents were founded and churches built. In New Spain by 1559 there were 802 Franciscans, Dominicans and Augustinians, and between them they had established 160 religious houses.[61]

For all the differences between the Orders, the religious in America, at least in the early years of evangelization, entertained high hopes of the prospects before them. Here was an opportunity to re-create among the uncorrupted and innocent peoples of the New World a church that would resemble the primitive church of the early apostles, untainted by the vices that had overwhelmed it in Christendom.[62] The programme for the evangelization of Spanish America was therefore launched on a wave of fervour and enthusiasm generated by members of the religious orders who saw in the New World incomparable prospects for the winning of new converts and the salvation of souls. It enjoyed, too, the full support of the crown, which normally bore the travelling costs of those religious who requested a passage to the Indies,[63] and would use the tithes conceded by the papacy for paying the salaries of those in charge of parishes, and for building and endowing churches and cathedrals. The programme began with the mass baptism by the Franciscans of vast numbers of Indians in the valley of Mexico and was followed up by preaching, catechizing and the founding of schools.

The word *doctrinero*, used first of the friars and in due course, also, of the parish priests working independently or alongside them in *doctrinas* or Indian parishes, is suggestive of the character of the programme that was now under way.[64] It was a programme to instruct, or indoctrinate, in the elements of Catholic Christianity, its belief systems, its sacraments and its moral code. Such an ambitious programme, conducted on so vast a scale, inevitably raised fundamental questions about the capacity of the Indians to understand and assimilate the new faith, and about the extent and sincerity of the 'conversion' hailed with such enthusiasm by the first Franciscans. Sceptics were soon able to point to some spectacular failures, like the discovery in 1539 of a cache of idols in the house of Don Carlos de Texcoco, a former prize pupil of the College of Santa Cruz in Tlatelolco, established by the Franciscans for the education of the sons of Mexico's indigenous elite.[65] In Peru, where the Andean peoples were to show themselves incorrigibly reluctant to abandon their *huacas*, or sacred objects and sites, the vicar-general of Cuzco in 1541 identified idolatry as the greatest obstacle to the establishment of the faith.[66]

The setbacks and the failures prompted a variety of reactions. They encouraged some ecclesiastics, like Bishop Diego de Landa in Yucatán, to make a bonfire of sacred texts which could only perpetuate among the indigenous population the memory of the pernicious beliefs and practices with which the devil had for so long held them in thrall.[67] But others responded in a more positive fashion. In the opinion of the Dominican Fray Diego Durán, 'a great mistake was made by those who, with much zeal but little prudence, burnt and destroyed at the beginning all their sacred pictures. This left us so much in the dark that they can practice idolatry before our very eyes.'[68] In other words, to extirpate idolatry one had first to understand it. This could only be achieved by a systematic attempt to explore and record for posterity the character and beliefs of a rapidly vanishing world – the world of the indigenous peoples of America before the arrival of the Spaniards.

The result was an intensive effort by a number of friars to understand the history and the customs of the peoples whom they were attempting to indoctrinate (fig. 11). In order to present the gospel, many of them had already laboriously mastered one or more native languages. Several of these languages were transcribed into the Latin alphabet, and grammars and dictionaries were compiled, like the Quechua dictionary published in 1560 by Fray Domingo de Santo Tomás.[69] At the same time native informants who still had some knowledge of life before the conquest were asked to interpret and flesh out the pictographic evidence provided by the surviving codices, and to answer carefully constructed questions about ancient practices and beliefs. Fray Bernardino de Sahagún's great *History of the Things of New Spain*, completed in 1579 in a bilingual text, Nahuatl and Castilian, may have been ethnography with a purpose – the more effective evangelization of the Indians – but it was ethnography none the less. Sahagún and his colleagues in the Spanish mendicant orders were the pioneers in Europe's attempt to study on a systematic basis the beliefs and customs of the non-European peoples of the world.[70]

While a growing knowledge of indigenous social and political organization before the coming of the Spaniards evoked admiration in some circles, and provided Las Casas with the ammunition he needed to argue for the rationality of the peoples of America and their aptitude for the gospel, it was insufficient to win over those who saw everywhere around them the footprints of the devil. It was firmly believed that the devil stalked the New World, and everything in native society that allowed him to work his diabolical contrivances had to be systematically eradicated if true Christianity were ever to take root.[71]

Yet it very quickly became clear that this involved far more than the eradication of pagan rites and superstitious practices. It was one thing to put an end to the practice of human sacrifice which had so horrified the Spaniards on their arrival in Mexico, but it was quite another to overthrow the belief-systems and cosmologies which had given rise to such barbarities. The friars sought as best they could to fill the spiritual vacuum created by the destruction of the old gods and their priests, and provided their charges with new rites and ceremonies, new images, and a new liturgical calendar that would help to reconnect them to the sacred.[72] It also became apparent that the imposition of Christian morality implied major changes in social habits and traditional ways of life, and it was not always easy to draw the line between what should be abolished and what allowed to remain. So far as marriage customs were concerned, it was clear that polygamy, practised among the ruling class of pre-conquest Mexico, must be banned, and concepts of incest be revised to conform to Christian notions.[73] But in matters of dress there was more room for latitude. The *maxtlatl* or loincloth worn by Mexican men offended Christian notions of decency, and gradually lost out over the course of the sixteenth century to trousers; but traditional women's dress, seen as more modest, was allowed to survive.[74] Although the friars might struggle to prevent their flocks from being contaminated by European vices, the whole programme of conversion carried with it an inexorable subtext of hispanicization, as spiritual and social pressures alike pushed the Indians into the orbit of the Europeans, and notions of Christianity and civility became hopelessly entangled. Sahagún might be critical of those who wanted to 'reduce' the Indians to 'the Spanish way of life', but the whole rationale of conquest culture was to compel them to live, in the words of Bishop Landa, 'incomparably more like men'.[75]

In practice many Indians, especially in central Mexico and the Andes, were to adapt with remarkable speed to the culture of the conquerors, soon equalling or surpassing them in some areas of craftsmanship, and assimilating, often with apparent enthusiasm, those elements of Christianity which would enable them in due course to rediscover their own route to the sacred.[76] But because they moved at their own pace and in their own ways, clinging fast to practices which branded them as unregenerate idolaters in European eyes and obstinately failing to conform to Spanish notions of civility, they became the objects of increasing disparagement, pity or contempt. Between the heady days of early evangelization and the later sixteenth century, the image of the Indian changed, and changed for the worse. Partly this was a result of changes among the Indians themselves, as traditional social disciplines and norms of behaviour crumbled in the aftershock of conquest. But it was also a reflection of lowered expectations bred by closer acquaintance, and perhaps too by a generational change among the friars themselves. Where the first friars brought with them something of the optimism and curiosity of Renaissance Europe, the second generation came to maturity in the age of the Reformation and Counter-Reformation, deeply imbued with Augustinian notions of original sin. This more pessimistic attitude, already apparent in the campaign led by the Dominicans for the evangelization of Peru, induced a greater wariness in the approach to conversion, together with a reduced estimate of the capability of the Indians to assimilate the faith. The Indians no doubt responded in kind.

The result was the gradual emergence of a new, and depressing, consensus about the nature of the Indian, far removed from the generous enthusiasm of Las Casas and his friends. The College of Santa Cruz came to be regarded as a failure, and strong opposition closed the entry of Indians to the priesthood.[77] With the Indians regarded as unfit for ordination, the Spanish church in America was to remain a church run by the conquerors on their own terms. The scepticism about the aptitude of Indians for the priesthood came to pervade the whole missionary enterprise. Where Las Casas saw the mind of the Indian as a *tabula rasa* on which it would not be hard to inscribe the principles and precepts of Christianity,[78] others increasingly saw him as an intellectually feeble and inconstant creature with an inherent inclination to vice. Deficient in rational capacity, did he not conform all too well to Aristotelian notions of natural inferiority?

To the plaudits of the encomenderos, the distinguished humanist scholar, Juan Ginés de Sepúlveda, argued that the deficiencies of the indigenous peoples of America condemned them to the status of natural slaves.[79] Others insisted that at best they were children, who should be fed only the simplest rudiments of the faith. As children, they needed guidance and correction, as Fray Pedro de Feria, the Bishop of Chiapas, argued before the third Mexican provincial council in 1585: 'We must love and help the Indians as much as we can. But their base and imperfect character requires that they should be ruled, governed and guided to their appointed end by fear more than by love.'[80] Wayward children cried out for a paternalist approach.

Whatever the disappointments involved in the evangelization of Spanish America, the fact remained that, to European eyes, millions of lost souls, formerly wandering in the darkness and subject to the tyranny of Satan, had now been brought into the light. The Spanish achievement was impressive enough for William Strachey to hold it up as an example to his compatriots as they embarked on the colonization of Virginia: 'Have we either less means, fainter spirits, or a charity more cold, or a religion more shameful, and afraid to dilate itself? or is it a lawful work in them, and not in us? . . .' The opportunities, as he saw it, were great. The Indians were 'simple, and innocent people', and – using the image of the *tabula rasa* employed by Las Casas – he described their minds as 'unblotted tables, apt to receive what form soever shall be first drawn thereon . . .'[81]

Whether the English had 'fainter spirits', a 'charity more cold, or a religion more shameful' than the Spaniards are matters for debate, but they certainly had 'less means'. With the coming of the Reformation to England, the religious orders disappeared. There was no cadre of militant evangelists in the home country ready to take up the challenge of converting the peoples of North America to the faith. Nor was the Anglican church in the early seventeenth century in a position to devise and implement a Spanish-style programme of evangelization, enjoying full and effective support from the crown. It was still struggling to establish itself and its doctrines at home, and had neither the energy nor the resources to devote much attention to the opportunities that awaited it overseas.

The first meeting of the Virginia Assembly in 1619 endorsed the Church of England as the legally authorized religious establishment in the colony,[82] but it was neither quick nor very effective in establishing itself. In 1622 there were forty-five parishes to be cared for, and only ten ministers in residence.[83] Gradually a church was created in the colony, with the parish as a vital element in local life, but it was a church far removed from the hierarchy in England and one controlled by the planters themselves. Institutionally, therefore, the Anglican church failed to transfer its authority across the ocean, and there was to be no bishop in Virginia, or indeed in any part of British North America, before the Revolution.[84] Not surprisingly, in view of this absence of authority and direction, no systematic programme was developed for Christianizing the Virginian Indians, and Henrico College, founded in 1619 for the education of Indian children, closed its doors even before it ever got round to opening them.[85]

But it was not simply the organizational weaknesses of the Anglican church that hampered its missionary effort in British America. It also possessed no monopoly of religious life. Unlike Spanish America, the English settlements would become an arena for competing creeds. Although Maryland was designed as a haven for Roman Catholics, they were outnumbered from the start by Protestants, and the colony survived its early years by having no established church (which meant, uniquely for British as well as Spanish America, having no compulsory tithes or other more or less compulsory forms of contribution for the support of the clergy), and adopting a pragmatic form of toleration which made religion a private affair.[86] It was only after the Glorious Revolution, in 1692, that the first moves were made to establish the Church of England as Maryland's official church. In New England the purpose behind the founding of Puritan settlements was to promote a purer form of religious life and worship than seemed possible under the Anglican church as currently established, and their founders were pre-eminently concerned with constructing in the New World a church of visible saints.[87]

This preoccupation did not necessarily preclude a mission into the wilderness to convert the Indians, although in practice it did much to complicate the enterprise. The very fact that the seal designed for the Massachusetts Bay Company in 1629 displayed an Indian with a scroll emerging from his mouth bearing the legend 'Come over and help us', borrowed from the vision of St Paul in Acts 16:9,[88] indicates an initial commitment to missionary activity which promised more than it eventually delivered (fig. 7). In the early years there was a shortage of pastors even to minister to the needs of the settlers, and the difficulty of mastering Indian languages was to be a further obstacle to progress in the British colonies, as in the Spanish. But some individuals, in British as in Spanish America, made a determined effort to overcome this obstacle. Roger Williams, whose 'soul's desire', as he wrote, was 'to do the natives good', published his A Key into the Language of America in 1643.[89] In 1647 Governor Winthrop reported in his Journal that the pastor of Roxbury, the Reverend John Eliot, had taken 'great pains' to learn Algonquian, 'and in a few months could speak of the things of God, to their understanding'.[90] At the same time Thomas Mayhew, who had settled on Martha's Vineyard, achieved some important conversions and was acquiring proficiency in the native language. The 1640s, then, saw the beginning of a major effort, although small-scale by Spanish standards, to win the North American Indians to Christianity.[91]

This effort benefited from the triumph of the parliamentarians in the English Civil War, which created a more favourable official climate in the home country for the support of Puritan missionary enterprise overseas. In 1649 the Rump Parliament approved the founding of a corporation, the Society for Propagation of the Gospel in New England, to promote the cause of the conversion of the

Indians by organizing the collection and disbursement of funds.[92] The enterprise was therefore dependent on voluntary contributions from the faithful – a reflection of the growing tendency in the English world to rely on private and corporate initiative and voluntary associations to undertake projects which in the Hispanic world came within the official ambit of church and state.

As in Spanish America the missionary effort supported by the Society involved the compilation of dictionaries and grammars, and the preparation of catechisms in the native languages.[93] It also included something that did not figure on the Spanish agenda – the translation into a native Indian tongue of the Bible, a heroic enterprise completed by Eliot in 1659 and published in 1663. The fundamental importance of the written word to Protestantism strengthened the arguments for the schooling of Indians, and considerable effort – including the construction of an Indian College at Harvard in 1655 – was to be devoted to the teaching of Indian children.[94] But the most spectacular, if not the most successful, feature of the New England missionary enterprise was the establishment of the 'praying towns' – the fourteen village communities set up by Eliot in Massachusetts for converted Indians.[95] The practical purpose behind their foundation was similar to that which inspired the creation of the so-called *reducciones* in the Spanish colonial world from the mid-sixteenth century: it was easier to indoctrinate Indians and to shield them from the corrupting influences of the outside world if they were concentrated in large settlements, instead of living dispersed. The Spanish policy of concentrating Indians in *reducciones* led to massive forced resettlement in Mexico and Peru.[96] Although there were none of the forced movements of population which dramatically altered the demographic landscape of the Spanish viceroyalties, the praying towns were *reducciones* writ small, the visible manifestations of the conviction that, if only the Indians could be isolated and brought under the exclusive tutelage of ministers and pastors, they might one day be fitted to join the community of saints.

The results, in both instances, failed to correspond to the high hopes with which the experiment had been invested. Many of the Peruvian Indians fled the *reducciones* as soon as they could, while some of Eliot's praying Indians were to join King Philip's warrior bands.[97] The praying towns had to face not only the scepticism of many of the colonists, but also the derision and hostility of Indian tribes which remained impervious to the appeal of Christianity; and the very proximity of these hostile tribes made the praying towns less safe from attack than *reducciones* that lay in the heartlands of the Spanish viceroyalties. The towns did, however, achieve some important successes. Where the Spanish church turned its back on the ordination of Indian ministers, the Puritans succeeded in training a number of converts for the ministry, some of whom in turn went out to carry the gospel to unconverted tribes.[98] Their contribution was all the more important because the first obligation of Puritan ministers was to their own communities of the elect, and, unlike the friars in Spanish America, they could not devote themselves full time to evangelization among the Indians.

Against the blanket 'conversion' of the indigenous population under Spanish rule, must be set the conversion of some 2,500 Indians – perhaps 20 per cent of the Indian population of New England – by the time of the outbreak of King Philip's War in 1675.[99] The fact that New England was still a frontier society with relatively few Indians living within the borders of the settlements made conditions very different from those that prevailed in the Spanish viceroyalties. It was one thing, for instance, to establish a college for the sons of an old-established indigenous nobility in the urbanized environment of Mexico City, and quite another to persuade young Massachusetts Indians to abandon their open-air existence for the sedentary life and unfamiliar diet of a colonial grammar school. The Indian College at Harvard, not surprisingly, was no College of Santa Cruz in Tlatelolco, which, in the early years after its foundation in 1536, enjoyed a resounding success in creating a new and hispanicized native elite, allegedly capable of producing Latin sentences of a Ciceronian elegance that astonished Spanish visitors. Very few Indians actually went to the Indian College, and scarcely one of them survived the ordeal of exposure to life at Harvard. The college was eventually demolished in 1693.[100]

The character of the Puritan message, moreover, played its own part in adding to the uphill nature of the task. Puritanism was an exclusive, not an all-embracing, form of religion, and it depended for conversion on the working of God's grace. For this reason, there could be no imitation of the Spanish policy of *compelle eos entrare* – 'compel them to come in'. On the contrary, the colony's policy, as John Cotton wrote in the 1630s, was 'not to compel' the Indians, 'but to permit them either to believe willingly or not to believe at all'.[101] Puritan theology was complex, and no doubt the complexity was all the greater for a population still being initiated into the fascinating mysteries of the written word. Moreover, as a religion without images, and one which prided itself on the simplicity of its worship in the barest of churches, it offered little in the way of the visual and ceremonial that seems to have appealed to the indigenous populations of Mexico and Peru. Only the singing of hymns and psalms tempered the rigour of the message.[102]

The new faith also demanded changes in social behaviour even more exacting than those required by the Catholic Church in Spanish America. The doctrine of election carried with it strict adherence to a set of norms which left little latitude for manoeuvre where standards of 'civility' were concerned. 'I find it absolutely necessary', wrote Eliot, 'to carry on civility with Religion.'[103] Conversion to Christianity meant in effect conversion to an English way of life, and in the praying towns the Indians were expected to abandon their wigwams for the allegedly superior comforts of English-style houses, built with little regard to the climatic conditions of New England.[104] Anglicization extended even to attempts to persuade Indians to abandon their traditional custom of wearing their hair long. 'Since the word hath begun to worke upon their hearts,' wrote a minister, 'they have discerned the vanitie and pride, which they placed in their haire, and have therefore of their own accord . . . cut it modestly.'[105] In Peru, where the long hair of the Indians outraged Spaniards as much as it outraged the Puritans of New England, a Spanish official, Juan de Matienzo, showed more sensitivity. He could see no great objection to long hair, except perhaps on grounds of cleanliness, and wrote that 'to make them change their custom would seem to them a sentence of death.'[106]

The willingness of the New England converts to face the derision of their unconverted fellow Indians and reconstruct their way of life, even to the extent of adopting the dress and hairstyles of the Europeans, suggests that, for some tribes at least – perhaps those whose lives had been especially disrupted by the advent of the Europeans and their diseases – the new faith, for all its complexity, met a real need.[107] Yet these converts remained a small minority, precarious clusters of believers in a pagan ocean, and even then their conversion was regarded with scepticism by many of the settlers, who remained convinced that the whole notion of conversion and civilization of the Indian was 'meere fantasie'.[108] One or two, like Thomas Morton, might even affect to question its desirability, finding 'the Massachusetts Indian more full of humanity, than the Christians',[109] but Morton was a notorious maverick.

Although John Eliot shared with Bartolomé de las Casas the name of 'Apostle to the Indians',[110] he was a Las Casas in a minor key. Las Casas devoted a large part of his long life to campaigning, lobbying and writing on behalf of the Indians against their detractors in America itself and at the Spanish court. Confronted by a settler community which justified its exploitation of the Indians by arguments based on their natural inferiority as human beings, he sought to end the oppression by working for the abolition of the encomienda and arguing that the Indians had the spiritual aptitude to assimilate true Christianity if they were removed from the hands of the encomenderos and placed directly under the benevolent rule of the Spanish crown.

The agitation of Las Casas and his fellow Dominicans on behalf of the Indians was sufficiently powerful to persuade Charles V, on the recommendation of the Council of the Indies, to order in 1550 that all further expeditions of conquest in the New World should be suspended until a junta of theologians had pronounced on the moral issues involved. The junta, convened in Valladolid in September 1550, and holding a second session in May 1551, was confronted with the opposing arguments of Las Casas, Bishop of Chiapas, and Sepúlveda, the emperor's chaplain, who had no personal knowledge of American Indians but on the basis of his reading of Aristotle had asserted their natural inferiority in his treatise, *Democrates secundus*. It was this inferiority, in Sepúlveda's view, that justified making war upon them.[111]

The judges, no doubt battered and bruised by Las Casas's five-day reading of his inordinately long Latin treatise of apology for the Indians, never delivered their verdict. Yet if Las Casas and his supporters failed in their prime purpose of elevating the status and conditions of life of the Indians, they did succeed in creating a moral climate in which the crown was forcefully reminded of its obligation to defend them against their oppressors and do what it could to improve their lot. In 1563 the Indians were formally classified as *miserabiles*. This classification gradually acquired a juridical content, as special judges were appointed to handle Indian cases in the viceroyalties of New Spain and Peru, and legal assistance was provided for Indians who wished to lodge complaints.[112] Subsequently, in 1573, Philip II promulgated a long set of ordinances, drawn up by the President of the Council of the Indies, Juan de Ovando, that were designed to regulate any further territorial expansion.[113] The ordinances came late in the day, and new-style 'pacification' often proved to be little more than a euphemism for old-style 'conquest'. Both the convocation of the Valladolid debate, however, and the legislation that followed it, testify to the Spanish crown's commitment to ensuring 'justice' for indigenous subject populations – a commitment for which, in its continuity and strength, it is not easy to find parallels in the history of other colonial empires.

Las Casas was primarily known in other parts of Europe for his harrowing *Brief Account of the Destruction of the Indies*, which first appeared in English translation in 1583. A new translation, dedicated to Oliver Cromwell, was published in London under the emotive title of *The Tears of the Indians* in 1656, following the conquest of Jamaica and the outbreak of war with Spain.[114] The name of Las Casas was therefore well known to English readers, and not least to John Eliot, who to some extent would follow consciously in his steps. But there was less opportunity for the emergence of an effective Las Casas in the British world, where there was no encomendero class exploiting a large work-force of nominally free Indians, and no powerful group of missionaries to keep up the pressure on the secular authorities. Nor, in a world of colonial legislative assemblies, was there an over-arching system of royal control which would allow the crown to intervene, by legislative and executive action, on the Indians' behalf.

Those Indians who found themselves living within the confines of English settlements were gradually brought within the legislative purview of colonial societies. During the first decades of settlement in Puritan New England an effort was made to ensure fair treatment for the Indians under English law. Notions of fairness and reciprocity were deeply rooted in both Algonquian Indian and Puritan society, even if their interpretation could well differ in specific instances, and Algonquians, although holding to their own legal autonomy, would on occasion turn of their own free will to the colonial courts, especially for mediation in disputes. In 1656 Massachusetts appointed a commissioner for Indian affairs – a post comparable to that of Protector of the Indians with which the Spaniards experimented in the early stages of the colonization of the mainland[115] – and by the 1670s juries composed of six Indians and six whites were pronouncing on criminal cases that arose between Algonquians and settlers.[116] But after King Philip's War of 1675–6 the Indian courts set up by the New England colonists were dismantled, 'overseers' were assigned to deal with Indian affairs, and Indian legal rights were steadily eroded.[117] Spanish justice, on the other hand, gave Indians at least a chance of fighting for their rights all the way to the summit of the judicial system; and Spanish judges, who personally administered justice and enjoyed a high degree of discretion in the hearing and assessing of evidence and the choice of punishment, showed a flexibility in their approach to crime, whether the case was one of drunken disorder or domestic violence and homicide, that contrasted sharply with the severity of New England's courts.[118]

King Philip's War undid much of the work done by Eliot and other apostles to the Indians in establishing in the English mind the worthiness of native Americans to be considered for eventual inclusion within the fellowship of the visible saints. For the Indians, the war was a disaster. Large numbers of those who had surrendered or been captured were sold into foreign slavery on the pretext, still much used by Spaniards on the fringes of empire, that they had been taken captive in a 'just war'. Eliot's seems to have been the sole voice raised in moral protest, and – in striking contrast to the decision taken by Charles V to convoke the Valladolid debate – his protest was apparently ignored by the governor and council of Massachusetts, and went no further. In so far as Eliot played the part of a Las Casas, there was no one prepared to give him a hearing.[119]

Among the settlers there was a growing consensus that the Indians were, and always had been, degenerate barbarians, bereft of 'any religion before the English came, but merely diabolical'.[120] It was the same consensus as had come to prevail in Spanish America, and was accompanied by a similar blend of paternalism and contempt. But among the settlers of New England there was a further, and disturbing, element, the element of fear – fear not just of the enemy roaming on the fringes of their settlements, but also of a yet more hidden enemy, lying deep within themselves.

Coexistence and segregation

Europeans who settled in America found themselves living side by side with people who neither looked, nor behaved, like themselves. Nor did they even bear much resemblance to other peoples of whom at least some of them had earlier experience. They were not, for instance, black, as Columbus noted of the first Caribbean islanders he saw: 'They were all of good stature, very handsome people, with hair which is not curly but thick and flowing like a horse's mane. They all have very wide foreheads and hands, wider than those of any race [generación] I have seen before; their eyes are very beautiful and not small. None of them is black, rather the colour of the Canary islanders, which is to be expected since this island lies E–W with the island of Ferro in the Canaries on the same latitude.'[121]

Although colour was normally explained by sixteenth-century Europeans by reference to the degree of exposure to the sun, and was therefore nominally neutral as a form of categorization, blackness carried with it strong negative connotations for many Europeans, and certainly for the English.[122] The peoples of the New World, however, were not black. The Spanish royal cosmographer Juan López de Velasco described them in 1574 as being the colour of 'cooked quince', and William Strachey in 1612 as 'sodden quince'.[123] One chronicler at least dismissed climatic explanations of skin colour. In his History of the Indies López de Gómara wrote that the colour of the Indians was the result of 'nature, and not nakedness, as many believed', and pointed out that peoples of different colour could be found in the same latitudes.[124] The English, too, were to find in the light of their American experience that the traditional classical theory of climatic influence did not seem to correspond to observable facts.[125] But the general tendency was to cling to the traditional paradigm. As long as this prevailed, and climate was regarded as the prime determinant of colour, tawny-skinned Indians were the beneficiaries, since the colour of their skin was free of many of the emotional overtones with which blackness was so heavily charged.

Civility, not colour, was the first test used by Europeans in their assessment of the indigenous peoples of America. Where civility was concerned, the dispersed nature of Indian settlement patterns in the areas of British colonization enhanced the disparities that European colonists normally expected to find between themselves and the indigenous population. In promoting colonization, however, Richard Eburne denied that the English faced a greater challenge than the Spaniards: 'The Spaniard', he wrote, 'hath reasonably civilized, and better might if he had not so much tyrannized, people far more savage and bestial than any of these.'[126]

But the pattern of relationships in America was determined by past experience as well as present circumstance. The Christians of medieval Spain had for centuries lived alongside an Islamic civilization with which they enjoyed a complicated and ambiguous relationship. If they fought against the Moors, they also borrowed extensively from a society which in many respects was more refined than their own. Although religion was a decisive barrier at many points, and especially where the possibility of intermarriage was concerned,[127] personal contacts were numerous, and increased still further as large Moorish populations were left behind in Christian territory by the southward advance of the Reconquista. In these reconquered territories a toleration born of necessity rather than conviction prevailed for many years, although it came under increasing pressure in the fifteenth century as the Reconquista moved towards its triumphant conclusion. During the sixteenth century Spaniards came to despise and distrust the morisco population which continued to live among them, and whose conversion to Christianity was no more than nominal. But nothing could quite obliterate the experience of their long and often fruitful interaction with an ethnically different society that could not easily be regarded as culturally inferior to their own.[128]

The medieval English, in seeking to establish their lordship over Ireland, had no doubt of their own superiority to the strange and barbarous people among whom they were settling. Before Henry II's invasion in 1170 the native Irish, it was asserted, 'did never build any houses of brick or stone (some few poor Religious Houses excepted)', nor did they 'plant any gardens or orchards, enclose or improve their lands, live together in settled villages or towns, nor made any provision for posterity'.[129] Given what seemed to the English to be the vast disparity between their own culture and that of a Gaelic population whose way of life was 'against all sense and reason', they sought to protect themselves from the contaminating influence of their environment by adopting policies of segregation and exclusion. Marriage or cohabitation between the English and the Irish was forbidden by the Statutes of Kilkenny of 1366, in the belief that mixed marriages would tempt the English partner to lapse into degenerate Irish ways.[130]

The very fact that legislative measures against cohabitation were thought to be necessary suggests that English settlers in Ireland did indeed succumb to the temptation to go native.[131] The choice made by these renegade settlers could only have reinforced the latent English fears of the dangers of cultural degeneration in a barbarian land. In the sixteenth century the Irish remained for the English a barbarous people, whose barbarism was now compounded by their obstinate determination to cling to papist ways. When the English crossed the Atlantic and again found themselves living among, and outnumbered by, a 'savage' people, all the old fears were revived.[132] In the circumstances, the equation between the Indians and the Irish was easily made. In the New World of America the English came across another indigenous population which did not live in houses of brick and stone, and failed to improve its lands. 'The Natives of New England', wrote Thomas Morton, 'are accustomed to build them houses, much like the wild Irish . . .'[133] As Hugh Peter, who returned to England from Massachusetts in 1641, was to observe five years later, 'the wild Irish and the Indian do not much differ.'[134]

The instinctive tendency of the colonial leaders was therefore once again to establish a form of segregation. While the danger of Indian attacks made it prudent for the settlers of Virginia to live inside a 'pale', the founders of the colony also had no wish to see their fellow colonists go the way of the Norman invaders of Ireland, most of whom, according to Edmund Spenser, had 'degenerated and grown almost mere Irish, yea and more malicious to the English than the very Irish themselves'.[135] While the pale, therefore, may initially have been devised by the settlers as a means of protection against the Indians, it was also a means of protection against their own baser instincts. In 1609, in the early stages of the settlement of Virginia, William Symonds preached a sermon to the adventurers and planters, in which he drew a parallel between their enterprise and the migration of Abraham 'unto the land that I will shew thee' in the book of Genesis. 'Then must Abram's posterity keep them to themselves. They may not marry nor give in marriage to the heathen, that are uncircumcised . . . The breaking of this rule, may break the neck of all good success of this voyage . . .', Symonds warned.[136] Not surprisingly, John Rolfe agonized over his prospective marriage to Pocahontas, recalling 'the heavy displeasure which almighty God conceived against the sons of Levi and Israel for marrying strange wives' (fig. 8).[137]

The fear of cultural degeneracy in an alien land was especially pronounced among the Puritan emigrants to New England in the 1620s and 1630s. Images of another biblical exodus, that of the Israelites out of Egypt, were deeply impressed on their minds,[138] and their leaders were painfully aware of the dangers that lay in wait on every side. The Indians were the Canaanites, a degenerate race, who threatened to infect God's chosen people with their own degeneracy. For this reason it was essential that the New England Israel should remain a nation apart, resisting the blandishments of the people whom they were in process of dispossessing of their land.[139] In large measure this seems to have been achieved. In New England, no marriage is known to have occurred between an English settler and an Indian woman in the period before 1676. In Virginia, where the sex ratio among the settlers was even more unbalanced, it was much the same story, although a 1691 law passed by the colonial assembly forbidding Anglo-Indian marriages suggests that such unions did in fact occur. [140] But if so, their numbers were small, as Robert Beverley would lament in his *History of the Present State of Virginia* (1705):

> Intermarriage had been indeed the Method proposed very often by the Indians in the Beginning, urging it frequently as a certain Rule, that the English were not their Friends, if they refused it. And I can't but think it wou'd have been happy for that Country, had they embraced this Proposal: For, the Jealousie of the Indians, which I take to be the Cause of most of the Rapines and Murders they commited, wou'd by this Means have been altogether prevented, and consequently the Abundance of Blood that was shed on both sides wou'd have been saved; . . . the Colony, instead of all these Losses of Men on both sides, wou'd have been encreasing in Children to its Advantage; . . . and, in all Likelihood, many, if not most, of the Indians would have been converted to Christianity by this kind Method . . .[141]

Beverley's vision was a belated lament for a world that might have been. Among the Spaniards the same vision inspired a series of proposals for inter-ethnic union at a time when colonial society was still in its infancy. In their instructions of 1503 to Nicolás de Ovando as the new governor of Hispaniola, Ferdinand and Isabella ordered him to 'try to get some Christian men to marry Indian women, and Christian women to marry Indian men, so that they can communicate with and teach each other, and the Indians can be indoctrinated in our Holy Catholic Faith, and learn how to work their lands and manage their property, and be turned into rational men and women.'[142] This policy seems to have met with mixed success. In 1514, 64 of the 171 married Spaniards living in Santo Domingo had Indian wives. Most of these Spaniards, however, were drawn from the lowest social stratum, and the marriages may primarily reflect the shortage of Spanish women on the island.[143] While Spanish women, even of low birth, were preferred as wives, there was, however, no compunction about taking Indian women for concubines.

By formally sanctioning inter-ethnic marriage in 1514,[144] the crown appears to have been reiterating its conviction that a union of Spaniards and Indians would help realize Spain's mission of bringing Christianity and civility to the peoples of the Indies. The idea was taken up again as large areas of mainland America fell under Spanish rule. In 1526 the Franciscans in Mexico wrote to the emperor Charles V urging that, to promote the process of conversion, 'the two peoples, Christian and pagan, should unite, and join together in marriage, as is already beginning to happen.'[145] Las Casas, advocating the foundation in America of colonies of Spanish peasants, envisaged the intermarriage of their families with those of the Indians as a means of creating 'one of the best republics, and perhaps the most Christian and peaceful in the world'.[146]

The two peoples had certainly been uniting outside marriage. The conquerors, beginning with Cortés himself, took and discarded Indian women at will. Marriage, however, was by no means ruled out, with rank being rated more important than ethnicity. After taking her as his mistress, Cortés married off Montezuma's daughter, Doña Isabel, to a fellow Extremaduran, Pedro Gallego de Andrade, and, following his death, she married Juan Cano, who was clearly proud of his marriage to such a high-born wife.[147] In arranging Isabel's marriage Cortés appears to have been pursuing a deliberate strategy for the pacification of Mexico, which led to a number of marriages between his companions and princesses of the ruling house or the daughters of Mexican caciques.[148] Such marriages, which were seen as no disparagement where the indigenous women were of noble birth, may well have helped to create a climate of acceptance among later settlers. A merchant in Mexico wrote in 1571 to his nephew in Spain telling him that he was happily married to an Indian wife, adding: 'Although back in Spain it may seem that I was rash to marry an Indian woman, here this involves no loss of honour, for the nation of the Indians is held in high esteem.'[149]

While it is possible that the merchant was putting the best gloss on his behaviour for the benefit of his Spanish relatives, it is also possible that the obsession with purity of blood in metropolitan Spain, springing from the insistence on freedom from any taint of Moorish or Jewish ancestry, was diluted by the Atlantic crossing. Initially at least, conditions in the New World favoured this dilution. With Spanish women still in short supply, forced or consenting unions with Indian women were accepted as a matter of course. As the first generation of mestizo children of these unions appeared, their Spanish fathers were inclined to bring them up in their own households, especially if they were sons. In 1531 Charles V ordered the Audiencia of Mexico to collect all 'the sons of Spaniards born of Indian women . . . and living with the Indians', and to give them a Spanish education.[150] But the existence of a growing class of mestizos created difficult problems of categorization in societies that instinctively thought in terms of hierarchy. Where did the mestizos properly belong? If they were born in wedlock there was no problem, since they were automatically regarded as creoles (Spaniards of American origin). For those born out of marriage but accepted by one or other parental group, assimilation within that group was the normal destiny, although illegitimacy was a lasting stigma, and the lack of full assimilation could leave an abiding sense of bitterness, as the career of the most famous of all mestizos, the Inca Garcilaso de la Vega, testifies. But there were also a rapidly growing number of mestizos rejected by both groups, and therefore unable to find a secure place in a hierarchically organized, corporate society.

No such problem apparently affected the English settler communities. While cohabitation between English men and Indian women inevitably occurred – and in 1639, to the horror of New England colonists, between an English woman and an Indian man[151] – it was not on anything like the scale to be found in the Spanish colonies and it is significant that the mestizos born of these unions have largely disappeared from the historical record.[152] Nor, apparently, was there any of the easy acceptance of the practice of cohabitation that was to be found in the Spanish colonies. Sir Walter Raleigh boasted of his Guiana expedition that, unlike the Spanish conquistadores, not one of his men ever laid hands on an Indian woman.[153] If his boast is true, their behaviour was a world away from that of the band of some seventy Spaniards travelling up the river Paraguay in 1537, who, on being offered their daughters by the Indians, called it a day, and settled down to found what became the city of Asunción.

Unique local circumstances made Paraguay an extreme example of the more general process that accompanied the colonization of Spanish America. The Guaraní Indians needed the Spaniards as allies in their struggle to defend themselves against hostile neighbouring tribes. For their part, the Spaniards, moving inland from the newly founded port of Buenos Aires a thousand miles away, were too few in number to establish themselves without Guaraní help. An alliance based on mutual necessity was sealed by the gift of Guaraní women as wives, mistresses and servants. The continuing isolation of the settlement, and the almost total absence of Spanish women, led to the rapid creation of a unique mestizo society. Mestizo sons succeeded their fathers as encomenderos, and races and cultures mingled to a degree unparalleled elsewhere on the continent.[154]

Everywhere in Spanish America, however, cohabitation took place, and the effect of it was to blur the lines of division which the Spanish authorities in church and state had originally planned to draw between the different communities. In Spanish eyes a properly ordered society was one that consisted of two parallel 'republics', each with its own rights and privileges – a 'republic of Spaniards' and a 'republic of Indians'. But the plan to keep the two communities apart was in danger of foundering even before the emergence of a generation of mestizos which straddled the borderlines between them. The upheavals of conquest and colonization threw Spaniards and Indians into daily, and often intimate, contact. Indian women moved into Spanish households as servants and concubines, while Indians whose lives had been disrupted by the conquest gravitated naturally to the new cities founded by the Spaniards in search of new opportunities in the world of the conquerors.[155]

The blending of races and cultures inherent in the process of *mestizaje* was therefore at work from the earliest stages of conquest and settlement, undermining the bipartite society which royal officials had fondly hoped that they could create and maintain.[156] The crown might legislate to keep encomenderos away from the Indian communities in their encomiendas; Indians might be herded into *reducciones* or compelled to live in special *barrios* or quarters of the cities reserved exclusively for them; their natural 'inferiority' might be ceaselessly proclaimed by the colonists; but in a world where they heavily outnumbered settlers who could not live without their sexual and their labour services, there was no lasting possibility of closing off the two 'republics' from each other by creating the equivalent of an Anglo-Irish 'pale'.

Royal policy came to reflect the same tensions between segregation and integration as those to be found in colonial practice. To some extent the encomienda acted as a barrier against integration, except in matters of religion, where it was designed to foster it. In 1550, however, even as the crown legislated to prevent unmarried Spaniards from living in or near Indian communities, it also took the first steps towards breaking down the linguistic separation between the two republics, by decreeing that the friars, in defiance of their traditional practice, should teach the Indians Castilian, 'so that they should acquire our civility and good customs, and in this way more easily understand and be indoctrinated into the Christian religion'.[157] Already the process of linguistic change was under way in New Spain, as Indians who moved into the cities picked up a working knowledge of Castilian, while Castilian words were simultaneously being incorporated into the Nahuatl vocabulary on a massive scale.[158] Large numbers of the Indian vassals of the Spanish crown, however, either resisted the imposition of Castilian or remained to all intents and purposes outside its orbit, while many friars were inclined to ignore the crown's decree. At the same time, creoles with indigenous nurses learnt in childhood the language of the conquered, and in the Yucatán peninsula, which had a high degree of linguistic unity before the conquest, the Maya language, rather than Castilian, became the lingua franca in the post-conquest era.[159] The crown, for its part, was driven in particular by religious considerations to recognize realities. In 1578 Philip II decreed that no religious should be appointed to Indian benefices without some knowledge of the language, and two years later he set up chairs of indigenous languages in the universities of Lima and Mexico City, on the grounds that 'knowledge of the general language of the Indians is essential for the explanation and teaching of Christian doctrine.'[160]

The English, on finding themselves confronted by the linguistic barrier between themselves and the Indians, at first reacted much like the Spaniards. Indians showed little inclination to learn the language of the intruders, and initially it was the settlers who found themselves having to learn an alien tongue, both to communicate and to convert. Indians in areas of English settlement had less inducement than those in the more urbanized world of Spanish America to learn the language of the Europeans, although by degrees they found it convenient to have some of their number who could communicate in the language of the intruders. As the balance of forces tilted in favour of the settlers, however, so the pressures on the Indians to acquire some knowledge of English increased, until the colonists were securing promises from neighbouring tribes to learn the language as a requirement for submission to their rule.[161] Here there was no question, as there was in Spanish America, of a policy of actively promoting, at least among a section of the colonial community, the learning of indigenous languages – a policy which had the concomitant, if unintended, effect of encouraging not only the survival but also the expansion of the major languages, especially Nahuatl, Maya and Quechua. The powerful impulse to Christianize that worked in favour of the toleration of linguistic diversity in Spain's American possessions simply did not exist in British America.

While their acquisition of pidgin English extended their access to the developing colonial society, Indians living within the confines of the British settlements tended to have the worst of every world. They remained unassimilated, but at the same time had difficulty in maintaining the degree of collective identity to be found in so many Indian communities in Spanish America. The reasons for this were partly numerical, since their numbers were relatively so much smaller than those of the indigenous population under Spanish rule. But the difference was also a reflection of the differing policies adopted in the British and Spanish colonial worlds. The Spaniards, having imposed their dominion over vast native populations, saw it as their duty to incorporate them into a society defined on the one hand by Christianity and on the other by the rights and obligations that accompanied the status of vassals of the Spanish crown. As converts and vassals the Indians were entitled to a guaranteed position within a social order that was to be modelled as closely as possible on the divine.[162] The hopes of achieving the incorporation of the Indians into an imagined ideal society by means of a strategy of separate development were constantly frustrated by colonial conditions – demographic pressures, the demands of the settler community for Indian services, the desire of many Indians themselves to take advantage of what the Europeans had to offer. But enough of the policy was retained to make it possible for Indian communities shattered by conquest and foreign domination to regroup themselves and begin adapting collectively to life in the emerging colonial societies, while striving with a measure of success to maintain that 'republic of the Indians' which the crown itself was committed to preserving.

Where the Spaniards tended to think in terms of the incorporation of the Indians into an organic and hierarchically organized society which would enable them in time to attain the supreme benefits of Christianity and civility, the English, after an uncertain start, seem to have decided that there was no middle way between anglicization and exclusion. Missionary zeal was too thinly spread, the crown too remote and uninterested, to allow the development of a policy that would achieve by gradual stages the often asserted objective of bringing the Indians within the fold. In so far as a 'republic of the Indians' was to be found in British America, it was to be found in the praying towns of New England. But the whole concept of such a 'republic' was alien to settlers who expected the Indians either to learn to behave like English men and women, or else to move away. Tudor and Stuart England, unlike Habsburg Castile, had little tolerance for semi-autonomous juridical and administrative enclaves, and no experience of dealing with substantial ethnic minorities in its midst.

Since so many Indians appeared resistant to assimilation, it seemed to many settlers preferable to remove them out of the way. This would enable the colonists to devote their efforts to more rewarding pursuits. 'Our first work', wrote Sir Francis Wyatt, the governor of Virginia, soon after the 'massacre' of 1622, 'is expulsion of the Salvages to gain the free range of the country for increase of cattle, swine &c, which will more than restore us, for it is infinitely better to have no heathen among us, who at best were but thorns in our sides, than to be at peace and league with them . . .'[163] Expulsion of the Indians had the double advantage of making space for further settlement, and removing 'thorns', or something sharper, from the settlers' sides.

In part, the English response was dictated by fear. If there was a progressive hardening of attitudes towards the Indians, both in Virginia and New England, in the wake of incidents of alleged Indian 'treachery' and armed confrontation, intimidation and violent revenge looked like the only options available to the frightened setters who were still greatly outnumbered by those whose lands they had taken.[164] Expulsion of the Indians, if it could be managed, at least seemed to offer infant settlements a degree of security. Yet, at a time when the settlers still needed the assistance of the indigenous population in keeping them fed, their reaction suggests that the English had less confidence than the Spaniards in their ability to bring the benefits of their own civilization to these benighted people.

This may be a reflection of their failures in Ireland, although Spain, too, effectively admitted failure when it resorted in 1609 to the expulsion of some 300,000 moriscos from the peninsula. The Spanish failure, however, could be disguised as a triumph for the purity of the faith, whereas the continuing obduracy of the Irish allowed the English no such easy sleight of hand. Inevitably there were some shocking examples of Spaniards going native in the Americas, like that of the sailor Gonzalo Guerrero who, after being cast ashore on the coast of Yucatán, was found by Cortés living contentedly among the Maya, with his nose and ears pierced and his face and hands tattooed.[165] Yet the Spanish in the early stages of colonization appear not to have had the same obsessive fear of cultural degeneration that afflicted the English on making their first contact with indigenous peoples. At least in the early years, it seems to have been confidently assumed that most Spaniards, if confronted by such a dilemma, would imitate not Guerrero but his companion, Jerónimo de Águilar, who had held fast to his faith during the trials and temptations of captivity, and, unlike Guerrero, seized the first opportunity to rejoin his compatriots. By contrast, there was a constant trickle of deserters from the Jamestown settlement. To the distress of the colony's leaders, the poorer settlers at least tended to prefer a carefree existence among the 'wild' Indians to the rigours of building a 'civilized' community under the direction of their social superiors.[166]

Even on the frontiers of settlement, where life remained precarious, there still seems to have been a strong confidence in the eventual triumph of Christian and Hispanic values. Friars and royal officials approached the nomadic or semi-sedentary tribes on the fringes of empire with a clear sense of the superiority of what they had to offer the 'barbarian' peoples. Over time, the combination of urbanized frontier settlements and missions brought peace and a measure of hispanicization to many of the frontier regions. This was particularly true of northern Mexico, where a shift in viceregal policy in the later sixteenth century away from fire and slaughter to the more subtle weapons of diplomacy and religious persuasion succeeded in pacifying the ferocious Chichimecs.[167]

Royal officials bribed the Indians on the borderlands with offers of food and clothing. Friars sought to dazzle them with their ceremonies, and woo them with their gifts.[168] The inhabitants of the advanced Spanish outposts – soldiers, cattle ranchers and miners – mixed their blood with that of the indigenous population.[169] Although tensions inevitably arose as friars, royal officials and settlers pulled in different directions, they all represented in their different ways a coherent and unified culture which was not afraid to interact with the surrounding population because it took for granted that sooner or later its values would prevail.

While the English displayed a similar sense of superiority, it does not seem to have been accompanied, at least in the early stages of settlement, by the same measure of confidence in the triumph of the collective values of their own society in an alien environment. Confidence was lacking both in their capacity to instil into the Indians their own cultural and religious values, and in the willingness of fellow Englishmen and women to remain true to those values when confronted with an alternative way of life. Religious differences, social differences, and the lack of unified direction may all have worked to lessen the coherence of the twin message of Christianity and civility that the English colonizing enterprise was supposed to bring to the Indians. This in turn brought failure, and as failures multiplied, exclusion rather than inclusion of the Indians became the order of the day. Once the Indians had been defeated, however, and relegated to the margins of their society, new generations of colonists could look out on the world with a new-found confidence based on a sense of power. In their own eyes at least, they might not have Christianized and civilized the 'Salvages', but they could claim a massive achievement, both for their forebears and themselves, in clearing the wilderness and transforming the land.

CHAPTER 4

Exploiting American Resources

Plunder and 'improvement'

The first European images of America were images of abundance – of a terrestrial paradise with sparkling rivers, fertile plains and luxurious fruits.[1] Above all, there was gold, first of all in the rivers of Hispaniola,[2] then in Mexico, and finally in Peru, where Atahualpa's ransom – a staggering 1,326,539 *pesos* of gold and 51,600 silver marks, by official, and no doubt undervalued, reckoning[3] – set the seal on the image of fabulous wealth. But, as the humanist chronicler Pedro Mártir de Anglería observed, 'it is to the South, not the icy North, that everyone in search of fortune should turn.'[4] And it was to the south that Sir Walter Raleigh duly turned in his futile quest for El Dorado.

The south – the central and southern mainland of America – offered not only the promise, and the reality, of gold and silver, but also the possibility of tapping into the labour supply and surplus production of indigenous societies which had exploited the resources of their local environments in ways that offered more points of convergence with European needs and expectations than were to be found in more northerly parts. The hunters and gatherers of the 'icy North' apparently had little to offer European newcomers, other than the furs which were to become the source of a flourishing Indian-European trade. In southern New England and further down the coast, the more agricultural life-style of the native population produced a food surplus that saved the life of many a colonist in the early days of settlement. It was also a life-style that involved the stripping of forests and the clearing of fields, thus effectively doing some of the work of clearing the land that would otherwise have fallen to the settlers in this heavily forested world. But Indians who moved their village habitats in accordance with the dictates of the seasons and the fertility of the soil, and whose way of life depended on the possession of little more than a few, easily transportable household objects, seemed distinctly unpromising as a source of labour or tribute.[5]

It was therefore not surprising that English colonists should have felt a certain sense of bafflement on their arrival in a world in which the abundance of nature seemed to offer a standing rebuke to a sparse and – to European eyes – poverty-stricken, population.[6] Much work was needed to 'improve' the land, and there was no indication that the Indians were either willing to undertake it, or capable of doing so. On the other hand, Spaniards arriving in Mexico and Peru found teeming populations organized into polities which, for all their strangeness, functioned in relatively comprehensible ways, and which had learnt how to mobilize large labour forces for the performance of tasks that went beyond meeting basic subsistence needs. While it was not easy to come to terms with the idea that feathers, or cacao beans, might be more highly valued than gold or silver, it still remained true that these were peoples whose disciplined polities, agricultural practices, and skills in arts and crafts could be turned into valuable assets for their conquerors.

The Spaniards, slipping easily into the position of the privileged elites they had vanquished, took immediate advantage of the glittering opportunities that opened up before them. While their first response to conquest was to seize and share out the portable booty, they also moved quickly to make themselves the masters of economic and tributary systems that were still in relatively good working order in spite of the disruptions caused by the conquest. To satisfy their own overwhelming greed they were all too soon to wrench these systems out of context, especially in Peru, where they inherited forms of labour organization and redistributive systems carefully designed to provide an adequate food supply for populations living at different altitudes and in a diversity of ecological environments, rising from the sea-coasts to the high peaks of the Andes.[7] In effect, for the first twenty or thirty years after the conquest of Mexico and Peru, the conquerors heedlessly ran a form of plunder economy, although endowing it with a spurious respectability by the institution of the encomienda, which was supposed to carry with it certain spiritual and moral obligations, but was liable to be no more than a licence to oppress and exploit.[8]

If the Spanish conquerors were happy to live off the backs of the peoples they had conquered, they were also anxious to lead a life-style that conformed as closely as possible to that of the privileged classes in their native land. Their tastes and expectations had been formed in Castile, Extremadura or Andalusia, and now that riches had come their way, they were not about to abandon them. 'The desire of the Spaniards to see the things of their native land in the Indies', wrote the Inca Garcilaso de la Vega, 'has been so desperate and so powerful that no effort or danger has been too great to induce them to abandon the attempt to satisfy their wishes.'[9] They yearned for their glasses of wine, their oranges and other familiar fruits; they wanted dogs and horses, swords and guns; they wanted the luxuries that they had possessed, or at least coveted, at home; and they wanted their traditional staples, meat and bread.

The satisfaction of these wants would entail massive changes to the economies they had inherited – changes that in turn would transform the ecologies of the lands they had settled. The civilizations of the Americas were maize-based. It was above all maize, capable of a yield of sixty or more (some chroniclers spoke of as much as 150) to every seed planted, as against a return of six to one for wheat in Early Modern Europe, that had allowed the societies of Mesoamerica and the Andes to sustain such large populations and produce an agricultural surplus.[10] The Spanish settlers, however, although gradually accustoming themselves to maize tortillas,[11] still insisted on having their wheat loaves, to which they retained an obstinate attachment throughout the colonial period. Coarse bread therefore remained the staple of poor colonists, while the better-off ate *pan blanco* at twice the cost.[12] English settlers to the north seem to have shown a greater degree of adaptability, perhaps by force of circumstance. Indian corn became an essential part of their diet, and was considered preferable as a crop to English cereals because it was easier to grow and produced a higher yield. The New England climate proved unpropitious for wheat production, and although wheat, barley, oats and rye were beginning to be cultivated in the Chesapeake colonies in the later seventeenth century in sufficient quantities to allow for modest exports, their 'chiefest Diett' consisted of maize, and not wheat.[13]

In the regions settled by the Spaniards, with the exception of the Caribbean islands, where all attempts to cultivate wheat proved abortive,[14] large areas of land were brought under the plough for the purpose of wheat production. Since the Indians persisted in their diet of maize, the wheat-fields which began to transform the landscapes of Mexico and Peru were exclusively devoted to production for the conquerors and settlers. With land becoming abundant as the indigenous population declined, viceroys were prepared to make land grants (*mercedes de tierra*) to interested parties,[15] and the growing towns and cities provided a ready market for the produce from the new landed estates.

Simultaneously, the land was transformed even more dramatically by the introduction and proliferation of European livestock – cattle, sheep, horses and goats. The appearance of this livestock, immensely damaging to Indian agriculture as the animals trampled the maize plots and ate the vegetation, provided another set of opportunities for entrepreneurially minded settlers as they took to stock raising, again with the growing domestic market in mind. A pastoral economy was developed in the viceroyalty of New Spain, where the Spanish institution of the *Mesta* was taken as a model for the organization of the sheep-owners.[16] Horse breeding and cattle ranching provided a further stimulus to the formation of great estates – known as *haciendas* or *estancias* – especially in northern Mexico and the Peruvian sierra.[17] By means of a modest system of land grants to poorer settlers, the viceregal authorities in Peru seem to have hoped to encourage the rise in the coastal regions of a class of small farmers, comparable to that which would later develop in New England and the Middle Colonies. But all too often their farmsteads or *chacras* proved not to be economically viable, as a result of lack of capital and limited market outlets. By the end of the sixteenth century many of them were being swallowed up by the larger landowners.[18]

The development of commercial agriculture, cattle farming and sheep raising, together with viticulture in Chile and Peru, soon began to reduce the initially overwhelming dependence of the settlers on the home country for essential food-

Mesta – powerful assoc. of sheep owners.

stuffs. Until as late as 1570–80, however, Spanish agrarian products – corn, wine and oil – remained the preponderant element in transatlantic shipments from Seville.[19] Somehow the settlers had to find ways of paying for these essential commodities, as well as for the luxury items – high-quality textiles and articles of clothing, metal objects, furnishings and books – for which they craved. This required the identification and development of suitable commodities to sustain an export trade.

English settlers in North America would be faced with a similar desperate search for 'commodities' – for items in short supply at home that would justify the investment of capital and resources in overseas enterprise. William Wood's *New England's Prospect* (1634) told its own story. Where fertility was concerned, 'for the natural soil, I prefer it before the country of Surrey or Middlesex, which if they were not enriched with continual manurings would be less fertile than the meanest ground in New England. Wherefore it is not impossible, nor much improbable, that upon improvements the soil may be as good in time as England.' Turning to prospects for the subsoil, Wood wrote: 'For such commodities as lie underground, I cannot out of my own experience or knowledge say much . . . but it is certainly reported that there is ironstone . . . And though nobody dare confidently conclude, yet dare they not utterly deny, but that the Spaniards' bliss [i.e. gold] may yet lie hid in the barren mountains.' As for other possible resources, 'the next commodity the land affords is good store of woods . . .'[20] In terms of the mother country's requirements, New Englanders were to discover that the region they had settled did not offer the most promising of prospects.

In the initial stages of their colonization of the mainland the Spaniards would fare considerably better. Their first instinct, having looted what they could, was to go for commodities which required the minimum of processing or development: placer gold, in the first instance, but also pearls, first found by Columbus off the Cumaná coast of Venezuela, and acquired by barter from the natives until pearl fisheries based on the island of Cubagua began to be systematically developed.[21] Dyestuffs, too, were in much demand at home. In 1526 the first shipment from Mexico of cochineal, the source of a red dye greatly superior to the traditional 'Venetian scarlet', marked the beginnings of what was to become a highly profitable transatlantic trade.[22] This was followed later in the century by the development in central America of indigo as an export crop, although indigo production, unlike that of cochineal, required mechanical processing.[23] Other indigenous crops, too, began to find a European market, and most notably cacao. Early settlers in New Spain acquired from the indigenous population a taste for chocolate, and it was to meet the needs of the growing Mexican market that settlers in the Izalcos region of northern central America, desperate to find some rapid source of wealth, began producing cacao in the middle decades of the century.[24] Boom was followed by collapse, but by the end of the sixteenth century New Spain in turn was exporting cacao to metropolitan Spain, where Mexican chocolate became an addiction among the elite and a cause for grave moral concern among those of tender conscience.[25]

[handwritten margin note: The land in New England was not very fertile and they had a hard time growing food]

There were profits to be made, too, from exports based on Old World trans-plants to the Indies – hides and skins from the livestock now roaming Spain's Caribbean islands and the mainland colonies, and sugar, originally brought by Columbus to Hispaniola on his second voyage. Hides and sugar, indeed, were to become the mainstay of Hispaniola's economy as the tide of colonization moved on to the mainland, leaving the island half-abandoned and desolate, with its indigenous population dying out. In the 1520s wealthy encomenderos with a stake in Hispaniola's future began to invest in sugar mills, with the help and encouragement of royal officials. This marked the modest beginnings of a plan-tation economy in the Spanish Antilles which in 1558, at its peak, produced 60,000 *arrobas* of sugar for export to Seville, before it was outpriced on the Iberian markets by sugar produced more cheaply in other parts of the Americas.[26] Within a few years of the conquest of Mexico sugar production moved to the mainland when Hernán Cortés established sugar mills at Tuxtla and Cuernavaca. Most of this sugar was for export, and the Cortés plantations survived, with fluctuating fortunes, throughout the colonial period.[27]

Throughout the Spanish American world, therefore, plunder began to give way to development as easy booty became a diminishing asset, and it began to dawn on the conquerors and early immigrants that they were unlikely in the immediate future to be returning to their homeland laden with American riches. Their out-look was no doubt different from that of those early settlers of New England who had come in search of an alternative home, and, in William Wood's words, 'look not so much at abundance as at competency'.[28] Many of these were content with a step-by-step development of arable farming and animal husbandry on their modest farmsteads, although from the earliest days New England had its entre-preneurs like John Pynchon, who threw himself into commercial and industrial enterprises and dominated the economic and political life of his native town of Springfield, Massachusetts, founded in 1636 by his father, William.[29] In both instances, however, the sheer pressure to survive forced the immigrants to think in terms of the best ways to develop local resources and exploit the opportunities provided by the growth of the settler communities.

A continent that to European eyes appeared unimproved, or undeveloped, offered immense possibilities to the resourceful, and to those willing to take risks. But conditions tended to favour those who already had resources at their disposal, in the form of capital or labour, or both. Their privileged position made it possi-ble for them to advance credit, or to engage personally in new ventures, like the textile workshops (*obrajes*) that began to be established in the viceroyalties of New Spain and Peru.[30] After the initial investment of Spanish and European cap-ital in the colonization of the Spanish Caribbean, further development in the Spanish American world had to depend largely on local capital and resources. A substantial, if erratic, supply of gold, and the flow of Indian tribute and labour that followed the defeat of the pre-Columbian empires, made the first stages of capital formation easier in Spanish than in British America. Merchants, encomenderos and royal officials with access to these sources of wealth were especially well placed to take advantage of the new opportunities presented by the need to refashion the New World to meet Old World requirements.

It was, however, the discovery in the 1540s of the great silver deposits of northern Mexico and the Andes that dramatically altered the prospects of Spain's American possessions, and transformed them into far more than mere appendages to Europe's trading networks. Although the first silver strikes in New Spain were made within a decade of the conquest, the decisive event was the finding in 1546 of silver ores on the northern plateau at Zacatecas, to be followed by discoveries of further deposits in the same region in the following decades.[31] Already in the previous year Spaniards in Peru had come across the extraordinary silver mountain of Potosí in the eastern range of the Andes. As a result of these spectacular discoveries, silver took the place of the dwindling supply of looted gold as the most valuable mineral resource of Spain's empire in America.[32]

Although subsoil rights in Spain and its overseas territories belonged to the crown,[33] the imposition of a state monopoly on the development of mining in the New World was out of the question. The crown needed silver urgently, and if new deposits were to be found and effectively exploited, this could only be achieved through private enterprise. The crown was therefore ready to grant prospecting and mining rights, in the form of what came to be a permanent concession, to those who came forward to request them. Those who received the concession were obligated in return to hand over to treasury officials a proportion – commonly a *diezmo*, or tenth – of all the silver they mined.[34] It was this waiving by the crown of its subsoil rights that made possible the rapid development of the mining economies of New Spain and Peru, although at a high price in terms of deception and fraud.

The beginnings of large-scale silver production in the two American viceroyalties had a galvanizing impact on their economies and societies, and one that would spread outwards in a ripple effect to other parts of Spanish America where precious metals were sought but not often found. There was an immediate stimulus to mining technology and production techniques, first of all in New Spain, where, as against the Andes, there was little by way of a native metallurgical tradition to which the Spaniards could resort. The most important technical advance came in New Spain in the 1550s when the process of drawing silver from the ore by the use of an amalgam of mercury was pioneered. There was a delay of some twenty years before the amalgamation process was transferred to the Andes, probably because Spanish entrepreneurs in Potosí were happy to cut costs and win quick profits by leaving it to Indian miners to follow their old and well-tried techniques.[35] When the new refining procedure was eventually introduced, it made possible spectacular increases in silver production – increases facilitated by the fortunate discovery in 1563 at Huancavelica, in the mountains south-east of Lima, of mercury deposits that would provide a partial alternative to the mercury that had to be shipped across the Atlantic from the Spanish mines at Almadén.[36]

The introduction of large-scale mining operations required a concentration of capital and technical expertise, bringing to the mining areas speculators and merchants from Spain and other parts of the Indies who would advance goods and credit to the miners, and receive raw silver in return. The rush to find new reserves of silver was the principal dynamic behind the creation of new settlements and towns in northern Mexico, while Potosí, located 13,000 feet above sea level in the rarefied air of the Andes, grew into one of the largest cities of the western world, with a combined indigenous and Spanish population exceeding 100,000 by the start of the seventeenth century (fig. 12).[37] The development of large centres of population acted in turn as a stimulus to agriculture and livestock farming, with food and supplies being drawn from an ever wider radius as the population grew. Potosí was eventually drawing on a catchment area that extended from the Pacific coast of Chile – a source of fish, grapes and sugar – to Paraguay and the province of Buenos Aires, from which it obtained the cattle and sheep needed to keep it provisioned with meat.[38]

The production and minting of silver introduced at least a partial monetary economy to expanding areas of Spanish America. The conquerors and settlers of Mexico needed a means of exchange in a land where cacao beans, bales of cloth and various other artefacts had served as currency before they appeared on the scene. The coin supply from Spain was fitful and inadequate, and, after growing agitation, a mint was established in Mexico City in 1536. This was authorized to strike silver and copper coins, although minting of the latter ceased in 1565 when it was found that the Indians were misusing them.[39] A second mint in the Americas was founded in Lima in 1565, and then transferred to Potosí, where in 1574 the Casa de Moneda, situated on the south side of the Plaza Mayor, began striking the silver coins that would soon be circling the globe.[40]

Very soon after its introduction, Indians began to use specie in Mexican markets alongside their cacao beans.[41] The growing familiarity of the indigenous population with coins and complex financial transactions played an important part in the inexorable process by which the Spaniards would realize their aim of drawing it into a monetary economy. 'Giving them their own lands and money in payment for their work,' wrote a Spanish judge in Peru in 1567, 'so that they can purchase for themselves locally produced sheep, and cattle from Spain and other items for themselves, they will become interested in working, and by this means civility will begin to get into them.'[42] The chink of coins would herald the coming of 'civilization' to the Andes.

The absence of silver mines in the areas of English settlement left the British colonies at an obvious disadvantage in providing settlers with specie as a circulating medium. From the 1620s tobacco became the common currency of the Chesapeake, even if accounts were kept in pounds, shillings and pence.[43] A mint was set up in Massachusetts in 1652 but was closed some thirty years later, following the imposition of the Dominion of New England.[44] Thereafter, colonial English America would have no mints. The gold and silver coins that circulated in the colonies were Spanish and Portuguese, with the Spanish silver piece of eight (the dollar) considered the most reliable coin because of its milled edges.[45] These silver pieces filtered in to the American mainland through contraband trade and exchanges with the Spanish Caribbean islands, and there were never enough to meet the demand. As a result, local shortages of gold and silver coins remained a persistent problem throughout the colonial period, with individual colonies seeking to attract the coins in circulation by giving them a higher value than their neighbours. With specie draining away to England to pay for British imports, barter and commodities continued to be used for many local transactions, although by the end of the seventeenth century paper money, in the form of bills of credit, was becoming increasingly common as a medium of exchange, and would do much to limit the consequences of a money-short economy.[46]

Thanks to its mines, Spanish America naturally developed a more monetized colonial market. Yet, for all the abundance of silver, it too tended to suffer from serious currency deficits as pieces of eight became a global currency. A royal order of 1556 that half of all the silver minted in Mexico City should be retained for use in New Spain inevitably failed to prevent the clandestine export of silver coins. Where these were insufficient for local transactions, traders would often have recourse to unminted bullion, in spite of the crown's efforts to put an end to a practice which defrauded it of revenue.[47] There were great opportunities for personal enrichment, both open and clandestine, in these silver-rich societies, and leading merchants in Mexico City and Lima, after accumulating large stocks of silver, found it expedient and profitable to deploy their reserves to finance local enterprise. Throughout the colonial period credit played a central part in the financial and commercial life of Spanish America. In the absence of formal banking institutions the gap was filled by merchants, who, together with the church, became the principal source of loans.[48]

Since sixteenth-century Europe possessed an insatiable thirst for silver, which it needed both for its own transactions and to balance its chronic trade deficit with Asia, its outflow from the Indies was a foregone conclusion. Even if anything from a quarter to a half would remain in the viceroyalties,[49] whether in the form of coins, unminted silver or artefacts – altar frontals and candlesticks in the churches, caskets and tableware in the houses of the wealthy – Mexican and Peruvian silver propelled the Spanish Indies inexorably towards integration into the developing economies of Europe. From the mid-sixteenth century, Spanish America became pre-eminently a silver-based empire, furnishing successive Spanish rulers with a significant proportion – 20 to 25 per cent – of their revenues, while providing a stream of bullion which helped to lubricate Europe's economic activities and enabled the colonial societies to acquire from Europe the commodities they were unwilling or unable to produce locally.[50]

Spain's empire of the Indies therefore became heavily dependent for its export trade to Europe on a single staple which accounted for 80 to 90 per cent of the value of its annual exports to Seville in the final decades of the sixteenth century and the opening decades of the seventeenth.[51] A similar dependence on a single staple export trade would be characteristic of the economies of other colonial societies in the Americas in the early stages of development, although New Spain and Peru would be unique in their development of an extractive economy until gold was struck in large quantities in eighteenth-century Brazil. Outside the silver-producing regions, it was a question of finding and developing a suitable crop for large-scale export. While New England and the Middle Colonies failed to achieve this, the story would be very different in the Caribbean islands and the Chesapeake colonies. Both regions were to provide fertile soil for one or other of the two crops that were to prove most in demand in overseas markets – sugar and tobacco. To these would be added rice and indigo as the Lower South (the Carolinas and Georgia) was developed in the eighteenth century. In Spanish American cacao would become an increasingly strong export staple over the course of the seventeenth century, to the particular benefit of the planters of Caracas in what had until then been a relatively marginalized Venezuela.[52]

The realization that the soil was suitable for the cultivation of tobacco and that the home country would pay a good price for the 'weede' proved to be the salvation of the Jamestown colony. Extensive cultivation got under way in Virginia in the 1620s, and would spread in the 1630s and 1640s to the newly founded colony of Maryland. As tobacco exports grew, so also did the population – from 2,500 in Virginia in 1630 to a total of 23,000 for the two colonies in 1650, and up to 100,000 by the end of the century.[53] Tobacco cultivation came to dominate the life of the Chesapeake region, shaping its dispersed settlement patterns along the waterways, and the character of its labour supply.

Sugar had a comparable transforming effect on the economy and the prospects of the island of Barbados, which was annexed in 1625 by a passing British captain, and then colonized as a commercial venture sponsored by a London syndicate until Charles I granted its proprietorship, along with that of the Leeward Islands, to the Earl of Carlisle.[54] The original sponsors had planned to develop the island as a tobacco colony, but the crop proved disappointing, and the struggling planters were saved by the discovery that the soil was ideal for the cultivation of sugar. In the 1640s and 1650s, as the techniques of cane production were imported from Portuguese Brazil, Barbados's sugar production shot up, with spectacular consequences for immigration rates and for the price of land and foodstuffs.[55]

The export of sugar, supplemented by that of cotton, made Barbados easily the richest English possession in the Americas in the second half of the seventeenth century (fig. 10). While its population was little more than half that of Virginia, the value of its exports was almost 50 per cent more.[56] Like the silver of Mexico and Peru, the sugar of Barbados created a febrile prosperity, encouraging those who benefited from the production and export of a commodity in high demand in Europe to make the most of their good fortune and indulge in a life-style consonant with their newly acquired affluence. But, as the relatively simple life-style of the Chesapeake tobacco planters in the later seventeenth and early eighteenth centuries makes clear, there were other possible reactions to the potential riches of a natural resource.[57] A sense of the fragility created by dependence on a single export staple in fluctuating markets could provoke diametrically different responses, ranging from lavish spending and conspicuous consumption to a prudential approach in the face of an uncertain future in an impermanent world.

Many considerations would enter into the fashioning of these diverse responses – inherited cultural traditions, the nature of the resource, and the relationship of the elite to its production and marketing. One way or another, however, the overwhelming dependence on a single resource inevitably shaped the perceptions, attitudes and behaviour of the emerging elites in colonial societies wherever it occurred. Their lives, and with them the character of their societies as a whole, would revolve around the fluctuations in the production of, and demand for, their staple commodity. These fluctuations would be dictated both by local and European conditions, and by the continuing provision of an adequate labour supply at a realistic cost.

Labour supply

The labour systems developed in Spanish and British America for the production of their staple commodities were heavily conditioned by the degree to which they were populated by Indians capable of being put to productive work by the colonists. The Spaniards were exceptionally fortunate in that their silver-producing regions lay either within, or relatively close to, densely populated regions of indigenous settlement. This made it possible, by one device or another, to recruit a native labour force for working in the mines. The first areas of English settlement lacked any such advantage. In the absence of a densely settled and usable local population, the settlers and their sponsors were forced to come up with other solutions to the problem of providing a continuing labour supply for growing and processing their staple crop.

The challenge confronting the Spanish colonists and colonial authorities was how to mobilize the potentially vast indigenous labour force without infringing too blatantly the letter of the law. Ferdinand and Isabella had laid down the fundamental principle that the indigenous inhabitants in the new overseas territories of the Crown of Castile were vassals of the crown, and, as such, were not to be enslaved. 'What power of mine does the admiral hold to give my vassals to anyone?' asked Isabella in 1498 on being told that Columbus had allowed every returning settler from Hispaniola to bring a slave back to Spain. All the slaves were forthwith to be freed.[58] There were, however, exceptions, and the conquerors and early settlers were quick to exploit them. In 1503 Isabella permitted the enslavement of man-eating Caribs, 'because of the crimes they have committed against my subjects'[59] – a provision that effectively gave carte blanche to the Hispaniola settlers to engage in slave-raids on the neighbouring islands. They could also resort to the rules of 'just war', as developed in medieval Christendom, by which infidels who persisted in resisting Christian forces and fell into their hands could legitimately be enslaved. In the circumstances surrounding Spanish expansion into America, this provision was open to obvious abuse. It was in the hope of curbing this abuse, and laying down the ground rules for establishing whether the Spaniards were justified in launching an attack, that the device of reading aloud the *requerimiento* to bemused Indians had been devised.[60]

As Las Casas and others were quick to point out, the conquerors and first settlers made a mockery of the *requerimiento*,[61] which in effect became a sanction for committing illegalities under the guise of legitimacy. The Caribbean islands, and the heavily populated central American mainland region between Mexico and Panama, became a vast catchment area in which Spanish raiders seized Indians for enslavement, using specious arguments of 'just war' as their pretext, and salving their consciences by pointing to the existence of slavery among the Indians themselves. The new slaves were then transported to regions where labour was needed – New Spain, Guatemala and, increasingly, Panama and Peru.[62]

Under Charles V, the crown sought to limit the abuses by further legislation. This culminated in a decree of 1542, subsequently incorporated into the New Laws later that same year, ordering that nobody in future should enslave Indians, 'even if they are taken in just war'. Indians were neither to be purchased nor otherwise acquired, but were to be treated, as the New Laws put it, 'like our vassals of the crown of Castile, since that is what they are'.[63] The founding in 1543 of a new court, the Audiencia de los Confines (later to become the Audiencia of Guatemala), brought some improvement, but the decline of Indian enslavement in central America after the middle years of the century was largely caused by the extinction of much of the potential slave population. Elsewhere, enslavement continued wherever royal authority was weak or officials were willing to turn a blind eye. This was particularly true of the lawless border areas on the fringes of empire, like Chile and New Mexico, whose conqueror and first governor, Juan de Oñate, razed the village of Acoma in 1599 and sentenced adult captives to two decades of personal servitude. The leading families of seventeenth-century New Mexico would all have their Indian bondsmen and women, many of whom were in reality slaves.[64]

In the principal regions of Spain's American empire, however, the prohibition of Indian slavery made it necessary to devise alternative methods of recruiting indigenous labour. Initially this was achieved through the encomienda system, which was supplemented, and in some regions gradually replaced as a source of labour, by the repartimiento, or short-term allocation of Indians by royal officials to non-encomenderos for different forms of compulsory service.[65] In the middle years of the sixteenth century, when vast new reserves of labour were needed for working the newly discovered silver deposits, the sharp fall in the size of the indigenous population was already beginning to undermine the foundations of the encomienda system. In the eyes of the colonial authorities silver production came to take precedence over all other requirements, including those of the encomenderos. As an early viceroy of Peru put it, 'if there are no mines, there is no Peru.'[66] Although the crown remained reluctant to reverse its policies and sanction a system of forced Indian labour, its local officials were driven by necessity to devise their own strategies, which they tailored to meet local circumstances.

In Peru, Don Francisco de Toledo, who arrived as viceroy in 1569, oversaw the elaboration of a forced labour system based on a combination of Inca precedent and recently developed Spanish practice. Using as their model the *mita* employed by the Incas for public works, the Spaniards arranged for the provision of a continuous labour supply for the Potosí mines by means of a rota system, under which one-seventh of the adult male Indians from a wide catchment area in the Andean highlands were drafted for a year's labour in Potosí. The *mitayos*, although miserably remunerated, were accorded basic rates of pay. Towards the end of the sixteenth century their labour was increasingly supplemented by that of voluntary workers, known as *mingas*, who were drawn to Potosí by the prospect of the wages that were offered.[67] Their presence brought the system closer to that employed in New Spain, where the mines were located too far away from the large sedentary population of central Mexico to make a forced labour system feasible. Instead, Zacatecas and the other mines made use of migrant Indians who were lured to the north by the offer of salaried labour. Gradually but inexorably, in both New Spain and Peru, the indigenous population, considered to be congenitally idle by the Spaniards – themselves generally regarded as something of an authority on the subject – was being sucked into a European-style wage economy.

The prime solution to the labour problem in Spanish America, therefore, was found in a combination of forced and 'voluntary' indigenous labour. As the indigenous population shrank, however, it was increasingly incapable of meeting the numerous demands imposed upon it. Since it was unthinkable that settlers and their descendants should engage in menial labour, the only remaining option – unless the Spanish crown was prepared, as it was not, to open its American territories to immigrants from other European states – was to import a coerced labour force from overseas. The richest and most accessible source of supply was black Africa.[68]

Precedents were well established. At the beginning of the sixteenth century the Iberian peninsula – especially Andalusia and Portugal – possessed a substantial population of Moorish and African slaves, working both in the fields and in domestic service. It was therefore a logical extension of current Iberian practice for Ferdinand to authorize the despatch in 1510 of fifty slaves to work in the Hispaniola gold mines. In 1518 his successor, Charles, not yet elected to the Imperial title, granted one of the members of his Flemish entourage, Laurent de Gorrevod, an eight-year licence, which he then sold for 25,000 ducats to the Genoese bankers, to import black slaves into the Indies.[69] Hitherto, the slaves sent to the New World had mostly been drawn from the peninsula, and were therefore Spanish-speaking, as were the black servants or slaves who crossed the Atlantic with the conquistadores, and made a valuable contribution to expeditions of discovery and conquest.[70] They were also Christian converts, since the crown was not prepared to run the risk of having its overseas territories infiltrated by Islam.[71] Following the grant to Gorrevod, the traffic in slaves to the Indies acquired a new dimension. The prohibition on the introduction of Muslims into America remained at least nominally in place, but with the granting of the first of the *asientos* or contracts issued under a monopoly system for the regulation of the Atlantic slave trade, the way was open for slaves to be transported direct from Africa to the Indies, without necessarily experiencing a period of acculturation on Iberian soil.

In the years up to 1550, some 15,000 African slaves were officially recorded as arriving in the Spanish Indies, and a further 36,300 between 1550 and 1595,[72] but the real numbers, swollen by a growing contraband trade, must have been substantially larger. In the six years following the introduction in 1595 of a new monopoly contract between the Spanish crown and a Portuguese merchant, Pedro Gomes Reinel, who ran the Angola slave trade, there was a sudden massive upsurge in the number of Africans shipped to Spanish America. The 80,500 transported in those five years may have pushed the total for the sixteenth century to 150,000, excluding the further 50,000 taken to Brazil.[73]

The dominance of the Atlantic slave trade achieved by Portuguese merchants in the last quarter of the sixteenth century at the expense of their Genoese rivals followed logically from the establishment of Portuguese trading bases down the coast of West Africa during the fifteenth and early sixteenth centuries, and the rise to pre-eminence of Lisbon as the slave trade capital of the western world.[74] The Portuguese acquired a further advantage following the union of the crowns of Castile and Portugal in 1580. As the subjects of Philip II they were now well positioned to negotiate profitable deals in Madrid, and they seized their opportunity. In the years during which they held the monopoly contract, between 1595 and 1640, Portuguese merchants shipped between 250,000 and 300,000 Africans into Spanish America, thousands of them clandestinely through the port city of Buenos Aires, refounded by the Spaniards in 1580.[75] From here they were sent on to Peru, where their labour was needed to supplement that of the Indians in the mines and the fields. Other ports of entry were Santo Domingo, Havana, Vera Cruz and, above all, Cartagena, which received more than half the total number of slaves legally shipped to Spanish America between 1549 and 1640.[76]

By the early seventeenth century, therefore, the mechanisms of an international Atlantic slave trade had been firmly established. Sir William Alexander, in his *An Encouragement to Colonies* of 1624, would castigate the shipping of slaves from Angola and other parts of Africa to the Spanish Indies as 'an unnatural merchandise',[77] but in principle the way was open for the English in America to follow suit. Whether they did so would depend on their own labour requirements and the consideration of relative costs.

Spain's empire of the Indies offered numerous examples of the large variety of ways in which African slaves could be employed. Once on the mainland, they were first established in substantial numbers in the capitals of the two viceroyalties, Mexico City and Lima. Although slavery would soon spread to the countryside, urban slavery was to be a continuing feature of life in a society in which African slaves would come to constitute anything between 10 and 25 per cent of the populations of major cities like Lima, Mexico City, Quito, Cartagena and Santa Fe de Bogotá.[78] Large numbers of Africans, both slave and free, were employed as household servants; others became skilled craftsmen, at a time when artisans of Spanish origin proved unable to keep pace with the growth in demand.[79] Many arrived from Spain in the entourage of officials and other Spanish dignitaries.[80] Once in the Indies, the presence of such retainers enhanced the prestige of their masters, both Spanish and creole, as they travelled by coach through the streets or took the evening air. 'The gentlemen', wrote the English renegade, Thomas Gage, when describing Mexico City in 1625, 'have their train of blackamoor slaves, some a dozen, some half a dozen, waiting on them, in brave and gallant liveries, heavy with gold and silver lace, with silk stockings on their black legs, and roses on their feet, and swords by their sides.'[81]

In the Caribbean islands, and later in New Spain, slaves were employed in the cultivation of sugar cane. The five hundred contracted by Cortés in 1542 to work on his Mexican sugar estates[82] were the harbingers of the thousands upon thousands whose backs would bear the burden of working the plantation economies of the Caribbean islands and mainland America in a later age. While extensively employed on the haciendas of encomenderos, African slaves were also drafted into the textile workshops of New Spain and Peru to supplement the native workforce of sweated Indian labour. In the lowlands of New Granada, they replaced a dwindling indigenous population as members of labour gangs panning for gold in the rivers and creeks.[83]

There was also a growing and unsatisfied demand for enslaved or free black labour in the mines of northern Mexico as Indian workers succumbed to European diseases. By the end of the sixteenth century, blacks and mulattoes (the offspring of Spanish men and African women) had become indispensable to the mining economy of New Spain: as the saying went in Zacatecas, 'bad to have them, but much worse not to have them.'[84] But expense remained a problem. It was more costly to employ imported African labour than indigenous Indian labour in the mines. In the silver workings of Potosí, for which an indigenous work-force, habituated to working at such an altitude, could be mobilized from the surrounding regions, the relative labour costs proved an overwhelming deterrent to royal officials anxious to relieve the exploitation of Indians by abandoning the *mita*.[85] In other areas of economic activity in Peru, however, black slaves and their descendants came to play a vital role, especially in Lima and the coastal zone, where the Indian population decreased faster than it did in the highlands. They not only supplied a large part of the urban artisan labour force, but they also worked on the irrigated plots that sprang up round the towns. They tended the livestock on the large estates and drove the ox and mule carts on which the transportation system introduced by the Spaniards into America depended.[86]

African labour, therefore, whether slave or free, made a decisive contribution to economic activity in Spanish America, although it varied in scale and character from region to region. The greatest concentrations of Africans were to be found in the tropical and sub-tropical zones – the Antilles, the coastal regions of the two viceroyalties, and in New Granada and Venezuela.[87] The sheer numbers of those

[Handwritten margin note: Slaves were used more and more as the native people died from European disease.]

of African descent in the two viceroyalties as a whole – in 1640 some 150,000 in New Spain and 30,000 in Peru, of whom 20,000 lived in Lima[88] – suggest something of their indispensability to the functioning of the colonial economy, although the silver production on which the fortunes of Spain's empire of the Indies ultimately turned would have been impossible without the toil of the Indians working in the mines of New Spain and Peru.

In British America inadequate numbers, unsuitability for the kind of systematic labour expected by Europeans, and deep distrust – who in Virginia would be willing to take Indians into domestic service after the terrible events of 1622? – all played their part in preventing the early English settlers from systematically building up an indigenous work-force on the Spanish model. The Maryland settlers found that male Indians, unwilling to accept the routine of daily labour in the fields, simply disappeared into the interior when the summer months approached.[89] Had it been worth while, institutionalized forms of compulsory Indian labour service would no doubt have been developed in the English settlements, as in the Spanish, although it is hard to know whether they would have assumed the character of outright slavery.

It would have been awkward for the Jamestown settlers to defy Virginia Company policy by enslaving an indigenous people who were to be brought to the faith,[90] although, in the absence of a strong religious lobby and a concerned crown, it seems unlikely that scruple would for long have prevailed over necessity. During the course of the seventeenth century, in the absence of any imperial policy on slavery like that developed for Spanish America, individual colonies made occasional moves in the direction of Indian enslavement. They resorted, too, as in New England following King Philip's War, to the pretext of 'just war' to turn Indians into slaves, and displayed no scruples about purchasing Indians taken captive by some rival tribe. South Carolina, indeed, between the time of its foundation in 1670 and the end of the Yamasee War in 1713, made the Indian slave trade a major business, in defiance of the objections of its lords proprietors. Its white inhabitants indulged, like those of Spanish border societies, in raids deliberately conducted to enslave Indians, and engaged in the large-scale exchange of European goods for Indians made captive by fellow Indians. While some of these slaves were kept in Carolina itself – there were 1,400 of them in the colony in 1708 – many more were exported, primarily to the West Indies plantations, although they were also sold to the northern colonies for domestic service. As many as 30,000 to 50,000 may have been enslaved over the course of the colony's first fifty years, before the supply trickled away.[91]

Yet there were deterrents, both practical and legal, to Indian enslavement as a long-term solution to the shortage of labour in British America. Outside the West Indies it was too easy for slaves to abscond when Indian country was so near at hand. They could also be a dangerous presence. In the early eighteenth century the northern colonies, worried about the impact on their own Indians of slaves imported from South Carolina, imposed an import ban. Yet at the same time New Englanders were forcing growing numbers of their own native population into involuntary servitude. Changes to legal codes led to an expanded sentencing of Indian men and women into labour service for criminal activities and debt. Once indentured, they were liable to be bought and sold, and their children placed in forced apprenticeships on terms less advantageous than those enjoyed by white apprentices. By the middle of the century bound Indian workers, suffering from the imposed stigma of racial inferiority, were to be found throughout the region in substantial numbers.[92]

The whole question of slavery, however, was fraught with legal ambiguities, and some Indians at least managed to secure redress in the courts. The word 'slave' had no meaning in English law when the first settlers moved across the Atlantic, even though slavery did make a brief appearance in Protector Somerset's abortive Vagrancy Act of 1547.[93] Yet while slavery itself was unknown to English law, English society was well accustomed to various degrees of unfreedom, ranging from villeinage, or serfdom, to indentured service. It was to indentured white servants from the British Isles that the colonies first turned in their search for additional sources of labour, and it was as indentured servants that the majority of white emigrants crossed the Atlantic in the seventeenth century.[94] But, as many of them were to find on arrival, the conditions under which they were forced to work their four- or five-year stints made them, in their own eyes, little better than slaves. In one revealing incident, when a Spanish expedition attacked English settlers on Nevis in 1629, servants in the militia threw away their arms crying 'Liberty, joyfull Liberty', preferring collaboration with the Spaniards to subjection to tyrannical English masters.[95]

A shortage of white indentured servants, combined with difficulties in managing men and women whose only thought was to finish their period of service and strike out on their own, encouraged English settlers, both in the Caribbean and on the southern mainland, to turn to the most obvious remaining source of labour – imported Africans. Bermuda, granted to the Virginia Company in 1612 and run by the Bermuda Company from 1615, imported its first blacks in 1616. In its first half-century, however, Bermuda's economy was not heavily dependent on black slave labour.[96] The story was very different in the short-lived colony of Providence Island. However reluctant Puritan investors may have been to jeopardize the establishment of a godly community by filling it with slaves, relatively accessible sources of supply made it considerably cheaper to import blacks than white indentured servants to cultivate the tobacco crop. Considerations of godliness therefore lost out to harsh financial realities. By 1641, when its eleven-year existence was abruptly terminated, the Providence Island colony had become an authentically slave society – the first such society in British America.[97]

Elsewhere, the turn to slavery was slower. If godly arguments proved stronger in New England than on Providence Island, this may have been because the combination of a good supply of immigrants with high survival and reproductive rates, the absence of a staple crop, and the widespread use of family labour, all reduced the necessity for importing slaves. Africans therefore never constituted more than 3 per cent of New England's population.[98] Virginia began importing

African slaves soon after Bermuda. In 1619 John Rolfe reported the purchase of '20. and odd Negroes' from a Dutch man-of-war – an early indication of the important part that Dutch carriers and traders would play in the seventeenth-century Atlantic economy.[99] It was only at the end of the seventeenth century, however, that the Chesapeake colonies began to turn massively to African slaves to meet their labour requirements, and to look directly to Africa rather than the West Indies as their source of supply. Before then they had relied heavily on indentured labour, and white servants worked side by side with blacks, both slave and free, in the tobacco fields. The situation began to change in the 1680s, at a moment when a decline in the supply of indentured servants from the British Isles coincided with a fall in the cost of importing slaves. By 1710, 20 per cent of Virginia's population were slaves.[100]

It was Barbados in the 1640s and 1650s that would provide the model and set the trend. As sugar became the staple crop, the drawbacks of dependence on indentured labour became increasingly clear to the planters. Not only did white servants often prove unruly and rebellious when they found themselves condemned to effective servitude on the sugar plantations, but they were naturally reluctant to continue as wage-earners when their period of indenture expired. Some of the Barbados planters had seen African slave gangs at work in Brazil, and began to realize that African labour, even if initially more expensive, offered long-term advantages, since slaves would provide life-long service and could be more cheaply clothed and fed. Best of all, their condition as bondsmen made them absolute servants of their masters, as no white man could be.[101] As the demand for sugar soared, and with it the pressure to produce, so too did the numbers of imported blacks. By 1660 there were as many blacks as whites on the island – perhaps 20,000 of each race – and by the end of the century Barbados, along with its companion slave societies of Jamaica and the Leewards, had absorbed 250,000 slaves from Africa.[102]

Condemned by the 'curse of Ham' and set apart from the beginning by the colour of their skin, blacks stood little chance in societies which had as yet no developed code of law relating to slavery, and which, with little or no Indian labour available, were otherwise overwhelmingly white. As Virginia's House of Burgesses realized in the wake of Bacon's rebellion in 1676, it was in the interests of masters to prevent the development of an alliance between aggrieved indentured servants and slaves by drawing a sharper dividing line between them in terms of legal status, a process already under way before the rebellion began.[103] Gradually the legal shackles were tightened round the Africans, and British America moved inexorably towards the establishment of chattel slavery.

This chattel slavery would make possible the development of plantation economies on the British American mainland whose nearest Iberian equivalent was to be found not in the territories settled by the Spaniards but in Portuguese Brazil.[104] In principle, the Spanish Caribbean islands – Hispaniola, Cuba, Puerto Rico and Jamaica – might have seemed to offer the same potential in the sixteenth century for the development of monocultures based on slave labour as that which was to be realized in the British island of Barbados in the seventeenth century, or indeed in Spain's own possession of Cuba in the later eighteenth. But, after the early years of plunder and ruthless exploitation were over, the Spanish Caribbean became something of an economic backwater. The more ambitious settlers moved on in search of richer prizes on the mainland, and with their departure the white population of the islands stagnated or declined. The sugar estates of Hispaniola and Cuba, although enjoying some initial successes, found it increasingly hard to compete with the sugar produced in New Spain and Brazil. It was cheaper and easier to concentrate on the less labour-intensive activity of cattle herding and ranching to meet the steady demand in Spain for hides. Moreover, the consequences for Spanish American economic life of the primacy of silver mining in the mainland viceroyalties extended to the Caribbean. As Havana became the port of departure for the annual silver fleets, it was understandable that islanders should lose their enthusiasm for the development of local products for export. There were quicker profits, illicit as well licit, to be made out of Havana's growth as the emporium of a transatlantic trade that was now attracting the predatory interest of Spain's European rivals.[105]

It was Brazil, not the Spanish Caribbean, that offered the first, and most spectacular, example of the enormous wealth to be made from large-scale plantations worked by black slave labour. Serious colonization had begun only in the 1540s after the Portuguese had become alarmed by reports of French designs on the vast region that had nominally come into their possession after its accidental discovery by Pedro Alvares Cabral on his expedition to India in 1500. Initially appreciated for their brazilwood trees, which produced a highly prized reddish-purple dye, the coastal regions of the Brazilian north-east, thinly settled by Portuguese colonists, turned out to be well suited to the growing of sugar cane. As the Portuguese crown moved in the years leading up to the union with Spain in 1580 to establish a tighter grasp over its promising new territory, it also began to take a close interest in the creation of a sugar industry. The Tupinambá Indians failed to live up to expectations as a work-force for the new plantations, whether as chattel slaves or as European-style wage-labourers, and large numbers were wiped out by European diseases. With the European demand for sugar expanding, the response to the labour shortage was the same as it was in the Spanish Indies. From the 1560s growing numbers of African slaves were imported to supplement or replace an unsatisfactory and diminishing Indian work-force, and by the end of the century Brazil, now dependent on African labour, had become the world's largest supplier of sugar.[106]

The production techniques responsible for Brazil's spectacular success in growing and exporting sugar could not be kept secret indefinitely. When the Dutch West India Company seized Pernambuco from the Portuguese in the 1630s, the information fell into the hands of their Protestant rivals; and when the settlers chased the Dutch out of Brazil in the course of the decade following Portugal's recovery of independence from Spain in 1640, Sephardic Jews anxious to escape the attention of the Portuguese Inquisition fled Pernambuco for the Antilles, where they instructed the islanders in Brazilian production and processing techniques.[107] With Dutch merchants happy to provide the settlers of Barbados with African slaves, the necessary ingredients were at hand for the dramatic expansion of the slave-based sugar plantations of the British Caribbean.

As Virginian tobacco growers came to imitate the example of the Barbadian sugar producers, so the English word 'plantation' became more narrowly and specifically defined.[108] When the Reverend John Cotton preached a sermon in 1630 on the departure of Winthrop's fleet for New England, he chose as his text a passage from the book of Samuel: 'Moreover, I will appoint a place for my people Israel, and I will plant them.'[109] The Irish 'plantations' of the sixteenth century were essentially plantations of people, which would flourish in the right soil, and offer scope for infinite possibilities. Sir Philip Sidney, as an Irish planter, could write that he had 'contrived' a 'plantation' that would be 'an emporium for the confluence of all nations that love or profess any kind of virtue or commerce'.[110] But, a hundred years later, the developments of the intervening century had begun to accustom people to think of 'plantation' as an overseas settlement producing a cash crop for export, and as an emporium for the confluence of nations that professed the least virtuous of all kinds of commerce – the commerce in slaves.

The conditions of that commerce, as it was developed by the Portuguese and then appropriated by the Dutch and the English, were uniformly barbaric, although the ministrations of members of the religious orders at the ports of entry in the Iberian world did something to mitigate the sufferings of the sick and dying as they sought the salvation of their souls. If the seventeenth-century Anglo-American world had its equivalent of the Jesuit Fray Pedro Claver, who embraced the slaves on their arrival in Cartagena and even went down into the stinking holds of the slave-ships,[111] his deeds remain unsung. For those who survived the ordeal of the Atlantic crossing, and subsequently of exposure to the unfamiliar disease environment of the New World, prospects were bleak. Their fate was described in vivid and moving words by Claver's colleague and fellow Jesuit, Alonso de Sandoval, in a work first published in Seville in 1627. Denouncing the treatment to which the new arrivals were subjected, he described how they would be made to work in the mines 'from sunrise to sunset, and also long stretches of the night', or, if they were bought as house-slaves, would be treated with such inhumanity that 'they would be better off as beasts'.[112]

Yet, for all the horrors of their situation, African slaves in Spain's American possessions seem to have enjoyed more room for manoeuvre and more opportunities for advancement than their counterparts in British America. Uprooted and far from home, they were regarded as representing less of a potential security threat than the indigenous population. This meant that Spanish settlers tended to use them as overseers or auxiliaries in dealing with the Indian work-force, thus raising them a rung on the increasingly complicated ladder of social and ethnic hierarchy.[113] The settlers' confidence was frequently misplaced, and marauding bands of *cimarrones*, or fugitive slaves, sometimes operating in collusion with local Indians, became a danger to Spanish settlements, especially in the Caribbean and Panama.[114] Yet the ambiguous status of slaves placed among a population itself subjected to a form of servitude offered opportunities that the shrewd and the fortunate could turn to their advantage.

Paradoxically, slaves in Spanish America also benefited from the fact that peninsular Spain, unlike England, possessed a long experience of slavery. This had led to the development of a code of law and practice which, at least juridically, tended to mitigate the lot of the slave. On the grounds that 'all the laws of the world have always favoured liberty',[115] the thirteenth-century code of the *Siete Partidas* laid down certain conditions governing the treatment of slaves. These included the right to marry, even against the wishes of their masters, and a limited right to hold property. The code also opened the way to possible manumission, either by the master or by the state.

The transfer of slavery to the Spanish Indies inevitably brought departures from peninsular practice.[116] In the vast areas under Spanish rule it was not easy to enforce the more generous provisions of the *Siete Partidas,* even when there was a will to do so, and the lot of the slave inevitably varied from region to region and from master to master. Yet the rules relating to marriage, manumission and the holding of property allowed slaves some latitude, and urban slaves in particular quickly became adept at exploiting the rivalries between the different institutions of control, together with the openings offered by the law. In principle, as Christians, they enjoyed the protection of the church and the canon law, and as vassals of the crown could seek redress from royal justice. No doubt many were in no position to take advantage of these possibilities, but the numerous cases that came before the courts in New Spain suggest that, in common with members of the indigenous population, they soon learnt to play the game by Spanish rules.[117] As they battled to establish their rights to marriage or their entitlement to freedom, they managed, with the help of church and crown, to erode the claims of masters to hold them as mere chattels and dispose of their bodies as they wished.

Since children took their mother's and not their father's status, *zambos* – the offspring of African slave fathers and Indian mothers – were free-born, although in practice this might mean little more than exchanging one wretched life-prospect for another, since they now became subject to the tribute and labour demands imposed on the Indian population. Legally, however, their status was superior to that of the slave, and although the colonial authorities frowned on the growing number of Afro-Indian unions, the crown refused to break with a custom which favoured a libertarian trend.[118] Slavery, after all, ran counter to natural law, and natural law exercised a powerful hold over the Hispanic imagination.

Not surprisingly, therefore, manumission was more easily obtained in Spanish than in British America, where various possible avenues to freedom would come to be blocked one by one. The British American colonies increasingly restricted the master's power to free his slaves, whereas in general the territories of the Spanish crown were free of such restraints.[119] In Spanish America it was not uncommon for masters – particularly in their last wills and testaments – to grant freedom to their slaves, especially female slaves and the sick and elderly, although this can also be seen as a device that enabled them to avoid the expense of continuing maintenance.[120] It was possible, too, for slaves who met the appropriate criteria to win their freedom in the courts, something which seems to have been more difficult to achieve in North America, at least outside New England, although there were always variations between colony and colony and between statute and practice.[121] The majority of manumitted slaves in the Spanish territories, however, appear to have gained their freedom by purchasing it with monies saved from earnings on the side.[122]

With a constant trickle of manumissions adding to the pool of free Africans already settled in the Indies, the free black population grew rapidly, especially in the cities, and already in early seventeenth-century New Spain the free African urban labour force was beginning to outnumber that of slaves.[123] Jointly with artisan slaves owned by artisan masters, free Africans and mulattoes set up confraternities – nineteen in Lima alone in the early seventeenth century[124] – and established an uneasy foothold for themselves in a Hispanic American colonial world reluctantly prepared to accept their presence within its stratified society. British America, too, had its free blacks, but as slavery tightened its grip on the southern mainland colonies, the environment in which they lived became progressively less congenial. The advent of the plantation was accompanied by a deepening social and racial degradation, which affected them all.[125]

Transatlantic economies

✳ The exploitation of the New World's resources by European settlers, drawing – as circumstances suggested and new opportunities presented themselves – on their own labour, that of the indigenous population, and imported African slaves, was based on the recognition of reciprocal needs. Europe needed, or believed that it needed, the products of America, with gold and silver at the top of the list. The colonists needed European commodities that, for one reason or another, they could not supply for themselves. Until sound growth rates were established, they also needed a constant replenishment of people. The interaction of these mutual necessities promoted the rapid development of transatlantic commercial networks, in conformity with patterns dictated in the first instance by the winds and currents of the Atlantic, but also by metropolitan practices and requirements, and by their adjustment to local American conditions. ✳

Through a combination of intuition and seafaring skills Columbus discovered the transatlantic route that would become the norm for the first and most elaborate of the commercial networks linking Europe and America – that between Andalusia and the tropical America of the Caribbean. Taking maximum advantage of the prevailing winds, the route described an elliptical arc, with the outgoing ships from Andalusia making the crossing after stopping over at the Canaries, and returning by more northerly latitudes by way of the Florida Strait and the Azores. If all went well, the outward passage, from Seville's port of San Lúcar de

Barrameda to Portobelo on the isthmus of Panama, could be done in something like 91 days, while the return journey, always much slower, would take some 128.[126] Sailing times were shorter for the London–Jamestown route, although not as short as might appear from Captain Seagull's understandably over-enthusiastic response to the question 'How far is it thither?', put by one of his drinking companions in Chapman's *Eastward Ho*: 'Some six weeks' sail, no more, with any indifferent good wind'. The average was in fact 55 days, although the return journey could be done in 40 (see map 2, p. 50).[127]

The natural laws governing navigation in the age of sail carried with them certain ineluctable consequences, prescribing ideal times, routes and seasons for sailing, and giving preference to certain points of departure at the expense of others. If Andalusia – in effect Seville and its port complex of San Lúcar and Cadiz – acquired a monopoly of transatlantic sailings at an early stage of Spain's overseas expansion, this was not simply the result of bureaucratic machinations or human caprice. If sailings had taken place instead from Spain's northern coast, sailing times would have been 20 per cent longer, and the voyage would have cost 25 per cent more.[128] The Andalusian monopoly would in time become the object of bitter criticism, but it is a reflection of these unpalatable logistical facts that when in 1529 sailings to the Indies were authorized for a whole string of ports, ranging from Bilbao in the north to Cartagena on the east coast of Spain, little use seems to have been made of the authorization, which became a dead letter long before it was formally revoked in 1573.[129]

There was therefore a geographical logic to the early selection of Seville as the organizing centre for Spain's Atlantic trade, with the creation in 1503 of the Casa de la Contratación – the House of Trade – to supervise sailings to the Indies. As an inland port Seville had serious shortcomings, which would become increasingly apparent as the Guadalquivir silted up and river navigation grew hazardous. Yet as a city in the royal domain in an Andalusia pocketed with large seigneurial enclaves, and as the busy metropolis of a rich agricultural hinterland well capable of provisioning the Indies fleets, Seville's case for selection was overwhelming, on both political and economic grounds.

In founding the Casa de la Contratación Ferdinand and Isabella had in their minds the example of the *Casa da India* in Lisbon, with which the Portuguese crown sought to regulate and control Portugal's lucrative Asian trade. In the circumstances of the early sixteenth century such a regulatory approach appeared entirely logical, on grounds both of national security and narrower state interests. The secrets of transatlantic navigation had to be guarded, and foreigners excluded from trade with, and emigration to, the Indies, if Castile's new overseas possessions were not to fall into the hands of its rivals and the fruits of its enterprise be lost. After its long struggle to uphold its own prerogatives at home the crown was also extremely anxious that its authority, and with it the possibility of potentially great financial benefits, should not be unnecessarily jeopardized by allowing uncontrolled access of its own subjects to its transatlantic possessions. Those benefits soon became apparent. As increasing quantities of American gold and silver began to be shipped home, there was clearly an unanswerable case for channelling shipments from the Indies through a single port of entry where bullion could be properly registered and the remittances for the crown be set aside under lock and key.

Seville's monopoly, therefore, born of logic and convenience, and responding well to the political and international needs of the early sixteenth century, was very quickly reinforced by the security requirements of a transatlantic trade in which silver was so overwhelmingly the most valuable commodity shipped back from the Indies. These same requirements, too, came to determine the distinctive structure of the Indies trade – the *Carrera de Indias* – as it developed over the course of the sixteenth century. To counter the growing threat from privateers, armed escorts had to be provided. Isolated sailings were too expensive to protect and too vulnerable to attack, and an incipient convoy system attained its definitive form in 1564 when two separate fleets were organized – the *flota*, leaving in April or May for Vera Cruz in New Spain, and the *galeones* sailing in August for the isthmus of Panama, with the combined fleets returning to Spain the following autumn, after meeting up in Havana. This would become the annual pattern for Spanish transatlantic crossings.

Unless periodically pruned back, however, monopolies tend to grow. In 1543 the merchants of Seville were incorporated into a *Consulado*, or Merchant Guild, which came to exercise a growing dominance over the Indies trade as the century progressed. By the end of the century the trade was enveloped in a closely meshed web of commercial and financial interests linking a dominant group of merchants in the Consulado with royal bankers, officials of the Casa de la Contratación, and ministers and officials of the Council of the Indies. These various interest groups, enjoying the support of the municipal authorities of Seville, would fight tenaciously to preserve the monopoly, and resist any initiative that might threaten to subvert it.[130]

While the perpetuation of the monopoly introduced rigidities that would make it difficult for the Spanish transatlantic system to adapt to the evolving requirements of the colonial societies, the Sevillian mercantile–financial complex never possessed a complete stranglehold over the colonial trade. Foreign merchants, beginning with the Genoese, found innumerable ways of infiltrating the system; smuggling and contraband became endemic; and the slave trade, even if channelled through Seville, was in the hands of Portuguese merchants, who had their own separate networks, and exploited the system for their own private ends.[131] Members of Sevillian mercantile families, like the Almonte,[132] moving to and fro between Spain and America, would share business with local merchants in New Spain, Panama or Peru. By the later sixteenth and early seventeenth centuries this new breed of American merchants was becoming rich and powerful enough for its members to act as independent participants in the Spanish Atlantic trading system, and influence Seville in their turn.[133]

The business houses of Seville were anyhow overstretched, and large areas of commercial activity in the New World lay beyond their reach. While European imports into the Americas fell within Seville's monopoly and had to be consumed in the province to which they were consigned, there was, as a rule, no restriction on inter-regional trades in colonial produce. Venezuela, for instance, enjoyed a lively trade with neighbouring regions, and from the 1620s was exporting large consignments of cacao to Mexico.[134] Throughout the sixteenth century there was also an unrestricted trade between the Pacific coast ports of New Spain and Peru. This was finally ended by the crown in 1631, in a bid to curb the consequences of a trans-Pacific trade that had developed in the 1570s between the Mexican port of Acapulco and Manila in the Philippines, and was draining off to China large quantities of American silver that had been destined for Seville.[135]

The regulation of trade in the name of national interest and through the mechanism of privilege and monopoly rights was a standard weapon in the armoury of Early Modern European states, which operated in an environment where the correlation of bullion, prosperity and power was regarded as axiomatic. Considerations of profit and power were as dominant in the formulation of economic policy in Tudor and Stuart England as they were in that of Habsburg Spain, with mercantile interests looking to the crown to devise strategies for the protection and enhancement of trade, and the crown in turn looking to the merchant community to provide it with a continuous flow of revenue from its overseas activities. It was on the basis of just such a mutual accommodation that Seville acquired and preserved its monopoly, while the crown collected its dues.

Such a tight system of control, however, would have been difficult, if not impossible, to introduce into the trading activities of the English Atlantic world, especially in the early stages of transatlantic colonization. The North Atlantic maritime routes moved to a different rhythm from that of the Spanish Atlantic, and the products shipped home imposed different imperatives. The first routes were navigated high up in northern waters as English, French and Basque fishermen arrived to exploit the international fishing grounds off the Newfoundland coast. The English Atlantic was at its narrowest between the British Isles and Newfoundland, but the inhospitable nature of the country was not conducive to extensive settlement, while the nature of the trade – conducted from English outports in the most perishable of commodities – hardly lent itself to close regulation.[136] Further north, in the remote and icy region of Hudson Bay, settlement was an even less attractive prospect, but furs, unlike fish, were a staple that lent itself to company exploitation, and in the late seventeenth century, as the trade expanded, were to provide the basis for the lucrative monopoly granted by Charles II to Hudson's Bay Company.

Two main routes existed for trade and communication between the British Isles and the principal colonies of British settlement, running from New England to the Caribbean. The more northerly of the two, cold and foggy, involved a five-week westward crossing and a three-week return crossing by way of the Newfoundland Banks. The more southerly route, hot and humid, went by way of Madeira, the Azores and Barbados, eight weeks' sailing time to and from England; but more direct passages, avoiding the need for a West Indies landfall, were sought and found as the tobacco trade with the Chesapeake developed.[137] The variety of routes, leading to a variety of settlements yielding a very diverse range of produce, made it difficult to think in terms of a Spanish-style system of fixed annual sailings in convoy. But, as the staple trades developed, so also did the need to reduce the risks of potentially heavy losses at the hand of pirates or enemy vessels. It was the French wars of the later seventeenth century which forced the English to follow the Spanish example, at least in part. During the years of war, regular sailing dates had to be arranged for the sugar and tobacco fleets, so that they could proceed in armed convoy with protection provided by the state. In determining these dates, the interests of London merchants prevailed over those of the outports.[138]

To achieve such a Spanish-style level of organization and defence, however, required a combination of circumstance, capacity and commitment which simply did not exist during the first half-century of English overseas settlement. Although Charles I cherished a vision of a well-ordered empire with all its component parts moving in majestic unison,[139] the process of overseas colonization during his reign remained obstinately haphazard. While Virginia was transformed in 1625 into a colony under direct royal government, the granting elsewhere of colonial charters to corporate and individual proprietors for the planting of new settlements ruled out the possibility of establishing uniform royal control. Similarly, Charles might announce his intention to take over the tobacco trade,[140] but he had no means of enforcing his wishes. The state simply lacked the resources and apparatus to impose firm central direction on overseas trading and colonizing ventures that were characterized by fierce competition between rival interest groups in London and the outports, and an overwhelming urge for short-term gain at the expense of long-term planning. But the state's failure may well have been the essential precondition for the eventual success of England's overseas enterprise, which depended on the mobilization of the widest possible range of financial and human resources – a mobilization that would have been very difficult to achieve through royal directives. The very inability of Charles's government to impose such directives left room for the free play of enterprise. This in turn made it possible to experiment with differing forms of 'improvement' in settlements that resembled each other only in the absence of the three elements – precious metals, an adequate supply of local labour, and immediately accessible staple commodities of uncontested importance to the national economy – of which one at least was commonly regarded by mercantilist thinkers as essential for their long-term survival.

Although publicists made the case for English overseas colonization in terms of draining off surplus population and opening new markets for home manufactures, the apparent inability of the settlements to produce local commodities that would complement the weaknesses of the home economy made it difficult to devise a coherent economic strategy for them along sound mercantilist lines. One or two tropical islands and a scattering of coastal settlements offering what seemed very limited possibilities of advantage to the mother country hardly looked like the foundations of a British empire in America comparable in value to that of Spain. By the middle years of the seventeenth century, however, Barbados sugar and Virginia tobacco were beginning to suggest that these remote American outposts might after all be turned to good account. Yet Cromwell's Western Design of 1655, with Hispaniola as its target, testified to the continuing hold exercised over the English imagination by the Spanish silver empire.

While the Western Design proved a disappointment for which the acquisition of Jamaica appeared to offer little by way of compensation, it was at once a testimony to recent achievements and a portent of things to come. This was the first time that the British state had organized a transatlantic military operation in pursuit of imperial interests.[141] As such, it was evidence both of the resurgence of state power under Cromwellian rule, and of a new determination on the part of the state to use that power for the promotion of economic as well as strategic ends. The Western Design can be seen as part of a larger national design, in which the state sought to realize the nation's potential, and that of its overseas settlements, in order to maximize power in its great international struggle against England's rivals – the Spanish, the French and the Dutch.

The construction of a powerful navy after 1649 was critical to the success of this grand design, as also was the Navigation Act of 1651, which was equally intended to strengthen the nation's power at sea.[142] The unexpected success of the English fleet in the first Anglo-Dutch war of 1652–4 demonstrated beyond a doubt that England now possessed a formidable capacity for maritime and colonial expansion.[143] It would be for the restored monarchy of Charles II, in the years after 1660, to build on the foundations laid by the Republic by introducing its own Navigation Acts of 1660 and 1663, and setting up in 1660 a Council for Trade and Plantations.

Compared with the Spaniards, the British state was slow in developing a coherent approach to the exploitation of American resources, and in seeking to impose its own regulatory control over the movements of transatlantic trade. The creation of the Casa de la Contratación came only a decade after Columbus's return from his first voyage, while almost half a century elapsed between the founding of Jamestown and the first effective measures taken by the British crown to ensure that overseas trade was directly regulated by state power. Partly this was a reflection of the nature of the resources themselves. The early discovery of gold in the Spanish Caribbean introduced an urgency into the establishment of some form of state control which was not felt in a British Atlantic world that seemed to offer little more than fish, furs, timber and a few bales of tobacco. Partly, too, it was a reflection of the inability of the English crown under the Tudors and early Stuarts to develop a significant bureaucratic apparatus – something that would have been much more feasible if a regular supply of New World bullion had been flowing into its coffers. Private initiatives, reinforced by charters and monopoly grants, therefore became the order of the day in the development of England's overseas possessions. As the state grew stronger in the middle years of the seventeenth century, it could begin to challenge these monopolies, whereas the Seville monopoly, dependent on a complicated collusion of mutually reinforcing state and mercantile interests, proved impervious to reform.

⨯Both imperial powers, however, were operating over the course of the sixteenth and seventeenth centuries within the same set of assumptions about the proper relationship of overseas settlements to the mother country. This was to be a relationship in which the interests of the settlements were ruthlessly subordinated to those of an imperial metropolis bent on identifying and developing in its transatlantic possessions those economic assets that most nearly complemented its needs. The supply of those assets would then be controlled and regulated in ways that would bring fiscal benefits to the state and maximize national power in a world of bitter international rivalries – rivalries that already, from the mid-sixteenth century, were extending to the Americas as the Atlantic was transformed into a European lake.⨯

Certainly there might well be disagreements about which assets were most greatly to be prized. By the mid-seventeenth century silver was becoming more than a little tarnished. Observers noted how all the silver of America had failed to bring prosperity to Spain, although there were still bullionists, like George Gardyner, who saw the principal aim of English commerce as to bring as much silver and gold into the country as possible, while carrying as little as possible out. For him, 'the trade of America is prejudicial, very dishonest, and highly dishonourable to our Nation.'[144] By 1651, however, such views were becoming more than a little eccentric, and overseas empire, even if it lacked gold and silver, was coming to be seen as an indispensable appendage to every self-respecting state. The problem, as perceived from the centre of empire, was how best to manage overseas possessions in such a way as to yield the maximum benefits to the mother country. The challenge of constructing an effective imperial framework had long exercised Spanish minds. In the age of Cromwell and the restored Stuarts it would also begin to exercise the minds of those who cherished the vision of an empowered British state.

PART 2

Consolidation

CHAPTER 5

Crown and Colonists

The framework of empire

On 13 May 1625, following the dissolution of the Virginia Company in the previous year and the imposition of direct royal rule on the struggling colony, Charles I issued a proclamation stating that Virginia, the Somers Islands and New England formed of right a part of 'Our Royall Empire, descended upon Us and undoubtedly belonging and pertaining unto Us'. 'Our full resolution', the proclamation continued, 'is to the end that there may be one uniforme course of Government, in, and through, our whole Monarchie . . .'[1]

'Our Royall Empire' . . . These were high-sounding words, with a portentous, if somewhat ambiguous, ancestry. In 1533 Henry VIII had proclaimed the Realm of England to be an 'Empire', a term which seems to have been intended as an assertion not only of national sovereignty but also of claims to territorial authority over England's neighbours, most immediately the Irish and the Scots.[2] The first known use of the term 'British Empire' dates from 1572, and evoked a historic empire of the British Isles lost in the mists of antiquity; but it was a notion that could be expanded without excessive difficulty to embrace overseas settlements in America.[3] When Charles I spoke of 'Our Royall Empire' he would seem to have had in mind his own benign government over an empire of British communities, consisting primarily of the kingdoms of England, Scotland, Ireland and the principality of Wales, but now stretching across the Atlantic to include the new American plantations. Between them these constituted 'our whole Monarchie', which he envisaged as being ruled by 'one uniforme course of Government'.

This was more a matter of aspiration than of fact. Like Habsburg Spain, Great Britain, as united under the rule of James VI and I, was a composite monarchy. In common with its continental counterparts the British composite monarchy of the early Stuarts – 'our whole Monarchie' – consisted of different realms and territories with their own distinctive traditions and forms of government, although subject to one and the same monarch.[4] But an overseas settlement governed not by the crown but by a chartered company, even if its charter had been granted by the crown, was an anomaly among such territories; and for a monarch who cherished the vision of 'one uniforme course of government' and had a passion for tidying up loose ends, the subjection of Virginia to direct royal rule in the year before his accession no doubt represented a source of considerable satisfaction. Yet although Charles's assertion of a direct interest in overseas settlements clearly showed that he regarded them as something more than mere commercial ventures, his reign did not see much progress in the matter of bringing the American territories under 'one uniforme course of government'. The crown did, however, insist that investors and potential colonizers must first secure royal authorization for their projects, and made clear its intention to maintain a general oversight over their activities, which, if properly regulated, could add substantially to national power and prosperity.

While the foundation of the Massachusetts Bay Company in 1629 suggested that, in spite of its failure in Virginia, the chartered company might still have an American future, the trend was towards the establishment not of royal, but proprietary, governments – a system under which land grants and rights of jurisdiction were made to well-connected patron proprietors who possessed privileged access to the monarch and were well placed to mobilize capital and potential settlers. Barbados became a proprietary colony in 1629 as one of a number of West Indies islands that fell within the patent of the Earl of Carlisle,[5] while George Calvert, Lord Baltimore, was granted the proprietorship of the proposed new settlement of Maryland, with a royal charter being issued to his son, Cecilius Calvert, in 1632, conferring on him powers of government similar to those traditionally exercised by the prince bishops of Durham. With almost regal powers vested in the proprietors, the medieval model of palatinates in the marchlands bordering Scotland and Wales seemed at first sight a promising model for the frontier societies springing up in British America.[6] Experience, however, was soon to suggest otherwise.

With the British colonizing enterprise still at an experimental stage, and little prospect of rapid returns from investments, it is not surprising that colonial ventures under the early Stuarts should have assumed a variety of forms, resulting in a patchwork of different styles of government and jurisdiction. Although a Commission for Regulating Plantations was set up under the chairmanship of Archbishop Laud in 1634,[7] the crown was not strong enough, and the colonial economies themselves not developed enough, to allow the imposition of any significant degree of uniformity, or even of central direction. Survival was the first priority, and it was only in the middle decades of the seventeenth century, as the colonies took firm root and the Britain of the Commonwealth and the Restoration established itself as a major maritime and commercial power among European states, that it became possible to think in practical terms of developing a genuinely imperial policy and a more systematic framework for the government of overseas empire. Significantly, it was in this period that the terms 'the British [or English] Empire *in* America' or '*of* America' came into use. The more general term 'British Empire', used to designate a unitary political body of England,

Ireland, Scotland and the colonies, does not seem to have made an appearance before the second quarter of the eighteenth century, following belatedly in the wake of the Anglo-Scottish union of 1707. Even then, however, the term was slow to make its way into print. Before 1763 it appeared in only sixteen titles, with a further 108 added between then and 1800. 'Colonies' and 'plantations' remained overwhelmingly the terms of first choice.[8]

The relatively slow and haphazard British moves towards the imposition of empire stood in marked contrast to the speed with which Spain's American territories were formally incorporated within an effective imperial framework. Again, however, the terminology proved ambiguous. When their monarch was elected Holy Roman Emperor in 1519, under the name of Charles V, the Castilians made it clear that for them he was, and remained, primarily King Charles I of Castile.[9] Castile had no intention of being submerged within a universal empire, a concept towards which it was traditionally hostile. Its king, however, was now not only the Emperor, but also the ruler of a vast composite monarchy, of which Castile was one member, although increasingly *primus inter pares*, in a complex of kingdoms _A first among equals_ and territories that included the Crown of Aragon, the Netherlands and Spain's Italian possessions. On Charles's abdication in 1556, his son Philip II of Spain was left with the bulk of his composite monarchy, but not the imperial title, which went to Charles's brother Ferdinand.

Eventually a name would emerge for the collectivity of lands owing allegiance to Philip and his descendants – the *monarquía española*, the Spanish Monarchy. But along the way various suggestions were made to endow Philip with a title which would give him clear precedence over his closest European competitor, the King of France. In 1564, for instance, he received suggestions that he should style himself Emperor of the Indies, or of the New World.[10] This was in line with the argument originally put forward by Hernán Cortés that Charles could legitimately style himself 'emperor' of New Spain[11] – an argument which he ignored, probably on the grounds that Christendom traditionally knew only one Emperor, the titular head of the Holy Roman Empire. In rejecting the new suggestion, Philip was presumably moved by the same considerations as his father, and especially by the desire not to give unnecessary offence to the Austrian branch of his family. But as early as 1527 Gonzalo Fernández de Oviedo had written of 'this occidental empire of these Indies',[12] and Philip's seventeenth-century successors on the Spanish throne would be dignified in various publications with the title of 'Emperor of the Indies' or 'Emperor of America'. Neither the title, however, nor the term 'empire of the Indies' ever quite attained official status during the two centuries of Spanish Habsburg rule.[13]

While not formally constituting an empire, the transatlantic territories of Spanish settlement were early endowed with their own distinctive juridical status within the Spanish composite monarchy. Nominally, this monarchy consisted of realms and dominions of two types, those acquired by inheritance and dynastic union, and those acquired by conquest. The first type, which were joined in partnership on an equal footing (*aeque principaliter* in the juridical terminology), would continue to be ruled in accordance with the laws and customs which prevailed at the moment of union. The second, as conquered territories, became subject to the laws of the conqueror. This, at least, was the theory, although in practice even kingdoms like Naples and Navarre which could be classified as 'conquered', tended to retain in large measure their customary forms of government.[14]

The Indies were indisputably conquered territory, and Alexander VI, in his bull of 1493, specifically stated that they were henceforth to be 'united with, and incorporated into, the crown of Castile and León'.[15] Faced with the options of maintaining the newly acquired transatlantic possessions – still only a few islands – as a separate entity or incorporating them into one or other of the crowns of the recently united Castile and Aragon, Ferdinand and Isabella chose the second option. There is no indication that they ever considered incorporating them into the crown of a now united Spain, of which they were joint monarchs. Their further decision to incorporate the Indies into the Crown of Castile rather than that of Aragon had an obvious logic. Andalusia, from which Columbus's expedition had set sail, formed part of the kingdom of Castile and León, and the recently reconquered kingdom of Granada had been incorporated into the Castilian crown. So, too, had the Canary Islands. Any further conquests among the islands of the Atlantic could therefore naturally be conceived of as an extension of Castilian and Andalusian space.

The papal bull of 1493 was addressed to both Ferdinand and Isabella, as joint rulers. On her death in 1504 Isabella bequeathed to her husband the lifetime usufruct of half the crown's revenues from the Indies and certain other dues, on condition that on his death all such revenues should revert to the heirs and successors of the couple on the throne of Castile and León. Ferdinand duly complied with this condition in the will drawn up before his death in 1516. Full rights over the Indies then devolved upon their daughter Juana, as Queen of Castile, and – in view of her mental incapacity – on her son Charles, the future emperor.[16] The juridical status of the new transatlantic possessions was spelt out in a decree issued by Charles V in Barcelona on 14 September 1519, which began: 'By donation of the Holy Apostolic See and other just and legitimate titles [a clear attempt to avoid exclusive dependence on papal donation as the legitimation of the royal title, by evoking claims based on conquest or first discovery], we are Lord (*Señor*) of the West Indies, Islands and Mainland of the Ocean Sea, both discovered and to be discovered, and they are incorporated into our Royal Crown of Castile.' The decree went on to state that the union with the Castilian crown was to be perpetual, and to prohibit any alienation or division of the territories in favour of another party.[17]

The incorporation of the Indies into the Crown of Castile had immense long-term consequences for the development of Spanish America. Technically this was to be a Castilian, rather than a Spanish, America, just as the territories of North America settled from the British Isles were technically to constitute an English, rather than a British, America. Although the kings of Castile were also kings of Aragon, and a number of Aragonese participated in the first stages of Spanish expansion into the New World,[18] there was to be a lingering uncertainty over the rights of natives of the Crown of Aragon to move to, and settle in, America. The sixteenth-century legal texts relating to the exclusion of foreigners from the Indies appeared then, as now, ambiguous and contradictory over the exact status of possible immigrants from Aragon, Catalonia and Valencia. In practice it seems that there were no serious impediments to their securing a licence to emigrate to the Indies, but, for geographical and other reasons, those who took advantage of the opportunity turned out to be relatively few.[19]

Much more immediately significant was the endowment of the new American territories with laws and institutions modelled on those of Castile rather than of Aragon. Although there was a strong tradition in medieval Castile, as in the Crown of Aragon, of a contractual relationship between monarch and subjects, and this had penetrated deep into Castilian political culture,[20] Castile emerged from the Middle Ages with weaker theoretical and institutional barriers against the authoritarian exercise of kingship than those to be found in the Aragonese realms. Fifteenth-century Castilian jurists in the service of the crown had argued for a 'royal absolute power' (*poderío real absoluto*), which gave wide latitude to the royal prerogative. The sixteenth-century rulers of Castile inherited this useful formula, which could obviously be used to override the crown's contractual obligations in real or alleged emergencies.[21] While the moral restraints on Castilian kingship remained strong, the potential for the authoritarian exercise of power was now established; and Charles V's suppression of the Comunero revolt in 1521 would effectively reduce still further the chances of imposing effective institutional restraints in a realm whose representative assembly, the Cortes of Castile, suffered from a number of grave, if not necessarily fatal, weaknesses.

With the Indies juridically incorporated into the Castilian crown as a conquered territory, the monarchs in principle were free to govern them as they liked. One institution that they were in no hurry to see transferred to the other side of the Atlantic was a representative assembly, or Cortes, on the Castilian, and still less on the Aragonese, model. The settlers themselves might petition for such assemblies, and viceroys and even the crown itself might occasionally play with the idea of introducing them, but the disadvantages were always held to outweigh the advantages, and the American territories never acquired Cortes of their own.[22]

Yet although the Indies were seen as a Castilian conquest, and were therefore united to the Castilian crown by what was known as an 'accessory' union rather than on a basis of equality, *aeque principaliter*, the fact remained that the conquerors themselves were the king's own Castilian subjects, and were evolving into *pobladores*, or settlers, although proudly clinging to their title of *conquistadores*. As conquerors, they understandably expected their services to be properly remembered and rewarded by a grateful monarch, who could hardly deny them and their descendants the kind of rights which men of their worth would expect to enjoy in Castile. Such a recognition might not extend to the formal establishment of a Cortes, but this did not preclude the development of other institutional devices and forums, notably the *cabildo* or town council, for expressing collective grievances. Moreover, it was clear that the status of the lands that their valour had brought under Castilian rule should receive some proper acknowledgement. The conquerors had overthrown the empires of the Aztecs and the Incas, and had dispossessed great rulers. In the circumstances, it was natural that the larger pre-conquest political entities which they had delivered into the hands of their monarch should have a comparable standing to that of the various realms – León, Toledo, Córdoba, Murcia, Jaén, Seville and, most recently, Granada – which constituted the Crown of Castile.[23] New Spain, New Granada, Quito and Peru would all therefore come to be known as kingdoms, and the conquerors and their descendants expected them to be ruled in a manner appropriate to their status.

While the crown was well aware of the dangers of unnecessarily bruising the susceptibilities of the conquistadores, especially in the early stages of settlement when the political and military situation remained very volatile, it was determined to impose its own authority at the earliest opportunity. Too much was at stake, in terms of both potential American revenues and the commitment entered into with the papacy for the salvation of Indian souls, to permit the kind of *laissez-faire* approach that would characterize so much of early Stuart policy towards the new plantations. Imbued with a high sense of their own authority, which they had fought so hard to assert in the Iberian peninsula itself, Ferdinand and Isabella moved with speed to meet the obligations incumbent on them as 'natural lords' of the Indies, while at the same time maximizing the potential to the crown of its new territorial acquisitions.

This required the rapid development and imposition on the Indies of administrative, judicial and ecclesiastical structures – a process that would be carried forward by Charles V and Philip II. From the first, expeditions of conquest had been accompanied by royal officials whose task was to watch over the crown's interests, and particularly its interests in the sharing out of the spoils. As an incorporated territory the Indies fell within the orbit of the supreme governing body of Castile, the Council of Castile, and in the early years the monarchs would turn for advice on Indies affairs to selected members of the council, and in particular to the Archdeacon of Seville and eventual Bishop of Burgos, Juan Rodríguez de Fonseca, who was effectively the supremo in the management of the Indies trade and the administration of the Indies from 1493 for almost the entire period down to his death in 1524.[24] By 1517 this small group of councillors was being spoken of as 'the Council of the Indies',[25] and in 1523 this became a formalized and distinctive Council within the conciliar structure of the Spanish Monarchy.[26]

The newly constituted Council of the Indies, with Fonseca as its first president, was to have the prime responsibility for government, trade, defence and the administration of justice in Spanish America throughout the nearly two centuries of Habsburg rule. Spain thus acquired at an early stage of its imperial enterprise a central organ for the formulation and implementation of policy relating to every aspect of the life of its American possessions. Had Charles I's regime survived, Archbishop Laud's Commission for Regulating Plantations might conceivably have evolved into a broadly similar omnicompetent body. As it was, it would take time, and various experiments, for an even remotely equivalent body – the Board of Trade of 1696 – to be established in England, and even then, as its name suggests, its primary concern was with the commercial aspects of the relationship between the mother country and its American colonies.

The immediate and most pressing task of the councillors of the Indies, following Cortés's conquest of Mexico between 1519 and 1521, was to ensure that it should be followed as quickly as possible by a second conquest – that of the conquerors by the crown. In the early years of the century the crown had fought tenaciously to strip Columbus and his heirs of what quickly came to be seen as the excessive powers and privileges granted to him under the terms of his original 'capitulations' with the Catholic Monarchs. With vast riches from the conquered empire of Montezuma in prospect, it was essential that Cortés, who in 1522 had been appointed governor, captain-general and Justicia Mayor of New Spain by a grateful monarch in recognition both of his services and of the realities of Mexico in the immediate aftermath of conquest, should have his wings clipped as those of Columbus had been clipped before him. As the bureaucrats descended on New Spain, the conqueror saw himself stripped of his administrative functions and subjected to a *residencia* – the normal form of judicial inquiry into the activities of servants of the crown against whom complaints had been lodged. Simultaneously harried and honoured – he received the title of marquis and the grant of substantial lands with 23,000 Indian vassals for his services – he eventually abandoned the struggle and left for Spain in 1539, never to return. Francisco Pizarro, too, was to be simultaneously rewarded with the title of marquis and harassed by treasury officials, and was on the verge of losing his governorship of Peru when he was assassinated by his disappointed rivals in 1541.[27]

While the conquistadores and the encomenderos were to be dispossessed as quickly as possible of effective powers of government, it was essential to create an administrative apparatus to fill the vacuum. To achieve this, the crown made use of institutions which had been tried and tested at home, and were now pragmatically adapted to meet American needs. The first *Audiencia*, or high court, in the New World had been established in Santo Domingo in 1511. As more and more mainland territory came under Spanish rule, so more Audiencias were set up: the Audiencia of New Spain in 1530, following a false start three years earlier; of Panama in 1538; of Peru and Guatemala, both in 1543, and of Guadalajara (New Galicia) and Santa Fe de Bogotá in 1547. By the end of the century there were ten American Audiencias.[28] As a judicial tribunal the Audiencia was modelled on the chancelleries or Audiencias of Valladolid and Granada, but, unlike its counterparts in the Crown of Castile, it would develop administrative as well as judicial functions, as an extension of its obligation to maintain a judicial oversight over all administrative activities in territories far removed from the physical presence of the monarch.

These administrative activities were initially carried out by governors (*gobernadores*), a title conferred on a number of the early conquistadores.

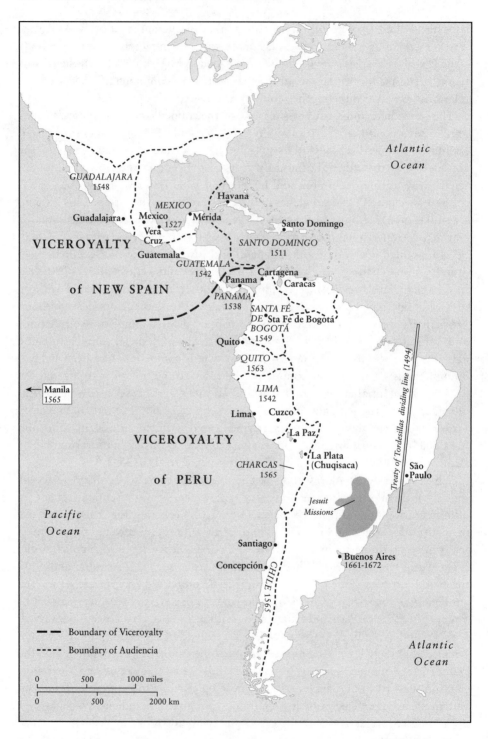

Map 3. Spanish American Viceroyalties and Audiencias (sixteenth and seventeenth centuries).
Based on Francisco Morales Padrón, *Historia general de América* (1975), vol. VI, p. 391.

viceRoyalty—territory goverened by a viceroy.

Governorships proved to be particularly useful for the administration and defence of outlying regions, and 35 such provincial governorships existed at one time or another during the course of the sixteenth and seventeenth centuries.[29] But the supreme ruling institution over large parts of Spain's empire of the Indies was to be the viceroyalty. This had originally been developed for the government of the medieval Catalan-Aragonese empire in the Mediterranean, and the appointment of Columbus in 1492 as viceroy and governor-general of any lands he discovered may have been modelled on the example of the government of Sardinia.[30] As a result of his failures in the government of Hispaniola Columbus was stripped of his viceregal title in 1499, and the viceroyalty went into temporary abeyance in the New World as the crown chose instead to appoint governors, captain-generals and *adelantados* (the title given to the men put in charge of newly conquered frontier regions during the reconquest of southern Spain from the Moors).

The conquest of Mexico, however, posed problems of administration on a scale hitherto unprecedented in the Indies. The government of New Spain between 1528 and 1530 by its first Audiencia proved a disaster, with the judges and the conquistadores at each other's throats. Although the new Audiencia appointed in 1530 represented a marked improvement in terms of the quality of government, it was clear that a new and better solution had to be found. In 1535 Don Antonio de Mendoza, the younger son of a prominent Castilian noble house, was appointed first viceroy of New Spain, and held the post with distinction for sixteen years (a length of tenure which would never be equalled, as the viceregal system consolidated itself, and tenures of six to eight years became the norm).

Mendoza's success encouraged the Council of the Indies to repeat the experiment in Peru, which was transformed into a viceroyalty in 1542. New Spain and Peru were to remain the sole American viceroyalties until the elevation in the eighteenth century of New Granada, with its capital in Santa Fe de Bogotá, and the region of Río de la Plata, with its capital in Buenos Aires, to the rank of viceroyalties. In the words of the legislation of 1542, 'the kingdoms of New Spain and Peru are to be ruled and governed by viceroys, who shall represent our royal person, hold the superior government, do and administer justice equally to all our subjects and vassals, and concern themselves with everything that will promote the calm, peace, ennoblement and pacification of those provinces . . .'[31]

In effect, therefore, the viceroy was to be the *alter ego* of a necessarily absentee ruler, and the living mirror of kingship in a distant land. Generally drawn from one or other of the great noble houses of Spain, a viceroy crossed the Atlantic – as befitted his rank – accompanied by a large entourage of family members and servants, all anxious for rich pickings in the New World during his tenure of office. His arrival on American soil, and his passage through his territory to the capital city, was as carefully staged a ritual event as if the king himself were taking possession of his realm. Each new viceroy of New Spain would follow the route to the capital taken by Hernán Cortés. On arrival at the port of Vera Cruz, he would be ceremonially received by the civil and military authorities, and spend a few days in formal duties, like inspecting the fortifications, before setting out on his triumphal progress towards Mexico City. Moving inland by slow stages, he would be greeted in towns and villages along the route by ceremonial arches, decorated streets, singing and dancing Indians, and effusive orations by Spanish and Indian officials. Arriving at the Indian city of Tlaxcala, which had loyally supported Cortés during the conquest of Mexico, he would make a ceremonial entry on horseback, preceded by the indigenous nobility, and followed by vast crowds of Indians to the accompaniment of drums and music. Having thus symbolically recognized the indigenous contribution to the conquest, and enjoyed or endured three days of festivities, he continued on his progress to the creole city of Puebla, to pay a comparable tribute to the Spanish conquerors. Here he spent eight days before moving on to Otumba, the site of Cortés's first victory after the retreat from Tenochtitlán. At Otumba he would be met by the outgoing viceroy, who, in a symbolic transfer of authority, presented him with the baton of command. The triumphal progress, part Roman triumph, part Renaissance royal entry, culminated in Mexico City itself, where the ceremonial arches were more elaborate, the festivities more lavish, the rejoicings more tumultuous, than anywhere else along the route.[32]

Once he had taken the oath of office and had been installed in the viceregal palace, the new viceroy found himself at the centre of a court where the etiquette and ritual replicated in microcosm those of the royal court in Madrid. As in Madrid, there was a palace guard to protect him.[33] For if the king himself was far away, he was also here, and the viceroy, as his living image, was entitled to a regal deference. At the same time, the monarch himself was an absent presence. The portrait of a new ruler would preside over each proclamation ceremony. Royal births and deaths were the occasion for elaborate commemorations in cathedrals and churches. The monumental catafalques for royal exequies again bore the image of the deceased, whose virtues and achievements were symbolically and emblematically depicted. On all these ceremonial occasions the viceroy occupied the centre stage, receiving in his palace delegations bearing congratulations or condolences, and upholding in his person the dignity and authority of his royal master.[34]

The viceroy was not only the supreme governor in the name of the king; he was also president of the Audiencias within his area of jurisdiction, but was not allowed to intervene directly in judicial business; he was head of the treasury system; and captain-general over the entire territory, although only exercising the duty in a supervisory capacity in those parts of his viceroyalty which possessed a captain-general of their own. He enjoyed considerable powers of patronage and appointment, although viceroy after viceroy would complain that these were not enough.

Subordinate to the viceroy were the governors of the various provinces within his viceroyalty, together with the officers of local government, *alcaldes mayores* (the title most commonly used in New Spain) and *corregidores* – equivalents of the officials in Castile who exercised local authority on behalf of the crown.[35] Municipal councils – the cabildos – formed an integral part of this administrative structure of the Indies, where the crown, starting from scratch, was better placed than in the Iberian peninsula, with its accretion of historic municipal privileges and corporate rights, to create a system of government directly dependent on royal and imperial control.[36] If the 'modernity' of the modern state is defined in terms of its possession of institutional structures capable of conveying the commands of a central authority to distant localities, the government of colonial Spanish America was more 'modern' than the government of Spain, or indeed of that of almost every Early Modern European state.

From the middle of the sixteenth century, therefore, an elaborate administrative chain of command existed for Spain's empire of the Indies. It ran from the Council of the Indies in Spain itself, to the viceroys in Mexico City and Lima, and then down to treasury and local officials and town governments. A parallel judicial system ran similarly from the Council of the Indies to the viceroys and the various Audiencias and judicial officers. The operations of this administrative and judicial bureaucracy were governed by a set of laws, dispositions and practices that again had been developed in Castile but were subsequently adapted, as the occasion demanded, to the special requirements of the Indies.

Since the Indies had been incorporated into the Crown of Castile, they were essentially to be ruled by the Castilian legal system. A Roman Law system, it incorporated some of the traditional law of Castile, and was codified by jurists schooled in Roman and canon law, in the great thirteenth-century legal compilation, the *Siete Partidas* of Alfonso X.[37] The monarch, as the supreme source of authority, was expected to maintain justice in accordance with divine and natural law on the basis of this compilation, which was extended and modified over time by royal decrees issued either on his own initiative or in the light of representations made by the Castilian Cortes. It soon became apparent, however, that laws compiled for Castile would not necessarily cover all the circumstances of life in America. Increasingly, therefore, the Council of the Indies found it necessary to make special provision for local situations in the New World, as it did when creating the American viceroyalties.

Even if the Indies were conquered territory, the Council of the Indies was not legislating in a total vacuum, since the Indian populations of the conquered territories – some of them loyal allies, like the Tlaxcalans of central Mexico, and therefore deserving of special treatment – possessed their own laws and customs. Naturally respectful of established custom, the immediate instinct of sixteenth-century Spaniards was to recognize the validity of existing Indian legal arrangements and practices where they did not openly conflict with Castilian law and requirements. But the indigenous law that survived the conquest was subject to an inevitable process of erosion as the character of Indian society was transformed by Christianization and the pressures of colonial rule. Pre-conquest records might continue to be used for the settlement of boundary disputes and for suits of Indian against Indian, but by the time that a General Indian Court of New Spain was established in 1585 it was more likely to be Spanish than Indian law that the Court found itself enforcing.[38]

As the Council of the Indies began to enact ever more special measures for the American territories, however, and as the viceroys drew up special regulations and provisions for their own territories, this Spanish law was no longer exactly that of Castile. Unlike the Anglo-American world, the Hispanic world was not governed by case law and judicial precedent, but by specific enactments and codified provisions. The result of this was a confusing tangle of enactments, which left the councillors of the Indies in growing doubt as to what was, or was not, the law. In the 1560s Philip II, with his habitual concern for close regulation and for the imposition of order on chaos, turned his attention to the Council of the Indies. A royal official, Juan de Ovando, was appointed to conduct a visit of inquiry into the Council, on which he was subsequently to serve as a great reforming president between 1571 and his death in 1575. Ovando identified as one of the Council's greatest problems the fact that 'neither in the Council nor in the Indies does information exist about the laws and ordinances by which those States are ruled and governed.'[39] He then set about reducing them to some sort of order, but the so-called *Código Ovandino* remained unfinished at the time of his death.

The work was not taken up again until the following century, when two councillors of the Indies, Antonio de León Pinelo and Juan de Solórzano y Pereira, both embarked on attempts at codification, which again remained uncompleted at the time of their deaths.[40] But eventually, in 1680, during the reign of Carlos II, these earlier efforts bore fruit in the publication of a vast compendium, *Recopilación de las leyes de Indias*, a belated companion to the *Recopilación* of the laws of Castile published by order of Philip II in 1567. In spite of the crown's desire to keep them unified, the laws of Castile and America were inevitably moving apart. Even this, however, was not the full extent of the process of fragmentation. By 1680 a universal code for the Indies had come to acquire a certain phantom quality. Five years after its publication, Peru significantly responded to the *Recopilación* by printing its own *Recopilación provincial*, a compilation of the provisions and ordinances issued by the Peruvian viceroys.[41] Each territory of Spanish America was gradually acquiring its own corpus of legislation tailored to suit its own special requirements.

The administrative and judicial apparatus imposed on Castile's conquered Indian possessions was accompanied by an increasingly elaborate ecclesiastical apparatus developed in response to the papacy's concession to the Crown of Castile of the Patronato of the Indies.[42] The Patronato gave the crown enormous powers in the Indies, which it exercised to the full. While the colonization of Spanish America was a joint church–state enterprise, it was one in which the crown from the first had the upper hand. The church in the Indies began as a missionary church, with the religious orders taking the lead in the work of evangelization, but the secular clergy followed in the wake of the friars, just as the bureaucrats followed in the wake of the conquistadores. Although the religious orders remained immensely powerful, and continued to receive strong royal support, the normal apparatus of formal church government was established bit by

The crown ruled then the church

bit under royal direction, initially almost in parallel to the mendicant structures. All ecclesiastical appointments were made by the monarch on the basis of recommendations by the Council of the Indies, which divided the territory into dioceses – 31 by the end of the sixteenth century, including the four archbishoprics of Mexico City, Lima, Santo Domingo and Santa Fe de Bogotá.[43] The affirmation of episcopal authority over the church in the Indies would fully conform to the requirements of the Council of Trent, but it also provided the crown with a means of reining in the mendicant orders, which by the middle years of the sixteenth century were well on the way to becoming a power unto themselves. Philip II was no more inclined to see his authority subverted by the friars than by the encomenderos, with whom the friars often acted in collusion.

In his *Ordenanza del Patronazgo* of 1574, Philip produced a code of orders designed to reinforce his own authority by subjecting the regulars to the bishops and placing secular clergy in parishes in the place of the friars.[44] This was to prove a long and contentious business, since the friars had no intention of abandoning their Indian flocks. The struggle between seculars and regulars would continue throughout the colonial period. But the institutional and legal structures were now all in place for the functioning of ecclesiastical life in the Indies under close royal control – so close, indeed, that no papal nuncio was allowed to set foot in America, and papal nuncios in Madrid were not allowed to meddle in American business.[45] The crown also enjoyed control over the financial arrangements of the American church, which depended on the collection and distribution of tithes by treasury officials. By royal orders of 1539 and 1541 half of the tithes, which were collected in kind and then put up for auction, were shared equally between bishops and deans and cathedral chapters, while the other half were divided into nine parts, of which four went to the payment of parish priests and their assistants, three to the construction and decoration of churches, and the remaining two were absorbed into the royal coffers.[46]

The mutually reinforcing relationship of church and crown cemented a structure of Spanish royal government in America so all-embracing that Juan de Ovando in the 1570s could justifiably speak of the *estado de las Indias*, the State of the Indies.[47] In less than a century since the beginning of the overseas enterprise, the Spanish crown had established in the New World a system of government and control that might well be the envy of European monarchs struggling to impose their own authority on recalcitrant nobles, privileged corporations and obstreperous Estates close to home.

For all the flaws and defects in the system – the built-in conflicts between competing authorities, the numerous opportunities for procrastination, obstruction and graft – this creation of a 'State of the Indies' was by any measure a remarkable achievement, not least because it seems to have defied successfully the normal laws of time and space. The viceroyalties of the Indies were thousands of miles, and an ocean, away. It could take two years for the government in Madrid, the capital of Spain's world-wide monarchy from 1561, to send a message to Lima and receive the reply. Yet, as Francis Bacon relates, 'Mendoza, that was viceroy of

Peru, was wont to say: That the government of Peru was the best place that the King of Spain gave, save that it was somewhat too near Madrid.'[48] An exchange of messages between London and Virginia might take a mere four months, but for the monarchs of Stuart England, struggling to bring a few thousand recalcitrant settlers within the framework of their 'royal empire', Spain's government of the Indies could only have looked like a triumphant assertion of the obedience properly due to kings.

Authority and resistance

Yet the Spanish crown had not imposed its authority without a long and bitter struggle, and at many times and in many places that authority would prove to be more nominal than real. When Castile and England exported their people to America, they also exported pre-existing political cultures which permeated both the institutions of government and the responses of the governed. Those distinctive political cultures produced two distinctive colonial worlds with profoundly different political characteristics, reflecting those of the metropolitan societies out of which they emerged. Yet amidst the contrasts there were also strong points of resemblance.

Driven by the twin imperatives of its thirst for precious metals and its obligations towards its new Indian vassals, the Spanish crown was interventionist from the beginning in its approach to the government of the Indies. It sought to mould the developing colonial society in accordance with its own aspirations, and its own high sense – fortified by university-trained jurists who had entered the royal service – of the all-commanding nature of its divinely ordained authority. Inevitably, however, as it embarked on the task of giving institutional expression to theoretical aspirations, it encountered resistance from those who harboured distinctive aspirations of their own. The friars yearned to establish in the New World a New Jerusalem, free from corrupting secular influences. The conquistadores, for their part, dreamed of exercising lordship over numerous Indian vassals, and so transforming themselves into a hereditary landed aristocracy as rich and socially dominant as the aristocracy of Castile.

The incompatibility of these differing aspirations meant that none of them could be realized in full, and the crown would find itself forced to make open or tacit compromises in its struggle to get its commands obeyed. In embarking on this struggle it began with an important advantage: the success of Ferdinand and Isabella in restoring royal authority in Spain itself, and the mystical prestige conferred on the crown by a miraculous succession of triumphs, including the recovery of Granada from the Moors and the discovery and acquisition of the Indies. The election of Charles in 1519 as Holy Roman Emperor, although it threatened to have unwelcome consequences for Castile, could also be read as a sign of God's continuing favour for the dynasty, as it was by Hernán Cortés, who saw himself benefiting, as Charles's loyal captain, from 'God's help and the royal fortune of Your Majesty'.[49]

The mystique of kingship, together with the realities of political life in the Spain created by Ferdinand and Isabella, therefore combined to inculcate in the generation that conquered America an instinctive sense of the deference that should be paid to the crown. Hernán Cortés, even when defying the authority of his immediate superior, the royal governor of Cuba, went to extreme pains to represent his action as being taken solely in order to promote the higher interests of his prince – as the prince himself would appreciate as soon as he was in possession of the facts. This identification of themselves with royal authority was to be a constant in the life of the conquistadores, and reinforced that sense of loyalty which was to be a trump card in the hands of royal officials determined to give reality to that authority three thousand miles from home.

At the same time, however, the crown's authority by no means went unchallenged, even in Castile itself. Cortés's conquest of Mexico coincided almost exactly with one of the greatest political upheavals in Castilian history, the revolt of the Comuneros, in which the policies and actions of the new king and his Flemish advisers were openly challenged by the cities of the Castilian heartland in the name of the community of the realm.[50] Although the Comuneros were defeated in battle in 1521, the beliefs and assumptions that informed their rebellion had been exported to America alongside the cult of loyalty, and they too would take deep root in the political culture of the emerging colonial world.

At the heart of these beliefs and assumptions lay the conviction that the well-being of the community depended on the proper functioning of a contractual relationship between the ruler and the ruled. Prince and subjects together formed an organic community, a *corpus mysticum*, designed to enable its members to live good and sociable lives according to their respective social stations, under the benevolent rule of a monarch who governed, following the dictates of his conscience, in accordance with divine and natural law. The good prince would not swerve into tyranny, and his subjects in return would serve, obey and advise him faithfully. These were the assumptions that found practical expression in the code of the *Siete Partidas*, well known to Hernán Cortés and his fellow conquistadores.[51] Deriving from Aristotle by way of Aquinas, they were reformulated at a theoretical level for sixteenth-century Spaniards by the neo-Thomist scholastics of the School of Salamanca.[52] They constituted the premise on which the Spanish patrimonial state in the Indies was constructed, just as they also constituted the premise underlying legitimate resistance to the actions of that state when it acted in ways that were deemed to run counter to the common weal, the *bien común*.[53]

The contractualist doctrines built in to Spanish theories of the state allowed for different levels of resistance. The first and most fundamental of these, which was to have a long and important life in the Indies, was articulated in the formula originally deriving from the Basques and subsequently embedded in later medieval Castilian law, of obeying but not complying. An official or an individual receiving a royal order which he considered inappropriate or unjust would symbolically place it on his head while pronouncing the ritual words that he would obey but not comply: *se acata* (or *se obedece*) *pero no se cumple*. This simultaneously demonstrated respect for the royal authority while asserting the inapplicability of royal orders in this particular instance. Appearances were thus preserved, and time was given to all parties for reflection. This formula, which was to be incorporated into the laws of the Indies in 1528, provided an ideal mechanism for containing dissent, and preventing disputes from turning into open confrontation.[54] Hernán Cortés took obedience without compliance one stage further when, on arriving on the coast of Mexico, he ignored the governor of Cuba's orders that he was to conduct an expedition of reconnaissance rather than conquest. Instead, he denounced him as a 'tyrant', and appealed over his head directly to the monarch.[55] The right of appeal was fundamental in this society, as was the right of the vassal to be heard by his prince, and between them they provided an essential device for conflict resolution.

The final recourse against what was perceived as 'tyrannical' government or unreasonable laws was resort to arms. The most explosive situation faced by the Spanish crown in America before the late eighteenth century was that created by the New Laws of 1542, and particularly law 35, forbidding the creation of new encomiendas and providing for the reversion of existing encomiendas to the crown on the death of the current holder. Faced with the prospect of a revolt by the encomenderos, the viceroy of New Spain, Antonio de Mendoza, in effect activated the process of obeying but not complying by persuading the royal official sent out to enforce the laws to suspend those relating to the encomienda until an appeal could be heard by the Council of the Indies.[56]

In the highly volatile Peru of the early 1540s the story took a different and more tragic turn. The conquistadores had fought a bitter civil war over the spoils of conquest, the governor, Francisco Pizarro, had been assassinated, and royal authority had yet to be firmly established. Blasco Núñez Vela, the first viceroy appointed to the newly created viceroyalty, was sent out to Lima in 1543 with instructions to enforce the New Laws. The news of the crown's intentions preceded him. An orchestrated response was prepared by the town councils, acting under the leadership of the cabildo of Cuzco. At the same time Gonzalo Pizarro, claiming the governorship of Peru in succession to his dead brother, stepped into the political arena as the leader of the encomenderos, who claimed that their services had been insufficiently recognized and rewarded. To cries of 'Long live the king and down with bad ministers' – the standard cry of protest in the Spanish Monarchy – Pizarro set out to recruit an army.

The justification for the revolt threatening the new viceroy on his arrival was the defence of the common weal. The jurists who lent their support to Pizarro argued that 'certain royal laws affecting these kingdoms had been made and decreed without their representatives being present' – a clear reference to the traditional formula that 'what affects all should be agreed by all.' The viceroy proved intransigent, and in the uprising that followed he was defeated in battle and executed on the battlefield. Gonzalo Pizarro, supremely confident both of his own popularity and of the rightness of his cause, then went far beyond the limits of an already dubious legitimacy by replacing the royal arms by the Pizarro arms on the standards carried by his army. He also did nothing to prevent his adherents from letting it be known that he would shortly be proclaimed king of an independent Peru. Such a proclamation was averted by the timely arrival and skilful manoeuvring of Núñez Vela's replacement, Pedro de La Gasca, who announced a general amnesty in advance of his arrival – an offer that Pizarro rejected. Having divided the opposition, La Gasca then defeated Pizarro in battle, and had him tried and executed for *lèse majesté* in 1548. Honour was subsequently satisfied all round, as Charles V, having already revoked the law abolishing the encomienda, accepted that the rebels, in appealing to him, had recognized his authority. Much of the blame could thus be laid on Núñez Vela for rejecting their supplication. In this way the ground was prepared for the consolidation of royal government in Peru on the basis of an act of oblivion, and of a tacit compromise that rested on the assumption of the fundamental loyalty of the encomenderos and settlers to their lawful monarch.[57]

Pizarro's rebellion was a highly unusual act of outright defiance to the authority of the crown in colonial Spanish America, just as the revolt of the Comuneros remained a unique act of large-scale armed insurrection in the history of Habsburg Castile. Both in Castile and in the Indies a heavy state apparatus was imposed on society in the name of royal authority. But the weight of this apparatus was to some extent alleviated by a political culture which, although lacking the more obvious institutional restraints on the arbitrary exercise of power, was postulated on the basis of a reciprocal relationship that required and expected a continuous process of negotiation between the monarch and his subjects. Lobbying and petitioning (fig. 13), compromise and counter-compromise, formed the everyday stuff of political life in Spain's empire of the Indies. Over the best part of three centuries this tacit compact between monarch and subjects did much to ensure a high degree of outward compliance to the orders of the crown. The settlers remained loyal to a distant monarch, who, they continued to believe, would respond to their complaints and redress their grievances once he was properly informed. It was a convenient fiction in which all parties participated during the period of Habsburg rule, and when it began to wear thin under the new Bourbon dynasty in the eighteenth century, the loyalty which held Spain and its overseas possessions together would be strained to the limits.

The combination of a bureaucratic state structure with a culture of loyalty that permitted resistance within certain understood limits gave colonial Spanish America the appearance of a politically stable society. Reality did not always coincide with appearance, but conflicts were in general resolved and crises contained. The political stability, however, had the effect of trivializing much of public life. With so many areas of government under the control of royal officials, a substantial amount of the colonial elite's time and energy in the Habsburg period was devoted to maintaining the outward and more symbolic manifestations of power and status. Although there were always unwelcome encroachments on local autonomy to be fended off, much political energy was expended in endless jockeying over rank and ceremonial within the narrow confines of municipal life.

Such matters would also occupy the colonial elites of British America. Here, however, the nature of colonial government allowed considerably more scope for the independent exercise of effective political power. This was a society whose political and administrative institutions were more likely to evolve from below than to be imposed from above. It was also a society that operated in a political culture more effectively grounded in notions of representation than the political culture transferred to America from Castile.

The absence of close control by the British crown in the early stages of colonization left considerable latitude for the evolution of those forms of government that seemed most appropriate to the people actively involved in the process of overseas enterprise and settlement – the financial backers of the enterprise and the colonists themselves – as long as they operated within the framework of their royal charter. Care was taken in drawing up the Virginia Company's charter of 1606 to guarantee to the colonists and their children all the 'liberties, franchises and immunities' enjoyed under English laws.[58] But the imposition of martial law in 1611 following the early troubles of the colony was hardly a source of encouragement to colonists or potential colonists looking to find themselves in possession of the 'liberties, franchises and immunities' of Englishmen. The 'Great Charter' of 1618 was designed to respond to their grievances by improving administration, settling the question of land tenure, and replacing martial law with English common law. The reforms included provision for the establishment of a Virginia Assembly, which met for the first time in 1619.[59] It was in 1619, too, that Nathaniel Butler arrived as governor in the faction-ridden island of Bermuda with instructions from the Bermuda Company to summon an assembly as quickly as possible, because 'every man will more willingly obey laws to which he hath yielded his consent.'[60] In stark contrast to Spanish America, therefore, representative forms of government came to British America within a few years of settlement.

The Virginia Assembly of 1619 and the Bermuda Assembly of 1620 were attempts to resolve problems relating to public order, local administration and the raising of taxes for public purposes by recourse to the well-tried English expedient of involving the 'political nation', and through it the wider community, in the processes of government. The 'political nation' in the colonial context, as in the metropolitan, meant property-holders, but the nature of that context was likely, especially in the initial stages of settlement, to favour a franchise that was wider than in England. As early as 1623 reports of 'democracy' in Plymouth Colony were causing concern at home, and William Bradford had to reassure the colony's supporters that women and children did not possess the vote.[61] Practice would vary widely from one colony to the next, but there were continuing uncertainties about the definition of 'freemen' on the farther shores of the Atlantic. In relation both to voting and to office-holding, these uncertainties enlarged the range of opportunities for many immigrants well beyond what they could have expected at home.

More significant, however, than variations in the character of the franchise was the sheer fact of representation through the institutionalized forum of representative assemblies, such as were not allowed to emerge in the viceroyalties of Mexico and Peru. Once the pattern had been established in Virginia and Bermuda there was every chance that it would be followed elsewhere as new colonies were founded. This was partly because voting was an established feature of joint stock companies, and was therefore likely to be transferred with relative ease to colonial settlements operating under company charters. The most striking example was provided by the Massachusetts Bay colony, which was unique in that both the charter and the government moved across the Atlantic with the first settlers. Once a year the adult free males of the Bay colony would assemble in their capacity as company stockholders to elect a governor and assistant governor for the coming year.[62] But, irrespective of the practices of company organization, there were other forces at work to push the new colonies towards the establishment of government by consent. At a time when some of the most influential leaders of the opposition to Charles I were involved in colonial ventures, and when the very existence of parliament itself was under threat from the crown, there was a strong natural predisposition to re-create in the colonies representative bodies modelled on an institution that had come to be identified with the preservation of traditional English liberties.

By 1640 eight such assemblies had been set up in the colonies, six of them during the period in which Charles I attempted to rule at home without a parliament: Massachusetts Bay, Maryland, Connecticut, Plymouth, New Haven and Barbados.[63] Pressure for the establishment of these assemblies tended to come from the colonists themselves, although Lord Baltimore's charter for the creation of his proprietary colony of Maryland had already empowered him to make laws with the advice of the assembled freemen.[64] Once a colony had been founded, however, it was difficult, as James, Duke of York, would eventually discover in his proprietary colony of New York,[65] to withhold permission for the summoning of an assembly when the other British colonies possessed them and were competing for settlers. The Special Court of Assize, petitioning the duke in 1681 against the burden of taxes which it condemned as arbitrary, complained that the inhabitants of New York were 'wholly shut out or deprived of any share, vote, or interest in the government . . . contrary to the laws, rights, liberties and privileges, of the subject; so that we are esteemed as nothing, and have become a reproach to the neighbours in other of his majesty's colonies, who flourish, under the fruition and protection of his majesty's unparalleled form and method of government, . . . the undoubted birthright of all his subjects.' With his colony in turmoil, his own position in England temporarily weakened, and English legal opinion coming out in support of the independence of local assemblies, James had no option but to give New Yorkers the assembly they demanded.[66]

New or potential colonists were thus likely to regard the possession of a representative assembly as a visible guarantee that settlement in the New World would not involve any diminution of their English liberties. For the proprietors, too, *noisy and difficult to control* ←

such assemblies offered certain advantages. While they might well prove obstreperous, they also offered the best means available for committing settlers to the financing and defence of their colony, and served as a convenient forum for the resolution of disputes.

Yet the creation of an assembly in a royal or proprietary colony was sooner or later bound to raise questions about the character and extent of its powers. Just as the Spanish crown could look on its American possessions as 'conquered' territories, so the British crown, taking the conquered kingdom of Ireland as a precedent, could regard the Caribbean and North American settlements in the same light. Naturally, British settlers were as eager as Spanish settlers to reject the inferior status implicit in the notion of a conquered territory, and to insist on their entitlement to the rights and privileges that they would have enjoyed had they stayed at home. Where Spanish colonists claimed these privileges by virtue of their own descent from the conquerors, or argued that the pre-conquest character of Mexico and Peru as kingdoms elevated them above mere 'colonial' status, English colonists were insistent that the 'vacant' lands they had settled fell outside the definition of 'conquered' territories. Yet this argument was never fully accepted in England itself, and as late as the 1760s Sir William Blackstone was asserting that not only Ireland but also the American plantations were conquered lands.[67]

While London might not be amenable to the colonists' arguments, a representative assembly offered them a forum in which they could press for their rights as Englishmen against governors disposed to trample on those rights. Even if English settlers could not resort to the Spanish symbolic procedure of obeying but not complying, it was still possible for them to refuse to comply with a royal order or a governor's instructions on the grounds that the king was misinformed.[68] A governor, as the chief colonial executive, found himself, moreover, in a considerably weaker position than a viceroy or governor in Spanish America, in spite of what often appeared on paper to be substantial powers.

Nominally, a governor in an English royal colony enjoyed extensive powers of appointment and patronage, including the authority to issue grants of land.[69] In practice he was liable, like his Spanish counterpart, to find these powers circumscribed by the determination of home officials to encroach on his patronage, and also by the stringent terms of his instructions.[70] The already detailed set of royal instructions for governors seems to have become even more constraining to independent action following an attempt at revision in 1752. Horace Walpole commented ironically on those issued in 1753 to Sir Danvers Osborn, the new governor of New York, that they were 'better calculated for the latitude of Mexico and for a Spanish tribunal than for a free rich British settlement'.[71]

An English royal governor was not normally surrounded by the pomp and circumstance of his Spanish viceregal counterpart, although one or two governors compensated for this by bringing a retinue of servants on a truly Spanish scale. James II's governor-general of Jamaica, the second Duke of Albermarle, was accompanied by 150 servants, but Joseph Dudley, appointed governor of

Massachusetts in 1702, seems to have found five sufficient.[72] A new governor on arrival would be greeted by a seventeen-gun salute from the harbour guns, and a receiving party on the wharf. There would be a procession to the statehouse along a route lined by the local militia, followed by a reading of the governor's commission and his swearing the oath of office. There might be illuminations and fireworks in the evening, but it was entirely in keeping with the relative informality of the proceedings, as compared with those in New Spain and Peru, that the day was likely to end with dinner and entertainment in a local coffee-house or tavern.[73]

British governors, like their Spanish counterparts, were well aware that they were the physical representatives on American soil of the person of the monarch, although few of them took the identification as far as Lord Cornbury, the governor of New York and New Jersey from 1702 to 1708, is alleged to have done. On the basis of contemporary charges of cross-dressing he has entered the historical record as having dressed up to resemble his sovereign, Queen Anne, but the atmosphere of early eighteenth-century New York politics was highly scurrilous, and charges of cross-dressing look like no more than attempts by his enemies to discredit him.[74]

While transvestism may have been a step too far, royal governors were expected to do everything in their power to embody in their own persons the figure of the monarch and sustain an appropriate degree of display. Cornbury himself travelled through his colonial domain in style, often accompanied by a train of local gentry. Everywhere he entertained on a generous scale, and he was careful to reciprocate in full the hospitality accorded him when he was met by Indian chiefs.[75] Of around three hundred governors or deputy-governors appointed by the crown during the period of colonial rule, one in every four was a peer, the son of a peer, or the holder of a title,[76] and such liberality was expected of men of rank.

From the later seventeenth century the English colonies were being absorbed into what was becoming a transatlantic network of patronage.[77] In Britain, as in Spain, high office constituted a form of outdoor relief for hard-pressed members of the aristocracy. 'Governours', wrote Lewis Morris Jr. to the Lords of Trade in 1729, 'do not come here to take the air', but '. . . to repair a shattered fortune, or acquire an Estate.'[78] They could look forward to some five years in office to achieve this happy resolution of their problems – a tenure approaching that of a Spanish viceroy, who could normally expect an initial three-year term of service to be extended for a further three years.[79] Military and naval service was also a passport to a colonial governorship in British America, while in Spanish America the Bourbons showed a willingness, unlike the later Habsburgs, to select for viceregal appointments members of the lower nobility and even the professional classes who had distinguished themselves in administrative or military service.[80] The Spanish crown, however, with its deep suspicion of creole aspirations, did not follow the British crown in countenancing the appointment of colonials to head colonial governments, like Sir Henry Moore, an eighteenth-century governor of New York.[81]

Suspicion, indeed, pervaded the attitude of the imperial authorities in Madrid to every aspect of the government of their American possessions. Too much was at stake for them to run any risks. There were endless opportunities for royal officials to enrich themselves, or to enter into tacit and mutually advantageous alliances with the creole elite. It was for this reason that Philip II ordered in 1575 that viceroys and judges of the Audiencias should not marry a wife from their area of jurisdiction, and Madrid would make desperate if doomed attempts over the years to ensure that the matrimonial prohibitions were upheld, and that royal officials should as far as possible be socially isolated from the surrounding population.[82]

Spain's officials in America, too, were subjected to numerous checks and controls. Viceroys would report on Audiencias and Audiencias on viceroys, and there was a permanent tension in their relationship which was perfectly capable of leading to a total breakdown of communications between the two, as happened in New Spain during the tumultuous viceroyalty of the Marquis of Gelves between 1621 and 1624.[83] All those who felt themselves aggrieved had the right to bypass the local authorities and make their complaints directly to Madrid, and this method of control by accusation and innuendo was reinforced by institutional checks. These took the form of *visitas*, or visitations, in which a visitor was sent out to inquire into the activities of an official, or group of officials, suspected or accused of irregularities. In addition, all officials at the end of their term of office would be subjected to a residencia, consisting of a judicial review of their conduct during their period of tenure.[84]

No British governor in colonial America had serious reason to fear such draconian proceedings. Slanders and innuendoes might fly to and fro across the Atlantic, but the casual attitude of successive British administrations to so many aspects of colonial life was far removed from the legalistic approach adopted by the Council of the Indies in Madrid, the majority of whose members were professionally trained Roman Law jurists. Yet even if a British governor was not exposed to the constant scrutiny and intrusive investigations from the imperial centre to which his Spanish counterpart was condemned, the authority he could command in his area of government was likely to be less.

He was expected to govern with the advice of a council, usually of twelve members, drawn from among the colonists, and also doubling as the upper house of colonial assemblies. Governors and councils often worked well together, but even when a governor's relations with his council were good, he had to move with caution, if only because the councillors were unlikely to approve measures prejudicial to their own interests and those of the colony's elite.[85] It was precisely to counteract this kind of local pressure that the Spanish crown had placed its restrictions on the judges of an Audiencia – the nearest equivalent to the governor's council – forbidding them to acquire land or marry in the area of their jurisdiction.

A British royal or proprietary governor was also at a serious disadvantage in matters of finance. In Spanish America, royal administration was financed by income from the crown's fifth of the production of precious metals and its share of the church's tithes. It could also count on the annual per capita tribute paid by the Indians, together with a set of dues levied on the transatlantic trade.[86] It was true that the settlers and their descendants were exempt from direct taxation as a reward for their services in conquering and settling the land, but, as the costs of administration rose, the crown sought to introduce various forms of indirect taxation. This process began in 1575 with the levying in New Spain of one of Castile's most important taxes, the *alcabala*, a sales tax initially set at 2 per cent. In 1591 the tax was extended to Peru, where its introduction provoked strong resistance.[87]

In Spanish America, as in Spain itself, the crown was forced to turn to merchant-financiers to advance funds in anticipation of revenues still to be received. In many respects, however, it was successful in developing an effective imperial fiscal system, particularly in terms of its ability to respond to changing requirements. A network of regional treasury offices (*cajas reales*) was set up, with royal officials controlling the collection and registration of revenue under the supervision of a principal treasury office located in a viceregal capital or a major administrative centre. Regional treasuries would pay their surplus funds into the principal treasury. By 1600 fourteen of these regional treasury offices were in existence, and a further seventeen were created in the seventeenth century. Each *caja* possessed its own area of jurisdiction, and treasuries were added, and sometimes eliminated, as circumstances changed. The discovery of new silver deposits, or new-found prosperity in some outlying region of empire, was likely to be followed by the establishment of a *caja real*. The system possessed a further element of flexibility in providing the opportunity for the transfer of cash from one region to another in the light of local needs. The Mexican treasury, for example, in addition to the annual remittance of 'surplus' funds to Spain, was called upon to subsidize some of the more impoverished outposts of empire, like the Caribbean islands, Florida and the Philippines, by the transfer of funds, known as *situados*. While the system lent itself to exploitation by merchants and local officials who were in the fortunate position of being able to lay their hands on the monies remitted to their region, in principle the mechanism for the redistribution of tax revenues made it possible to allocate resources, and especially resources for defence, in response to imperial priorities and requirements.[88]

Colonial government in British America, by contrast, lacked a strong and independent fiscal base, and there was no apparatus for the allocation of resources at the imperial level.[89] In the absence of silver mines and of a densely settled Indian tax-paying population, government had necessarily to be funded by the colonists themselves. Although quit-rents were payable to the crown in royal provinces where the king claimed an immediate title to the soil, they met only a fraction of the costs of government, even in the colonies where such rents were collected.[90] As a result, governors were forced to turn to colonial assemblies for money, including in some instances their own salaries. It was precisely to avoid this kind of financial dependence on the colonists that Ferdinand and Isabella had set themselves against the creation of parliamentary institutions in America.

Outside the New England charter colonies, representative assemblies for much of the seventeenth century were slow to find their feet, and were liable to be dominated by the governors and their councils.[91] Yet the potential for conflict existed from the start, as governors anxiously sought ways of covering the rising costs of administration and defence, while assemblies began to appreciate the political leverage offered by control of the purse strings. It was the same story as that of the House of Commons, with which the assemblies or their lower houses increasingly tended to identify themselves. In Virginia, where the governor's council had been the dominant element for the first sixty or seventy years of the assembly's existence, William Fitzhugh, a lawyer, proudly referred in 1687 to the House of Burgesses, now sitting as a separate branch of the assembly, as 'our Parliament here'.[92] By the eighteenth century, following the historical model of the House of Commons, the lower houses were seeking sole authority over the raising and disbursement of revenues, and were gradually eroding the legislative powers of the governors' councils.[93]

In contrast to Spanish viceroys and governors, British colonial governors were also handicapped by the absence of a royal bureaucracy. Without it, they were overwhelmingly dependent on local resources for providing the officers of government and justice, especially in the first decades of settlement when the patterns of administration were being laid down. While overall responsibility for administration in the colony rested with the governor and his council, they naturally looked to English precedents as they set about establishing a framework of government. Unable to count on a regular provision of judges and officials from Britain, equivalent to the stream of Spanish judges and officials travelling over to take up posts in the Indies, they had no choice but to rely on the co-operation of the local elite. As a result, the English system of local self-government at the king's command was transferred to the colonies.

One disadvantage of this was that for a large part of the seventeenth century, and in some colonies beyond it, elites were still in the making. This meant that there was no substantial pool of colonists with a tradition of administrative and judicial service, like the English country gentry, to occupy the posts that had to be filled. By the 1630s the first-generation elite of Virginia, heavily composed of immigrants drawn from the upper ranks of the English social hierarchy, had largely died out. It would take time in this ruthlessly competitive land-grabbing society to forge from among the successful planters a new and stable elite with the inclination, capacity and sense of service to discharge the burdens of office with dedication and competence.[94]

As plantations began to spread through the Tidewater, creating problems of communication over long distances, it ceased to be possible for the governor and his council to perform the tasks of local government, and new institutions were urgently needed to help maintain law and order and regulate disputes. Eight shires, or counties, were established in Virginia in 1634, 'which are to be governed as the shires in England. And Lieutenants to be appointed the same as in England, and in a more especial manner to take care of the war against the Indians. And as in England *sheriffs* shall be elected to have the same power as there; and *sergeants*, and *bailiffs* where need requires.'[95] By 1668, with a flood of immigrants pushing up Virginia's population from 5,000 to 40,000, the number of counties in Virginia had grown to twenty, each with its own county court consisting of justices of the peace, a sheriff with policing and tax-collecting duties, and a clerk and several minor officials.[96]

The operations of these county courts were modelled on English quarter and petty sessions, although with little of the splendour of their English originals.[97] Ceremonially, this was a pared-down version adapted to the more rugged requirements of early colonial society, but, as the General Assembly devolved more and more duties on them, the courts accumulated powers that came to extend beyond those to be found at the equivalent level in England. They became in effect units of government, with a wide range of responsibilities in the management of local life. In the absence of church courts in Virginia, the county courts took over a range of functions which in the home country fell within the sphere of ecclesiastical jurisdiction, like the right to probate wills. In many areas of concern, including those of public and private morality, they worked in close partnership with the vestries, the governing bodies of the parishes into which the county was divided.[98] In Spanish America the church–state partnership ran all the way down the administrative scale, with the institutional church heavily subordinated to royal authorities enforcing regalist policies. In the Anglican colony of Virginia, it operated primarily at the local level, with church business subject to management by the local planter oligarchies which came to dominate county life as a whole.

As the powers of jurisdiction of the county courts were continually augmented by the General Assembly, an essentially decentralized system of government and justice established itself in Virginia, as also in the neighbouring colony of Maryland. The governor and his council increasingly retreated from local government, and, with justices of the peace empowered to hear all cases in criminal law and equity after 1645, the council, sitting as a court, reduced the range of its activities until it was effectively transformed into a court of appeals. Nominally, appointment of justices of the peace rested with the governor, but from the 1660s he was doing little more than formally ratifying choices made at the local level as the planters competed for, and carved up, offices in the county courts among themselves.[99]

Some settlers, as 'new men' who had crossed the Atlantic in search of social betterment, had little or no experience of administering the law at home, although many would at some stage of their lives have come into contact with the courts in England, whether as jurymen, witnesses, plaintiffs or defendants. A number, however, had studied law at the universities and the Inns of Court. Yet even these were confronted on arrival in America with conditions very different from those they knew at home, and now found themselves called upon to meet the heavy challenge of devising and implementing laws that had to be shaped to conform to the needs of societies in the making.

They could only do this by making creative use of such legal traditions as lay to hand, combining them, as appropriate, with the injunctions of divine law and a strong dose of pragmatism. Renaissance England, like Renaissance Spain, was a country endowed not with one system of laws but several. In Spain, a land where Christian, Jewish and Moorish legal systems had coexisted in the Middle Ages, Christian and royal law, although now triumphant, was still hemmed in by customary law, in the form of regional and local juridical privileges, or *fueros*. It was also restricted by corporate privileges – the *fuero militar*, granting various immunities to soldiers, and the *fuero eclesiástico*, which confined a wide range of offences to the church courts, and shielded the clergy from secular jurisdiction. Legal pluralism was equally the order of the day in Tudor and early Stuart England. Not only did civilian lawyers continue to contest the claims of the common law to supremacy, but the common law courts competed in a crowded field with a multiplicity of courts, each with its own form of jurisdiction – church courts, admiralty courts, law merchant courts, local and manor courts, and prerogative courts like the Star Chamber.[100]

Out of this welter of legal systems the first settlers in each new colony had to fashion a legal and court system which would enable them to build civil societies in an alien environment and regulate their relations with the indigenous peoples into whose lands they had moved. In Spanish America, royal officials were quickly on the scene to impose royal justice and the laws of Castile. In the English settlements, on the other hand, the settlers were left largely to their own devices, and had to come up with creative answers of their own, drawing as best they could on legal memories, and guided by William Lambarde's *Eirenarcha* (1581), Michael Dalton's *The Countrey Justice* of 1619, and other essential handbooks for English justices of the peace.

The transplantation of cultures leads to selectivity, as emigrants, especially if drawn from different regions, are driven by circumstance to pare down to a single common denominator, or a few essentials, the forms and institutions of the mother country which will give order to their lives in an alien world. Not surprisingly, therefore, the multiplicity of courts to be found in England gave way in the colonies to a unified court system.[101] Yet at the same time the absence of central direction from England, and the presence of numerous different settlements along the eastern seaboard, tended to have an opposite effect when it came to drafting new legal codes. Each colony struck out on its own to shape a system of laws appropriate to its needs, and although colonies borrowed ideas from each other, their codes inevitably reflected the time of origin of the initial settlement, the character and aspirations of the first wave of settlers, and the situation they found on their arrival in America.

In early Virginia, for instance, the need to discipline a tumultuous colony found expression in a resort to the prerogative notions of English military justice and the judicial practices of the English border regions. Gradually, as the colony was stabilized, the colonists incorporated appropriate aspects of the common law, while at the same time the Virginia General Assembly displayed growing confidence in drafting statutes to cover novel circumstances.[102] The law-makers of Massachusetts, for their part, drew on a wide range of sources in addition to the common law, including the Scriptures, European concepts of civil and natural law, English and foreign local customs, and the law reform propos-als being advocated in the home country during the colony's early years. The outcome was the carefully devised Massachusetts legal code of 1648, which gained wide popular acceptance. The aggrieved were encouraged to take their chances at law, and, as a result, the Massachusetts courts provided a valuable forum for conflict resolution in a naturally contentious society.[103]

The plurality of the legal systems established in seventeenth-century English America, however, was to come under growing pressure during the second half of the century, as a consequence both of developments in the home country and of the determination of the imperial government under the later Stuarts to take the colonies in hand. In the Civil War period the English prerogative courts were abolished, and they were not restored when the monarchy returned in 1660. The church courts, although re-established, saw the scope of their jurisdiction reduced. The implications were clear. The common law was close to achieving definitive victory over its adversaries, and the effects of this were soon to be felt in the colonies. In the years immediately before and after the Glorious Revolution, imperial officials embarked on a strenuous attempt to bring colonial legal systems into line with the practices of the English common law. At the same time, the arrival in America of growing numbers of settlers who had been trained in the common law, and the increasing tendency of the settlers themselves to send their sons to England for a legal education at the Inns of Court, inevitably led to the gradual anglicization of colonial law and legal practice.

The progressive subordination of the diversified legal culture of the colonies to the uniformity of the English common law in the century between the 1680s and the 1770s necessarily involved the closing of several avenues for redress that had been open to suitors in the settler communities during the early years of settle-ment. At the same time, growing professionalization in the world of the common law led to rising costs of litigation, which in turn discouraged the poor from bringing suits.[104] Yet, as in Spain's American territories, the uniformity was far from absolute. In both colonial worlds, specific local circumstances continued to require local legislation; and the presence or proximity of Indians forced the settler societies into accommodation with indigenous customs and traditions, especially in the borderlands.

In British America, moreover, there were matters of great moment on which the common law was largely silent. These included slavery, questions of land-ownership and distribution, and the resolution of border disputes. On such sub-jects, each colony tended to develop its own rules and practices, or borrow them from others. A degree of legal pluralism therefore continued to survive within the tightening legal framework of a British Atlantic civilization. But by degrees that framework of shared Atlantic law and practices came to be prized in the

American colonies as guaranteeing the fundamental English liberties. One of the most fundamental of these liberties was the right to judgment by one's peers.

Trial by jury as a fundamental right of Englishmen had been extended to Virginia by the charter of 1606, but Tudor and early Stuart England had seen a trend to limit the use of juries in favour of more summary forms of justice. The resulting uncertainty in the mother country over the use of juries crossed the Atlantic with the settlers. In the Chesapeake colonies, with their thinly scattered population, it was difficult and expensive to assemble a jury, and for much of the seventeenth century juries tended to be dispensed with, even in civil cases. The magistrates of Puritan New England, whose reverence for biblical law exceeded their reverence for the English common law, showed a strong preference for summary justice – a preference not, however, shared by Rhode Island, whose settlers had moved there from the Bay colony in the hope of escaping from the rigours of magisterial justice, and who not unnaturally possessed a special fondness for juries. In the second half of the century, however, as freemen became increasingly resentful of magisterial domination, and as fears grew about threats to liberty under the later Stuarts, juries became an increasingly established feature of public life throughout the New England colonies, to the point that civil juries came to be used far more extensively than they were in England itself.[105]

Jury service, the holding of local office, voting for, and membership in, an assembly – all this exposed settlers in British America to a considerably wider range of opportunities in the management of their affairs than were available for the creole population of Spanish America. Spaniards found such active popular participation in matters of government and justice both alarming and odd, to judge from the reactions of one of them whose ship ran aground on Bermuda in 1639. 'As in England,' he noted, 'authority here is placed in the hands of the humblest and lowest in the Republic, and not entrusted to educated persons having an aptitude for office . . . The Judges and Governor appoint twelve persons of the Republic and instruct them to consider all matters and documents in the causes that have been heard in their presence, and to give their verdict. These twelve persons then leave the Sessions house and are conducted by one of the other officials to the church and are there left locked in with orders not to be let out until they have decided the cases.'[106]

Authority in Spain's American possessions could certainly not be described as being 'in the hands of the humblest and lowest in the Republic'. Instead, it was exercised by royal officials sent out from Spain, together with a select group of creoles. Until the sale of public offices allowed growing numbers of the creole elite to infiltrate the royal administration as the seventeenth century proceeded,[107] active creole engagement in government tended to be confined to the running of municipal affairs, and was characterized by a heavy bias towards oligarchical control.

The town of Popayán, the capital of the province of the same name in the kingdom of New Granada, offers a telling illustration of the restricted nature of municipal government, and of the uncertain relationship between a local elite and the royal authorities.[108] A town of some 150 permanent Spanish households in the seventeenth century, it had a mixed population of around 2,000 inhabitants, consisting of Spaniards, mestizos, Indians and blacks. Either the provincial governor, as the crown's representative, or, more frequently, his deputy, presided over the meetings of the cabildo, the town council, which consisted in 1612 of eight members – a number that varied over subsequent decades, depending on the readiness of the crown to create and sell new seats on the town council, and citizens to buy. The cabildo was composed of proprietary members who had purchased their seats from the crown, along with three elected members chosen annually by the proprietary members. Election did at least allow for the incorporation into the town's government of prominent newcomers, but control of the wide range of municipal business, both administrative and judicial, rested effectively with a handful of Spanish families who seem to have acquired greater internal cohesion as the century progressed. In principle, open town meetings – *cabildos abiertos* – could be convened, but only six are recorded for the entire seventeenth century. Yet for all the influence of Popayán's oligarchy at the provincial as well as the municipal level, the cabildo's powers were circumscribed by those of the governor, who had to authorize all but the smallest municipal levies. The degree of its influence therefore depended at any given moment on the oligarchy's success in forging an effective working relationship with the governor and his deputy. Not surprisingly, the ill-defined nature of the relationship between municipality and the imperial government meant that important business was at least as likely to be conducted through private negotiation as through public transaction. It is some indication of the closed, informal and personalized character of Popayán's town government that the cabildo never got round to producing a set of ordinances for the regulation of municipal business.

The extreme opposite of Popayán's method of conducting its business was to be found in New England, where, in spite of the existence of county courts, the town constituted the principal organ of local government. Town meetings of resident householders would take the major decisions, while electing a group of 'selectmen' to manage business between the meetings. Seventeenth-century Easthampton, for instance, was a small town on Long Island which, although transferred against its wishes from Connecticut to the province of New York, was shaped by its characteristically New England style of government.[109] Three selectmen, chosen by the householders, looked after the town's business for the year, sometimes with the help of an additional four, while a variety of officials, ranging from the recorder and constables to highway overseers and fence viewers, were responsible for different aspects of municipal life. In all this, Easthampton was typical of New England towns, as it was, too, in its recourse to *ad hoc* committees to deal with special issues.[110] In Spanish America, on the other hand, there is nothing to suggest that government by committee became a way of life.

New England, however, was not all British America, and the degree of popular participation in local government varied substantially from colony to colony. In the Southern Colonies in particular, local government was in the hands of self-selecting members of the planter elite. The city of New York held its first elections for aldermen and assistants in 1686, but the governor and council made the appointments to all the other city offices. Philadelphia, founded in 1681, possessed a broad suffrage, but the city charter of 1691 was modelled on that of closed English corporate towns, with the municipal corporation constituted as a self-perpetuating body, although elections were held annually for sheriffs, commissioners and tax assessors.[111]

Even in seventeenth-century New England the system of municipal government was liable to be less genuinely popular than it appears at first sight. Due deference tended to be paid to social status when it came to appointments, as in Easthampton, where committee memberships and major offices circulated among a small group of citizens, while half the remaining householders held no office at all.[112] Many New Englanders also found themselves excluded from active participation in town life, either because they did not conform to the requirements of church membership, or, as the seventeenth century proceeded, because they lacked the necessary property qualifications.[113]

Yet the nature of New England's system of town government did much to enhance each town's sense of its corporate identity as a close-knit community, and of the collective responsibility of the householders for the management of civic business. The effect was to place a powerful emphasis on stability, order and the maintenance of religious and moral values inherited from the past, while simultaneously fostering a strong commitment to independence from outside interference. The combination of corporate independence and individual obligation to the upholding of an ideal community was bound to create problems for the royal authorities as soon as they sought to intervene in colonial life. Obstinacy was to become second nature to colonial New England.

The potential for trouble was symbolically illustrated as early as 1634 when John Endecott, who had been the Massachusetts Bay Company's governor of the settlement at Salem, cut the red cross out of the royal ensign, on the grounds that it was a popish symbol. In spite of considerable concern that this would give 'occasion to the state of England to think ill of us',[114] Massachusetts managed to hold on to its own distinctive flag, shorn of the offending cross, until the last years of the century.[115] Such a degree of defiance would have been unthinkable in Spanish America once Gonzalo Pizarro's followers, after flaunting the Pizarro arms in place of the royal arms on their banners, had gone down to defeat. There was, however, a stand-off with the royal authorities in Mexico City, which never reconciled itself to the conventional coat of arms conferred on it by Charles V. As proud inheritors of the conquered Tenochtitlán, the city authorities appropriated the Aztec emblem of an eagle devouring a serpent and poised on a cactus, which they deftly placed above the new civic arms. In 1642, after eagles and serpents began to proliferate on municipal buildings, the viceroy, Bishop Palafox, took alarm at these idolatrous symbols and ordered their removal from the city's arms. But the serpent-devouring eagle was becoming a potent symbol of Mexico's distinctive identity, and – never entirely suppressed – it would once more come to rest on its cactus during the struggle for independence.[116]

Clinging obstinately to its flag, Massachusetts, both insolent and obdurate, was to prove a constant thorn in the side of the Stuarts. Already in the late 1630s, when Archbishop Laud's Committee on Plantations challenged the colony's charter, the General Court warned him that 'the common people here will conceive that his Majesty hath cast them off, and that, hereby, they are freed from their allegiance and subjection . . .'[117] In the event it was to be the English and the Scots in the next few years who would free themselves from 'their allegiance and subjection' to Charles I.

The English Civil War and the king's execution in 1649 raised, not only for Massachusetts but for all the colonies, major questions about the exact nature of their relationship with the mother country. Not only did the Civil War sharply reduce the inflow of capital and immigrants to the colonies,[118] but it also created fundamental problems of allegiance, and posed questions about the exact location of imperial authority that would hover over the Anglo-American relationship until the coming of independence. No comparable challenge would confront the Spanish empire in America until the Napoleonic invasion brought about the collapse of royal authority in Spain in 1808. The transition from Habsburgs to Bourbons in 1700, which brought conflict to the peninsula, provoked only a few passing tremors in the American viceroyalties.[119]

For the colonies, as for the British Isles themselves, the outbreak of the Civil War brought divided loyalties.[120] Virginia remained faithful to the king and the Anglican establishment; Maryland briefly overthrew its government in favour of parliament, and descended between 1645 and 1647 into a period of turbulence graphically known as 'the plundering time';[121] and many New England settlers went home in the 1640s to help establish the New Jerusalem in the mother country and join the parliamentary cause.[122] But the absorption of the English in their own affairs during the 1640s gave the colonies even more scope than they had previously enjoyed to go their own way. Governor Winthrop of Massachusetts made the most of the opportunity to press on with the creation of new settlements and to form a Confederation of the United Colonies of New England for mutual defence.[123] The colonies could not, however, count on being indefinitely left to their own devices. As early as 1643 the Long Parliament set up a committee under the chairmanship of the Earl of Warwick to keep an oversight over colonial affairs.

This committee, although interventionist in the West Indies in response to the activities of the royalists, and supportive of Roger Williams's attempts to secure an independent charter for Rhode Island, was generally respectful of legitimate authority in the colonies. But its activities raised troubling questions about whether the ultimate power in colonial affairs lay with king or parliament. As early as 1621 Sir George Calvert had claimed that the king's American possessions were his by right and were therefore not subject to the laws of parliament.[124] This question of the ultimate location of authority became acute after the execution of the king, since several of the colonies – Virginia, Maryland, Antigua, Barbados and Bermuda – proclaimed Charles II as the new monarch on his father's death. Parliament responded to these unwelcome colonial assertions of loyalty to the Stuarts by passing in 1650 an Act declaring that the colonies, having been 'planted at the Cost, and settled by the People, and by Authority of this Nation', were subject to the laws of the nation in parliament.[125]

When this Act was followed in the succeeding year by the Navigation Act, it must have seemed to the colonies that the Commonwealth represented at least as grave a threat as monarchy to their cherished rights. Parliament's bark, however, proved fiercer than its bite, and Cromwell turned out to be reluctant to interfere in colonial politics. The colonies therefore reached the Restoration of 1660 relatively unscathed. If anything, they emerged with enhanced confidence in their ability to manage their own affairs as a result of the uncertainties of the Interregnum and the impact of those uncertainties on the authority of royal and proprietary governors. Yet the growing economic importance of the colonies to the mother country, both as markets for English manufactures and as sources of supply for raw materials, meant that sooner or later the restored royal government was likely to make an effort to strengthen its authority over its imperial territories. It was in line with the sharpened perception of the colonies' value to England that the Earl of Clarendon urged on Charles II 'a great esteem for the plantations and the improvement of them by all ways that could reasonably be proposed to him'.[126]

Clarendon's concern for the future development of the colonies, expressed in the creation in 1660 of two advisory Councils, for Trade and Foreign Plantations,[127] harked back, as might be expected, to the age of Charles I and Archbishop Laud. But it also took into account the new naval and commercial realities of the Interregnum, and the growth of state power under Cromwell, whose conquest of Jamaica represented an important and potentially lucrative reinforcement of the British presence in the Caribbean. The government of Charles II, at once goaded and hampered by its perpetual need of funds, was to inch its way towards the formulation of a more coherent imperial policy, although this was constantly to be undercut by short-term considerations of immediate financial advantage. A government, for instance, that had ambitions to produce a more uniform pattern of colonial administration, had no hesitation in adding to its complexities by simultaneously creating new colonies on a proprietary basis in order to gratify friends and increase its revenues. Carolina, granted to eight proprietors including the future Earl of Shaftesbury, in 1663; New York, handed over to James, Duke of York, in 1664 after its capture from the Dutch; the Jerseys, transferred that same year by the Duke of York to Sir George Carteret and Lord Berkeley; and William Penn's settlement of Pennsylvania in 1681, were all set up as charter colonies. Only Jamaica, its long-term status still uncertain after its seizure from Spain in 1655, was incorporated into the English empire in America as a royal colony.

Yet in spite of a casualness in the disposal of territory that seems to belie its own perceived best interests, the crown under the later Stuarts was moving, however erratically, towards increased intervention in American affairs, prompted partly by considerations of profit and power, and partly in response to pressures from within the colonies themselves. In an age of system-building, whether in intellectual life or in politics, the creation of a rational and orderly imperial system seemed to offer the best hope of securing maximum benefits from the growing prosperity of the colonies. The France of Louis XIV provided an obvious model as it moved to consolidate and extend its presence in America. But it would be surprising if some at least of Charles II's ministers and officials were not also influenced in their formulation of the new system by the Spanish model, designed to integrate America into a tight imperial framework and to regulate colonial trade to the benefit of the metropolis. In the Council for Trade and Plantations of 1660, and its various successor bodies, culminating in the Board of Trade in 1696, can be seen an embryonic Council of the Indies; in the Navigation Acts and the attempts to enforce them, a Spanish-style monopoly of the transatlantic trade; and in the proposals for a Dominion of New England, which would take shape under James II, the first stage of an ambitious programme for the consolidation of the American colonies into three or four viceroyalties on the Spanish model.[128]

Under the new programme that was being slowly forged in London, the New World settlers, who for so long had been left to their own devices, would, for the first time in their collective experience, be brought face to face with the intrusive state. That collective experience, however, in some instances already reached back three generations, and this made the assertion of the royal prerogative in America by the later Stuarts a very different proposition from its assertion by the Spanish crown over the conquistadores and first settlers of Mexico and Peru. The Earl of Sandwich, himself recently returned from an extended embassy in Spain, recognized as much in his 'Comments upon New England' of 1671: 'They are at present a numerous and thriving people and in twenty years are more likely (if civil wars or other accidents prevent them not) to be mighty rich and powerful and not at all careful of their dependence upon old England.' For this reason he took 'the way of roughness and peremptory orders, with force to back them, to be utterly unadvisable. For they are already too strong to be compelled . . . And though I apprehend them yet not at that point to cast us off voluntarily and of choice: yet I believe if we use severity towards them in their Government civil or religious, that they will (being made desperate) set up for themselves and reject us.'[129]

'They are already too strong to be compelled.' The verdict was perhaps too gloomy. Changing conditions in New England in the 1670s and 1680s – King Philip's War, the threat from the French in Canada, the increasingly complex ties between Massachusetts merchants and the British commercial system – were to make the New England colonists more amenable to the imperial authority in the last years of the century than at the time when Sandwich delivered himself of his 'Comments'.[130] Yet the instinct to resist was strong, and this was true even of the new colony of Jamaica, which started its life under the British crown with a military government, and – as a conquered island on the model of Ireland – offered unique opportunities for the assertion of the royal prerogative. Already in 1660, with half of the island's British population consisting of settlers from the older colonies, the governor, Colonel D'Oyley, had to promise that taxes would be levied only by their representatives.[131] Jamaica's assembly was soon flexing its muscles, and at the end of the 1670s it successfully fought off attempts by the Privy Council to introduce Poyning's Law, a measure originally devised for Ireland and requiring the prior consent of the council to the passage of local legislation. 'It was', argued the Speaker, Captain Samuel Long, 'against law and justice to alter the constitution Jamaica had so long lived under.'[132] 'So long' amounted to some sixteen years of English rule, the earliest of them under military government. English liberties, it seemed, had rapidly taken root in fertile Caribbean soil.

So-called 'garrison government' by army officers might, if systematically pursued as a policy objective, have laid the foundations of a more autocratic system of imperial rule in British America.[133] This would have brought it more into line with French Canada than with Spanish America, where – outside Chile and the frontier regions – there was little military presence at any level before the eighteenth century. But it is easier to see in the appointment of military men to colonial governorships a form of outdoor relief for the superannuated and unemployed than a carefully thought-out design to impose royal power on the colonies, although professional soldiers certainly had their uses when colonists proved obdurate. The despatch of a thousand-strong expeditionary force from England to crush Bacon's Rebellion in 1676, for example, gave the crown the opportunity to curb the powers of the Virginia assembly, remodel the colony's system of government, and secure a grant of a perpetual duty on tobacco exports which yielded a substantial permanent revenue.[134] Yet if the crown was thinking in terms of continuing garrison government, it did not achieve its aims. In 1682, with their pay badly in arrears, the troops had to be disbanded.[135]

Government ministers and officials in the London of Charles II, however, were itching to get their hands on a greater share of American revenues, and were busily hatching schemes to secure a greater degree of royal authority over the crown's wayward transatlantic possessions. Sent out on a fact-finding mission to the colonies in 1676 by the newly established Privy Council committee, known as the Lords of Trade, Edward Randoph, who was to have an important career as a royal official in America, was horrified by the lack of respect shown to the crown in Massachusetts, and looked forward to the day when 'it shall please his Majesty fully to resolve upon the reducing this Plantation to their due Obedience'.[136] This day looked like dawning exactly ten years later, when Sir Edmund Andros, a military man and a former governor of New York for James, Duke of York, arrived in Boston as the first royal governor of the newly created Dominion of New England.[137]

The decision to consolidate the New England colonies into a single dominion under a royal governor was an attempt by the authorities in London to resolve through a dramatic intervention in colonial life the various problems that had exercised them since the Restoration.[138] The traditional lack of respect for the crown in Massachusetts; the perennial shortfall in the royal revenues; the desire to impose closer control over the increasingly lucrative transatlantic trade; the growing costs of colonial defence at a time of war with France – all these suggested the desirability of introducing some uniformity into the existing patchwork of colonial government, and of grouping the New England colonies together into a union under a single governor. Randolph's activities in the colonies in the early 1680s suggested that there were significant groups in colonial society, like the moderate Puritans and Anglican merchants, who would welcome reform and would be ready to co-operate with the royal authorities to bring it about.[139] If Andros played his cards well, he could capitalize on these divisions to strengthen royal influence through a centralized form of government, and similar policies might in due course be extended to the Middle Colonies and those of the South.

Yet the dangers were obvious, and had already been foreshadowed in the proprietary colony of New York, where the Duke of York had replaced Andros as governor by an Irish Catholic, Colonel Thomas Dongan, a former lieutenant-governor of Tangier. In conceding the New Yorkers an assembly, the duke tied the concession to a grant large enough to pay off the public debts and provide sufficient revenue to support the government and the garrison in perpetuity. When writs for the assembly were sent out in September 1683, Easthampton was one of the towns to instruct its representatives to stand up for the maintenance of 'our privileges and English liberties'. Drawing for its inspiration on Magna Carta and the 1628 Petition of Right, the assembly proceeded to draw up a 'Charter of Libertyes and Privileges', designed to establish the colony's government on a firm contractual basis. The charter was rejected by the Duke of York, and in October 1684, in what looked like the beginnings of a systematic assault by the crown on colonial charters along the lines of its assault on chartered corporations in England, the charter of Massachusetts was revoked.[140]

The accession of the Duke of York to the English throne in 1685 inevitably heightened the fears of the colonies that a Catholic conspiracy was afoot for the imposition of arbitrary rule in America. The instructions given Governor Andros by James II in 1686 for the establishment of the Dominion of New England included the introduction of major changes in the system of land tenure, the establishment of religious liberty, which could only be seen as a devious attempt to promote popery, and the abolition of representative assemblies. It was already too late for this. New revenue-raising attempts quickly ran into resistance, as in Essex County, where the town government of Ipswich voted that 'it did abridge them of their liberty as Englishmen'.[141]

New Englanders would not have found much cause for comfort in the response of Judge Joseph Dudley to one of the Essex County defendants: 'They must not think the privileges of Englishmen would follow them to the end of the world.'[142] The colonists, however, were well aware of the growing resistance to the government of James II in the mother country. In defying Judge Dudley and asserting their claims to equality of status with their English brothers and sisters, they transformed the English struggle for the preservation of English religion and English liberties into a common Atlantic cause. When news reached America of the Glorious Revolution of 1688 they were ready for action. Revolution in Britain was followed by upheavals in the colonies – most notably in Massachusetts, New York and Maryland – and the overthrow of the hated Andros, whose arrogant, arbitrary and secretive character had alienated even his natural supporters. The experiment of centralized government in a Dominion of New England had come to a humiliating end.[143]

The Stuart invasion of colonial liberties ended in failure, partly because the imperial policies pursued by the crown were inconsistent and erratically pursued, but also because of deep divisions within British political culture of the seventeenth century. The Civil War had exposed the fissures in English politics and society, and these fissures, although papered over, persisted after the restoration of the monarchy. The Lords of Trade, for instance, were divided between those who favoured a forceful assertion of royal prerogative and supported the Anglican establishment, and those who were inclined by conviction and tradition to support a strong parliament and to side with the dissenters.[144] Such political and religious divisions militated against the formulation and pursuit of a coherent policy designed to enhance royal control over the colonies, and gave the representative bodies already well entrenched in America room to manoeuvre when they felt themselves threatened by the power of the crown.

Where the Council of the Indies in Madrid, for all its factional divisions, was united in its determination to uphold the royal authority, some ministers and officials in London spoke the language of the prerogative while others spoke the language of liberty and consent. These divisions ultimately made it impossible for the later Stuarts to realize, by means of Whitehall's proposed system of Dominion government, Charles I's original ambition of introducing 'one uniforme Course of government' in the American plantations. The Revolution of 1688 decisively reaffirmed the primacy of the principle of representation on both sides of the English Atlantic. It also ensured the definitive acceptance, however reluctant, of religious pluralism as a necessary component of the political and social ordering of the British Atlantic community. For that community after 1688 there could be no turning back.

CHAPTER 6

The Ordering of Society

Hierarchy and control

Family and hierarchy were the twin pillars supporting the social structure of Early Modern Europe. The ordered family, under the control of the head of the household, patterned the state in microcosm, just as the state, under royal government, was a microcosm of the divinely ordered universe subservient to its Maker. Some in this universe were born to rule and others to obey; or, as John Winthrop expressed it in his famous sermon, *A Modell of Christian Charity*, said to have been preached on board the *Arbella*, but more probably in Southampton before the ship's departure: 'in all times some must be rich, some poor, some high and eminent in power and dignity; others mean and in subjection.'[1] The doctrine of degree, transplanted to Spanish America and more recently to the English dominion of Virginia, now crossed the north Atlantic again, this time in the *Arbella* to Puritan New England.

Yet the New Englanders would find, as Spanish Americans and Virginians had found before them, that old European certainties and new American realities did not necessarily coincide. During the Peruvian civil wars, Hernando Pizarro, in a rousing speech to his infantry soldiers before they engaged in battle with the army of his rival, Diego de Almagro, told them that he understood, 'they were saying among themselves that soldiers without horses counted for little when it came to the distribution of land; but he gave them his word that no such thought had ever crossed his mind, because good soldiers are not to be judged by their horses, but by the valour of their persons. Therefore whoever showed himself brave would be rewarded in conformity with his service; for not to possess horses was a matter of fortune, and no disparagement of their persons.'[2]

The extent to which such words represented a dangerous subversion of traditional notions of the proper ordering of society is suggested by a passage in a sermon preached by a New England minister, William Hubbard, in 1676: 'It is not then the result of time or chance, that some are mounted on horse-back, while others are left to travel on foot. That some have with the Centurion, power to command, while others are required to obey.'[3] God's design was clear, and was spelled out by an early viceroy of Peru when he wrote that, 'in conformity with other republics it is necessary that there should be persons of different quality, condition and estate, and that not all should be equal, just as for the good government of the human body not all members are equal.'[4] Yet could this grand design be as successfully sustained in the New World as in the Old? Hernando Pizarro's words gave an early warning of the difficulties.

Throughout the colonial period there was to be a persistent tension between the traditional image of the ordered society and the social practices and arrangements arising out of the conditions of conquest and settlement. No doubt in Europe too there were wide disparities between theory and practice, especially in periods like the sixteenth century when economic change brought accelerated social mobility. But, in general, social change in Europe would be contained and absorbed by the society of orders, which would only begin to be eroded in the late eighteenth century under the double impact of the French and Industrial Revolutions.[5] In America, it remained an open question whether the society of orders could even survive the Atlantic crossing, and, if so, whether it could be reconstituted in ways familiar to those who came from Europe.

Not everyone, however, necessarily wished for such an outcome. In the course of the great social and religious upheavals in sixteenth-century Europe, what passed for dangerously radical and egalitarian doctrines had risen alarmingly to the surface. In the Tyrol, Michael Gaismayr had put forward proposals for a drastic reordering of society along evangelical communitarian lines,[6] and the Anabaptists introduced forms of communal organization in Münster which were ruthlessly suppressed by the forces of law and order in 1535. In spite of the tragedy of Münster, Anabaptists, Hutterites and other splinter religious movements managed to keep egalitarian doctrines alive,[7] while the popularity of Thomas More's *Utopia* ensured that visions of an alternative organization of society based on community rather than hierarchy would not be lost from view. With the forces of repression in the ascendant in Europe, where better to establish a more just and egalitarian society than in the New World of America?

Although Bishop Vasco de Quiroga did indeed attempt to found communities inspired by *Utopia* on the shores of Lake Pátzcuaro in the mid-sixteenth century,[8] this was communal organization for the Indians, and not for European colonists. There is no indication that Spanish immigrants were infected by egalitarian or communitarian ideals. They came to better themselves – to 'be worth more' (*valer más*) in the language of the day – and to be worth more meant acquiring not only wealth, but also social status and honour, as understood and approved by the home societies to which many of them hoped one day to return.[9] Perhaps a quarter of the 168 men who followed Francisco Pizarro at Cajamarca could lay claim to some trace of gentle birth, but not one of them was legitimately entitled to use the prefix *don*, still nominally reserved in Castile for those with relatively close ties of lineage to the titled nobility.[10] Usage in the Indies, however, rapidly conferred the title of *don* on the leading conquistadores even before some of them received titles or offices from the crown, and within a generation the prefix was sufficiently common for the Mexican chronicler Baltasar Dorantes de Carranza to complain, no doubt with considerable exaggeration, that mere cabin boys and sailors would style themselves '*don Fulano*' as soon as they set foot on American soil.[11] Status – not its abolition – was the aspiration of Spanish settlers in the Indies.

If egalitarian notions were to take root in America, this was more likely to occur in the British than the Spanish settlements, because the natural carrier for such notions was Protestant sectarianism. The leaders of the Puritan emigration to New England were well aware of this, and were haunted by the memory of Münster and fears of levelling.[12] John Winthrop and his colleagues were concerned that reports of any levelling tendencies or communal experiments would discredit their fledgling Bay Colony in the eyes of its supporters in the home country, and were quick to stamp on the first signs of social or religious subversion. The unorthodox religious opinions of Anne Hutchinson, with their subversive message that God revealed Himself directly to the elect, were all the more dangerous because she was not only a woman but a woman of standing, as the wife of a substantial Lincolnshire merchant, with whom she had arrived in Boston, along with their eleven children, in 1634. The social esteem she enjoyed among the Boston women who gathered in her home for inspirational meetings compounded the challenge that her antinomian teachings presented to the Puritan clerical establishment. Subjected to a civil trial before the Massachusetts Bay General Court, and then to a trial by the Boston church, she was expelled from the colony in 1638.[13]

The proximity of a neighbouring settlement established on the principle of liberty of conscience – Roger Williams's new colony of Rhode Island, where Anne Hutchinson took refuge – inevitably added to the fears of the Massachusetts ministers. Rhode Island appeared to exemplify the breakdown of all social cohesion which in their eyes followed ineluctably from insistence on spiritual equality and the absence of ministerial control, and the colony was deliberately excluded from the Confederation of New England set up in 1643 for regional defence.[14] Worse still, the English Civil War opened a religious Pandora's box, releasing into the world a host of a crazed notions with dangerously radical intent. Winthrop noted in his Journal for 1645 how the Anabaptists 'began to increase very fast through the Country here, and much more in England, where they had gathered diverse Churches, and taught openly . . .'[15] Although Cromwell might suppress the Levellers, the damage had been done.

The effect of strict religious control in Massachusetts was simply to encourage settlers and new immigrants to settle in colonies more tolerant of dissenting opinions – not only Rhode Island, but also Maryland, which was openly accepting of toleration, and Virginia, where the Anglican establishment continued to be weak. Quakers began arriving in America in the 1650s, bringing with them notions and practices which seemed to represent a direct assault on the established foundations of family discipline, codes of honour and a society based on rank. How could society continue to function if hats were not doffed? Yet Quakers came to develop their own form of family discipline, even if it was one that conferred more authority on women in the household than was conventionally acceptable. When William Penn founded his colony of Pennsylvania in 1681, it became clear that spiritual egalitarianism was not after all incompatible with the demands of social hierarchy.[16]

In the early years of colonization the principal threat to a family-based society grounded in hierarchy and deference came, not from egalitarian doctrines imported from Europe, nor even from the notions of religious dissent that were beginning to permeate the Protestant world of the British colonies, but from the raw facts of life, death and patterns of immigration in the new societies. Of all the societies, British and Spanish, that established themselves in the New World of America, only that of New England managed in the early stages of settlement to replicate something approaching the family structure of the society from which the colonists were drawn. With nearly half its immigrants women, and a preponderance of immigrants travelling in family groups,[17] there was a good chance from the beginning that the accepted forms of family life could be reconstituted with reasonable fidelity in the relatively benign climatic environment of New England. The early settlers, however, saw things differently, and parents were deeply concerned that their children would succumb to the savagery of the forest world that surrounded them unless Christian and civilized values were inculcated from an early age by rigorous schooling.[18]

In the Chesapeake, with its overwhelmingly male immigration and its mortality rate of perhaps 40 per cent within two years of arrival,[19] the establishment of Old World patterns of family life came much more slowly and would be infinitely harder to achieve. Spanish America was affected by similar problems of acute gender imbalance among white settlers until the later years of the sixteenth century. The Spanish crown, concerned to promote stability in the settler community and prevent destitution in Spain, ordered that wives left behind in Spain should join their husbands in the Indies, and that unmarried men should find themselves wives.[20] The settlement of the Indies, however, would leave a trail of broken marriages, together with many prosecutions for bigamy.[21]

The early stages of settlement of British and Spanish America were therefore marked by the development of household structures which responded more to the dictates of demography and environment than to cultural differences. The northeastern colonies of British America were a world on their own – a world of essentially nuclear families, with high survival rates for children (fig. 14), and an average life expectancy of around seventy for those who reached adulthood. With land relatively abundant, and an inheritance pattern in which the house or farm was left to only one son, siblings were expected to leave the family home on marriage and set up on their own. The result was a community of separate households tied together by the relationships of an extended family network.[22] Servants were integrated into the family households, which were run on firmly patriarchal lines, and the status of wives, as in England, was strictly subordinate, although colonial conditions seem to have produced a certain flexibility, at least in practice, where their legal and property rights were concerned.[23]

In the Chesapeake and the Antilles, and throughout Spanish America, there was a much greater initial fluidity in social and household arrangements than there was in New England. With white women in short supply, and with such a large proportion of the Chesapeake population consisting of young male indentured servants who would need time to accumulate sufficient capital to establish a household, men married late, if they married at all. In southern Maryland, even in the second half of the seventeenth century, over a quarter of male testators died unmarried.[24] Illegitimacy rates in the Chesapeake were correspondingly high, with female servants particularly at risk, and when couples did marry the marriage was likely to be cut short by the early death of one or other of the partners. Second marriages were frequent, with widows enjoying a relative latitude for manoeuvre, while the many children who lost one or both parents moved into a world in which they were dependent for their support, and such education as they received, on an extended network of relatives, friends and neighbours.[25] There was a sharp contrast, therefore, between New England, with its tight parental control and its inherent tendency to generational conflict, and the shifting kaleidoscopic world of sexual and family relationships in the southern colonies.[26]

A similar looseness of arrangements prevailed in the Spanish colonial world, especially in the early stages of settlement. Here, too, illegitimacy rates were very high, largely as a consequence of illicit unions between Spanish men and Indian women. As a result, the word *mestizo* became virtually synonymous with 'illegitimate'.[27] The early absorption of many of these mestizo children, and especially the boys, into the father's household[28] could be no more than a palliative to the growing problem of how to integrate the mestizos into Spanish American colonial society. A comparable problem was to be presented in the British Caribbean islands and the southern mainland colonies by the mulatto children resulting from illicit unions between the colonists and black women drawn from the rapidly growing African labour force. Here the problem would be brutally solved by their largely automatic incorporation into the ranks of the slaves. The plantation complex could conceal a multitude of sins, although, as a group, the Caribbean planters may have shown a higher degree of paternal responsibility than their fellow planters on the mainland, perhaps influenced by the very smallness of the white minority in a largely black population.[29]

No doubt the haciendas that developed in the American viceroyalties created just as many opportunities as the British plantations for sexual profligacy and abuse; and the growing inequalities of Spanish American colonial society and the absence of effective religious or social control over Spanish–Indian sexual liaisons meant that, even with the reduction of the gender imbalance in the Hispanic community as more female immigrants arrived from Spain, the numbers of mestizo children continued to increase. Spanish American society, however, developed an important instrument for the preservation of social cohesion, in the form of *compadrazgo*, or co-godparenthood. This form of ritual kinship, although important as a method of social bonding in Andalusia, took on a new and vigorous life in the initially atomized world of colonial America. By creating a relationship of mutual trust and reciprocity between the godparents themselves, as well as between the godparents and their godchildren, it could bridge both social and racial divides, blurring the dividing lines and adding a useful integrating element to societies that were all too prone to fragmentation.[30]

If godparenthood acted as a stronger force for social cohesion in Spanish than in British America, both worlds placed a heavy reliance on the power relationships inherent in patriarchal authority – husbands over wives, seniors over juniors, masters over servants – to maintain the family household as the basic unit of society and to hold the forces of social dissolution in check. The members of the Virginia Assembly showed themselves as keen as the New England ministers to assert and reinforce the authority of the master of the household, and to ensure that he fulfilled his responsibilities in disciplining, instructing and watching over the conduct and morals of those entrusted to his charge.[31] The English common law that was adopted, and where necessary adapted, by the colonial societies, provided scope for this, not least by placing so much economic power in the hands of husbands and fathers. Wives were financially dependent on husbands; widows, although entitled to something like a third of their husband's real and personal estate, could find, at least in much of New England, that their right was not absolute; and the distribution of property among the children was dependent on the decision of the father, unless he died intestate.[32]

Castilian law, too, as embodied in the *Siete Partidas*, made strong provision, especially in the fourth Partida, for parental, and particularly paternal, authority, known as *patria potestas,* which went further than its equivalent in the Anglo-American world by giving parents legal authority over their adult children until the time of their marriage.[33] But both law and custom in Castile favoured women in ways that the English common law did not. Daughters inherited equally with sons a mandatory share of the estate, known as the *legítima*, and widows took back on the deaths of their husbands not only their dowries, and the sum known as the *arras* or bridewealth which the husband promised on marriage, but also half any property gains made jointly by the spouses.[34] In the control and division of assets, therefore, peninsular society possessed a tradition of equity between the sexes, even if this was tempered in the sixteenth century by the growing recourse of wealthy families to the use of primogeniture and entail (*mayorazgo*) to counter the inherent tendency in a partible inheritance system towards the fragmentation of the family estate.

The mayorazgo duly crossed the Atlantic to Spanish America, as Adam Smith noted with disapproval. 'In the Spanish and Portugueze colonies,' he wrote, 'what is called the right of Majorazzo takes place in the succession of all those great estates to which any title of honour is annexed.' He admitted that outside Pennsylvania and New England, 'the right of primogeniture takes place, as in the law of England. But in all the English colonies the tenure of the lands, which are all held by free socage, facilitates alienation, and the grantee of any extensive tract of land, generally finds it for his interest to alienate, as fast as he can, the greater part of it, reserving only a small quit-rent.' To Smith, the conclusions were obvious. A lively land market reduced the price of land and encouraged its cultivation. 'The labour of the English colonies, therefore, being more employed in the improvement and cultivation of land, is likely to afford a greater and more valuable produce' than that of Iberian and French America, 'which, by the engrossing of land, is more or less diverted to other employments'.[35]

Smith's information, however, was not entirely accurate, and his contrasts were too starkly drawn. While the church and the religious orders had extensive holdings of land in mortmain, thus restricting the unfettered circulation of landed property, entails developed relatively slowly in Spanish America. Some fifty entails had been established in the viceroyalty of New Spain by the 1620s,[36] and although with the passage of time the mayorazgo became more frequent among wealthy families, it never acquired the prominence it enjoyed among the upper and middle ranks of society in the Iberian peninsula itself. By the end of the colonial period something of the order of a thousand entails had been founded in New Spain, most of them fairly modest in scale. They seem to have been more prevalent here than in other parts of Spanish America, but in the important agricultural district of León in northern Mexico, for instance, there is no record of any estate being entailed, and under the system of partible inheritance estates changed hands by sale in almost every generation.[37]

In its desire to prevent the growth of an American aristocracy, the Spanish crown seems to have been careful not to concede too many licences to found mayorazgos. The inheritance laws, however, offered an alternative device which gave some of the advantages of an entail without the trouble and costs. This was the *mejora,* by which a parent could favour a particular child by increasing his or her share of the inheritance. The device was much favoured by the merchant elite of seventeenth-century Mexico, enabling them to ensure the perpetuation of the *linaje* – the lineage – by arranging for a substantial proportion of the family assets to pass intact from one generation to the next.[38]

Both the mejora and the entail were at least nominally gender-blind in the Hispanic world. In a society where the mother's surname as well as the father's was transmitted to the children, and might indeed be taken in preference to it, the transfer of property through a daughter was perfectly acceptable. While parents in British America no doubt did their best to ensure that their daughters were well settled,[39] the fact that the family name was transmitted in British society through the male bloodline naturally tended to favour male heirs. Although rigorous primogeniture appears never to have been particularly popular in British America, the custom of primogeniture and entail seems to have grown stronger in the Chesapeake colonies over time, and was the rule in all cases of intestacy. In Virginia, in particular, the great landed families of the eighteenth century, keen to take the English aristocracy as their model, tied up their estates with entails on a positively English scale, with the result that three-quarters of the land in the

Tidewater counties was entailed by the time of the Revolution.[40] Here at least the contrast with the Spanish colonial world was nothing like as sharp as Adam Smith suggested.

The relative abundance of land in the British mainland colonies meant that it was often possible for a father to leave the bulk of his property to one son, in the knowledge that enough remained for his siblings to gain a livelihood.[41] Yet if American space and American resources offered wider individual opportunities to those who in Europe would normally have found themselves cramped by the operation of inheritance laws, the lineal family, transmitting its name and property from one generation to the next, was central to the social and economic life of British America, as it was to that of Hispanic America.

Within the family, paternal authority was nominally supreme, although in practice many households were headed by widows, who became responsible on their husband's death for supervision of the estate and the transmission of the family property. Early remarriage, which was to be expected where substantial property was involved or where women were in short supply, was liable to limit the period when women held the family assets in their hands. There were also variations in law and practice between the different colonial societies which could have significant consequences for the degree of control enjoyed by women. In general, it would seem that this was greater in the seventeenth-century Chesapeake than it was in New England,[42] and greater still in Spanish America because of the distinctive legal identity and extensive property rights accorded women under Spanish inheritance laws. Spanish colonial widows could manage their husband's estates without first having to secure permission from the authorities, as was required in British America. They could also control the distribution of resources among the children, and could exercise the *patria potestas*, in the form of legal guardianship, over children who, under Spanish law, remained minors until the age of twenty-five.[43] Consequently, the wealthy widow was, and remained, an exceptionally powerful figure in the Hispanic colonial world. In Peru, whose richest woman in the immediate post-conquest period, Doña María Escobar, held three encomiendas, women still held sixty encomiendas as late as 1583.[44]

With women sometimes wielding power, if only on a temporary basis, the colonial family, like the European, was not invariably patriarchal, although settlers looked askance at the matrilineal organization of some of the Indian societies which they saw around them.[45] Parental authority in one form or another, however, was paramount. Yet this authority had its limits where the choice of marriage partners for children was concerned. Whereas the Protestant churches for the most part sought to reinforce the authority of parents, the Church of Rome, after much discussion at the Council of Trent, came down against mandatory parental consent, thus leaving the ultimate choice of partner to the children themselves. While many Catholic societies chose to defy or ignore this Tridentine legislation, it was strongly endorsed by the majority of theologians and moralists in Spain, where it accorded both with prevailing practice and with cultural values that traditionally insisted on the priority of individual consent.[46]

The Anglican church distanced itself from the approach taken by the Protestant churches on the continent, and, like the church in Spain, gave priority to the wishes of the children over those of their parents.[47] It struggled, however, although with only very limited success, to persuade couples to solemnize their unions in a church ceremony. The widespread popular willingness to accept as binding the informal arrangements that surrounded so many of these unions made it difficult for parents to assert their authority. The colonial settlements of English America, anxious to maintain social cohesion, sought to tighten up on the practice that prevailed in the home country, but they did so in ways that reflected the differing social structures of the settlements themselves. Where New England legislation was particularly concerned to insist on the need for the prior consent of parents to the marriage of their children, legislators in the Chesapeake colonies were more interested in securing the rights of masters to approve or veto the marriage of indentured servants in their charge. A combination of legislation and insistence on marriage in church would, it was hoped, bring the problem of 'secret marriages' between servants under control.[48]

The lack of success of these efforts at control is suggested by illegitimacy rates in the Chesapeake that were perhaps two or three times as high as the rates in England.[49] In Puritan New England, on the other hand, the prevailing religious and moral values, combined with close community control, made the rates of illegitimacy and pre-nuptial pregnancy low both by English standards and by those of the other colonies.[50] In the Hispanic world – both in the peninsula itself and in the colonies – illegitimacy rates were exceptionally high by European standards, with illegitimate births to Spanish women in one parish of Mexico City between 1640 and 1700 fluctuating at around 33 per cent.[51]

The explanation of such high illegitimacy rates in a Hispanic society which placed a special premium on sexual virtue in women still has to be found. Some of it must lie in the freedom given to children to choose their own partners, as also in the high value placed by society on verbal promises of marriage – the so-called *palabras de consentimiento*. Some of the taint of dishonour was removed if an unmarried woman gave birth after receiving such a promise; and under Spanish law the eventual marriage of the partners, so long as they were single, automatically legitimized any children born out of wedlock.[52] Since the honour code which infused Hispanic society was effectively designed to preserve the appearance of sexual virtue even after virtue itself had been lost, the unmarried woman who lost her virginity might well escape social censure, since friends and relatives would join in a conspiracy of silence. The church, for its part, was always anxious to legitimize unions when both partners were free, in spite of possible disparity in their social – and even occasionally racial – status.[53] Parents were often driven to acquiesce, however reluctantly, in such unequal marriages, in recognition of the binding force of verbal promises and of the social importance of preserving a daughter's reputation. Where parents remained recalcitrant but the couple themselves were determined to marry, church courts almost invariably pronounced in the couple's favour.[54]

If, as seems likely, these social conventions created an environment that did something to reduce the stigma of birth out of wedlock, the ecclesiastical and secular authorities alike became increasingly concerned by the large number of illegitimate births in colonial society, especially since so many of these births were of children of mixed race. In 1625 the viceroy of New Spain placed a ban on the legitimization of children born to couples who were not married,[55] but it is doubtful whether this measure had much effect other than to aggravate the problems already faced by the illegitimate children themselves. The church in the Spanish Indies, too, gradually began to move in the direction of giving increased weight to parental consent, although major legislative change came only towards the end of the colonial period. The growing assertion of state power over the church in Bourbon Spain was to have important consequences for matrimonial legislation in the Indies as well as in Spain itself. In 1776 Charles III issued a pragmatic which required parental consent in the selection of a marriage partner for all those under the age of twenty-five, while at the same time jurisdiction over matrimonial disputes was removed from the church courts to the civil courts. Two years later the new legislation was extended to the Indies, although with the stipulation that the necessity for parental consent applied only to the marriages of 'Spaniards', and not to those of blacks, mestizos, mulattoes and others of mixed race.[56]

While, in the sixteenth and seventeenth centuries at least, a combination of the law, social conventions and the attitudes of the church tended, in certain important areas, to weaken parental control in the Spanish American household, there were many informal ways of bringing pressure to bear on children's choices – ways that necessarily escape the historical record. Disinheritance, which was sanctioned by the *Partidas*, was a possible option, although there is no evidence that it was much used.[57] The manipulation of dowries, however, was a useful instrument of parental control.[58] Dowries in seventeenth-century New Spain might run to as high as 25,000 *pesos*, but Hispanic parents also enjoyed an option not open to their British American equivalents, the placing of daughters in convents, at a cost of a mere 3,000. Not surprisingly, the cities of Spanish America abounded in convents.[59] For all the initial fluidity that was only to be expected of societies in process of establishing themselves, the patriarchal family had its own ways of reasserting its control in the superficially more open environment of America.

Although the family gradually overcame such impediments as gender imbalance, high mortality rates and the startling availability of land, to reconstitute itself as the central unit of the new American societies, these societies themselves were unable to replicate in full the hierarchical ordering of the European societies from which they derived. This, however, was not for want of trying. Coming from a world in which an undifferentiated society was normally regarded as an invitation to anarchy, early settlers of Spanish and British America alike were anxious to see their own fledgling societies approximating as soon as possible to the orderly hierarchical societies they had known in their homelands.[60]

Yet if, in the new environment of America, ownership of a horse, as Hernando Pizarro conceded, was purely fortuitous rather than a natural consequence of birth and degree, troubling questions presented themselves about the criteria that should be adopted for the ordering of these new societies. Deference could most obviously be paid, or at least demanded, where deference was due – to the sixteen undoubted *hidalgos* among Cortés's 530 men, or the 36 gentlemen among the first 105 planters of Virginia.[61] Yet very quickly the waters became muddied, as the normal indicators of status in Europe lost much of their resonance, especially in a setting in which there was a large subservient population of non-whites. In 1594 Juan Cabeza de Vaca, a resident of Mexico City, wrote to his sister in Spain urging her and other relatives to come and join him. 'In this land', he wrote, 'they do not know what hunger is . . . and so poor people are much better off here than in Spain, because they always give the commands and never have to work personally, and they always ride on horseback.'[62] No doubt the picture he painted was excessively rosy, although an account of life in early seventeenth-century Lima gives a similar impression: 'everyone boasts of great nobility, there is nobody who does not claim to be a *caballero*, and they all go about the city on horseback except for a few who are very poor.'[63]

The social implications of this state of affairs were all too clear. Who was in command if all could give commands? At the top of a hierarchically ordered society there should have been a titled aristocracy. But the titled nobility itself did not participate in the conquest of Spanish America, and the crown, in its determination to prevent the development of a New World aristocracy, was for a long time to be extremely sparing in the granting of American titles. It was reluctant even to elevate the conquistadores to the status of hidalgos in reward for their services, and it was only after much agitation among the conquerors and their heirs, who saw themselves being displaced in the granting of offices and favours by new arrivals from Spain, that Charles V agreed in 1543 that those who had actually participated in the conquest of Mexico should be classed as 'first and principal conquistadores', and by virtue of this should be entitled to preferential treatment.[64]

If the first conquerors, many of them transformed into encomenderos, constituted at least an embryonic 'natural aristocracy' of Spanish America, it proved to be an aristocracy that had great difficulty in staying the course. Attrition rates, as a result of death or return to Spain, were high. Only 45 per cent of the encomiendas granted in New Spain are known to have stayed in the family line beyond the first recipient,[65] and the initial 'natural aristocracy' would require continuous replenishment by later arrivals who possessed the money or the connections to acquire land and encomiendas, or to marry the widow or the daughter of an encomendero or 'first conquistador'. The same was true of Virginia, where the death rate was devastatingly high among the first settler gentlemen.

Even in New England, where there was a much better chance than in the Chesapeake colonies or the Antilles of perpetuating the family line, the social order looked deficient and truncated by English standards. Few settlers had English titles, but painstaking efforts were made to retain such titular honours as existed. Deference was, and continued to be, a characteristic of New England life, but as time went on the niceties of English usage began to disappear, and *Gent.*, at first a relatively rare indicator of social rank, came into wider use in the later years of the seventeenth century as an indicator less of rank than of personal virtue.[66] New England, with its emphasis on a spiritual calling, was particularly propitious ground for waging a successful fight against the notion that honour was defined by lineage – a fight that was being fought right across Early Modern Europe. 'Pardon me', wrote Cotton Mather in 1701, 'if I say, any Honest Mechanicks really are more Honourable than Idle and Useless Men of Honour. Every man ordinarily should be able to say, I have something wherein I am occupied for the good of other men.'[67]

Hierarchies, then, if they were to be re-created, were likely to develop in ways that would differentiate them from those of the mother country. Too few members of the upper ranks of either Castilian or English society settled in the New World to allow of any simple replication, and New World conditions themselves, by offering unexpected opportunities for wealth and advancement to many who had little chance of either in the homelands they had left, created the potential for a social fluidity surprising to those accustomed to the more rigid hierarchical structures of Europe.

This fluidity found its counterpart in the eager pursuit of status symbols which would help to maintain distinctions of rank in societies where the dividing lines were all too easily blurred. The holding of public office conferred an obvious cachet, and the same was true of military command. In seventeenth-century British America, always on the alert against an Indian attack, military titles became a popular form of deferential address, just as the lure of a military title would induce many a young Spanish American creole to join the ranks when the militias were placed on a more regular footing in the eighteenth century.[68] At least the trappings of hierarchy remained pervasive in the British colonies until the coming of the Revolution, even if the notion was being hollowed out from within. In Virginia in the middle years of the eighteenth century a young clergyman recorded his alarmed reaction to the arrival of his patron: 'When I viewed him riding up, I never beheld such a display of pride in any man, . . . arising from his deportment, attitude and jesture; he rode a lofty elegant horse . . .'[69] In the plantation society of the southern regions of British America, as in the hacienda society of rural Spanish America, the man on horseback still held the upper hand.

Social antagonism and emerging elites

For all the arrogance of his power, the developing character of life in America none the less raised a continuing question over how long the man on horseback would remain firmly seated in his saddle. Inequality abounded in the colonial societies of America, and where inequality abounded, so also did resentment. Settlers who had come to the New World to improve their lot were unlikely to resign themselves uncomplainingly to a life of subordination when open spaces and new opportunities beckoned. Freshly arrived indentured servants were understandably desperate to throw off the shackles of servitude. In British America in particular there was an anti-deferential counter-current, born both of Old World religious and ideological inheritance and New World circumstance. This counter-current ran in parallel with the trend to the emergence and consolidation of elites. But in Spanish America, too, as oligarchies tightened their hold, the dispossessed and the disadvantaged found ways to make their voices heard.

In 1675, the year that saw the opening of King Philip's War between Algonquian-speaking Indians and the New England colonists, hostilities also erupted between Susquehanna Indians and aggressive and insecure frontiersmen in the Virginia–Maryland border region. The former governor of Virginia, Sir William Berkeley (fig. 17), who had been restored to the governorship on the return of Charles II from exile, was unsympathetic to the frontiersmen and had no wish to see the colony involved in a full-scale Indian war. The backcountry settlers, however, had other ideas. Many of them poor planters, they wanted land, and they wanted protection from Indian attacks. With Berkeley refusing to mobilize the colony's resources in their support, they had to rely on themselves and their muskets. But they needed a leader. They found him in the 28-year-old Nathaniel Bacon.

Cambridge-educated, quick-witted and plausible, Bacon – a member of the well-connected East Anglian family of that name – had been packed off to Virginia by his father in the previous year after the exposure of his involvement in a swindle. Although taken up by Berkeley, who appointed him to the Virginia council within a few months of his arrival on the grounds that he was a gentleman of quality, he fell out with his patron after Indians murdered his overseer on his James River estate. A group of armed volunteers, determined to settle accounts with the Indians, turned to him for leadership with shouts of 'A Bacon! A Bacon!', and in defiance of the governor's orders he led an expedition of reprisal, which ended in the butchering of numerous Indians. Berkeley responded by declaring him a rebel.[70]

Although the two men subsequently patched up their differences, relations remained tense, and the meeting of the Virginia assembly at Jamestown in June 1676 provided the occasion for a showdown. Berkeley was deeply unpopular in the colony that he had governed for too long. There were innumerable complaints of his allegedly pro-Indian policies and of the oppressive burden of taxation imposed during his long tenure of the governorship, and there were many who resented the way in which he and his friends dominated the political life of the colony. The frontier settlers, exasperated by the failure of the government to assist them against the Indians, saw their salvation in Bacon, who marched on Jamestown on 23 June at the head of 400 armed men.

As Berkeley fled, Bacon gathered widespread support for his defiance of the governor. Many gentry and burgesses, as well as the populace at large, wanted a reform of government, together with a campaign against the Indians that would make the border areas secure. Yet, for all his cleverness and charisma as a leader,

Bacon found it increasingly difficult to control the more hot-headed of his followers. As lawlessness spread, the rebels put Jamestown to the torch, and sacked
Berkeley's own plantation, Green Spring. Then suddenly, at the end of October,
Bacon died of dysentery. With the unexpected death of its leader, the rebellion fal-
tered and collapsed. When three royal commissioners, accompanied by a regiment of redcoats, reached Virginia from England in February 1677, they were
horrified to find that a vengeful Berkeley had already carried out a string of executions on his own initiative. In April, Colonel Herbert Jeffreys, the commissioner in command of the regiment of English troops, ordered Berkeley to
surrender his powers. Shortly afterwards the humiliated ex-governor sailed for
home, where he died before he could put his case to the king.

Bacon's intentions remain controversial, although his primary concern seems
to have been to persuade the king to sanction fundamental reforms in the colony's
government rather than make a bid for Virginian independence, as his enemies
alleged.[71] But beneath the political disaffection lay a deep social resentment, as
Bacon's 'Manifesto' makes clear: '. . . Let us trace these men in Authority and
Favour to whose hands the dispensation of the Countries wealth has been committed; let us observe the sudden Rise of their Estates compared with the Quality
in which they first entered this Country Or the Reputation they have held here
amongst wise and discerning men, And let us see wither [whether] their extrac-
tions and Education have not bin vile, And by what pretence of learning and
vertue they could [enter] soe soon into Imployments of so great Trust and consequence . . .'[72] Bacon, although himself a newcomer to Virginia and the immediate
recipient of favours from the governor, was lashing out against a new elite.

During the middle decades of the century a new ruling class had indeed been
emerging to replace the vanished group of gentlemen who constituted the first
leaders of the colony but had failed to transmit their leadership to a second generation. Along with thousands of indentured servants, a fresh wave of emigration
beginning in the 1640s had brought to the Chesapeake disinherited cavaliers and
younger sons of landed families from the losing side in the Civil War, many of
them encouraged to emigrate by Sir William Berkeley, himself a prominent social
figure whom Charles had selected for the governorship of Virginia in 1642. The
new influx of immigrants also contained men of mercantile and business origins,
like William Byrd, many of them connected by marriage with the landed gentry
of southern and eastern England, and already possessing financial interests in the
Chesapeake. These men formed part of a growing business community that
spanned the Atlantic, and could call on substantial funds as they sought to establish themselves in colonial life. It was out of this group, reinforced in the early
years of the Restoration by a further influx of younger sons of gentry families,
who went on to marry into planter families surviving from the first generation of
settlers, that the new elite was forged.[73]

This elite, acquiring and extending tobacco plantations, and taking over the
management of local government, may well have been tainted by its associations
with mercantile wealth, but it hardly looks as if it was composed of men of 'vile'

extraction and education, who so aroused Bacon's wrath. There were few, if any, former indentured servants in its ranks. Possibilities certainly existed, although more in Maryland than Virginia, for indentured servants – originally for the most part unskilled and illiterate rural labourers or artisans – to acquire land after securing their freedom, but most of those who succeeded in doing so became at best modest independent planters, and many sank back into poverty as tobacco prices began to fall sharply in the 1660s.[74] The effect of economic depression was to harden the social divisions and fuel the resentments on which Bacon capitalized as he embarked on his rebellion. The bulk of his army was made up of discontented free men 'that had but lately crept out of the condition of Servants'.[75]

While Bacon's attack was partly directed against that section of the new elite which was monopolizing local office, it had as its particular target a group who themselves were the object of hostility from these same local office-holders – the ruling clique of the governor and his council. The friends and relatives of Governor Berkeley, many of them drawn from the ranks of the new elite and benefiting from his patronage, had come to constitute a hated oligarchy, which was held responsible for corrupt practices and high taxation at a time of war with the Indians and widespread economic distress. Essentially this was a revolt for the restoration of good government and fundamental English rights rather than for the subversion of the social order, although increasingly extreme measures adopted by Bacon during the course of the rebellion, including the freeing of servants and black slaves recruited into his army, eventually cost him the support of most of his planter allies.[76]

The report delivered by the commissioners to Charles II placed the blame for the rebellion squarely on the misgovernment of Berkeley and his ruling clique. Their judgment gave the king and the Privy Council the opportunity they had long been awaiting to attempt some restructuring of Virginia's administration in ways that would ensure greater royal control. In particular, the assembly was induced to grant the king in perpetuity an export duty on tobacco to help defray the costs of government.[77] In future, Virginia's elite would need to tread more cautiously, showing a greater sensitivity on the one hand to pressures emanating from Whitehall, and on the other to the wishes of a populace which had made its voice heard, and had been prepared to resort to arms against an oppressive and avaricious oligarchy in defence of the rights of free-born Englishmen. A vote by the assembly to limit the privilege of wealthy planters to tax-free labour suggested that the elite had learnt its lesson.[78]

Yet although Bacon's revolt shook Virginian society to its foundations, the new social order in process of formation during the middle decades of the century emerged largely unscathed from the upheaval. Property qualifications for voters, rescinded when Bacon was in command, were restored by the assembly in 1677. If the poor white population lost their votes, however, they still kept their guns, and this was something the elite could not afford to forget.[79] Meanwhile, changing economic and social conditions in the two decades following the rebellion altered the dynamics of a society in which turbulence had formerly seemed endemic, and opened the way to a tacit, although initially fragile, accommodation between the rich and the poor in Virginia's white community.

The rise in tobacco prices after 1684 brought a new prosperity, which gradually improved the lot of the landless freemen who had responded in such numbers to Bacon's call to arms.[80] Legislation imposing chattel bondage on imported Africans had been initiated by the Virginia assembly in the 1660s, and as the planters turned more and more to the import of black slaves in preference to increasingly expensive white indentured servants,[81] the balance and composition of the colony's population began to change. In the 1690s, with the import of servants from England declining, the majority of Virginia's whites were Virginia-born for the first time in the colony's history.[82] The native American population of the Chesapeake region was rapidly dwindling – the process no doubt exacerbated by the hunting down and enslavement of Indians by Bacon and his men, and by the decision of the assembly in 1682 to lump together imported Indians and blacks as slaves for life, whether or not they became converts to Christianity.[83]

By now, Virginia was looking to Africa for its slaves at least as much to its traditional supplier, Barbados. In the 1680s some 2,000 Africans were landed in the colony.[84] In earlier years the free black population had lived and worked side by side with the white labouring force, but as the number of blacks increased, to reach perhaps 10,000 – some 15 per cent of Virginia's total population[85] – by the end of the seventeenth century, the assembly embarked on efforts to reduce the number of free blacks by forbidding masters to free their slaves unless they agreed to transport them out of the colony.[86] The assembly also sought to drive a wedge between whites and blacks by denouncing miscegenation and its consequences. Virginians were on the way to being classified by the colour of their skin.

Around 1700, therefore, a new dividing line emerged in Chesapeake society – a line in which the social antagonisms separating white from white were eclipsed, although by no means obliterated, by a growing racial divide between white and black. During the course of the following years, white Virginian society slowly began to acquire something of the cohesion it had lacked for so long. A common white male culture was emerging, based on a number of shared points of reference – gambling, horse-racing, cockfights and the tavern. This was to become a patriarchal society, under the leadership of an elite which took its duties of hospitality seriously, looked with a paternal benevolence on social inferiors, and accepted the need to let them assert their rights as free-born men when it came to election time.[87]

As dynastic marriages cemented the ties between leading families like the Byrds, the Carters and the Beverleys, Virginia in the opening decades of the eighteenth century entered on a prolonged era of stability, guided by a closely knit group of substantial planters who saw no incompatibility between speaking the language of liberty and holding large numbers of slaves. The need to maintain a common front against the interfering ways of royal governors helped to keep the principal families united among themselves.[88] But it was the rapid spread of

slavery that created the conditions for this new age of stability and for the dominance of the wealthy elite that presided over it. Privileged and underprivileged
whites were brought together by their common contempt for blacks, and by fears
that at any moment they might have to close ranks in the face of a mass uprising
of slaves.[89]

Chesapeake society was following in the wake of the slave societies of the
British Caribbean islands, although oligarchy here became even more entrenched.
After a comparable period of turbulence the big sugar planters of Barbados, the
Leeward Islands and Jamaica succeeded both in reaching a political accommodation with the government in London and in consolidating their dominance over
the social and political life of their islands.[90] Both in the islands and in the southern mainland colonies large-scale investment in slaves reinforced the wealth and
power of the top stratum of the planter class at the apex of hierarchically structured societies linked by ties of deference and subordination.[91] The ways in which
this elite used or abused its wealth and power would vary with both place and
time. Cultural cross-currents might, as in eighteenth-century Virginia, come into
play to check the inherent tendency to indulge in conspicuous consumption, but
all these elites shared an acute concern with honour and reputation.[92] By the early
eighteenth century nearly every Virginian family with any claim to status had
obtained its coat of arms.[93]

If a hierarchical order emerged in the plantation societies of the Chesapeake
and the British Caribbean, it was a relatively simple hierarchical order when compared with that which emerged in the viceroyalties of New Spain and Peru. The
black–white dichotomy of a largely agrarian world of planters and slaves saw to
this, even if the dichotomy was complicated by the presence of a population of
poor whites, and by the emergence in the Caribbean of a significant intermediate
sector of free blacks and mulattoes. There were, too, groups of subservient
Indians in the Chesapeake region. Over large parts of Spanish America, on the
other hand, the coexistence and interbreeding of different ethnic groups in a
much more urbanized environment than that of the British plantation societies
was reflected in the construction of a social order of far greater complexity.

Although the Spanish crown had set itself firmly against the creation of a New
World nobility, it was otherwise concerned to replicate the hierarchical and corporate system of social organization on which peninsular society was based. Only
an organic society headed and regulated by the crown – a society in which each
element recognized, and kept, its proper place – offered the security of a durable
political and social order that patterned the divine. But in the Indies this proved
much more difficult to achieve than in Spain itself, partly because of the crown's
own reluctance to validate the social pretensions of the conquerors, and partly
because of the difficulties encountered by the conquerors and encomenderos
themselves in perpetuating their lines and consolidating their position as a
natural elite.[94]

The creation of a clear-cut hierarchical order was further complicated from the
first days of settlement by the presence of large Indian populations, which would

be endowed with a distinctive corporate identity as a *república de los indios*. Nominally, therefore, two parallel social orders coexisted, one Spanish and one Indian, with its own hereditary nobility. This nobility was juridically entitled in Spanish eyes to the special treatment and privileges accorded to the nobility of Spain; and although, particularly in New Spain, the Indian nobility and its rights were whittled away during the course of the sixteenth century, a society of orders was considered as integral to the Indian republic as conceptualized by the Spaniards as it was to the *república de los españoles*.

In other respects, however, theory and practice soon parted company, as the barriers between the two republics began to break down, and growing numbers of Indians moved into the cities. Here they found themselves living alongside a growing Spanish population made up of first settlers, new immigrants and their descendants, who naturally saw themselves as members of a conquering race, even if they themselves had not participated in the conquest. The superior status of these settlers of Hispanic descent, who first began to be known as *criollos* in the 1560s,[95] was recognized in their exemption from the payment of taxes – the privilege enjoyed by nobles and hidalgos in Spain. It was this privilege that set the creoles apart from the tribute-paying Indian population, although many of them lived no better than their Indian neighbours.

The obsessive pursuit by the creoles of the outward marks of social distinction, including the title of *don*, reflected their deeply felt need to mark themselves out as belonging to the society of the conquerors and to place themselves on an equal footing with the upper strata of the colonial social hierarchy. 'Any white person,' wrote Alexander von Humboldt at the end of the colonial period, 'even though he rides his horse barefoot, imagines himself to be of the nobility of the country.'[96] Yet whiteness, like nobility, was to acquire its own ambiguities in a society where nothing was quite as it appeared on the surface.

By the later years of the seventeenth century, although the creoles retained their tax-exempt status and still nominally formed the society of conquest, the old distinctions between conquerors and conquered were coming to be blurred by racial intermingling and were being overlaid by new distinctions thrown up by the confusing realities of an ethnically diverse society. What became known as a society of *castas* was in process of formation – *casta* being a word originally used in Spain to denominate a human, or animal, group, of known and distinctive parentage.[97] The mestizos born of the unions of Spanish men and Indian women were the first of these castas, but they were soon joined by others, like *mulatos*, born of the union of creoles with blacks, or *zambos*, the children of unions between Indians and blacks. By the 1640s some parish priests in Mexico City were keeping separate marriage registers for different racial groups.[98]

As the combinations and permutations multiplied, so too did the efforts to devise taxonomies to describe them, based on degrees of relationship and gradations of skin colour running the full spectrum from white to black. In the famous series of 'casta paintings', of which over 100 sets have so far been located, eighteenth-century artists would struggle to give visual expression to a classificatory system designed to emphasize and preserve the social supremacy of a creole elite that felt threatened by contamination from below, even as it found itself dismissed as degenerate by officials coming from Spain. The elaborate efforts of these artists to depict in sets of exotic paintings family groups representing every conceivable blend of racial mixture and colour combination look like a doomed attempt to impose order on confusion (fig. 15).[99] In the 'pigmentocracy' of Spanish America, whiteness became, at least in theory, the indicator of position on the social ladder.[100] In practice, however, as time went on there were few creoles to be found without at least some drops of Indian blood, as newly arrived Spaniards (known to the creoles as *gachupines*) took pleasure in proclaiming.

Colonial society, like that of metropolitan Spain, was obsessed with genealogy.[101] Lineage and honour went hand in hand, and the desire to maintain both of them intact found its outward expression in the preoccupation with *limpieza de sangre* – purity of blood. In the Iberian peninsula, purity of blood statutes were directed against people of Jewish and Moorish ancestry, and were designed to exclude them from corporations and offices. In the Indies the stigma reserved in Spain for those 'tainted' with Jewish or Moorish blood was transferred to those with Indian and African blood in their veins. In effect, *limpieza de sangre* became a mechanism in Spanish America for the maintenance of control by a dominant elite. The accusation of mixed blood, which carried with it the stigma of illegitimacy – compounded by the stigma of slavery where there was also African blood – could be used to justify a segregationist policy that excluded the castas from public offices, from membership of municipal corporations and religious orders, from entry into colleges and universities and from joining many confraternities and guilds.[102]

Yet the barriers of segregation were far from being impassable, and were the subject of heated debate within colonial society.[103] In New Spain at least it was possible to remove the taint of Indian, although not African, blood over the course of three generations by successive marriages to the caste that ranked next above in the pigmentocratic order: 'If the mixed-blood is the offspring of a Spaniard and an Indian, the stigma disappears at the third step in descent because it is held as systematic that a Spaniard and an Indian produce a *mestizo*; a *mestizo* and a Spaniard a *castizo*; and a *castizo* and a Spaniard a Spaniard.'[104] Genealogies could be constructively rewritten to conceal unfortunate episodes in a family's history, and retrospective legitimation could be purchased for dead relatives.[105]

There were other ways, too, of circumventing the rigidities of a social ranking based on the colour of one's skin. A royal decree of 1662 relating to the mixed-blood society of Paraguay did no more than recognize realities when it stated that 'it is an immemorial custom here in these provinces that the sons of Spaniards, although born of Indian women, should be treated as Spaniards.'[106] Where mestizos were both legitimate and white, or nearly white, their chances of being passed off as creoles, with all the social advantages that this implied, were greatly improved. Already from the late sixteenth century it was possible for mestizos of legitimate descent to purchase from the crown a certificate classifying them as

'Spaniards', which meant that their descendants would have access to institutions of higher learning and to the more profitable forms of employment.[107] In the seventeenth century the so-called *gracias al sacar* permitted even mulattoes to move from black to white.[108] This kind of legalized ethnic flexibility, facilitated by the crown's perennial shortage of funds, was almost unheard of in Anglo-American colonial society. Only in Jamaica, it seems, was formal provision made for the social ascent of mulattoes, following legislation in 1733 to the effect that 'no one shall be deemed a Mulatto after the Third Generation . . . but that they shall have all the Privileges and Immunities of His Majesty's white Subjects on this Island, provided they are brought up in the Christian Religion.'[109]

Yet, for all the deceptions and ambiguities, colonial Spanish America evolved into a colour-coded society, although the equation between darkness of skin and social, as distinct from legal, status was by no means absolute. Black servants, the majority of them slaves, were legally inferior to pure-blooded Indians living in their communities, but in social and cultural terms they tended to rank higher, because their occupations in creole households or as hacienda foremen effectively made them members of the Hispanic world.[110] If Spanish American colonial society was fundamentally a three-tier society, consisting of 'Spaniards', castas and Indians, then the black population, unlike that of Barbados or the Chesapeake, occupied an intermediate position by virtue of its inclusion among the castas, even though Indian ancestry was rated superior to black ancestry when it came to contamination of the blood-line.

The complexities of these shades of ethnic difference, imperfectly superimposed on a traditional society of orders, inevitably made for a volatile society, especially in the cities. The poorer sections of the Spanish creole population, whose 'pure' blood placed them above the castas, clung to the status symbols that differentiated them from people of mixed ancestry who might well be better off than themselves. Simultaneously they resented the airs, and wealth, of the creole elite. In spite of attempts by the authorities to end their exemption, mestizos shared with creoles the privilege of paying no direct taxes. This gave them every inducement to differentiate themselves from tribute-paying Indians. Correspondingly, an Indian who could pass himself off as a mestizo stood to gain substantially because he escaped tribute payments. Yet in matters of the faith he was better off if he remained classified as an Indian, since Indians, unlike creoles and mestizos, were not subject to the jurisdiction of the Inquisition.[111]

Such confusing cross-currents in legislative and social practice gave rise to continuous uncertainties and ambiguities, victimizing some but creating opportunities for others. Inevitably, too, the imperfect fit between rank and colour afforded wide scope for social subversion. According to Humboldt, 'when some plebeian gets into an altercation with a titled personage, he will quite commonly say to him: "Do you think you are whiter than me?" – words which perfectly reflect the status and origins of today's aristocracy.'[112]

It is not therefore surprising that Spaniards and the upper ranks of the creoles lived in fear of an explosion among the ethnically mixed population that crowded the streets of the cities of New Spain and Peru. A popular insurrection in Mexico City helped topple the reforming viceroy, the Marquis of Gelves, in 1624. If the Indians made up the bulk of the rioters, these also included many mestizos, blacks and mulattoes, and not a few whites.[113] An urban underclass was in process of formation, indiscriminately drawn from a mixture of the different racial groups. Reflecting the hardening social divisions, the elite began to draw a distinction between its own kind – decent people (*gente decente*) – and the *plebe*, including the poor whites, just as the Virginia elite would seek to differentiate itself from the lower orders of white society by means of a social code based on the notions of gentility and respectability.[114]

In the rural society of Virginia accumulated social and economic resentments found their outlet in Bacon's rebellion of 1676. In the urban society of Mexico City they culminated in a brief explosion of popular violence in 1692. Following heavy rains and floods, maize prices that year reached their highest level of the century,[115] and on 8 June an infuriated populace vented its wrath on the symbols of authority, sacking and setting fire to the viceregal palace, the city hall and the town gaol, and looting the shops. Ethnic divisions between Indian, mestizo and Spanish artisans were momentarily forgotten in a concerted denunciation of 'the Spaniards and the *gachupines* who are eating up our corn'. The orgy of destruction was followed by a wave of repression and the rapid crumbling of the temporary unity achieved on 8 June. Economic hardship might produce a coalition of the poor and disadvantaged, but caste and colour consciousness helped to ensure that it was fragile and short-lived.[116]

The 1692 Mexico City insurrection, like Bacon's rebellion, proved to be an evanescent phenomenon, representing no lasting threat to an older and more firmly established elite than that of Virginia. Right across Spanish America urban oligarchies had been consolidating their hold over their cities during the second and third generations of the post-conquest period. At the heart of these oligarchies, which controlled the city councils and exercised a growing influence at the wider, provincial level, were those families of the conquerors that had managed to perpetuate themselves and hang on to the spoils of conquest. It was these families, for instance, which constituted the core of the urban elite of Santa Fe de Bogotá during most of the colonial period.[117] But they were replenished and renewed – as the elite of its fellow New Granada town of Popayán was renewed – by newcomers from Spain or other parts of the Indies who married into them and periodically revived the family fortunes with injections of new wealth.[118]

The new wealth came from trade, from mining and from the benefits of office. To the disgust of old conquistador families that had fallen on bad times, immigrants freshly arrived from the peninsula were all too often preferred in the allocation of posts in the central or local administration, and in the distribution of grants of land or labour. Viceroys would arrive from Spain with a large entourage of friends, relatives and retainers, all of them on the lookout for opportunities for enrichment during the tenure of their patron. Lines of influence and family connection stretched from the Iberian peninsula to Lima and Mexico City, where

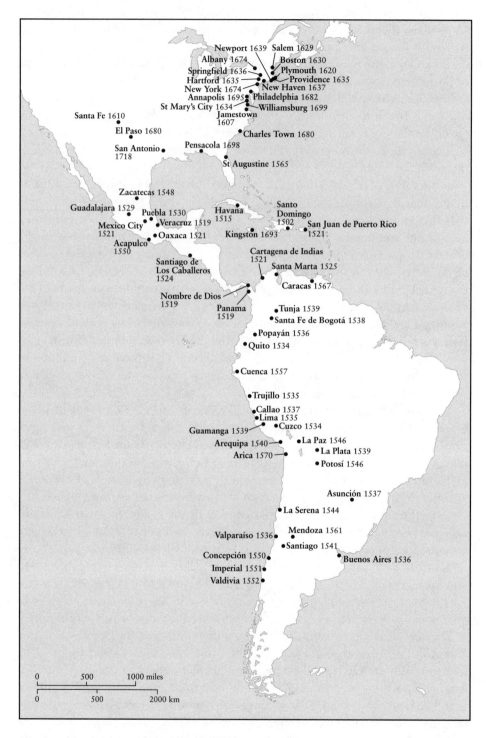

Map 4. Principal Cities and Towns of British and Spanish America, c. 1700.
Based on R. L. Kagan, *Urban Images of the Hispanic World, 1493–1793* (2000), fig. 2.5.

the viceroys dispensed patronage to their clients, and to those who could afford to pay. Don Luis de Velasco, a member of a junior branch of the powerful dynasty of the Constables of Castile, arrived in New Spain as its second viceroy in 1550, and held the post for fourteen years. His son, of the same name, was viceroy between 1590 and 1595, and again between 1607 and 1611, following an interim period as viceroy of Peru, before moving back to Spain to become President of the Council of the Indies (fig. 16). The more than twenty years of Velasco dominance in New Spain were to see a powerful reinforcement and consolidation of the viceroyalty's elite – an elite that included several members of the Velasco family who had married into the families of Mexican encomenderos or mining entrepreneurs.[119]

The upper echelon of the imperial bureaucracy – the presidents, judges and fiscal officers of the eleven American Audiencias, numbering 76 ministers and authorized officials by the late seventeenth century[120] – in theory represented a closed caste, which was expected to keep its distance from the population in the name of equitable government and even-handed justice. In practice its members soon found ways of circumventing prohibitions on marriage into local families or the acquisition of property in their area of jurisdiction, and by the seventeenth century the crown was increasingly ready to grant special marriage dispensations to judges who wished to arrange marriages that would unite themselves or members of their families to the local elites. These connections with elite families naturally redounded to the benefit of both parties. Judges and officials enriched themselves by marrying into wealth, while the families with which they were now linked by marriage secured special consideration in disputed cases and an inside track to patronage.[121]

Making use of their special connections to the royal administration, leading urban families built up their resources, established entails where it suited their purposes, and consolidated their dominance over the cities and their hinterland. They took advantage, too, of the crown's growing financial difficulties to buy their way into public office. Private traffic in *regimientos* – aldermanships – in city councils had long been standard practice, and from 1591 they were put up for public sale. From 1559 notarial posts were placed on the market, and these were followed in 1606 by almost all local offices. Philip II and Philip III had held the line against the sale of treasury offices, but in 1633 Philip IV began putting these, too, up for sale. Eventually, in the second half of the seventeenth century, even the highest posts came onto the market, with posts in the Audiencias being systematically sold from 1687. Creole families naturally moved to take advantage of these expanding opportunities, buying their way into local and central administration, and reinforcing their social and economic dominance in the process.[122]

A nexus of interests was thus built up, linking leading families to the royal administration, the church, mining and trade. Large profits were to be made, both in mining and the transatlantic trade, where Mexican and Peruvian merchants in the earlier seventeenth century looked for returns of 30 per cent or more.[123] Some of these returns were directed into mining, which required heavy capital investment;

others were used for dowries, thus enabling large-scale merchants to marry into landowning and administrative families. According to the Marquis of Mancera, viceroy of New Spain from 1664 to 1673, 'the merchants and traders, who constitute a large part of the Spanish nation in the Indies, approach close to the nobility, affecting their style and comportment, so that it is not easy to distinguish and segregate these two categories.' The penury of the old-established families, and the ambition of the new merchant families, led to intermarriage, 'so that it can be assumed that in these provinces the *caballero* in general is a merchant, and the merchant a *caballero*' – an outcome that, with Venice in mind, he regarded as being to the public benefit.[124]

While large-scale merchants did indeed come to form part of the elite, both in New Spain and Peru, Mancera was exaggerating. Even the wealthiest merchants continued to remain a distinctive social group, often maintaining their commercial interests by arranging for at least one son to go into trade; and they failed to penetrate the uppermost echelon of colonial society.[125] This echelon was now acquiring new badges of distinction. During the seventeenth century 422 creoles were admitted into the prestigious Spanish military orders of Santiago, Calatrava and Alcántara, compared with a mere sixteen in the preceding century.[126] Creoles were also beginning to receive titles of nobility from a crown which in the sixteenth century had been determined to prevent the creation of a New World aristocracy, but was now too financially hard pressed to be able to hold the line. Peru, where Francisco Pizarro's marquisate was the sole title of nobility in the sixteenth century, acquired thirteen marquises and fourteen counts during the reign of Carlos II, and a further 78 titles were added in the course of the eighteenth century.[127]

Although an increasingly exclusive group may have been forming at the summit of Spanish American colonial society, the willingness, or anxiety, of leading families to gain access to new sources of wealth by agreeing to marriage alliances with the families of office-holders, merchants and mining entrepreneurs, helped to ensure that the elite remained relatively open to new blood and new money. It was also an elite with a potentially wide geographical range. For all the localism of Spanish American society, it was conscious of forming part of a wider structure whose parameters were defined by the larger units of royal jurisdiction and extended to Spain itself. Within the two viceroyalties and in the jurisdictional areas of the Audiencias, the elites of the various cities and towns were in constant touch, and in planning their marriage strategies they would frequently operate at the viceregal rather than the purely local level. A leading family in Santiago de Chile might thus be linked by ties of marriage to families in Cuzco, Lima, La Paz and Tucumán.[128] Spain's American empire both created, and was held together by, a transcontinental web of inter-related families.

Here, as elsewhere, the all-embracing structure of royal government gave a greater underlying unity, and a greater degree of homogeneity, to the Spanish colonial societies than was to be found in the British societies to the north. There was certainly a significant element of movement between the different colonies in the formation of British America. Puritans from New England settled on the eastern shores of Maryland and Virginia from the 1640s, and during the second half of the seventeenth century thousands of Barbadians left their overcrowded island for a new life on the Chesapeake. Virginian merchants, too, would strengthen their trading connections by arranging marriages between their children and those of merchants in the other colonies with whom they did business.[129] Yet, with the partial exception of the eighteenth-century Middle Colonies – New York, New Jersey, Pennsylvania and the three Lower Counties (Delaware), where market ties and common business interests helped to encourage social and political interchange[130] – the mainland colonies of British America remained strongly self-contained communities, preserving and even reinforcing the distinctive characteristics that derived from the occasion and place of settlement, and from the local and regional English origins of their early settlers.

Spanish America, by contrast, had from its very beginnings been subjected to processes that pushed the colonists in the direction of uniformity rather than diversity. While the different regional origins of the conquistadores pointed to an initial diversity, this diversity was submerged in the common enterprise of conquest and colonization. Regional differences were pared away in a 'conquest culture', as the exigencies of conquest and settlement impelled a process of selection and simplification, whether of material objects, like ploughshares, or of cultural and linguistic traits.[131] This first process of homogenization was succeeded by another, as royal officials imposed a common administrative apparatus across the continent.

Although differences would soon begin to develop as the new colonial societies established themselves and made the necessary adaptations to local conditions, there remained an underlying social and cultural unity that was reflected in the character of the emerging elites. A member of the elite of Mexico City would have had no great difficulty in adjusting to life among the elite of Lima. Civic institutions were identical; the forms of worship the same. The story was different in British America, where differing local backgrounds, differing motives for emigration and differing religious beliefs and practices created a mosaic of communities settled at a diversity of times and in a diversity of ways. With little or no conquest process and no over-arching structure of intrusive royal government to impose unity on diversity, each colony was left free to develop in its own distinctive fashion. The result was a great gulf in character and life-style, especially between the New England colonies and those of the Caribbean and the Chesapeake. There was neither similarity, nor sympathy, between New England's Puritan establishment and Virginia's gambling and horse-racing gentry elite.[132]

Yet even a society, like that of New England, which clung fast to the beliefs and practices of its founding fathers, found itself inexorably subjected to the challenge of change. A successful entrepreneur like John Pynchon of Springfield, Massachusetts, would build a handsome mansion for himself which immediately singled him out from his fellow citizens, many of whom had become his employees or looked up to him as their patron.[133] Observing with alarm the changes going on around them, and contemplating with distress the corrupting effects of riches and the loss of civic virtue, the New England clergy of the second generation thundered out their jeremiads – the political sermons that cast the history of their settlements into a narrative of decline. While at one level these were sermons of despair, they were also rallying-calls to action, designed to recall the second and third generation to the spiritual errand that had inspired the thoughts and actions of their forefathers, and had marked out New England for its providential destiny.[134]

As New England society grew more complex, it was natural to wonder whether the spirit that had animated the errand into the wilderness could successfully be transmitted from one generation to the next. The creation of a close-knit community of the godly was, and remained, a powerful ideal. But from the first years of the Massachusetts Bay settlement there had been tensions between the Puritan leadership of the community and merchants who, even if they counted themselves among the godly, were liable to chafe at the restrictive authoritarianism of the ministers. In the second half of the seventeenth century, as Boston became a thriving port, and New England was increasingly integrated into the expanding commercial economy of the British Atlantic, the tensions multiplied. Where the clergy had gloried in New England's isolation, which they saw as a continuing guarantee of the purity of its mission, the merchants saw the future of New England in terms of closer ties with the mother country, on which they depended for investment and trade.[135]

These merchants, marrying into each other's families, were coming to form a distinctive and influential group in New England society, just as, half a century or so earlier, Mexican and Peruvian merchants with transatlantic trading interests had evolved into a distinctive and influential group in the colonial societies of New Spain and Peru.[136] In the two Spanish viceroyalties this mercantile elite, while never fully assimilated into the upper echelons of society, managed to imbue them with something of its own concern for enrichment through investment in mining, trade and real estate. But at the same time it all too quickly assumed many of the more restrictive characteristics of the corporate and hierarchical society that surrounded it. The Consulados of Mexico City and Lima, to which the leading merchants belonged, were exclusive, self-perpetuating corporations, occupying their own area of protected space in oligarchical societies of interlocking families closely bound by ties of patronage, clientage and interest to the dominant institutions of church and state.

While the New England merchants had to contend with the Puritan establishment, they were not enveloped, like their Hispanic counterparts, by a powerful existing complex of families drawing their wealth from land and office. This gave them a greater freedom of manoeuvre, not only to impart something of their own values to society, but also to influence its character and its political direction, by offering a different form of leadership with a distinctive set of priorities. From the standpoint of the Puritan establishment these merchants may have acted as the precipitants of 'declension', but by the final years of the seventeenth century they were beginning to emerge as the leading actors in an alternative narrative – a narrative, not of declension, but of progress and development.

This new mercantile elite, developing alongside the more traditional New England elite of respected professionals – lawyers, doctors, government officials and ministers of religion – was far from constituting a monolithic bloc. Some of its members were attracted by the Anglicanism of the Restoration Settlement, and complained bitterly of their disenfranchisement under a Puritan regime. Others remained Congregationalists, but Congregationalists who shared the desire of their Anglican colleagues for a more open and tolerant society, which they regarded as essential for the promotion of trade.[137] By the later years of the seventeenth century this loosely united group of merchants was therefore acting as a catalyst for change in New England society, challenging the political importance of church membership, and making its first priority the maintenance of a close and continuing relationship with the authorities in London.

Yet the merchants of Boston and their colleagues elsewhere would have a struggle to impose their own values on New England society and orientate public policy in ways conducive to business enterprise. On the one hand they were faced with the admonitions, exhortations and denunciations of influential ministers, like Cotton Mather, who deplored the new social mobility and the greedy pursuit of profit that accompanied it.[138] On the other, they were faced with an undertow of popular resentment as disparities of wealth became more marked.

Boston politics were still in large measure deferential in the later seventeenth century, with the most important offices being filled by persons of wealth and social standing.[139] But the city's elite could never afford to take matters for granted. Decisions were taken by majority vote on a large range of civic issues at regularly convened town meetings, which were open to all the city's inhabitants, irrespective of social and economic status or sex. Challenges, both to individuals, and to policies favoured by the elite, could therefore come at any moment. If Bostonians still accorded due respect to status, they remained wary of individuals whom they suspected of attempting to manipulate or monopolize power.

On 18 April 1689 the city erupted in revolt as news arrived of the successful landing of William of Orange in England. In a concerted movement of armed protest, led by magistrates, merchants and preachers, and supported by militias from the neighbouring towns, the population rose and overthrew the hated government of Sir Edmund Andros in a bloodless revolution.[140] Detestation of popery and tyranny had momentarily united all sections of Boston society, but the unity did not last. The overthrow of Andros was followed by popular demands for wider participation in the decision-making process, and an interim government had difficulty in maintaining control in the uneasy period during which the colony impatiently awaited news of its fate from the authorities in London.

The elite itself was divided over the form of government that was to replace the ill-fated Dominion of New England. The majority wanted a return to the old Bay charter, but the new government of William III had other ideas. In spite of tenacious resistance by the colony's representatives in London, the new royal charter granted to Massachusetts in 1691 curbed the autonomy hitherto enjoyed by the colony, along with the power of its Puritan establishment. For the new class of wealthy Boston merchants, however, the new charter possessed many attractions. By guaranteeing liberty of worship to all but Roman Catholics, and transforming the governorship of the colony into a royal appointment, it offered the promise of stability, tolerance and prosperity under benign royal rule.

The events of 1689–90 in Boston brought to the surface social antagonisms and resentments which, although largely contained, made it clear that the elite could not automatically count on the passive acquiescence of the mass of the inhabitants. Men of property warned darkly of 'levelling' tendencies, which all too easily could plunge the city into anarchy.[141] The anxieties felt by the Boston establishment over the dangers of mob rule could only have been enhanced by the news of more violent upheavals in New York, another seaport city boasting a vigorous merchant class that had made its wealth in the Atlantic trade. In New York social and religious tensions were compounded by antagonism between the English and the Dutch.[142] The city's population, a mosaic of different creeds and nationalities, had little more in common than a detestation of popery. The city differed from Boston, too, in lacking a tradition of participatory politics. Not surprisingly, therefore, when the authority of James II's lieutenant-governor, Colonel Francis Nicholson, was challenged by the local militia and his government collapsed, it proved impossible to reach any consensus on what should happen next.

The void was filled by a militia captain, Jacob Leisler, a former soldier of the Dutch West India Company, a fanatical Calvinist, and now a middling merchant. He and his fellow militia captains set up a committee of public safety which took it upon itself to proclaim William and Mary king and queen. Although the Leisler regime could lay claim to having saved New York from popish tyranny, it was living on borrowed time. It lacked legitimacy, in spite of a letter from William III, received in December 1689, which, as read by Leisler, gave him authority to run the government. The heavily Dutch composition of his new city council inevitably aggravated the already sharp tensions between the English and the Dutch. At the same time, while the leading New York families, Dutch and English alike, resented the dominance of this upstart merchant, Leisler himself was being pushed from beneath by artisans and labourers. These had earlier vented their feelings by attacking the town houses of wealthy city merchants, and they saw in the new regime a chance to end government by oligarchy.

With the city deeply divided and its politics radicalized, the position of Leisler looked precarious by the time that William III's new governor arrived in the spring of 1691. His enemies were quick to claim that the city had fallen into the hands of the mob. Tried on trumped-up charges of treason, Leisler and his son-in-law, Jacob Milborne, were executed, and the old elite returned to power. But Leisler's legacy lived on. His friends and partisans rallied to the memory of their martyred leader, who remained as controversial in death as in life. For the next two decades Leislerians and anti-Leislerians would fight bitter battles to win control of the city government. The factional tradition of popular politics in New York had been well and truly launched.

Even if in 1689–90 events took a different course in Boston and New York, the uprisings in the two cities had several points in common. In both of them, the trigger for action was provided by the crisis into which the British Atlantic community had been plunged by the policies of James II and the invasion of England by an army of liberation under William of Orange. This great imperial crisis, perceived in terms of a cosmic struggle against tyranny and popery, was played out in miniature in the transatlantic colonies, where it naturally became embroiled with political and religious conflicts at provincial and local level. It came at a time of sharpened social antagonisms, as elites strengthened their hold over local and municipal life, only to find themselves being simultaneously challenged, on the one hand by new mercantile wealth, and on the other by a growing underclass resentful of the dominance of the privileged few. The resentment, which a few years earlier had exploded into rebellion in the Virginia of Berkeley and Bacon, was particularly acute in the urban environment of the Atlantic seaport towns, where growing profits from trade and the accelerating pace of social change combined to nurture a sense of relative deprivation.

By the standards of Spanish America these towns were still very small. Mexico City at the time of its insurrection in 1692 had a population of at least 100,000.[143] Boston, by contrast, had some 6,000 inhabitants, New York City 4,500, and Philadelphia, founded in 1681, a mere 2,200.[144] Nor, in spite of the presence of free and enslaved blacks, did their populations have anything like the ethnic complexity of a Mexico City or a Lima, where the whole spectrum of colour and castas was on daily display in the crowded streets and market-places (fig. 20). If the North American towns had their poor, their poverty was relative by the standards of contemporary England,[145] and it is doubtful whether anybody starved. There was certainly none of the grinding poverty of Mexico City, where a sudden sharp increase in the price of maize could make the difference between life and death.

Yet, as the uprisings in Boston and New York showed, even small cities could become breeding-grounds for unrest and insurrection. Seaports, with their transitory populations of sailors and immigrants, were especially vulnerable. But for those immigrants who had moved to the New World in the expectation of a better life, disillusionment could be bitter, and all the more so if they arrived imbued with the radical ideas that had risen to the surface in England during the revolutionary years of the mid-seventeenth century. Privilege and hierarchy, they soon discovered, had crossed the Atlantic too.

For all the disappointment and disillusionment, however, both the political culture of British North American societies and their urban arrangements offered more latitude to the discontented than was to be found in their Spanish American equivalents, where the populace could do little more than take to the streets with cries of 'Long live the king and down with bad government!' The concept of 'English liberties' was a powerful one, and sufficiently flexible to allow substantial room for judicial and political action. The revolutionary upheavals in seventeenth-century England had encouraged wide-ranging public debate over fundamental issues, and in the process had helped to consolidate in the British Atlantic community a strong sense of the people's rights.

In North America the notion of a degree of popular participation in government found practical expression at the provincial level in the elections to assemblies, in which suffrage requirements of £40 freeholds were apparently low enough, or at least liberally enough interpreted, to allow a majority of free adult males in Massachusetts, New York and Pennsylvania to exercise the right to vote.[146] Relatively wide urban electorates that had grown accustomed to participating in assembly elections were likely to find ways of making their voices heard, even where, as in New York and Philadelphia, they were initially faced with largely closed systems of city government. If they found their wishes blocked, they could take to the streets side by side with the unenfranchised, to demand proper recognition of their rights as a free people.

The effect of the overthrow of unpopular governors in Boston and New York in 1689 was to reinforce the people's sense of their own power, and consequently to strengthen their claims to a more active role in the making of decisions which would affect their lives. In September 1693 a Connecticut magistrate, Samuel Wyllys, was sufficiently alarmed by the strength of the new demands to express the hope that the new monarchs would 'please to declare that persons of mean and low degree be not improved in the cheifest place of civill and military affairs, to gratifie some little humors, when they are not qualified nor fit for the King's service'. The proper rulers of the colony, in his view, were 'persons of good parintage'.[147] The turmoil in Boston politics during the first two decades of the new century, however, made it clear that, as in New York, 'persons of good parintage' could no longer count on having everything their own way.[148] Others, of less good parentage, were becoming insistent that they, too, should have a share of power.

By the beginning of the eighteenth century in British North America, therefore, ideas and practice had jointly set in motion a dynamic that, once unleashed, could mount a powerful challenge to the exercise of power and privilege by the few. It is hard to detect, in the hierarchical society of Spanish America, forces capable of mounting a comparable challenge to the power of oligarchy. In June 1685 the Rye House plotter, Colonel Richard Rumbold, went to the scaffold in London after making an eloquent speech which found its place in the radical tradition of the British Atlantic community. While paying due deference to the wisdom of a God who had ordered different stations in society, he also uttered words that would not be forgotten: 'None comes into the world with a saddle on his Back, neither any Booted and Spurr'd to Ride him.' Nearly a century and a half later Thomas Jefferson would write in the last letter of his life: 'The general spread of the light of science has already laid open to every view the palpable truth that the mass of mankind has not been born with saddles on their backs, nor a favored few booted and spurred ready to ride them legitimately by the grace of God.'[149] British Americans had succeeded, sometimes in spite of themselves, in creating a society in which the booted and spurred could no longer take for granted a divine right to command.

CHAPTER 7

America as Sacred Space

America was thought to be the promised land by several religions

God's providential design

For Protestants and Catholics alike, America held a special place in God's providential design. 'The overruling *Providence* of the *great God*', wrote Cotton Mather, the Puritan divine, in 1702, 'is to be acknowledged, as well in the *concealing* of America for so long a time, as in the *discovering* of it, when the fulness of time was come for the discovery . . .' For Mather the coincidence of the discovery with the 'Reformation of Religion' in Europe was part of God's providential plan. With America now revealed, 'the *Church* of God must no longer be wrapped up in Strabo's cloak; *Geography* must now find work for a *Christiano-graphy* in regions far enough beyond the bounds wherein the *Church* of God had, through all former ages, been circumscribed . . .'[1]

That same 'Reformation of Religion', which was central to the Protestant story of the redemption of the human race, also helped Catholics to locate the conquest and colonization of America within their own alternative story of the unfolding of God's design. Giovanni Botero, in his highly influential *Relazioni universali* of 1595, declared that it was divine providence which brought about the rejection of Columbus's proposals by the kings of France and England, whose countries would subsequently fall prey to the supreme heresy of Calvinism. Instead, God placed America in the safe hands of the Castilians and the Portuguese and their pious monarchs.[2] Franciscans engaged in the evangelization of the Indies made an even closer association between the conversion of the New World and religious upheaval in the Old. Luther and Cortés, asserted Fray Gerónimo de Mendieta, had been born in the same year. No matter that his dates were wrong. Hernán Cortés was the new Moses who had opened the way to the promised land, and the losses suffered by the church to heresy in Europe had been offset by the winning of innumerable souls in the new lands he had conquered for the faith.[3]

Mendieta, who stood in much the same temporal and psychological relationship to the first evangelists of New Spain as Mather to the first settlers of New

England,[4] represented a late flowering of a spiritual Franciscan tradition which located America, as the Puritans would seek to locate America, in both time and space. The twelve Franciscan 'apostles' who, at the request of Hernán Cortés, embarked on the enormous task of winning the peoples of Mexico to the faith, were the heirs to an apocalyptic tradition permeated by the eschatological ideas of the twelfth-century Cistercian abbot, Joachim of Fiore. In Joachimite prophecy, the first two ages, those of the Father and the Son, would be followed by a third age, the age of the Holy Ghost. This third age, as the Franciscans saw it, was about to dawn. The New Jerusalem would be established on earth, and the conversion of the world would be the prelude to its end.[5]

In this scheme of things, as interpreted by the Franciscan apostle, Fray Toribio de Benavente – known as Motolinía, 'the poor one', by his Nahua flock – America was to be the theatre in which the great drama of salvation was played out. According to Motolinía, the twelve apostles, as the sons of the 'true Israelite, St. Francis', came to Mexico 'as to another Egypt, not hungering for bread but for souls, which are to be found in abundance'. The Indians, to whom they were bringing the Christian evangel, had been struck down for their sins by plagues more cruel even than those that once afflicted Egypt – by the diseases that accompanied the conquest, and by the heavy labour and tributes imposed by the conquerors. But the evangelists had come to lead them on their exodus out of the land in which their souls had been held in pharaonic captivity by the devil.[6] As these redeemed people embraced the true faith with simple fervour, it would become possible – and indeed was already becoming possible – to restore the church of the apostles in its pure and primitive form. In this Franciscan 'Christiano-graphy', to borrow Cotton Mather's term, America thus became a supremely sacred space, with the conversion of the Indians presaging the imminent coming of the age of the Holy Ghost.

This millennial vision of the first Franciscans was by no means universally shared, even among members of the Franciscan Order itself. Not only was there scepticism about the sincerity of the mass Indian conversions, but there were those like the Dominican Las Casas who held firmly to the Augustinian doctrine that salvation was not for the masses but was reserved for the elect.[7] Spanish America, however, was large enough to provide the setting for a variety of holy experiments. In the 1530s, in a bellicose region of Guatemala that was to be rechristened Verapaz, Las Casas launched his own ultimately abortive experiment for the peaceable winning of the Indians to the faith, placing them directly under royal rule and keeping the encomenderos at arm's length.[8] It was in this decade, too, that Vasco de Quiroga, the Bishop of Michoacán, set up his famous 'pueblo-hospitals' of Santa Fe, on the shores of Lake Pátzcuaro. An important source of inspiration for these Indian communities, in which religious indoctrination was combined with six hours a day of labour for the common weal, was Thomas More's *Utopia*, which Quiroga had read with admiration. But alongside this humanist vision, Quiroga also shared the Franciscan ideal of the restoration in the New World of the primitive Christian church.[9]

As the sixteenth century drew to a close, millenarian expectations among the friars were on the wane, and just as Mather was to lament the 'declension' of New England from the high ideals of its pioneering generation, so Mendieta looked back in bitterness on the fall of the Mexican New Jerusalem, corrupted and destroyed by the vices of the conquerors.[10] But in fact the most ambitious of all holy experiments in Spanish America was yet to come, undertaken by the Jesuit Order among the unsubdued Guaraní Indians in the remote jungle borderlands between Brazil and Paraguay. Here, from 1609, the Jesuits began to establish their famous mission settlements, after obtaining from the royal authorities a prohibition against the entry of Spanish colonists into the region, like that secured by Las Casas for his Verapaz experiment.[11]

In their aspiration to control both the spiritual and the temporal activities of the Indians who inhabited them, these Jesuit mission settlements resembled the *reducciones* – the village communities created by Viceroy Toledo's forcible relocation of the Peruvian Indians in the later sixteenth century. But, unlike the *reducciones*, these communities were unconnected with encomiendas, and Indians paid their tribute through the Company of Jesus directly to the king. The exclusion of encomenderos and other Europeans, which owed at least as much to the remoteness of the region as to any royal prohibition, allowed the Jesuits to conduct their holy experiment on their own terms. In their period of maximum prosperity, in the opening decades of the eighteenth century, the thirty communities, covering some 100,000 square kilometres, had a population of perhaps 150,000 Guaraní Indians who had been persuaded to abandon their previous semi-nomadic existence and to live tightly disciplined lives regulated by the liturgical calendar and strictly supervised by the Jesuits.[12] Economically self-supporting, and organized to defend themselves against raids by the *bandeirantes* from neighbouring Brazil, these proved themselves to be viable communities over a period of a century and a half, yielding the Jesuits both a healthy income and a rich harvest of souls. But, as transformed by a European imagination nourished by Jesuit newsletters, they were to be much more than this. The Jesuits, it seemed, had created nothing less than a Utopia in the forests of America.

The Jesuit 'state' of Paraguay, as interpreted by the Europe of the Enlightenment, represented the secularization of a spiritual ideal. But, as with the other holy experiments conducted on American soil, the spiritual and the secular were closely intertwined. Spiritual communities withdrawn from the world were, by their nature, exemplary communities holding out an alternative vision of how the world might be if it would only change its ways. It was the peculiarity of these exemplary communities of Hispanic America, beginning with the millennial kingdom of the Franciscans in New Spain and culminating in the Jesuit 'state' of Paraguay, that they all revolved around the conversion of the Indians, in fulfilment of what were seen as the spiritual obligations inherent in God's choice of Spain to conquer and settle these pagan lands. By contrast, the Indians were marginal to the greatest holy experiment in British America, the creation of Puritan New England as a 'city upon a hill'.

It was of course true that the conversion of the Indians had figured on the agenda of the English since the beginnings of settlement – although it was to be conversion, argued Robert Johnson in his *Nova Britannia* of 1609, not in the Spanish manner 'with rapier's point and musket shot . . . but by fair and loving means, suiting to our English natures . . .'[13] This was the animating spirit behind Eliot's 'praying villages', the Protestant answer to the Jesuit missions, and the most visible reminder of a continuing if erratically pursued commitment to the propagation of the gospel on American soil.[14] There was no doubt that the spiritual and moral well-being of the Indians formed part of God's providential design for the English settlement of America, as Cotton Mather noted in relation to the report of the healing of a Christianized Indian in Martha's Vineyard, whose withered arm was restored through prayer. Quoting with approbation the words of a fellow minister, 'who can or dare deny but that the calling of those Americans to the knowledge of the truth, may seem a weighty occasion to expect from God the gift of miracles?', he added his own triumphant conclusion: 'Behold, reader, the expectation remarkably accommodated!'[15]

One of the ironies inherent in Mather's comment is that the friars in Spain's American dominions had agonized over the absence of miracles to support and validate their efforts. Not all were convinced by Mendieta's argument that 'Miracles according to St. Paul are for the infidels and unbelievers, and since the Indians of this land received the Faith with such readiness and desire, miracles were not necessary in order to convert them.'[16] Mather and his colleagues were untroubled by any such doubts. Theirs was a world not of miracles but of 'especial providences of God', in which an event like the healing of an Indian's withered arm constituted but one small fragment of the providential order of a God-centred universe.[17]

According to the Protestant apocalyptic tradition as it developed in Tudor and early Stuart England, all the territories in America settled and to be settled by the English had their predestined place in God's grand design, since the English themselves were an elect nation chosen by the Lord. For John Rolfe, as for others who pioneered the settlement of Virginia, their migration across the Atlantic was the going forth of 'a peculiar people, marked and chosen by the finger of God, to possess it, for undoubtedly he is with us'.[18] As one of the sermons preached before the Virginia Company at the time of the founding of Jamestown declared, England possessed a divine warrant to establish a 'new Britain in another world'.[19] America thereby assumed its position as a new battleground in the unrelenting struggle between the forces of light, represented by the Protestant Reformation, and the satanic forces of darkness, which had their seat in Rome.

Yet if, in accordance with this cosmic vision, all British America acquired the character of sacred space, one part of it, at least in the eyes of its committed inhabitants, was sacred above all others: 'that English settlement', as Cotton Mather put it, 'which may, upon a thousand accounts, pretend unto more of *true* English than all the rest, and which alone therefore has been called New-England . . .'

Here, looking back over the course of the seventeenth century, he could proudly record 'some feeble attempts made in the American hemisphere to anticipate the state of the New Jerusalem, as far as the unavoidable vanity of human affairs and influence of Satan upon them would allow of it . . .'[20]

Not everyone was willing to accept Mather's version of the story, even in New England itself. The maverick Roger Williams, for one, rejected the notion that New England, or for that matter old England or any other nation, qualified as elect because of a covenant with God.[21] Others, more secularly minded, would have no truck with the idea that they had come to America to build an approximation of the New Jerusalem. When a minister attempted to persuade a group of listeners in northern New England to mend their ways because 'otherwise they would contradict the main end of planting this wilderness', one of them cried out: 'Sir, you are mistaken: you think you are preaching to the people at the Bay; our main end was to catch fish.'[22] But if the image of New England as new Canaan held little appeal for those who had gone there merely to catch fish, many saw the unfolding of God's plan in the story of its settlement.

The story, as told by Mather, began with the providential landfall in 1620 of the Pilgrim Fathers at Cape Cod, which 'was not the port upon which they intended', and not the 'land for which they had provided. There was indeed a most wonderful providence of God, over a pious and a praying people, in this disappointment! The most crooked way that ever was gone, even that of Israel's peregrination through the wilderness, may be called a right way, such was the way of this little Israel, now going into the wilderness . . .'[23] The children of Israel had set forth on the tortuous journey that would lead them to the promised land.

John Winthrop's crossing in the Arbella in 1630 added to the already potent image of an exodus into the wilderness[24] another, and eventually even more potent image, that of a 'city upon a hill'.[25] 'The eyes of the world are upon us', as he told his companions in his address on board ship. The covenant among the participants in the Great Migration to build their city on a hill in New England rather than old England was an explicit recognition of the failure of the Puritans to conform the Anglican church to their wishes and to create in their home country the godly society for which they had yearned and striven for so long. God's wrath was about to descend on England for its sins. 'I am verily persuaded,' wrote John Winthrop, 'God will bring some heavy Affliction upon this land and that speedily.' America thus became a place of refuge for those whom God 'means to save out of this generall callamitie'.[26]

The providentialist vision therefore transcended the Protestant-Catholic divide, giving America, in the eyes of Franciscans and Puritans alike, its assigned place in the great drama of judgment and salvation. But where the Franciscans made the conversion of the Indians the centrepiece of this drama, the Puritan version of it was exclusive, not inclusive, and was framed in terms of the salvation of the elect. The church to be established in Massachusetts Bay was to be a gathered church of visible saints, those who had experienced the transforming touch of God's grace. Whether Indians would be numbered among the saints was in the disposition of God, not of man. For this reason, the mission to the Indians came a poor second to ministering to the elect.

Yet it was possible that the Indians had special claims to the attention of the New England ministers, for reasons that were both historical and providentialist – or so the 'Apostle' John Eliot came to believe. Ever since the conquest of Mexico there had been suggestions that its inhabitants might be descended from the lost tribes of Israel. How else explain what seemed to a number of friars, like the Dominican Fray Diego Durán, the remarkable parallels between some of the rites and experiences of the Israelites as related in the Bible, and those of the Aztecs, a people whose history was also that of an exodus to a promised land?[27] In the middle decades of the seventeenth century, possible affinities between the Jews and the indigenous peoples of America again became the subject of excited debate, this time among the Protestants, duly impressed in the prevailing climate of millennial expectation by Manasseh ben Israel's identification of the Indians with the ten lost tribes in his *Spes Israelis*.[28]

Just as the identification had lent credibility in the sixteenth century to the notion that the Indians were capable of conversion, and had thus given a providentialist context to the activities of the friars, so, a century later, similar doctrines gave a new impetus to Eliot's missionary endeavours. In two series of public lectures on biblical prophecy the Boston preacher John Cotton had expounded in the 1640s a millenarian doctrine which can be traced back, like that of the Franciscans of New Spain, to the teachings of Joachim of Fiore. The New England saints were to stand ready for a period of great convulsions, in which the destruction of the Church of Rome would be followed by the conversion of the Jews, the dawn of the millennium and the redemption of the gentiles, among whom he numbered the American Indians. Eliot was one of those deeply influenced by Cotton's millenarian beliefs, although they offered no hope for anything more than a few scattered conversions of the New England Indians until there had first been a mass conversion of the Jews. But if, as Eliot began to believe at the end of the decade, the peoples of America were not after all of gentile but of Jewish origin, then – if the millennium was indeed imminent – the mass conversion of the Indians must be much nearer than was thought. While the execution of Charles I indicated that England was to provide the setting for the inauguration of the new millennial order in the west, New England now became, in Eliot's eyes, the setting for its inauguration in the 'east'.[29]

In 1651, at Natick, on the Charles River, he established his first Indian community. Like Vasco de Quiroga's 'pueblo-hospitals' on the shores of Lake Pátzcuaro, the settlement was a civil and religious polity, and Eliot planned its governance by means of rulers of one hundred, as prescribed by his understanding of the millennial order.[30] Yet although the missionary work itself made great strides in the following years, and thirteen more praying towns were eventually to be founded, the founder himself gradually retreated from some of his more extreme positions. The Restoration of the monarchy in England cast doubt on the anticipated time-scale for the coming of the millennium, and further study made the Hebrew origin of the Indians less certain than it had seemed at the peak of Eliot's millenarian zeal in the early 1650s. Others never shared his millenarian views, and had always harboured doubts about the spiritual aptitude of the Indians. Especially afer the trauma of King Philip's War of 1675–6, New England ministers were inclined to agree with the conclusion to William Hubbard's *General History of New England* (1680): 'here are no footsteps of any religion before the English came, but merely diabolical.'[31] The same conclusion had long ago been reached by friars and clerics in Spanish America, who castigated Indian 'idolatry' as active devil worship, and had become convinced that any resemblances between indigenous ceremonial practices and those of Judaism were deceptions by the devil rather than the acting out of vague ancestral memories of distant Hebrew rites.

For the devil stalked Spanish and British America alike. 'That old usurping *landlord* of America', Cotton Mather called him, the prince of darkness who hoped that 'the gospel of the Lord Jesus Christ would never come here to destroy or disturb his *absolute empire*'.[32] In a European mental world 'structured by opposition and inversion',[33] it was taken for granted that the devil operated by means of a cunning mimesis of the supernatural order, turning the world upside down. The friars were therefore not surprised to find that the rites and ceremonies of the indigenous societies mimicked, sometimes frighteningly, the rites and ceremonies of the Christian church.[34] Faced with a world of invisible forces, of sorcery and enchantment, they wrote manuals to alert converts and their confessors to the stratagems of Satan, and the history of the church in Spanish America was to be characterized by a series of campaigns, like that of Archbishop Villagómez in seventeenth-century Peru, for the 'extirpation of idolatry'.[35]

Such campaigns were in effect a contest for the sacralization of American space, and nowhere more literally than in the Andes, where the Spaniards sought to destroy the *huacas* – the sacred objects, the sites and the shrines of the Indians – and erect on the site of every *huaca* a cross, a shrine or a church. A similar contest for mastery was enacted in New England, where

> upon the arrival of the English in these parts, the Indians employed their *sorcerers*, whom they call *powaws*, like Balaam, to *curse* them, and let loose their demons upon them, to shipwreck them, to distract them, to poison them, or in any way to ruin them, . . . but the devils at length acknowledged unto them, that they could not hinder those people from their becoming the owners and masters of the country, whereupon the Indians resolved upon a good correspondence with our new-comers; and God convinced them that there was no *enchantment* or *divination* against such a people.[36]

The gradual spread of settlement, and the establishment of new congregations of the saints, displaced the devil, along with the Indians, to the New England forests.[37] But he was, and remained, terrifyingly close, and was forever walking abroad in pursuit of his nefarious designs. Not only did he hold the Indians in his thrall, but he was also working to seduce the godly, who must be on constant guard to defend themselves against his wiles. 'Wilderness' was closely equated with temptation in the minds of the godly, for had not Christ struggled with the tempter in the wilderness?[38] In a world that was perceived to be dominated by supernatural forces – where the ways of providence were expressed not only in extraordinary expressions of God's favour, but also in sudden calamities, in storms and crop failures and prodigies of nature – the dividing line between the angelic and the diabolical was a narrow one. For this reason it was all too easy for even the elect to be deceived.

The resort to magic was one way both to secure access to, and to seek to control, the occult forces at work in the universe. Although the ministers set themselves firmly against recourse to magical practices, these were widespread in Puritan New England, as in the other British settlements.[39] At the best of times it was not easy to distinguish between orthodox and magical remedies for the cure of ailments. In the New World the difficulty was compounded by the profusion of hitherto unknown plants with potential medicinal qualities, and by the proximity of an indigenous population with its own traditional healing arts, that in European eyes were all too likely to smack of superstition and sorcery.

In principle the challenge might seem to have been even greater in Spanish America than in the English settlements, as a result of the cohabitation and racial intermingling of Europeans, Indians and Africans, all furnished with their own ample stock of folk beliefs and practices. The settlers, through their nursemaids and servants, learnt new healing arts from the Indian *curanderos*, whose resort to 'superstition' and to hallucinogenic plants was a source of indignation to doctors trained in European practices, like Juan de Cárdenas in later sixteenth-century New Spain.[40] Sorcery and magic among the creole, mestizo and mulatto population fell within the ambit of the tribunals of the Inquisition, which were set up in Lima in 1570 and in Mexico City in 1571. But the Mexican tribunal displayed a relatively limited interest in them, to judge from the number of prosecutions that it undertook.[41] The Lima Inquisition, at least from the 1620s, seems to have shown considerably more interest than its Mexican counterpart, possibly because of the growing preoccupation of the authorities with the apparent failure of Christianization to uproot superstitious and idolatrous practices in Andean society, and the seductive power of Inca revivalism, among non-Indians as well as Indians, as the age of the Incas receded into the mists of the past.[42] The extensive use of coca, not only for curing but also for divining, inevitably added to the uneasinesss of the authorities. With the possible exception, however, of the Lima region and the Andean highlands in the age of the 'extirpation of idolatry' campaigns, the general impression is of a broad tolerance in the racially mixed society of Spanish America for practices that lent themselves to a benevolent interpretation as offering cures for ills.

Even in New England, although the ministers condemned magic as the work of the devil, many of them were inclined to regard it as the outcome of ignorance and 'simplicity', rather than of premeditated sin.[43] In the 1680s, however, the

New England ministers became increasingly preoccupied by the prevalence of malefic magic, which had been the subject of sporadic indictments since the first witch trials and executions in the late 1640s and early 1650s. The northern colonies had been passing through difficult years. King Philip's War had brought massive destruction in 1675–6, and further tension and uncertainty had been created by the attempts of the crown to tighten its control by revoking the Massachusetts charter in 1684 and establishing the Dominion of New England. In the midst of these various trials and tribulations the ministers were deeply troubled about the 'declension' they detected from the high spiritual standards set by the first generation of their ministerial predecessors. Their own authority was facing a growing challenge, both from within their congregations and from the rising strength of Anglicans, Quakers and Baptists. Increasingly beleaguered, they saw in the prevalence of magic further evidence of the machinations of the devil, who was visibly gaining ground in his attempts to overthrow the city on a hill.[44] 'Satan', declared the Reverend Deodat Lawson, preaching in Salem Village, Massachusetts, in 1692, 'is the grand enemy of all mankind . . . He is the original, the fountain of malice, the instigation of all contrariety, malignity and enmity . . .'[45] Prayer and repentance, not diabolically inspired magic, were the only effective answer to satanic wiles.

Lawson's bleak warning was indicative of the climate of anxiety and condemnation that had gripped Salem and the surrounding region since the launching of its famous witchcraft trials in February 1692. The crisis began in January when the niece and daughter of the Reverend Samuel Parris of Salem Village were seized by convulsive fits.[46] Under questioning, it transpired that a woman neighbour had resorted to countermagic in an attempt to cure the girls, and had instructed Tituba, a household slave, to prepare a 'witchcake' for them. There are strong indications that Tituba was an Indian, not an African slave, and a later account describes her as having been 'brought into the country from New Spain', which may suggest that she originally came from Spanish Florida.[47] The girls were not cured, and the reports of diabolical practices multiplied as more and more girls and young women in the community were similarly affected by convulsions, and identified their tormentors by name from among their neighbours. Once the process had begun, it became unstoppable. More and more unfortunates – men as well as women – were denounced and prosecuted as being in consort with the devil. The hysteria gripped not only Salem but also the neighbouring town of Andover, both in Essex County. By November, when the campaign had largely run its course, and fifty-four 'confessions' had been forthcoming, at least 144 people (38 of them men) had been prosecuted, and fourteen women and five men had been hanged.[48] Then, as doubts spread about the handling of the cases in the Salem courtroom, and scepticism grew about the credibility of the graphic testimony presented by the afflicted girls, the trials collapsed as swiftly and dramatically as they had begun. Belief in the existence of witches and witchcraft still remained strong, but after the turn of the century there would be no further witch trials in New England.

What remains unclear is why a generalized sense of anxiety about the activities of the devil should have come to a head in this particular area, Essex County, Massachusetts, and at this particular moment. The years 1690–2 seem to have been a time of particular stress and tension, even in relation to what had come before. A smallpox epidemic in 1690 had set nerves on edge.[49] In 1691 the worst fears of Congregational ministers were confirmed when the new royal charter permitted freedom of worship to dissenters from Congregationalism, thus officially sanctioning the religious competition they had long struggled to contain. At the more local level, there were tensions between Salem Village and the nearby Salem Town. The strong Quaker community located between them was a visible threat to old-established ways.

Perhaps most potent of all was the sense of crisis generated by the outbreak of a second Indian War in 1688, only ten years after the ending of King Philip's War. Settler society suffered from a deep and persistent fear of the 'redskins', those half-present, half-absent Indians who peopled the imaginations of the whites in the northern frontier regions even more than they peopled in reality its dark woods and forests. The Wabanakis were once more on the warpath, in collusion with the French Canadians, whose popery made them as threatening as the Indians. They raided the town of Andover in 1689, and when the colonial militia tried to stop the raids and launch a counter-attack on Montreal its efforts were rewarded with humiliating failure. Maine in particular suffered further devastation, and the inflow of refugees from the border areas was a stark reminder to Essex County of the constant menace of attack, although whether it received more refugees than other parts of Massachusetts is far from clear. But it is significant that some confessions of spectral sightings of the devil depicted him as being 'tawny', like an Indian. Tituba and her witchcake had brought the devil out of the forest and into the home.

Private grudges, manipulation, mass hysteria all played their part in the terrible collective drama which, as it developed in these fear-stricken communities, showed increasing signs of sparing not even the ministers themselves. Even the judges of Salem's Court of Oyer and Terminer, a class of men who in the past had tended to be sceptical when presented with cases involving witchcraft, succumbed to the hysteria, perhaps out of genuine conviction that only the machinations of the devil could explain the failure of the military operations led by their friends and relatives against the Indians and the French.[50]

Mass hysteria, however, was not confined to this small corner of the American continent. By an odd coincidence a not dissimilar, if less tragic, drama was being played out at almost exactly the same moment thousands of miles away, in the Mexican City of Querétaro.[51] In 1683, at a time when the New England ministers were agonizing over the backsliding of their flocks, a new branch of the Franciscan Order, known as Propaganda Fide, set up a college in Querétaro. The aim of these ascetic Franciscans, many of them new arrivals from Spain, was to bring the gospel to unevangelized rural areas, while also conducting a spiritual ministry in the towns – a ministry which would bring about a 'universal reformation of customs'.[52] Like the ministers in New England, the Franciscans had found themselves faced with growing competition – in this instance from rival religious orders, the Dominicans, the Augustinians and the Jesuits, whose activities had subverted traditional Franciscan primacy in the evangelization of New Spain.[53] Like the ministers in New England, they needed to recover the initiative with a powerful message, and they found it in their cause of ascetic reform. Whipping up popular enthusiasm through preaching and processions they imposed a puritanical regime on the city, putting a stop to public games, dances and other unsuitable festivities. Both sexes were affected by their preaching, but women proved to be especially susceptible, and by the end of 1691 disturbing reports were reaching the tribunal of the Inquisition in Mexico City that women who had taken the Franciscan habit and frequented the missions in Querétaro were showing signs of diabolical possession. They screamed, insulted the Virgin Mary, spat on crucifixes and holy relics, and went into convulsions. On receiving these reports, the Inquisition moved swiftly into action, formally accusing the demoniacs of pretending to be possessed, simply as a pretext for blaspheming and uttering heresies. Some of the Franciscans most closely involved in the affair were reprimanded, and the episode ended almost as soon as it had begun.

Querétaro and Salem were very different worlds, but there were certain obvious similarities in the dramas that engulfed them, like the apparent susceptibility of women to messages of warning and redemption, and allegations of diabolical possession of children, who played such an important part in the Salem trials. One of the cases adduced by the Franciscans was that of a ten-year-old girl, alleged to have been whisked through the air to a distant hill. Here the witches sought to persuade her to make a compact with Satan, that would enable her to visit Spain and Rome at will. This, after all, was a devil operating under Catholic, not Protestant, auspices. More significantly, the allegations of diabolical possession, both in New England and Querétaro, coincided with campaigns to raise the level of religion and morality. In both instances, the effect of these campaigns seems to have been to fill congregations with a deep sense of spiritual inadequacy. Commenting on the Franciscan mission in Querétaro, a Carmelite wrote: 'Men are disconsolate, women are afflicted and souls are everywhere riddled with doubt.' The over-zealous Franciscans, by attempting to turn their followers into saints overnight, had generated strains which had led them to indulge in bizarre behaviour and develop 'strange illnesses'.[54] In Roman Catholic New Spain, as in Puritan Massachusetts, religious professionals proved to be prime purveyors of anxiety.

For all the differences between Protestantism and Tridentine Catholicism, their shared theological inheritance inevitably led to many points of convergence, and not least on questions relating to magic and diabolism. This was particularly true of their common reliance on the teachings of Saint Augustine, which, by sharply separating the natural from the supernatural, could easily lead on both sides of the confessional divide to perceptions of a God so omnipotent as to be a capricious tyrant, using the devil for His own providential purposes. In playing down the Querétaro episode the inquisitors, while no doubt motivated, as the New England ministers belatedly came to be motivated, by an awareness of the role of malice and deceit in witchcraft accusations, seem to have been as anxious to preserve the credibility of a malign devil as of a just God.[55] In New England it was the credibility of spectral evidence, rather than of the devil himself, that came to trouble the ministers and the magistrates.[56] The winds of the new sceptical philosophy may have been blowing in America as well as Europe by the late seventeenth century – both the Mexican savant, Sigüenza y Góngora and, with considerably more hesitation, Cotton Mather, opted for natural rather than supernatural explanations of the comet they observed passing through the skies in 1680[57] – but down on earth the devil, even if not necessarily each and every spectral sighting, remained unnervingly believable.

Religious teaching that stressed, in New Spain and New England alike, the divine intention to test and increase the merits of the faithful through satanic trials and temptations while also emphasizing the relationship between personal responsibility and personal misfortune, helped to intensify the sense of vulnerability in a world where so much seemed to be beyond individual control. But where the sense of vulnerability among the faithful in Counter-Reformation societies may have been alleviated by belief in the countervailing power of ritual, this recourse, although by no means absent, was less obviously available for Protestants standing in an unmediated relationship to an all-powerful God.[58] Fasting, public confession and penitential rites, however, played a major part in the life of New England congregations, providing collective reinforcement against the temptations of the devil. Yet the very practice of public confession in the Congregational churches must also have encouraged members to make the confessions of demonic possession that unleashed the witchcraft trials.[59]

While the conjunction of mentality and circumstance may have contrived to give greater prominence to malefic magic among the settler population of later seventeenth-century New England than of New Spain, Spanish American churchmen, had they known of it, would have had no cause to quarrel with John Foxe's assertion that 'the elder the world waxeth, the longer it continueth, the nearer it hasteneth to its end, the more Satan rageth.'[60] But those same churchmen could call on powerful allies in their battle to defend American space from the hosts of Satan. There were, to begin with, the angels and archangels, who were seen as the soldiers and guardians of the new Catholic empire of the Indies. An ancient and doctrinally suspect tradition, transmitted by way of the spiritual Franciscans to the Jesuits, endowed the archangels Michael and Gabriel with five archangelic companions, each with a name and a specific heavenly assignment. Corresponding to the seven virtues, these were pitted against seven named devils, who corresponded to the vices. Nowhere was this struggle between the forces of good and evil fought out more fiercely than in Peru, where, in representations from the later seventeenth century onwards, artists took to depicting the seven archangels like members of a heavenly corps de ballet, dressed in elaborate lace-trimmed uniforms, and with muskets in hand (fig. 18).[61]

While the archangels were fighting on their side, the clergy and the faithful also had recourse to intercession by the Virgin and a battery of saints. The 'local religion' of sixteenth-century Spain, with its proliferation of chapels, shrines and images for which a local community felt a particular devotion,[62] transferred itself to the Indies, where towns and villages acquired their own special patron as space was Christianized.[63] Some images were brought over from Spain, allegedly in the saddle-bags of the conquistadores, like the Virgin of Los Remedios, who was named the patron of Mexico City in 1574.[64] Some were crudely carved by local Indians, and subsequently acquired an unearthly beauty, like the Virgin of Copacabana, a Christianized Indian sanctuary on the shores of Lake Titicaca – an image which, beginning as an object of local devotion, came to be specially venerated throughout the viceroyalty.[65] Others were discovered hidden in some cave, or were miraculously revealed by an apparition.

The most famous of all such apparitions of the Virgin Mary was that to a poor Mexican Indian, Juan Diego, in 1531. The story went that, on receiving her instructions to gather up flowers, he carried them in his cape to the bishop, who was astonished to find her likeness painted on the cloth. The veneration of this image, first established as a local cult after a shrine was built for it at Guadalupe, near Mexico City, began to spread as miracles were reported. But it was a veneration largely confined to Indians. It was only during the seventeenth century, at a time when the creole population of New Spain was struggling to establish a sense of its own place in the world, that the cult was also taken up by creoles, and the Virgin of Guadalupe was effectively launched on the spectacular career that would eventually transform her into the symbol of 'Mexican' aspirations and a 'Mexican' identity.[66]

The Virgin of Copacabana never quite achieved the same transcendence in viceregal Peru, but on the other hand the viceroyalty was to secure the first American saint, a creole visionary called Isabel Flores de Oliva (1584–1617), who, in her struggles with the devil, subjected herself to extraordinary mortifications and was canonized in 1671 as Santa Rosa of Lima.[67] The cult of Santa Rosa was to spread throughout Spanish America, of which, on her canonization, she was named patron saint. In a powerful painting in the cathedral of Mexico City she was depicted locked in the devil's muscular embrace (fig. 19).[68] Transcending local, and even viceregal, boundaries, this striking image, pitting the spiritual serenity of the saint against the malignity of the devil, epitomizes what was perceived as a cosmic struggle between the forces of light and darkness throughout Spain's dominions in the Indies.

The sacralization of space reflected in the appropriation of saints and images by different localities right across the Spanish Indies was accompanied by the sacralization of time, as their feast-days were celebrated in massive demonstrations of popular devotion. Taking Sundays into account, over 150 days a year in seventeenth-century Peru were given over to festivities in celebration of important events in the life of the church and of the Spanish crown.[69] This made a striking contrast with the calendar of Puritan New England, where traditional Christian holy days, like Christmas and Easter, were rigorously suppressed, and only Sundays were kept. Yet the routine of the day's work in Massachusetts could be disrupted at any moment if a minister were moved by the spirit to give a lecture or sermon, and the General Assembly found it necessary in 1639 to ask the clergy to cut down on their preaching. There was a proliferation, too, of special prayer days, of days of fasting and thanksgiving, both in New England and elsewhere. New England is said to have observed 664 fast days and days of thanksgiving for 'providential events' over the course of the seventeenth century. With Sundays included, this meant that some sixty days a year – compared with Peru's 150 – were set aside for religious purposes. In Anglican eyes this was inadequate. In 1681 royal pressure forced the General Council of Massachusetts Bay to repeal its law against the celebration of Christmas, and Governor Andros encouraged the observance not only of the major Christian feast-days but of nearly twenty annual saint's days.[70]

Removing ritual from time, the Puritans of New England also removed it from space. 'Holiness of Places', wrote Cotton Mather, 'is . . . no more believed among them, than it was in the Days of Clemens Alexandrinus, who says . . . *Every Place is in truth holy, where we receive the knowledge of God.*'[71] With no specifically sacrosanct spaces in Puritan 'Christiano-graphy', the ministers, unlike the friars in Spanish America, made no effort to adapt places revered as sacred by the Indians to Christian purposes. It was true that their religious buildings – simple, unadorned meeting-houses, not churches – were situated at the centre of settlements, but their position was dictated as much by civil as by religious considerations, and meeting-houses and cemeteries conferred no special sanctity on the ground they occupied.[72] If the New England congregations duly developed their own rituals, in the form of public and private prayers, fasting and confessions, and took communion from silver vessels,[73] they were engaged in a ritualism whose credentials remained firmly anti-ritualistic.

For those who did not share the sense of participating in an errand into the wilderness, and had no wish to see their settlements transformed into cities on a hill, the Puritans of New England were likely to give the impression of profaning the sacred and sacralizing the profane. But even the luminous churches that began to embellish the countryside of Anglican Virginia from the late seventeenth century were places of civil as well as of religious encounter.[74] No special shrines, no local saints, no holy images – the spiritual landscape of British America, outside a few Roman Catholic places of worship in Maryland, was coming to bear the imprint of the Protestant Reformation, just as the spiritual landscape of Spanish America had come to bear the imprint of the Catholic Reformation and Counter-Reformation, with Spanish local religion and hybrid forms of Indian religion thrown in for good measure.

The church and society

A primitive Christian church built on Indian foundations or a republic of the saints? The two most radical dreams for the spiritual appropriation of America –

one cherished by the first generation of friars in New Spain, the other by the Puritan communities established in New England – were to prove equally difficult of realization. The Indians turned out to be wayward and dissembling; the saints showed an alarming proclivity for backbiting and backsliding. In both instances, the requisite response appeared to lie in the direction of more discipline and control. The friars fought to establish an exclusive control over their erring Indian charges; the Puritan ministers to impose and preserve their authority over recalcitrant congregations. But discipline brought institutionalization, and institutionalization, in turn, was all too prone to quench the fervour of the spirit. Mendicants and ministers who struggled to preserve the original vision in all its pristine purity had to do so in an environment in which it soon became clear that they held no spiritual monopoly. The authority of the mendicants was to be challenged by a state church that rapidly consolidated the institutional basis of its power, while the New England ministers were to find themselves in competition not only with an increasingly assertive Anglican establishment but also with religious groups claiming to have received their own distinctive revelation. The sacred soil of America lent itself all too well to turf wars.

[handwritten margin note: Christian religious order that adopted a lifestyle of poverty]

The mutually reinforcing alliance of throne and altar in Spanish America created a church whose influence pervaded colonial society. Philip II, in his capacity as Vicar of Christ, and using the enormous powers granted him under the Patronato, shaped an institutional church which he sought to conform to the requirements of the Council of Trent while ensuring that it remained strictly subordinate to royal control.[75] Authority was firmly placed in the hands of the bishops, all of them chosen by the crown. But the colonial church that was constructed on the twin foundations of the royal Patronato and the Tridentine decrees was to be neither as monolithic nor as subservient to royal control as Philip would have wished.

Just as royal government in Spanish America was made up of different power centres – viceroys, Audiencias, and royal officials with visitorial powers – all of them with competing and overlapping areas of jurisdiction, so the clerical establishment was divided among competing bodies, with their own priorities, interests, and areas of autonomy. A fissure ran down the centre of the colonial church between the secular clergy and the religious orders, which in turn were divided by their own institutional affiliations and traditional rivalries. During the sixteenth century the crown turned primarily to the religious orders to fill the bishoprics, pursuing a policy that reflected the primacy of the regulars in the evangelization of the Indies. Of the 159 bishops who took up their appointments in Spain's American territories between 1504 and 1620, 105 were members of the religious orders (52 of them Dominicans), and 54 were secular clergy.[76] For the remainder of the seventeenth century the numbers were more evenly balanced, before tilting in favour of the secular clergy in the eighteenth century.[77]

The acrimonious rivalries between the regular and the secular clergy over episcopal appointments were repeated at ground level across the Indies as the crown, against fierce mendicant opposition, sought to comply with the provisions of the

Council of Trent by 'secularizing' many of the parishes (*doctrinas*) run by the friars, replacing them with secular priests. But by the end of the sixteenth century the crown's campaign was stalled, and a large and impressive mendicant establishment – some 3,000 in mid-seventeenth-century New Spain alone, as against some 2,000 secular clergy[78] – largely succeeded in holding its own until the mid-eighteenth century, when the campaign was renewed with more success under Bourbon auspices.[79]

In fighting their stubborn rearguard action the religious orders could draw on their record of success with their Indian charges, on the support they enjoyed among influential circles in Rome and Madrid, on the goodwill of their devotees among the creole population, and on their own rapidly growing resources as they accumulated property through gifts and endowments. But, in common with other sections of the clerical establishment, they exploited the internal divisions within the structures of royal government to defend their position and promote their cause. The result was a continuous interplay of ecclesiastical and secular disputes in Spain's American territories throughout the colonial period, as religious issues shaped and distorted political alignments.

A classic example of this process occurred in New Spain during the troubled viceroyalty of the Marquis of Gelves. Arriving in Mexico in 1621, Gelves embarked on a programme of root-and-branch reform that polarized colonial society. Sudden and unexpected alliances were formed as church and state were split down the middle. Gelves' decision to support the friars over the secularization of parishes antagonized the Archbishop of Mexico, Juan Pérez de la Serna, who had been supportive of his campaign to reduce corruption among royal officials. He now made common cause with his old enemies among the judges of the Audiencia. Finding their interests threatened by the viceroy's moves against corruption, the judges reversed their position and came out in support of control of the parishes by the secular clergy. The religious orders, as was to be expected, ranged themselves behind Gelves, with the exception of the Jesuits, traditionally at loggerheads with the mendicants, and the Carmelites, who had no Indian parishes of their own. The Inquisition, for its part, was on bad terms with the viceroy, and may have conspired against him behind the scenes, although the inquisitors attempted to pacify the menacing crowds by going in procession to the central plaza with crosses uplifted. But passions were running high, and on 15 January 1624, in the famous 'tumult' of Mexico City, the mob attacked and looted the viceregal palace, forcing Gelves to flee for his life.[80]

The overthrow of Gelves, whose recall to Spain was made inevitable by the public humiliation he had suffered, vividly illustrates how even a church–state partnership drawn up on the state's own terms was unable to guarantee the crown's supreme representative immunity from clerical attack. 'Thus', observed the renegade English Dominican Thomas Gage of the role played by Archbishop Pérez de la Serna in the Gelves affair, 'did that proud prelate arrogantly in terms exalt himself against the authority of his prince and ruler ... trusting in the power of his keys, and in the strength of his Church and clergy, which with the rebellion of the meaner sort he resolved to oppose against the power and strength of his magistrate.'[81] A dependent church still possessed considerable room for manoeuvre in a corporate society in which each corporate body and institution enjoyed a semi-autonomous status and its own permitted sphere of action. Yet the church itself rarely spoke with one voice, thanks to the conflicting character and interests of its different constituent parts. While acting, or claiming to act, in pursuance of the highest ideals, these different branches of the clerical establishment were also responding to the more mundane pressures created by the nature of their relationship with the society in which they were embedded.

The consolidation of creole society in the viceroyalties of New Spain and Peru during the later sixteenth and early seventeenth centuries inevitably generated pressures for the 'creolization' of the institutions of both church and state. In the early stages of colonization the Iberian peninsula had necessarily provided the bulk of recruits for the regular and secular clergy, but an increasing supply of qualified candidates became available among the children and grandchildren of the colonists as seminaries were founded in the Indies in accordance with the provisions of the Council of Trent. At the same time, Philip II's policy of secularizing parishes increased the availability of benefices for creoles entering holy orders, especially as Indians, and, for the most part, mestizos, were denied ordination.[82] Since Spanish-born secular clergy showed little interest in making a career in the Indies at the parish priest level, the lower and middle ranks of the clerical establishment in the Indies came to be occupied largely by creoles. Bishops for the most part continued to be appointed from Spain, but the numbers of native-born bishops began to rise from the reign of Philip III (1598–1621), who appointed 31 of the 38 creoles occupying American sees between 1504 and 1620.[83]

The secular church, therefore, offered an important extension to the employment possibilities open to creole youth, with the younger sons of the elite securing privileged access to the richer parishes and cathedral benefices. The extraordinary proliferation of religious houses across the continent also opened up new opportunities, this time for daughters as well as sons. Nunneries – a number of them, like Santa Clara in Cuzco, first intended primarily for the illegitimate mestiza daughters of the encomenderos – were conveniently appropriated by wealthy creoles for the accommodation of their female relatives, who brought dowries to the community in which they professed.[84] Yet if the houses of the female orders established in town after town of Spanish America were locally founded institutions, designed to meet the needs of creoles and, to a lesser extent, of mestizos, the relationship of the creole community to the majority of the male religious orders was much more problematic.

The mendicants recruited heavily in Castile and Andalusia, and had an organized system for the despatch of their members to the mission field.[85] Having pioneered the evangelization of the Indies, the several orders – Franciscans, Dominicans, Augustinians, Mercedarians – showed no enthusiasm for passing the spiritual baton to American-born colleagues, whose training for mission work and standards of religious discipline seemed to them to leave much to be

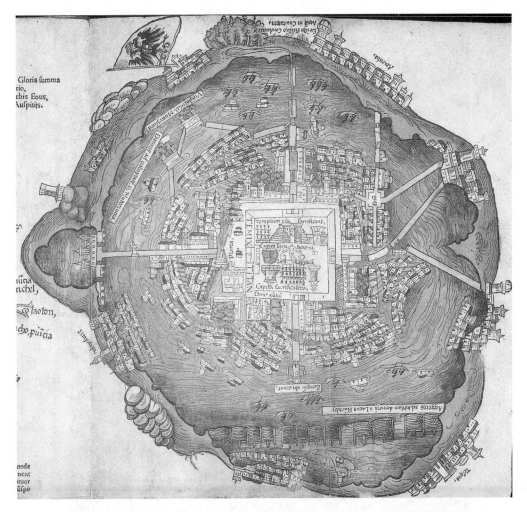

1 This map-view of 'the great city of Tenochtitlán' is a woodcut illustration to the Latin edition of Hernán Cortés's second letter to Charles V, published in Nuremberg in 1524. On 8 November 1519 Cortés and his men crossed Lake Texcoco by the Ixtapalapa causeway, shown on the left, to make their entry into the city. At the centre of the map is the Temple of the Sun, with the *Plaza Mayor* beneath it.

2 Antonio Rodríguez (attrib.), Portrait of Moctezuma (Motecuhzoma II) (c.1680–97). Although this portrait of the emperor was made in Mexico in the late seventeenth century, the artist based his representation on images to be found in sixteenth-century codices.

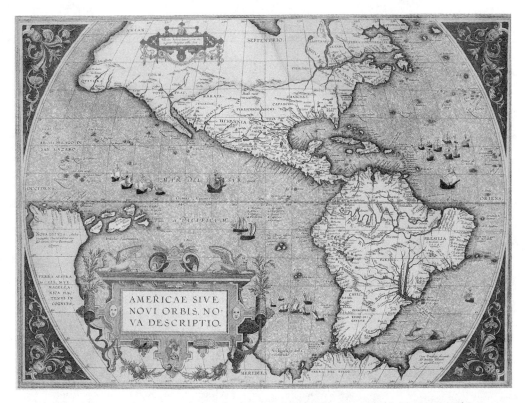

3 'New Description of America' from Abraham Ortelius, *Theatrum Orbis Terrarum*. This map, from the 1592 edition of Ortelius's Atlas, published in Antwerp, shows the New World as it was known to Christopher Newport. Chesapeake Bay, shown on the map, was discovered in 1585 by a party of colonists from Roanoke Island led by Ralph Lane.

4 John White, Indians Fishing (water-colour, 1585?). John White was sent to Roanoke Island in 1585 by Sir Walter Raleigh to record the appearance of the people of Virginia. This watercolour is one of a number of vivid depictions of the life of Carolina Algonquians, which constitute the best visual record made by a European of any of the indigenous peoples of sixteenth-century America.

5 New England Natives Greeting Bartholomew Gosnold. Engraving from Theodor de Bry, *America*, book XIII (Frankfurt, 1628). Bartholomew Gosnold was captain of the *Godspeed*, one of the three ships on Christopher Newport's 1607 Jamestown voyage. Five years earlier he had made a reconnaissance of the coast of New England, which provides the setting for this idealized reconstruction of Algonquian Indians eager to trade with the newly arrived English, offering them strings of wampum, or beads made with shells, in return for knives. Once in Jamestown, Gosnold, like so many of his companions, succumbed to sickness and died within a few months of the colony's foundation.

6 Powhatan's mantle. Deerskin with shell decoration. Although known as a mantle, this deerskin may be a representation of the tribes or villages over which Powhatan ruled. Now preserved in the Ashmolean Museum at Oxford, it is first recorded in 1638 as 'the robe of the King of Virginia'. Originally it formed part of the famous collection of antiquities and exotica, known as 'The Ark', made by John Tradescant, gardener to King Charles I.

7 The Seal of the Massachusetts Bay Company. The seal emphasizes the commitment of the company to the conversion of the Indians. In the engraving, an Indian echoes the words spoken by 'a man of Macedonia' in a vision of St Paul: 'Come over [into Macedonia], and help us.'

8 Simon van de Passe, Portrait of Pocahontas, engraving (1616). Following her famous encounter with Captain John Smith, Pocahontas, the daughter of Powhatan, was sent by her father on various occasions to the Jamestown settlement to act as an intermediary. Converted to Christianity and given the baptismal name of Rebecca, she was married in 1614 to John Rolfe and accompanied him to England with their infant son in 1616. Much fêted in London, she fell ill and died in the following year while awaiting the departure of the ship that would take the family back to Virginia. Her marriage to one of the early settlers pointed to the path not taken in British America, where interethnic union was to remain relatively rare by comparison with the process of racial mingling in Spanish America.

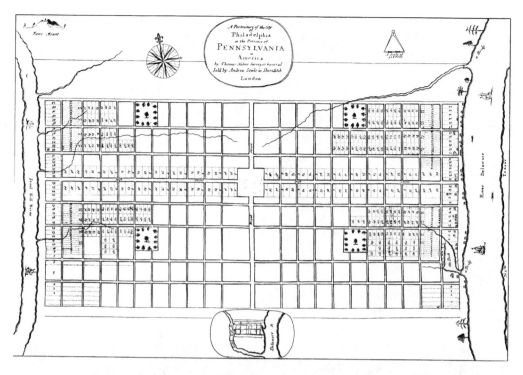

9 Thomas Holme, *A Portraiture of the City of Philadelphia in the Province of Pennsylvania in America* (London, 1683). As can be seen from this 1682 town plan of Philadelphia, the grid-iron pattern of urban design, extensively used in Spanish America, was adopted by William Penn for the capital of his new colony. Penn stipulated that the streets should be fifty to a hundred feet wide, and that the houses be placed in the middle of their lots, thus setting a pattern that would be widely followed in North America.

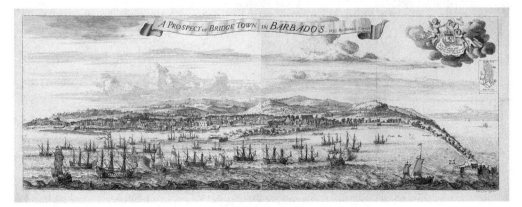

10 Samuel Copen, *A Prospect of Bridge Town in Barbados*, engraving (1695). This, the first large panoramic view of an English colonial settlement, depicts the thriving seaport of Bridgetown, which had been largely reconstructed after a hurricane in 1675. Warehouses for the storage of sugar line the waterfront.

11 New World ethnography in the making. The *Relación de Michoacán* (1539–40) provides a rich account of the history and customs of the Tarascan Indians of west-central Mexico in the period before the Spanish conquest. The author, possibly the Franciscan Jerónimo de Alcalá, is shown presenting his manuscript to the viceroy, Don Antonio de Mendoza.

12 Gaspar de Berrio, *Description of the Cerro Rico and the Imperial Town of Potosí* (1758). The Cerro Rico, or silver mountain, rises in the background, while the town itself, built to a grid-iron plan, is laid out before it. To the left are the artificial lakes and dams constructed by the Spaniards to power the mills for refining the silver. While work goes on in the mines, a procession comes down the hillside carrying the banners of a religious confraternity. Situated in the high Andes, 13,000 feet above sea level, mid-eighteenth-century Potosí had a population of under 60,000, well down from that in 1600, when a population of over 100,000 made it one of the largest cities of the western world.

13 José de Alcíbar, *St Joseph and the Virgin* (1792). Celestial bureaucracy in action. The Virgin and St Joseph act as intercessors, passing up petitions to Christ for decision. While earthly kingdoms were supposed to be modelled on the divine, this painting suggests that the Hispanic world modelled its image of the celestial kingdom on that of the hierarchical structure of a bureaucratized Spanish Monarchy with its elaborate processes of lobbying and petititioning, motivated by the assumption that services would in due course be appropriately rewarded by a grateful monarch.

14 Anon., *Mrs Elizabeth Freake and her Baby Mary* (c. 1671–74). Elizabeth Clarke was born in 1642, the daughter of a prosperous merchant from Dorchester, south of Boston. In 1661 she married John Freake, a recent immigrant, who became a substantial Boston merchant, and whose portrait by the same artist made a companion piece to this picture. The couple had eight children, the youngest of whom, born in 1674, was the baby daughter shown in the painting. Following her husband's death in an accident in the following year, Elizabeth Freake made a second marriage and survived until 1713. The double portrait of mother and child can be seen as a testimonial to the fruitfulness expected of the Puritan family, while Elizabeth's lace collar, silk dress and jewellery testify to the affluence of the mercantile elite in late seventeenth-century New England.

15 Andrés de Islas, Four Racial Groups (1774). These four works, taken from a series of sixteen *casta* paintings by a Mexican artist, are typical of a genre that was highly popular in the eighteenth century. They illustrate well the attempt to devise a taxonomy for the gradations of racial mixture to be found in the viceroyalty of New Spain. *Top row:* 1. From a Spaniard and Indian is born a *mestizo*; 2. From a Spaniard and a *mestiza* is born a *castizo. Bottom row:* 3. From an Indian and a *mestiza* is born a *coyote*; 4. From a *lobo*, or wolf (the result of a union between an Indian man and an African woman) is born a *chino*.

16 Anon., Don Luis de Velasco the younger, marquis of Salinas (1607), second son of Don Luis
de Velasco who governed New Spain as its second viceroy from 1550 to 1564. Educated at
Salamanca University, he was a member of the entourage that accompanied the future Philip II to
England in 1554 for his marriage to Mary Tudor. In 1560 he joined his father in New Spain,
where he married the daughter of one of the conquerors of Mexico, Don Martín de Ircio, a
wealthy encomendero. In 1590 Philip II appointed him to his father's former post as viceroy. In
1611 he was recalled to Madrid to become president of the Council of the Indies, a post from
which he retired in 1617, dying the same year. Smoothly ascending to the highest levels of the
imperial bureaucracy, he exemplified, like his father before him, the extensive deployment of
patronage by American viceroys to reward relatives and dependants and form profitable
connections with the creole elite.

17 Sir Peter Lely, Portrait of Sir William Berkeley. Governor of Virginia from 1641 to 1652, and again from 1660 to 1677, Sir William Berkeley (1605–77) stamped his personality on a troubled and faction-ridden colonial society, for which he harboured great ambitions. Like Don Luis de Velasco he had strong personal interests in the land and society over which he presided, and, again like Don Luis, governed through a circle of friends and dependants chosen from among the creole elite. His career, however, unlike that of Don Luis, ended in failure and disgrace. Resentment at his style of governance helped provoke Bacon's rebellion, and led to his recall in 1677 to England where he died, a broken man, before being able to clear his name.

18 Anon., *Angel Carrying Arquebus*. Peru, Cuzco school (eighteenth century). Andean artists developed in the later seventeenth century a unique iconography representing a celestial militia composed of elegantly attired angels and archangels, many of them sporting arquebuses. Alongside the biblical archangels, Michael and Gabriel, the series frequently showed apocryphal archangels, whose inclusion, regarded as heterodox in Europe, passed without challenge in America. The origins of the iconography remain uncertain. It could well reflect the teachings of Christian missionaries in the Andes, but depictions of a militant heavenly host carried echoes of pre-conquest religious beliefs which may help to account for its popularity among the peoples of the Andes. The angelic manoeuvres with the arquebus are borrowed from engravings of drill movements taken from Jacob de Gheyn's *Exercise of Arms*, first published in the Netherlands in 1607.

19 Anon., *Santa Rosa of Lima and the Devil*. Santa Rosa of Lima (1584–1617), canonized in 1671, was the first American to be made a saint. Although a native of Peru, her cult spread to other parts of Spanish America, including the viceroyalty of New Spain, as demonstrated by this late seventeenth-century painting from a retablo in the cathedral of Mexico City.

20 Anon. *Plaza Mayor de Lima* (1680). The painting testifies both to the splendour and preeminence of the viceregal capital, and to the diversity of the city's population. Behind the fountain at the centre of the *Plaza Mayor* rises the cathedral, with its baroque facade. Beside it stands the archbishop's palace, and, to the left of the painting, on the north side of the square, the viceregal palace. The proximity of the two palaces suggests the close union of church and state. The numerous figures in the *plaza* cover the spectrum of Peruvian colonial society, from members of the Spanish and creole elite, in carriages or on horseback, to Indian women selling food and fruit in the market and African water-sellers filling their jars.

21 A representation (1653) of the transfer in 1533 of the image of the Virgin of Guadalupe to its first chapel in Tepeyac, outside Mexico City. The two 'republics' of Spaniards and Indians are clearly distinguished. In the Virgin's first miracle an Indian is cured, after being accidentally wounded by an arrow in a mock battle of Aztecs against Chichimecas. Her image is shown in the background being brought across the causeway to Tepeyac.

22. Anon., *Return of Corpus Christi Procession to Cuzco Cathedral* (c. 1680). The Spanish American city as the scene of open-air religious theatre. One of a series commissioned by the bishop of Cuzco showing different stages of the procession, which took place in a period of renewed civic confidence and splendour following the city's recovery from a devastating earthquake in 1650.

desired.[86] As a result, religious houses became an early battleground in the conflict between creoles and *peninsulares*, or *gachupines*, which was to become a permanent feature of Spanish American colonial life. Thomas Gage, moving from one religious house to another in Mexico and Guatemala during his ten years in America from 1627 to 1637, was eyewitness to the bad blood which turned the religious houses into warring communities: 'they told us plainly that they and true Spaniards born did never agree.'[87]

The antipathy was liable to come to a head during the elections periodically held for the appointment of priors, provincials and their councils. During the seventeenth century these elections came increasingly to pit creoles against *peninsulares*, and aroused the most intense passions not only in the religious houses themselves but throughout a society in which everyone had a relative in the religious life. 'Such were their various and factious differences', wrote Thomas Gage of the election of a provincial for the Mercedarians, 'that upon the sudden all the convent was in an uproar, their canonical election was turned to mutiny and strife, knives were drawn, and many wounded. The scandal and danger of murder was so great, that the Viceroy was fain to interpose his authority and to sit amongst them and guard the cloister until their Provincial was elected.'[88]

Both locally and in Rome the Spanish-born friars fought hard to prevent their orders in the Indies from being taken over by the creoles, and found a weapon to hand in the *alternativa*, which could be used to impose the regular alternation of creoles and *peninsulares* in election to office. The *alternativa* – or, for the Franciscans, a *ternativa*, stipulating the succession in turn of a *peninsular* who had taken the habit in Spain, a *peninsular* who had taken it in the Indies, and a creole – was to become a source of growing irritation to the creoles as they became the majority element in the orders. It also became an important political issue as viceroys sought to impose the system of alternation on different religious communities in a desperate attempt to keep the peace.[89]

Regular versus secular clergy, order against order, creole against native-born Spaniard, a state-controlled church all too often impervious to state control – these different sources of tension, conflicting and combining, ran like a series of electric charges through Spanish American colonial life. Storms could blow up very rapidly, as they did again in New Spain twenty years after the downfall of Gelves, when the Bishop of Puebla, Juan de Palafox, renewed the campaign for the secularization of parishes in his diocese, and became embroiled in a violent dispute with the Jesuits over their refusal to pay tithes. Once again the viceroyalty lurched into a major political crisis, with Palafox receiving the acclaim of the creoles, not least for his efforts to open up to them parishes controlled by religious orders which too often seemed unresponsive to creole aspirations.[90] Yet, if animosity and vituperation abounded, the church could call on vast reserves of loyalty in a society where the Inquisition – less energetic than its peninsular counterpart[91] – exercised its policing activities over a colonial population well insulated from the danger of competing faiths by geography and the strict control of emigration in Seville.

The loyalty was inculcated from an early age by a church whose doctrines and ceremonial were woven deeply into the fabric of daily life. The wealth generated by the mining economies of the two viceroyalties made it possible to sustain a continuing programme of church building and refurbishing. In the nine years following his nomination as Bishop of Puebla in 1640, Palafox brought to a triumphant conclusion the construction of the city's magnificent cathedral, with the use of a labour force of 1,500 and at a cost of 350,000 pesos. This most austere of men had no compunction in devoting massive resources to a building that would proclaim to the world the glory of God and the power of His church.[92] Everywhere, elaborate altarpieces and a profusion of images were the order of the day. Of the churches in Mexico City in the 1620s Thomas Gage wrote:

There are not above fifty churches and chapels, cloisters and nunneries, and parish churches in that city, but those that are there are the fairest that ever my eyes beheld. The roofs and beams are in many of them all daubed with gold. Many altars have sundry marble pillars, and others are decorated with brazilwood stays standing one above another with tabernacles for several saints richly wrought with golden colors, so that twenty thousand ducats is a common price of many of them. These cause admiration in the common sort of people, and admiration brings on daily adoration in them to these glorious spectacles and images of saints.[93]

The spectacle was carried out of the church doors into the streets in the innumerable processions which filled the liturgical year. Writing of the cult in Lima in his *Compendium and Description of the West Indies*, the early seventeenth-century cosmographer Antonio Vázquez de Espinosa observed that 'in few parts of Christendom is the Holy Sacrament brought out to such an accompaniment, both of priests . . . and populace . . . all in a vast concourse, and with universal devotion at whatever hour of day or night . . .' (fig. 22).[94] The participation in these great processions not only of the civil and ecclesiastical authorities but also of the guilds and confraternities, competing with each other in the liberality of their contributions and the splendour of their floats, helped further to lock great sections of the populace into the ceremonial apparatus – and, with it, the ideology – of a state church in a church state.[95]

Inevitably the construction and adornment of churches, the maintenance of the cult and the upkeep of a large and imposing clerical establishment made continuing demands on the energy and resources of colonial society, of a weight and on a scale simply not to be found in British North America. Tithes, conceded in perpetuity by the papal bull of 1501 for the upkeep of the church in the Indies, were the foundation of the church's finances.[96] Even if there was continuing uncertainty and confusion over the liability for tithes of land held by Indians,[97] the growth of a prosperous agricultural economy meant a large and continuous flow of funds into the coffers of the church. These were supplemented by the usual fees for baptisms, weddings, funerals and other ecclesiastical services. The religious orders were dependent on alms-giving and charity, and their activities were financed by a vast outpouring of donations and pious bequests from creoles, mestizos and Indians alike.[98]

The willingness of this population to found chaplaincies and convents, endow masses in perpetuity and leave property in its wills for the support of religious and charitable activities was both an expression of its devotion to a particular order or cult, and a form of spiritual investment promising longer-term if less immediately tangible benefits than the appropriation of wealth for secular activities. Founders and patrons of convents, for instance, could expect constant prayers to be offered up for the salvation of their souls and those of their family. In a society, too, in which identities were affirmed and status measured by conspicuous expenditure, spectacular expressions of piety performed an essential social function. Religion, status and reputation were intimately related and mutually reinforcing in Spanish American colonial society, and the pious benefactions which created a close association between a family and a particular religious institution bought for it not only spiritual benefits but also social prestige.[99]

But there were other, and more easily calculated benefits, too, to be gained from investment in the faith. As a result of the continuous flow of gifts and legacies, the church, in its various branches, became a property-owner on a massive scale. By the end of the colonial period 47 per cent of urban property in Mexico City belonged to the church,[100] and the religious orders, with the exception of the Franciscans, acquired large tracts of profitable land through donations, purchase and transfers.[101] By the time of their expulsion in the eighteenth century the Jesuits, as the most successful landowners of all, owned over 400 large haciendas in America, and controlled at least 10 per cent of the agricultural land of what is now Ecuador.[102] Religious institutions thus became involved, either directly or indirectly, in estate management, and were often liable to find themselves with funds surplus to their immediate needs. With money to spare, once they had met the obligation imposed on them by the Council of Trent to be self-financing, they naturally sought outlets for the investment of their surplus capital. As a result, even in seventeenth-century Peru, unique in Spanish America for its seven public banks founded between 1608 and 1642, the church emerged during the course of the seventeenth century as a major – and frequently *the* major – supplier of credit in a society short on liquidity.[103] Landowners, merchants and mining entrepreneurs would turn to ecclesiastical institutions for loans, in order to invest in new enterprises or simply to keep afloat, and those already possessing close family links with some religious foundation – through patronage, endowments and the presence of relatives as friars and nuns[104] – clearly enjoyed privileged access to the facilities they could offer.

Since church teaching on usury made it impossible for convents and other religious institutions to advance money on interest, an alternative device – the *censo al quitar* – was imported from Spain. The prospective borrower, offering the institution a *censo* or fixed rent on a piece of property, effectively contracted to provide it with an annual return, disguised as an annuity payment, on the sum advanced. The rate of return, which was fixed by the crown, stood at 7.14 per cent in the later sixteenth century, but was reduced to 5 per cent by a royal decree of 1621.[105] The collateral was provided by real estate. This had major implications for the colonial economy. The owners of haciendas and rural estates might find up to 60 or 70 per cent of the value of their properties swallowed up in payments to the church.[106] Not all of this burden was the result of borrowing. A significant portion came from the encumbering of properties with *censos* established for the upkeep of *capellanías* or endowed chantry funds which would pay a priest to say a number of masses every year for the soul of the founder and other family members.[107] But in both instances the effect was to channel rural wealth into the cities for the upkeep of urban clerics; and failure to meet the annual payments on loans could result in the passing into ecclesiastical hands of the property used as a collateral.

Already by the end of the sixteenth century concern was being expressed about the massive accumulation of real estate by the church,[108] but it was not until the eighteenth century and the introduction of the Bourbon reforms that its power and resources would be clipped. The effects of mortmain, however, were not as uniformly negative as the eighteenth-century reformers liked to assert. If the various agencies of the church absorbed a substantial proportion of colonial resources, these at least remained in the Indies themselves, whereas the bulk of the crown's American revenues were remitted to Spain.[109] Within the Indies, the church's assets could benefit the local economy in various ways. It was in its own right a large-scale employer of labour, for the construction of cathedrals, churches and convents, while the credit facilities that it was able to offer could be used to finance economically or socially productive projects. The religious foundations, too, could be highly efficient landowners. In general they placed their rural estates in the hands of administrators, but the Jesuits preferred to involve themselves directly in exploiting the possibilities of the agricultural and grazing lands that passed into their possession, and proved themselves shrewd business managers when it came to developing important enterprises like sugar mills and textile workshops.[110]

The income generated by these various activities was used to support not only the religious houses themselves but also hospitals, charitable works, missions and colleges. The educational system in Spanish America was overwhelmingly in clerical hands. The first university in the Americas, that of Santo Domingo, was a Dominican foundation of 1538. The universities of San Marcos in Lima (1551) and of Mexico City (1553), although royal foundations, were also the outcome of initiatives by the religious orders and were intended both as bastions of orthodoxy and as training-grounds for the clergy. On the model of the university of Salamanca, however, they contained faculties of law, medicine and arts, in addition to the faculty of theology.[111] At the level of primary education, while the religious orders made an intensive effort to provide instruction for the indigenous population, and especially for the sons of the Indian nobility,[112] their schools and colleges also played an important part in the education of the sons (and to some extent also the daughters) of creoles. These were supplemented by private schools, perhaps set up by unbeneficed clerics and bachelors of arts newly arrived from Spain.[113]

Much of the teaching probably consisted of little more than instruction in the catechism, accompanied by the rudiments of reading and writing. The educational scene in Spanish America, however, was transformed by the arrival of the Jesuits in the later sixteenth century. With indigenous education already in the hands of the mendicant orders, the Jesuits turned their attention to the cities and to the unsatisfied demand of the creoles for instruction for their children. Moving into territory that had until now belonged largely to the Dominicans, the Jesuits created a network of colleges that spanned the cities and towns of Spanish America. These colleges were designed to provide creole boys, and especially the sons of the elite, with secondary education to a high standard, but many also included provision for elementary education where existing teaching arrangements were considered inadequate. The Jesuits' domination of creole education, often from the earliest years to university level, meant that a substantial section of the elite in the Spanish viceroyalties emerged from their years of schooling solidly grounded in the forms of learning and thinking prescribed by a fixed pedagogical system, the *ratio studiorum*. Uniformity of method was accompanied by uniformity of content, which assimilated the humanist tradition of classical studies within an officially approved theological framework. Whatever its other merits the system was not one that provided space for dissenting opinions or for individual responses to the challenge presented by exposure to disturbing new ideas.[114]

Education and the confessional enabled the secular clergy and the religious orders, assisted by the Inquisition, to keep a close watch on the movement of thought. The high premium placed on conformity in the Spain of the Counter-Reformation was carried over by a natural extension to its transatlantic possessions, as constituent territories of a global *monarquía* which saw its mission as the defence of the faith against the assaults of Protestantism, Judaism and Islam. The religious culture of the American viceroyalties therefore tended to replicate, often in extravagant form as if they were struggling to assert their own distinctive identity through the display of exemplary orthodoxy, that of the mother country to which they were intellectually, emotionally and psychologically tied. The printing press, it was true, came relatively early to Spanish America. At the request of Fray Juan de Zumárraga, Bishop of Mexico, the house of Cromberger in Seville agreed to set up a press in Mexico City in 1539, eighteen years after the conquest.[115] Lima acquired its first publishing house in 1583, and was followed by La Paz in 1610 and Puebla in 1640,[116] two years after the first press in British North America was set up in Cambridge, Massachusetts.[117] These presses, however, were primarily devoted to the printing of religious manuals, catechisms, grammars, dictionaries and other works needed for the evangelization of the Indians, and the reading public remained overwhelmingly dependent, both for its religious and secular literature, on books imported from Spain.

The transatlantic movement of books, like that of people, was regulated in Seville with much bureaucracy and not a little inefficiency. Popular and fictional literature came under the purview of the secular authorities, which, notoriously, placed a ban in 1531 on the export of romances of chivalry to the Indies as being likely to corrupt the minds of the Indians.[118] The Inquisition, for its part, was solely concerned with the circulation of books prohibited on theological grounds. Inevitably conflicts of jurisdiction arose between the officials of the Holy Office and those of Seville's House of Trade. The frequent repetition of orders controlling and restricting the shipment of books, together with surviving inventories of the contents of private libraries in the viceroyalties themselves, make it clear that the orders were widely ignored. Even a decree of 1550 ordering that in future officials of the House of Trade should register books item by item rather than simply by bulk consignments failed to stop the contraband, and the operation continued to be undermined by laxity and fraud among the officials of the agencies involved in the inspection and registration of books for the Indies.[119]

By licit or illicit means, therefore, peninsular booksellers were able to supply their lucrative market in the Indies with most of the books, permitted and forbidden, which circulated covertly or openly in Spain itself. But, as in Spain, restrictions and prohibitions, combined with the dangers and difficulties of access to theologically unacceptable works, had the effect of closing off to the reading public wide areas of religious thought. Protestant writings, unless they were to be used by select individuals for the purpose of refutation, were ruled out on principle. So, too, was the Bible in the vernacular. Clerics and select laymen, however, were allowed access to the Bible in Latin, the Vulgate.[120] Yet even this seems to have reached the Indies in relatively small quantities. In 1584 a Spanish bookseller, Ricardo Boyer, was in negotiation with an agent in Mexico City for the sale in the Indies of two hundred copies of the Bible with notes and commentaries by François Vatable, published in Salamanca that year, out of a stock of one thousand that was entirely in his hands. But the agent seems to have found the price of fourteen ducats high, and Vatable's commentary ran into serious problems with the Inquisition.[121] In any event, Bibles did not figure heavily in the large amount of religious literature exported to the Indies – only three copies were included among the books registered in 1583 to 1584[122] – and the mass of the laity is likely to have acquired only at second hand, through sermons and the reading of selected texts and commentaries, such biblical knowledge as it possessed.

By doing its best to seal off its American possessions from heterodox opinions, the Spanish crown in alliance with the church effectively instilled into them the sense of forming part of a moral community resting on the immutable principles of divine and natural law. The character and boundaries of this community were determined by the Aristotelian and neo-Thomist philosophy which was the dominant cast of thought in Counter-Reformation Spain. It was a philosophy that was deeply sceptical of innovation, and heavily reliant on a set of authoritative texts. It placed a high premium on unity and consensus – a consensus based on the precepts of natural law rather than the movements of individual conscience, and which had as its overriding aim the furtherance of the common good. It elevated order above liberty, obligations above rights, and entrusted the maintenance of justice and good government within a hierarchically structured society to a monarch in whom the people had vested their sovereignty but who remained bound in conscience to conform to the dictates of divine and human law.[123]

These beliefs, and the attitudes and assumptions that sprang from them, shaped the mental universe of Spanish American society during the three centuries of colonial life. It was a universe in which a variety of opinions could be, and were, expressed – for instance on such controversial issues as the status of the Indians. But they were opinions that emerged from, and remained within, a frame of reference that had been patiently constructed by generations of theologians and moralists, and given its definitive form by the Council of Trent. The dogma, once proclaimed, was immutable, and would be sustained in Spain and its American territories by the full weight of ecclesiastical and secular authority.

A plurality of creeds

The authority that was stamped across the face of Spanish America had no counterpart in the British territories to the north. The Protestant Reformation which gave them their religious colouring had begun as a movement of protest against one supreme authority, that of Rome, in the name of a higher authority, that of the Word. The outcome was a variety of creeds and confessions, which, even if seeking to impose their own authority by such devices as the creation of a new clerical elite and dependence on the coercive powers of the state, were themselves consistently open to challenge from those who found justification for their objections in their own unmediated interpretation of the Scriptures. At the same time, the newly emerging doctrinal traditions, Lutheran, Calvinist and Anglican, had been forced to take into account the diversity of interpretations to which certain key passages in the Scriptures lent themselves, and in the effort to accommodate them had constructed orthodoxies rich enough to allow of a range of possibilities on such fundamental questions as grace and salvation. This offered endless scope for debate, disagreement and creative construction among ministers and laity, thus complicating still further the task of maintaining a rigid control over the movement of inquiry and belief.[124]

The fissiparous character of Protestantism was compounded in British America by the fissiparous character of the process of settlement and colonization. Two distinctive forms of English religion laid claim to official status in their respective territories during the first decades of settlement, Anglicanism in Virginia and Congregationalism in New England. The terms of their charter made it impossible for the Roman Catholics to do the same in Maryland, where in any event they were in too much of a minority to be able to impose their faith. This left the way open in the colony for the coexistence of several different creeds.

Although Anglicanism was to be the official faith of Virginia, the crippling weakness of the Anglican establishment during the formative years of the colony[125] ruled out any possibility that the institutionalization of religion would proceed under strong clerical leadership. The late seventeenth century would see the beginnings of an Anglican renaissance in Virginia and several other colonies,[126] but by that time the nature of the church–state union which governed Virginia's religious life had already been determined. It was a union in which the initiative rested with the laity in their capacity as vestrymen, and not with the parsons, who – under a system unique among the mainland colonies except for Maryland – depended for their salaries on a colony-wide church tax.[127] Few in number, and coming, as the majority of them did, directly from England, they lacked the support that might have been provided by local knowledge and connections, and were not well placed to shake Virginian society out of the spiritual torpor which had settled upon it during the early stages of the colony's development.[128]

Writing in 1697, James Blair, a Scot who had been appointed commissary of the Bishop of London in a bid by the Anglican church to revitalize its establishment in America, reported scathingly on the temper of life in Virginia: 'For well-educated children, for an industrious and thriving people, or for an happy government in church and state, and in short for all other advantages of human improvements, it is certainly . . . one of the poorest, miserablest, and worst countries in all America that is inhabited by Christians.'[129] In fact, even as he wrote, the 'improvements' for which he hankered were already under way. These owed much to his own efforts, and to the support that he received from the Bishop of London. But they also reflected the desire of the emerging planter elite to establish their volatile society on firmer foundations. In 1693 the College of William and Mary was founded under royal charter, with Blair as its first president. 'It was a great Satisfaction to the Archbishops and Bishops', wrote Robert Beverley in his *History and Present State of Virginia* a few years later, 'to see such a Nursery of Religion founded in that New World; especially for that it was begun in an Episcopal Way, and carried on wholly by zealous Conformists to the Ch. of England.'[130]

The Anglican church now had its own seminary in America for the training of clergy 'in an Episcopal Way', potentially creating a rival establishment to New England's Harvard College, which had been producing Puritan ministers since its foundation in 1636. As with the first universities in New Spain and Peru, the religious impetus behind the foundation of the two colleges did not exclude provision for the education of the laity. The lack of towns and the dispersed nature of settlement presented particular problems for the provision of adequate schooling in Virginia. Although some parents would continue to send their sons to England to be educated, the College of William and Mary, benefiting from the transfer of Virginia's capital in 1699 from the insalubrious Jamestown to what became the handsome new capital of Williamsburg, offered a socially acceptable and less expensive answer to the educational needs of the colony's elite. The sons of the new planter class emerged from their schooling as good Anglican gentlemen whose very visible presence at Sunday morning services made it clear to clergy and congregation alike who were the masters in colonial Virginia. As a seminary, however, for the training of Anglican clergy to minister to the spiritual needs of the Chesapeake region, it failed to live up to the hopes of its founders. An anti-clerical Board of Visitors entertained more secular ambitions for Virginia's only college.[131]

If a godly state was to be founded in British America, it would not be on the Chesapeake, but further to the north. The Puritans brought with them from England to the northern settlements a clear vision of the kind of community they wished to see established, although a much less clear one of the character of the relationship between ministers and laity on which its success would depend. In conformity with Calvin's own teachings, a godly state postulated a system in which church and state were two equal but separate entities, although harmo-niously conjoined in the common enterprise of serving God's purpose. The immi-grants' unhappy experience of the consequences of mixing the spiritual with the temporal in the country they had left behind them only served to reinforce their determination to prevent the re-creation in America of the apparatus of ecclesi-astical power within a church–state alliance, of the kind which had caused them such suffering at home. Ministers, therefore, were – at least in principle – to exer-cise no temporal power, and the church handed over to the state such functions as the regularizing of marriages and the probating of wills, which in England fell within its province. For its part, the civil government of Massachusetts would have a broad jurisdiction over religious and moral offences, but would exercise it independently of the churches, and would not interfere in the disciplining of church members, which was the responsibility of the churches themselves.[132]

Discipline was regarded as fundamental if the errand were not simply to dis-solve in the wilderness, but how it was to be maintained was not entirely clear. Reproof and correction were powerful moral sanctions in churches where the evi-dence of saving grace was a requirement for membership; but excommunication involved no civil penalties, and merely added the excommunicated to the large numbers outside who for one reason or another were deemed unworthy of taking their place among the ranks of the saints.

In a system which thus relied essentially on self-imposed and collectively rein-forced discipline, the spiritual leadership and moral authority of the ministry acquired particular importance. In early New England, congregations which had been through deep waters with their ministers had a natural tendency to look to them for guidance. As a result, they often came to dominate their churches, some of them acquiring in the process the arrogance of power.[133] But what was their exact status and the extent of their authority? All of them were elected by their congregations, but at the heart of the Protestant tradition lay an unresolved dilemma as to how far a minister drew his authority from his congregation and how far he derived it from membership in a sacred order.[134]

This question became acute as the New England churches were caught up in vigorous internal debate about the criteria for church membership and about whether the ministry should devote its efforts to converting the unregenerate or to nurturing the spiritual growth of the members themselves.[135] Discord rent the churches of Massachusetts and Connecticut as congregations accustomed to exercising their own authority in the running of their churches came into conflict with ministers who claimed that they were entitled to a unique position by virtue of the ministerial call. Any attempt by ministers to determine controversial questions in occasional ministerial meetings and synods was liable to lay them open to the charge that they were subverting the cherished ideal of congregational independence. The presence in New England of a vociferous Presbyterian minority added substance to the fears that the Congregational way could be replaced by the Presbyterian system of church government, with its hierarchy of presbyteries, synods and assembly above the congregations.[136]

The doctrinal disagreements, the feuds and the quarrelling came against a backdrop of falling church membership, the result partly of the rise in New England's population and partly of the discouraging obstacles to membership imposed by the churches themselves. By 1650 half the adult male population of Boston was outside the church.[137] The Half-Way Covenant of 1662 was designed to remedy this disturbing situation by making church membership more accessible, but was rejected by congregations concerned that the new proposals would lead to a relaxation of the high standards that they themselves had met. As membership fell, and the churches increasingly turned in on themselves in their preoccupation with maintaining their denominational purity, the new generation of Harvard-trained ministers laid the blame for setbacks on the failings of their congregations, while themselves being uneasily conscious of the distance between their own spiritual stature and that of the heroic generation of ministers that was now passing away.[138]

If many ministers still retained their dominance over their congregations, the spiritual leadership of a whole society which they had once envisaged was slipping from their grasp. Too many of them could agree neither with each other nor with their congregations, while the world around them was visibly being transformed. On the one hand they were confronted by religious indifference among too many of the new immigrants, and on the other by the growing religious pluralism of the surrounding society. Not only had the Restoration of 1660 given the Church of England a new assertiveness, but the sects that had sprung to life and flourished in England during the Civil War period – notably the Quakers and the Baptists – had crossed the Atlantic to provide increasingly vigorous competition to the Anglican and Congregational churches alike.

The very character of settlement in British North America made it impossible in the long run for orthodoxy, whether of the Anglican or the Congregationalist variety, to hold the line against the encroachment of new sects and new beliefs. Already in the 1630s Roger Williams, following sharp disagreements with his colleagues, had removed from Massachusetts to found a settlement in Rhode Island that promised full liberty of conscience. This alone, he believed, could guarantee the true separation of church and state, in place of the equivocal form of separation that he deplored in the Bay Colony. North America provided ample space for religious initiatives of this kind, and each new colony had its own religious climate, which could well prove attractive to those who for one reason or another were dissatisfied with what they found on offer in their own place of settlement. A trickle of colonists from Massachusetts, for instance, began moving into the Connecticut River Valley in 1635–6 under the leadership of Thomas Hooker, who objected to the restrictiveness and rigidity of the approach to church membership that was being adopted by John Cotton of Boston and his fellow ministers.[139] A generation later a further migration from Massachusetts occurred, this time of Presbyterians into neighbouring New Netherland/New York, where the Dutch Reformed Church offered them a system of church government more to their liking.[140]

The method of founding colonies through the grant of a royal charter provided obvious openings for minority faiths, as the Catholic proprietors of Maryland had demonstrated before the Civil War. In the 1670s the Quakers sought to take advantage of the proprietary system in East and West Jersey. They did so again, and to considerably greater effect, when William Penn secured a charter from Charles II for the founding of his new colony of Pennsylvania in 1681. There were many 'holy experiments' on American soil, running from the millennial kingdom of the Franciscans in New Spain and the Jesuit missions in Paraguay to New England's 'city on a hill' and the ideal communities that began to proliferate from the late seventeenth century onwards with the arrival in America of Protestant evangelical and pietist sects – Mennonites, Amish, Moravians and others. Pennsylvania, however, stands out for the breadth and practicality of its original conception, and the potential that it offered for creative change in the society that surrounded it. The tendency of 'holy experiments' is to create closed systems as a result of their single-minded pursuit of a supreme ideal. Penn's holy experiment had the opposite effect of encouraging the development of an open and tolerant society. The result was an impact that would eventually be felt throughout the western world.[141]

In the eyes of William Penn and his fellow Quakers the 'Inner Light' that guided them was not simply reserved for a select few but was to be found in everyone. This meant that the new colony, unlike Massachusetts, was designed from the start not only as a place of refuge for persecuted members of a single religious group but for all believers in God who wished to live together in harmony and fellowship. Liberty of conscience was to be its guiding light. The idealism, however, was accompanied by a strongly practical approach. In founding his colony, Penn could draw on his close connections with the world of the court and of business, and also on previous colonial experience through his proprietary interest in Quaker settlements in West Jersey. Although a strong partisan of liberty, he had somehow to devise a frame of government for his new colony that would balance the conflicting demands of liberty, order and his own interests as proprietor. This was something that the Fundamental Constitution prepared for Carolina by the Earl of Shaftesbury and John Locke in 1669 had failed to achieve, and it was a goal that he, too, would find frustratingly elusive.

Earlier attempts at colonization had made clear the need for substantial and continuing investment from the mother country during the early stages of settlement, and Penn's skilful promotional campaign netted six hundred investors.[142] Both they and potential immigrants had to be assured that economic prospects for the future colony were sound. The 45,000 square miles of land so cavalierly signed away to him by Charles II under the flattering name of Pennsylvania proved to be ideal for attracting the kind of hard-working, self-reliant and godly settlers whom he saw as the mainstay of his colony. The fertile soil of the Delaware Valley and the Piedmont hills offered perfect opportunities for the farmers, who, as small landowners, would constitute the backbone of his agrarian utopia. They would also need an Atlantic port to export their produce and receive supplies from Britain. The excellent location of Philadelphia on the banks of the river Delaware promised easy trading connections with the West Indies and the wider Atlantic world.[143]

Drawing on his close relationship with the extended Quaker merchant community, Penn was able to launch his new colony in style, with the despatch over the course of 1682–3 of some fifty ships carrying four thousand settlers and ample supplies. He was concerned from the start to build up peaceful relations with the native Americans by negotiating land deals, in advance of any settlement, with the sparsely settled Delaware Indians, whom he described as 'a Careless, Merry People yet in Property strict with us'.[144] If planning alone could build a New Zion in America, then the one now being founded on the banks of the Delaware had a better chance of succeeding than any of its predecessors.

In the event, many of the high expectations, including those of Penn himself, were to be defrauded. The cumbersome Frame of Government that he drew up in 1682 failed to create the kind of well-ordered but free society which he had envisaged. Faced with a virtually unlimited expanse of rich and fertile land, Quakers succumbed as easily as less godly settlers elsewhere in North America to the fever of land hunger and land speculation. An elite of merchants and larger landowners emerged to block the founder's efforts to shape and control the development of the infant colony; and the anti-authoritarian attitudes inherent in the religious culture of the Society of Friends was hardly sympathetic to direction from above. As Penn discovered to his cost, it was not easy to be the proprietor of a colony in which access to the Inner Light was regarded as a universal birthright. Nor did political and social harmony follow automatically from the Society's practice of seeking consensus by way of long and scrupulous deliberation. There was feuding between Quakers and Anglicans, and bitter disagreement between the elite and those who discovered that, even in a society based on spiritual equality, socially at least some were more equal than others.[145] Religiously, too, an already divided community was subjected to further splintering soon after a Scottish Quaker, George Keith, arrived from the Jerseys in 1689 to become the head of Philadelphia's Latin School. By directly challenging the authority of travelling Quaker ministers, known as Public Friends, with his plans for stricter discipline and his insistence on the importance of the Scriptures to salvation, he plunged the Society into schism.[146]

Yet for all the turmoil in Pennsylvania's politics and religion in the 1680s and 1690s, the colony, if not exactly a New Zion, had at least the makings of an unusual and promising experiment. Penn had travelled through the Rhineland as a missionary in 1677, and his recruitment campaign in the early 1680s was directed not only to the British Isles but also to Holland and Germany. The Quaker network, extending to continental Europe, was to prove crucial for establishing the future direction of the colony. Leaving the continent through the port of Rotterdam, a group of Quakers and other religious dissenters from German-speaking territories established a settlement at Germantown in 1683. The signal had been given. Pennsylvania stood ready to welcome all those who wanted to escape the constraints of the Old World for the sake of a better life in the New, irrespective of their creed or nationality.

Although the name 'Germantown' was symbolic of what the future held in store, Germans would not in fact begin immigrating in large numbers until the late 1720s, many of them attracted to Pennsylvania as much by its economic as its religious possibilities.[147] From the start, however, Pennsylvania offered itself as a haven both for the economically aspiring and the religiously distressed. As the news spread back in Europe, a growing stream of immigrants, many of them arriving with their families, landed in Philadelphia to build for themselves new and better lives – British and Dutch Quakers, Huguenots expelled from the France of Louis XIV, Mennonites from Holland and the Rhineland, Lutherans and Calvinists from south-west Germany. As prospective settlers they looked forward to establishing their own independent family farms, which they would build up through hard work and mutual support. As God-fearing Protestants, they would enjoy, many of them for the first time, the right to worship as they wished, without fear of persecution.

In embarking on a 'holy experiment' for the harmonious coexistence of peoples of different nationalities and adherents of all faiths, Penn was foreshadowing the religiously and ethnically pluralist society that British North America would in due course become. At the time of Pennsylvania's foundation, toleration in many colonies was at best only grudging, but the lack of any effective mechanism for the enforcement of orthodoxy left them with no option but to move, however hesitantly, down the road that would lead, as in Pennsylvania, to free religious choice.

The great changes in England produced by the Glorious Revolution and the Toleration Act of 1689 provided additional sanction for the route that was being taken. It is true that the Toleration Act was a strictly limited measure. In Maryland in the wake of the Glorious Revolution, Roman Catholics were progressively barred from public life, and eventually, in 1718, lost their right to vote. Similarly, in 1705 the Pennsylvania assembly was forced by pressure from the crown to exclude Roman Catholics, Jews and non-believers from the enjoyment of political rights.[148] Yet the Act represented a grudging recognition that uniformity of belief and practice was no longer regarded as indispensable for the survival of the British polity. As such it reflected what had long been the reality on both sides of the Atlantic. Dissenting Protestants had come to stay. So too, it seemed, had the Jews, whose tacit readmission to England by Cromwell had not been reversed by Charles II.

Since the middle years of the seventeenth century small communities of Sephardic Jews had been establishing themselves on mainland North America, initially in New Netherland, and then in 1658 in Newport.[149] The majority of them came by way of the British and Dutch Caribbean, to which a number had fled from Brazil after the Portuguese recovered it from the Dutch in 1654. The acceptance of their presence in the British colonies provided a neat counterpoint to the fate which overcame them or their brethren in the Iberian New World. Although from the beginnings of colonization the Spanish crown had prohibited the entry of Jews or New Christians (*conversos*) into its American possessions,[150] a continuous trickle of New Christians – among them the seven brothers of St Teresa of Avila[151] – managed to get through. Following the union of the crowns of Spain and Portugal in 1580 the policy of exclusion became virtually unworkable. New Christians, many of them covert Jews, had not only settled in Brazil but were also the dominant element among the Portuguese merchants who controlled the transatlantic slave trade, and they seized the opportunity offered by the union of the crowns to establish themselves in the Spanish American ports of Vera Cruz, Cartagena and Buenos Aires.[152] From here they infiltrated the viceroyalties of New Spain and Peru, where they became a significant presence, particularly in Lima.

Although the objects of constant suspicion by the Inquisition, which was always on the lookout for signs of Jewish practices, the New Christians clearly felt that the risks were well worth taking. There was obvious scope for profitable commercial activity in the silver-rich viceroyalties, and for at least sixty years after 1580 they made an important contribution to Spanish American economic life, some of them simply as small traders, shopkeepers and artisans, but others as wealthy merchants. Both as Portuguese and as suspected Jews, however, they were disliked and distrusted in the Spanish territories, where opinion hardened against them in the 1620s and 1630s. In 1639 Lima was the scene of an impressive *auto de fe*, and their vulnerability increased dramatically when the Portuguese revolution of 1640 dissolved the union of the crowns and anyone of Portuguese origin was liable to be regarded as a traitor. In Mexico alone some 150 'judaizers' were seized by the Inquisition in the early 1640s, and the anti-*converso* campaign reached its climax in the terrible 'great *auto de fe*' held in Mexico City on 11 April 1649, when thirteen of them were burnt at the stake, and twenty-nine abjured.[153]

Although sporadic trials of suspected crypto-Jews would continue into the eighteenth century, the great days of the clandestine Jewish presence in Spanish America were at an end. But, in part at least as a consequence, Jews were to find a fresh field for their enterprise and skills in a British America where there was no Inquisition to harass them, and no necessity to conceal their faith. Their coming, like that of the Quakers, added yet another distinctive piece to the patchwork quilt of creeds and cults that was beginning to cover the north Atlantic seaboard.

With a growing diversity of faiths, British American religion at the end of the seventeenth century stood in a very different relationship to both society and the state from that which prevailed in the American territories of the Spanish crown. Orthodoxy, whether of the Anglican or Congregationalist variety, had failed to impose itself. The apparatus of an ecclesiastical establishment, in the form of a clerical hierarchy, church courts and a regularized system of taxation for the payment of the ministry and the propagation of the faith, was notable by its absence. Religious pluralism, more or less tolerated, was becoming the order of the day. As a result, the clergy were having to compete with each other in an increasingly crowded market-place. Nor was it easy for them to assert their authority in a diversified and often vociferous lay society, some of whose members resolutely refused to recognize them as special conduits of grace and found in the inspiration of the Holy Word, or an Inner Light, a sufficient guide to salvation.

The implications of all this for the development of colonial society were profound. Religious diversity reinforced the political diversity that was already such a striking feature of British American colonial life. The collective Puritan ideal of ordered liberty, which was enshrined in the 'Body of Liberties' adopted by the General Court of Massachusetts in 1641, inspired a style of political life very different from that of Anglican Virginia, where 'liberty' involved, at least for the governing class, a minimum of restraint.[154] In the Middle Colonies religious diversity, coming on top of a growing social and ethnic diversity as Scottish, Scottish-Irish, French and German immigrants began arriving in increasing numbers, contributed to the political instability of the region as a whole.[155]

The unstable combination of religious and political diversity enhances the impression of British America as an atomized society in a continuous state of turmoil. At first sight this appears truer of the Middle Colonies and the Chesapeake than of New England, where the collective values and ideals of a covenanted people had struck deep roots, and where the magistrates continued to take with extreme seriousness their duty to support the church and ensure that the people remained true to the terms of the covenant. Yet even New England had never been the tranquil society which its own historians liked to depict, and the collective discipline of a godly state was always fragile and precarious.[156]

The turmoil and confusion, however, also reflected the vitality of New World Protestantism, made up as it was of unresolved tensions – between institutionalized authority and the free movement of the spirit, between the aspirations of individuals and those of the group with which they had entered into a voluntary association. These tensions offered the prospect both of continual spiritual turmoil and of no less continual spiritual renewal as the pendulum of religious life swung between institutional attempts to impose discipline and spontaneous outbursts of revivalist enthusiasm imbued with millenarian hopes.

In so far as the tensions were capable of resolution, they would find it in the shared biblical culture that was the foundation of religious life in British North America. The Bible was to be found everywhere – in the libraries of Virginian gentlemen, and in the households of New England, which might possess it in two formats, 'great' and small.[157] Since the university presses of Oxford and Cambridge held the monopoly printing rights, colonial printers were not allowed to publish it, although the newly founded press in Cambridge, Massachusetts, exploited a loophole in the legislation to produce in 1640 the first printing of what was to be the extremely popular 'Bay Psalm Book'.[158] Virginia had no permanent printing press until 1730 and, like New England, imported its Bibles, along with much other religious literature, from England.[159] If the high cost of book imports kept sales down, the Bible was an overwhelming priority. The language and the culture of the colonies were infused with biblical references and turns of phrase, and white children in eighteenth-century Virginia would use Bibles for their reading primers.[160]

A biblical culture encouraged literacy and gave an impetus to schooling, both private and public. Behind the laws passed in Virginia and New England in the 1640s for the promotion of schooling there may well have lurked an anxious preoccupation with the upholding of standards of civility in a remote and savage environment,[161] but religion was integral to civility. 'If we nourish not learning,' wrote John Eliot as plans for the foundation of Harvard College were being mooted, 'both church and commonwealth will sink.'[162] The prime responsibility for the training of the young lay with the family, as the Massachusetts statute of 1642 made clear in reminding parents and the masters of servants of their duty to ensure that the young were able 'to read and understand the principles of religion and the capital laws of this country'. Further legislation in the same decade ordered that each family should engage in weekly catechizing, but also made provision for formal schooling in every town of over fifty families.[163]

The early commitment to education in New England and Virginia, as reflected in their legislation, left an enduring legacy,[164] but its effects are difficult to measure. In Virginia, where schooling was so difficult to organize, literacy among white males, as measured by the ability to sign rather than simply make a mark, rose from 46 per cent in the 1640s to 62 per cent around 1710.[165] In New England, by the same criterion, 60 per cent of adult men and 30 per cent of adult women were literate in 1660, although this form of measurement would class as 'illiterate' many who, if they could not write their names, may well have learnt the rudiments of reading.[166] By 1750 literacy in New England would approach 70 per cent among men and 45 per cent among women – exceptionally high figures by the standards of contemporary Europe.[167] Unfortunately, no literacy figures are available for the creole population of the Spanish American viceroyalties. Letters from sixteenth-century settlers writing home to friends and relatives make a point of emphasizing the opportunities for immigrants who could read and write;[168] but for all the efforts of the Jesuits it seems doubtful whether, even in the cities, where education was at its strongest and literacy was seen as a means of social ascent, literacy rates among creoles approached those attained in the British colonies by the late seventeenth century.

A biblical culture obviously provided the mass of the population with a strong incentive to achieve an entry into the world of print. A member of the party of

Spaniards shipwrecked on Bermuda in 1639 noted how 'men, women, youths, boys and girls, and even children all carry their books to church' for Sunday morning and evening services. It is impossible to know how many of the congregation were actually able to follow on the printed page the passage read aloud by the minister, but the sight was a novel one to the Spaniard, who was impressed by the 'silent devoutness' of the congregation.[169]

If the surprise expressed by the shipwrecked Spaniard testifies to Hispanic ignorance of the character of the Protestant society that was emerging in British North America, British North Americans were at least as ignorant of the Hispanic societies to the south of them. Contacts between the two worlds were becoming more frequent, especially as clandestine trading relations developed with the Spanish Caribbean islands; and the founding of South Carolina meant that a group of British settlers now found themselves closer to Spanish St Augustine than to the Chesapeake settlements of their own compatriots. 'We are here in the very chaps of the Spaniard,' wrote a settler to one of the Carolina proprietors, Lord Ashley, the future Earl of Shaftesbury.[170] But greater proximity did not necessarily bring with it a greater understanding.

Mutual perceptions had been shaped by stereotyped images developed over the course of a century of Anglo-Spanish conflict and were liable to be periodically reinforced by some new incident or publication.[171] Oliver Cromwell, whose anti-Spanish attitudes were those of an Elizabethan gentleman, was encouraged in his ambitious Western Design by Thomas Gage, whose *The English-American* first appeared in 1648, and was subsequently republished three times before the end of the century.[172] Partly no doubt to reinforce his credentials as an enthusiastic convert from Rome to Anglicanism, Gage misleadingly presented Spanish America as a fruit ripe for the picking. But he also gave a vivid first-hand account of life in New Spain – the first such account of any substance to come from a non-Spanish source. His descriptions of convent life were appropriately lurid, and amply confirmed Protestant assumptions about the scandals and depravity of the Roman church.

One New Englander who owned a copy of Gage was Cotton Mather.[173] Reading the book, Mather could hardly fail to be struck by the contrast between the sobriety of his own society, for all the many failings that he so constantly lamented, and the episodes of wickedness and debauchery retailed by Gage in the course of his travels in central America, where 'worldliness' was 'too too much embraced by such as had renounced and forsaken the world and all its pleasures, sports, and pastimes'.[174] To a man of Mather's spirit, the contrast could only have opened up a vista of new opportunities. 'I found in myself', he wrote in 1696, 'a strong inclination to learn the *Spanish* language, and in that Language transmitt Catechisms, and Confessions, and other vehicles of the Protestant-Religion, into the *Spanish* Indies. Who can tell whether the Time for our Lord's taking possession of those Countreys, even the *sett Time* for it, bee not come?'[175]

In due course, after the Lord had wonderfully prospered him in his undertaking, Mather wrote and printed a tract, *La religión pura*, designed to bring the light of the gospel to the peoples of that benighted Spanish world.[176] In 1702, after he had been 'much engaged both in public and private Supplications, that the Lord would open a way for the Access of His glorious Gospel into the vast regions of the *Spanish America*', he received with excitement the news of the Grand Alliance against Bourbon France and Spain, with the commitment of the English and the Dutch to make themselves the masters, if they could, 'of the Countreys and Cities under the Dominion of Spain in the Indies'.[177] The day of redemption was surely close at hand.

Mather's hopes were not, after all, to be realized. There was more resilience in Spain's American possessions than he, or the Protestant world in general, could appreciate. Nor were all the comparisons necessarily to the advantage of the British colonies. Uniformity of faith had given Spanish America, for all its social and ethnic diversity, an inner cohesion that still eluded the British colonies. But could a society based on uniformity of faith adjust to new ideas? On the other hand, could a society with a diversity of creeds achieve stability? As the eighteenth century opened, the test was yet to come.

CHAPTER 8

Empire and Identity

Atlantic communities

On 20 October 1697, Samuel Sewall, who shared the hopes of his friend and fellow Bostonian, Cotton Mather, for the speedy conversion of Spain's dominions in America, went to Dorchester to wait on the Lieutenant Governor: 'breakfast together on Venison and Chockalatte: I said Massachuset and Mexico met at his Honour's Table.'[1] This gastronomic encounter of British and Spanish America at a Massachusetts breakfast table was a small, but symbolic, indicator of a larger process of transformation that was by now well under way: the creation of an integrated Atlantic world. It was a world in which the rivalries of European states increasingly impinged on the colonial societies of the Americas, and in which new relationships, both transatlantic and hemispheric, were being forged in response to the combined, and frequently conflicting, requirements of trade and war.

The accelerating process of contact and conflict within the framework of a developing Atlantic community sprang from developments on both sides of the Atlantic. In Europe, the middle and later decades of the seventeenth century were marked by profound shifts in the international balance of power. In the Americas, which found themselves caught up in the consequences of those shifts, they saw the consolidation of colonial societies as distinctive polities with their own unique characteristics – characteristics that differentiated them in important ways from the metropolitan societies that had given birth to them, and gave rise to fundamental questions of identity which would become increasingly insistent during the opening decades of the eighteenth century.

The massive change in the relationships of the great powers of Europe in the middle years of the seventeenth century was succinctly summarized by the English publicist and political theorist, Slingsby Bethel, in his *The Interest of Princes and States* (1680):

Formerly the affairs of Christendom were supposed to be chiefly swayed by the two great powers of Austria (wherein Spain is understood) and France: from whom other Princes and States derived their Peace and War, according to the several parties they adhered unto. But now the puissance of the former being so much abated, that it deserves no rank above its Neighbours, France of the two remains the only formidable Potentate, of whose greatness, all Princes and States are as much concerned to be jealous, as formerly they were of Austria.[2]

The revolts of the 1640s in Catalonia, Portugal, Sicily and Naples had shaken the Spanish Monarchy to its core. While it eventually managed to weather the storm, although at the expense of the permanent loss of Portugal and its overseas empire, its 'puissance', as Bethel observed, was 'much abated'. The signing of the Peace of the Pyrenees in 1659, which ended almost 25 years of Franco-Spanish conflict, marked the emergence of the France of Louis XIV as the dominant military power in Europe. 'Having now got the advantage of Spain,' wrote Bethel, France was aiming to 'improve it to an universal monarchy, as Spain formerly designed.' Great Britain and the Dutch Republic were understandably anxious. They had not fought for so long against Spanish world domination simply to exchange one tyrannical Roman Catholic power for another as the arbiter of Europe.

New confirmation of Spain's loss of global supremacy was to be found in the terms of the Anglo-Spanish Treaty of Madrid of 1670, in which, for the first time, Spain officially conceded full British 'sovereignty, ownership and possession' of 'all the lands, regions, islands, colonies and dominions, situated in the West Indies or in any part of America' held at that time by 'the King of Great Britain and his subjects'. This included Jamaica, seized by Cromwell fifteen years before.[3] The New World monopoly conferred on the Iberian monarchs by Alexander VI in 1493 thus lost its last shreds of international legitimacy. While the Spanish crown might still retain the bulk of its possessions on the American mainland, and the treasure fleets continue to return year after year to the Iberian peninsula with impressively large cargoes of silver, there was a widespread impression that Spain itself was in terminal decline.

Foreigners, following in the path of the Spanish *arbitristas*, made their own diagnoses of what had gone wrong. 'Spain', wrote Slingsby Bethel, 'is a clear demonstration that Mis-government, in suffering all manner of Frauds, and neglecting the Interest of a Nation, will soon bring the mightiest Kingdoms low, and lay their honour in the dust.'[4] In the eyes of Bethel and other contemporary British observers, misgovernment included a failure to grasp the nature of the relationship between population, prosperity and liberty. As Bethel pointed out with reference to the recent successes of the Dutch and the English, 'industry and ingenuity are not the effects of the barrenness of a country, oppression of the People, or want of Land . . . but the effects only of Justice, good laws and Liberty.'[5] The Spaniards had flouted the essential principles of good government by disregarding this fundamental truth, and were paying the inevitable price.

If Spain in the sixteenth century had furnished the model to be followed, now in the later seventeenth it was the model to be shunned. The encouragement of commerce, so neglected by the Spaniards, was coming to be seen as central to Britain's true interest. With the encouragement of commerce went a growing appreciation of the potential value to the mother country of its transatlantic colonies, although not everyone was persuaded of this. The pamphlet entitled *A Discourse of Trade* published by Roger Coke in 1670 feared that England was set on the same ruinous path as Spain. 'Ireland and our Plantations', he wrote, 'Rob us of all the growing Youth and Industry of the Nation, whereby it becomes weak and feeble, and the Strength, as well as Trade, becomes decayed and diminished . . .'[6] Sir Josiah Child found himself having to launch a counter-attack against 'gentlemen of no mean capacities', like Coke, who argued that 'his Majestie's Plantations abroad have very much prejudiced this Kingdom by draining us of our People; for the confirmation of which they urge the example of Spain, which they say is almost ruined by the Depopulation which the West-Indies hath occasioned.'[7] Far from weakening a nation, overseas plantations augmented its strength, although Child found himself wrestling with the problem of New England, notoriously unable to supply the mother country with those raw materials and commodities that justified colonies in the eyes of good mercantilists.

In practice, however, the new wealth brought to the metropolis in the second half of the seventeenth century by the rapid growth of the colonial market, and the economic stimulus provided by a buoyant transatlantic trade, spoke louder than any number of economic tracts.[8] The genuine if erratically pursued concern of later Stuart governments to regulate the colonial trade and reorganize colonial administration[9] was a measure of the degree to which the American settlements were beginning to assume their place in the national consciousness as imperial outposts integral to the development of England's power and prosperity.

Britain's empire was therefore to be a maritime and commercial empire. As such it came to think of itself as the antithesis of Spain's land-based empire of conquest, the alleged cause of its ruin. The Glorious Revolution of 1688, in securing the Protestant succession in England and confirming its character as a parliamentary monarchy, contributed new layers of religious and political ideology to this dawning imperial vision. Commercial enterprise, Protestantism and liberty were now to be enshrined as the mutually reinforcing constituents of a national ethos which, in the long and exhausting wars against the popish tyranny of Louis XIV, would win the ultimate sanction of military success. Piece by piece, the various components of an eighteenth-century ideology of empire were being fitted into place.[10]

The Glorious Revolution and its aftermath – the forging by William III of his grand anti-French coalition, and the global conflict with France culminating in 1713 in a peace settlement at Utrecht which set the seal on British claims to supremacy on the high seas – had profound if ambiguous consequences for the transatlantic colonies.[11] It was only right that subjects of the crown who had settled overseas should enjoy the many benefits of an empire of liberty. Consequently there would be no Stuart-style attempts to interfere with the system of representative government operating through colonial assemblies, although continuing uncertainty over the relative powers of governors and assemblies would leave ample scope for conflict in the years ahead.[12]

In general, the government of William III looked more benignly on the Caribbean colonies than on the mainland settlements, if only because of the growing importance of the sugar interest, and the need to assist the plantations as they sought to defend themselves against French attack.[13] But it proved unable to tackle effectively the continuing problem of the survival of the proprietary colonies. Even in Massachusetts, the imposition of a royal governor under the new charter of 1691 was accompanied by a compromise which left the legislature in a potentially stronger position relative to the governor than that enjoyed by the assemblies of other royal colonies.[14]

Yet, even as the colonies were confirmed in their possession of institutions and liberties conforming to the broad principles of the Revolutionary Settlement, the growing recognition of their economic value to the imperial metropolis encouraged an interventionism from London in the management of trade that pointed to the potential for future conflict between the requirements of an empire of commerce and an empire of liberty. In the years immediately following the Glorious Revolution, the crown was too preoccupied with its domestic and international concerns to pursue a consistent policy towards the American settlements. But the creation in 1696 of the Board of Trade and Plantations in succession to the Lords of Trade was evidence of its determination to tighten London's control over the transatlantic trade. This seemed all the more necessary at a time when the diversionary effects of the war with France had made it easier for Scottish and Irish shipowners to break into the English monopoly created by the Navigation Acts, and sail directly to the Chesapeake and Delaware.[15]

The creation of the Board of Trade was accompanied by the establishment in the colonies of vice-admiralty courts to try offences against the Navigation Acts. In spite of the setbacks to governmental control represented by the colonial upheavals of 1688–9, the hand of bureaucracy was reaching out towards America. By 1710 there were 42 permanent customs officers in the British colonies seeking to ensure that the Acts were observed.[16] The number might be small, but the appearance of these officials was a portent. Spain's American possessions had long been accustomed to the prying activities of royal inspectors and customs agents. Where empire was established, regulation was never far behind.

At the turn of the seventeenth and eighteenth centuries, therefore, the presence of empire was making itself increasingly felt in England's Atlantic possessions, although imperial policy lacked the coherence and effectiveness that senior officials in London like Sir William Blathwayt would have wished. Colonial affairs inevitably took second place to the prosecution of the war in Europe. Consistency in the government's colonial policies, however, was also hampered by the divisiveness of British politics under William III and Anne. Bitter political feuding between Tories and Whigs gave an opening to colonial societies and their spokesmen in London to exploit the party political divisions in England for their own purposes. Individual colonies had begun to follow the example of Massachusetts in appointing a permanent agent to keep an eye on their interests in court and parliament. The activities of these agents and of pressure groups that emerged to defend one colonial interest or another complicated the attempts of Board of Trade officials to develop and implement a grand strategy. Colonial lobbying in London was beginning to influence the formulation of imperial policy.[17]

By force of circumstance, England and its colonies were being inexorably drawn into a closer relationship. The process of imperial integration was strongly driven by the expansion of the transatlantic trade – by 1700 there were at least 1,000 London merchants trading with America, and the steadily expanding British demand for sugar and tobacco was rapidly increasing the volume of transatlantic shipping. If in the 1680s fewer than 500 ships a year made the crossing from England, their number had more than doubled by the 1730s.[18] Not only was transatlantic communication growing in both frequency and regularity, but the development of intercolonial trade between the mainland settlements and the West Indies, and between the various mainland settlements themselves, meant that by the 1730s British and European news was arriving more promptly, and being disseminated more widely, than fifty years earlier. In 1702 a bold wartime initiative was launched for the organization of a monthly transatlantic packet service to the West Indies, making the round trip in 100 days. Although the new service failed to survive the coming of peace, eighteenth-century correspondents on both sides of the Atlantic could write their letters with a growing confidence that they would reach their destination with a reasonable degree of predictability.[19]

If improved communications did much to further the integration of an Anglo-American Atlantic polity, so also did the advent of war. As England and its continental allies embarked on all-out war with France, the European struggle spread to the far side of the Atlantic, and the colonies found themselves embroiled in what was fast becoming a global conflict. King Philip's war of 1675–6 proved to be the last Indian war without external intervention. As the British settlements and the authorities in French Canada jockeyed for support among the independent Indian tribes, Indian–settler conflicts were subsumed into the wider conflict of the two colonial powers. Along the borders of New England and New York, townships were pillaged and razed by the French and their Indian allies.[20]

All the colonies, however, were affected to a greater or lesser extent, as London sought to induce them to unite in self-defence, while colonial governors struggled to persuade their assemblies to vote money and quotas of men for the prosecution of the war. Arms and ammunition were needed from England, and the help of the royal navy was required for the protection of the North Atlantic trade. The experience of war between 1689 and 1713 made the colonists more aware of their dependence on the mother country, while also stimulating pride in their own efforts and in the new closeness of their partnership with their English cousins. 'It is no little Blessing of God', wrote Cotton Mather in 1700, 'that we are part of the *English Nation*.'[21]

While the bonds of empire were being more tightly drawn in the British Atlantic polity, the relationship between Spain and its empire of the Indies seemed to be moving no less inexorably in the opposite direction. The difference reflected the divergent trajectories of English and Spanish power during the second half of the seventeenth century. As England rose to a position of commercial and maritime supremacy, the military and economic weakness of metropolitan Spain during the final years of Philip IV and the agonizingly prolonged reign of his sickly and feeble-minded son Carlos II (1665–1700) had the effect of loosening the control of Madrid over its American territories, and giving their creole societies new and expanded space for manoeuvre.

'As the weaknes of *Spain* is such at home,' wrote Roger Coke in 1670, 'so it is the more in his *Indies*, from whence his Wealth and Riches flow . . .'[22] The effects of metropolitan weakness were felt at many points, and most obviously in the seizure by the English, the Dutch and the French of a string of islands in the Caribbean and of toeholds on the American mainland – the English in Belize and the Mosquito coast of Nicaragua, and all three powers in the Guiana region. These European outposts served as ideal bases for piracy and trade. Between the 1650s and the 1680s buccaneers swarmed through the Caribbean, raiding the Spanish American mainland and preying on Spanish ships. Jamaica in particular was a hornets' nest of pirates. Acting in collusion with the island's governor, Thomas Modyford, and in wilful disregard of the Anglo-Spanish peace treaty of the preceding year, Henry Morgan launched a devastating raid on Panama in 1671.[23]

Trade and piracy were liable to be synonymous in this lawless Caribbean world of the later seventeenth and early eighteenth centuries, and buccaneers, merchants and planters became fickle accomplices in the enterprise of stripping the Spanish empire of its assets. New England merchants seized control of the export trade in central American logwood (for dye-making) from the Gulf of Campeche, and fortunes were made in Rhode Island by Newport merchants who happily combined commerce with attacks on Spanish shipping.[24] Spain's islands in the Antilles were poor and vulnerable imperial outposts, requiring heavy and continuous subsidies from the Mexican treasury for their fortification and defence. The larger the subsidies that had to be remitted from New Spain to the Antilles, the less would be the silver available for shipment to Seville. By contrast, Britain's Caribbean islands, with their developing plantation economies, were to be the jewels in the crown of its American empire.

Jamaica, ideally located at the heart of the Spanish Caribbean and blessed with a splendidly sheltered harbour at Port Royal, was better placed than the Dutch island of Curaçao for managing the collective larceny of Spain's overseas assets. Britain's possession of the island gave English merchants, and their New York and Boston counterparts, the edge over their Dutch competitors for domination of the contraband trade with the Spanish Indies. From their Jamaican vantage-point Anglo-American merchants infiltrated and subverted the Spanish trading system, supplying the Spanish islands and mainland with smuggled goods which they could otherwise only obtain at inflated prices when the fleets put in from Spain, or else not obtain at all. Spanish officials would wink at this illicit trade once their palms had been greased, but there were occasions when sheer necessity forced

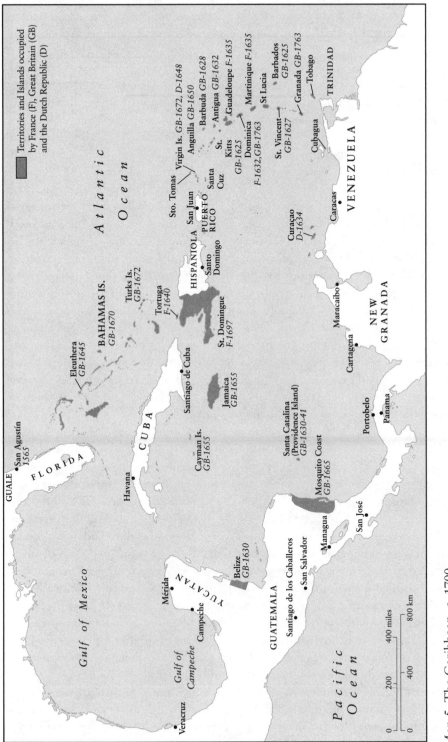

Map 5. The Caribbean, c. 1700.
Based on Guillermo Céspedes del Castillo, *América hispánica, 1492–1898* (1983), map xiv; *The New Cambridge Modern History*, Vol. XIV, *Atlas* (1970) pp. 229 and 230.

them to issue official import licences. African slaves especially were in short supply. As a result, Jamaica in the 1680s became a major supplier of slaves for despatch to Spanish America by way of Havana, Portobelo and Cartagena.

This Jamaican trade in slaves and other commodities brought handsome returns. The silver siphoned off by merchants or seized by buccaneers percolated through the Anglo-American Atlantic economy, and helped reduce Britain's trading deficit with the Far East. Jamaica became the principal supplier of bullion to the North American colonies, mitigating their endemic monetary difficulties and enabling them to purchase not only essential British commodities, but also Spanish American luxuries, like the Mexican chocolate which Samuel Sewall sipped for breakfast in Dorchester, Massachusetts, on 20 October 1697.[25]

While European penetration of the Caribbean was eroding Spain's monopoly of the American trade at its receiving point, a vast breach had also been opened at its point of origin in mainland Spain itself. For a century and a half this had been located in Seville. From the 1670s, however, Cadiz was beginning to replace Seville as the entrepot of the American trade, as the Guadalquivir silted up, and ships found it increasingly hazardous to navigate the river. In 1717 the Spanish crown, bowing to geographical realities, would make the transfer official, and both the House of Trade and the Consulado removed to Cadiz.[26] Taking advantage of the privileges negotiated under special treaty arrangements with a weakened Spanish crown, the foreign merchants operating from the two port cities freighted the outbound fleets with large quantities of the manufactures that Spanish industry was unable to supply. These goods, fetching high prices in the American market, were exchanged for the American silver on which Britain, France and the Netherlands relied to keep the wheels of their economies turning.[27]

French, Flemish, Dutch and English merchants were not the only beneficiaries of the inability of Seville's Consulado to sustain its monopoly of the American trade – a monopoly undermined by massive fraud at every stage of its operations. As early as the late sixteenth century creole merchants in the Americas, and most notably those of Mexico City and Peru, had glimpsed lucrative possibilities for themselves in the structure and functioning of the Indies trade. As they appreciated, not even the elaborate mechanisms set in place by Seville could dictate every detail of a trading system spanning the Atlantic. The growing quantities of silver produced by the American mines gave them a strong hand, further strengthened by the opening of the trans-Pacific trading route from Acapulco to Manila in the late sixteenth century. This offered new opportunities for making large profits by supplying creole elites with the oriental luxuries like silks, porcelain, lacquer ware and Japanese screens, for which they developed an insatiable appetite. The purchase of these luxuries was paid for by the diversion to their Asian suppliers of silver which might otherwise have been remitted to Seville.[28]

By making use of their ties of contract and kinship with Sevillian trading houses, and by participating in the fairs held at Vera Cruz, Portobelo and elsewhere on the arrival of the fleets from Seville, the merchants of New Spain and Peru became important players in both the official and the unofficial economy of the Spanish Atlantic. In the opening and middle decades of the seventeenth century they proved strong enough to challenge Seville's dominance of the colonial markets, manipulating prices to suit their own purposes, and exploiting the numerous opportunities for engaging in contraband trade.[29]

The new-found strength and confidence of the merchant communities of the American viceroyalties was a reflection of the wider shifts that were occurring in the economic relationship between the metropolis and its American possessions. The exploitation of the continent's mineral resources, the development of agriculture and manufactures – especially textiles – to meet the needs of a growing creole and mestizo population, and the growth of home-based shipbuilding, all helped to lessen the economic dependence of the viceroyalties on the imperial metropolis.

There was also a steady growth of inter-regional trade, hinting at the emergence of a partially autonomous Hispanic American economy. Mexico City had become the centre of an informal but widespread trading system. Horizontally this ran along an axis from Manila in the Philippines to Havana in the Caribbean. There was also a north–south axis which, in spite of the 1631 ban on trade between Mexico and Peru,[30] linked the Pacific coast port of Acapulco to the ports of northern Peru, and then ran on to Lima, with a spur to Potosí. The Peruvian complex had trading links with Panama, to the north, and with Chile in the south, which was vastly increasing its production of wheat in response to Peruvian demand. Another route, reluctantly authorized by the crown in the early seventeenth century, ran overland from the Peruvian mines, by way of Tucumán and Córdoba, to the growing port city of Buenos Aires, 63 days on horseback from Potosí (see map 7, p. 354).[31] At this point, internal trading systems tapped into the increasingly internationalized Atlantic economy, as foreign traders descended on the La Plata region with supplies of slaves and European manufactures to exchange for illegally exported Peruvian silver.[32]

Although dependent on Portuguese and other foreign merchants for a steady supply of African slaves, and still relying on Europe for luxury products and essential commodities like paper and hardware, the economies of New Spain and Peru were therefore becoming more self-sufficient, and, as a result, less vulnerable to the vagaries of Spanish and European economic movements.[33] This does not, however, mean that they were untouched by recession. Devastating floods struck Mexico City in 1629, and New Spain experienced serious economic difficulties over the following three decades. In the years between 1635 and 1665 there was a slump in the output of the Mexican silver mines, but production picked up strongly again in the 1670s, at a time when the indigenous population was at last beginning to recover from the demographic disaster of the century of conquest.[34]

The Peruvian economy seems to have escaped sustained recession in the middle years of the century, but only to run into serious trouble in the wake of the devastating earthquakes which hit central Peru in 1687. Silver production in Potosí, which reached a peak around 1610, moved in the second half of the century into a prolonged period of decline, which continued at least until the 1730s, although with moments of recovery.[35] Downward trends in Peru, however, were offset by the mining revival in New Spain, where production began to outstrip that of Peru in the late seventeenth century.[36] Although the registered imports of American silver into Seville slumped dramatically in the second half of the century, there are strong indications that the drop was more the result of a massive increase in fraud and contraband than of an over-all diminution of production. Enormous quantities of silver, sometimes arriving in larger consignments than during the peak period of the late sixteenth century, continued to be remitted to Europe, in spite of the retention of considerable quantities for defence and other purposes in the viceroyalties themselves, and of a constant drain of silver to the Far East by way of the Acapulco galleon and the Manila route.[37]

The balance of evidence, therefore, indicates that the Spanish and Spanish American economies moved in opposing directions during the seventeenth century, with the latter by now sufficiently self-supporting to be insulated from the worst effects of the economic depression that afflicted much of central and southern Europe in the era of the Thirty Years War.[38] Partly because of the capture by foreign merchants of such large swathes of the transatlantic trade, and partly because of the process of transition and expansion within the viceroyalties themselves, the economic ties between Spain and its American possessions were being loosened at the very time that economic growth on both sides of the British Atlantic was tightening the relationship between England and its Caribbean and mainland colonies.

If America, however, had less need of Spain, Spain never stood in greater need of America than now. By the mid-seventeenth century, the fiscal difficulties that perennially beset the Spanish crown had become acute. The prolonged struggle with the Dutch and the French, the revolts of the 1640s and Philip IV's increasingly desperate attempts to recover control over the newly independent kingdom of Portugal, placed enormous strains on a treasury perennially incapable of meeting the demands made upon it. The resulting fiscal crisis forced the crown to resort to every kind of financial expedient, both in metropolitan Spain itself and in its overseas possessions. The crisis exported itself to the royal treasuries in Mexico City and Lima, where the viceroys faced growing difficulties in raising the additional revenues demanded by Madrid.

As the economies of the two viceroyalties became more diversified, so the enforcement of new fiscal expedients became more problematic. The difficulties in raising more revenue in societies where the white and mestizo population were exempt from direct taxation were compounded by the dishonesty of the treasury officials. In Peru, traditionally a more lucrative source of revenue for the crown than New Spain, high-ranking treasury offices began to be offered for sale on a systematic basis from 1633. As the crown's difficulties multiplied, so too did the number of offices created and put up for sale. While the sale of offices proved to be a highly profitable source of revenue, it was acquired at a heavy political price. Offices that came onto the market were snapped up by creoles or by Lima merchants with strong local connections. Large sums were diverted into private pockets by corrupt officials, and viceroys watched in despair as the sale of office drastically reduced both the efficiency of the administration and their own powers of patronage, which they considered essential for the effective exercise of viceregal authority.[39]

The natural beneficiaries of this process were the creole elite, for whom the crown's troubles fell as manna from heaven. The purchase of offices and titles to land, the acquisition of new credit opportunities as royal revenues failed to cover costs, and informal alliances struck with corrupt royal officials for the clandestine distribution of state resources, enabled oligarchies throughout Spanish America to entrench themselves still further. By the middle years of the seventeenth century the crown was putting provincial governorships up for sale, and under Carlos II the last dam was breached when the crown began systematically selling the judicial posts in the eleven Audiencias of the Indies. Between 1687 and 1695, 24 such sales occurred, 18 of them in the jurisdiction of Peru. The control of justice as well as administration was beginning to slip from the hands of Madrid.[40]

Consequently, by the time of Carlos II's death in 1700, it was not only the economic ties between metropolitan Spain and its overseas possessions that were unravelling. Under the cover of continuing deference to the royal authority, the creole elites, taking advantage of the crown's continuing fiscal needs, had sidled into a semi-detached political relationship with Madrid. In principle, a highly regulated transatlantic trading system and a vast body of legislation belatedly codified in the *Recopilación de las leyes de Indias* held Spanish America in a tight metropolitan grip. In practice, the spread of systematized corruption endowed the imperial structure with a flexibility that its rigid framework appeared to belie. Corruption facilitated social mobility in a hierarchically structured society, and enlarged the space in which the creole elites were able to manoeuvre.[41]

It is not therefore surprising that the proclamation of a Bourbon successor to Carlos II, in the person of Louis XIV's grandson, Philip V, passed off almost without incident in America, in sharp contrast to the turmoil that the events surrounding the Glorious Revolution of 1688 brought to the British colonies, where the growing interventionism of the later Stuarts had awakened dark fears of tyranny. Only in Caracas did a small group of pro-Austrian supporters, incited by a Habsburg *agent provocateur*, proclaim the Archduke Charles, the rival, Austrian candidate to the Spanish throne, to be the rightful monarch under the name of 'Carlos III'.[42] While mainland Spain would soon be plunged into civil war by the conflict of loyalties, there seemed no good reason in the American viceroyalties to contest the terms of Carlos II's last will and testament. The creole elites already possessed much of the reality, if not the appearance, of power.

Yet inevitably a question-mark hung over the new dynasty. Although the creoles constantly complained of the way in which they were treated by native-born Spaniards, they had generally fared well under the government, and misgovernment, of the House of Austria. Could they expect an equally benign treatment from a French-imported dynasty? The France of Louis XIV had already engineered for itself a dominant position in Spain's Atlantic trade. On top of this,

French ministers and advisers were now descending on Madrid, carrying plans for radical reform in their baggage. Was Spain to become a mere appendage of its traditional enemy? Even if not, there was always the danger that it might be subjected to French notions of government. The auguries were far from promising in 1713 as Philip V emerged victorious over his Austrian rival at the end of the long and destructive War of the Spanish Succession.

Over the course of almost two hundred years of government the Habsburgs had in general respected the innate diversity of the realms that made up their Monarchy. Philip V, by contrast, used his victory over his rebellious territories of the Crown of Aragon to sweep away those fundamental laws, liberties and institutions which had allowed them to retain their separate identities. The eastern provinces of the peninsula were now to find themselves incorporated into a nominally unified and centralizing state controlled from Madrid – a 'vertical' Spain in place of the 'horizontal' Spain of the House of Austria.[43]

The forced incorporation of the Crown of Aragon between 1709 and 1716 contrasted sharply with another contemporary union, that of England and Scotland in 1707. Although the Scots negotiated from a position of weakness, they secured important advantages from their incorporation into the parliamentary monarchy of a United Kingdom of Great Britain. The disaster of the Darien expedition of 1698 had brought home the high price to be paid for any attempt to establish independent Scottish overseas settlements in an America to which the larger European powers had already laid effective claim. Instead, the Scots now obtained unrestricted access to the commercial and other opportunities offered by an empire that was henceforth to be not English but British. In this they had the advantage of the Irish, and of the North American colonies themselves, since their freedom of manoeuvre would cease to be limited by the Navigation Acts and other mercantilist legislation imposed by a United Kingdom parliament.[44]

While the British colonies might chafe under the trading arrangements dictated from London, they at least possessed, unlike Spain's American territories, barriers against the intervention of the imperial state, in the form of their own representative institutions. In the absence of such assemblies, Spain's overseas territories had been forced to rely on the crown's continuing willingness to recognize the inherent diversity of the Monarchy, and on the opportunities for manoeuvre offered by the endemic rivalries between the organisms that competed for power under the Habsburg system of conciliar government. But how far would these opportunities continue to exist under a Bourbon regime determined to modernize the structures and administrative methods of an *ancien régime* society? While the Council of the Indies survived, even if its functions were gradually reduced to those of a purely judicial tribunal, much of the old conciliar system was dismantled, and power began to be concentrated in the hands of a new breed of secretaries of state, including, from 1714, a secretary of the navy and the Indies.[45] Most significant of all, the new regime was adopting a French-inspired language of reform. The authoritarian terminology of Louis XIV and the centralizing mercantilist terminology of Colbert were now beginning to colour the traditional, contractualist language of composite monarchy inherited from the Habsburgs.

The Indies, however, were to secure a reprieve that would last for half a century. The new dynasty was too preoccupied with the problems of domestic reform, and with the recovery of the European territories lost to Spain in 1713 at the Treaty of Utrecht, to be able to devote itself to any systematic programme of reform in America. Such changes as did occur, like the creation of a third viceroyalty, that of New Granada, fleetingly in 1717, and then definitively in 1739, were responses to immediate problems of defence and administration, rather than part of a larger strategy of reform.[46] The crown's military commitments in Europe meant that it remained as short of money as ever, and, in spite of its attempts to return to the practices of an earlier age, offices in the Indies, including the judicial posts in the Audiencias, continued to be put up for sale, almost as if Carlos II were still the King of Spain.[47]

Yet there was also a growing awareness in Madrid that the Indies held the key to Spain's recovery. Salvation lay in the command of both silver and trade, and each had largely slipped from the grasp of the crown. Although the War of the Spanish Succession ended with Spain retaining its American empire territorially intact, it left the French pulling the strings of the transatlantic trade.

In the aftermath of the Treaty of Utrecht, this French dominance was subject to growing challenge from the British, to whom the treaty had awarded the extremely valuable slave-trade contract, the *asiento de negros*, previously held by the Portuguese and the French. The concession included the famous annual 'permission ship', a South Sea Company vessel authorized to unload its cargo in Vera Cruz or Portobelo at the time of the arrival of the Seville/Cadiz fleet and the resulting trade fair. This represented the first breach of the Spanish Atlantic trading monopoly officially authorized by the crown itself.[48]

The authorization vividly symbolized the new economic realities. As the Spanish Atlantic became internationalized, Spain's closed world of the Indies was rapidly being cracked open. If not yet offering unrestricted access to European goods, it seemed to be headed in that direction, unless the new dynasty could find ways of reversing the trend. Not only were Spanish America's ties to the peninsular economy unravelling, but the southward advance of the British mainland settlements was creating new openings for the development of an illicit hemispheric trade between the colonial possessions of the two imperial powers. In 1717 oranges grown in Spanish Florida were being shipped to Charles Town, and by the 1730s they were being enjoyed by the residents of Philadelphia and New York.[49]

In Spain itself there was mounting resentment at the foreign penetration of the Indies trade. The Colbertian mercantilism that the French were attempting to establish in the peninsula stopped short of policies, such as the encouragement of Spanish manufacturing, that were likely to prove prejudicial to France's national interests.[50] Understandably, reform-minded Spaniards like Gerónimo de Uztáriz, the author of a highly influential treatise published in 1724 on 'the theory and practice of trade', wanted their own comprehensive Colbertian programme, with no selective omissions favouring the British and the French.[51]

The extraordinary buoyancy of Britain's commercial empire during the first half of the eighteenth century galvanized reform-minded ministers and conscientious royal officials like Uztáriz, and prompted vigorous debate about ways in which Spain's American possessions might be made more profitable to the imperial metropolis. One outcome of this debate was a decision to charter a number of monopoly trading companies, on the model of those of France, England and the Dutch Republic, as a means of checking the flow of American contraband goods to foreign merchants. These companies, of which the first was the Royal Guipúzcoa Company for trade with Caracas, founded in 1728 and with its seat in Bilbao, were also intended to benefit the economies of the Iberian periphery, judged to have been prejudiced by the restriction of the transatlantic trade to Seville and Cadiz. Since, however, the new companies were only allowed to trade with marginal regions of America, like Venezuela, which were not directly supplied by the transatlantic convoys, the Andalusian monopoly – considered essential for the retention of control over the silver remittances – remained largely intact.[52]

While changes might be introduced on the margins of the transatlantic trading system, the debate really concerned the whole character of Spain's American empire and its relationship to Spain itself. Uztáriz himself devoted little direct attention to this, although the question was implicit in his treatise. In 1743, however, José del Campillo, a man with personal experience of American administration who had been appointed secretary of the navy and the Indies in 1736, composed a manuscript in which he attempted a full-scale reassessment of Spain's system of government in America.[53] 'A new method of government', Campillo argued, was needed 'in that great portion of the Spanish Monarchy', in order that 'such a rich possession should give us advantages'. At present the islands of Martinique and Barbados brought more benefits to their imperial owners, the French and the British, than all its vast American territories brought to Spain. Why should this be? 'Our system of government', he wrote, 'is totally vitiated.' 'Economic government', as distinct from 'political government', had been neglected, and the 'spirit of conquest' had been intemperately maintained, with its preference for dominion taking precedence over the advantages and utilities of trade. The empires of England and France, unlike that of Spain, had realized the need to give their colonies 'freedom and space, removing the shackles and restrictions oppressing their industry, and first giving them the means to enrich themselves before enriching their mother'.[54]

Campillo's interpretation of the colonial policies of France and Britain was no doubt excessively rose-tinted, but his treatise, for all the ambiguities of its recommendations and the circumspect terms in which it was couched, is an indication of the way in which Spain's empire was coming to be conceptualized by ministers in Madrid in terms of its potential as a British-style empire of commerce. Sooner or later the new priorities would lead to a systematic reforming effort in the Indies, especially if military and naval expenses generated by continental and overseas wars continued to mount.

The War of Jenkins' Ear, arising in 1739 out of Spanish efforts to cut down on contraband in the West Indies, began as an Anglo-Spanish naval conflict in the Caribbean before being swept up in the wider European conflict over the Austrian succession. On both sides, the costs of war would encourage already existing attempts to tighten the bonds of empire and rethink imperial relationships. In Britain, the war unleashed a patriotic frenzy that turned to triumphalism as the news arrived in March 1740 of Admiral Vernon's capture of Portobelo. Britain's empire of the seas was resoundingly confirmed, and fittingly commemorated in the first singing of Thomas Arne's rendering of 'Rule Britannia'.[55] The War of Jenkins' Ear, however, generated more than a localized patriotism. It reinforced the sense of a British transatlantic community, by giving the colonies the conviction that they were participating in a joint enterprise, both Protestant and free. In so doing, it strengthened the psychological and emotional bonds that were at least as powerful as the influence of interest groups and the bonds of patronage and commerce in tying them to the mother country.[56] Yet at the same time it raised awkward questions about whether the existing structure of empire was adequate to meet the expectations, and satisfy the aspirations, of either the imperial metropolis or the colonies.

In the Spanish Atlantic community, the period of warfare which ended in 1748 with very mixed results could hardly be expected to generate such positive emotional responses. But it brought with it important changes, including the licensing, in response to the hazards of wartime shipping, of transatlantic sailings by single ships in place of the traditional fleets. Even if the monopoly-minded merchants of Seville and Cadiz succeeded in 1757 in reviving the *flota* to New Spain, the days of the great transatlantic convoys were over. So too were the days of the American trading fairs which traditionally followed the arrival of the fleets.[57] Policy and circumstance had combined to introduce a new, if still limited, flexibility into the commercial arrangements of Spain's Atlantic empire.

Except where matters of commerce and war were involved, however, the governments of both Britain and Spain showed no great disposition during the first four decades of the eighteenth century to tamper with the prevailing political and administrative relationship between the imperial centre and its transatlantic possessions. Inertia, bordering on neglect, appeared to be the order of the day – a neglect that was salutary or pernicious according to the perspective adopted.[58] But the growing appreciation in both Britain and Spain of the commercial benefits of their Atlantic empires, coupled with the growing costs of imperial defence in an age of great-power conflict on land and sea, meant that the neglect could not continue indefinitely.

Yet change imposed from the imperial metropolis was likely in both instances to aggravate the latent tensions that had existed between the colonial communities and the mother country ever since colonization began. These communities saw themselves, and were seen by the metropolitan societies from which they derived, as constituent parts of polities that spanned the Atlantic – polities more closely integrated in some areas than in others, but none the less united by a common heritage and a whole complex of loyalties and interests. Over their mutual relationship, however, hovered a puzzling question. Were these overseas communities respectively British and Spanish, or were they really something different?

Creole communities

In 1567 Lope García de Castro, the interim governor of Peru, informed the President of the Council of the Indies: 'Your Excellency should understand that the people of this land are different from what they were before, because most of the Spaniards who depend on it for their livelihood are old, and many are dead and have been succeeded in the *repartimientos* [of the Indians] by their sons, and have left many children. As a result, this land is full of *criollos*, who are those who were born here . . .'[59] To the new generation which succeeded that of the conquistadores, the Indies, not Spain, was the only home they knew. They were *criollos* – 'native-born' – a word first used in the mid-sixteenth century of black slaves born in the Indies, rather than in Africa.[60] In the last twenty or thirty years of the century *criollo*, as applied to American-born Spaniards, began to catch on in peninsular Spain, to some extent displacing *indiano*, a term also used to describe someone who returned home from the Indies, having made his fortune. Its growing popularity reflected the existence in America of a new breed of Spaniards, who in some respects might differ from their Spanish-born relatives.

By the early seventeenth century, some form or other of the word *criollo* had entered the English language, but it was still an unfamiliar term. William Strachey found it necessary to explain its meaning in his *The Historie of Travell into Virginia Britania* of 1612, when, writing of 'the *Indian-Crollos*', he added in parenthesis '(*Spaniards* born there)'.[61] In the middle years of the century Thomas Gage's racy account of his experiences in Mexico no doubt helped popularize the word among English readers, while also acquainting them with the antipathy between creoles and new arrivals from Spain, the so-called *gachupines* or *peninsulares*.[62] It seems, however, to have been only in the 1680s that English officials, or newly arrived immigrants, began to apply the term *creole* to their own compatriots born either in the Caribbean or the mainland colonies, or long settled there. Even then, there was some uncertainty about the usage, since *creole* could equally be applied to American-born blacks.[63]

Criollo and *creole* were words more likely to be employed by others to describe European settlers and their descendants, than used by native-born white Americans as a form of self-description. In a famous pamphlet of 1764 the Boston lawyer, James Otis, appended an explanatory note: 'Those in England who borrow the term of the Spaniards, as well as their notions of government, apply this term to all Americans of European extract; but the northern colonists apply it only to the islanders [i.e. the West Indies settlers] and others of such extract under the torrid Zone.'[64] The descendants of English settlers of America thought of themselves as quintessentially English, just as, in their own eyes, settlers of Spanish descent in the Indies were *españoles*, as distinct from *indios, mestizos* and *negros*. The term *creole*, moreover, rapidly acquired a set of negative connotations. Even those who could boast pure Spanish descent, without any admixture of Indian blood, were widely believed among peninsular Spaniards to have gone to seed in the Indies. The seventeenth-century jurist Solórzano y Pereira, coming to their defence, blamed those who, through ignorance or a malicious desire to exclude creoles from offices and honours, liked to claim that they 'degenerate so much as a result of the constellations and temper of those provinces, that they lose all the good effects that derive from the influence of Spanish blood', with the result that they were 'scarcely worthy of being described as rational beings . . .'[65]

This notion that those who settled in the Indies ran the risk of degeneration was not confined to the Spanish world. Cotton Mather, in the annual election sermon of 1689 which he preached on the occasion of the opening of the Massachusetts General Court, spoke ominously of 'the too general want of education in the rising generation, which if not prevented will gradually but speedily dispose us to that sort of Criolian degeneracy observed to deprave the children of the most noble and worthy Europeans when transplanted into America'.[66] Such fears had dogged English settlers since the early days of their migration to a New World environment for which John Winthrop and others claimed an essentially English character, in spite of the climatic evidence to the contrary.[67] 'For the country itself,' he wrote to his son, 'I can discern little difference between it and our own . . .'[68] But the growing realization that New England was not old England, just as New Spain was not old Spain, opened up the disturbing possibility of Mather's 'Criolian degeneracy'.[69]

If settlers did indeed degenerate in their new transatlantic environment, one plausible explanation was their proximity to the Indians. The fear of cultural degeneration through osmosis was one that had haunted the English in their dealings with the Irish, and they carried it with them in their cultural baggage when they crossed the Atlantic.[70] Spanish settlers who had consorted with Indians and grown used to Indian ways seem to have been less exercised by this fear than their English counterparts, but their unwillingness to protect themselves from contaminating Indian influences made them vulnerable to disparaging comments from officials and clerics who had recently come from Spain and did not like what they saw. Criticism was levelled in particular at the employment of Indian nurses and wet-nurses in creole households, not only because, in conditions of such intimacy, these women were likely to instil Indian habits into their creole charges, but also because – on the assumption that a child will 'extract the inclinations which it imbibed with the milk' – its 'inclinations' would naturally be perverse if the milk was Indian.[71] With the creole elite already living a life of idleness and luxury, what hope was there that their children, and in due course their grandchildren, would escape the corrupting consequences of such perverse inclinations?

Above all, however, it was the climate and the constellations that were held responsible for the perceived failings of the creoles. Fray Bernardino de Sahagún, a sympathetic observer of the Indian scene, declared that he was not surprised by the blemishes in the character of the Indians of New Spain, 'because the Spaniards who live in this land, and much more those born in it, acquire these evil inclinations. Those who, very like Indians, are born there, resemble Spaniards in appearance, but not in their nature and qualities, while native Spaniards, if they do not take great care, become different people within a few years of their arrival in these regions. I ascribe this to the climate or the constellations of this land.'[72]

This climatic determinism, a legacy of the classical world of Hippocrates and Galen, and given a fresh impetus in sixteenth-century Europe by the writings of Bodin, was to cast a long shadow over European settlers in America and their descendants.[73] It implied that they were doomed to Mather's 'Criolian degeneracy', a tendency to descend to the level of the Indians in their manners and morals. This assumed process of creeping Indianization was capable not only of arousing deep anxieties among settlers, but also of creating unflattering stereotypes in the minds of European visitors and observers. A Quito-born creole bishop, Gaspar de Villarroel, who spent nearly ten years in Madrid, wrote in 1661 of his indignation when a Spaniard expressed surprise that an *americano* should be 'as white, and well-formed, as a Spaniard, and speak Castilian just as well'.[74]

All such stereotypes took as their starting-point the fact, or the assumption, of *difference*, a difference that was cultural rather than racial, although there was some suspicion that the American environment might in due course lead also to actual physical differentiation. There was anxious debate, for instance, as to whether the descendants of Spaniards who had settled in the Indies would eventually acquire hairless bodies, like those of the Indians.[75] It was in response to such concerns about the impact of environment on physique as well as temperament that seventeenth-century creole writers in Spanish America began to develop racialist theories about the Indians, in an effort to differentiate the descendants of the conquerors and settlers from the indigenous population whose environment they shared. It was 'nature', not environment, that made Indians what they were; and it was nature that would prevent the environment from turning American-born Spaniards into Indians.[76]

English settlers, for their part, were keen to deny that the American climate had any adverse impact on their physique, and claimed that English bodies positively flourished in a New World environment, unlike those of the indigenous inhabitants who were dying of disease in their thousands. As Cotton Mather's remarks on 'Criolian degeneracy' indicate, however, they were less confident when it came to the cultural consequences of living in America.[77] The fear of being tarnished by the slur of cultural degeneration made it important to draw sharp distinctions between themselves and the indigenous population. English colonists seem for a long time to have been reluctant to apply to themselves the epithet *American*, perhaps because, at least for the Founding Fathers of New England, the 'Americans' were the Indians. It is not clear whether the same holds true for Spanish America.

Bishop Villarroel, using the word *americano* in 1661, immediately adds the confusing gloss, 'that is, Indian' (*indio*), although he is clearly referring to creoles. The word *americano* does not appear in the Spanish Dictionary of Authorities, published in 1726, which suggests the infrequency of its use at that date. As in British America, the association of *American* with *Indian* may well have made the word problematic. In spite of occasional use from the later seventeenth century onward, it would only be in the second half of the eighteenth century that the creole inhabitants of both British and Spanish America began to sport *American* as a badge of pride.[78]

The attempts by the creoles to disassociate themselves in the minds of their Old World cousins from the non-European inhabitants of America failed to have the desired effect. They were unable to eradicate the perception of difference – a perception that to some extent accorded with reality. It was not simply the presence of indigenous or African populations which made the difference, although this certainly counted for much. As colonial societies were consolidated, they developed their own special characteristics, which began to mark them out in significant ways from the parent society. When, as in the Chesapeake region in the early eighteenth century, immigration from the mother country tapered off and those born on the American side of the ocean came to constitute the majority of the white population, memories of how life was lived in the homeland inevitably grew fainter, and new generations slipped naturally into the patterns of life developed by their parents and grandparents as they adapted to New World conditions.[79]

Self-interest, however, might well exaggerate allegations of difference in ways prejudicial to settler societies. In seventeenth-century Spanish America there was fierce competition for administrative and ecclesiastical posts between native sons and new arrivals from Spain, and it was to the obvious advantage of the newcomers to harp on the inadequacies of the creoles with whom they were competing. Even if recurrent intermarriage between Spaniards and creoles took the edge off some of the rivalry by uniting *peninsulares* and old-established settler families in a nexus of interests,[80] there is widespread evidence of bitter hostility. Commenting on the tendency of creole women to prefer as husbands poor Spaniards to rich creoles, a Neapolitan traveller who visited Mexico City in 1697 claimed – no doubt with more than a touch of Mediterranean hyperbole – that antipathy had reached a point where the creoles 'hate their own parents because they are Europeans'.[81]

With many fewer administrative posts in the gift of the British than the Spanish crown, one major cause of friction in the relationship between newcomers and colonists was correspondingly reduced in the British Atlantic world, although it was by no means eliminated. Settlers in the Caribbean islands and on the American mainland had constantly to struggle against charges of difference similar to those levelled by the Spaniards against their creole cousins. Disparagement began with slurs on their origins. '*Virginia* and *Barbados*', wrote Sir Josiah Child, 'were first peopled by a Sort of loose vagrant People, vicious and destitute of Means to live at Home . . . and these I say were such as, had there been no English foreign Plantation in the World, could probably never have lived at home to do service for this Country, but must have come to be hanged, or starved, or died untimely of some of those miserable Diseases, that proceed from Want and Vice . . .'[82]

Early negative images were compounded by scandalous reports of the life-style of the settlers. By the early eighteenth century the planters in the Caribbean islands had become a byword for extravagance and debauchery:

Barbadoes Isle inhabited by Slaves
And for one honest man ten thousand knaves . . .[83]

Nor did the more sober New Englanders escape disparagement. '*Eating, Drinking, Smoking* and *Sleeping*', wrote Ned Ward in 1699, 'take up four parts in five of their Time; and you may divide the remainder into *Religious Exercise, Day Labour,* and *Evacuation.* Four meals a Day, and a good Knap after Dinner, being the Custom of the Country . . . One Husband-man in *England*, will do more Labour in a Day, than a *New-England* Planter will be at the pains to do in a Week: For to every Hour he spends in his *Grounds*, he will be two at an *Ordinary* [i.e. tavern].'[84]

Such slurs left the more sensitive settlers with deeply ambivalent feelings. While rejecting the criticisms as coming from malevolent or ill-informed outsiders, they simultaneously worried that they might perhaps be true. This led either to excessively strident rebuttals, or to the kind of defensiveness displayed by the historian of Virginia, Robert Beverley, when he sought to forestall criticisms of his prose style by explaining to the reader in his preface: 'I am an *Indian*, and don't pretend to be exact in my Language . . .'[85] The very charge of 'Indianization' – the charge that British settlers of the mainland feared most of all – was thus self-deprecatingly turned into a weapon of defence.

The first line of defence among the creoles, whether English or Spanish, was to emphasize their inherent Englishness or Spanishness, qualities which neither distance, climate nor proximity to inferior peoples were capable of erasing. Ignoring the juridical inconvenience that the Indies were conquests of the Crown of Castile, the creole inhabitants of the kingdoms of New Spain or Peru claimed comparable rights to those enjoyed by the king's subjects in his kingdoms of Castile or Aragon. Faced with new levies and imposts, they would have had no difficulty in identifying with the Barbadian planter in 1689 who complained that Barbadians were being 'commanded as subjects and . . . crusht as Aliens'.[86] Any imputation that they were in some sense alien was deeply offensive to those who regarded themselves as entitled by birth to the status and rights of metropolitan-born subjects of the crown.

Insinuations of inferiority were particularly offensive to those creoles who claimed legitimate descent from the original conquerors of Spanish America. As the conquest itself receded into the distance, and the descendants of the conquistadores found that newcomers were preferred before them in appointments to offices, they grew increasingly embittered. 'We are Spaniards – *somos españoles*', wrote Baltasar Dorantes de Carranza in the early seventeenth century, as he lovingly recorded the names of the conquistadores and their descendants, and claimed that, since he and his like belonged to the 'harvest and government' of Spain, they should be governed by its laws and customs.[87] Because of the heroic achievements of their fathers and grandfathers, such men should be honoured and rewarded, not rejected and excluded. Yet their petitions and complaints were ignored.

Although officers of Cromwell's expeditionary force who remained on the island as planters liked to refer to themselves as 'the conquerors of Jamaica',[88] British America, unlike Spanish America, could claim no conquering elite. But this did not prevent the emerging class of Virginia planters from seeking to establish their claims to gentility on the model of the English gentry, just as the descendants of the conquistadores sought to model their own life-styles on the real or imagined life-styles of Castilian *señores*. When Virginian planters travelled to London they acquired coats of arms and had their portraits painted; and when they returned home to Virginia they built themselves handsome new brick houses, and displayed all the enthusiasm for horse-racing of their English counterparts.[89] Unlike Spanish settlers in the Indies, some of them, like William Byrd I, sent their sons back to the mother country for their education, although never on the scale of the West Indian planters, large numbers of whom chose an English education for their sons.[90] The experience, at least as far as William Byrd II was concerned, seems to have led to a deep ambivalence. Never quite accepted by his fellow schoolboys at Felsted, he did his best to become the perfect English gentleman. Yet somehow his colonial origins thwarted all his efforts. Too colonial to be entirely at ease in England, and for a long time too English to be entirely at ease in his native Virginia, he was caught between two worlds without truly belonging to either.[91]

The sense of exclusion, experienced to a greater or lesser degree by Byrd and his fellow colonials who visited the mother country or came into contact with unsympathetic representatives of the crown, was especially painful because it implied second-class status in a transatlantic polity of which they believed themselves to be fully paid-up members. Just as Dorantes de Carranza complained in 1604 that the descendants of the conquistadores were not enjoying the equal treatment with native-born Castilians to which they were entitled by the laws of Castile, so, exactly 100 years later, Robert Beverley complained on behalf of Virginia's House of Burgesses that 'it's laid as a crime to them that they think themselves entitled to the liberties of Englishmen.'[92] The rights of Castilians and the liberties of Englishmen were being denied them by their own kith and kin.

Yet even as they demanded full recognition of those rights, not least as evidence of a shared identity with their metropolitan cousins, they could not shake off the uneasy suspicion that the community of identity was perhaps less complete than they would have wished. The revealing comment of a sixteenth-century Spanish immigrant to the Indies suggests that some of them at least were conscious of a

difference in themselves. In a letter to a cousin in Spain he wrote that, on returning home, he would not be what he had previously been, 'because I shall return
so different (*tan otro*) from what I was, that those who knew me will say that I am
not I . . .'[93] His comment was an unsolicited testimonial to the transforming
power of the American environment, for good or for ill.

Since metropolitan observers seemed in little doubt that the transformation
was for ill, it was natural that the creoles, even as they proclaimed their identity with their Old World kith and kin, should seek to counter charges of
inevitable degeneracy by loudly singing the praises of their New World environment. In the American viceroyalties a succession of writers sought to depict
their American homeland as an earthly paradise, producing the fruits of the
earth in abundance, and climatically benign. New Spain and the kingdoms of
Peru, wrote Fray Buenaventura de Salinas, 'enjoy the mildest climate in the
world'. It was a climate that ennobled the spirit and elevated the mind, and so
it was not surprising that those who lived in Lima should do so 'with satisfaction and pleasure, and look upon it as their *patria*'.[94] The pride of place – a
place uniquely blessed by God – was to be the cornerstone of the increasingly
elaborate edifice of creole patriotism.[95]

During the seventeenth century the creoles of New Spain began to develop a
strong sense of the location of their own distinctive space in both the geographical and the providential ordering of the universe. To the east lay the Old World of
Europe and Africa. To the west lay the Philippines, that distant outpost of
Hispanic and Christian civilization which formed an extension to the viceroyalty
of New Spain, and served as a natural gateway to the fabled lands of the East.
Their homeland, therefore, was situated at the centre of the world.[96] Historically,
too, as well as geographically, they bridged the different worlds. Had not the
apostle Saint Thomas, coming from Jerusalem, preached the gospel in the Indies
as well as in India, and might not Saint Thomas be identified with Quetzalcóatl,
the bearded god-hero of the ancient inhabitants of central Mexico, as the great
Mexican *savant* Carlos de Sigüenza y Góngora affirmed?[97] Even if the identification was disputed, there was no doubt in creole minds that their *patria* enjoyed a
providential status. Following the publication in 1648 of a treatise by Miguel
Sánchez recounting the miraculous origins of the Virgin of Guadalupe, her cult
acquired a wide following among the creole population of New Spain. The
Virgin, it seemed, had graciously cast her protective mantle over their beloved
patria (fig. 21).[98]

The increasingly regionalized American *patrias* of the creoles came to be
located not only in space, but also in time. The conquest and conversion of the
Indies were decisive and heroic achievements, worthy of eternal remembrance.
But while they marked a decisive new beginning, it was not a beginning *ex nihilo*.
The presence of such large numbers of Indians, and the survival in Mexico and
the Andes of so many relics of the Indian past, drew attention to a more distant,
if largely barbarous, antiquity. It clearly suited the self-image of the conquistadores as a warrior caste to dwell on the heroic qualities of the peoples they had

vanquished.[99] With the Indians safely defeated, the way was open, at least in New Spain, to idealize certain aspects of the pre-Columbian civilization that Cortés had overthrown.

If writers like Bernardo de Balbuena, in his poem of 1604, *Grandeza mexicana*, celebrated the beauties of the Mexico City built by the Spaniards, they were also very conscious of the vanished splendors of its Aztec predecessor, the great city of Tenochtitlán, once described by Hernán Cortés in such glowing terms. There was an increasing tendency to emphasize the continuities between the old and the new, as in the depiction on the city's banner, as well as on prominent buildings, of the Mexica's device of the eagle perched on a cactus with a serpent in its beak.[100] This process of appropriating selected features of the Aztec past and incorporating them into the history of the creole *patria* reached a climax in the famous triumphal arch designed by Sigüenza y Góngora for the entry into Mexico City of the new viceroy, the Marquis of La Laguna, in 1680. The arch carried statues of the twelve Mexica emperors since the foundation of Tenochtitlán in 1327, with each emperor representing a different heroic virtue, as if they were so many heroes of classical antiquity. Even the defeated Montezuma, and Cuauhtémoc, the defiant defender of Tenochtitlán, were accorded their place in the pantheon.[101]

A Mexican-style appropriation of the pre-Columbian past in order to endow the creole *patria* with a mythical antiquity was more problematic in Peru, where indigenous resistance was more persistent and more menacing than in New Spain. The mestizo Inca Garcilaso de la Vega, nostalgically writing the history of his homeland in far-away Andalusia, constructed for it a developmental narrative in his *Royal Commentaries of the Incas*. Primitive Peru with its multiplicity of gods had given way to the sun-worshipping Incaic Peru of his ancestors, only to be replaced in turn by the Peru of his own times, to which the Spaniards had brought the inestimable knowledge of the one true God.[102] Garcilaso offered a vision of the Andean past – and with it of a utopian future – that was to prove highly attractive to an indigenous nobility which survived better under Spanish rule than its Mexican counterparts. But equally this vision held fewer attractions for a creole society uneasily aware of the influence exercised by the local Indian leaders (the *curacas*) over the sullen indigenous population of the Andes, and afraid that one day it might rise in revolt to restore the empire of the Incas. Slowly, however, attitudes began to change. It became fashionable among Peruvian creoles in the later seventeenth century to possess complete portrait series of the Inca rulers, but it was not until the eighteenth century that a patriotic ideology embracing the period of Inca rule began to attract sections of the creole population.[103]

Treacherous or warlike Indians needed to be remote, in time and space, before they could be safely appropriated into creole patriotic mythology. In much of British America they were neither. Those of Virginia, described by Beverley in the early eighteenth century as 'almost wasted',[104] lacked the ancient grandeur of the civilization of the Mexica, while the Indians of New England were all too close. When writing their narratives of the Indian wars of the later seventeenth century the New England Puritans defined themselves in terms of their relationship with their adversaries, the pagan Indians and the papist French.[105] This self-imagining reinforced their sense of their own Englishness, and of the Englishness of the world they had created for themselves in the wilderness. 'As we went along', wrote Mary Rowlandson, in her poignant narrative of captivity among the Indians, 'I saw a place where English cattle had been: that was comfort to me, such as it was: quickly after that we came to an English path which so took with me, that I thought I could have freely laid down and died.'[106]

The creole inhabitants of the Spanish American heartlands, who had no need to fortify their towns against Indian attack, could afford to distance themselves somewhat from the mother country and begin fashioning a distinctive and partially 'American' identity, incorporating, if necessary, an Indian dimension in ways still impossible for the colonists of New England. For these, the only safe Indian had become a dead Indian. Only during the course of the eighteenth century, as the Indian menace started to recede, would a few Indians begin to be silhouetted by the colonists on the skyline of their imagined American landscape, as exemplifications either of Roman martial virtues or of unspoilt natural man.[107]

Unable to endow their communities with the respectability of time stretching away into a distant Indian antiquity, British settlers needed to find other arguments to support their cause when confronted by metropolitan disparagement and contempt. As long as it remained faithful to its origins, New England could justify itself in terms of its self-proclaimed mission as a city on a hill. This gave a strong providentialist and religious cast to an emerging local patriotism which in this respect had obvious affinities with the local patriotism of the creole communities of the Spanish Indies. For other colonies, the task of identity construction was harder, and it proved easier to look to the future than to dwell on the past. The appropriate note was struck by Robert Beverley in *The History and Present State of Virginia* when he wrote: 'This part of *Virginia*, now inhabited, if we consider the Improvements in the Hands of the *English*, it cannot upon that Score be commended: but if we consider its natural Aptitude to be improv'd, it may with Justice be accounted one of the finest Countries in the World.'[108] English settlers had the duty of improving and transforming the land with which they had been blessed.

The expression of such aspirations fitted well with the developmental ideology of the commercial society of eighteenth-century England, where it could help to reinforce the metropolitan commitment to overseas colonization and legitimize the activities of the colonists. This was all the more necessary because of the widespread assumption in the mother country that all too many of the colonists, especially in the Caribbean, were mere lay-abouts. The planters and settlers therefore seized on the language of improvement as a useful device for justifying their record, in an attempt to rebut the slanderous allegations made against their lifestyles. Richard Ligon, in his *True and Exact History of the Barbadoes*, neatly turned the tables: 'Others there are that have heard of the pleasures of *Barbadoes*, but are loth to leave the pleasures of *England* behind them. These are of sluggish humour, and are altogether unfit for so noble an undertaking . . . So much is a sluggard detested in a Countrey, where Industry and Activity is to be exercised.'[109] This language of industry, activity and improvement was ubiquitous in the British transatlantic world of the late seventeenth and early eighteenth centuries. No longer restricted to turning the land to good account, 'improvement' now had a wide range of connotations, which ran from making a profitable investment to cultivating one's character. It implied, too, the process of acquiring gentility or civility – a process which, for members of settler communities, could be equated with the construction of their societies on a model resembling as nearly as possible that of the mother country.[110]

At the turn of the seventeenth and eighteenth centuries the challenge to replicate the norms and customs of the mother country was especially strong in the Caribbean colonies, where the social structure of the island communities, with white minorities asserting their mastery over rapidly expanding black populations, bore little relation to that of the English society that they sought to emulate. For this reason the planters found it all the more necessary to prove that they had not degenerated in tropical climes and lost their Englishness. 'They being *English*', wrote Sir Dalby Thomas in 1690, 'and having all their commerce from *England*, will always be imitating the Customs, and Fashions of *England*, both as to Apparrell, household-Furniture, *Eating* and *Drinking* &c. For it is impossible for them to forget from where they come, or even to be at rest (after they have arrived to a Plentifull Estate) untill they settle their Families in *England* . . .'[111]

Many Caribbean planters were inclined to think of themselves as transient residents of islands from which they would return to the mother country to live as country gentlemen once their fortunes were made. This distinguished them from the mass of settlers in the mainland colonies, whose prime commitment was American. But even as these mainland settlers came to identify themselves with the land which they and their forefathers had 'improved', they too remained anxious to display their English credentials and to share in the refinements of the polite and commercial society of eighteenth-century England. The scale of the black population in the southern colonies, and the menacing presence of the Indians in the forests of the north, were standing encouragements to maintain and strengthen ties with an English homeland which diminishing numbers of them had ever seen.

As Sir Dalby Thomas indicated, one way of asserting Englishness was to imitate the latest metropolitan fashions. Since the beginnings of colonization the settlers had looked to the mother country for inspiration as they constructed their transatlantic lives, and for the supply of such material objects as they could not produce themselves. As the ties of commerce were strengthened, it was natural that the colonies, as cultural provinces of Britain, should share the aspirations of growing numbers of Britons for more genteel forms of living and an increasing array of comforts.[112] The process began at the top of the social scale in the late seventeenth and early eighteenth centuries as rich merchants and planters built their new brick mansions on the latest English pattern, with a parlour taking the place of the old hall, and the creation of an open stairway ascending to the second floor as the central feature of the house.[113] Often, especially in the Caribbean, fashion tended to win out over practical considerations, as planters constructed houses in the most fashionable English style, with little regard for the difference between an English and a tropical climate. Sir Hans Sloane noted the difference in Jamaica between Spanish houses, with their tiled floors, shuttered windows and great double doors, and those built by the English, which 'are neither cool, nor able to endure the shocks of Earthquakes'.[114]

In practice, most colonial houses remained, as in Maryland,[115] simple frame or log constructions, but the new or remodelled mansions helped to set new standards for gracious living, as their occupants surrounded themselves with growing numbers of chairs and tables, plates and glassware, knives and forks.[116] What once were seen as luxuries were coming to be regarded as necessities, although there was, and remained, a counter-current in the culture of the mainland colonies which favoured plain living over luxurious new refinements. 'This man', wrote a diarist of Robert Beverley in 1715, 'lives well; but though rich, he has nothing in or about his house but what is necessary . . .'[117] The kind of austerity practised by Beverley was likely to have more resonance in a society which, even while becoming acquainted with the pleasures of refinement, spoke the language of hard work and improvement, than in one where, as in the Spanish viceroyalties, there was no effective rallying cry against the values exemplified by conspicuous consumption.

While church and state in Spanish America fought a long but losing battle to maintain an ordered, hierarchical and respectable society through the regulation of codes of dress, the blurring of the lines of social and ethnic distinction produced by inter-ethnic marriage or cohabitation tended to encourage extravagance in dress and adornment. 'Both men and women', wrote a disapproving Thomas Gage, 'are excessive in their apparel, using more silks than stuffs and cloth . . . A hat-band and rose made of diamonds in a gentleman's hat is common, and a hat-band of pearls is ordinary in a tradesman. Nay, a blackamoor or tawny young maid and slave will make hard shift, but she will be in fashion with her neck-chain and bracelets of pearls, and her ear-bobs of some considerable jewels.'[118] As creoles, mestizos, mulattoes and blacks bedecked themselves with an extravagance that shocked and dismayed the authorities, it is clear that the population at large had come to see richness of apparel as a fairer measure of social status than the colour of one's skin.

By contrast, in the North American colonies, where black was black and white was white and there was little in between, those who chose to cultivate austerity on religious or ethical grounds were not haunted by the fear that the choice of a frugal life-style would undermine their social worth. Indeed, as Beverley's comportment suggested, frugality might send out as powerful a social message as conspicuous consumption. Yet, in British America too, the pressures to consume were growing, as the colonial societies found themselves caught up in an expanding commercial empire, an 'empire of goods'. From the 1740s, as British manufacturers, in their search for profitable markets, turned their attention to the possibilities offered by a rapidly expanding American population and made available to it an increasing number and range of goods at affordable prices, the rush to consume in the mainland colonies became vertiginous. Growing supply was matched, or exceeded, by growing demand.[119]

The response of the North American colonists indicated that it was not only hierarchically organized societies, like those of Spanish America, that were driven by the urge for conspicuous consumption. A rough equality of status generated its own pressures to keep ahead of one's neighbours. The desire to follow the latest metropolitan fashions, however, also responded to a collective psychological need. The colonists needed to prove to themselves, as well as to their parent societies, that they had triumphed over the innate barbarism of their New World environment. Yet it would not be easy to persuade sceptical Europeans that their efforts had transformed America into an outpost of civility.

Cultural communities

The British and Hispanic communities that bridged the Atlantic were at least as much cultural communities as political and commercial. Spanish colonization, however, was driven, far more strongly than British colonization, by the urge to raise the indigenous inhabitants of America to the levels of civility which Europeans claimed as unique to themselves. From the start, this gave Spain's colonial enterprise a strong religious and cultural dimension that did much to shape the development of its transatlantic possessions. The priority given by church and crown to *policía* – civility – made it natural for the creoles, from an early stage, to point with pride to their cultural achievements. In 1554, only a generation after the conquest, Francisco Cervantes de Salazar, one of the first teachers in the newly founded university of Mexico, published a set of Latin dialogues in which two citizens pointed out to a newcomer some of the sights of Mexico City – its broad and regular streets, its handsome houses, its viceregal palace adorned with columns of Vitruvian proportions. The dialogues, dwelling with special pride on the university, gave the author an opportunity to blow his own trumpet. As one of the participants in his dialogues explained, Cervantes de Salazar had done his best to ensure that 'young Mexicans', by the time they left the university, should be 'erudite and eloquent, so that our illustrious land should not remain in obscurity for lack of writers, who until now have been in short supply'.[120]

By 1700, Spanish America could boast nineteen universities, as against the two colleges in British America – Harvard and William and Mary – rising to three with the founding of the future Yale University in 1701.[121] Although many of them were at best mediocre, the Spanish American universities were a source of intense regional pride, and seventeenth-century creole writers lovingly listed the names of the luminaries they had produced.[122] Yet, as Bishop

Villarroel complained in 1651, the merits of their graduates were ignored by the Spanish authorities. It seemed to be assumed in Madrid that only in the university of Salamanca were the letters and learning requisite for service to church and state to be found.[123]

Such complaints reflect the uneasy relationship normally to be found between a metropolitan centre and its cultural provinces. The provinces receive, and seek to imitate, the high styles of the metropolis, only to find their efforts dismissed as 'provincial' and crude. Imitation, however, is only a part, and not necessarily the most important part, of a relationship that is often too complex to be summarily reduced to questions of mimesis and influence. Distance from the sources can inspire creative transformation, as the artistic achievements of colonial Hispanic America amply testify.[124]

The 'Spanish' culture transmitted to the societies of the Indies by way of Seville was itself a hybrid culture. In religion, literature and the visual arts, peninsular Spain was exposed to a variety of influences, and most immediately those coming from its dominions in the Netherlands and Italy. As the centre of a world-wide empire – a centre dominated by a highly formalized court, a powerful church and a wealthy and cultivated elite – it sought to accommodate those influences to its own tastes and needs, while passing on to the outlying parts of its empire fashions and styles that arrived with the cachet of metropolitan approval.

The most direct transmitters of peninsular styles and techniques to Spanish America were the painters, architects and craftsmen who crossed the Atlantic to use their skills in a new and potentially rewarding environment – artists like the sixteenth-century Flemish painter Simón Pereyns, or the Aragonese artist and architect, Pedro García Ferrer, who travelled with Bishop Palafox to New Spain in 1640 and played a crucial part in the completion of the bishop's most durable monument, Puebla cathedral.[125] Styles and images were primarily diffused across America, however, through books, engravings and imported works of art. Many of these were specifically intended for the American market, like the canvases produced in Zurbarán's workshop in Seville, or Flemish engravings and paintings on canvas or copper, done initially in the mannerist style and subsequently assuming baroque forms under the influence of Rubens.[126]

Inevitably there was a time-lag. This was especially true of architecture, since many of the great cathedrals, like those of Mexico City, Puebla, Lima and Cuzco, were begun to designs drawn by Philip II's architects, but often had to wait for their completion until well into the seventeenth century.[127] By the last third of the seventeenth century, however, Spanish America was using with growing assurance the visual and architectural language of Spanish baroque, itself a hybrid language with strong Italian and Flemish components. To this were added further, more specifically American, and even oriental, components, in response to local tastes and requirements. *Biombos*, for instance, the Japanese-inspired folding screens which divided up the spaces in upper-class Mexican houses, reflected the Asian influences introduced into New Spain through the Acapulco galleon trade with Manila (fig. 23). Indigenous craftsmen in the sixteenth century, working with materials traditional to their own culture, like feathers, were quick to appropriate European models and then reinterpret them in their own fashion, manipulating the visual language of the conquerors to reshape it as their own (fig. 24).[128] Now, a century later, and more fully integrated into urban life, they continued to bring their own stylistic traditions to a baroque culture that sought to enfold within its capacious embrace all the ethnic and social groupings of an increasingly variegated and complex society.

American expressions of this baroque culture, whether in its visual or literary manifestations, might well be too naïve, or too overwrought, to meet with the approval of those whose tastes had been formed in Seville or Madrid. To peninsular Spaniards the turns of phrase employed by the creoles could appear as convoluted as the gilded wooden retablos that framed the altars of their churches.[129] Yet between 1670 and the 1760s the viceroyalties of New Spain and Peru succeeded in creating a distinctive Hispano-American culture that transcended replication, and represented a genuine transmutation of the forms and images borrowed from Spain (fig. 25).

This distinctive culture was to be seen in the vast theatrical canvases of the greatest of Mexican baroque painters, Cristóbal de Villalpando, and in the depictions of elegant arquebusier angels and archangels by anonymous painters of the Cuzco school (figs 27 and 18).[130] It was to be seen, too, in the ornate work of Peruvian silversmiths (fig. 28),[131] and in the spectacular churches that arose in New Spain and the Andes, with their elaborate baroque façades and their interior surfaces intricately decorated by Indian and mestizo craftsmen and dazzling with gold. It found expression in the scintillating poems written in her Mexico City convent by Sor Juana Inés de la Cruz, described in the second (1690) edition as 'the unique *American* poetess, the tenth muse . . .' (fig. 29)[132] and in the ingenious erudition of Sor Juana's friend and admirer, Carlos de Sigüenza y Góngora, mathematician, natural scientist, historian and philosopher.[133]

Literary and artistic tastes in Spain's American cultural provinces suggest that the creoles had set themselves to outperform the productions of the mother country in their pursuit of an idiom that would express their own distinctive individuality. At the same time, however, the kind of culture they were in process of creating possessed an internal coherence which suggests that it was well attuned to the characteristics of the racially mixed societies now developing in the Indies. It was, above all, a culture of show, in which imagery was called upon to promote the social and political aspirations of these increasingly complex communities. The sense of theatre was everywhere. Essentially urban, and overwhelmingly religious, this was a creole-dominated culture, which found its most popular expression in the fiestas and processions that formed a constant accompaniment to city life. These great ceremonial events, marking significant occasions in the life of the church and the monarchy, were so orchestrated as to create the illusion of an integrated society, every section of which was entitled to its own carefully delineated space. Ethnic and social tensions found miraculous, if temporary, resolution as all ranks of society came together to express their allegiance and devotion to the higher powers that ruled their lives – God and the king. Through these celebrations the authorities could remind the people that they were participants in a universal order. Yet the universal found its counterpoise in the particular, as creole elites used the celebrations to proclaim the unique glories of their various *patrias*.[134]

There was nothing comparable to all this in the contemporary cultural life of the British colonies, although, in so far as Britain itself participated in an international culture of the baroque, North America, too, felt its influence. The self-conscious erudition of Cotton Mather, with its philosophical speculations deeply rooted in theological certainty, had something in common with that of Sigüenza y Góngora, his contemporary in New Spain (figs 30 and 31).[135] The morbid and the miraculous were far from being the exclusive prerogative of Hispanic, or Latin, civilization, and the Puritan culture of Massachusetts was not without its own tendencies towards 'baroque' excess. Nor were the reading tastes of the two colonial worlds widely dissimilar, as a comparison of the inventories of book dealers in Boston and Mexico City in 1683 reveals. Readers in both cities, while turning to the classics and history, showed a strong preference for devotional works, sermons and moral disquisitions. Only where dramatic literature was concerned was there a real parting of the ways. Spanish America, where companies of actors gave public performances of plays written by Spanish or local playwrights in the major urban centres, was an enthusiastic participant in the theatrical culture of the metropolis. New England was not, and its hostility to the theatre was shared by Quaker Pennsylvania, where in 1682 the assembly prohibited the introduction of stage plays and masques. Although small troupes of actors from England toured the southern colonies with some success in the opening decades of the eighteenth century, it was not until the 1750s that the theatre in any sustained form arrived in North America, and hostility remained deeply rooted in Philadelphia and New England.[136]

If Spanish America far outshone British America in the coherence and sophistication of its cultural life at the turn of the seventeenth and eighteenth centuries, there were good reasons for this. Spanish America, unlike British America, had created an urban civilization, in which civic elites, largely Jesuit-educated[137] and with time on their hands, spoke a common religious and cultural language that spanned the continent. The viceregal courts of Mexico City and Lima transmitted to the New World the latest fashions in the court culture of the Old, and provided the patronage and the setting for the kind of activities that lay at the heart of baroque culture – dramatic spectacles, masquerades and literary jousts, in which competitors sought to outdo each other in elaborate conceits and ingenious word-play. Above all, a rich and powerful church had not only stamped its authority on society, but deployed its massive resources to convey its message to vast populations through spectacle and imagery.

The scattered populations of British America possessed neither the resources nor the political and religious cohesion to follow suit. The majority of Britain's colonies were still struggling societies, far younger than those of the Spanish

Indies. Only in 1743 was Benjamin Franklin able to write that 'the first Drudgery of Settling new Colonies, which confines the attention of People to mere Necessaries, is now pretty well over; and there are many in every Province in Circumstances that set them at Ease, and afford Leisure to cultivate the finer Arts, and improve the common Stock of Knowledge.'[138]

Over the preceding three decades certain sections of colonial society had in fact already transcended 'the first Drudgery of Settling new Colonies' and revealed a quickening interest in acquiring the refinements of life, as their increasing expenditure on clothes and furnishings from England made clear. Their civic projects, too, had become more ambitious, although, in contrast to Spanish America, ceremonial considerations tended to take second place to commercial. Sir Christopher Wren's plans for the rebuilding of London in 1667, themselves inspired by French town-planning, may partly have inspired the design of Annapolis. Planned by Governor Francis Nicholson of Maryland in 1694, this was intended to be a characteristically baroque city, its principal streets radiating outwards from two circles, which housed respectively the centre of colonial government and the Anglican church. It was Nicholson, too, who as governor of Virginia, projected the colony's new capital of Williamsburg, where the governor's 'palace', begun in 1706 in the manner of Wren, helped set the fashion for 'Virginian baroque' – the style chosen by planters and gentry for the mansions they constructed in the following decades.[139]

Even the grandest of these mansions, however, were small-scale affairs when compared with the magnificent country houses that the English nobility were building for themselves (fig. 32).[140] If these testified to a wealth beyond compare, it was none the less true that substantial wealth was to be found on the American seaboard, both among the southern planters and in port cities like Philadelphia, where the urban professional classes built their town houses in the style made fashionable in the home country by Wren. But the colonies were as yet no more than distant cultural provinces of a Britain still establishing its own criteria for gentility. Colonial patrons remained uncertain about the fashions they should follow, while craftsmen who commanded the latest styles and techniques remained in short supply.

It is not therefore surprising that the cultural achievements of Britain's American colonies around the turn of the seventeenth and eighteenth centuries were a good deal less independent of their sources than those of their Spanish American counterparts. In general, the English colonies were still at the stage of imitation, and had yet to transmute metropolitan influences into distinctive and original styles of their own. The very absence, indeed, of an indigenous workforce, of the kind to be found in the Spanish viceroyalties, may have reduced the chances for originality and innovation, although the presence of Dutch and German colonists offered the possibility of creative alternatives to predominantly British tastes and fashions.

Nevertheless, a distinctive British American culture did begin to emerge as the eighteenth century progressed. When contrasted with Spanish America's culture of show, it could fittingly be described as a culture of restraint (fig. 26). Although the pursuit of English-style gentility by the wealthier colonists meant that they were happy to fill their houses with growing quantities of English luxury goods, and to deck themselves out in the latest English fashions with printed cottons, linen, ribbons and lace imported from Britain, their taste, more classical than exuberantly baroque when it came to the construction of their houses or to their locally produced furniture, tended towards the simple, the convenient and the practical. This taste, which gave rise to a degree of stylistic uniformity through the mainland colonies, no doubt drew its inspiration both from New England's traditional culture of moderation, and from a Chesapeake culture that had long emphasized the virtues of simplicity, perhaps as a form of self-protection against English gibes about the backwardness of the colonies in the arts of civilization.[141]

A similar restraint was apparent in the approach of the North American colonial elite to commissioning and acquiring works of art. There was a brisk market in prints imported from England, but the only paintings on their walls were likely to be portraits of themselves and family members. Painted for the most part in a highly formulaic manner by artists who travelled through the colonies in search of commissions, these family portraits were a mark of social status and a record for posterity of personal and family achievement (fig. 33). To the frustration of the more talented artists there was no market for still lifes, landscapes or genre scenes. Nor, in a Protestant society, was there any demand for the devotional paintings which provided a living for so many artists in the Hispanic world, although biblical scenes were popular subjects for the prints with which the colonists decorated their walls. Lacking the patronage provided in Spanish America by the church and the viceregal courts, and restricted to the endless production of family portraits, it is not surprising that the more ambitious North American artists of the eighteenth century – Benjamin West, Charles Willson Peale, John Singleton Copley and Gilbert Stuart – should have set their sights on London. They went, not only in search of fame and fortune, but also to study the works of the great European masters and enjoy the wider creative possibilities that were not available to them at home.[142] By contrast, large numbers of original Spanish and Flemish paintings were available in Spanish America for studying and copying,[143] and Mexican and Peruvian artists apparently felt no comparable need to travel to Madrid.

Artists and craftsmen in Spanish and British America alike, however, were caught between conforming and not conforming to Old World conventions. When artists, writers and artisans produced their own innovative variations on the styles reaching them from Europe, fidelity to the original still remained the measure by which Europeans judged their cultural attainments. Creoles, for their part, believed that the more closely they approached the levels of civilization of the mother country, the stronger would be their claims for inclusion in a partnership of esteem. Yet, even as they struggled to assert those claims, they were striving to find and assert an identity that was distinctively their own.

Not surprisingly, the effort to reconcile these conflicting aspirations proved to be a source of tension and anxiety. The stronger the determination of creole communities to demonstrate their similarity to the mother country, the more obvious it became, not only to Europeans but also to themselves, that the resemblance fell short. This paradox had far-reaching implications both for their own future and for that of their parent societies. If ever the moment should arrive when, in an act of collective rejection, they should choose to base their identity, not on the expectation of similarity but on the assertion of difference, they would be turning their backs on that larger community in which their fondest dream was to be accepted as full partners by their transatlantic cousins.

PART 3

Emancipation

CHAPTER 9

Societies on the Move

Expanding populations

When two Spanish naval officers, Jorge Juan and Antonio de Ulloa, were ordered by Madrid in 1735 to accompany a French scientific expedition to the kingdom of Quito, they were instructed to gather information on the character and condition of Spain's Pacific coast territories. Their report, written in 1747 on their return after ten years of travel, contained a devastating account of administrative corruption and the ill-treatment of the Indians. But the two men also commented on the enormous wealth, both mineral and agricultural, of the viceroyalty of Peru, and described in their prologue the countries of the Indies as 'abundant, rich and flourishing'.[1] Any mid-eighteenth-century visitor to the great viceroyalties of New Spain and Peru would certainly have been struck, not only by the splendour and obvious wealth of Mexico City and Lima, but also by the evidence of entrepreneurial activity, commercial vitality, and social mobility over large areas of territory.

Underlying the prosperity noted by eighteenth-century visitors to the two viceroyalties was the new-found buoyancy of their mining economies after a difficult seventeenth century.[2] The recovery of Peruvian production, where the Potosí silver mountain may have accounted for 80 per cent or more of total output in the viceroyalty in the early colonial period,[3] was slower and more hesitant than that of New Spain. This had the benefit of a larger number of mining centres, higher-grade ore, a lower level of taxation by the crown, and lower labour costs. Presented with greater opportunities, the mining entrepreneurs of New Spain and their merchant backers had stronger incentives to take risks than their Peruvian counterparts. As a result, New Spain was to maintain its lead over Peru for the entirety of a century in which total Spanish American bullion production would achieve a fourfold increase, with Peruvian production up by 250 per cent and that of New Spain by 600 per cent.[4]

Apart from the development of subterranean blasting techniques, this impressive increase in output seems to have owed less to any major technological improvement than to changes in working methods and the employment of labour. The increase in production was a response to the apparently insatiable European demand for American silver, together with a greater availability of mercury from Spain for the process of refining, the opening of new shafts, and the willingness of entrepreneurs to sink their capital into risky but potentially highly lucrative enterprises. The entrepreneurs benefited, too, from the growth of population, which helped to keep wages down – a consideration that was particularly important in the mines of New Spain, always less reliant on forced labour than those of Peru.[5]

The wealth and activity generated by the eighteenth-century development of their extractive economies – especially of silver rather than gold[6] – had a pervasive influence across Spain's American territories. The proportion of their population directly engaged in mining activities was not in fact large – perhaps 0.5 per cent of the total labour force in New Spain.[7] The numerous men, women and children, however, who flocked to the mining centres had to be clothed and fed, and the mines themselves required a steady stream of tools and supplies, many of which had to be brought long distances over arid and difficult terrain.

All this activity could have a dramatic impact on local economies. Landowners who enjoyed relatively easy access to mining communities were given a powerful incentive to increase their production of maize, wheat and livestock in response to the market demand. Nowhere were the consequences more striking than in the Bajío region of northern New Spain, formerly a remote and scantily populated frontier area.[8] The growing prosperity of the mining region of Guanajuato – the most productive of all the eighteenth-century mining areas of Spanish America – made it a magnet for large numbers of people from central Mexico. By the end of the eighteenth century the city of Guanajuato, with its surrounding villages, had a population of over 55,000. A major beneficiary of this growth was the agricultural region round the nearby town of León, traditionally a region with many small proprietary farmers. Some of these took advantage of rising land values to sell out to the great estate-owners, while others succeeded in accumulating enough holdings to become hacienda owners in their own right. In the ownership and use of land, as in the development of the textile workshops of Querétaro, another rapidly growing city in the Bajío, the expansion of urban markets created by the mining boom was a powerful promoter of social and economic change.

The priority placed on the production of silver, however, and its overwhelming preponderance in the export trade, gave silver mining a disproportionate influence over other types of economic activity in the two viceroyalties. Its also tended to concentrate wealth in very few hands, with spectacular fortunes being made, and lost. Elites able to tap in to the various stages of silver extraction and export were avid consumers of luxury goods imported from Europe and from Asia by way of the Philippines trade. The extractive economies of New Spain and Peru were therefore in some respects comparable to the plantation economies of the British Caribbean and the southern mainland colonies, where the concentration of wealth in the hands of a small class of planters encouraged the consumption of foreign luxuries and militated against the expansion of a home market because the mass of the population lived in poverty.[9]

The analogy, however, is not perfect, since, unlike sugar or tobacco, silver – unless it all went directly for export – was the instrument for monetizing colonial economies, generating new activity in the process as it passed from hand to hand.[10] Unfortunately it is impossible to determine the quantity of silver retained in Spanish America instead of being exported, but it may have been as much as half.[11] In addition to the portion held back after minting to meet the requirements of domestic commerce, there was a continuous unauthorized seepage of minted and unminted silver into the local economies. This silver energized the internal trade circuits of Spain's American empire; and although part of it went to the Spanish crown in payment of dues and taxes, or was siphoned off to Europe and Asia for the purchase of imports, enough remained to finance the church building and the urban improvements of the eighteenth century, which gave visitors their impression of opulence and growing prosperity.[12]

Growth and development were visible, too, in the eastern regions of Spanish America, away from the extractive economies of New Spain and Peru, but increasingly locked into the Atlantic economy. Cacao from Venezuela and hides from the La Plata region were being exported to Europe in growing quantities. This in turn brought a new prosperity and population growth to Caracas and to Buenos Aires, which was already benefiting from its position on the silver conduit running from the mines of Peru.[13] Yet for all the signs of economic progress and social change in Spanish America over the first half of the eighteenth century, a contemporary visitor returning to both Americas after a prolonged absence would probably have found them less startling than the transformation of British America during the same period.

This was hardly surprising. The British colonies had been settled much later than the Spanish, and several of them were still struggling to become viable communities when the eighteenth century began. New colonies had been settled in the closing decades of the preceding century. The colonization of Carolina began with the founding of Charles Town – uncomfortably close to the Franciscan missions of Spanish Florida – by planters from Barbados in 1670.[14] Carolina's northern province, Albermarle County, which had been settled from Virginia, emerged as a distinct entity under the name of North Carolina in 1691. The Delaware counties broke off from the proprietary colony of Pennsylvania, founded in the 1680s, to form a colony of their own in 1702. Georgia, the last of the pre-revolutionary thirteen mainland colonies, would only begin to be settled in the 1730s.

Traditionally, the founding of new colonies in British America had been a response to political, religious or economic pressures in the mother country. But, as the foundation of North Carolina suggested, local American circumstances were now beginning to play an important part in a process hitherto largely governed by metropolitan preoccupations. The most powerful of these local circumstances was land hunger. From the later seventeenth century the population of

British America was rising dramatically, and its rapid growth would generate powerful new pressures affecting every aspect of eighteenth-century colonial life. Population increase was partly the consequence of natural growth on a scale that was spectacular by contemporary European standards, and partly of the influx of white immigrants and African slave labour.[15]

Between 1660 and 1780 the total population of the mainland colonies grew annually at a rate of 3 per cent.[16] A combined white and black population for all the American colonies of some 145,000 in 1660 and 500,000 in 1710, increased to nearly 2 million by 1760. Of these 2 million, some 646,000 were black, almost half of them working on the Caribbean plantations.[17]

Natural increase accounted for anything from two-thirds to three-quarters of this spectacular population growth. The eighteenth-century North American mainland was relatively free of the periodic harvest failures which brought famine to Europe. Fertility rates were high, and infant mortality rates far lower than in Europe. Much of the population, too, enjoyed the benefits of reasonable conditions of peace and security for a good part of the period.[18] There were, however, wide regional variations in the rate and degree of population increase. The average annual rate of growth on the mainland was twice that on the islands. Of the mainland colonies, the Chesapeake settlements outpaced New England's 2.4 per cent, while the Lower South registered 4.3 per cent.[19]

The statistics of increase were pushed up by immigration, both voluntary and involuntary. It is estimated that some 250,000 men, women and children arrived in the English mainland colonies from overseas between 1690 and 1750. Of these perhaps 140,000 were black slaves, transported either from Africa or from the Caribbean plantations. The reproductive rate of the slave population settled on the mainland was significantly above that in the Caribbean islands, where mortality rates were higher, and the fertility rate lower, for reasons that still have to be fully explained.[20]

Forced removal to America was not restricted exclusively to blacks. Some 50,000 of the English immigrants to eighteenth-century America were convicts, following the passage of a new law in 1718 providing for their systematic transportation overseas. Most of these involuntary immigrants were shipped in chains to three colonies – Pennsylvania, Maryland and Virginia – under conditions little better than those aboard the African slave-ships.[21] As far as voluntary emigration from England was concerned, this was substantially less in the eighteenth than the seventeenth century. With an expanding economy taking up some of the slack in the population at home, it was now the skilled, rather than the desperate, who were leaving for America. They did so in search of the higher wages and wider opportunities offered by a rapidly expanding market for skilled labour in the colonies. Some skills, however, were in more demand than others. William Moraley, a spendthrift from Newcastle who ran into difficulties at home and took sail for the colonies in 1729 as an indentured servant, was warned – correctly – that watchmaking, in which he had been trained, was 'of little Service to the *Americans*', and that the 'useful trades' in the colonies were 'Bricklayers, Shoemakers, Barbers, Carpenters, Joiners, Weavers, Bakers, Tanners, and Husbandmen more useful than all the rest'.[22]

If English and Welsh immigration was less intense than in the preceding century – under 100,000 in the period 1700–80, as compared with 350,000 in the seventeenth century[23] – this was to some extent offset by the growing number of Scots and Scots-Irish immigrants. Somewhere between 100,000 and 150,000 Scots-Irish arrived before 1760, and many more would follow in the succeeding decades, driven overseas by population pressure and the lack of employment opportunities at home.[24] To these Celtic immigrants were added swelling numbers of immigrants from continental Europe, whose presence added new and variegated pieces to the mosaic of peoples which British American colonial society was in process of becoming. Besides Huguenot refugees fleeing the France of Louis XIV, a tide of German-speaking immigrants – more than 100,000 by 1783 – streamed into the country, driven from the Rhineland and other regions of Germany by hardship or political instability, or attracted by glowing reports of the success of the Pennsylvania Quakers in creating space for religious minorities to live their own lives.[25]

The majority of these German immigrants landed in Philadelphia. Some moved onwards, but many remained in Pennsylvania, where they found themselves in what William Moraley described as 'the best poor Man's Country in the World', borrowing a phrase that seems already to have been in common usage.[26] The Middle and Southern colonies in particular were embarking in the eighteenth century on a dramatic phase of expansion, but everywhere through mainland America the buoyancy of the British Atlantic economy was creating opportunities for a new, and better, life.

There was nothing comparable in the Hispanic world to this massive movement of white immigrants into British North America during the first half of the eighteenth century, not least because of the crown's continuing formal prohibition on non-Spanish immigration, although a number of Irish and other foreign Catholics had been allowed to settle in the Indies during the seventeenth century, and officials showed a growing disposition in the eighteenth to relax the rules. A steady stream of Spaniards, however, continued to migrate, although apparently it flowed less strongly than in earlier times.[27] As with British emigration in the eighteenth century, new tributaries were joining this stream. Just as, as in the eighteenth century, the British periphery was producing a growing share of the total number of white immigrants, so too the Spanish periphery was playing a larger part than before. During the seventeenth century increasing numbers of Basques, in particular, had joined the Castilians, Andalusians and Extremadurans who had preponderated in the first century of colonization. Eighteenth-century emigration saw the increased representation of immigrants from the northern regions of the peninsula – not only Basques but also Galicians, Asturians and Castilians from the mountain region of Cantabria – together with Catalans and Valencians, from the east coast of Spain.[28]

Some at least of this new wave of immigration from the periphery was encouraged and assisted by the Spanish crown. As the borders of Spain's American empire were pushed forward in the eighteenth century to counter the encroaching presence of the English and the French, great open spaces had somehow to be filled. There was little enthusiasm in Spain for migration to these remote outposts of empire, and successive governors of an underpopulated and ill-defended Florida begged Madrid to send them colonists. The crown responded by offering free transportation and other facilities to peasants from Galicia and the Canary Islands. The Galicians, clinging to their small parcels of land at home, were reluctant to be uprooted, but the crown enjoyed greater success with the Canary Islanders, whose tradition of emigration to America reached back to the earliest years of colonization. From the 1670s, as the population of the Canaries approached saturation point, islanders began to emigrate in significant numbers, in particular to Venezuela, with which the islands had maintained their connection since Cumaná was conquered in the sixteenth century.[29]

The Canary Islanders tended to emigrate in family groups, and a number of families were resettled in the 1750s in St Augustine, the principal town of Florida. A small contingent of islanders had earlier been despatched to another distant outpost, San Antonio in Texas. The numbers of these government-sponsored immigrants, however, remained disappointingly few. As so often, Spanish bureaucracy proved the graveyard of good intentions.[30]

Apart from the Spanish crown's policy of excluding the nationals of other European countries, there were good reasons why its transatlantic possessions should have proved less of a magnet to potential emigrants in the eighteenth century than those of the British crown. Although the population of Spain was growing again – from 7.5 million in 1717 to rather over 9 million in 1768[31] – it would take time to make up for the catastrophic losses of the seventeenth century, and especially those experienced in the realms comprising the Crown of Castile. Growth was stronger on the Spanish periphery than at the centre, and in so far as emigration was a response to population pressure at home, it was in the peripheral regions that the pressure was most likely to be felt.

In spite of new signs of economic vitality in many parts of Spanish America, the opportunities it offered for an immigrant population at this stage of its development are likely to have been less than those awaiting immigrants to the British colonies. As in British America, the import of African slaves – much of it in the hands of British merchants following the Treaty of Utrecht in 1713 – ensured a steady supply of labour for the haciendas and plantations. One reckoning of the number of Africans imported into Spain's American dominions between 1651 and 1760 puts the figure as high as 344,000.[32] Growing numbers of slaves were needed to provide labour for territories on the fringes of empire, like New Granada, whose combined gold-mining and agricultural economy had become dependent on Africans to supplement a rapidly dwindling Indian population.[33] In the cacao-growing province of Caracas in Venezuela black slavery was the predominant form of labour during the boom years which stretched from the 1670s to the 1740s.[34] Another outpost of empire, Cuba, had a slave population of some 30,000 to 40,000 by the mid-eighteenth century. The mass importation of slaves into the island only began in the years after the brief British occupation of Havana in 1762, and was a response to the dramatic spread of the sugar plantations as sugar overtook hides and tobacco as Cuba's principal export.[35]

While the import of black slaves helped to meet local demands for unskilled labour in regions where indigenous labour was non-existent or in short supply, the older-established areas of Spanish settlement on the American mainland were less dependent on external sources of skilled labour than the majority of the British mainland colonies. As in British America, the eighteenth century was an age of population growth, and increasing numbers of Indians, mestizos and free blacks helped to swell an artisan class catering for an urban demand that was expanding, but was still limited by the poverty of all but a small elite.[36]

In the viceroyalty of New Spain, in particular, the total population showed a marked increase, from some 1.5 million in 1650 to 2.5–3 million a hundred years later – a figure larger than that of the total population of all the British American colonies combined.[37] Across Spanish America, however, there were wide regional variations in the rate and extent of growth, just as there were also wide ethnic variations between the increase in the numbers of creoles and mestizos on the one hand, and Indians on the other. The Indian population of Peru, and still more of New Spain, was beginning to recover in the middle or later decades of the seventeenth century from the cataclysm that had overtaken it in the aftermath of conquest and colonization, but the recovery, while strengthening, continued to be fragile. In spite of improved resistance to European diseases, Indians remained vulnerable to waves of epidemics, like the one that ravaged the central Andes in 1719–20 or the typhoid fever that hit central Mexico in 1737. Indian mortality rates – and especially child mortality rates[38] – remained significantly higher than those of the white and mestizo population. The recovery, too, would falter in the later eighteenth century in areas where the food supply was unable to keep pace with population increase.[39]

The creole population was also increasing. In Chile, where the Indian population continued its decline until it constituted under 10 per cent of the total population by the late eighteenth century, the creole community was growing at the rate of 1 per cent a year in the first half of the century, and the pace of growth would accelerate as the century proceeded.[40] The figures for creole demographic increase were certainly assisted by the inclusion of those who, although not of pure Spanish descent, managed to pass themselves off as white. The most marked feature of eighteenth-century Spanish American life, however, was the rapid growth of the mixed population of castas.[41] Its results were everywhere apparent, although less, for instance, in Chile than in New Granada, whose population by 1780 was 46 per cent mestizo, 20 per cent Indian, 8 per cent black, and 26 per cent 'white' (creole and peninsular Spaniard). Creoles, for their part, constituted no more than 9 per cent of the total population of New Spain in the 1740s, although this rose to 18–20 per cent (no doubt including many mestizos) around 1800. In Peru in the 1790s 13 per cent of the population was creole, as against some 76 per cent in Chile.[42] New Granada society was consequently more fluid than that of

Andean Peru or the heavily settled regions of New Spain, where Indians accounted for 60 per cent or more of the population, and where the two 'republics' of Spaniards and Indians continued to enjoy more than a purely nominal existence, at least outside the cities.[43] Yet in New Spain and Peru, even if to a lesser extent than in New Granada, the growth of an ethnically mixed population was also changing the character of society and unleashing new forces which would sooner or later undermine traditional distinctions and erode Indian communities that had hitherto preserved a fair measure of integrity and autonomy.

One important consequence of eighteenth-century population growth throughout the Americas was an increase in the size of urban populations in both the British and the Hispanic colonial societies. Estimates suggest that the population of the five leading cities of mainland North America rose in the period 1720 to 1740 from between 29 per cent for Boston to 57 per cent for New York and 94 per cent for Charles Town. While this increase was impressive, these remained very small urban populations when compared with those of some of the major cities of the Spanish American world.[44]

1742 (to nearest thousand)		*1740s to 1760s* (to nearest thousand)	
Boston	16,000	Mexico City	112,000
Philadelphia	13,000	Lima	52,000
New York	11,000	Havana	36,000
Charles Town	7,000	Quito	30,000
Newport	6,000	Cuzco	26,000
		Santiago de Chile	25,000
		Santa Fe de Bogotá	19,000
		Caracas	19,000
		Buenos Aires	12,000

The growth of cities did not in itself mean a progressive urbanization of society. Indeed, as the population grew and spread outwards to cultivate new areas of land, so the proportion of town-dwellers in British America tended to decline. Even on the eve of independence, only 7–8 per cent of the mainland population lived in towns of more than 2,500 inhabitants.[45] In Spanish America, too, population growth also seems to have led to a fall in the urban share of the population. With an estimated 13 per cent living in cities of 20,000 inhabitants or more in 1750, however, it was far above the North American percentage, and in line with European levels, although the cities of Spanish America were far more thinly distributed over space than their European counterparts.[46]

Even in the still relatively small cities of British America, urban growth brought in its train an expanding underclass, whose existence gave rise to mounting civic concern.[47] In Boston, where the problem of poverty emerged for the first time on a serious scale during the war of 1690–1713 – a war which created many war widows and fatherless children, and left seamen and carpenters jobless when it ended – a quarter of the population were living below the poverty line in 1740.[48] This was a problem with which Spanish American towns had long been familiar. The insurrection in Mexico City in 1692 was an unpleasant reminder of what could happen when a large and ethnically diverse population, living at or below the poverty line in crowded tenement houses and insalubrious conditions, was suddenly confronted with sharp rises in the price of maize and wheat.[49]

In the Hispanic world there was a well-established tradition of charitable giving, and the founding of convents and hospitals from the early years of settlement offered the possibility of relief for some at least of the poor and homeless. By the late seventeenth century, too, a network of municipal granaries had come into existence across the continent to hold down food prices and respond to sudden shortages. But the 1692 Mexico City riots were an indication that more drastic measures would be needed to tackle the problems of poverty, vagabondage and urban lawlessness, all of which increased as the cities of Spanish America expanded and hovels and shanties multiplied. During the eighteenth century both the imperial administration and municipal governments began to turn away from reliance on indiscriminate charity and move in the direction of more interventionist policies, confining the distribution of alms to the 'deserving poor', and setting up institutions to confine the indigent.[50]

The Protestant world of the North American colonies lacked the institutional safety net of religious foundations and charitable fraternities which offered a measure of relief in Spanish America to the needy and abandoned. Heirs to the ethos of Elizabethan England, the colonists regarded idleness as a major cause of poverty, and carried with them to America the harsh corrective traditions of the Elizabethan poor laws. Indeed, poor law legislation in Massachusetts was even harsher than its English original. Stern measures were taken to set the poor to work, and 'warn out' unwanted paupers and exclude undesirable immigrants, especially the Scots-Irish, when shiploads of them began arriving in Boston in the second and third decades of the eighteenth century.[51] Yet the colonists also brought with them from their homeland an appreciation that the care of the 'impotent poor' was a communal responsibility. They devoted money, in increasing quantities, to poor relief. In Anglican Virginia, in particular, the costs of welfare rose dramatically in the early eighteenth century, and charitable grants and other relief measures placed a growing burden on the parishes.[52]

While vestrymen and churchwardens struggled to keep pace with the increasing numbers of paupers, especially in the seaport towns, philanthropic associations sprang up to provide additional sources of relief.[53] The responses to the problem of poverty in the Spanish and British colonial worlds did not therefore differ as much as their differing religious traditions might suggest. During the eighteenth century there appears to have been a growing convergence of attitudes to a common problem, as Spanish America, better endowed with religious and charitable foundations, moved in the direction of more interventionist and authoritarian measures, while British America, even if initially inclined to impute poverty to individual failings, displayed a growing awareness of the need to supplement restrictive legislation with communal and individual charity.

It seems plausible to assume, however, that poverty was proportionately much more widespread and acute in the teeming urban world of Spain's American territories than in the far smaller coastal towns of the British mainland colonies. There was always the safety valve of an expanding agrarian frontier in the British colonies, offering space and opportunity to indigent immigrants prepared to try their luck. The poor of the overcrowded Spanish colonial cities had fewer possibilities for escaping and making new lives for themselves, in a world where so much land was concentrated in the hands of large lay and ecclesiastical landowners, or was reserved for the use of Indian communities.

The chances of employment in the cities of the Spanish Indies depended on a demand for goods and services which was determined by the spending capacity and tendency to conspicuous consumption of relatively small urban elites. Although fine craftsmanship and the products of skilled labour were always in demand in the viceregal capitals and the great mining centres, the demand was liable to fluctuate with the fluctuations of a mining economy, and life remained precarious for an artisan class that displayed an amazing ethnic diversity. In contrast to British America, where guilds either failed to take root or were few and generally ineffectual in controlling the market,[54] craft and trade associations developed early in Spanish America, and exercised considerable control over the regulation of wages and labour and the quality of the finished products. If these guilds, some of which admitted Indians as well as creoles, gave their members status in urban society, they also had the effect of restricting the range of possibilities open to skilled craftsmen who found themselves excluded. Guilds were not intended for mestizos and blacks.[55]

Yet in this complex Hispanic American society, nothing was ever quite as it seemed, and the urban labour market was frequently less restricted than would appear at first sight. Guilds were less powerful in some towns than others, and even in the older cities, where guilds for the different trades and crafts had commonly sprung up during the sixteenth century, ambitious master artisans found ways of evading guild restrictions. It was open to those who could afford it, whether creole, Indian or free black, to purchase black slaves. Slave labour had the advantage of permitting a greater flexibility of working methods and was not subject to the usual guild restrictions on hours and conditions of employment. As a result, a number of trades, like building, came to depend heavily on their slave labour force.[56]

Where British America provided numerous opportunities for immigrants with skills in what were described to William Moraley as the 'useful trades', immigrants from the Iberian peninsula to the Spanish American viceroyalties were therefore liable to find that their dreams of a better life on the far side of the Atlantic were doomed to disappointment. There was already an ample supply of labour, both free and unfree, in the cities, and immigrants would find themselves competing for employment with creole, African and Indian artisans. Outside the cities, the natural growth of the population was reducing opportunities for securing employment and acquiring land. The Indian communities soon began to experience the impact of this population increase, as growing numbers of outsiders encroached on their communal lands in defiance of the law.

The Indians did their best to resist these encroachments and fought back with all the legal weapons at their disposal where they could.[57] The legal rights they enjoyed, even if increasingly infringed, continued throughout the eighteenth century to maintain what amounted to internal frontiers in Spanish America. British America, too, had its frontiers, but these were primarily external, and under the pressure of a rapidly expanding settler population they were being relentlessly eroded.

Moving frontiers

As each new generation of settlers outnumbered the generation that preceded it and immigrants swarmed into the mainland colonies of British North America, the frontiers of settlement were constantly being pushed forward in the search for new land. But what constituted a frontier?[58] Even in the Europe of the later seventeenth century, the concept of territorial demarcation through precisely defined linear boundaries was not yet fully established.[59] Boundary lines in the Americas were correspondingly more obscure. Frontiers, whether between Europeans and Indians or between the colonial settlements of rival European states, were little more than ill-defined zones of interaction and conflict on contested ground.[60] The assertions made on paper by mapmakers caught up in the work of imaginary colonization at the behest of European ministers were unlikely to bear much relation to American realities.[61] These were determined by the colonists themselves, as they surged outwards from the old areas of settlement until checked by some geographical barrier, or by the presence of unsubmissive Indians or rival Europeans.

The most formidable physical barrier to the westward expansion of the British colonies was the Allegheny Mountains, and it was only in the middle years of the eighteenth century, with the founding in 1747 of the Ohio Company of Virginia, that a serious attempt would be made to embark on projects for the settlement of the vast and unknown regions beyond the Alleghenies.[62] This was 'Indian Country', and no European colonial society on the North American continent could hope to exercise any form of control over the interior unless it drew on the support and co-operation of powerful groups among the competing Indian peoples who inhabited it.[63]

The prize had for long been the fur trade of the Great Lakes region. Conflict over the control of this trade had pitted the Iroquois against Algonquian-speaking peoples and the French against the English, with corresponding combinations and permutations of political alliances. During the first half of the eighteenth century the French sought to hem in the English colonies along the Atlantic seaboard, while forming a chain of trading settlements that would link Canada to their newly established colony of Louisiana at the mouth of the Mississippi. In the central decades of the eighteenth century, as the demand for agricultural land among the English colonists became greater than the demand for fur and hides,[64] the frontiersmen had to contend not only with the physical barrier of the Alleghenies, but also with the alliance system put in place by the French. Westward expansion from the Middle Colonies could only be achieved by military victory over France and its Indian allies.

Further north, the New Englanders, by crushing the Algonquian Indians in King Philip's War of 1675–6, had won for themselves more room for settlement, although the ending of the war also saw the drawing of firmer boundaries between English and Indian land.[65] Conflict continued along the frontier areas until the Treaty of Utrecht in 1713, when a temporary equilibrium was established between British America, French America and the Five Nations of an Iroquois Confederacy that had learnt from experience the advantages of neutrality.[66] Calmer conditions during the three decades that followed the Treaty of Utrecht allowed New England settlers to flow westward in growing numbers towards the boundary lines. In this, they enjoyed more room for manoeuvre than their fellow colonists in New York. These found their hopes for expansion into the area of the Great Lakes blocked not only by the buffer territory of the Iroquois,[67] but also by the unwillingness of the great New York proprietors to sell, rather than lease, portions of their land. The effect of this was to make land settlement and cultivation within the confines of the colony a relatively unattractive proposition for potential yeoman farmers.[68]

The mass of new migrants – the Germans and the Scots-Irish – therefore tended to concentrate in the Middle and Southern Colonies, pressing westwards in Pennsylvania into Lancaster County and the Susquehanna River Valley, casting covetous eyes on the vast but still inaccessible expanses of the Ohio Country, which were claimed both by Pennsylvania and Virginia,[69] and moving south-east from the Shenandoah towards the backcountry of North Carolina. Their arrival meant further displacements of indigenous tribal groupings, whose way of life had already been profoundly disturbed by the spread of English colonial settlements in the Carolinas in the 1670s and 1680s. As the colonists set Indian against Indian, and occupied new swathes of land, so the tensions multiplied. In 1711 the Tuscarora Indians struck back against the colonists of North Carolina; in 1715 it was the turn of the Yamasees of South Carolina. These had been military allies and trading partners of the English, whom they helped supply with the 50,000 or so deerskins that were now being exported to England each year.[70] Their grievance was less over the occupation of their land than over the behaviour of the Carolina traders on their expeditions into the interior, where they carried off Indian poultry and pigs, exploited Indian carriers, and traded illegally in Indian slaves. In their exasperation the Yamasees launched a series of attacks on their former allies, and in the war that followed it looked for a moment as if the colony faced extinction. The eventual defeat and expulsion of the Yamasees opened up more land for settler occupation.

The displacement and destruction of Indian tribal groupings generated an enormous volatility in the interior of the continent, precipitating mergers and alliances of enemies as well as friends, as the indigenous peoples struggled to hold on to their lands and hunting grounds in the face of growing European encroachment. Like the settler societies that had intruded upon them, the native American societies, too, were societies on the move. They responded to the dangers that faced them in different ways. The Iroquois resorted to diplomacy. They had negotiated the confederation of the Covenant Chain with the English colonists in 1677, and they played skilfully on Anglo-French rivalry to sustain their own territorial interests and extend their influence or hegemony over other Indian peoples in the West and the South (fig. 35).[71] Other groups resettled well away from the intruders, or, like the remnants of the defeated Yamasees of South Carolina, changed sides. A generation earlier, the Yamasees had allied with the English to wipe out the Spanish mission province of Guale – 'Wallie' to the English[72] – on the Georgian coast. Now they moved south into Florida to seek the protection of their former Spanish enemies.[73]

The upheavals created by European imperial rivalries and internal colonial pressures were not confined to the North American continent. Frontiers with the Indians grew up in South America wherever pacification or military conquest failed. The earliest and most obvious of these was the military frontier in southern Chile along the river Biobío, designed to keep the Araucanian Indians at bay. In the late seventeenth and eighteenth centuries another Indian frontier emerged, this time in the Río de la Plata region. Once horses crossed to the other side of the Andes in the late seventeenth century, mounted Pampas Indians, attracted by the livestock, became a serious threat to the growing number of stock-raising settlements, forcing the Spaniards to take defensive measures.[74]

But in this region, and up much of the eastern side of the continent, the Spaniards also had European rivals to worry about. In an attempt to demarcate the respective spheres of interest of the crowns of Spain and Portugal, the Treaty of Tordesillas of 1494 had allotted to Spain all lands and islands in the Atlantic falling to the west of a line running 370 degrees west of the Cape Verde Islands, while those to the east of it went to Portugal. The land of 'Brazil' found by Pedro Alvares Cabral in 1500 thus fell automatically within Portugal's area of jurisdiction. Juridically speaking, the straight line drawn on a map made the frontier of Brazil the most clear-cut frontier in all the Americas, but nobody in the seventeenth or early eighteenth century had any accurate idea of where in practice Portuguese territory ended and the Spanish viceroyalty of Peru began.

Although Portugal's overseas possessions legally kept their separate identities in the sixty years following the union of the crowns in 1580, the eastwards expansion of settlers from Peru and the westwards expansion of Portuguese and mixed-race colonists from the coastal settlements into the Brazilian interior brought convergence as well as conflict. By the mid-seventeenth century there would be many Castilian names among the inhabitants of São Paulo.[75] But the frontier was also the setting for violent confrontation. As the Spanish Jesuits advanced their mission settlements eastwards from Asunción, armed gangs of *bandeirantes* from São Paulo raided deep into mission territory to seize slaves for work on the landed estates of the São Paulo region and the sugar plantations of Pernambuco and Bahía. By the time Portugal recovered its independence in 1640 the Spanish crown had been forced to abandon its traditional Indian policy and consent to the arming of the Guaraní Indians living in the Jesuit missions so that they would be in a position to defend themselves. By then, however, the Guairá missions, with their 10,000 remaining Indians, had been driven to relocate to a safer region east of the River Uruguay.[76]

The ruthless depredations perpetrated by the Paulista *bandeirantes* checked the process of Spanish expansion from Asunción, clearing the way for eventual occupation of the disputed territory by settlers from Brazil. The Spaniards, for their part, founded Montevideo, at the mouth of the River Plate, in 1714, as a base from which to extend their control over the hinterland and check the southward expansion of the Portuguese.[77] In the following decades the Spanish-Portuguese frontier remained a still undefined and shifting zone of conflict and commercial interchange, with a shrinking indigenous population caught in the middle.

Some peoples, like the Pampas Indians of the Río de la Plata region, were more effective than others at keeping the Europeans at bay. When the Jesuits sought to complete their ring of missions round Portuguese territory by establishing themselves on the Upper Orinoco, they were compelled to withdraw after their missions were attacked and destroyed by Guayana Caribs in 1684. Along with other religious orders they moved back again into the Orinoco region in the 1730s. This time the forward movement of the missions was backed up by a support system of Spanish civil settlements and a line of fortifications. But even then their situation remained precarious in the face of an alliance between the Caribs and the Dutch, who had begun settling in Guayana in the later seventeenth century. The Caribs, like the Iroquois, had learnt to play the European game.[78]

At the Treaty of Madrid of 1750 Spanish and Portuguese ministers and map-makers made an effort to define Brazil's borders all the way from the Orinoco basin in the north to the ranching region of the Banda Oriental, the eastern edge of the Río de la Plata estuary, in the extreme south-east. Except where concessions were mutually agreed, each party was to retain possession of territory already occupied. This effectively relegated the line drawn at Tordesillas to the realm of myth. Instead of a geometrical abstraction, natural boundaries were now sought wherever possible. These followed the contours of the Brazilian river system, as politicians turned to geography rather than astronomy to determine frontier lines.

The treaty, however, which involved the exchange of considerable areas of land between the two crowns, proved ephemeral. It was welcomed neither on the Portuguese side, nor by the Jesuits and their Guaraní charges, who rebelled against the transfer. It was also premature, in the sense that the new line ignored a vast central and northern belt of territory inhabited solely by Amazon tribes. With Portuguese and Spanish settlements still far away, this was a territory that

Brazil would start to colonize and incorporate only in the nineteenth century.[79] In those areas along the new frontier where Spanish and Portuguese settlements were in striking distance of each other, the frontier line itself remained little more than a vague point of reference, and the borderlands continued to be what they had always been, a law unto themselves, regulated, in so far as they were regulated at all, by the prospects of commercial advantage, a mutuality of interests, and the power of the gun.

Where frontier areas were tamed along this great Brazilian border, this tended to be a consequence of the activities of the religious orders, which effectively created new frontiers, as they penetrated into regions as yet unsettled by Europeans, and then imposed upon them their own brand of Christian peace. It was a method of colonization also employed by the French, but alien to the ways of a British colonial world that had no religious orders and all too few ministers willing to dedicate their lives to the conversion of the Indians. Its extensive use by the Spaniards, not only on the borders of Brazil, but also in pushing forward the boundaries of Hispanic culture into the far north of Mexico and Florida, gave the borderlands of Spain's empire in America a dynamic distinct from that of the British American borderlands.

The mission frontier system developed by the Spaniards – initially by the Franciscans, but increasingly during the seventeenth century by the Jesuits, who began moving into areas, like Arizona and the western coastal regions of North America, that the Franciscans had not reached – was a form of cultural activism intended to transform the indigenous peoples on the fringes of Spain's empire, and bring them into the orbit of Spanish civilization. While there were disagreements both between and within the religious orders as to the desirability or necessity of turning Indians into Spanish speakers,[80] their aim was to acculturate them to accept Spanish Christianity and Spanish norms of civility. Where possible, the initial approach was that of more or less subtle persuasion,[81] but the end result, which involved the relocation of Indian converts into new settlements or *reducciones*, was to turn their world upside down. Drastic changes to that world had already been occurring as a result of contacts, either at first or second hand, with European intruders into indigenous territory. The coming of the missions, however, effectively meant a system of forced acculturation designed to bring them within the frontiers of an alien Spanish world.

The friars and the Jesuits were the advance agents of a Spanish frontier policy that sought to be a policy of inclusion, absorbing and assimilating the indigenous population, in contrast to the frontier policy of exclusion that had become the norm among the British colonies to the north.[82] But the policy of inclusion had its limitations and its failures, of which the Chilean frontier with the Araucanian Indians along the river Biobío was for long the most glaring example.[83] After failing lamentably to subdue the Araucanians in their wars of the sixteenth and early seventeenth centuries, the Spaniards found themselves compelled in the middle of the seventeenth century to reinforce their defensive system of frontier garrisons. The costs of maintaining a standing army of some 1,500 men were high, and the soldiers' pay, as in all Spanish *presidios*, was pitifully inadequate. They therefore supplemented it by a brisk trade in Indian captives. These could legally be enslaved since the Araucanian war was deemed to meet the criteria of a 'just war', and this lucrative traffic provided every inducement to perpetuate the conflict. It was only in 1683 that the crown ceased to authorize the enslavement of the Araucanians, but it would take more than a decree from Madrid to stamp out such a well-established practice in one of the remotest outposts of Spain's global empire.

Yet increasingly the Araucanian war became a phantom war, as trading and personal contacts across the frontier multiplied. Simultaneously, conflict was being reduced by alternative methods of pacification. The missions played their part, although the process of Christianization proved frustratingly slow, not least because it was hard for the religious to disassociate themselves from the activities of the military. More effective in reducing tension was the development from the mid-seventeenth century of regular 'parliaments' between the Spanish authorities and the Araucanians, comparable to the discussions that William Penn held with the Pennsylvania Indians in his pursuit of an enlightened Indian policy. These could lead to the signing of formal treaties between the two parties.[84] But more than the missions, or regular discussions between Spanish officials and Indian caciques, it was the evolution of forms of coexistence based on mutual need which gradually tamed the Chilean border zone. Not war but trade and *mestizaje* would finally subdue the people whose heroic defence of their homeland had so moved European readers of Alonso de Ercilla's sixteenth-century epic *La Araucana*.

In spite of periodic raids by Dutch and other foreign vessels on the Pacific coast of South America, there was little to suggest that Spain's attempt to bring the Araucanians within the confines of their empire would be seriously compromised by the activities of Spain's European enemies. In this respect the Chilean frontier differed both from the Spanish–Portuguese frontier in Brazil and from the borderlands of northern New Spain, although there was always a lurking fear of enemy intervention in support of the Indians even in the remote Pacific coastal regions, and in the middle years of the seventeenth century some 20 per cent of the revenues of the Lima treasury were having to be allocated for coastal defence.[85]

The defence of northern New Spain was to become by the end of the seventeenth century a growing preoccupation for Mexican viceroys and the ministers in Madrid. The northwards advance of New Spain had been a hesitant and often faltering process ever since the creation of the vast new province of Nueva Vizcaya in 1563.[86] In 1598 Juan de Oñate, leading an expedition from the new province, took possession of the Pueblo Indian territory of New Mexico in the name of the King of Spain, and went on to find the mouth of the Colorado River at the head of the Gulf of California. The settlements that sprang up in New Mexico were hundreds of miles from those of Nueva Vizcaya, and unlike Nueva Vizcaya, where silver mines were discovered, the far northern borderlands seemed to have little to offer potential Spanish settlers. The Pueblo Indians, living in their scattered villages, were not easily brought under control, while the rugged and desert landscape of the American Southwest was uncongenial territory, difficult to reach either from Nueva Vizcaya or New Mexico. For much of the seventeenth century, therefore, New Spain's northern borders remained only lightly populated by settlers, a frontier territory of missions and military outposts. Slowly, however, the Hispanic population of New Mexico, with its capital at Santa Fe, began to grow, and agricultural and ranching settlements started to spread.[87]

Each new advance of the northern frontier, however faltering, brought the Spaniards into closer proximity to hostile Indian peoples, like the Apaches, whose mastery of the horse would convert them into formidable adversaries.[88] The extension of the frontier regions also increased the possibilities of eventual confrontation with the settlements of European rivals, like those of the French at the mouth of the Mississippi and the English in the Carolinas.

Like New Mexico, Florida was another isolated outpost of empire, consisting of little more than the presidio or garrison town of St Augustine and the Guale missions. In the later years of the seventeenth century both these frontier provinces came close to being obliterated. Carolina settlers, supported by non-mission Indians who had been alienated by Spanish labour demands, were on the offensive in Florida from 1680 onwards, and forced the Franciscans to abandon their Guale missions. They failed, however, to capture St Augustine, which was strongly enough fortified to beat off the attacks by land and sea launched by Governor James Moore of Carolina in 1702.[89] In New Mexico in 1680, four years after the ending of King Philip's War in Massachusetts, the Pueblo Indians of New Mexico launched a concerted attack on the Spaniards. Already suffering from the loss of herds and crops through the effects of drought and the raids of Navajos and Apaches, they turned on a settler population only some 3,000 strong, which had continually oppressed them with labour demands. Their rebellion, too, was the cry of protest of a people whose way of life was being eroded by Spanish attempts to impose new cultural practices and religious beliefs.[90] Here as elsewhere along the margins of Spain's empire in America, the missions were just as likely to be part of the problem as of its solution.

The Pueblo rebellion, when it came, took the Spaniards by surprise. Santa Fe was surrounded and destroyed, and the surviving Hispanic population of New Mexico was driven back to El Paso. The whole northern frontier caught fire as the rebellion spread beyond Pueblo country to engulf other Indian peoples under Spanish rule. Spain and New Spain alike lacked the people and the resources to establish well-defended frontiers along the borderlands of empire.

Yet strategically the northern frontier was too important to be abandoned for long. Indian raids deep into the viceroyalty were a standing danger to the mining camps of Nueva Vizcaya, while the presence of the English and the French in the region posed a growing threat. Silver fleets making their homeward journey from the Caribbean through the Bahama Channel had to sail uncomfortably close to English settlements in the Carolinas.[91] As for the French in the Gulf of Mexico, there was the prospect that one day they would be strong enough to seize the silver mines of northern New Spain, although the danger receded when a Bourbon monarch ascended the Spanish throne. The French and the English, too, had access to a wider range of European goods than the Spaniards for trading with the Indians, and could turn this to advantage when seeking Indian allies.

The requirements of defence, therefore, at least as much as the need to acquire more land for agriculture and ranching and the urge to win more converts for the faith, pushed Spain to strengthen and extend its North American borders at the turn of the new century. In the 1690s a campaign began to reoccupy New Mexico. Little by little a shrinking Pueblo population was worn down, until eventually an accommodation was reached, and relative calm at last descended on the Pueblo–Spanish borderland.[92]

In the 1690s, too, Spain embarked on sporadic efforts to forestall the French in the Gulf of Mexico. In 1691 the viceroy of New Spain appointed the first governor of the province of Texas, where a Franciscan mission had just been founded to evangelize the Indians.[93] Seven years later the Spaniards built a small fort at Pensacola in West Florida, but Pensacola Bay proved no substitute for the mouth of the Mississippi as a base from which to control the river system that led to the interior. While the emerging French colony of Louisiana drove a wedge between New Spain and Florida, the expanding French presence in the region also threatened Texas, with its fragile Spanish missions. In 1716 the viceroy was sufficiently alarmed by the threat to despatch a small military expedition to reoccupy East Texas. With this expedition the permanent Spanish occupation of Texas began. A new outlying province was added to Spain's extended empire of the Indies – a thinly settled province of garrisons, missions, and struggling settlements vulnerable to attack by the Apaches. But the beginnings of cattle ranching around San Antonio at least hinted at the possibility of less bleak times to come.[94]

Florida, Texas and the other outposts that straggled along the northern borders of the viceroyalty of New Spain were, and remained, the orphans of Spain's empire in America. Madrid accepted them only reluctantly, and ignored them as far as it could. The tripartite struggle between England, France and Spain for the domination of the vast area of territory that lay to the south and south-east of the North American continent made their acquisition and defence an unpleasant necessity. They represented a constant and unwelcome drain on resources, and they were also unattractive to emigrants, who preferred to make for the more settled regions of New Spain and Peru.

The occasional importation of Canary Islanders to populate the frontier regions had little impact when compared with that made by the influx into British America of the Scots-Irish, who were encouraged by the colonial authorities to settle the frontier areas on the assumption that their experiences in Ulster had uniquely equipped them to deal with barbarous frontier tribes. Writing in 1720 about the grant two years earlier to Scots-Irish settlers of a tract of land in Chester County, where they founded the border township of Donegal, the provincial secretary of Pennsylvania explained that, in view of apprehensions about the

Indians, he 'thought it might be provident to plant a settlement of such men as those who formerly had so bravely defended Londonderry and Enniskillen as a frontier against any disturbance'.[95] His use of the word 'frontier' was itself suggestive. In this region of encounter between European and non-European a defensive barrier made up of doughty fighters was regarded as a prerequisite for successful settlement. The Indians, however, were not Irish, in spite of traditional assumptions to the contrary,[96] and 'defence' was all too liable to be a euphemism for the most naked forms of offence.

The British American borderlands, unlike the Spanish, were constantly being replenished by fresh streams of immigrants, many of them brutal in their disregard for the Indians and their rights, but most of them ready and willing to employ their energy and skills in clearing the ground and 'improving' the land. Such people were in short supply on the northern frontiers of Spain's empire in America. As a result, the Hispanic frontier territories found it hard to generate the kind of economic activity that would create self-sustaining wealth, unless – as in the missions or the mining camps – they had a docile Indian labour force at their command.

The lot of the governors of such outposts, therefore, was not a happy one. Dependent on remittances of money that arrived only irregularly from the New Spain treasury and were in any event inadequate, the governors of eighteenth-century Florida – all of them military men, who lacked experience of government and could call on none of the administrative support systems enjoyed by the viceroys of New Spain and Peru – were expected to fight off attacks by the English and the French, strengthen the defences, maintain the missions and the clergy, and turn this outpost of empire into a going concern. Not surprisingly the colony languished, staggering from crisis to crisis, and surviving, if barely, with the help of small permanent garrisons, sporadic injections of defence subsidies, and illicit trade.[97]

There was an obvious contrast, therefore, between these Spanish northern borderlands, envisaged primarily as buffer zones against European rivals and hostile Indians, and the border regions of the British mainland colonies which were pushing forward in response to the pressure of colonists hungry for land or anxious to extend their trading contacts with the Indian peoples of the American interior. Yet for the British, too, strategic requirements became an increasingly important consideration in the forward movement of the frontiers, as they looked to ways of responding to the growing threat posed by France's empire in America. The founding of the new colony of Georgia on the southern flank of South Carolina in the 1730s may have been inspired by the philanthropic ideals of James Oglethorpe and his friends, but it also met an urgent strategic need by creating a buffer against the expansionist tendencies of the French and Spanish settlements.[98]

London, however, was as reluctant as Madrid to take on long-term military commitments in outlying frontier regions.[99] The imperial authorities therefore left it to the individual colonies to settle their border arrangements as best they could. Some, like New York and Pennsylvania, resorted to diplomacy to remain on good terms with the Indians. Others made attempts to improve their military capability. As it became necessary for larger numbers of soldiers to travel greater distances, the colonial militias began to be supplemented by volunteer forces, paid and provisioned by colonial assemblies. Advancing frontiers called for extended means of protection.[100]

Irrespective of the different motivations, military, economic, demographic and religious, that were driving frontiers forward – motivations that varied within the colonial empires themselves, as well as between them – those of British and Spanish America possessed certain common characteristics. Even where protected by a string of forts and garrisons, like the arc of Spanish forts running from the top of the Gulf of California across southern Arizona and on to El Paso and San Antonio,[101] the frontiers were not boundary lines but porous border regions – lands neither fully settled by, nor integrated into, the colonial European societies that aspired to possess them, nor as yet wholly abandoned by their indigenous inhabitants. As such, they were zones of contact, conflict and interaction on the periphery of empire, where the requirements of survival on both sides found expression in violence and brutality, but also in co-operation and mutual accommodation.

As far as the Indians were concerned, these frontiers were first and foremost frontiers of disease. Wherever the Europeans – sometimes perhaps even a single lone trader – came into contact with an Indian population hitherto protected by a degree of isolation, the ravages of disease were all too prone to follow. The Pueblo Indians of New Mexico may have numbered some 80,000 when the Spaniards reached the banks of the Rio Grande in 1598. By 1679 their numbers were down to an estimated 17,000, and fourteen years later to 14,000, following the revolt.[102] A million Indians may have been living east of the Mississippi on the eve of the English settlement of North America. By the end of the colonial period only 150,000 were left. A sudden lethal attack of smallpox or influenza could wipe out an entire people. Alternatively, recurring bouts of epidemics over two or three generations could lead to a similar disaster, played out in slow motion.[103] With their tightly packed concentrations of converts, the Spanish missions were breeding-grounds for disease,[104] and warfare completed the work that epidemics left undone. Not surprisingly, 'the Indians generally choose to withdraw, as white people draw near them', as an English official remarked in 1755.[105]

Consequently, the frontier regions were often regions of withdrawal and retreat, and not only for Indians desperate to escape the scourge of European-born diseases. The settlers, too, might be forced to pull back in the face of Indian attacks, as in New England during King Philip's War, or in the Spanish mission provinces of Guale and East Texas. The advance of the European frontier may have been inexorable, but it was never irreversible. Yet even as frontiers, whether British or Spanish, shifted to and fro, new human relationships were all the time being forged, as a consequence of coercion, mutual necessity, or a combination of the two.

Coercion was obviously at its highest in areas with a military presence, like New Mexico. Here Spanish soldiers, who were in effect soldier-settlers, were dominant figures in an evolving and highly stratified society, consisting of missionaries, a sparse settler population living in three or four towns and a number of farming villages, and large numbers of subjugated Pueblo Indians. The 'Kingdom of New Mexico', as it was officially styled, possessed a small landowning nobility of fifteen to twenty families, some of them descended from the conquistadores and settlers of the late sixteenth century. Priding themselves on their Spanish ancestry, which was much less pure than they liked to boast, they lorded it over a population of mestizo landed peasants, and the so-called *genízaros* – janissaries. These were either detribalized Indians taken in 'just wars' and pressed into domestic and military service, or captive Indians acquired from other tribes. New Mexico's was a rough, callous and highly status-conscious society of conquerors and conquered, dependent for its survival on coerced Indian labour, and constantly oscillating between barter and warfare with the surrounding Indian peoples.[106]

But it was also a society in which whites and Indians, even if nominally in the ranks of the excluded, found themselves in daily contact, and in which such Spanish blood as existed was being constantly diluted as a consequence of marriage and concubinage, so that by the end of the seventeenth century almost the entire population was racially mixed.[107] In New Mexico, as in all the borderlands of empire in the Americas, exploitation and interdependence threw together peoples of very different background and traditions to create a world, if not necessarily of shared blood, at least of shared experience. A fort protecting the Spanish or English 'frontier' might be a symbol of oppression to some and of protection to others, but at the same time it was likely to be a meeting-point for the exchange of goods and services and for human intercourse. In this way, each party learnt something of the customs and characteristics of the other, and began adapting to new contacts and conditions, and to an environment that itself was being transformed as it was brought within the ambiguous category of 'frontier' territory.

Propinquity and mutual need served as an encouragement to move towards a 'middle ground' in which the actions and behaviour of both parties would become mutually comprehensible.[108] Some trod this middle ground with greater ease than others – traders, for instance, who were liable to take an Indian 'wife'; interpreters, whether European or Indian, who had learnt the other's language; men and women who had once been captives, and had acquired some understanding of the ways of an alien society during the years of their captivity.[109] Trade was among the strongest of inducements to search out a middle ground; and trade, which came to occupy a central place in the lives of the Indian societies of North America as they were drawn into contact with Europeans, became a prime instrument for securing the Indian alliances that were indispensable for the Europeans as they fought among themselves for hegemony. Colonial officials, therefore, in pursuit of such alliances were also liable to become denizens of the middle ground, like the trader and army contractor William Johnson (1715–74), who negotiated with the Six Nations on behalf of New York, took a Mohawk common-law wife, and in 1755 was appointed superintendent of Northern Indian affairs.[110]

The middle ground, however, was treacherous territory, where a false step could prove fatal. Violence, after all, was a permanent fact of life over large stretches of the borderlands of empire. The individualism that featured so prominently in Frederick Jackson Turner's vision of the frontier and its impact on the evolution of the United States was therefore tempered by a powerful urge towards mutual assistance and co-operation among European settlers who were seeking to carve out new lives for themselves in the isolation of an unfamiliar and frequently intimidating environment.[111] Many settlers must have seen themselves living, in the words of William Byrd in 1690, at 'the end of the world', although not many of them did so in the relative comfort of a Virginia plantation.[112] In Pennsylvania and the Appalachian borderlands, home was more likely to be a cabin of rough-hewn logs, the type of housing favoured by Scandinavian and German settlers in the region, and later adopted by the Scots-Irish immigrants.[113] Not surprisingly, these settlers banded together for help. Almost within earshot of their settlements and clearings lay 'Indian Country', whose inhabitants they contemplated with a mixture of unease, contempt and fear. How many of them, like the Massachusetts minister, Stephen Williams, taken captive as a child, must have passed restless nights filled with 'disquieting dreams, about Indians'?[114]

If all frontiers in America shared certain common features, they were also very different. William Byrd's frontier in Virginia was not that of Stephen Williams in Massachusetts, and neither was it the frontier of New Mexico or Brazil. While their very remoteness from the major centres of settlement made them laws unto themselves, this does not mean to say that they shared a common lawlessness. Garrisons and missions imposed their own forms of discipline. There was, too, the communal discipline that was all too often needed for survival, and a self-discipline that might be instilled by religion or prompted by the desire to maintain standards of gentility in regions that looked out over a 'barbarian' world. At the same time, there was a widespread perception in the more settled parts of the colonies that it was the dregs of humanity who moved into the frontier regions, 'the Scum of the Earth, and Refuse of Mankind', as the settlers of the Carolina Backcountry were described by a contemporary.[115] Scots-Irish immigrants were regarded in Pennsylvania as turbulent and disorderly people, squatting on land to which they had no legal right, and 'hard neighbours to the Indians'.[116] Many of these frontiersmen lived in conditions of abject poverty. As happened in Spanish New Mexico or in those parts of North America where the land speculators were the first to arrive, a frontier region could just as easily be a setting for the most acute inequality as for the equality later hailed as the defining characteristic of frontier life.[117]

Over time, the ethos of the settled regions of the colonial world in America was more likely to impress itself on the borderlands than was the ethos of the borderlands to impress itself on the heartlands of colonial societies. This became all the more true as colonies were consolidated, elites emerged, and eighteenth-century

European concepts of refinement spread to the Americas. By the middle of the eighteenth century country stores were making European commodities available even in remote frontier areas of North America.[118] The very fact that frontiers were advancing into territory formerly occupied by heathen and 'barbarians' itself represented a gain for European notions of civility.

The contrast between these claimed or reclaimed regions and the 'Indian Country' lying beyond them was, to white settlers, both obvious and painful, and created a genre of literature which was to enjoy vast popularity in British North America – the narratives of captivity among the Indians. While accounts of the Indian wars, like Increase Mather's *A Brief History of the War with the Indians in New England* (1676), could always be assured of a wide readership,[119] their popularity would be eclipsed by that of personal narratives recounting the experiences of those who had been held prisoner by the Indians. The number of such captives ran into the thousands – 750 are recorded as having been taken by Indians to French Canada alone between 1677 and 1750.[120] Many captives were in due course redeemed, but others never returned, either because they died in captivity, or, more alarmingly, because they had assumed the life-style of their captors, and, for one reason or another, were unwilling to abandon it. These were the 'White Indians', many of them taken captive as children, and so successfully assimilated into Indian societies that they forgot their European ways and even their native tongue.[121]

To white settlers imbued with fears of cultural degeneration brought about by contact with the Indian[122] it was deeply disturbing that their own kith and kin should go so far as to choose barbarism over civilization. Yet this appeared to be happening with unnerving frequency as men, women and children were taken captive during the French and Indian wars of the later seventeenth and early eighteenth centuries. For Puritan New England in particular, voluntary defections to the Indians raised fundamental questions about the character and the efficacy of the errand into the wilderness of their forebears and themselves.[123] To some extent they found their answer in captivity narratives – morality tales, evoking in vivid detail the dangers and ambiguities of a frontier existence, offering solemn warnings, and providing the spiritual consolation that came from seeing the dangers overcome.

Captives might well face torture and death, but they also faced the more subtle danger represented by the temptation of turning their backs on a Christian way of life. The most popular and famous of all the captivity narratives was *The Soveraignty and Goodness of God*, Mary Rowlandson's graphic account of her life among the Indians.[124] Running through three editions in Massachusetts and another in London in 1682, the year of its publication, it conveyed an appropriately inspiring message of how the grace of God enabled a lone but pious woman in the clutches of 'atheisticall proud, wild, cruel, barbarous, bruitish (in one word diabolical) creatures', to survive the many adversities and dangers that beset her. Many other such accounts would follow, containing elevating stories of redeemed captives to set against the distressing news that some, like Eunice

Williams (renamed A'ongote by her Mohawk captors), obstinately chose to remain unredeemed.[125]

In 1673, nine years before the publication of *The Sovereignty and Goodness of God*, a Chilean soldier, Francisco Núñez de Pineda y Bascuñán, put the final touches to a manuscript recounting his six months' captivity among the Araucanian Indians over forty years earlier. Entitled 'Happy Captivity' – *Cautiverio feliz* – it would not find its way into print for another two centuries. It was not only in its publishing history that it differed from Mary Rowlandson's account. The two writers responded in very different ways to the ordeal of their captivity.[126]

The differences cannot simply be put down to the differences between the Nipmuck Indians and the Araucanians. Both writers, indeed, depicted the Indians as cruel, and Núñez de Pineda had to watch while his captors 'sacrificed' one of his companions and devoured his heart. But where Mary Rowlandson misses no opportunity to express her revulsion for her captors' way of life, Núñez de Pineda gives every impression of bonding with the people into whose hands he had fallen. He would sup with them 'with great pleasure', and was treated as if he were the cacique's adopted son, a status that could have been his for the asking. The temptation to remain among his captors was clearly strong, and it was with regret that he eventually parted from them and returned to 'Christian country' and his elderly father.[127] For all the cruelty of the Indians, they were – unlike the Spaniards – men of their word, true descendants of the noble and heroic people portrayed a century earlier in Alonso de Ercilla's epic poem, *La Araucana*. Happy the captive of such a race!

Mary Rowlandson, too, was well treated by her captors, not one of whom 'ever offered me the least abuse or unchastity to me, in word or action'.[128] The Algonquians, like the Araucanians, were keen to adopt captives to replenish their numbers, and Rowlandson, like Núñez, could easily have done what many others of her compatriots did in a similar situation, and remained. But if ever the temptation to do so came upon her, she went to enormous pains to conceal the fact, and was keen to express her revulsion for the way of life of the 'diabolical' Indians, and her nostalgia for the English world she had lost. Hers was an unhappy captivity, although at the same time a truly redeeming experience, in that her afflictions made her wonderfully aware of the overwhelming power of God.

It was on the point of religion that the Calvinist Rowlandson and the Catholic Núñez, so different in their responses to life among the Indians, were most closely united, at least when it came to addressing themselves to their readers. To emphasize his spiritual steadfastness when among the heathen, Núñez makes much play of how he resisted the temptation to sleep with the women offered him by his hosts, and how he seized such opportunities as he could to teach his captors Christian prayers. At the end, both the redeemed captives joined in offering up thanks to God for their safe return. But if one of them on returning left the frontier wide open, the other did her best to ensure that it remained tight shut.

'Happy Captivity' – for so long unpublished – represents the captivity literature that Spanish America otherwise lacks, with the exception of the famous sixteenth-century narrative, *Los naufragios*, by Núñez Cabeza de Vaca.[129] One reason for this may be that until the eighteenth century there were few places on the fringes of Spain's empire of the Indies, other than Chile, where it is possible to speak of military borderlines and a more or less permanent state of 'war'. As the eighteenth century proceeded, the situation would change, and the number of captives would increase as the frontiers of the empire were pushed forward into hostile country. The accounts of their sufferings, however, were to be found in petitions to the monarch rather than, as in British America, in narratives that made their way into print.[130]

The unwillingness of Spaniards who had been taken prisoner to go public with an account of their experiences may well reflect a feeling of shame at the sheer fact of captivity among 'barbarous' Indians. A stigma was now attached to them, although Núñez de Pineda went some way to expunging it by presenting his captors in a favourable light, especially when their behaviour was set against that of corrupt and self-serving royal officials sent out from Madrid. In the circumstances, it was not surprising that his manuscript had to wait two centuries before seeing the light of day. The authorities were unlikely to license publication of any work that would draw attention to failings and deficiencies in a great imperial enterprise whose rationale was to bring Christianity to pagan peoples and incorporate them into a civilized Hispanic polity. Readers, both in Spain and the Indies, may well have shared these inhibitions. It was unpleasant to be reminded of the barbarians still at the gates. For readers in Britain and colonial America, on the other hand, captivity narratives like that of Mary Rowlandson served a useful didactic purpose, reminding them of the need for fortitude in the face of adversity, and the wonderful workings of Providence.

The different responses to the ordeal of captivity among the Indians, however, are also likely to reflect different attitudes to 'the frontier' in the two colonial societies. The northern borderlands of New Spain were remote and thinly populated regions, far removed from the densely settled heartland of Mexico, and neither before nor after the coming of independence did they carry the kind of emotional charge associated with 'the frontier' in the minds of British colonists, for whom it conjured up visions of hard labour and heroic enterprise in hostile Indian territory. The psychological frontiers separating the colonial societies from 'Indian country' were also less sharply drawn in Spanish than in British America, and the deep concerns about the temptations of 'Indianization' that so troubled English settlers were apparently not shared by Spanish settlers, many of whom already had Indian blood in their veins. The elite of New Mexico might be concerned to preserve the already suspect purity of their blood-lines, and uphold their status by ostentatiously sporting Spanish dress,[131] but *mestizaje* nevertheless proceeded more or less unchecked. Secure in their value-systems and beliefs, the settlers on the borderlands, while boasting of their Spanish descent, could allow themselves some latitude in the way they lived their daily lives.

The colonists of British North America, and especially those of Puritan New England, where the Indian wars were most intense and prolonged, seem to have been less well equipped to deal with the psychological consequences of life on the borders of 'Indian country'. The Indian had been demonized for too long, and ambiguities are hard to accept in a world where mental polarization is the order of the day. In the face of the insecurities generated by defections to the way of life of the enemy, the narratives of redeemed captives offered some assurance of the ultimate triumph of religion and civility.

Yet the creation and expansion of new frontiers in the Middle and Southern Colonies, and the acquaintance of growing numbers of settlers with the life on the borderlands, gradually began to prompt a change of attitude.[132] There was to be an increasing sense of affinity with the American landscape, no longer as much of a 'wilderness' as it had originally seemed. With this came the beginnings of a reassessment of the Indian, as his way of life, apparently so well attuned to American nature, came to be better known and understood. The eighteenth century was rediscovering 'natural man' in the forests of America, Indians who possessed the primitive virtues of an uncorrupted people. The Iroquois, as described by Cadwallader Colden in his *History of the Five Indian Nations* (1727), were like the early Romans in their devotion to the ideals of republican liberty. 'Indeed', he wrote, 'I think our Indians have outdone the Romans' – a comparison already made in the sixteenth century, and also to the advantage of the Indians, in Ercilla's *La Araucana*.[133]

In this mid-eighteenth-century world of changing sensibilities, the frontier was becoming broad enough to accommodate two ideal types – Indians still uncorrupted by the vices that civilization brought in its train, and settlers who were not 'the Scum of the Earth', but upright and hard-working farmers, living close to God and nature as they cleared spaces in the forests and met the challenge of the wild. The two races inhabited a bountiful land of rugged beauty, a land whose savagery would in due course be tamed by the honest toil of a people no longer European but 'American', at one with an American environment they had made their own. The myth of the frontier was in process of creation.

Colonial Spanish America, it seems, could do without this particular myth. There was less urgency than in British America to bring under cultivation the often arid land on the borders of empire, and hence less need for the heroic pioneer. A mythology, too, already existed – a mythology woven from the memories of conquest, and in which the conquered as well as the conquerors came to participate, as they re-enacted on festival days the battles of Moors and Christians, or of Christianized Indians against the 'barbarian' Chichimecas of the northern frontier of New Spain.[134] The English settlers, by contrast, had no conquest to celebrate. Nor could they very convincingly celebrate that massive winning of Indian souls for the faith, which to the creoles of Spanish America conferred upon their *patrias* a special place in God's providential plan.[135]

While it was true that Puritan New England, too, could lay claim to a special place in God's providential plan, the vision had lost some of its cogency by the eighteenth century, and in any event was not immediately and obviously applicable to colonies which had been founded at different times from New England, and under very different auspices. The captivity narrative might serve to reanimate the vision, but in a society subjected to strong new secularizing influences and being peopled by immigrants from many different lands, the mythology of the frontier could help to extend the range of imaginative possibilities by creating the collective image of a pioneering society on the move.

Yet if the 'backcountry', as the North American borderlands were coming to be called, symbolized the future for thousands of colonists, its existence also posed a multitude of problems for the more settled territories of the Atlantic seaboard. There was the increasingly urgent problem of how best to defend these outlying regions at a time when border relations between settlers and Indians were being subsumed in the great struggle between the rival European powers for the control of a continent. There was also the fundamental question of the nature of the relationship between the populations of the maritime regions, proud of their increasing refinement and civility, and the hordes of backcountry farmers and squatters, regarded by many inhabitants of the eastern seaboard as beyond the pale. Independent-minded people, with a taste for liberty, these backcountry dwellers would not take easily to discipline or any form of institutional control.[136] This was a problem that would face all the mainland colonies to a greater or lesser degree, and its solution was made no easier by the fact that, under the pressure of immigration and population expansion, so many of them were themselves in a state of flux.

Slave and free

If the increase in population affected all the British American mainland, its impact was most strongly felt in the Middle and Southern Colonies, where immigration, whether voluntary or involuntary, was strongest. It was not only a matter of numbers, but also of growing ethnic, religious and racial diversity, as more and more immigrants streamed – or were shipped – into the country, changing the face of society wherever they appeared. By the middle of the eighteenth century a heterogeneous British America was in the making, although its heterogeneity was different from that of Spanish America, where the survival and slow recovery of substantial Indian populations had created an astonishing racial mosaic of white, red and black, and every shade in between.

In the British-controlled areas of North America the drastic diminution of the indigenous inhabitants meant that the red had in many parts dwindled to the point of invisibility. The black, on the other hand, was daily becoming more prominent. Among the whites, colonists of English origin were now liable to find themselves in a minority, swamped by Scots-Irish and continental Europeans. By 1760 settlers of English origin would constitute no more than 45 per cent of all the residents of New York, and only some 30 per cent of those of Pennsylvania.[137] 'Unless', wrote an alarmed Benjamin Franklin in 1753 of the German immigrants flooding into Pennsylvania, 'the stream of importation could be turned from this to other colonies . . . they will soon outnumber us, that all the advantages we have, will in my opinion, be not able to preserve our language, and even our government will become precarious.'[138]

Although the arrival of so many non-English whites, many of them without a knowledge of the language, created obvious problems of assimilation for the receiving societies, these could not compare in magnitude with the lastingly divisive issues raised by the growth of the black population, most of it enslaved. By 1740 Africans and Afro-Americans constituted 28.3 per cent of the population of the Upper South, and 46.5 per cent of that of the Lower South. In the Middle Colonies and New England the percentages were 7.5 per cent and 2.9 per cent respectively.[139] From as early as the second decade of the eighteenth century Virginia's slave population was beginning to grow from natural increase – the first time this had happened in any New World slave population – and during the 1740s American-born blacks in the Chesapeake colonies came to outnumber those imported from Africa, allowing slave-owners to replenish their labour force from their own stock.[140] With the growth of an African population that had no memory of Africa, black, as well as white, society was undergoing a decisive transformation.

Both in the Chesapeake region, and in North and South Carolina, societies based on chattel bondage were in the making. The only exception in the Lower South was the new colony of Georgia, whose trustees held out against the introduction of slavery until 1751, the year in which they surrendered the colony to the crown.[141] The model for these slave societies, which Georgia would join after 1751, was provided by the British West Indies islands, with their forced plantation labour. These in turn had found their model in the sugar-producing slave plantations of Portuguese Brazil.[142] If the plantation societies resembled each other, however, in depending on forced labour by a work-force whose members were no more than chattels to be exploited and disposed of at the whim of their masters, the effect of differing ecologies, demographic patterns, and social and cultural attitudes was to create significant differences between them. In the West Indies, where, in the 1740s, 88 per cent of the population was black,[143] there was likely to be a different dynamic, both between white and black societies and within them, from that to be found in a mainland region in which some 70 per cent of the population was still of European descent.[144]

On the North American mainland the differing characteristics of the Chesapeake region and the southern Lowcountry led to marked divergences in the development of their slave societies and of society as a whole.[145] The tobacco culture of Virginia and Maryland[146] created a rhythm of work and patterns of labour organization different from those to be found in South Carolina, where the discovery in the late seventeenth century of the potential of the wetlands for rice production set in motion an economic revolution. Once rice was established as the colony's staple crop, its production and export from Charles Town became the predominant preoccupation of the emerging planter class (fig. 36).

Labour in the Carolina rice fields was intensive, and the length of the growing season of rice as compared with that of the tobacco plant left little or no time for the pursuit of other activities, and the consequent diversification of labour, as in Virginia. Tobacco in the Chesapeake could be cultivated by a planter working on his own, or with only one or two slaves to help him, whereas profitable rice production required large plantations with labour forces at least thirty strong. More slaves, therefore, lived on large plantations in Carolina than in Virginia. As a result, personal relationships with masters were liable to be less close than in Virginia, where the great planters developed patriarchal attitudes to the slaves born and bred on their estates; and the constant need for slaves newly imported from Africa to replenish a black population less healthy and less fertile than that of Virginia made it more difficult for Carolina slaves to develop the kinship and community ties that were gradually being woven by their counterparts in the Chesapeake.

Yet if, as seems likely, Carolina slaves were treated with greater brutality than those of Virginia, the relative proximity of Spanish territory meant that Carolinian slave-owners still needed to take care that they did not drive their slaves to desperation. In 1693 black fugitives from Carolina who managed to reach St Augustine were offered their freedom by the Spanish crown on condition that they converted to Catholicism. From then onwards Carolina's growing black slave population glimpsed a beacon of hope shining away to the south.[147] Following two abortive revolts, many Carolina slaves joined the Yamasee Indians in 1715 in their war against the English settlers, and during the 1720s and 1730s increasing numbers of runaways made their escape to Florida. These included Portuguese-speaking slaves from the central African Christian monarchy of Kongo. In 1738 the governor of Florida gave them permission to establish an autonomous black Catholic settlement, Gracia Real de Santa Teresa de Mose, two miles north of St Augustine. As news of the foundation of Mose spread through the South Carolina plantations, groups of slaves broke loose and tried to make for Florida, among them a group of Angolans who revolted near Stono in 1739. After killing more than twenty whites most of them were themselves killed as they headed south for Mose.

For all the degradation and horrors of life on the Carolina plantations, the very size of the plantations meant that the slaves lived in a world that was overwhelmingly black, and in which they were able to preserve customs and traditions they had brought from Africa (fig. 37). Unlike the often absentee West Indian planters, their masters maintained a direct personal interest in their plantations, and they were less inclined than the Virginia planters to break up slave families by selling surplus slaves, or giving them away. There were opportunities, too, to escape from rural servitude. The planters' desire to escape the malaria season on their plantations by spending much of the year in the handsome mansions they built for themselves in Charles Town led to the emergence of a class of urban slaves in domestic service. Like the black slaves to be found in Mexico City and Lima, many of them became skilled carpenters, cabinet-makers and silversmiths, and their accumulated earnings allowed them, like their Spanish American counterparts, to enjoy a fair level of prosperity, copying the life-styles and clothing fashions of the white elite.[148]

The lines of racial division, however, remained brutally sharp in these southern colonies, and the number of free blacks was small in comparison with those to be found in the viceroyalties of New Spain and Peru. Eighteenth-century New Spain had the largest free population of African descent in the Americas, and although it was subject to specific restrictions and obligations it enjoyed a recognized status within the casta system. One consequence of this was that, since the early seventeenth century, Mexican free blacks had been allowed to form their own militia units. The survival of these units until the later eighteenth century not only provided them with valuable corporate privileges but also tended to reinforce their sense of racial identity.[149] In Virginia, by contrast, gun ownership for free blacks was banned after Bacon's rebellion, although it was only in 1723 that the colony's legislature formally prevented them from joining the militias.[150] There was a world of difference between arming a black population that constituted under a tenth of the total population, and one that ranged from a quarter to a half.

'It appears absolutely necessary to get a sufficient Number of white Persons into this Province,' asserted a committee of the South Carolina Assembly in 1739, as it proposed legislation to compel large landowners to import and maintain white soldiers in proportion to the acreage that they held.[151] In societies where blacks constituted such a large portion of the total population, the spectre of slave rebellion haunted the whites. It also worked, however, to generate among them a sense of solidarity that helped in the Chesapeake region to bridge the social divide between the great planters on the one hand and the middling planters, small landowners and tenant-farmers on the other.

Yet although white and black stood in sharp contradistinction to each other, they were also connected by an intricate web of visible and invisible ties. For all the depth of the divide between the status of master and that of slave, they were bound together in a relationship from which neither could escape. Slavery and freedom coexisted in close symbiosis, with liberty itself becoming the most precious of commodities in a society based on servitude.[152]

If this led the planter elite of Virginia to develop a political culture with liberty at its heart, it also encouraged the slaves to make the most of every chink and crack in the carapace of constriction that contained their lives. They held fast to ancestral rituals and practices that linked them to a world that whites could not enter; they fostered, as best they could, the new bonds of kinship and community that the circumstances of their lives had allowed them to establish; and they exploited the needs and the weaknesses of the white society around them in order to gain access to some of the opportunities and advantages which that society had to offer. In doing so they reached out to a world that had become dependent on their services, shaping that world even as it, in turn, shaped their own.

As the eighteenth century progressed, this mutual interaction of black and white, stronger in some parts than others of the Chesapeake and the Lower South, led to the construction of a new world of shared experiences and shared patterns of behaviour.[153] Just as, in post-conquest Mexico, the presence of indigenous servants in conquistador households came to exercise a deep influence on the life-styles of subsequent generations,[154] so the presence of black nursemaids and domestic servants produced a comparable process of acculturation in the planter households of Virginia. 'I have none but negroes to tend my children – nor can I get anyone else – ,' wrote the Virginian planter, Landon Carter, in his diary for 1757, 'and they use [accustom] their own children to such loads of Gross food that they are not Judges when a child not so used to be exposed to different weathers – and not so inured to exercise – comes to eat. They let them [Carter's children] press their appetites as their own children did and thus they are constantly sick.'[155]

Yet the often close personal relationships could not bridge the vast gap dividing master from slave, nor do much to mitigate the brutality and sheer savagery that constituted the daily fare of plantation slaves.[156] Dissatisfied with the work of the men deputed to thresh the oats, Landon Carter, who prided himself on his paternalist concern for the slaves on his Sabine Hall plantation, noted in his diary, as if it were a simple matter of routine, 'They have been severely whipd day by day.'[157] Sexual exploitation of women slaves, too, was a commonplace of plantation life, although there is no evidence that Carter himself indulged in this. Casual sex and long-term sexual relationships between planters and slaves were taken for granted in the great houses and on the plantations, although Lowcountry planters seem to have been more willing than their Chesapeake counterparts to recognize and provide for their mulatto children, even if they remained generally unwilling to free them.[158] No distinctive mulatto caste developed here, as it did in the corporate society of Spanish America and, to a lesser extent, in the British Caribbean. Instead, the mulattoes were simply absorbed into the slave population.

While the eighteenth-century plantation complex shaped slave and white society in the Chesapeake and the Lower South in ways that were to set a permanent imprint on the entire region, slavery was also becoming more common in the north, in response to the fluctuating labour requirements of an eastern seaboard caught up in the rapidly expanding Atlantic economy.[159] Even New England, whose population was expanding faster than the capacity of the land to offer productive employment, looked to unfree labour in the form of black slaves or indentured servants to meet the deficit in its labour needs. Boston's slave population rose from 300 to 400 in 1710 to over 1,300 in 1742; by 1750, blacks constituted a tenth of the population of Rhode Island, where Newport was emerging as a major centre of the shipbuilding industry.[160]

The port towns of the Middle Colonies were still more reliant than those of New England on unfree labour. By 1746, 21 per cent of the population of the city of New York consisted of black slaves, and weekly slave auctions were held at various points in the city.[161] Philadelphia, too, had a sizeable black population. Here, as in other seaboard cities, the upper ranks of society acquired blacks as household servants. At the same time, slavery was also spreading to the countryside.

Yet there were also potential constraints, both voluntary and natural, on the growth of slavery in this central region. A wave of slave unrest, accompanied by arson, moved up the eastern seaboard, hitting New York in 1741, and creating a general sense of unease. This could only encourage a preference for white labour, free or indentured, although the ultimate decision was likely to turn on its availability and relative cost. There was, too, a diffused, if still weak, anti-slavery sentiment in some parts of white society, and during the 1750s Philadelphia Quakers began to campaign actively against slave ownership. Practical considerations also came into play. In spite of the growth of rural slavery in the Middle Colonies, the absence of a labour-intensive staple crop – sugar, tobacco or rice – militated against the development of the kind of plantation economies that institutionalized black slavery in the West Indies and the southern colonies. Perhaps most important of all, the sheer flood of white immigrants, coupled with natural population increase on a remarkable scale, meant that, even if localized shortfalls in times of economic boom created a temporary demand for imported labour, the upward surge of population proved sufficient to respond to ordinary needs and was even beginning to create a labour surplus.[162]

A similar phenomenon was visible in those parts of the Spanish American mainland where, by the mid-eighteenth century, the irregular recovery of the Indian population and the rapid growth of a racially mixed population was tilting the balance in favour of a home-grown 'free' labour force. This was happening, for instance, in the *obrajes*, or textile workshops, the nearest the Spanish American colonial economy came to possessing a factory system. These workshops, employing anything from twenty to 200 workers apiece, and operating either in, or on the outskirts of, cities and towns, were a response to the clothing requirements of a population which could not afford the high prices of textiles imported from Europe. Dependent on Indian labour when they were first set up in the sixteenth century, the *obrajes* of New Spain subsequently resorted to African slave labour to supplement a diminishing indigenous labour force. In the eighteenth century, however, they turned increasingly to Indian or mixed-race workers, who were forced to labour in conditions that made them little better off than slaves.[163]

All the societies of the Americas had in fact to weigh the relative costs of African slaves and of the alternative sources of labour available. The calculation had to include not only the price demanded at the auction block by slave-traders and merchants, as set against that of free labour or other forms of unfree labour currently on offer, but also the estimated profitability, reliability and productivity of slaves over the term of their lives when compared with the alternatives. It also had to take into account the type of occupation for which they were required. An African slave might be better than an Indian for overseeing workers on a Mexican hacienda, but unsuited for labour in the mines.

On this basis, the terms of the equation seem to have swung against the acquisition of black slave labour over significant areas of the Spanish American mainland during the eighteenth century. This was certainly true of New Spain, where the slave population, which stood at 35,000 in the mid-seventeenth century,[164] had dwindled to no more than 10,000 in a population of almost 6 million by the last years of the eighteenth. A high rate of manumission, which is likely to have been influenced by assessments of profitability at least as much as by religious considerations, helped to swell Mexico's already large free black population, and with it the domestic – and multi-ethnic – pool of free labour. On the other hand, demand for African labour remained high in the coastal regions of Peru, and, to a lesser extent, on the cacao plantations of Venezuela. Both had African populations of around 90,000 at the end of the eighteenth century, of whom 40,000 in Peru and 64,000 in Venezuela were slaves.[165]

There were therefore wide variations in the pattern of slave-holding – variations that reveal potential limits to the institutionalization of chattel bondage, although it still remained unclear in the middle decades of the century, both in British and Iberian America, how strong the demarcation lines would be between slave and free societies, and where those lines would eventually be drawn. Slavery is too easily equated with the presence of plantation economies, and urban slavery remains an underrated and understudied phenomenon.[166] In the event, in spite of the extensive use of slaves in the cities of the British Atlantic seaboard, and the spread of slavery to rural New York and Pennsylvania, the Middle and Northern Colonies of North America would not follow the path taken by the Caribbean islands, the Southern Colonies and Brazil. After a period of prevarication the mid-Atlantic colonies, with their rapidly expanding white populations and their very varied employment needs, opted for a wage-labour system that proved cheaper than bound labour. Rural New England, for its part, remained firmly wedded to its system of family labour supplemented by hired help.[167]

While all the colonies along the North American seaboard responded to the growth of population and the opportunities arising from the rapid expansion of the British Atlantic economy by increasing their total output,[168] the extent of the social and political dislocation created by economic development and demographic change varied from place to place and region to region. In general, the Northern and Southern Colonies displayed greater stability than the mid-Atlantic Colonies, which struggled over the middle decades of the century to find an equilibrium.[169]

Between 1720 and 1750 the total white and black population of New England rose from around 170,000 to 360,000, largely through natural increase rather than as the result of immigration, but it experienced much less of an economic transformation than the other mainland regions.[170] It already possessed a closely integrated commercial economy, based on farming, fishing, and trade in animal and timber products. Although the buoyancy of the Atlantic economy benefited New England's ship construction and its coastal and carrying trades, the region's growth was held back by its inability to increase the agricultural output of the stony New England soil sufficiently to keep pace with the growth of population.

New England's currency troubles threw into sharp relief the economic problems confronting the region. Its permanently adverse balance of trade with

Britain meant a constant drain of specie, which colonial legislatures attempted to offset by an over-enthusiastic printing of paper notes. The crisis came to a head in Massachusetts in the years around 1740, when an acute shortfall in the monetary supply led to the revival of a scheme for backing the issue of paper currency through a privately funded Land Bank. The proposal, which led to the new Land Bank releasing bills without first securing legislative approval, set off a bitter debate in a society in which the traditional values of the common weal had long been locked in battle with the self-interested and acquisitive instincts of an increasingly commercialized society.[171]

The tensions generated by the region's economic difficulties were felt most acutely in the teeming port city of Boston, which was particularly vulnerable to the fluctuations produced by the wartime expansion of 1739 to 1748 and the post-war depression that followed. Political and social unrest was compounded by the wave of religious revivalism, later to be known as the Great Awakening, that swept through the Northern Colonies in the mid-1730s and early 1740s, challenging traditional authority and bringing to the massed audiences of George Whitefield and his fellow revivalist preachers the exciting message of the primacy of individual choice.[172] Yet in spite of sporadic manifestations of unrest in the streets of Boston and some lively pamphleteering, Massachusetts in the middle years of the century retained a high degree of stability. New England's communal traditions were firmly based, town meetings and regular elections provided an opportunity for the organized expression of dissent, and the well-entrenched image of the 'godly ruler' helped maintain a measure of deference to the region's governing elite.[173]

The Southern Colonies, too, enjoyed a high degree of stability, although this would come to be challenged, particularly in South Carolina, as new tides of immigrants moved inland to settle the backcountry. The stability here, however, derived from the successful dominance by the planter elite of a hierarchical society with slavery at its base. In Virginia, where perhaps 70 per cent of adult free males qualified for the franchise, the elite took its responsibilities seriously, and was careful to court electors when election time approached. There were obvious tensions in this patriarchal world, but they were successfully contained.[174] In South Carolina, which became a royal colony in 1720, the relatively new elite of planters and merchants was anxious to prove, not least to itself, its worthiness to be accepted as a virtuous ruling class on the model of Whig England. With its social and political power firmly concentrated in Charles Town, the elite maintained an authority which became increasingly ragged the further away from the coastal region the frontiers of settlement moved.[175]

It was in the Middle Colonies – New York, New Jersey, Pennsylvania – that the achievement of political order and social stability proved most elusive. This was the region of the North American mainland that displayed the greatest ethnic and religious diversity. New immigrants, Germans, Scots and Scots-Irish, jostled with older-established populations, not only the English, but also the Dutch in the Hudson Valley and Scandinavians around the Delaware. Some of the new immigrant communities, especially the Huguenot French, blended easily with the surrounding population, but others did not.

Ethnic or national antagonisms were compounded by religious animosity. Feuding between Quakers, Presbyterians, Anglicans and the newer evangelical sects had a profound impact on the struggle for power and influence in both New York and Pennsylvania.[176] There were also sharp clashes between the Dutch Reformed Church and the Church of England. The English and the Dutch had long had a strained relationship, reaching back to the English conquest of New Netherland in 1664 and before. The continuous pressure on the Dutch of New York to accept the anglicization of their culture was intensified by the founding of the Society for the Propagation of the Gospel in 1701 and the development of a more aggressive Anglicanism. Dutch children were taught the Anglican catechism in the Society's schools, and Anglican missionaries worked hard to win converts from the Dutch Reformed Church. A letter from Lord Cornbury, as governor of New York, points to the collusion between church and state in the promotion of anglicization. 'This', he wrote, asking for a minister to be sent to Albany County, 'will be a means to make the growing Generation English men.'[177]

In the aftermath of Leisler's rebellion,[178] many lower-class Dutch left New York City and Long Island for the Hudson Valley and northern New Jersey, where they clung to a religious and cultural tradition that was eventually absorbed by the pietism of the Moravian immigrants and the enthusiasm of the revivalist sects. Yet in spite of the departure of this disaffected sector of the Dutch population from New York, the traditional antagonism between the Dutch and English communities continued to colour New York city politics. By mid-century, however, the campaign for anglicization had largely succeeded. Especially at the elite level, Dutch culture had conceded defeat.[179]

For all its disruptive effects, and the factional politics to which it so often gave rise, pluralism also created an environment conducive to the generation of new ideas and new forms of political organization.[180] The sheer attempt to impose order on potential anarchy forced members of the elite to bid for popular support in a highly competitive political and religious arena. Over the first half of the century, the persistent erosion of the authority of the royal governors of New York by the assembly[181] meant that provincial and city politics were conducted within an increasingly autonomous framework. In order to seize power, or buttress their position, rival New York families, like the Morrises and the Philipses, turned to artisans, shopkeepers and labourers to provide them with electoral support. On the model of contemporary British politics, they engaged in heated political warfare through the medium of pamphlets and the press, and developed during the 1730s party platforms and incipient party organization in their efforts to mobilize on their behalf a volatile and unpredictable urban electorate.[182] The Quakers of Philadelphia were faced with the same necessity if they were to hold on to power, and turned especially to the new German immigrants to secure additional political support as they found themselves being outnumbered by adherents of other faiths.[183]

By grouping the disparate units of a fragmented urban society under the banner of a cause, the resort to such tactics had its own stabilizing effects. The 'Quaker party' succeeded in dominating Pennsylvania's political life from the late 1730s to the mid-1750s, and in the same period New York's politics were dominated by the Anglican-based DeLancey coalition, which reached out to leaders of the Dutch Reformed Church. Stability, however, was not the same as stagnation. In couching their appeals to the electorate in terms of the people's rights, the elite were unleashing a force which they might one day find themselves unable to control.

The message of political liberty was reinforced by the message of religious liberty carried through the Middle Colonies by the revivalist movements of the Great Awakening. Some of these were inspired by German pietism, others by the activities of the Baptists, and others by the movement for renewal within Calvinism itself, at a moment when Calvinist immigrants from Scotland, Ireland and continental Europe were flocking into Pennsylvania. In an already competitive religious environment, evangelical revivalism, with its insistence on the conversion experience and the achievement of personal salvation, sharpened the edge of competition between the churches, while also generating schisms within churches of the same faith. Enthusiasm was a heady experience, and the thousands who turned out in New Jersey and Pennsylvania in 1739–40 to hear the rousing sermons of George Whitefield were caught up in a movement that may have risen and fallen like the waves of the sea, but which changed many individual lives and had a lasting impact on colonial society as a whole.

Given the diversity of religion, politics and society in colonial British America, the effects of this revivalist movement were as varied and contradictory as its origins, and could as easily strengthen as weaken the authority of the churches.[184] At heart, however, the revivalism represented a return to the radical tradition within the Protestant Reformation, with its egalitarian and democratizing tendencies.[185] This was a tradition calculated to appeal to the small farmers, shopkeepers, artisans and labourers who were trying to carve out new lives for themselves in America, and resented the dominance of wealthy urban elites and powerful country landowners, like the great barons owning estates along the Hudson River. As the course of the Protestant Reformation in Germany two centuries earlier had already demonstrated,[186] demands for political liberty and social equality are liable to flourish in a radical religious environment.

The original settlers from England had brought with them a powerful conviction of their 'right' to English liberties – a conviction contested in vain by Judge Joseph Dudley in that dangerous year 1687 when he asserted that 'they must not think the privileges of Englishmen would follow them to the end of the world.'[187] As new waves of immigrants arrived, carrying with them little or no feeling of allegiance to the British crown, the God-given rights of Englishmen were permeated, and ultimately transcended, by a conviction that rights were God's gift to humanity as a whole – the right to religious choice, personal freedom, social justice, and happiness on earth. The immigrants, and the communities they joined, shared the conviction that they were endowed with the right to make what they could of their own lives, untrammelled by authority. It was a conviction that linked Benjamin Franklin in Philadelphia, with his message of self-improvement, hard work and personal responsibility, to the urban artisan, the Pennsylvania farmer and the backcountry settler. While the pursuit of individual liberty and the wish for independence could represent divisive forces in a society already splintered into a multitude of ethnicities and faiths, they were also capable, if the situation required it, of generating mutual association and solidarity in support of a common cause.

The inherent sense of liberty permeating the mainland colonies in the mid-eighteenth century stopped short of the rapidly increasing black population on North American soil. Freedom and servitude, it seems, were doomed to walk hand in hand. Yet for all their shortcomings – the sharpening racial divisions, the growing social inequalities, and the strident acquisitiveness of people on the make – the societies of mid-century British America possessed a political vitality and a religious effervescence that differentiated them from the Spanish American societies to the south. Racially, these societies might be more mixed, but religiously and politically they tended towards the monochrome. While the first half of the eighteenth century saw accelerating movement – demographic, social and economic – throughout the hemisphere, the sheer diversity of peoples, creeds and traditions that distinguished the mainland societies of British America suggested that here, more than anywhere, change was in the air.

CHAPTER 10

War and Reform

The Seven Years War (1756–63) and imperial defence

The great international conflict known to the colonists as the French and Indian War, and to Europeans as the Seven Years War, was a struggle for global primacy between Britain and France. In that struggle, in which Bourbon Spain was to be directly involved in its closing stages, the fate of North America would be decided. Not only were the lives and prospects of millions of North Americans – the Iroquois and other Indian peoples, French Canadians, colonial Britons, West Indian planters and their slaves – to be changed for ever by the conflict and its aftermath, but its impact would be felt throughout the hemisphere, even in Spanish territories as far away as Chile and Peru. War, even war at second or third remove, was to be the catalyst of change in British and Spanish America alike.

The conflict on North American soil in fact began in 1754, two years before the formal outbreak of war in Europe, when Governor Robert Dinwiddie of Virginia sent a military expedition under the 21-year-old Lieutenant-Colonel George Washington to the further side of the Allegheny mountains in a bid to challenge the assertion of French sovereignty over the Ohio Valley.[1] As was to be expected, the expansionist plans of the recently formed Ohio Company of Virginia[2] had collided with those of the French to establish a permanent presence for themselves and their Indian allies in the vast area of territory between their settlements in Canada and in the Mississippi Valley, and so to block British expansion into the interior. Washington's crushing defeat at Fort Necessity was followed by the despatch in 1755 by the Duke of Newcastle's ministry of Irish infantry regiments under the command of Major-General Edward Braddock – 'two miserable battalions of Irish', as William Pitt described them in a speech to the House of Commons[3] – to expunge the chain of French forts. His expedition, like that of Washington, ended in disaster at the hands of the Indians and the French.

The Duke of Newcastle hoped to confine the conflict to North America, but the dramatic reversal of great-power alliances in Europe created the conditions and the opportunities for a struggle that was to be global in scale. England

Map 6. British America, 1763.
Based on *The New Cambridge Modern History*, Vol. XIV, *Atlas* (1970), pp. 197 and 198;
Daniel K. Richter, *Facing East from Indian Country. A Native History of Early America*
(2001), p. 212.

declared war on France in May 1756, as French warships sailed up the St Lawrence
with troops for the defence of Canada under the command of Montcalm.[4]
Montcalm's energetic direction of military operations forced the English and
colonial forces on to the defensive, and it was only after William Pitt was
entrusted by a reluctant George II in 1757 with the effective running of the war
that vigour and coherence were injected into the British war effort, and the run of
defeats was succeeded by an even more spectacular run of victories.

By establishing British naval superiority in the Atlantic, and making North America the principal focus of Britain's military effort, Pitt was able to turn the war around. During the course of 1758 General Amherst captured Louisbourg on Cape Breton Island, commanding the mouth of the St Lawrence,[5] and Anglo-American forces took and destroyed the strategically commanding Fort Duquesne at the forks of the Ohio. The year 1759 was to be the *annus mirabilis* of British arms. A naval force in the West Indies seized the immensely profitable sugar island of Guadeloupe; a campaign fought with the help of the Iroquois, who realized that the time had come to switch their support to the English, captured the French forts in the Lake Ontario region; and Quebec capitulated to the troops of General Wolfe. When the last effective French Atlantic squadron was defeated two months later at Quiberon Bay, the chances of French recovery in North America were gone, and with the surrender of Montreal in the summer of 1760 the conquest of Canada was complete. The young George III, ascending the British throne in October of that year, had entered into a rich and vastly expanded imperial inheritance. On both sides of the Atlantic his triumphant peoples could celebrate an unprecedented succession of victories around the world; and there were more to come, both in India and America, where the remaining islands of the French West Indies, including Martinique, fell to British attacks in 1761–2.[6]

When Charles III succeeded his half-brother Ferdinand VI on the Spanish throne in 1759, the year before the accession of George III, it was already obvious that the balance of global power had tilted decisively in favour of Great Britain. Although courted by both sides, Spain had remained neutral during the opening years of the Anglo-French conflict, but the run of British victories was cause for growing concern to Madrid, and in 1761 the French and Spanish Bourbons renewed their Family Compact. Although this was nominally a defensive alliance, the British government got wind of a secret convention promising Spanish intervention in the conflict after the safe arrival of the treasure fleet, and in January 1762 Britain pre-emptively declared war on Spain.[7]

Spain's ill-judged intervention was to prove a disaster. In a pair of audacious military and naval operations that testified to the new global dimensions of eighteenth-century warfare, a British expeditionary force sailing from Portsmouth, and joined in the West Indies by regular and provincial troops from North America, besieged and took Havana, the pearl of the Antilles, while another expeditionary force, despatched from Madras to the Philippines, seized Manila, the trading entrepot where Asia and the viceroyalty of New Spain touched hands.[8]

The almost simultaneous fall of these two port cities – one the key to the Gulf of Mexico and the other to the trans-Pacific trade – was a devastating blow to Spanish prestige and morale. No peace settlement would be possible without the return of Havana to Spain, but the security of Florida and central America was now endangered, and the French minister, Choiseul, was keen for negotiations to begin. Although Britain had achieved a crushing naval superiority, its finances were stretched, and Choiseul found a war-weary British government willing to respond. The Treaty of Paris, which came into effect in February 1763, involved a complex series of territorial exchanges and adjustments that, while recognizing the extent of the British victory, would, it was hoped, give reasonable satisfaction to all three powers involved. Britain retained Canada but restored Guadeloupe and Martinique to France; Spain, in exchange for the return of Cuba, ceded Florida – the entire region east of the Mississippi – to Britain, abandoned its claims to the Newfoundland fisheries, and made concessions on logwood cutting along the central American coast; and the French, to sweeten the pill for their Spanish allies, transferred to Spain their colony of Louisiana, which they themselves were no longer in a position to defend. With France now effectively expelled from North America, Britain and Spain were left to face each other across thinly colonized border regions and the vast expanses of the Indian interior.[9]

For both these imperial powers, the war itself had exposed major structural weaknesses, which the acquisition of new territories under the terms of the peace settlement would only compound. In London and Madrid alike, reform had become the order of the day. Britain might be basking in the euphoria of victory, but, as ministers in London were painfully aware, its power was now so great that it could only be a question of time before France and Spain again joined forces to challenge its supremacy. How long that time would be depended on the speed with which Charles III's secretaries of state could implement a programme of fiscal and commercial reforms that had been the subject of constant discussion in official circles, and which the government of Ferdinand VI had taken the first steps to introducing in the 1750s. The failure of the defending forces at Havana and Manila brought a new urgency to their task. 'The secretaries', it was reported, '. . . are working like dogs. They are doing more in a week than they previously did in six months.'[10] The long siesta was drawing to a close.

The most pressing problem for both the British and Spanish governments was the improvement of measures for imperial defence. For the victors as for the vanquished, the strains and stresses of war had thrown the inadequacies of the existing system into sharp relief. The central issue for both London and Madrid was how to achieve a fair distribution of defence costs and obligations between the metropolis and the overseas territories in ways that would produce the most effective results. Both empires had traditionally relied heavily on colonial militias for the protection of their American possessions against either Indian or European attack, but as frontiers expanded during the first half of the eighteenth century, and European rivalries on the American continent intensified, the drawbacks of the militia system became glaringly apparent.[11]

The Spanish authorities already made use of regular or veteran troops to man the expanding network of *presidios* or frontier garrisons, finally numbering 22, along the vast northern frontier of the viceroyalty of New Spain. They also turned to regulars for the protection of the vital harbour of Vera Cruz on the coast of Mexico, raising an infantry battalion in 1740 to reinforce its defences. Over the middle decades of the eighteenth century in the viceroyalty of New Spain, therefore, a small number of regular troops – perhaps 2,600 in all, and widely dispersed on garrison duty – came to supplement the urban and provincial militias on which the viceroyalty's defence had traditionally depended. In spite of an attempt at reform in the 1730s, these militias, which were open to all classes except for Indians, and included companies of *pardos* (all or part black),[12] were neither organized nor disciplined, and could offer little effective resistance in the event of attack.[13] The story was similar in other parts of Spanish America. It was true that over vast areas of the interior of the continent, far removed from the dangers posed by hostile Indians or European rivals, there was little cause for concern. The disasters of 1762, however, exposed the hollowness of a defence system ill prepared either for serious frontier warfare or for amphibious attack.

In the British colonies, with their long frontiers bordering on potentially hostile French, Spanish or Indian territory, and their own growing populations in expansionist mode, the militias were more likely to be put to the test than their Spanish American counterparts. By the eighteenth century, however, their military effectiveness had taken second place to social respectability. Not only Indians, as in New Spain, but also blacks and mulattoes were excluded from the mainland militia companies, and the citizens who manned them were naturally reluctant to commit themselves to the lengthy periods of service demanded by a frontier war that grew dramatically in scale in the 1740s. As a result, the militias had increasingly to be supplemented by volunteer units, drawn from among the poorer whites, and unwillingly paid for by colonial assemblies which had a visceral dislike of voting taxes.[14]

Although the colonies made an intensive effort in the 1740s to get their militias and volunteer units out on campaign, their military record was mixed, and looked even less satisfactory when subjected to the cold critical scrutiny of British professional soldiers and government officials. Where the viceroys of New Spain and Peru, although with limited financial resources at their disposal, could make, in their capacity as captains-general, such provisions for defence as they considered necessary, the thirteen governors of the mainland colonies of British North America had the difficult preliminary task of negotiating with assemblies that were all too likely to be truculent. The Board of Trade was growing increasingly concerned that Britain's American empire was in no position to repulse a sustained onslaught from New France. Provincial politicking and the ineptitude of military amateurs were putting Britain's valuable North American empire at risk. In deciding in the 1750s, therefore, to commit regular troops to the defence of its transatlantic possessions the British government embarked on a major change of policy. By the end of the decade twenty regiments from the home country were to be stationed in America.[15]

In spite of the growing British commitment to the defence of North America, there was a not unreasonable expectation that the king's American subjects should do more to defend themselves. This involved a much greater degree of mutual co-operation than they usually managed to achieve. While in the northern colonies the danger from the French and the Indians had fostered a tradition of mutual assistance in emergencies, the intensity of inter-colonial jealousies and rivalries made it difficult, if not impossible, for all thirteen colonies to act in unison. Even before the formal outbreak of war between Britain and France in 1756, however, the urgency of the need for common defence measures was becoming apparent to observers on both sides of the Atlantic. In June 1754 the Board of Trade was informed that the king thought it highly expedient that 'a plan for a general concert be entered into by the colonies for their mutual and common defence', and ordered the Board to prepare such a plan.[16] In America itself, Benjamin Franklin, who had become the eager apostle of a great British empire in America, drafted a 'Plan of Union' for submission to a congress convened in Albany in 1754 on the instructions of the Board of Trade for the co-ordination of the Indian policies of the different colonies. Franklin's plan was ambitious – too ambitious for colonies historically jealous of their own rights and traditions, and deeply suspicious of any scheme involving the surrender of some of the most cherished of those rights to a 'Grand Council' of the colonies, meeting annually and empowered not only to negotiate on their behalf with the Indians, but also to levy taxes and raise troops for colonial defence. When the plan was brought before the colonial legislatures, most of them rejected it out of hand, and some did not even consider it.[17] The idea of unity was not one that came instinctively to societies born and bred in diversity.

Exasperation in London went hand in hand with relief at the inability of increasingly prosperous and independent-minded colonies to join together in a common endeavour that might conceivably be one day directed against the mother country itself. At present, the very danger posed by the French and the Indians was an inducement for them to stay in line. But at the same time the inability of the colonists to set aside their differences in the face of this danger persuaded the Duke of Newcastle of the need for more direct and consistent intervention from London. Already he had decided to appoint a commander-in-chief for North America, and this was to be followed by the appointment of two superintendents for Indian affairs, for the northern and southern colonies respectively, to bring some order and uniformity to the anarchic American scene.[18] The failure of the Albany congress was confirmation, if any were still needed, that colonial defence was too serious a matter to be left to mere colonials.

First-hand experience during the course of the war did not enhance the admiration of British officials and military commanders for the attitude and behaviour of these provincial Americans. 'The delays we meet with in carrying on the Service, from every parts [sic] of this Country, are immense', wrote the commander-in-chief, the Earl of Loudon, in August 1756. 'They have assumed to themselves, what they call Rights and Priviledges, totally unknown in the Mother Country, and [these] are made use of, for no purpose, but to screen them, from giving any Aid, of any sort, for carrying on, the Service, and refusing us Quarters.'[19]

Collaboration would improve considerably as Pitt took over the direction of the war and introduced a system of reimbursement for the military expenses of the colonies. But the haggling and procrastination of the colonial assemblies, and the indiscipline of provincial troops who had little use or respect for the rigidities of European military professionalism and hierarchies of rank, gave rise to constant complaint. The exasperation of the British authorities was further compounded by the systematic disregard shown by colonial merchants for the regulations prohibiting trade in Dutch, French and French-Caribbean commodities.[20] 'It is not easy to imagine', wrote Governor Clinton of New York in 1752, 'to what an enormous hight [sic] this transgression of the Laws of Trade goes in North America.'[21] The inhabitants of the British colonies displayed a positively Spanish American enthusiasm for the smuggling of enemy goods.

The conquest of Canada added further complications to the logistical and practical problems of defending the British empire of America. A vast new area of territory had been added to the king's dominions, and more would be added with the transfer of Spanish Florida to British rule by the peace settlement of 1763. The French threat might for the moment have been eliminated, but France would certainly be seeking revenge. The Spain of Charles III, too, was a far from friendly power, and the Indian nations along the borderlands were a continuing preoccupation. By the later stages of the war 32 regiments containing over 30,000 British regular soldiers were serving in the Americas, at enormous expense to the British tax-payer, who was paying 26 shillings a head for imperial defence, as against a shilling a head paid by the colonists.[22] If some of these regiments were to remain on American soil after the return of peace, it would be necessary to devise ways of financing them.

George III, guided by the Earl of Bute and imbued with all the enthusiasm of a novice king, took a direct personal interest in the question. By the end of 1762 he had reached the conclusion that a large British army would have to remain in the colonies. His ministers endorsed what they called 'his majesty's plan', and prepared to present it to the House of Commons. Under the plan, as outlined to the House in March 1763, 21 battalions, totalling some 10,000 men, were to be permanently stationed in North America in order to maintain authority over the Indians of Canada, 'not familiaris'd to civil government', as well as over '90 thousand Canadians'. The American colonists were to assist with the upkeep of these troops, although the method and quantity of their contribution was, for the time being, left open.[23] When the great Indian rebellion, led by the Ottawa war leader, Pontiac, broke out in the spring of 1763, and one after another of the British forts around the Great Lakes and in the Ohio valley fell to Indian attack, the wisdom of 'his majesty's plan' could hardly be contested.

While George III and his ministers were grappling with the consequences of victory, Charles III and his ministers were grappling with the implications of defeat. The naval construction programme undertaken by his predecessor had given Charles III a relatively strong fleet, and his government, dominated at this early stage of the reign by two Italians, the marquises of Esquilache and Grimaldi, pressed ahead with the shipbuilding programme on both sides of the Atlantic, turning to the French for technical expertise.[24] But the most urgent task facing the administration was a radical overhaul of the whole system for defence of the Spanish Indies. A secret junta, consisting of Grimaldi, Esquilache and the secretary for the Indies and the navy, Julián de Arriaga, was set up late in 1763 to consider not only questions of defence, but also of government and revenue in the American viceroyalties, and the Indies trade. By early 1764 the junta was ready with its proposals for the improvement of American defences, while another junta was entrusted with the task of preparing proposals for increasing trade and revenue.[25]

The fortifications of the American Atlantic ports – Vera Cruz, Havana, Campeche and Cartagena – were to be massively strengthened, at great expense. But, as with George III's plan, the principal recommendation was for the sending of metropolitan forces to improve the security of the American territories. The existing permanent garrisons and the urban and provincial militias had both proved themselves largely useless. The solution appeared to lie in the professionalization of the military in America, with the formation of well-trained and well-equipped regiments, established on a permanent footing. If only on grounds of cost, the new field army, however, would be much more dependent on colonial participation than the British army in America. It was to consist in large part of units of volunteers, recruited in the Indies, but commanded and trained by Spanish officers. These 'fixed' units, as they were called, would be reinforced by peninsular regiments sent out to the Indies for a maximum of four years' service. Their presence would provide, or so it was hoped, a model of modern military methods in time of peace, and the nucleus of a professional army in time of war. At the same time, the old colonial militias would be augmented, reorganized and professionally trained by a cadre of Spanish officers, to furnish an auxiliary force for use in emergencies.[26]

The captain-general of Andalusia, Lieutenant-General Juan de Villalba, arrived in New Spain in November 1764 at the head of two regiments, carrying with him instructions to implement the programme of military reforms. Predictably he soon found himself in conflict with the viceroy, jealous of his own prerogatives as captain-general of New Spain. Moreover, as in the British colonies, differences of attitude and approach created endless possibilities for misunderstanding and antagonism between professional soldiers sent out from the metropolis and the colonial population. The Spanish officers, like their British counterparts, looked down on the creoles and were frustrated by the inadequacies of the militias they had been sent to reorganize. Their presence, therefore, increased the already existing tensions between creoles and *peninsulares*. Although the Spanish authorities were haunted by fears of a rebellion supported by the militiamen, just as the British authorities were perturbed during the Seven Years War by manifestations of 'a general disposition to independence',[27] the creoles in fact showed very little inclination for military activities and resisted calls to enlist. Villalba's high-handed approach did not help his cause. He affronted creole sensibilities by mixing whites and castas in the infantry companies, and found that members of the creole elite were unwilling to apply for commissions.

The military reform programme in New Spain therefore got off to a rocky start. Although, on Villalba's figures, the viceroyalty had an army of 2,341 regulars and 9,244 provincials by the summer of 1766, only one of the six provincial regiments was properly armed and uniformed, and the quality of the recruits was low. Yet at least the structure of the army of New Spain was now in place, and the pattern established in the viceroyalty would be followed across the continent. By the end of the decade it was estimated that some 40,000 men, in different categories, were stationed across Spanish America.[28]

Spanish officers brought a new military professionalism to the Indies, with encouraging results. In 1770, for instance, the governor of Buenos Aires was able to expel the British from the Malvinas – the Falkland Islands – where they had established a fishing and naval station. For diplomatic reasons, however, his success was to be short-lived. In the following year a British ultimatum forced Charles III to abandon the islands, since the French, whose alliance with Spain was essential for successful defiance of England, were unwilling to come to his support.[29]

Over the next two or three decades, as Spanish America acquired a permanent military establishment, creole attitudes to military service changed. Madrid had always hoped that military titles and uniforms would prove a magnet to a creole elite hungry for office and honour. But its hopes were dashed when young men of good colonial families showed themselves unwilling to serve under Spanish officers. Service in the militia, however, began to look rather more attractive when – as in New Spain in 1766 – full privileges under the *fuero militar* were extended to officers in provincial units, and partial privileges to enlisted personnel.[30] Traditionally, in the corporate society of metropolitan Spain, the military, like the clergy, constituted a distinctive corporation, possessing the right or *fuero* of jurisdiction over its own members. By extending immunity in criminal and civil cases to officers serving in the provincial militias, the *fuero militar* effectively set them apart from the mass of the population. Across the continent, from Mexico City to Santiago de Chile, the sons of the creole elite, resplendent in their uniforms, would constitute just over half the veteran officer corps of the army of America by the last decade of the eighteenth century.[31] The first seeds of the militarization of the states of nineteenth- and twentieth-century Latin America were sown by the Bourbon military reforms of the late eighteenth century.

The contemporaneous reforms in the system of British imperial defence were destined to have an opposite effect. The British government's decision to provide an army for America composed of regiments sent from the home country arose out of a perception of colonial realities that failed to factor colonial sensibilities into the equation. There were vast territories to be defended, and their experiences with provincial units during the Seven Years' War had left British commanders with a low opinion of American fighting capabilities. The authorities in London were therefore inclined – unwisely as it later transpired – to write off the militias as being of little value, and particularly those of New England which had been most heavily involved in the Canada campaign.[32] Where the Spanish authorities – driven more by financial stringency than by any high regard for the fighting qualities of the creoles – chose to integrate reorganized and retrained local militias into the new system of imperial defence, their British counterparts, with large numbers of unemployed soldiers on their hands after the signing of the peace, saw the solution to their domestic and American problems in a standing army imported from England.[33]

The very notion of a standing army, however, smacked of continental tyranny to a colonial population that took for granted its entitlement to English liberty. During the war it had seen for itself how the argument of military necessity could ride roughshod over rights.[34] For the time being, Pontiac's rebellion made them grateful for the continuing protection afforded by the redcoats. But grounds for apprehension already existed, and the subsequent actions of the ministers in London would do nothing to assuage them.

The drive for reform

The problem of security was to be the precipitant of change in both the British and the Spanish empires. Increased security meant increased costs, as ministers in Madrid and London were painfully aware. Britain emerged from the war saddled with an enormous burden of debt, and it now had to find an estimated £225,000 a year[35] to maintain an army in America. It seemed reasonable to expect the colonists, whose current contribution to the costs of empire came from inefficiently collected customs dues, to take a fair share of paying for an army intended for their protection. Ministers in Madrid were moved by similar considerations. The defences of outlying and exposed regions, like the Caribbean islands or the central American coast, represented a continuous drain on the resources of hard-pressed treasuries, and if the Indies were better administered they could surely do more to meet the costs of their own protection. Fiscal and administrative reform therefore appeared to follow naturally from the requirements of a modernized system of imperial defence.

Other, and related, considerations were also impelling British and Spanish ministers in the direction of a general reassessment of their colonial policies. There was, in particular, the question of territorial boundaries. For Britain the acquisition of New France and Florida meant the addition to its American empire of large new territories with their own distinctive legal and administrative systems, and with Roman Catholic populations. How could they be satisfactorily incorporated, and what rights could their populations be safely allowed at a time when English Catholics were excluded from participation in political life? The defeat of the French also meant the removal of the most effective barrier to trans-Appalachian expansion by a land-hungry population hemmed in along the Atlantic seaboard. Were the colonists now to be permitted to swarm into the Indian interior, thus provoking new Indian wars, with all the additional strain on financial and military resources that this would involve? The Spaniards, too, were faced with difficult boundary problems. The long northern frontier of New Spain was only thinly settled. Should it be extended still further northwards to form a barrier against the English, thus provoking further conflict with the Indians, and again adding to the costs of defence? The dilemma that confronted both Britain and Spain was that of an empire too far.

Their problems were exacerbated by the fact that the imperial territories they already possessed appeared to be in danger of slipping from their control. The consolidation of creole oligarchies, and the accelerating infiltration of their members into high judicial, administrative and ecclesiastical posts,[36] had left Spanish ministers and viceroys with a growing sense of impotence in the face of creole opposition. For all the talk of reform, and serious efforts between 1713 and 1729 to return to traditional standards of appointment, 108 creoles secured positions in the Audiencias during the reign of the first two Bourbons, and it was only in 1750 that the crown felt able to end the practice of putting these posts up for sale. By then, creole judges were in the majority in the Audiencias of Mexico City, Lima and Santiago, and retained it for a further two decades.[37] By no means all the creole judges were local sons, but, where they were, the strength of their local connections hardly guaranteed an impartial enforcement of royal justice and an effective implementation of royal decrees.

In the British colonies, royal governors found themselves hamstrung by their lack of financial independence, with colonial assemblies dictating appointments through their control of salary appropriations. 'The ruling faction has obtained in effect the nomination to all offices,' complained Governor Clinton of New York in 1746.[38] The Seven Years War only served to increase the opportunities for political leverage by the assemblies. By the end of the war all the lower houses in the British colonies had effectively secured an exclusive right to frame money bills, and were becoming accustomed to thinking of themselves as local equivalents of the House of Commons.[39] Until now, the presence of the French had helped to restrain those inclinations to independence which ministers in London suspected the colonists of harbouring. With that presence removed, how could continuing loyalty be assured?

These were the kind of problems that had long preoccupied George Montagu Dunk, Earl of Halifax, President of the Board of Trade between 1748 and 1761, who had tried to push successive administrations into paying more attention to American affairs and had presented them with far-reaching proposals for administrative reform.[40] They also bulked large in the minds of the reformist ministers whom Charles III had gathered round him in Madrid. The temper of the age in continental Europe was running strongly towards the strengthening of the state and the rationalization of administration in line with the scientific principles of the Enlightenment. Ministers and officials were anxious to take their decisions on the basis of the most up-to-date information available. This meant applying the methods of science to government and ensuring that reliable statistics were collected. Ministers therefore launched surveys and promoted scientific expeditions that would furnish them with the facts and figures on which to base their policies. Even English ministers were not immune to the new breezes blowing from the continent. Halifax exemplified this new rationality as he sought to devise a programme of colonial reforms that would enable London to create a cost-effective empire.[41]

It was one of the ironies of the 1760s that Spanish ministers should have taken Britain's commercial empire in America as a model for their own at a time when the British themselves were becoming increasingly attracted by the idea of a more centrally controlled empire on the model of the Spanish. Madrid wanted to see Spain's American possessions transformed into British-style 'colonies', a rich source of staple products and a market for its goods, but it was under no illusions as to the scale of the reforms that would be needed. The loss of Cuba, however, and its recovery under the terms of the Peace of Paris, presented ministers with an opportunity that they were quick to seize. The urgent need for a radical overhaul of the island's defences made Cuba an ideal laboratory for trying out a programme of comprehensive reform that might later be extended to the mainland territories.[42]

Following the return of the island to Spain, the Count of Ricla was sent out as governor and captain-general to retake possession and reorganize the system of defence. He arrived in Havana in June 1763, accompanied by General Alejandro O'Reilly, who was deputed to oversee the plans for refortifying Havana harbour, expanding the garrison, and reconstituting the island militia as a disciplined force. The costs of implementing the plans, however, would be high, and government revenues in the island were low. The *alcabala*, which in other American territories was a substantial source of income consisting of 4–6 per cent payable on sales, had only recently been imposed on domestic transactions, and was set at a meagre 2 per cent. Although the Mexican treasury would contribute to the cost of constructing new fortifications, there was still a heavy shortfall, and the challenge facing Ricla was to generate more income in the island itself.

Ricla embarked on a round of astute negotiations with the tobacco and sugar planters, the ranchers and the merchants who constituted the island's elite. Access to British markets during the months of British occupation had brought home to them the benefits to be gained from a more liberal trading system than the highly regulated system that still prevailed in the Spanish colonial trade, in spite of recent attempts at relaxation. Ricla's best hope of success therefore lay in hinting at the possibilities of a change in the commercial regime as compensation for acceptance by the islanders of an increase in taxes. Such a change, however, would mean the government's defying the formidable Consulado of Cadiz merchants, who were determined to preserve their monopoly of the American trade.

In April 1764, following a recommendation by Esquilache's reforming junta, the crown raised the Cuban *alcabala* from 2 to 4 per cent and placed levies on brandy (*aguardiente*) and rum. An anxious period of waiting followed on the island, as the Spanish crown considered a Cuban petition for liberalization of the trading laws. During this period Esquilache was engaged in facing down conservative-minded ministers and officials and the lobbying of the Cadiz Consulado. By October 1765 he was ready to act. In a decisive break with the practice of channelling the principal Indies trade through Cadiz, permission was granted to nine Spanish ports to trade directly with Cuba and the other Spanish Caribbean islands, and the ban was lifted on inter-island trade. A second royal decree modified and consolidated the island's tax system, raising the *alcabala* in the process to 6 per cent.

Esquilache himself was toppled from power five months later by a popular insurrection in Madrid directed against the Italian reformist ministers of Charles III and covertly encouraged by highly placed government officials.[43] But the Cuban fiscal and commercial reforms that Esquilache had devised in partnership with Ricla not only survived but were sufficiently successful to lay the groundwork for Cuba's future prosperity as a sugar-producing colony. At the same time, the appointment in 1764 of an intendant to handle the island's fiscal and military affairs – the first time that one of these new-style officials, introduced into Spain by the Bourbons, had been appointed outside the peninsula – represented a first, tentative, experiment towards endowing the Indies with a modern, professional bureaucracy.[44] The institution of these various measures, even if on the small scale of an island setting, suggested how reformist ministers, playing their cards skilfully within the traditional Spanish political culture of bargaining and mutual concessions, could defuse opposition and find a compromise solution acceptable both to themselves and to a colonial elite with a list of grievances to be redressed. It was an example that the ministers of George III would prove unable to replicate.

Even before they could be certain of the outcome of the Cuban reforms, Charles III's minsterial team decided to apply their reformist brushstrokes to a wider canvas. In 1765 José de Gálvez, a lawyer in Esquilache's circle with a dry personality and a fanatical zeal for reform, was sent out to conduct a general visitation of the viceroyalty of New Spain. His six-year visitation was to be decisive both for his own career in the service of the crown, and for the future of the reform programme in Spain's American possessions as a whole. The success of his mission was to lead to similar visitations of the viceroyalties of Peru in 1777 and New Granada in 1778. Gálvez himself, created Marquis of La Sonora by a grateful monarch, was appointed secretary of the Indies in 1775, and exercised a dominant control over American affairs up to the time of his death in 1787.[45]

The reform projects associated with the name of Gálvez, involving fiscal, administrative and commercial innovation on an unprecedented scale, testify to the extent of the transformation of attitudes and assumptions about Spain's empire of the Indies that had been gathering strength in Madrid over the middle decades of the eighteenth century. The reforms were bold, but Charles III and his closest advisers had reached the conclusion that the case for reform was overwhelming. There was no doubt in their minds that, in the predatory international world of the eighteenth century, the survival of Spain's American empire could no longer be taken for granted. The loss of America, with its great reserves of silver and its large population – probably now approaching, and soon to overtake, the population of peninsular Spain with its 9 million inhabitants[46] – would mean the end of Spain's pretensions to be counted among the great powers of Europe.

Although Britain might have won the war, British ministers in London were as anxious as their Madrid counterparts about the future of their overseas empire. The population of British America still lagged far behind that of Britain itself: in the 1750s the mainland colonies had some 1,200,000 inhabitants and the West Indies 330,000, while the population of the British Isles now stood at around 10 million.[47] It was generally acknowledged, however, that the value of the commodities produced for Great Britain by the colonies, and their rapidly growing potential as a market for British goods, had made their retention central to British policy. But they had to be retained in such a way as to prevent them from becoming a permanent burden on the British tax-payer, and this could not be achieved without major reforms in colonial management. In the spring of 1763 Bute observed: 'We ought to set about reforming our old colonies before we settled new ones.'[48]

The fall of Bute and the appointment in April 1763 of George Grenville as first Lord of the Treasury in his place, placed government in the hands of a man with an obsessive determination to balance the books. His financial expertise, coupled with the American expertise of Halifax, who three months later was made secretary of state for the South, promised a determined attempt to reduce colonial affairs to order.[49] This involved large-scale territorial reorganization, undertaken in the autumn of 1763. The newly acquired Spanish Florida was reconstituted as two separate colonies, East and West Florida.[50] These were to have royal governors and elected assemblies, and be made subject to the English legal system. French Quebec similarly became a British colony, while the territory south of the St Lawrence estuary was added to Nova Scotia, a British colony since 1713.[51] It was also necessary to give the benefits of royal protection to the king's new Indian subjects, together with his new French subjects and the handful of Spaniards who chose to remain in Pensacola and Florida after their transfer to the English crown. Halifax attempted to resolve the border question and pacify the Indian peoples by creating a demarcation line that would exclude settlers from the American interior. A royal proclamation of October 1763 established the famous Proclamation Line, drawing a boundary along the line of the Appalachian mountains – a boundary that was supposed to be policed by the colonial army, but that settlers and land speculators would rapidly come to ignore.[52]

This redrawing of the American map by ministers and officials in Whitehall was accompanied by the raft of measures between 1763 and 1765 which were to make the name of Grenville famous, or infamous, in Anglo-American history: the attempt to enforce the collection of customs dues by strengthening the system of vice-admiralty courts, originally established in 1697;[53] the 1764 Currency Act, curtailing the emission of independent currencies by the colonies;[54] the American Duties (Sugar) Act;[55] and the notorious Stamp Act of March 1765, imposing a duty on legal documents, books, newspapers and other paper products – a form of taxation which, under the name of *papel sellado*, had been levied in the Spanish Indies since the 1630s.[56] 'The great object', said Grenville in a speech in the House of Commons in 1764, 'is to reconcile the regulation of commerce with an increase of revenue.'[57]

This was equally the object of the Spanish crown, which was simultaneously accelerating its own campaign to secure higher returns from its American possessions. At the heart of this campaign was the move by royal officials to assume direct administration of the collection of excise and other dues previously farmed out to the highest bidder, and the establishment or reorganization of state monopolies on major articles of consumption, notably brandy and tobacco.[58] These fiscal measures were to be accompanied by a more rational and better regulated system for the transatlantic trade, which would both encourage its development through some liberalization of the existing laws, and reduce the opportunities and the pretext for contraband – a source of deep concern to Madrid as it was to London.

In comparison with the measures taken by Madrid, those taken by Grenville and his ministerial successors, although infused by a determination to establish firmer metropolitan control over wayward colonies, look more like a set of pragmatic responses to the military, financial and administrative problems created by the Seven Years War than the building blocks of a coherent programme of reform.[59] It was true that the sheer scale and complexity of the demands on the British military establishment in North America presented Whitehall with a formidable array of difficulties. As its commander-in-chief, General Thomas Gage, was painfully aware, his army was expected simultaneously to garrison an internal continental frontier against Indian attack, prevent colonists from jeopardizing relations with the Indian nations of the interior by flooding across the Proclamation Line, and keep a watchful eye on seaboard colonies that seemed strangely ungrateful to the mother country for all that it had done to defend them during the recent war. The costs of this programme were massive. Army estimates for America came to £400,000 a year, while the colonies themselves were yielding less than £80,000 in revenue annually.[60]

Government policy in the years following the Peace of Paris, however, lacked consistency of direction. The Quartering Act of 1765, specifying the services to be provided to the troops, was a typically botched piece of work, precipitating conflicts with colonial assemblies and unrest and violence in New York.[61] British ministers, having decided that something must urgently be done, give the impression of acting without having thought through their policies or calculated the impact on colonial sensibilities of measures that would inevitably challenge deeply ingrained practices and assumptions. Charles III's ministers in Madrid, by contrast, showed greater wisdom in their first moves to bring change to America. The pilot project successfully carried through in Cuba by the Count of Ricla suggests at once a more systematic approach to reform in the Indies, and a greater consistency in its implementation.

The greater coherence of Iberian reformist policy in America can be partly attributed to the presence of a dominant figure in the affairs of the Indies over a long stretch of time. The volatility of British domestic politics in the 1760s, and running disputes between the President of the Board of Trade and the Secretary of State for Southern Affairs, left American policy in an uneasy limbo. As Lord

Chesterfield observed in 1766: 'if we have no Secretary of State with full and undisputed powers for America, in a few years we may as well have no America.'[62] It was only in 1768 that a new office of Secretary of State for the Plantations was created, with the Earl of Hillsborough, a hard-liner in his approach to the colonies, as the first holder of the office. For all his American expertise, the Earl of Halifax was never given the opportunity to evolve into a José de Gálvez, who made his career by identifying himself with the cause of reform, first in America itself during his visitation of New Spain between 1765 and 1771, and subsequently in Madrid, as secretary for the Indies.

With a team of like-minded officials to support him, Gálvez displayed an unrelenting commitment over more than two decades to the reconstruction of a system of government that he regarded as antiquated, corrupt and ineffectual.[63] He found an America in the hands of old-style local officials, the *corregidores* and *alcaldes mayores*, and left it in the hands of new-style bureaucrats, the intendants. He found, too, a transatlantic commercial system straining under the rusty machinery of Habsburg regulation, and oversaw its replacement by a new and modernized version that was to operate under the famous ordinance for 'free trade' – *comercio libre* – of 1778.

Yet for all the drive and determination of a powerful minister backed by a resolute monarch, there were also strong underlying political and ideological forces pushing the Spanish reform programme forward. Unlike Britain, powerful in its new-found economic and maritime strength, Spain was a country convalescing from a long period of debilitating weakness. While the slow process of recovery was by now under way, there was still far to go. Royal officials who spoke the new language of political economy, like José del Campillo,[64] or the rising star of the royal administration, Pedro Rodríguez de Campomanes,[65] had left the king and his ministers in no doubt of the fundamental importance of the Indies and the American trade to that process. The political and administrative recovery of the Indies was a *sine qua non* for the internal and international recovery of Spain. The continuity which this assumption gave to Madrid's American policy over the following decades was reinforced by the continuity in office or in positions of influence of ministers who might differ in their ideas and approaches, but who were all committed to the goal of reform both in the Indies and in Spain itself – not only Gálvez, but also the three principal ministers of the reign of Charles III after the fall of Esquilache, the counts of Aranda, Campomanes and Floridablanca.

Reform in the peninsula had been directed over half a century to removing the obstacles to the creation of a powerful state capable of generating the wealth and mobilizing the resources that would enable it to hold its own in a ruthlessly competitive international system. In the eyes of the crown and its advisers this entailed the dismantling of much of the old order inherited from the Habsburgs. It meant the suppression of the old regional laws and institutions, and the dissolution of the Habsburg corporate society with its immunities and privileges – privileges which, in the view of Madrid, impeded the effective exercise of royal authority and obstructed the development of agriculture, trade and industry, the prerequisite of national power and prosperity. All private interests were to be subordinated to the common good – the *bien común*[66] – and every group in society must be subjected to a uniformity of dependence on the crown. 'As a magistrate', wrote Campomanes in 1765, 'I cannot abandon the *bien común*, hide the abuses that obstruct it, or fail to call on the support of the laws against them, and if some of these laws have fallen out of use or have been forgotten, to propose their renewal or improvement.'[67]

The sole object of loyalty was henceforth to be the unified nation-state – the *cuerpo unido de nación*[68] – embodied in the person of the monarch. In place of the regional patriotisms of the Habsburg composite monarchy, a new and genuinely *Spanish* patriotism was required. In the words of the famous Aragonese exponent of Enlightenment doctrine, Benito Jerónimo Feijóo (1676–1764), 'the *patria* . . . which we ought to value above our own private interests is that body politic in which, under a civil government, we are united beneath the yoke of the same laws. Thus Spain is the object of the love of the Spaniard.'[69]

In a campaign designed to extend state control over every aspect of public life, the church, with its enormous wealth and its corporate rights and immunities, inevitably came to occupy the attention of the reformers. In practice, regalist policies were nothing new, and had long been pursued by the Habsburgs, but they were resumed with a new vigour by the ministers of Charles III, who launched a determined assault on clerical privilege in their efforts to complete the work begun by the Concordat of 1753 and ensure the clear subordination of the church to the throne.

The American church had a somewhat different relationship to the crown from that of the church in Spain. Royal control of ecclesiastical appointments under the Patronato had made it a dependent, if not always reliable, junior partner in the government of the Indies. Questions of clerical immunity and of the excessive wealth of bishops and cathedral chapters, however, were universal in the Hispanic world. In the Indies, as in Spain, both the church and the religious orders could be represented as impediments to the effective exercise of a royal power operating in the name of the 'common good'. From the 1760s to the end of the century colonial officials therefore worked with varying degrees of success to curtail or abolish the immunities of the American clergy, while an obedient episcopal hierarchy sought to raise the level of ecclesiastical discipline, using provincial councils as the instruments of reform.[70]

The religious orders, for their part, presented special problems in the Indies, as a result of their pre-eminent position in the work of evangelization. Bourbon reformers, with their regalist notions, had little love for independent-minded members of religious communities enjoying a semi-autonomous status, and were therefore inclined to support the efforts of the bishops and the secular clergy to limit their influence. A new impetus was given to the campaign that had been waged since the late sixteenth century for the secularization of the parishes, a process that the religious orders systematically opposed in the courts.[71] By the 1760s they found themselves on the defensive, and in 1766 the Jesuits, the most powerful and intransigent of them all, finally lost their long legal battle against paying the 10 per cent of tithes on the produce of their properties, which the laity and the other orders paid to the cathedral chapters.[72]

This setback to the Jesuits in Mexico was to be overshadowed by the catastrophe that overtook the entire order in the following year, when Charles III, following the example of the kings of Portugal and France, decreed its expulsion from all his dominions. He had his own reasons for disliking the Jesuit order, which he saw as a dangerously powerful international organization unamenable to royal control, and which he suspected, with some reason, of being in collusion with the interest groups involved in the recent overthrow of his reforming minister, Esquilache.[73] A decree, however, that was warmly welcomed by adherents of the philosophy of the Enlightenment also received the support of 'Jansenist' elements in the Spanish church, which questioned the value of the religious orders and looked to a pastoral clergy and an internalized religion for spiritual reformation. This more austere form of Spanish Catholicism, which found its architectural and visual counterpart in the replacement of exuberantly ornate baroque church decoration by simple neo-classical interiors, was well suited to the temper of a regime that expected the church to confine itself to spiritual concerns, unless or until otherwise directed by the crown.[74]

The expulsion decree of 1767, dramatic as it was for metropolitan Spain, left a still more gaping hole in the fabric of Spanish American life. The enforced departure of some 2,200 Jesuits, many of them creoles,[75] meant the abandonment of their frontier missions, including the famed Indian communities in Paraguay. The order owned a total of some 400 large haciendas distributed through New Spain, Peru, Chile and New Granada. This massive amount of well-managed real estate was now transferred to the crown, and eventually from the crown to private purchasers.[76] In addition, the expulsion produced a major upheaval in the educational system of Spanish America, where Jesuit colleges had formed generation after generation of the creole elite, and it deprived the Indies of dedicated pastors and teachers, many of whom would carry with them to Europe a deep nostalgia for the world they had left behind them. Their precipitate departure provoked immediate and violent outbreaks of protest. José de Gálvez, busy with his visitation of New Spain, used the newly arrived regiments to crush the riots, hanging 85 of the ringleaders, and condemning hundreds more to imprisonment.[77] While the immediate protests might have been stifled, the long-term repercussions of the expulsion were to be as revolutionary as the decree that drove the Jesuits out.

There could have been no better symbol of the ruthless determination of the Caroline reformers to break decisively with the past than the expulsion of the Jesuits. When taken in conjunction with the administrative and fiscal reforms now gathering pace, it suggested to anxious creole elites that the world was fast changing around them. At the heart of that world had been an apparently stable relationship between the crown and its American subjects, governed by the predictability that came from the belief that each party to the relationship would abide by the rules. Now suddenly the very foundations of that relationship appeared to be crumbling. Far away to the north, the no less anxious subjects of the British crown were reluctantly arriving at the same conclusion.

Redefining imperial relationships

Ministers in Madrid and London were taken aback by the strength of colonial reactions to what seemed to them to be their entirely justified measures for fiscal and administrative reform. A comment made in 1766 by the fiscal attorney of the Audiencia of Quito was as applicable to the American subjects of George III as to those of Charles III of Spain: 'there is no American who does not reject any novelty whatsoever in the management of taxation.'[78] The words were written with feeling. Quito in 1765 was the scene of the first great outbreak in Spanish America of violent protest against the Caroline reform programme – an urban insurrection that dwarfed in length and intensity the Mexico City food riots of 1692.[79]

In conformity with the programme for increasing American revenues, although apparently acting without direct orders from Madrid, the viceroy of New Granada, Pedro Messía de la Cerda, gave instructions for the removal of the administration of the *alcabala* sales tax and the brandy monopoly from the hands of private tax-farmers. Instead, it was to be taken over by royal officials, whose loyalty and dedication would, he hoped, substantially increase the returns to the treasury. The effect of this proposed reform was to unite in opposition to the new measures a large number of disparate social groups in the city. The creole elite saw its economic interests directly affected by the changes. This was especially true of landowners who grew the sugar that was distilled into brandy. The elite also bitterly resented any attempt by the authorities to introduce fiscal innovations without prior consultation with the city council. For their part, householders, small tradesmen and artisans would be hit by more rigorous collection of the sales tax at a time of acute depression in the local textile economy, which had long been suffering from foreign competition and was further hit by the influx of cheaper, European, cloths at the end of the Seven Years' War. With the encouragement of members of the clergy and the religious orders – the Jesuits, among others, had sugar-producing estates – and with the approval of the Audiencia, the city council decided to resort to the old Hispanic tradition in times of trouble of convening an expanded town meeting – a *cabildo abierto* – in which representatives of different sections of the urban community would have the opportunity to air their views.

Acting, again following tradition, in the name of the public good – a *bien común* conceived rather differently from that put forward by royal ministers – the meeting resolved to oppose the reforms and petition the viceroy to this effect. De la Cerda had no intention of changing his plans. His officials, having successfully introduced the changes to the brandy monopoly, proceeded to push ahead with the scheme for taking the *alcabala* into administration. On 22 May 1765 large crowds, mostly mestizo in composition, came out onto the streets from the different *barrios*, or quarters, of the city, probably encouraged by clerics and members of the creole elite. There were no troops in the city, the militia companies were conspicuously invisible when their presence was needed, and the crowds, which were joined by Indians, ransacked and destroyed the *alcabala* office.

Once the weakness of the authorities had been exposed, the confidence and the radicalism of the protesters increased. The viceroy had chosen a peninsular Spaniard to introduce the Quito reforms, and strong anti-Spanish feelings began to rise to the surface, with placards being posted demanding the expulsion of all the *peninsulares* in the city. On St John's night, 24 June, a party of armed citizens headed by the *corregidor* and including peninsular Spaniards tried to reassert control by firing on the crowd, killing two young men. As the news spread, large numbers swarmed into the streets and congregated in the Plaza Mayor, where they attacked the palace of the Audiencia, the citadel of royal authority. The rioters were now in control, and the Audiencia, under pressure, had no choice but to order the expulsion of all peninsular Spaniards who were not married to creoles. The expulsion decree was read out in a public ceremony in the Plaza Mayor, and the crowd celebrated its victory with shouts of 'Long live the king!'

The royal government in Quito had effectively collapsed, and although the Indian communities in the immediate countryside remained quiet, the unrest spread southwards to the city of Cuenca, and northwards as far as Popayán and Cali. In Quito itself order was maintained by an increasingly precarious coalition of plebeian leaders and prominent creole citizens, who were becoming alarmed at the level of violence. By degrees, as the coalition crumbled, the urban patriciate and the Audiencia recovered control. When royal troops sent by the viceroy from Santa Fe de Bogotá finally entered the city in September 1766 they met with no resistance. The Audiencia, which had been so closely identified with the collapse of royal authority, was purged, and early in 1767 the brandy monopoly was restored. The crown had no intention of forgoing a valuable source of revenue, or of abandoning its reforms.

The Quito rebellion was an anti-tax revolt, which temporarily united the different strata of urban society in a common cause. It provided an outlet for the strong anti-Spanish sentiments that ran through so much of colonial society in eighteenth-century Spanish America, but if some of the rebels envisaged full autonomy for the kingdom of Quito there was no general intention of overthrowing royal government. The insurrection, however, was also a form of constitutional protest, in the conventional constitutionalist style of the Spanish Monarchy. Even if the American viceroyalties had no representative assemblies, the cities had their cabildos, and creole patriciates expected to be consulted by the authorities before innovations were introduced. In the absence of such consultation, the calling of a *cabildo abierto*, which extended the process of deliberation to embrace the urban community as a whole, was the logical next step in the organization of protest, and a preliminary to organized resistance.

Since the resistance on this occasion was to a reform programme that Madrid planned to extend to all its American territories, it could be regarded as presaging a general opposition throughout the continent. Quito, however, was a remote city in the Andean highlands, living in a world of its own. Although the kingdom of Quito had been incorporated into the viceroyalty of New Granada when it was re-established in 1739, it retained a substantial degree of autonomy and was some eight to ten weeks' travelling distance from New Granada's capital of Santa Fe de Bogotá. If anything, its links were closer to Lima and to the viceroyalty of Peru, to which it had formerly belonged.[80]

Given the city's remoteness, the events in Quito might have seemed a localized phenomenon, and one likely to have only limited repercussions. News, however, had a way of percolating through the Hispanic world, and it duly reached New Spain, where, in the autumn of 1765, rumours of an increase in taxes provoked an assault by the populace on soldiers in the garrison of Puebla.[81] More significantly, in Spain itself the rebellion provided yet another argument for use by the enemies of Esquilache. Already highly unpopular for his monopoly of power and office, his radical reforming policies, and his dictatorial ways, he could now be accused of pursuing a programme that threatened to lose Spain its American empire.[82] In so far as the accusation played its part in the movement that led to his overthrow on 23 March 1766, the uprising in Quito marked the moment at which events in America first began to influence Spanish domestic politics. Spanish ministers were starting to find, as British ministers were also finding, that the Atlantic was narrower than it looked.

In Spanish America itself, however, the varied timing of the reforms, depending on the region involved, helped reduce the chances of co-ordinated resistance by colonial populations across jurisdictional and administrative boundaries. The general visitation of Peru, for instance, by José Antonio de Areche, the natural sequence to that of New Spain by Gálvez in the 1760s, would only begin in 1777. This staggered approach to reform, a logical consequence of the vast areas of territory to be covered, gave the Spanish imperial authorities an advantage over their British counterparts when it came to responding to opposition, as the 1765 Stamp Act crisis in the British Atlantic community was to demonstrate.

Although early responses in the British colonies to Grenville's measures were muted, they provoked a groundswell of uneasiness. The plans for the rigorous enforcement of customs duties under the 1764 Sugar Act were deeply disturbing to merchants all down the Atlantic seaboard, and Governor Bernard of Massachusetts reported that 'the publication of orders for the strict execution of the Molasses Act has caused a greater alarm in this country than the taking of *Fort William Henry* did in 1757 . . . the Merchants say, There is an end of the trade in this Province.'[83] But the concern extended far beyond the mercantile community, badly hit by the post-war slump.[84] The colonies had emerged from the war proud of their contribution to a victory which had seen the glory of the British Empire – *their* empire – raised to unparalleled heights. Looking back more than half a century later to the early years of the war and the arrival of General Amherst and his redcoats in Worcester, Massachusetts, on their way to Fort William Henry, John Adams wrote: 'I then rejoiced that I was an Englishman, and gloried in the name of Britain.'[85] Now, at the moment of triumph, after the colonists had played their own part by raising some 20,000 men a year and paying half the cost themselves,[86] they saw their contribution to victory disparaged, a standing army stationed on their soil, and new revenue-raising measures being introduced without prior consultation or approval by their own elected assemblies.

News of the Stamp Act spread through the colonies in April and May 1765, around the time when the people of Quito were deciding to take the law into their own hands against the fiscal measures being imposed by the Spanish authorities. Initial responses were again muted, but on 29 May, in the Virginia House of Burgesses, Patrick Henry made the electrifying speech in which he argued for the passage of five resolutions outlining the House's constitutional objections to the Act.[87] Like the petitions put forward by the creoles in Spanish America, who used the historical argument of their descent from the conquistadores and first settlers to justify their claims to rights contested by the Spanish crown, so the Virginia resolutions also argued from history in favour of the colonists' rights:

> *Resolved*, that the first Adventurers and Settlers of this his Majesty's Colony and Dominion of Virginia, brought with them, and transmitted to their Posterity, and all other his Majesty's subjects since inhabiting in this his Majesty's said Colony, all the Liberties, Privileges, Franchises and Immunities, that have at any Time been held, enjoyed, and possessed, by the people of *Great Britain*.[88]

By including 'all other his Majesty's subjects', this resolution was nominally more all-inclusive than comparable Spanish creole assertions of their historical legitimacy, but it did not include two-fifths of Virginia's population, its 200,000 black slaves.

It was the fifth resolution, subsequently rescinded by the House of Burgesses but spread through the colonies by newspapers and gazettes with the addition of two spurious resolutions to the original five, that provoked uproar in the House and an upsurge of excitement far beyond it:

> *Resolved* Therefore that the General Assembly of this Colony have the only and sole exclusive Right and Power to lay Taxes and Impositions upon the Inhabitants of this Colony and that every Attempt to vest such Power in any Person or Persons whatsoever other than the General Assembly aforesaid has a manifest Tendency to destroy British as well as American Freedom.

Here was a direct challenge to the right of the British parliament to tax the colonies, and a challenge mounted, moreover, in the name of British as well as American liberty. As such, it provided a rallying cry for protest, and it was in Boston on 14 August 1765 that direct action first followed on protest.

Boston's population of some 16,000 was around half that of Quito, estimated at 30,000 in this period.[89] Boston, too, had been badly affected by sluggish economic conditions, exacerbated at the beginning of 1765 by what John Hancock called 'the most prodigious shock ever known in this part of the world' – the collapse and flight of a merchant banker, Nathaniel Wheelwright, with whom small-scale merchants, shopowners and artisans had deposited their money.[90] The Boston riots, like those of Quito that summer, were the work of a well-orchestrated mob, whose leaders, the Loyal Nine – soon to rename themselves the Sons of Liberty – were acting with the connivance or collusion of members of the civic elite.[91] The Loyal Nine were largely artisans and shopkeepers, the kind of people badly hit by the depression and the banking collapse. As in Quito, the first target of the rioters was the office from which it was expected that the hated new tax would be administered, and this was followed by the ransacking of the house of the designated stamp distributor, Andrew Oliver, who promptly resigned a post to which he had not yet received his official appointment. Twelve days later, the mobs turned their attention to the houses of the comptroller of customs, the register of the vice-admiralty court, and the wealthy lieutenant-governor of Massachusetts, Thomas Hutchinson. Running through the acts of looting and violence, as in Quito, was the animosity of the impoverished against rich citizens, some of whom had grown substantially richer on the profits made during the war by military contracting and other activities. According to the governor, Francis Bernard, 'a War of plunder, of general levelling and taking away the distinction of rich and poor', was only narrowly averted.[92] He himself retired to the safety of Castle William. With no regular soldiers stationed in Boston there was nothing he could do. British imperial authority in Massachusetts was as impotent as Spanish imperial authority in New Granada, but where the latter would eventually get its way, the former failed to do so.

The reasons for this were various, and were related to both local and wider colonial circumstances, and to the metropolitan context. Whereas the highland economy of Quito, although possessing remote access to the Pacific through the port of Guayaquil, left it relatively disconnected from the outer world, Boston was a normally flourishing port city, a busy hub of inter-colonial and transatlantic trade, closely and influentially connected with the other mainland colonies and those of the West Indies. It was also, as William Burke described it in his *Account of the European Settlements in America*, published eight years earlier, 'the capital of Massachusetts bay, the first city of New-England, and of all North America'.[93] The Massachusetts interior did not always march in step with its bustling capital, but on this occasion the city radicals effectively persuaded the colony's freehold farmers, with their 'very free, bold, and republican spirit', of the justice of their cause. 'In no part of the world', wrote William Burke, 'are the ordinary sort so independent, or possess so many of the conveniences of life.'[94] Flaunting their independence and flying their flag in the name of liberty – the birthright of every subject of the British crown – they united with the city-dwellers in an expression of outrage that resonated through all colonial America. Its effectiveness was revealed as rioting spread to other cities, and groups calling themselves Sons of Liberty sprang up in colony after colony.

Whether the different colonies could actually co-ordinate their opposition to the Stamp Act remained an open question. The emergence of a popular press during the preceding decades had raised the level of awareness in individual colonies of what was happening in the others, but the past record of inter-colonial co-operation had not been impressive, although the shared struggles and triumphs of the Seven Years War are likely to have fostered the sense of a wider American community to which all the colonies belonged. Eventually nine of the thirteen colonies attended the congress specially summoned for New York in October 1765. This itself was a remarkable display of unity, and all the more so since three of the absentees, Virginia, North Carolina and Georgia, were prevented from participating by the refusal of their governors to convene assemblies for the election of delegates.[95]

While the delegates to the Stamp Act Congress were anxious to reaffirm their loyalty to the British crown in the statement they prepared to draft on colonial rights and privileges, they were equally anxious to affirm their conviction that powers of taxation over the colonies were vested exclusively in their own elected assemblies. They accepted that legislation in matters of trade rested with parliament in London, but were faced with the awkward fact that Grenville's measures raised the problem of deciding where trade regulation ended and the levying of new taxes began. With opinions divided over tactics and wording, the final statement was inevitably somewhat ambiguous, but its general tenor was clear. Americans, by virtue of their rights as Britons, could not and should not be subjected to taxation voted by a British parliament in which they were not represented.

One lesson suggested by the Stamp Act Congress was that there was more to unite than divide the colonies. In the words of Christopher Gadsden, the representative of South Carolina: 'There ought to be no New England men, no New Yorker, &c., known on the Continent, but all of us Americans . . .'[96] Resistance to the Stamp Act, spreading – although in largely muted form – to the West Indies,[97] helped to strengthen ties of solidarity, enhancing a sense of American identity among people loudly proclaiming that they were Britons to the core. This community of feeling and action bridged social as well as inter-colonial divisions. Social groups that were disaffected or had hitherto played little or no part in colonial politics now became active participants in the cause of liberty. 'Such an Union', wrote John Adams triumphantly, 'was never known before in America.'[98]

The passionate dedication of the colonists to liberty, as manifested in the riots in the seaboard cities and the successful staging of an inter-colonial congress, found practical expression in the development of an unprecedented weapon of political opposition for bringing pressure to bear on the British ministers and parliament – the boycotting of British goods. Under the Stamp Act, merchants would need to pay stamp duty to clear their goods through customs. A group of New York merchants took the initiative in pledging to cancel all orders for manufactured articles until the Stamp Act was repealed.[99] Their action was publicized in colonial newspapers; merchants' orders were cancelled in Boston, Philadelphia and elsewhere; and consumers were exhorted to refrain from purchasing British luxuries.

In some respects the initiative taken by the New York merchants and imitated by their colleagues in the other port cities was self-serving. Times were depressed, import merchants had overstocked inventories on their hands, and the market for English goods was temporarily saturated. As it turned out, compliance with the boycott was patchy, but the colonists had hit on a form of leverage against the mother country with enormous potential. If the rapidly expanding consumer society of colonial America was heavily dependent on imports from Britain, the American market in turn had become of crucial importance for the industrializing British economy. Some two-thirds of the new industrial goods exported by Britain – linens, cottons, silks, metalware – were by now being exported to America.[100] At the beginning of the century, North America took 5.7 per cent of all British domestic exports; in 1772–3, the figure was 25.3 per cent.[101]

Virginia and Maryland financed the purchase of these British goods primarily through their tobacco exports to Britain, while New England and the Middle Colonies did the same by supplying timber, grain, flour and meat to the West Indies plantations. Any disruption to this delicately poised British Atlantic system could obviously have the most serious repercussions both for the British imperial economy and for domestic industrial production in Britain, as the chairman of an organization of London merchants warned the Marquis of Rockingham. When the colonists refused to participate in any commerce requiring stamps, as he expected them to do on 1 November, 'our sugar islands will be deprived of their usual supplies of provisions, lumber etc.' The West Indies planters would then be 'disabled from sending home their produce or even subsisting their slaves', with obvious and disastrous consequences for the economy of the mother country. He warned, too, that a stoppage of American trade would prevent merchants collecting their debts, thus threatening them with ruin, while those who survived would stop buying manufactured goods for export to America. 'It naturally and unavoidably follows that an exceedingly great number of manufacturers are soon to be without employ and of course without bread.'[102]

Any British parliament was likely to be acutely sensitive to such a threat to national prosperity, and not surprisingly the House of Commons took notice when confronted by petitions from 25 trading towns urging repeal of the Stamp Act because of the distress they were suffering as a result of the fall in exports to America.[103] It was the novel character of Britain's commercial empire of the eighteenth century – an 'empire of goods' – that made non-importation such a potentially effective weapon. For Spain's American colonists such a weapon was unimaginable. Not only did Spain lack a representative body in which commercial and industrial interests could publicly voice their concerns, but the backwardness of Spanish industry meant that Spanish American consumers were largely dependent on non-Spanish manufacturers for the luxuries they craved. Their insatiable appetite for European goods, whether legally or clandestinely imported, was far more harmful to the mother country than any boycott could ever be. In the Spanish Atlantic system, contraband, not boycotting, was the most effective form of protest against unpopular policies emanating from Madrid, and the purchase of contraband goods had become second nature to these overseas subjects of the King of Spain.

Through consumer boycotts and street protests alike, the Stamp Act, formally introduced on 1 November 1765, was to all intents and purposes a dead letter from the start. Mass resistance on this scale took ministers in London by surprise, and presented them with a dilemma from which there was no obvious escape. But Grenville's removal from office that summer had provided the opportunity for at least a temporary retreat if this should be needed. The new Rockingham administration's expectation that the Stamp Act would be self-enforcing was dashed when it received in early December a report on the imminent danger of rebellion in New York. Already aware of the logistical problems in the way of reinforcing from England the army in America to levels which would enable it to contain the rising tide of disorder, the administration rightly came to the conclusion that the act was unenforceable.[104] Imperial authority, however, must somehow be upheld. The government's solution was to repeal the Stamp Act in February 1766, but to follow the repeal with a Declaratory Act affirming the sovereignty of parliament over the colonies. It was in conformity with this act that Charles Townshend would introduce his project of colonial taxation in 1767, and thus unleash a new, and graver, crisis in the increasingly fraught relationship between London and the colonies.

The Stamp Act crisis exposed, as never before, the fragility of the imperial hold over North America in the face of violent and more or less co-ordinated resistance throughout the colonies to measures deemed unacceptable by their populations. But beyond this it also exposed fundamental ambiguities in the constitutional ordering of the empire itself. As a result of these ambiguities the metropolis and the colonies had come to view their relationship through very different lenses. The same was true of Spain and its American empire, but the ambiguities were not the same, and the problems they created, although severe, were not so immediately intractable.

The crisis that overtook the Anglo-American community in the 1760s can be seen in constitutional terms as the crisis of the British composite monarchy in the form it had come to assume by the middle of the eighteenth century.[105] Where Bourbon Spain had turned its back on the idea of composite monarchy and was moving firmly in the direction of an authoritarian monarchy based on a vertical articulation of power,[106] Hanoverian Britain was set on a course that had led to a partially composite parliamentary state. The events of 1688 had established the sovereignty of king in parliament, and the incorporating union of Scotland with England in 1707 had given the Scots parliamentary representation at Westminster in compensation for the loss of their own parliament in Edinburgh. Both Ireland and the colonies, however, remained outside this incorporating parliamentary union, and retained elected assemblies of their own.

This left open the question of the relationship between these assemblies and the Westminster parliament, at least until 1720, when it passed a Declaratory Act asserting its authority over the Irish parliament. But the Westminster parliament refrained from exercising tax-raising powers over the Irish, and was careful to obtain the agreement of the Irish parliament before legislating on Irish matters.[107] Until the 1760s it was similarly circumspect in questions relating to the internal affairs of the American colonies, although it showed no such scruples where the regulation of trade was concerned. But if the question of the ultimate location of sovereignty were to be directly put, there was no doubt at Westminster what the answer should be. Sovereignty was indivisible, and it lay with the English parliament. While rejoicing in American resistance in his famous speech on the Stamp Act of 14 January 1766, William Pitt described the constitutional position with brutal clarity: 'When two countries are connected together, like England and her colonies, without being incorporated, the one must necessarily govern; the greater must rule the less . . .'[108]

For a parliament, rather than the monarch, to assert sovereignty over the component parts of a composite monarchy, all of which had their own representative assemblies, constituted a novelty in the history of composite monarchies. Pitt and his fellow parliamentarians therefore found themselves navigating in uncharted waters. But the very notion of the indivisibility of sovereignty left them with little room for manoeuvre. The dominant interpretation of the status of colonies in terms of the historical example of the Romans, who (it was incorrectly believed) considered their colonies to be imperial dependencies, in contrast to the Greeks, merely strengthened their conviction of the correctness of their course.[109] As Charles Townshend observed in replying to Grenville, if parliament were ever to give up the right of taxing America, then 'he must give up the word "colony" – for that implies subordination.'[110] 'Subordination' was automatically taken to mean subordination to the English legislature.

An incorporating union between Britain and the colonies on the Scottish model would have brought American representatives to the Westminster parliament. This was an idea that Benjamin Franklin, as Pennsylvania's agent in London, toyed with at the height of the Stamp Act crisis, but soon abandoned on hearing the latest news from America. 'The Time has been', he wrote, 'when the Colonies, would have esteem'd it a great Advantage as well as Honour to them to be permitted to send Members to Parliament; and would have ask'd for that Privilege if they could have had the least hopes of obtaining it. The Time is now come when they are indifferent about it, and will probably not ask it . . .'[111] They would have no truck, either, with the argument devised by Thomas Whately during the course of the crisis, that the colonists, like those residents of Britain who did not possess the vote, nevertheless enjoyed 'virtual representation' in parliament, a notion described by a Maryland lawyer as 'a mere cob-web, spread to catch the unwary, and intangle the weak'.[112] They had been endowed with their own representative assemblies, modelled on the English House of Commons, and the copies should surely replicate the original, not only in its workings but also in its powers.[113] Their assemblies provided not only a guarantee of the right they enjoyed by virtue of their English descent to reject all taxation to which they had not given their prior consent, but also the only proper forum for consent to new taxes when new taxes were required.

Loyalty to the person of the British monarch remained unshaken, and the colonists continued to take pride in their participation in a British Empire that was an empire of the free. But the incompatibility between their perception of their British rights and the British parliament's perception of its own uncontested sovereignty as the necessary condition for the effective running of that empire created a constitutional impasse. This impasse was, if anything, made all the more difficult to negotiate by the sense of shared identity and shared ideals. Occasional references might be made in England to Americans as foreigners,[114] but many would have agreed with William Strahan, a London printer, when he wrote: 'I consider British Subjects in America as only living in a different Country, having the self-same Interests, and entitled to the self-same Liberties.'[115] 'Every drop of blood in my heart is *British*', wrote the Pennsylvania attorney, John Dickinson, in 1766, as if in confirmation.[116] It was precisely because they saw themselves as British that the Americans would stand up for their rights. This left little room for compromise in a constitutional framework which entrenched in representative institutions rights regarded as fundamental on both sides of the Atlantic.

The effective absence of such institutions in Spain's Monarchy and empire inevitably created a different dynamic from that which determined relationships in the British Atlantic community. But in the Spanish Atlantic community also there was a growing divergence in assumptions and perceptions on the two sides of the Atlantic that similarly presaged major troubles ahead. Spain's American territories, like the British colonies, continued to see themselves as members of a composite monarchy at a time when Madrid's terms of reference had changed. But where the British colonies now found themselves confronting a parliamentary regime that – even as it proclaimed its own absolute authority – still half spoke the language of composite monarchy, of liberty and rights, Spain's American dominions were faced with a monarch and ministers for whom the very notion of composite monarchy had become anathema. As a result, the two sides of the Spanish Atlantic were speaking different languages, whereas the languages spoken by Britain and British America were confusingly, and dangerously, the same.

The language spoken in official circles in Spain was now that of the unitary nation-state with an absolutist monarch at its head – a monarch who received his power directly from God without any mediation by the community.[117] This was the language used by the viceroy of New Spain, the Marquis of Croix, in his 1767 viceregal proclamation ordering absolute submission by all classes and conditions of Mexican society to the royal decree for the expulsion of the Jesuits: '. . . the subjects of the great monarch who occupies the throne of Spain should know once and for all that they were born to keep silent and obey, and not to discuss or express opinions on high matters of government.'[118]

In the authoritarian centralized monarchy of Charles III's ministers and viceroys there was no room for the semi-autonomous kingdoms and provinces of which a composite monarchy was traditionally composed, nor for the compacts that guaranteed the preservation of their distinctive identities. Instead, they must be integrated into the unitary state. But the creole elites of the kingdoms of Peru and New Spain, of Quito and New Granada naturally clung to the historic privileges and traditions of the lands that had become their *patrias*. These privileges and traditions, as they saw it, were now under growing threat from the interference of meddling reformers, and they expected their protests to be heard, and their grievances to be addressed, in the ways they always had been – through petitioning and bargaining, until an acceptable compromise was reached.

The reformers, however, showed alarming signs of being unwilling to play the old game, as the intransigent reaction of the New Granada authorities to the Quito riots made all too clear. In the more politically sophisticated creole community of New Spain, José de Gálvez's visitation between 1765 and 1771 provoked similar alarm. Taken in conjunction with the expulsion of the Jesuits, his attitudes and behaviour provided eloquent evidence of the new spirit that prevailed in Madrid. He had come with a clear mandate for reform, and the reform included plans for sweeping administrative changes, that would effectively put an end to the management by creoles of their own affairs. In 1768, in line with the experiment introduced in Cuba four years earlier, he proposed a new system of government for the Mexican viceroyalty, which would be divided into eleven intendancies, thus bringing it into uniformity with the administrative system established by the Bourbons in Spain. The plan envisaged the disappearance of the 150 district magistracies – the *alcaldes mayores* – which had allowed creoles to gain control of large areas of local government, with consequent opportunities for the exploitation of the Indian population.[119]

At the same time as Gálvez was drawing up his scheme for the undercutting of local interests through the professionalization of the American bureaucracy, ministers in Madrid were considering the government of the Indies in the light of reactions in the Indies to the expulsion of the Jesuits. On 5 March 1768 an extraordinary council, presided over by the Count of Aranda, president of the Council of Castile, met to discuss ways of strengthening the ties between Spain and its American possessions at a time when the expulsion had subjected them to heavy strain. The Council of Castile's two attorneys, Campomanes and José Moñino, the future Count of Floridablanca, drew up the report.[120] The tenor of their proposals was reminiscent of those put forward in the 1620s by the count-duke of Olivares for the closer integration of the Spanish Monarchy,[121] but while it still carried overtones of the age of composite monarchy, the temper of the document belonged to the new age of the unitary state.

Where Olivares had written of the need to end 'the separation of hearts' between the various kingdoms of the Monarchy,[122] the committee was concerned with the problem of how to induce the king's vassals in the Indies to 'love their mother, who is Spain', when they lived at such a distance from her. Nothing was being done to make them 'desire or love the nation', and there was little chance of this happening as long as they saw the *peninsulares* crossing the Atlantic to enrich themselves at creole expense. 'Those countries', said the report, 'should no longer be regarded as simple colonies (*pura colonia*) but as powerful and considerable provinces of the Spanish Empire.' One way to treat them as such was to bring over young creoles to study in Spain, reserve places in the Spanish administration for them, and establish a native American regiment in the peninsula. At the same time the policy should be maintained of

> always sending Spaniards to fill the principal posts, bishoprics and prebends in the Indies, but appointing creoles to equivalent offices in Spain. This is what would strengthen friendship and union [the words might have come straight from the Count-Duke's pen] and [an eighteenth-century touch] would create a single national body (*un solo cuerpo de nación*), with the creoles over here as so many hostages for the retention of those lands under the gentle dominion of His Majesty.[123]

This and the other proposals in the report were approved by the council, which saw them as a device for binding the Indies to the mother country with ties of mutual interest 'in order to make this union indissoluble'. The Indies were, in effect, to become provinces of Spain, and, as a further measure of integration, it was proposed that each of the three American viceroyalties, together with the Philippines, should be allowed to appoint a deputy to join those of Castile, Aragon and Catalonia in the standing body, or *diputación*, which had taken the place of Cortes now defunct. The object would be for them 'to confer and humbly represent suitable measures for the utility of those dominions'. This was the nearest that an absolute monarchy could permit itself to come to the suggestions being entertained in London for the inclusion of American representatives in the House of Commons.

Impelling the 1768 report was the fear, always latent in Madrid as in London, that the American territories might at some moment attempt to break loose. A few months earlier the fiscal attorney of the Council of the Indies had remarked that 'although they have been the most peaceful of our dominions since their discovery, it is never wise to assume that they are entirely safe from the danger of rebellion.'[124] But could the plans for closer integration now being discussed in Madrid quieten the unrest of the creoles by addressing their complaints? It soon became apparent that they could not.

With Gálvez missing no opportunity to display his contempt for the creoles, there was a growing suspicion in New Spain that Madrid had embarked on a systematic policy of filling the higher judicial and administrative offices in the viceroyalty with peninsular Spaniards. At present, six of the seven judges of the Mexican Audiencia were creoles.[125] Were those born and bred in New Spain no longer to hold positions of trust in their own land? In 1771 the Mexico City council commissioned one of the creole judges, Antonio Joaquín de Rivadaneira y

Barrientos, to draw up an official protest for submission to the crown.[126] Rivadaneira responded with an eloquent statement of the creole case for preferential treatment in appointment to office – a statement that moved beyond the standard argument, endlessly repeated since the sixteenth century, that such treatment was owed them by virtue of their descent from the conquerors and first settlers of New Spain.

Any attempt, Rivadaneira warned, to exclude 'American Spaniards' from high office 'is to seek to overturn the law of peoples. It will lead not only to the loss of America but to the ruin of the state.' 'Natural reason', he argued, and 'the laws of all kingdoms' dictated that 'foreigners' should not hold offices to the exclusion of natives. 'European Spaniards', even if sharing the same sovereign, should be considered foreigners 'by nature, if not by law' – a prudent qualification in view of the fact that the Indies had been constitutionally incorporated into the Crown of Castile by right of conquest. 'The truth is that while these people may not be considered foreigners in the Indies from a constitutional point of view, in fact they do not derive their identity from the Indies. They have their homes, their parents, their brothers and sisters, and all their ties in Old Spain, not in New Spain.' As a result, 'they regard themselves as transients in America whose prime purpose is to return wealthy to their own home and their native land.'

An awareness of the constitutional objections to his case had driven Rivadaneira to resort to the argument from 'nature' – an argument couched in terms of incipient national identity, and in this respect more radical than any yet advanced by the North American colonists. He had in effect turned Spaniards' criticisms of creoles against themselves. It was not the creoles but the Spaniards who were the 'foreigners', ignorant of the land they had been sent out to rule and stayed to exploit. Innate loyalty and political prudence, however, made him also well aware of the need to avoid any suggestion that Spanish Americans were determined to split the Hispanic community in two. 'We cannot cut out the Europeans altogether. This would mean seeking to maintain two separate and independent bodies under one head, something of a political monstrosity.' But there was an element of bathos when he went on to ask: 'do they have to receive all the higher appointments?'

Rivadaneira was engaged in a difficult balancing act. On the one hand he had to affirm the essentially Spanish character of the creoles, while at the same time he had to establish their right as natives of their *patria* to be the real masters in their own land. By placing so much emphasis on the *patria*, however, in an attempt to counter the relative weakness of their constitutional case, the creoles ran into problems that could be at least temporarily evaded by the North American colonists, who were similarly wrestling with the implications of a dual identity. British Americans could dwell on the constitutional rights to which they considered themselves entitled as Britons, while turning a blind eye to the presence of Indians and black slaves in their midst. But the presence of other races, and especially of large indigenous or mixed populations, was less easily ignored by Spanish creoles intent on defending their *patrias* against metropolitan attack.

Metropolitan Spaniards had persistently flung at the creoles the charge that they had not only degenerated in an American environment but had also been contaminated by continuous miscegenation. Rivadaneira therefore had to protect his flank by preserving a sharp differentiation between creoles and Indians, 'born to poverty, bred in destitution, and controlled through punishment'.

His words only serve to underline how the creole *patria* had been constructed as essentially the preserve of those who had conquered and settled it, men and women of incontestable Spanish lineage. 'We have to make it clear', he wrote, 'that America consists of a large number of Spaniards whose blood is as pure as that of Spaniards from Old Spain.' In the face of Spanish disparagement of all things American, the creole claim to purity of blood (*limpieza de sangre*), with all the resonance those words enjoyed in the Hispanic world, carried a heavy weight of psychological baggage. It might be deployed in support of the same underlying argument about the fundamental unity and equality of metropolitans and colonials, but it went well beyond the purely symbolic character of John Dickinson's proud boast that 'every drop of blood in my heart is *British*.'[127] For the creoles of Spanish America, blood, in the most literal sense of the word, was the source of rights.

Long before the imperial innovations of the 1760s the notion of the *patria* had been well rehearsed in the Spanish American territories – much more so than in British America, even if, on the classical analogy of the *patria*, there was some talk here too of 'country', as applied to individual colonies.[128] The ambivalence running through the petition of the Mexico City council reflects the ambivalence in combining loyalty to the Hispanic community with loyalty to the *patria*. Traditionally that community had been defined in terms of a composite monarchy, in which the *patria* possessed its rights on the basis of a contract agreed with the monarch – a contract which, at least in the eyes of creoles, placed their territories on an equal footing with the other kingdoms and provinces of the Spanish Monarchy. Even if that claim had never been fully accepted by Madrid as far as its American possessions were concerned, practice – as distinct from theory – had given it some validity over the course of a century or more.

Now the practice, as well as the theory, was in the course of being rejected by royal ministers. Mexico City's petition fell on deaf ears. By a decree issued in February 1776, the crown ordered, in accordance with the proposals of the extraordinary council of 1768, that 'to strengthen further the union of those kingdoms and these', creoles should be recommended for clerical and judicial positions in Spain. At the same time, a third of the posts in American Audiencias and cathedral chapters should be reserved for creoles. Consequently, peninsular candidates could be appointed to the remaining two-thirds. The Mexico City council immediately protested, and once again its protest was ignored.[129]

Creoles, still thinking in terms of the consensus political culture of a composite monarchy, now found themselves faced with the authoritarian responses of an absolutist regime. As Madrid sought to strengthen its grasp on its American territories in the 1770s and 1780s, the scope for conflict was obvious.

But the authoritarianism of the Bourbon monarchy did not, in the last resort, preclude the possibility of manoeuvre and compromise. It was always possible for the crown to jettison an unpopular minister or dismiss an over-zealous official without permanently diminishing the authority of a monarch cast in the role of the benevolent protector of his subjects. No great constitutional principle was at stake. With an absolute parliament, on the other hand, matters were different. In spite of themselves, Britain and its American colonies had become inextricably involved in that most intractable of all forms of conflict, the conflict over competing constitutional rights.

CHAPTER 11

Empires in Crisis

In the space of ten years, between 1773 and 1783, a series of convulsions transformed the political landscape of the Americas. In British America the Boston Tea Party of December 1773 opened a new and dangerous phase in the deteriorating relationship between Britain and its mainland colonies, that would descend in the next two years into rebellion and war. The colonists convened their first Continental Congress in September 1774. In April 1775 British troops and colonial forces clashed at Lexington and Concord. The first shedding of blood was followed by the summoning of the second Continental Congress, the proclamation by the British crown that the colonies were in rebellion, the colonists' Declaration of Independence of 1776, and a war in which thirteen mainland colonies, assisted by France and Spain, would emerge victorious when Britain recognized their independence as a sovereign republic in 1783. The crisis that overtook Britain's empire in America over these years proved nearly terminal.

Political convulsions, however, were not confined to North America. In South America, rebellion came to both Peru and New Granada in the early 1780s. Unlike the revolt of Britain's mainland colonies, neither Túpac Amaru's Andean rebellion of 1780–2, nor the 'Comunero' revolt, which first erupted in the New Granada town of Socorro in March 1781, were to result in independence from the imperial power. Both revolts were suppressed, and another generation would pass before Spain's possessions in central and southern America would follow in the footsteps of the British American colonies. In Spanish America, unlike British America, the crisis was contained.

Both these crises of empire were played out against a background of shifting ideas and ideologies. Comparable forces were operating in favour of change in the two colonial worlds, although at the same time there were profound differences – logistical, structural, human – between them, creating very different patterns of action and response. In neither instance was a break between colonies and metropolis a foregone, or even initially a desired, conclusion. But once it occurred in British North America, unexpected possibilities would begin to present themselves to Spanish Americans too.

Ideas in ferment

The revolution that impelled the thirteen mainland colonies of North America to break their bonds of loyalty to the British crown in 1776 was a revolution of disappointed expectations. In the aftermath of the Seven Years War, the Britain which they had supported on its road to victory failed to behave in the way that their image of it had led them to expect. Where were the gratitude and generosity to which their wartime sacrifices entitled them? Could such men as Grenville and Townshend really be representative of the nation they had been taught to revere as the cradle of liberty? What had become of that perfectly balanced British constitution, with all its checks and balances, when a legislature that had gloriously overthrown tyrants itself became tyrannical? Why did the king, the natural protector of his peoples, not assist them in their hour of need?

These agonizing questions burned their way into the minds of innumerable British Americans in that critical decade 1765–75. They were questions that brought them face to face with unpleasant realities, and impelled them towards personal decisions of a kind which, a few years earlier, they could never have dreamt that they would be called upon to face. Living at a time of far-reaching intellectual, cultural and social change, some of them responded to the pressure of unfolding political events by clinging to old certainties, while others were driven by temperament, conviction or circumstance to look for salvation to the new.

Among the creoles of Spanish America, too, the policies of the king's ministers provoked a sense of outrage and deep disillusionment. The expulsion of the Jesuits had come as a devastating shock, and the determination of the ministers to press ahead with unpopular reforms threatened to turn the creoles' world upside down. The sense of loyalty to the monarch was deeply ingrained in the overseas subjects of Charles III, but in the 1760s and 1770s, in the Spanish as in the British Empire, it is possible to detect a process of psychological distancing between the American territories and the mother country.

There is a difference, however, between distancing, and reaching the decision to snap the bonds of empire. Traditionally, separatism was always more feared by royal ministers in Madrid and London than discussed, or even contemplated, by the overseas settlers and their descendants. When the fiscal attorney of the Council of the Indies observed of Spain's American territories in 1767 that 'it is never wise to assume that they are entirely safe from the danger of rebellion',[1] he was merely the latest in a long line of ministers and officials consumed with similar anxieties since the days of the Pizarro rebellion in Peru, or indeed since Cortés conquered Mexico.

Similar preoccupations were to be found in Whitehall. When the Earl of Sandwich prophesied in 1671 that within twenty years New Englanders would be 'mighty rich and powerful and not at all careful of their dependence upon old England',[2] he was voicing fears already expressed at the time of the Puritan migration in the reign of Charles I. Such fears were reinforced by analogies with

Greek and Roman colonization made by seventeenth-century politicians and officials in the light of their reading of the histories of classical antiquity and the works of contemporary political theorists.

In his *Oceana* (1656), James Harrington compared colonies to children passing through different stages of development: 'For the colonies in the Indies', he wrote, 'they are yet babes that cannot live without sucking the breasts of their mother-cities'; but he would be surprised if 'when they come of age they do not wean themselves'. The reference to 'mother-cities' was no doubt inspired by Athens and Rome. The American colonies were more properly the offspring of a 'mother country'. The expression helped to popularize the image of colonies as children, wayward or disciplined, but still under tutelage as they made their way to adulthood.[3] What would happen when they reached it? In one of the radical Whig papers of 1720 to 1723 assembled under the title of *Cato's Letters*, and widely read in colonial North America, John Trenchard argued that the colonies would in due course grow up, and could not then be expected 'to continue their subjection to another only because their grandfathers were acquainted'. Partnership, not parental discipline, would be needed to preserve the family relationship.[4]

By the 1750s there was a growing belief in Whitehall that, unless discipline were soon applied, colonies that had grown so rich and populous would choose the path of separation. Ministers were strengthened in this belief by what they regarded as colonial recalcitrance during the Seven Years' War. In addition, they feared that the effect of the conquest of Canada would be to weaken the ties of dependency, perhaps fatally, since the colonies would no longer see any need for British military protection against the French. According to the Board of Trade in 1772, one of the intentions behind the 1763 Proclamation Line and its policing by British garrisons was 'the preservation of the colonies in due subordination to, and dependence upon, the mother country'.[5]

As questions about the strength and permanence of the imperial relationship came to be openly discussed in Whitehall and aired in British pamphlets and the press, it was hardly surprising if suspicions grew among the colonists themselves that a conspiracy was afoot to deprive them of their liberties. How else to explain the new coercive policies? Once they began to sense that the imperial government was motivated by the fear that Britain stood in danger of losing its American empire, the notion of independence, which had been the last thing on their minds at the start of the Seven Years War, began to emerge on the horizon as a cloud, still no bigger than a man's hand, but a portent of the future. When this happened, the fears of Whitehall were on their way to becoming self-fulfilling prophecy.

The absence of open discussion in Madrid on the crown's American policies reduced the chances of a comparable reaction in the Hispanic world, if only because there was less information in the public domain on the attitudes and intentions of ministers. Yet the creole population was affected by something of the same sense of alienation felt by the British colonists, and for much the same reasons. Not only were Madrid's policies alarming in themselves, since they seemed to betray a total misunderstanding of what the creoles believed to be the true nature of their relationship with the crown, but they were accompanied by a general disparagement of all things American that was far from new,[6] but was all the more disconcerting because it now came dressed in the fashionable garb of the European Enlightenment.

In a volume of his *Histoire naturelle*, published in 1761, the great French naturalist, the Comte de Buffon, had represented America as a degenerate, or alternatively as an immature, world, whose animals and peoples were smaller and weaker than their European counterparts. The same year saw the partial publication in French of the *Travels* through the North American colonies of a Swedish naturalist, Peter Kalm, in which he followed tradition by depicting the settlers as a population that had degenerated in the American climate. Cornelius de Pauw, in his *Recherches philosophiques sur les Américains*, published in 1768, was even more disparaging, and two years later the Abbé Raynal produced a virulently anti-American 'philosophical history' of European settlements and trade in the Indies.[7]

Faced with this bombardment, it is not surprising that British and Spanish Americans should have considered themselves under siege from a Europe that claimed to be enlightened. The slanders and misconceptions abounding in works written by authors most of whom had never even set foot in America provoked the ire of Benjamin Franklin, and drew responses from Spanish American creoles that ranged from the bombastic to the erudite. The polemic continued for the best part of a generation, to the accompaniment of reverberations that echoed around the Atlantic, and provided a noisy, but significant, background to the political battles of the age.

American Jesuits in their European exile hurried to the defence of their lost American *patria*, most notably Francisco Javier Clavijero, who was scathing in his denunciation of 'the monstrous portrait of America painted by Pauw', and sought in his *Historia antigua de México* (1780–1) to prove that neither the birds, nor the animals, nor the inhabitants of America were in any way inferior to their European equivalents.[8] In North America Thomas Jefferson, composing his *Notes on the State of Virginia* just as Clavijero was publishing his History of Mexico, scrutinized and refuted the facts and figures with which Buffon sought to prove the inferiority of American flora and fauna, and mounted a spirited defence of 'the race of whites, transplanted from Europe', who had been condemned by Raynal as failing to produce 'one good poet, one able mathematician, one man of genius in a single art or a single science'. Given the relative youthfulness of these transatlantic societies, Jefferson argued, and the size of their populations, how fair was the comparison with France or England? And what of Franklin, 'than whom no one of the present age has made more important discoveries'?[9]

If such responses suggest an understandable sensitivity to denigration by ill-informed or prejudiced European commentators, they also point to the turning away of the New World societies from the Europe that had engendered them. In the end, attack proved to be the best form of defence. The New World's

23 View of Mexico City (c.1690). Folding screen. Painted Japanese folding screens, imported in the Acapulco galleon returning from Manila, achieved great popularity among the creole elite of seventeenth-century New Spain, and inspired patrons to commission, and craftsmen to produce, local versions, which became indispensable elements in the furnishing and decoration of creole houses. Many of these screens depicted city views or scenes of life in Mexico City, in a clear manifestation of pride in the *patria*. The panorama depicted on this screen is designed to create the impression of a vast and perfectly ordered metropolis, which the creoles of New Spain regarded as the centre of the world. Along the lower right runs the aqueduct of Chapultepec, a hispanicized echo of the Roman aqueduct in Segovia, although Aztec in origin.

24 The Mass of St Gregory (1539). Feathers on wood. This piece of Mexican featherwork, commissioned for presentation to Pope Paul III by Montezuma's nephew and son-in-law, the Spanish-appointed governor of San Juan, Tenochtitlán, illustrates the survival of pre-conquest techniques of craftsmanship, and their rapid adaptation to the requirements of the post-conquest world. 'Every day', wrote Las Casas, 'they make images and altarpieces and many other things for us out of feathers . . . And with no prodding on our part, they make borders for chasubles and capes . . .' According to the legend a doubting St Gregory saw Christ present himself bodily on the altar at the moment of the host's consecration. Indigenous feather-workers would have based their design on a European print.

25 A culture of display. Exterior view of the church of Our Lady of Ocotlán, Tlaxcala, Mexico (c. 1760).

26 A culture of restraint. Interior of Christ Church, Philadelphia (1727–44).

27 Cristóbal de Villalpando, *Joseph Claims Benjamin as his Slave* (1700–14). One of a set of six canvases depicting scenes from the biblical story of the life of Joseph, and painted by the creole artist Cristóbal de Villalpando (c. 1649–1714). Villalpando's work betrays the influence of the great Venetian masters and of Rubens, whose dynamic compositions would have been known to him primarily through engravings.

28 Potosí silver used for ornamental purposes. Silver gilt tray (1700–50), probably from Upper Peru, and characteristic of the rich and intricate work of Andean craftsmen.

29 Miguel Cabrera, Portrait of Sor Juana Inés de la Cruz (1750). The best of the many posthumous portraits of 'the unique American poetess, the tenth muse'. Sister Juana Inés de la Cruz (1648–95), born out of wedlock to a creole mother, grew up as an exceptionally precocious child, interested in all branches of learning, including mathematics. At the age of sixteen she was given a place in the viceregal court in Mexico City, where for five years she served as lady-in-waiting to the wife of the viceroy, the marquis of Mancera, before taking her vows in 1669 as a nun in the convent of San Jerónimo, where Carlos de Sigüenza y Góngora and other leading Mexican writers and scholars would pay her visits. Her many poems and theatrical pieces made her the most famous poet of her age in the Hispanic world. Eventually silenced by clerical pressure, she sold off for charity the books that surround her in this portrait, and engaged in acts of penance and mortification which may have hastened her death in the Mexico City epidemic of 1695.

30 Peter Pelham, mezzotint Portrait of Cotton Mather (c. 1715). Cotton Mather (1663–1728), the son of Increase Mather, a Boston minister, and himself a minister in his turn, was the most important figure in the intellectual life of the New England of his age. A prolific author, he was faced with the challenge of reconciling the new science to the old theology, and the struggle took its toll.

31 Portrait of Don Carlos de Sigüenza y Góngora, from his *Mercurio volante* (1693). A poet, mathematician, historian and geographer, Sigüenza y Góngora (1645–1700), appointed professor of Mathematics and Astrology in the University of Mexico in 1672, was a gifted scientist and astronomer, and a man of encyclopaedic learning who, like his New England contemporary, Cotton Mather, sought to find a way between the new experimental philosophy and the teachings of the church.

32 Westover House, Charles County, Virginia, (1732). The seat of the Byrd family of Virginia, Westover, was built by William Byrd II to replace his father's house overlooking the James River. A red-brick mansion, built in the classical style of the houses Byrd had seen in England where his father sent him for his education, it was one of the first of the new manor houses built by the eighteenth-century Virginia gentry – houses that, however handsome, could not compete in scale and grandeur with those of the English aristocracy on which the Virginian elite sought to model itself.

33 William Williams, *Husband and Wife in a Landscape* (1775). William Williams (1727–91) was an English painter who sought to make a living in America, where he painted somewhat naïf conversation pieces for colonial families in imitation of those being made in England for the nobility and gentry. In Philadelphia he befriended the young Benjamin West, who in turn would move to England to become the first native-born British North American to acquire fame as an artist.

Matheo Vicente de Musitu y Zalvide   y su Esposa Dª Mª Gertrudis de Salazar y Dua

34 José Mariana Lara, *Don Matheo Vicente de Musitu y Zavilde and his Wife* (late eighteenth century). Rural tranquillity for the creole elite in late colonial New Spain. Don Vicente and his wife were the owners of a sugar mill near Cuautla.

35 Jan Verelst, Portrait of Tee Yee Neen Ho Ga Row. The Five Nations enter the world of international diplomacy as they manoeuvre between Britain and France. In 1710, when the English colonists were anxious to secure help from the mother country to conquer French Canada, they persuaded this Mohawk chief and three fellow Mohawks to go on an embassy to London to advance their cause. The four 'Indian kings' made a great impression and were enthusiastically received at court. It was also hoped that the ambassadors would be sufficiently impressed by what they saw in England to persuade the rest of the Iroquois Confederacy to join the attack. In the event, many Iroquois volunteers joined the English expedition mounted against New France in 1711, but it ended in disaster at the mouth of the St Lawrence even before the attack was launched.

36 Bishop Roberts, *Charles Town Harbour*, watercolour (c. 1740). By the time the harbour of Charles Town (the future Charleston) was depicted in this watercolour by a resident artist, the city had become a flourishing Atlantic port. The rice grown on the plantations of South Carolina was shipped from here to Europe and the West Indies. The colony's rice exports paid for the imported luxury goods eagerly sought by the planter elite for the adornment of their mansions and persons.

37 Anon., *The Old Plantation*, watercolour (c. 1800). The survival of African culture in a New World environment. Plantation slaves, probably from a South Carolina plantation, appear to be celebrating a wedding with music and dancing.

A North-West Prospect of Nassau-Hall, with a Front View of the Presidents House, in New Jersey.

38 Henry Dawkins, *A North-West Prospect of Nassau Hall with a Front View of the President's House*. An engraving of 1764, which shows the College of New Jersey (the future Princeton University) eighteen years after its foundation in 1746.

39 Paul Revere, The Boston Massacre. This engraving, with its dramatic depiction of the moment on 5 March 1770 when a party of eight British soldiers turned their guns on a hostile crowd, circulated widely through the colonies and helped inflame the passions that would lead to revolt.

Labels within the painting:
La nusta
D. Diego faui [...]
D. [...] tupa panaqui
D. Martin de Lo-
iola Governador de Chi-
le sobrino de N.P.S. Ignacio
cuyde su herm. maior D. Bel-
tran de Loiola caso con D. Beatris Nusta hered. y Princ. del Peru como hija de D. Diego ynga
su ultimo Rey, y aver muerto sin hija
su herm. D. Phel. ynga de D. Mart. y D.
D. Beat. nacio D. Lorenza nusta del P[...]
icleq paso a Esp. el orden de sus Ca-
tholi. Rey, y la casaron el R. con el
Ex.S.D. Iuan de Borja hijo de S.
Fr. del B. ansiac. del S.R. D. Phel.
2. a Alem. y forti. con esta Ma-
trimonio fe en parenci. con
la R.J. Caza de Loyoga[...]
de 1718

Adiutae Regule
rem Societa
tis
Gloriae 1556

D. Martin d Loiola
D. Beatris Nusta Princ. del Peru
D. Iuan d Borja.
D. Lorença nusta de Loiola

40 Anon., *Union of the Descendants of the Imperial Incas with the Houses of Loyola and Borja* (Cuzco, 1718). The painting commemorates a double union between the Inca and Spanish elites. On the left, St Ignatius Loyola's nephew, Don Martín García de Loyola, governor of Chile, who was ambushed and killed in the Araucanian wars in 1598, and his wife, Doña Beatriz, the daughter of Sairi Tupac, who succeeded to the imperial rights of the Incas. Beside them is St. Ignatius holding the constitutions of the Jesuit Order. Above them to the left are shown the bride's parents, along with Tupac Amaru I, in the centre, who was executed by the Spaniards for rebellion in 1572. In the foreground on the right, the daughter born of this marriage, Doña Lorenza, is depicted with her husband, Don Juan de Borja. The bridegroom was the son of St Francis Borja, who stands behind him holding his emblem, a skull. The painting, depicting marriages that had occurred more than a century before, testifies to the pride of the eighteenth-century nobility of Cuzco in their ancestral past.

41 William Russell Birch, *High Street from the County Market Place, Philadelphia*, engraving (1798). One of twenty-nine views of post-revolutionary Philadelphia, engraved by a British artist who arrived in America in 1794. The engravings were intended to serve as an advertisement 'by which an idea of the improvements of the country could be conveyed to Europe'. They give a lively impression of the handsome and prosperous city in which the First and Second Continental Congresses were convoked, and the Declaration of Independence signed.

42 Patriots and Liberators 1. George Washington (1732–99) painted by Gilbert Stuart in 1796.

43 Patriots and Liberators 2. Simón Bolívar (1783–1830), miniature on ivory of 1828, after a painting by Roulin.

youthfulness, which European critics liked to adduce as a source of weakness, could be depicted instead as its greatest source of strength. Where the Old World stood for the past, the New World stood for the future. American innocence offered a standing rebuke to European corruption, American virtue to European vice. These contrasting images imprinted themselves on collective creole consciousness. Under their influence, the leaders of revolution, first in British, and later in Spanish America, would find it easier to distance themselves from their mother countries and break the emotional and psychological bonds of empire.

While British and Spanish American colonists in the later decades of the eighteenth century shared a growing disillusionment with their mother countries and with the Old World itself, the British proved to have a more impressive armoury of ideological weapons at their disposal for resisting the political assault that now confronted them. The population of the British colonies had long enjoyed access, through books, pamphlets and other forms of ephemeral publication imported from England, to a wide spectrum of political opinions. These ran from the high Tory opposition views of a Bolingbroke, through the orthodox doctrines of a Whig establishment comfortably settled on the constitutional foundations established by the Glorious Revolution, to the radical and libertarian doctrines of the seventeenth-century Commonwealthmen and their reformulation by eighteenth-century publicists like John Trenchard and Thomas Gordon.[10] These divergent approaches to the ordering of politics and society were readily available because the fault-lines created by the upheavals of the Civil War and the Glorious Revolution still ran through the British Atlantic community. Each time the tectonic plates shifted there would be a new eruption of political and religious debate.

There was little scope for such public debate in the more controlled environment of the Spanish Atlantic world. An unpopular royal minister, like Esquilache, might be overthrown by the action of the Madrid mob, but there was no opportunity in the Spain of the 1760s for a John Wilkes to emerge and mount a sustained challenge to authority through the spoken and written word. Lacking the ammunition provided by a metropolitan literature of opposition, creoles who were critical of royal policies therefore remained dependent on the theories of contractualism and the common good propounded in medieval Castilian juridical literature and the works of the sixteenth-century Spanish scholastics. During the first half of the eighteenth century the Jesuits updated this scholastic tradition by assimilating to it the natural law theories of Grotius and Pufendorf,[11] but the political culture of the Hispanic world lacked the benefit of rejuvenating injections provided, as in Britain, by parliamentary and party conflict.

The opportunities for informed political discussion in the American viceroyalties were also narrowed by local constraints. Following the expulsion of the Jesuits in 1767, a royal decree forbade the teaching of doctrines of popular sovereignty as expounded by Francisco Suárez and other sixteenth-century Jesuit theologians.[12] The censorship of books was a further obstacle. It was normal practice in the Spanish Indies that no book could be printed without the granting of a licence by viceroys or presidents of the Audiencias. Such a licence would only be issued after its contents had been approved by the local tribunal of the Inquisition.[13] Even if the process of inquisitorial vetting was often perfunctory, and the system of licensing by the civil authorities was open to corruption, bureaucratic controls inevitably impeded the circulation of ideas in a continent where vast distances and problems of transportation made inter-regional communication laborious and slow.

The British colonies, too, were subjected to constraints on publishing, although these were weakened by the lapse in 1695 of the Licensing Act in England. The instructions issued to royal governors authorized them to exercise supervision over the public press, while colonial assemblies, although frequently in conflict with the governors, had an inclination to support them when it came to controlling publications which might be similarly subversive of their own powers and privileges. Printers, too, tended to tread warily, since they were in competition for the lucrative post of government printer in their respective colonies.

When legislation or more informal kinds of pressure failed, the authorities could still make use of the law on seditious and blasphemous libel. Resort to the courts, however, brought with it no guarantee of success. Massachusetts juries were notoriously reluctant to prosecute in cases of seditious libel, and in New York skilful advocacy and a populist jury produced a 'Not guilty' verdict in 1735 in the trial of John Peter Zenger for material printed in his *Weekly Journal*. Although the authorities showed no inclination to abandon recourse to censorship in the wake of the Zenger verdict, the outcome of the case illustrated the effectiveness of a defence strategy that linked freedom for printers, publishers and authors with the wider cause of liberty. While a free press might not yet be a natural right, at least it had become a natural right in waiting, and one that was explicitly recognized some thirty years later when the Massachusetts House of Representatives declared in 1768 that 'the Liberty of the Press is a great Bulwark of the Liberty of the People.' As the events of the 1760s and 1770s were to show, the existence of a jury system furnished the British colonists with a potential weapon for resistance to royal power that their Spanish American counterparts lacked.[14]

Not surprisingly, the more favourable conditions in the British colonies for the reception and dissemination of information gave them a substantial advantage over Spain's colonies when it came to the founding of newspapers and periodicals.[15] In New Spain a semi-official monthly gazette, the *Gaceta de México*, first briefly established in 1722, was relaunched in 1728 and survived until 1742. Lima too had its own gazette from 1745, but periodical publications in Spanish America continued to be irregular and ephemeral throughout the century.[16] By contrast, the British colonies, where the first newspaper, the weekly *Boston News-letter*, was founded in 1704, were already supporting twelve newspapers by 1750, although the first daily papers would only appear after the end of the War of Independence.[17]

In spite of their heavy London content, these newspapers, while reinforcing a sense of local and regional identity, helped simultaneously to encourage inter-colonial mutual awareness by reprinting scraps of information from other colonial papers.[18] Improvements in the internal postal services worked to the same effect. Benjamin Franklin, as postmaster in Philadelphia from 1737and colonial deputy postmaster general from 1753, increased the frequency of services, and managed to reduce the time for delivery and reply between Philadelphia and Boston from three weeks to six days.[19]

As the political atmosphere grew tense during the 1750s and 1760s, the flow of news through the colonies made it easier to fashion a common response to acts of perceived British injustice. The activities of printers, publishers and post-masters – and Franklin was all three at once – widened the opportunities for envisaging a British colonial America as a single body politic with a shared concern for liberty. Newspapers, periodicals, pamphlets provided material for lively discussion in taverns and coffee-houses, and in the dining clubs and societies that sprang up in the cities of the eastern seaboard in the pre-revolutionary years. It was by incessantly talking politics in the taverns and coffee-houses of Boston that Samuel Adams cut his teeth as a revolutionary.[20]

As the Stamp Act crisis developed, newspapers, voluntary associations and the boycott of British goods all involved widening sections of the colonial population in the process of political debate. In Spain's American possessions, on the other hand, distance and size made it much harder to fashion, or even envisage, anything approaching the degree of co-ordinated response found in the British colonies. The surface area of the empire of the Indies was more than 5 million square miles. Spanish South America alone covered nearly 3.5 million square miles, as against the roughly 322,000 of the thirteen mainland colonies of British North America.[21] It took two months to travel overland from Buenos Aires to Santiago de Chile, and nine months by horse, mule and river transport from Buenos Aires to the port of Cartagena in New Granada.[22] While the printing press made the Atlantic crossing soon afer the beginnings of colonization, even so important a city as Santa Fe de Bogotá, the capital of New Granada, did not acquire a press of its own until the late 1770s.[23] With local newspapers rudimentary or non-existent, and inter-colonial trade still to receive the impetus that would follow the introduction of 'free trade' in the years after 1774, there was no frequent or rapid network of communication between the various viceregal and provincial capitals.

The problems involved in mobilizing and co-ordinating resistance over large areas of territory were therefore of an entirely different order to those likely to be experienced in the mainland territories of North America. Here, for all the diversity of the colonies, their bickering and rivalries, there existed the potential, and to some extent the means, for rallying the white population across colonial boundaries to defend a common cause. Whether this would in fact happen would depend both on the actions of the British government following the repeal of the Stamp Act, and on the capacity of the colonists themselves to sink their differences and find a common will to resist.

If they did so – and it would not be easy – it would be around a set of common assumptions and beliefs. These assumptions and beliefs were deeply rooted in the experiences of the early colonists, but gathered shape and cogency over the decades before the crisis of the 1770s. The process, however, was inevitably complicated by the diversity of background and religion of the colonial population in a society where immigration was not officially confined, as it was in Spanish America, to persons of a single nationality or religious faith. If the open nature of British American society as compared with that of Spanish America made for the easier circulation of news and ideas and a greater freedom of debate, it also had the disadvantage of raising the general level of disputatiousness.

Yet while its diversity made the white population of British America contentious, its members were at least united in their fundamental conviction that the transatlantic lands in which they or their forebears had settled offered them the prospect of better lives than those they had lived, or might have lived, in Europe. They were the inhabitants of a genuinely New World – a world whose very newness promised them the freedom to worship as they wished, or, alternatively, not to worship at all; the freedom to settle and work a plot of land and keep the profits of their labour for themselves; the freedom to live their lives as they liked, without the need to defer to those whose claims to social superiority rested solely on the accident of birth; and the freedom to choose, reject, and hold accountable those in positions of authority.

These were precious freedoms, and the nature of eighteenth-century British Atlantic culture was such as to reinforce rather than undermine them. Politically, it was a culture firmly grounded in the principles of the Revolution Settlement of 1688–9, which had enshrined as central to the British constitution the virtues of representation, freedom from the exercise of arbitrary power, and (limited) religious toleration. Intellectually, it was a culture increasingly infused with pre-Enlightenment and Enlightenment notions of the supreme importance of reason and scientific observation for unlocking the secrets of the universe.

The heroes of the story were Newton and Locke. Once Newton's conceptualization of the laws of the universe, and Locke's political, educational and philosophical theories had been absorbed in their homeland, they automatically came to form part of British Atlantic culture, even if their reception and acceptance on the American side of the Atlantic involved something of a time-lag. Before the 1720s few in America had apparently read, or even seen, Locke's two *Treatises of Government*, and it seems to have been primarily his reputation as a philosopher that brought his political theories to such public attention as they received in the following two or three decades.[24] By the 1720s and 1730s, however, his moral philosophy and the new science were winning increasing numbers of adherents both among the professional and business classes in the Northern and Middle Colonies, and the slave-owners of the South. The Virginian planter, Landon Carter, inherited from his father the 1700 folio edition of Locke's *Essay Concerning Human Understanding*, and his annotations show him quite prepared to engage in debate with 'this great man'.[25]

The new notions naturally provoked opposition from the redoubts of orthodox religion. Tensions had already surfaced in later seventeenth-century New England, where the founding of Yale College in 1701 was intended to counter the dangerously latitudinarian tendencies of Harvard. As the new ideas and approaches became more diffused, so the religious opposition became more vocal. Conservative Calvinists on the one hand and evangelical revivalists on the other inveighed against deists and sceptics who subverted the truths of religion. Splits in the Presbyterian church led to the founding in 1746 by New Light Scottish Presbyterians of an interdenominational institution, the College of New Jersey, the future Princeton University (fig. 38). Anglicans responded in 1754 by founding King's College, which would later become Columbia University.[26]

In spite of the resistance to innovation, by 1750 the moderate Enlightenment, pragmatic and inquiring, had largely triumphed over Protestant scholasticism in the colleges of America. The leaders of revolution in the 1770s were formed in its mould.[27] Their mental world was characterized by a new, and generally more secular, rationalism based on scepticism and doubt; a belief in the capacity of the individual and society to achieve progress through an understanding of the laws of a mechanistic universe designed by a benevolent Creator; a confidence that human industriousness and the application of scientific knowledge could harness the forces of nature for human benefit; and, as a corollary, the conviction that it was incumbent on governments, drawing their legitimacy from the consent of the governed, to protect life, liberty and property, and enhance the happiness and prosperity of their peoples.

More slowly, and in the face of more entrenched resistance, Enlightenment ideals were also finding adherents in the Hispanic world. While the advent of the Bourbons gave an impetus to the renovation of Spanish intellectual life, which had already shown glimmerings of revival in the later years of Carlos II,[28] new ideas, especially if they were foreign, were all too likely to fall foul of the church, the Inquisition and the universities. This antagonism set the scene in the peninsula for a prolonged struggle between traditionalists and innovators, with the innovators gaining ground in the middle years of the century, especially after Charles III's accession in 1759.[29] This metropolitan struggle was replicated on the other side of the Atlantic, where, however, the inherited traditions of baroque scholarship still showed themselves capable of creative innovation.[30] Scholasticism was powerfully entrenched in the more than twenty universities of Spanish America, but as early as 1736 the Jesuits of Quito were teaching Descartes, Leibnitz and Spinoza.[31] Jesuit dominance over the education of the sons of the creole elite meant that by the middle decades of the century modest pockets of Enlightenment were to be found in all the major cities of the Indies, and in the long run even the universities would prove more accommodating to innovation than their peninsular counterparts.

In spite of these advances, the Spanish American Enlightenment lagged behind its British American equivalent, and its impact would only begin to be widely felt during the last two decades of the century, partly as a result of the additional spur applied by royal officials impatient with the slow pace of change. It was an

Enlightenment, too, that lacked the dimension of political dissent. In British America the conjunction of moderate Enlightenment principles with those inculcated by a British political culture imbued with notions of liberty and rights was to prove a heady mixture.

During the early years of the reign of George III that political culture was in process of transformation. Britain's victories in the Seven Years War and its commercial and maritime dominance had generated a more aggressive nationalism, British as well as English, that pointed towards more authoritarian styles of imperial management.[32] The rhetoric of this British nationalism might be the rhetoric of liberty, but at the same time it seemed to the Americans (as the British were now increasingly inclined to call the colonists),[33] that this was a rhetoric from which they were deliberately being excluded. Simultaneously, recent political developments in Britain itself were raising questions, in British as well as American minds, about the degree to which freedom was indeed entrenched in a country that gloried in its self-image as the homeland of liberty.[34]

In the young George III Britain had acquired a 'patriot king' who aspired to transcend and extirpate the traditional party divisions that had bedevilled political life during the reigns of his two Hanoverian predecessors. With the downfall of the Old Whigs after forty years of ascendancy, British politics – and with it political debate – acquired a new vigour and fluidity. The alleged attempt of the crown to reassert powers that it had lost in the Glorious Revolution and reinstate a Stuart tyranny provided a rallying-cry for Whig politicians who had lost out in the struggle for power, and allowed them to claim that the English liberties won in the seventeenth-century struggles were once again imperilled. At the same time, there was growing resentment, both in London and the provinces, at the corruption of public life resulting from aristocratic dominance and the system of patronage and influence that had developed during the Whig ascendancy. This resentment stimulated a movement for parliamentary and governmental reform, associated on the one hand with the popular politics of John Wilkes and his followers, and on the other with the dissenters, and the adherents of the radical version of the Whig tradition which traced its ancestry to the seventeenth-century 'Commonwealthmen' – notably Milton, Harrington and Algernon Sidney – and their eighteenth-century successors.

To American colonists following intently the British domestic debate, this seemed to have an immediate relevance to their own situation. They too saw themselves as the victims of the arbitrary exercise of power by an arrogant and unrepresentative parliament, and their reading of British history and British political tracts like *Cato's Letters* encouraged them to find the explanation of that arbitrary power in the deformation of the constitution by the corruption that had taken hold of the British body politic. In the writings of the radical Whigs in defence of the Old Cause they sought and found a source of inspiration for the fighting of their own battles.

The doctrines of the Commonwealthmen were an amalgam of intellectual and religious traditions: the classical republicanism of ancient Greece and Rome, the rational moral philosophy of Plato, Aristotle and their heirs; the English common law and natural law traditions; and the religious traditions of the Protestant Reformation and Christian humanism.[35] Out of these traditions, to which the new century would add Enlightenment rationalism, the Commonwealthmen fashioned their vision of a republic grounded in the virtue of citizens who placed the common good above the pursuit of mere self-interest. For the eighteenth-century successors of the Commonwealthmen, self-interested politics were sapping the foundations of the finely balanced constitutional arrangements achieved through the heroic struggles of the seventeenth century, and had brought about the corruption and degeneracy of the present age. Only a virtuous citizenry could ward off the evils of corruption and thus wage the eternal war in defence of liberty.

The exercise of public virtue therefore came to be seen as the only effective answer to the evils of the age. Some were now beginning to fear that Britain might already be sunk too deep in the mire of corruption to recover its virtue,[36] but on the American shores of the Atlantic the battle could still be fought and won. The patronage machines of royal governors, the nefarious activities of royal officials and the parasitic spread of their network of dependants,[37] and the pursuit of factional and personal interest in electoral contests in New York, Pennsylvania and elsewhere,[38] indicated that the corruption that had taken hold of British public life was beginning to infect the colonies. In the face of this alarming threat to liberty, it was incumbent on the property-owning elite to exercise the self-restraint required if the common good were to be elevated above the politics of interest. All, however, had their part to play in the unfolding struggle. In his tracts published as *Letters from a Farmer in Pennsylvania,* the Philadelphia lawyer John Dickinson adopted not only the language of the Whig opposition in his assaults on British policy, but also the persona of the independent yeoman farmer who represented, in the Harringtonian world-view, the epitome of patriotic virtue.

The opportunity for a colonial-wide expression of patriotic virtue was amply provided by the sequence of events that followed the repeal of the Stamp Act. In May 1767 Charles Townshend, as Chancellor of the Exchequer, introduced in the House of Commons a bill imposing new duties on a variety of goods on their entry into colonial ports. The object was to raise revenue to defray the expenses of colonial administration and provide an emergency fund to improve the salaries of governors and judges so that they would be less dependent on the colonial assemblies. It was a project that Townshend had cherished since serving many years earlier in the Board of Trade under Halifax. As a device for securing a more effective deployment of imperial power it made good sense, especially as it was to be accompanied by a reorganization of the totally inadequate American customs administration.[39] In its assumption that the colonists objected only to internal rather than external duties, however, it was hardly attuned to colonial sensibilities at this delicate moment in the transatlantic relationship.

There was some initial hesitation in the colonies over how to respond to the Townshend duties, but Dickinson's *Letters from a Farmer,* published over the winter of 1767–8, did much to rally opinion in favour of constitutional and legal methods of resistance, rather than open confrontation. Following unsuccessful petitioning for relief from the Townshend Act, the colonists reverted to the strategy that had served them so well in securing the repeal of the Stamp Act, and turned again to the use of non-importation agreements.[40] Between 1768 and 1770 innumerable groups sprang up to monitor the activities of merchants, many of whom showed themselves less keen to boycott British goods than in 1765–6, when goods were overstocked. The New England town meeting, which provided an ideal forum for decision-making and collective action, was imitated in other colonies, and large public meetings were held in New York, Philadelphia and Charles Town.[41]

The non-importation movement involved both open and covert coercion. As during the Stamp Act embargo, it acquired some of its momentum from those who stood to gain personally from rallying to a patriotic cause – smaller merchants resentful of the wealth and power of their more successful colleagues, artisans who saw the possibility of turning their hands to the manufacture of goods that had hitherto been imported, and debt-ridden southern gentry who saw in the boycott a convenient device for cutting down on conspicuous consumption while gaining the plaudits of the public.

Yet if the non-importation movement was inspired by mixed motives, and tended to be unevenly observed and inconsistently enforced, it evoked, in both its scale and its rhetoric, an impressive display of that civic virtue which lay at the heart of the republican tradition. It helped to politicize American women,[42] and to involve the lower orders of colonial society in anti-British protests. The denial of luxuries had always played a part in programmes for the reformation of morals and manners, but the ideals of classical republicanism, when added to the traditional moralizing appeal for self-restraint, ensured that, in clothing themselves in homespun, the colonists also donned the virtuous garb of Greek and Roman patriots. 'These are efforts of patriotism', claimed one publicist in 1769, 'that Greece and Rome never yet surpassed, nay not so much as equaled.'[43]

In capturing the public imagination and encouraging co-operation among the colonists, the movement reinforced the sense of a united struggle in the cause of liberty. The unexpected strength of colonial resistance, coupled with the failure of the Townshend duties to generate the anticipated revenue, persuaded the new government of Lord North to sound the retreat. On 5 March 1770 he announced his intentions to the House of Commons, and in April all the duties were repealed except for that on tea, which was retained as a symbolic assertion of parliamentary supremacy.

Leaders on both sides of the Atlantic now hoped for a return to calm. For a time at least, calm did indeed return. Yet mutual distrust ran deep. The ministry of Lord North, having retreated, had also determined on the point at which it must stand firm. There must be no yielding of the sovereignty of parliament. For their part, the conflicts of the 1760s had given the colonists a sense of common purpose against a common oppressor. Equally important, those conflicts had also given them them a chance to assemble the arguments and burnish the language on which they would need to draw in any final confrontation to save their cherished rights.

A community divided

On 5 March 1770, the day on which Lord North announced in parliament that the Townshend duties would be withdrawn, eight soldiers of the 29th Regiment guarding the Boston custom house responded to taunts and a volley of missiles from a hostile crowd by opening fire and killing or mortally wounding five civilians. At the subsequent trial, where the accused soldiers were ably defended by John Adams, Samuel's younger second cousin, a fair-minded Boston jury acquitted six of the eight soldiers, and found the remaining two guilty only of manslaughter. The radicals, however, seized on the incident as proof that the British would stop at nothing in their determination to destroy colonial liberties. Blood was running in American streets, and the 'Boston Massacre' was duly inscribed in the glorious annals of revolutionary history (fig. 39).[44]

The Massacre was only the latest in a long line of street riots and acts of violence against customs officials and recalcitrant merchants that marred what was supposed to be a peaceful boycott of British goods. Colonial governors and British ministers saw the hand of the radicals in these disorders. They suspected street leaders, like William Molineux in Boston,[45] of acting as intermediaries between the rioters and members of the colonial elite. Yet there were bound to be tensions between popular agitators and elites imbued with deep-seated fears about the dangers of unleashing mob violence,[46] and the extent of collusion is difficult to gauge. Samuel Adams, who is said to have been persuaded as early as 1768, when British troops arrived in Boston, that there was no alternative to independence, seems to have been connected with most of the major street actions in Boston in the years after 1765. But he covered his tracks well, and it is far from clear whether this passionate defender of the people's liberties was taking the initiative in order to advance his chosen policy, or riding a tiger that he found impossible to control.[47]

In New York, as in Boston, the presence of British soldiers gave rise to street fights and brawls,[48] but that same presence also acted as a reminder of the weakness of British imperial authority. If little or no blood was shed by American mobs in the pre-revolutionary years, this may largely have been because they met with no resistance.[49] Like other colonial governors, Francis Bernard, the governor of Massachusetts, simply did not have at his command an administrative apparatus for maintaining public order, and the institutions of imperial authority had no natural constituency of support in American society. For his part, General Gage lacked both the will, and the military resources, to restore authority by force of arms in Massachusetts. His weakness allowed Samuel Adams to negotiate the removal of the troops from the city to an island in Boston harbour. Adams's plan, however, to maintain the pressure on London by keeping the non-importation movement in being was to end in failure. With the British in an apparently conciliatory mood, the merchants along the eastern seaboard proved increasingly reluctant to participate, and by the autumn of 1770 the movement was everywhere unravelling.[50]

The moment of the radicals seemed to have passed, but this was to reckon without the pretensions of parliament, the intransigence of British public opinion, and the miscalculations of Lord North and his cabinet colleagues. The Tea Act remained in force, and colonial grievances unredressed. During the Stamp Act crisis and the agitation over the Townshend duties, 'correspondence committees' had sprung up in the different colonies to share information and co-ordinate resistance. In May 1773 the Massachusetts House established a revived and strengthened committee to maintain correspondence 'with our sister Colonies'. With Samuel Adams at its head, the Boston committee assumed leadership of a campaign against the Tea Act.[51]

In December of that year a bunch of colonists disguised as Mohawks threw £10,000 worth of East India Company tea overboard into Boston harbour. Lord North's government responded between March and May 1774 by enacting a series of punitive measures. The Coercive, or Intolerable, Acts closed Boston harbour to commercial shipping, gave the governor the right to appoint and remove inferior judges, sheriffs and justices of the peace, and partially abrogated the colony's 1691 charter by placing appointments to the council in the hands of the London government. The commander-in-chief in North America, General Gage, who replaced Bernard's discredited successor, Thomas Hutchinson, as governor of Massachusetts, was authorized to use his four regiments to impose submission by force if necessary.[52]

The events which followed over the following two years – the convening of the first and second Continental Congresses (1774 and 1775–6), the Declaration of Independence, and the resort to arms – saw the metamorphosis of increasingly generalized resistance into revolution, a revolution that within nine years would transform the thirteen rebellious mainland colonies into an independent republic. In September 1774, when the first Continental Congress convened in Philadelphia, this outcome would have been difficult to predict, and none of the stages by which it was reached was a foregone conclusion. It was not inevitable that Massachusetts should win the support of the other colonies, nor that the leaders of those colonies should unite to renounce their allegiance to the crown. Nor was it inevitable that they would succeed in mobilizing their populations for war, and still less that the war would end in victory. For Spanish Americans, who would follow their example a generation later, it would take up to twenty years of savage warfare to achieve a comparable result.

When Massachusetts, under pressure from the Coercive Acts, appealed to the other colonies for help, its appeal was far from being assured of success. While war and politics during the past two decades had brought the mainland colonies closer together and had forged personal friendships and a better mutual understanding, Massachusetts had a reputation for abrasive and precipitate behaviour, and the destruction of £10,000 worth of private property in the waters of Boston harbour could well be construed as another rash act by New Englanders that could only inflame passions and play into the hands of the imperial authorities.

The Coercive Acts, however, profoundly changed the political atmosphere in the colonies. Although the Acts were designed to punish Massachusetts, the coercion of one colony implied a potential threat to all. For George Washington, writing from his home at Mount Vernon on 4 July 1774, there was clearly a 'regular, systematic plan' to destroy American freedom.[53] Lord North's government contrived to strengthen this suspicion by a fortuitous piece of bad timing, when it secured the passage of the Quebec Act at the end of June. This replaced the current military administration in Canada with a civil administration. Quebec was to retain French civil law, and, for the time being, was not to be given a representative assembly. The Act managed simultaneously to offend the religious sensibilities of Protestants by conceding special privileges to the Roman Catholic church, and the territorial sensibilities of New York, Pennsylvania and Virginia by extending Quebec's provincial boundaries into the Mississippi Valley as far as the Ohio River. Coinciding as it did with the Coercive Acts, and coming at a time of renewed apprehension about alleged plans to establish an Anglican bishop in America,[54] it inevitably evoked in the overheated imaginations of colonists the twin spectre of political and ecclesiastical tyranny which, they fondly thought, the Glorious Revolution had banished. This was a society, and an age, in which conspiracy theory seemed to provide the most rational explanation of otherwise incomprehensible conjunctions of events.[55]

Yet the colonial elites had good reasons for proceeding with caution. Outright confrontation with the imperial power would not only be damaging to trade but could well produce upheavals in societies where the rapid growth of population, the influx of new immigrants, and the restrictions imposed by the Proclamation Line on westwards expansion, provided standing opportunities for outbreaks of social and political unrest. In 1764 Scots-Irish immigrants, the 'Paxton Boys' of Pennsylvania, attacked the Christian Indians in the settled areas and then marched on Philadelphia, accusing the assembly of not protecting them from Indian border raids. In New York's Hudson County the pent-up discontents of tenants against their landlords erupted in 1766. In the two Carolinas in the 1760s and early 1770s, the backcountry settlers – the 'Regulators' – exasperated by the failure of the colonial legislatures to provide law and order in the borderlands, took the law into their own hands and turned on their legislatures and the local agents of authority. In the northern seaport cities, where the presence of soldiers and the lack of employment in the post-war years added new elements of volatility, street brawls could easily turn into mob riots and disrupt an always fragile civic order.[56]

While colonial elites had been eagerly adopting the characteristics of eighteenth-century English aristocratic life-styles, they had long been aware, even in the more stable colonies of New England and the south, that they could not count on English-style deference from their social inferiors. Back in 1728 William

Byrd, on a tour of South Carolina, noted how the residents, many of them small property-holders, 'were rarely guilty of Flattering or making any Court to their governors, but treat them with all the Excesses of Freedom and Familiarity'.[57] If colonists arrived from the British Isles or the continent with their deferential instincts still intact – and those most resentful of enforced deference may well have been among the most eager to up stakes and emigrate – the opportunities and conditions of life awaiting them on crossing the Atlantic militated against the survival of such Old World attitudes. Access to the ownership of freehold land was a great social leveller. In a society where two-thirds of the white population owned land, it would be hard to sustain indefinitely the notion of deference to rank, even if rank itself was being vigorously asserted by the upper echelons of colonial society.[58]

The value placed by the evangelical revival on the individual may also have helped to subvert the notion of a deferential society.[59] Although rank, precedence and deference still ran through the fabric of colonial societies,[60] appearances could be deceptive. The elites who found themselves staring into the abyss in 1774 as they contemplated the alarming prospect of conflict with Britain, were uneasily aware that any precipitate move on their part might be the signal for their inferiors to throw over the remnants of deference and plunge the community into anarchy.

The awareness was especially acute among the elites of the Middle and Southern Colonies. All of them had assimilated the ideas and the rhetoric of Whig constitutionalism, and New York and Pennsylvania had been pioneers in appropriating the language and the methods of the opposition groups in England to provincial politics.[61] In so doing, they paved the way to a future based on coalition-building and party-political organization. At this moment, however, the two colonies held back. The Quaker ethos in Pennsylvania, and a strong Anglophile tradition in New York, militated in the minds of the dominant groups against a final break with Britain. But above all, having constructed with difficulty a form of coalition politics that would hold together their religiously and ethnically fragmented societies, they feared the chaos that was likely to ensue as imperial issues intruded into provincial politics and dissolved the coalitions on which public order, and their own power, rested.[62]

The Southern Colonies, no less imbued with notions of liberty than the Middle Colonies, also had reasons to fear the future. While the presence of large slave populations helped bring greater cohesion to white society than was to be found in the Middle Colonies, even if that society was structured on hierarchical foundations, it also raised the spectre of mass slave uprisings in the event of political upheaval. As perhaps the most Anglophile of all the colonies, South Carolina, in particular, had cause to emphasize its loyalty. From the middle years of the century the sons of the planter and merchant elite were making their way in growing numbers to England to complete their education, and the closeness of trading ties with England encouraged the Charles Town elite to ape the ways of London.[63]

Of all the southern colonies, it was Virginia that was most likely to risk the present for the sake of an uncertain future. Not only was its elite steeped in the Whig tradition, but it had achieved a level of social stability still lacking in colonies of more recent foundation.[64] In the event, the role of the planters of Virginia would be crucial in deciding whether Massachusetts would receive the support for which it urgently appealed in the summer of 1774. The decision of a group of Virginian colonial leaders, subsequently endorsed by a convention of planters, was to stand shoulder to shoulder with Massachusetts. If the king should attempt to 'reduce his faithful Subjects in America to a State of Desperation', they would forcefully respond.[65]

Their expression of support, which was accompanied by a decision to revive the defunct association of 1769 for the non-importation of British goods, may at some level have been influenced by financial strain. Tobacco had been afflicted by severe marketing problems since the middle of the century, and plantation-owners had run up huge debts to British middlemen and merchants. Although indebtedness was a fact of life in this colonial world, George Washington for one had been sufficiently preoccupied by his accumulating debts to look for more profitable alternatives to tobacco planting, and to convert to wheat instead.[66] Yet if personal and financial frustration were conducive to a spirit of rebelliousness, the resolve shown by the Virginia planters in confronting the imperial crisis was deeply rooted in the culture of the agrarian society in which they had been raised.

As the beneficiaries, and to some extent the victims, of a particularly demanding form of export culture liable to sudden fluctuations, Washington and his fellow planters were naturally well accustomed to calculating risks. To avoid the shipwreck of their fortunes they had always had to keep a close eye on the management of their plantations, conscious that their reputations rested on their ability to meet their obligations to their inferiors and the community at large. Their vast estates identified them in their own eyes with the great British landowners, overlooking the inconvenient fact that the estates of British landlords were not worked by slaves. In the same vein, they saw themselves as a benevolent natural aristocracy, whose right to rule derived not only from their wealth but also from their intelligence and learning.[67] While proud of the horses in their stables, many of them were no less proud of the books in their libraries. Yet if their reading in history and the classics encouraged them to envisage themselves in the stern and virtuous mould of republican Romans, it was primarily as the historic guardians of English liberties on the model of the Whig aristocrats that they now faced the world. In their eyes the America of 1774 was on the brink of 1688.

The Virginian elite, whose leadership was to be critical to the successful defiance of the British crown in the 1770s, seems to have had no contemporary equivalent elsewhere in the Americas in the way it combined the practical experience of local self-government and the personal management of great estates with a self-conscious awareness of its inherent duty to defend a set of values that it saw as fundamental for the survival of the community at large. Long before a republic had come to be envisaged, the royal governor, Robert Dinwiddie, described members of Virginia's House of Burgesses as 'very much in a Republican way of thinking'.[68] Theirs was a republicanism *avant la lettre*, inspired by civic consciousness – what Landon Carter called 'Social Virtue'[69] – and a sense of participation in a grand tradition.

Far away to the south, in Venezuela, another slave-holding class of plantation-owners had reacted to its own moment of crisis twenty years earlier in a very different way. Cacao haciendas were more easily managed than tobacco plantations. Leaving them to be run by overseers, the owners of the large plantations lived not on their estates, like the Virginia gentry, but in handsome town houses in Caracas, with large household establishments and an army of slaves. Here they served as members of the cabildo, engaging in municipal politics and participating in the usual rituals of Spanish American urban life. Their income, and with it their social status, depended on the profits earned from the sale of their cacao, large quantities of which were exported to Mexico, the Antilles and metropolitan Spain.[70]

In the 1730s and early 1740s, however, cacao prices collapsed, in part at least because of the new controls and regulations instituted after the creation in 1728 of the first of Spain's new monopoly companies, the Royal Company of Guipúzcoa. The company was run by Basque merchants who used their monopoly to acquire a stranglehold over the Venezuelan economy, forcing down the price of cacao, while forcing up the price of the European imports carried in their ships. Some at least of the larger planters fell heavily into debt, but it was the smaller planters, many of them recent immigrants from the Canary Islands, who were the principal sufferers. In 1749 bands of cacao farmers and rural labourers marched on Caracas in protest against the Company's economic domination. Led by a local official, Juan Francisco de León, they enjoyed at least the covert support of many of the large planters. An open meeting of the Caracas cabildo voted overwhelmingly against the government-supported monopoly. But as the royal governor of Venezuela fled Caracas, and resistance threatened to turn into rebellion, the leading families of Caracas pulled back.[71]

Although they sympathized with the protest, the great plantation-owners were primarily swayed by fears of a slave revolt. As a result of their long experience in the cabildo of negotiating with royal officials, moreover, they may also have sensed that their disagreements with the Basques could be resolved in the traditional manner by mediation and legal manoeuvring.[72] A royal judge, accompanied by troops, was sent from Santo Domingo to undertake an inquiry, and was followed by a new governor, who arrived from Cadiz with reinforcements of 1,200 men. The extent of the opposition persuaded him to offer a general amnesty, and with the Basque monopoly temporarily suspended, peace was restored. His successor, however, arrived in 1751 with instructions to restore the company's monopoly and ensure the submission of Caracas. León and other leaders of the revolt were hunted down by the troops, many were executed, and León himself was sent to Spain to stand trial. The authorities subsequently demolished the León family house in Caracas, and had salt scattered on the ruins as a mark of infamy. Repression, it seemed, had won the day, but the royal authorities, in one of those juggling acts at which they were so practised, proceeded to impose restraints on the company's monopoly and create a junta to regulate cacao prices on an annual basis. In this more acceptable form the company maintained its nominal monopoly status until the crown rescinded its contract in 1781 as part of its new policy of free trade.

The Virginia planters, firmly committed to what they saw as fundamental principles where liberty was threatened, were a more intransigent body than their Venezuelan counterparts. Their natural instincts were not to negotiate but to stand up for their rights, and their defiant stance in the summer of 1774 helped to stiffen opposition throughout the colonies. Between them, Massachusetts and Virginia made a formidable alliance, but it was by no means assured of success when the first Continental Congress met in Philadelphia in September 1774. Many of the 55 delegates, like Joseph Galloway, the most powerful figure in Pennsylvania politics, were deeply worried by the threat of a general breakdown of order. A lawyer with a deep respect for the British constitution, he submitted to the Congress what in retrospect appears as a last-ditch attempt at an accommodation between the colonies and Britain, in the form of a proposal for an organic union: 'the colonies ... most ardently desire the establishment of a Political Union, not only among themselves but with the Mother State ...'[73] It was the same plea for treatment on an equal footing that the creoles of Spanish America were making, and involved the establishment of a common colonial legislature which would act in concert with the British parliament for all legislation affecting colonial life.

Galloway and his Pennsylvania delegates were widely distrusted in the Congress, but the narrowness of the vote by which his 'Plan of Union' was defeated suggests how strong the desire remained to avoid a total rupture with the mother country.[74] The Congress, however, had assembled in Philadelphia to petition for redress of grievances, and the delegates were determined to push ahead with a clear statement of colonial rights.[75] While the Grand Committee appointed by the Congress was still at work drafting a Bill of Rights and List of Grievances, the delegates agreed on 20 October 1774, after difficult discussions, to set up a Continental Association that would impose a more wide-ranging embargo on trade with Britain than any yet attempted. Non-importation of British goods was to go into effect on 1 December 1774. Non-consumption would follow on 1 March 1775, and non-exportation to Britain on 1 September of that year. Local 'associations' would enforce a policy common to all.

The rich associational life of the cities of British America – richer, it is to be suspected, than that of contemporary Spanish American cities, for all their religious confraternities – now proved its value. Across the colonies a network of voluntary groups sprang into action to organize the new stoppage of trade.[76] These local associations formed part of a wider movement that was already well under way, whereby colony after colony experienced a dramatic shift in the location and balance of power. Royal governors, together with the proprietary governors of

Pennsylvania and Maryland, watched helplessly as their authority dissolved before their eyes. As elections were held across the colonies for Association committees, members of the old elites observed with consternation the eruption of popular elements into political life. The new committees, acting in the name of Congress, set about tracking down dissidents to the non-importation agreement, and offenders found themselves exposed to summary justice by an angry populace. The old dominant groups, like Joseph Galloway and his cautious colleagues in the Pennsylvania Assembly, saw themselves under growing pressure from insurgency in the streets. Imperial and local politics had become hopelessly intertwined, and each colony was embarking on revolution in its own way.[77]

Any chance of reconciliation was rapidly slipping away. What Franklin, writing from London, had earlier described as 'the idle Notion of the Dignity and Sovereignty of Parliament, which they are so fond of',[78] made it almost impossible for Lord North to grant concessions under pressure. Similarly, the more radically minded in the Congress, like John Adams of Massachusetts and Patrick Henry of Virginia, had no confidence in a British parliament which they regarded as irredeemably corrupt. As he prepared for his return to his native country in the early spring of 1775, even Franklin, who had struggled for so long to keep alive his vision of an empire of liberty, had lost all real faith in the possibilities of union and reconciliation between Britain and the colonies: 'when I consider the extream Corruption prevalent among all Orders of Men in this old rotten State, and the glorious publick Virtue so predominant in our rising country, I cannot but apprehend more Mischief than Benefit from a closer Union . . . To unite us intimately, will only be to corrupt and poison us also.'[79]

As the colonies trained their militias and built up stocks of arms and ammunition in preparation for a war they did not want, there was still a lingering hope that, in standing firm for their British rights, they would save those rights not only for themselves but also for a mother country too deeply mired in corruption to see how far its liberties had been eroded by the tyrannical exercise of power. Even now it was not too late for the British to awake from their sleep. But the opposition groups at Westminster failed to rise to the occasion, and no British revolution came.[80] The second Continental Congress, convened in May 1775 after Lexington and Concord, would have to address the consequences of the unpalatable truth that, with no help to be expected from Britain, the colonies would be forced to fend for themselves. For its part, the British government, for too long misled by over-optimistic colonial officials into underestimating the gravity of the situation in the colonies, was now belatedly awaking to the fact that they were in a state of rebellion. By the middle of June it had accepted the reality of war.[81] That same month, Congress appointed George Washington to take command of the Massachusetts citizen army that had been fighting General Gage and his men, and entrusted him with the task of converting it into a genuinely continental, and professional, force.

The appointment of a Virginian as commander-in-chief was not only a practical but also a symbolic move, uniting under a single military leadership the fighting men of colonies very different in composition and outlook, and keenly aware of those differences. The Middle and Southern Colonies were congenitally suspicious of New Englanders. 'We are well aware', a merchant once remarked, 'of the intentions of the New England Men, they are of the old King Killing breed.'[82] In commenting on the structure of the new army, John Adams, on the other hand, noted the difference of character from the standpoint of a New Englander. Unlike the New England yeomen, he considered that the common people of the South were 'very ignorant and very poor', while southern gentlemen were 'accustomed, habituated to higher Notions of themselves and the distinction between them and the common People, than We are'.[83] The continuing challenge would be to hold this disparate coalition together, and the most effective of all the forces making for unity would be the experience of war.

The decision of Lord North's government to wage war on the Americans as if they were a foreign enemy, deploying against them the full panoply of British naval and military power, forced the Congress inexorably towards a radical reassessment of the relationship between the colonies and the king. Their dispute had traditionally been a dispute with a British parliament that made unacceptable claims to intervene in their affairs. Their loyalty, however, was not to a corrupt and self-aggrandizing parliament but to the monarch, whom they regarded as the sole source of legitimate authority. 'He it is', wrote Alexander Hamilton, 'that has defended us from our enemies, and to him alone we are obliged to render allegiance and submission.'[84] But disillusionment was spreading, and the convenient image of a benevolently disposed monarch could not indefinitely withstand the uncomfortable realities of 1774–5. George III, by all accounts, was adamant for war. He showed no inclination to accept petitions from his American subjects, and in the aftermath of the battle at Bunker Hill was reported to be busily negotiating with his European fellow monarchs for the recruitment of mercenaries to fight in America.[85] By proclaiming in August 1775 that the Americans were rebels, and ordering war against them, he had effectively destroyed the compact that bound them to their king.

Yet residual loyalty remained strong, just as, some forty years later, it would remain strong in Spanish America when the creoles were similarly faced by evidence of the complicity of Ferdinand VII in ordering their oppression.[86] Washington acknowledged this continuing loyalty as late as April 1776: 'My countrymen I know, from their form of government, and steady attachment heretofore to royalty, will come reluctantly into the idea of independence.'[87] The radicals had their sights fixed – some of them since 1774 or even earlier[88] – on independence as the only way out of the impasse. There were many, however, like John Dickinson of Pennsylvania, who still hankered after a return to an imagined golden age before 1763. The first Continental Congress expressed this hope in its 'Address to the Peoples of Great Britain': 'Place us in the same condition that we were at the close of the last war, and our former harmony will be restored.'[89] But to increasing numbers the escalation of conflict in the spring of 1775 was now making independence look like the only alternative to surrender. 'The middle way', wrote John Adams, 'is no way at all. If we finally fail in this great and glorious contest, it will be by bewildering ourselves in groping for the middle way.'[90]

Congress in effect was already operating as a sovereign authority, but as Washington wrote in May 1776: 'To form a new Government, requires infinite care and unbounded attention; for if the foundation is badly laid the superstructure must be bad . . .'[91] This foundation was to be laid in the following weeks, although it had first to be preceded by the work of demolition. Tom Paine's *Common Sense*, anonymously published as the work of 'an Englishman' in January 1776, achieved the required explosive result. In its first three months, according to Paine, it sold 120,000 copies.[92]

The clarity of Paine's argument and the forcefulness of his rhetoric swept everything before them. Drawing equally on John Locke's minimalist ideas about the purpose of government – to provide 'freedom and security' in Paine's words, including security not only for property but also for the free practice of religion[93] – and on the radical tradition of the Commonwealthmen, he began with a blistering attack on monarchy and hereditary succession, and was dismissive of 'the so much boasted constitution of England'.[94] In the opinion of John Adams, the author had 'a better hand at pulling down than building'.[95] Yet after tearing down the edifice with a ferocious enthusiasm well calculated to play on popular emotions and incite to violent action, Paine went on to mount a powerful case for independence and union that was equally well calculated to appeal to the large body of moderate opinion which still hesitated to take the plunge. His argument was all the more effective for being set in a world-historical context:

> The sun never shined on a cause of greater worth. 'Tis not the affair of a city, a country, a province, or a kingdom, but of a continent – of at least one eighth part of the habitable globe. 'Tis not the concern of a day, a year, or an age; posterity are virtually involved in the contest, and will be more or less affected, even to the end of time, by the proceedings now. Now is the seed time of continental union, faith and honor.[96]

The logic of these stirring words pointed inexorably to the establishment of an independent republic – '. . . the most powerful of all arguments, is, that nothing but independence, i.e. a continental form of government, can keep the peace of the continent and preserve it inviolate from civil wars.'[97] To establish a republic on a 'continental' scale, however – a republic in which 'the law is king'[98] – would mean a massive leap into the unknown.[99] Those European republics still surviving in a monarchical age – Venice, the Swiss Confederation, the Dutch Republic and a clutch of city states – were relatively small polities. They were also thought to be constitutionally prone to descending into venal oligarchy or succumbing to the power of the mob. In spite of the successes of the Dutch Republic, the precedents hardly appeared encouraging.[100] Paine, however, was a man who had no use for precedents. At a time when the British constitution, which had once dazzled by its glory, was losing its halo among growing numbers of colonists,[101] Paine described it as fatally vitiated by the corrupting presence of monarchy and hereditary rule. His sights were set on the future, not on the past. 'We have it in our power to begin the world over again.'[102]

A vision cast in terms of the future could be expected to resonate powerfully in colonial American society. For the best part of two centuries preachers had encouraged New Englanders to see their country as occupying a special place in God's providential design.[103] The evangelical preachers of the Great Awakening gave millenarian wings to this message as they carried it through the colonies. Was not the millennium likely to begin in America, as Jonathan Edwards proclaimed?[104] Millennial prophecy, with its vision of a state of bliss to come, rode well in consort with a republican ideology designed to begin the world again. Underlying both images was the perception of the New World of America as a genuinely new world. The ill-informed criticisms of European commentators were an inducement to Americans to open their eyes to see and appreciate the unique nature of their land. That uniqueness would in due course find expression in a novel and constitutionally unique form of political community.

It was the dangerous, and potentially disastrous, developments of the spring and summer of 1776 that produced the convergence of revolutionary energy and revolutionary ideas needed to break the ties of empire and bring a self-governing American republic into being. The military campaign launched by Congress in 1775 to bring Canada into the union was collapsing, leaving the northern frontiers of New York and New England exposed to British and Indian attack; British land and naval forces were massing against New York; and George III, insisting on the reassertion of royal authority before there could be any talk of peace, was reported to have contracted for Hessian mercenaries to reinforce his army in America.[105]

Faced with the collapse of civil authority, individual colonies, led by New Hampshire and North Carolina, were already starting to write their constitutions, and on 15 May 1776 Congress recommended 'the respective Assemblies and Conventions of the United Colonies . . . to adopt such a government as shall . . . best conduce to the happiness and safety of their constituents in particular, and America in general'.[106] On the same day, the Virginia Convention instructed its delegates in Philadelphia to propose that Congress 'declare the United Colonies free and independent States'.[107] With varying degrees of enthusiasm and reluctance, and driven forward by a combination of popular pressure, political manipulation and the sheer momentum of events, one after another of the United Colonies fell into line.

The conservative-dominated Assembly of Pennsylvania, whose foot-dragging over the move to independence had so enraged John Adams and his fellow radicals in the Congress, was an early casualty. Philadelphia, with its vibrant artisan culture, was already a strongly politicized city when Thomas Paine arrived there from England in the autumn of 1774 (fig. 4). Ten years earlier Franklin had mobilized the city's mechanics, craftsmen and shopkeepers in his campaign to replace proprietary with royal government, and the non-importation movement in the early 1770s stirred a fresh round of agitation among artisans who resented the dominance of the merchant oligarchs and wanted protection against competition from British manufactures. These were people who had a strong sense of the importance of self-improvement and self-help, and Paine's *Common Sense*, with its plain man's arguments for independence presented in a plain man's prose, had an enormous impact on them as they snapped up their freshly printed copies and rehearsed its arguments in taverns and coffee-houses. Service in the militia companies and participation in the various civic committees that sprang up in 1775–6 were giving them a growing sense of empowerment. When a group of radicals, including Paine, seized the initiative and launched their challenge to the dominance of the Pennsylvania Assembly and the merchant elite, the artisans and lower orders made their power felt at public meetings and on Philadelphia's streets.[108]

With a well-spring of popular support in Philadelphia, and in a Pennsylvania west country which had long resented its political marginalization, the radicals exploited the congressional resolution of 15 May to press forward with their plans for a Convention. This met on 18 June. By the time the Pennsylvania Assembly met again in mid-August after an adjournment, a new constitution had been drawn up by the Convention, which had effectively seized control of government. The most radical and democratic of all the new American constitutions, it followed Paine in rejecting the British principle of balanced government, created a unicameral legislature, and gave the suffrage to all tax-paying freemen over the age of 21.[109] In New York, by contrast, the congressional resolution, combined with the landing of British troops at Staten Island, gave conservatives the opportunity to outmanoeuvre the radicals to their left and the Tory loyalists to their right, and to seize the initiative in moving towards independence on their own terms.[110]

The Convention called by Virginia, the fourth colony to avail itself of the congressional authorization to devise a new form of government, adopted its new constitution on 29 June 1776, after approving earlier in the month a Declaration of Rights. This, like the Bill of Rights adopted by the first Continental Congress in 1774, was inspired by the English Declaration of Rights of 1689, which had formally ended the reign of James II and inaugurated that of William and Mary.[111] In searching for a legitimate device for terminating one form of government and installing another, colonial elites looked instinctively to the Whig constitutional tradition in which they had been raised.

As colony after colony in the spring and summer of 1776 moved to declare its independence and embark on the task of establishing a new form of government, an irresistible momentum built up for a formal Declaration of Independence by the Continental Congress. Individual colonies had taken the law into their own hands, but the United Colonies lacked any internationally acceptable legal standing, and they desperately needed the military assistance that only France could supply to keep their rebellion going. The stark truth was spelled out on 2 June by Richard Henry Lee of Virginia: 'It is not choice then but necessity that calls for independence as the only means by which foreign alliances can be obtained.'[112] Five days later, on the instructions of the Virginia Convention, he put forward a resolution in the Congress, seconded by John Adams, that 'these United Colonies are, and of right ought to be, free and independent States.'

Following the passage of the resolution the Congress set up a drafting committee to prepare a Declaration of Independence, with Thomas Jefferson, the newly arrived Virginia delegate, as one of its five members. He had recently prepared a draft constitution for Virginia, and it was to him, with his 'peculiar felicity of expression', as John Adams put it, that the final wording of the proposed Declaration was entrusted, although the political advantage of involving a southerner in an enterprise which might otherwise have smacked too much of New England radicalism is likely to have weighed at least as heavily as considerations of literary skill.[113]

After much editing by the Committee of Five, Jefferson's text, which did indeed display his 'peculiar felicity of expression', was delivered to Congress on 28 June. On 2 July, after unanimously affirming that 'these United Colonies are, and of right, ought to be, Free and Independent States', Congress turned itself into a Committee of the Whole, for further discussion and amendment of the text – a process that caused its author growing distress. The most substantive change, introduced on the urging of South Carolina and Georgia, was the removal of a lengthy paragraph on the 'execrable commerce' in slaves.[114] The wording of the text was finally accepted by Congress on 4 July, a date that would prevail over 2 July as the official anniversary of independence.[115] Four days later in Philadelphia the United Colonies ceremonially announced to the world that henceforth they were to be regarded as free and United States. Copies of the Declaration were circulated and reprinted, and the symbols of royalty were torn down across the colonies.

The document declaring the colonies to be independent of British rule represented an eloquent amalgam of the traditions, assumptions and ideas that had animated the resistance to imperial measures over the preceding two decades.[116] In providing a long list of 'injuries and usurpations' allegedly committed by the king, the Declaration, like the earlier Declaration prepared by Jefferson for the Virginia Convention, drew on the precedents provided by the English Declaration of Rights of 1689. Now it was George III instead of James II who was bent on 'the establishment of an absolute tyranny', and who had ignored all petitions for redress. The consequence in this instance, however, was the termination of allegiance, not simply, as in 1688–9, to the monarch of the moment, but to the British crown itself. 'All political connection' was to be dissolved between the United Colonies – now to become the 'United *States* of America' – and the 'State of Great Britain'. In thus dissolving the connection between two polities the Declaration resembled less the Bill of Rights of 1689 than the Act of Abjuration of 1584 by which the States General of the Netherlands renounced their allegiance to Philip II of Spain.[117]

The American colonists, like the Dutch and the English before them, were resorting in their Declaration of Independence to that standard recourse for

rebels in the western world, the idea of a contract between a ruler and his subjects. Hispanic Americans, when opposing some measure of which they disapproved, traditionally resorted to the same device. While contractualism itself was
common to the peoples of both colonial societies, and was firmly rooted in their
shared natural law tradition, distinctive national histories and religious traditions
inevitably shaped the context in which it was deployed. The Comuneros of New
Granada in 1781 were the spiritual heirs of the Comuneros of Castile in 1521,
who themselves looked back to the Castilian constitutionalist tradition embodied
in the medieval law code of the *Siete Partidas*. In 1776, Jefferson and the representatives assembled in the Congress consciously took their place in a distinguished historical line of resistance to tyrants that was embodied in Magna
Carta, and then ran forward through the Protestant Reformation and the revolt
of the Netherlands to seventeenth-century Britain, and eventually to themselves.
Buttressed by the English legal tradition with its heroic record of defending
English liberties, resistance doctrines drew their theoretical support from the
writings of a succession of political philosophers, among them Locke and the
radical Whig upholders of the Old Cause.

   In the Declaration of Independence, however, the historical and legal case for a
separation between the colonies and the British state was subsumed, as it was in
Paine's *Common Sense*, within a larger moral case of universal import: when a government behaves tyrannically, the people have a duty to sever their connection with
it.[118] Lurking in the background of this argument was the classical republican tradition, as transmitted through the Commonwealthmen, with its emphasis on
morality in the shape of civic virtue, as the sole defence against the loss of liberty.
More immediately important, however, was the determination of Jefferson and his
colleagues to relate the cause of independence to the 'self-evident truths' revealed
by the Enlightenment.

   Although Jefferson, in enunciating the self-evidence of these truths, may have
been inspired by the writings of eighteenth-century Scottish philosophers,[119] they
were deeply grounded in Lockean morality. While there was a tension between the
organic view of society inherent in classical republicanism, and the individualism
inherent in Locke's political philosophy, the unanimity with which the
Declaration of Independence was received and approved suggests that the two
forms of discourse remained at this stage mutually compatible. The strain of radical individualism in Locke's thinking had yet to be asserted at the expense of its
other components, and the men of 1776 drew on a common culture that found
space for classical republicanism while being imbued with Lockean principles.[120]

   At the heart of those principles was the belief in a benevolent Deity who created men and women as rational beings, capable of coming together to form civil
societies based on consent. The eighteenth-century colonists had become
Lockeans almost without realizing it, accepting in principle the notion of a fundamental equality, at least for themselves, although not for Indians and Africans;
tolerating a wide variety of opinions as necessary to the successful functioning of
a society that must be based on mutual trust; and applying themselves to

industrious pursuits with the purpose and expectation of improving their own condition and that of the society in which they lived.

In doing so, they looked to government to protect what the Declaration called 'certain unalienable rights', among them 'life, liberty and the pursuit of happiness'. While the more normal formulation was 'life, liberty, and property', Locke himself, in book 2 of the *Essay Concerning Understanding*, had written several times of 'the pursuit of happiness'. For Locke, happiness was what God desired for all His creation, and was the earthly foretaste of His goodness. The Swiss jurist and philosopher Burlamaqui and the thinkers of the Scottish Enlightenment, with whose writings Jefferson was well acquainted, had similarly emphasized the right of human beings to be happy.[121] So fashionable, indeed, had the notion become that eighteenth-century rulers conventionally pronounced the promotion of happiness to be one of their aims. The governor of Massachusetts, Jonathan Belcher, picking up on the language of the age, spoke in an address to the General Assembly in 1731 of laying the foundation for laws that 'would greatly promote the Happiness of this People'.[122] As used in the Declaration of Independence, however, the notion of happiness acquired its full resonance, as the inalienable right of God's creatures to enjoy to the maximum their liberty and the fruits of their labours, unmolested by government as they went about their business and their pleasures.

The Declaration of Independence, by setting the particular within the context of the universal, and transmuting British into natural rights, resonated far beyond the English-speaking world. It appeared in French in a Dutch journal within a month of publication. German translations were to follow, and there would be at least nine more French translations before 1783.[123] Spain, however, was more circumspect. Readers of the *Gaceta de Madrid* on 27 August might have noticed, buried among various items of news, a report that 'The Congress has declared independent of Great Britain the twelve [*sic*] united colonies, with each one forming its own government while a common regency system is planned for all of them.' The Spanish government was not anxious to see its subjects, and least of all its subjects in the Americas, more than minimally informed.[124]

It was the French reaction, however, not the Spanish, that mattered to the men in Philadelphia. It was to France above all that the new republic looked for the immediate moral and practical support essential to victory in their fight for liberty. It was a fight which, in the bleak winter of 1776, looked as if it could only end in defeat for the Patriot forces. They had as yet no allies, and they had pitted themselves against an imperial power that only a decade earlier had defeated the combined forces of France and Spain. Moreover, in renouncing their allegiance to George III, they had torn the British Atlantic community apart, and in the process had left themselves dangerously exposed. Away to the south, East and West Florida were firmly in British hands. To the west of the rebel colonies, the Indian nations sought to maintain an increasingly precarious neutrality in this white, fratricidal conflict, anxious to be on the winning side when it finally ended, but more likely to come out in support of the British as offering the better hope of recovering lost community lands.[125] To the north, Canada and Nova Scotia, following the defeat of the invading American army in 1775, stayed loyal to the crown, and became an important base of operations against the rebels.

The British West Indies, too, although sharing many similarities with the southern colonies, showed no inclination to join the revolt. In a society where whites were massively outnumbered by blacks, fears of a slave rebellion acted as a strong deterrent, although similar fears in the American South, where the balance of races was more even, had proved insufficient to discourage the planters from defying the British crown. Unlike their Virginian counterparts, however, many of the Caribbean plantation-owners were absentee landlords, and therefore more tenuously connected to their estates. In the face of competition from the French sugar islands, the West Indies, too, were totally dependent on a protected British market. Already in the disputes over imperial legislation in the 1760s the West India lobby had found it convenient to play the card of loyalty in the hope of reinforcing the islands' preferential status. Submission was a price worth paying, both to keep the sugar exports flowing and to be asssured of British military assistance if the slaves revolted.[126]

If the thirteen colonies failed to carry with them significant portions of Britain's Atlantic empire, they also failed to carry a substantial section of their own populations. While the Declaration of Independence did much to mobilize enthusiasm for the revolutionary cause, for a large minority it proved a step too far. Some who had famously championed the cause of American liberty, like John Dickinson of Pennsylvania, pulled back from the brink.[127] Others, intimidated into silence, waited for the arrival of British troops before showing their hand. As always in revolutions, there were many who were neutral or uncommitted, hoping simply to ride out the storm. But perhaps as many as 500,000 in a white population of around 2,200,000 remained loyal to the British crown. Of these loyalists 19,000 joined up as volunteers in the 'provincial' corps of the British army in America, while perhaps 60,000 emigrated to Canada or England.[128]

This, then, was a civil war as much as a revolution, although one in which the loyalist 'Tory' opposition proved notably unsuccessful in winning the initiative or providing that continuity of leadership which was to be such an important element in the eventual victory of the Patriot cause. If that cause for a time looked hopeless, British military errors, and the grim determination of Washington and his men to hold on, slowly turned the tide. Congress, for its part, never withdrew its support from Washington, even when the military situation was at its bleakest. Always careful to defer to the civilians, Washington himself developed into a genuinely national leader, whose wisdom and steadfastness in the face of adversity came to symbolize, for contemporaries as for posterity, the tenacity and high ideals of the American Revolution.[129]

It was the British surrender at Saratoga in 1777 that transformed the prospects for the fledgling United States. The American victory persuaded France to enter the war in 1778. In June 1779 Spain, still smarting from the loss of Florida, and anxious, as always, to recover Gibraltar, followed suit.[130] What had begun as a rebellion of disaffected colonists was now transformed into a global conflict, in which the rebels were no longer fighting on their own.

When General Cornwallis surrendered at Yorktown in October 1781 an exhausted Britain lost the will to win a war in which it had never quite been able to believe. By the terms of the treaty of Versailles of September 1783 it retained Canada, but returned the Floridas to Spain, and formally recognized the independence of the thirteen rebel colonies. Only nine years had passed since Samuel Adams had written to the London agent of Massachusetts that he wished for a permanent union with the mother country, 'but only on the principles of liberty and truth. No advantage that can accrue to America from such an union can compensate for the loss of liberty . . .'[131] In the end, the American Patriots placed 'liberty' above the union they had initially hoped to re-establish on more equitable foundations. The effect of their victory was to break the British Atlantic community in two. It remained to be seen whether a Spanish Atlantic community experiencing many of the same tensions would fare any better.

A crisis contained

While Britain was struggling in the 1770s to retain hold of its American empire, Spanish imperial policy during the same decade displayed an assertiveness that owed much to the reforming drive of José de Gálvez, in his capacity, first as visitor general of New Spain, and then, from 1775, as secretary of the Indies.[132] Determined to protect the northern frontier of New Spain and the Pacific coast from British incursions, and from the growing threat posed by Russian expansion down the coast from Alaska, he embarked on an ambitious expansionist programme. This was intended not only to strengthen Spain's hold on the provinces of New Vizcaya, Sonora and the Baja California peninsula, but also to establish a firm Spanish presence up the Californian coastline. In 1770 Spain planted garrisons at San Diego and Monterey, and in 1776 San Francisco was founded as the third Californian *presidio*. Just as the British were losing their North American colonies, the Spanish were acquiring, in 'New California', a brand new American colony of their own.[133]

The assertive imperialism of the Spain of Charles III was accompanied by an effort, comparable to that of Philip II but inspired by the scientific spirit of the Enlightenment, to survey and document the physical features and natural resources of the crown's overseas territories. During the last three decades of the century, the crown sponsored a series of exploratory and scientific expeditions to different regions of Spain's American territories and the Spanish Pacific, culminating in Alejandro Malaspina's great expedition of 1789–94, which sailed all the way up America's Pacific coast from Cape Horn to Alaska, before proceeding to the Philippines, China and Australia and returning to Cadiz by way of Cape Horn.[134]

While these expeditions were evidence of the crown's determination to dispel the image of Spanish backwardness, they were also integral to the Bourbon

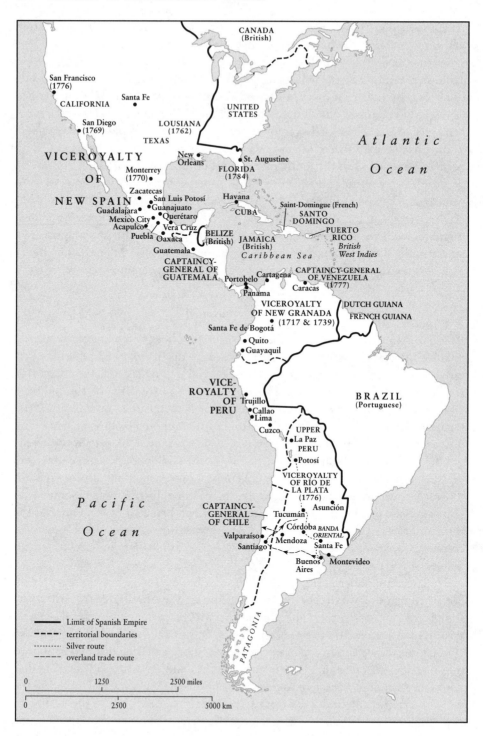

Map 7. Spain's American Empire, End of the Eighteenth Century.
Based on Guillermo Céspedes del Castillo, *América hispánica, 1492–1898* (1983), vol. 6, map xv; *The Cambridge History of Latin America*, vol. 3 (1987), p. 6.

programme for a more effective exploitation of American resources. It would only be possible to sustain the mounting costs of imperial defence and expansion if more wealth could be extracted from the American territories. In 1770 revenues from the Indies constituted around 23 per cent of the total revenues of the Spanish treasury.[135] With the crown imposing new pressures and providing new incentives, silver production in the mines of New Spain and Peru grew in the years before 1780 at an annual rate of some 1.2 per cent[136] – an increase that not only brought relief to the Spanish treasury but also helped to stimulate trading contacts around the Atlantic basin. In November 1776 the Congress of the newly independent United States effectively recognized the dominance of Spanish American silver by adopting the Spanish *peso*, under the name of 'dollar' (from the German *Thaler*), as the unit of currency.[137] Whatever the political transformations under way, the British and Spanish Atlantic economies were becoming increasingly interdependent.

The overseas revenues that allowed Spain to sustain, if somewhat precariously, its great power status, resulted not only from rising silver production, but also from the efforts of royal officials to rationalize the American fiscal system and raise more revenue by way of taxes and monopolies. These efforts, however, imposed massive strains on American populations and on the social fabric of American communities. At the beginning of the 1780s Gálvez and his colleagues were brought face to face with the uncovenanted costs of their programme of reform. While the thirteen mainland colonies of North America were slipping from Britain's grasp, Spain found itself in danger of losing a vast area of South America, some 500,000 square kilometres in extent, in the southern Andes.[138]

The coincidence did not escape the notice of Alexander von Humboldt as he introduced his readers to Túpac Amaru's rebellion, which he believed was 'little known in Europe': 'The great revolt of 1781 was on the point of snatching from the King of Spain all the mountainous region of Peru at the same time as Great Britain was losing almost all its colonies in the continent of America.'[139] The Andean rebellion of 1780 to 1783, easily the largest and most dangerous to have occurred in well over two hundred years of Spanish rule in America, originated at Tinta, in the Vilcanota valley to the south of Cuzco, and at one time or another extended over large parts of Peru and modern Bolivia to reach New Granada and Venezuela to the north, and Chile and the north-western regions of today's Argentina to the south.[140] Faced simultaneously with an independent, but not entirely unconnected, insurrection in New Granada, which at one point saw 20,000 rebels moving on the capital of Santa Fe de Bogotá,[141] Madrid as much as London appeared to be on the point of losing its American empire. Of all its major territorial possessions on the American mainland, only the viceroyalty of New Spain remained relatively tranquil (fig. 34).

The precipitating cause of both these regional rebellions was Madrid's programme of administrative and fiscal reform, now made all the more pressing by the new expenses arising from Spain's entry into the war against England in 1779. In Peru, the sales tax of the *alcabala* was raised from 2 to 4 per cent in 1772, and to 6 per cent in 1776, and three years later was extended to coca, a product that the Indians consumed in large quantities. These tax increases were rigorously implemented by the authoritarian and inflexible visitor-general Antonio de Areche, who arrived in the viceroyalty in 1777 with instructions from Gálvez to implement the reforms. Like the offices of the customs collectors in the British colonies, the customs houses he built through the southern Andes became the visible symbols of imperial oppression.[142] Similar reform processes were also at work in the viceroyalty of New Granada, where another visitor-general, Juan Francisco Gutiérrez de Piñeres, arrived in 1778, and immediately set about reorganizing the tax apparatus in an attempt to extend the fiscal net.[143]

The colonial societies of Spanish South America, like those of British North America, were now confronted with the unenticing prospect of being brought within the confines of the new-style European fiscal-military state. For all the differences in their political cultures, large areas in both colonial worlds responded with protest, riot and rebellion. Their rebellions, however, took different forms, and followed different trajectories, reflecting the deep differences that divided British American from Spanish American colonial society, and British imperial power and practice from their Spanish counterparts.

In reality, there was no more a single colonial society in Spanish America than there was in British America. Each colonial world contained a multiplicity of societies, leading in turn to a multiplicity of reactions. The British West Indies and the mainland colonies reacted to the policies of the mother country in very different ways. Similarly, although there were innumerable local riots in eighteenth-century New Spain, the viceroyalty, for reasons still to be fully explored, did not experience the great upheavals that shook Spanish power to its foundations in New Granada and Peru.[144] In the areas of revolt there were significant divergences, too, between the Andean insurrection of Túpac Amaru II and the rebellion of the Comuneros of New Granada. The story of both, however, highlights aspects of Spain's empire of the Indies which bring into sharper relief the character of Britain's American empire and of the revolt of the thirteen colonies.

The Andean revolt led by Juan Gabriel Condorcanqui, the self-proclaimed Inca Túpac Amaru II, was primarily, but by no means exclusively, the revolt of a large and exploited indigenous population which had been given a glimpse of a better future in the context of an idealized past. In 1763, when British troops and colonists were challenged by the massive uprising known as Pontiac's 'rebellion', they had faced a movement of Indian peoples living on the frontier of empire, whose lands had been encroached on by British settlers, and whose political bargaining power had been destroyed by the elimination of France's American empire.[145] Túpac Amaru's revolt, on the other hand, was that of a subject population which had been living under oppressive Spanish rule for over two centuries. Changing circumstances over the last few decades had alleviated some of its burdens, like the *mita* service in the mines,[146] but had added, or aggravated, others. There was particular resentment at the expansion of the *reparto*, or the system of forced sale of goods at inflated prices to the indigenous population by local officials, the *corregidores*, who would act in collusion with estate-owners and influential merchants. As a result, the debts of the Andean peasantry piled up and could only be paid off by service in the mines and the textile workshops, or by work on the haciendas.

Following the legalization of the *reparto* in 1756, local revolts against the *corregidores* and the native chiefs or *curacas* operating on behalf of the state became endemic, but usually ended, as they began, as minor and strictly local movements of protest.[147] The indigenous population of the Cuzco region was far from homogeneous, and Spanish rule had led to a progressive fragmentation of Andean rural society into numerous small peasant communities living their own lives and nursing their own communal grievances.[148] But the *reparto* system touched them all, as also did the fiscal changes introduced by Areche. The tax demands were all the harder to bear because they came at a time when the new and sustained growth of the Andean population had left Indian communities with a scarcity of resources and had generated bitter disputes over property rights with hacienda owners and members of the native nobility who had taken advantage of the long period of population decline to encroach on communal lands. The Andes had always been a cruel world, and from the 1740s onwards they were the scene of constant rural disturbances.[149]

In 1776 a major administrative change provoked further disruption. Following the decision to create the viceroyalty of La Plata, Upper Peru (modern Bolivia) was detached from the Peruvian viceroyalty, and incorporated into the new viceroyalty, which was governed from Buenos Aires. Since the Potosí mines formed part of the transfer, this sharply reduced the viceregal revenues in Lima. It also had the effect of weakening the economy of the Cuzco region, now artificially divided from its traditional regional market of Upper Peru, which gravitated into the orbit of Buenos Aires. When the viceroyalty of La Plata was permitted to trade directly with Spain in 1778 as part of the crown's new 'free trade' policy, Potosí's silver remittances to Cadiz were re-routed through Buenos Aires. Cuzco was thus deprived of its traditional source of silver supply, and its producers were left exposed to competition from cheap European goods introduced into the region by Buenos Aires merchants.[150]

It was against this background of fiscal oppression and economic dislocation that Candorcanqui launched his challenge to the established order. The Jesuit-educated son of a cacique of Inca royal lineage, he had been fighting a long and frustrating battle in the Lima courts in the 1770s to establish his claims to recognition as the legitimate descendant of the last Inca, Túpac Amaru, executed after the capture of the Inca redoubt of Vilcabamba by Spanish troops in 1572. As a member of an Indian elite sufficiently well established and wealthy to interact on equal terms with people of Spanish origin, he made useful connections in Lima with creoles and mestizos who were critical of Areche and Spain's imperial policy. The *Lima Gazette* would have allowed him to follow the course of events in British North America, and he had a mestizo friend in Lima who had travelled in France, Spain and England. But his essential point of reference was the world of the Andes, and he seems to have been deeply influenced by his reading of the Inca Garcilaso's *Royal Commentaries*. The prologue to the second edition, published in 1723, included an Indian prophecy related by Sir Walter Raleigh that Inca rule would one day be re-established with help from the English.[151]

Smarting from his own personal experiences of Spanish injustice in Lima and his native Tinta, and fired by his reading of Garcilaso's evocation of the lost golden world of the Incas, Candorcanqui became a man with a mission. In November 1780, under the name of Túpac Amaru II, he called out the Andean peasantry in rebellion, and found a suitable symbolic victim in the oppressive *corregidor* of Tinta, Antonio de Arriaga, whom he seized and executed.

In proclaiming revolt, Túpac Amaru tapped into a rich vein of cultural pride and collective Andean consciousness, which looked for the creation, or re-creation, of a utopian social order under Inca rule. Prophecies clustered around the mystical numerals of the year 1777, creating expectations of the return of the Inca to restore order and harmony to a world purged of Spaniards.[152] The outbreak of Pontiac's rebellion in North America had occurred in a similar climate of prediction and expectation, as the Delaware prophet Neolin urged his fellow Indians to turn their backs on the world of the whites. At the same time, Neolin's anti-European message, like the message now spreading through the Andes, bore the strong imprint of European religion. Its resort to Christian notions of sin, heaven and hell betrayed the growing religious syncretism of the Delaware Indians, a people whose exposure to Christianity did not begin to equal in length and intensity that of the population of the Andes, where the Catholic priest occupied a dominant position in village life, and extensive campaigns had been undertaken for the extirpation of idolatry.[153]

Parish priests in the Andes, resentful of Bourbon reforms which reduced their perquisites, patronage and prestige, had good reason to sympathize with the sense of injustice felt by their local communities. They lived among their Indian parishioners, they often spoke their language, and they had become integral to the new ritual and ceremonial system that had developed in the communities after the arrival of Christianity. At the same time, however, their extortion of money from their parishioners had made many of them hated.[154] This made them deeply ambiguous figures. Both the depth of their unpopularity and their essential role, in the eyes of their parishioners, as participants in a cosmic system that combined a continuing belief in the ancient supernatural forces of the Andean world with the rituals and belief systems of Spanish Catholicism, were tellingly revealed in an exchange that occurred in the village square of Livitaca between Túpac Amaru and the town's inhabitants, shortly after the outbreak of revolt. On arriving in the square he was greeted with the words: 'You are our God and Lord and we beseech you that there should be no priests to importune us.' He replied that this was not possible because then there would be 'nobody to attend to them at the moment of death'.[155]

Túpac Amaru, like Pontiac, found himself juggling with a variety of discordant elements in his efforts to extend the appeal of his movement. Unlike Pontiac, however, he was having to appeal not only to different Indian groupings, but also to a non-indigenous population of creoles and mestizos. The resulting eclecticism, which no doubt also reflected his efforts to combine the disparate elements of his own cultural background, makes his ultimate objectives far from clear. If he claimed for himself the royal status of Inca, he appears to have envisaged a Peru cleared of peninsular Spaniards, but still owing allegiance to the Spanish crown. Whether this was merely tactical, however, or was an integral part of his policy remains uncertain, since different manifestos sent out different messages.[156] If his movement was anti-European and anti-Spanish, he was also anxious to include not only the mestizos but also the creoles, for they too, like the Indians, suffered from what he called 'the perverse impositions and threats made by the kingdom of Europe' – a formulation that hardly reflects a very clear notion of political geography.[157] Although his rebellion was suffused with Andean concepts of Inca revivalism, these had acquired such a strongly Christian colouring that he proposed to govern Peru with the help of the Bishop of Cuzco.[158]

As a cacique in the Vilcanota valley who owned a string of mule trains, Túpac Amaru had a wide range of local contacts, and was well placed to mobilize the support of fellow caciques in order to raise the indigenous population in revolt across the Cuzco region.[159] His rebellion could also draw on the support, often tentative and opportunistic, of creoles and mestizos whose lives had felt the impact of the Bourbon reform programme. Yet it was a disparate coalition to hold together, and it never coalesced into a genuinely multi-ethnic movement against the viceregal government. In particular, Túpac Amaru signally failed to carry with him the old Inca nobility of Cuzco, to which the rebels laid siege at the end of December 1780. Charles V had issued Spanish patents of hereditary nobility to the Inca nobles in the 1540s, and through skilful exploitation of the Spanish system of government in the Andes by means of indirect rule, together with persistent recourse to the courts of law, the Indian nobility of Cuzco and its environs had established themselves in the top flight of Cuzco's social hierarchy. While periodically intermarrying with the creole elite (fig. 40), these nobles retained a powerful sense of their historic position as descendants of the natural lords of the Peru of the Incas. They looked down on Túpac Amaru as a mere rural *curaca* whose claims to Inca kingship they totally rejected, and while they shared his general aspirations for the Andean community as a whole, their historical experience led them to place a strong faith in the legal and bargaining processes inherent in the Spanish imperial system, and in the King of Spain as a just ruler who would right their wrongs.[160]

Timely reinforcements from Lima enabled Cuzco to withstand the attack of the insurgent forces, and as Túpac Amaru broke off the siege to campaign to the north and east of Cuzco, the cracks in his coalition began to appear. Humiliated by the failure of the siege of Cuzco, and enraged by what he regarded as the treachery of creoles and mestizos who had been unwilling to support him, Túpac Amaru seems to have abandoned his policy of protecting his non-Indian supporters, and gave orders for the summary execution of peninsular Spaniards, creoles and mestizos, as well as of corrupt native lords. Only priests were to be spared, to play their part in the new, purified society that was to rise from the ashes of the old. Not surprisingly, any remaining creole supporters were alienated by the savagery of peasants who looted and destroyed haciendas and textile workshops and took ferocious revenge on *corregidores* and *curacas*. This had ceased to be a generalized uprising against an oppressive imperial government, and was fast turning into a bloody racial conflict.[161]

Following the raising of the siege of Cuzco, royalist forces, consisting of regular soldiers, militias and loyalist Indians, went in pursuit of Túpac Amaru, and captured him in early April 1781, along with his wife and a number of his closest companions. While the revolt continued to spread, he was tried on charges of rebellion and other crimes. He was then sentenced by an implacable Areche to witness the execution of his wife and son and the other rebels taken prisoner, before being drawn and quartered in the great plaza of Cuzco. The horrific public spectacle was carefully calculated to symbolize the death of Inca kingship.

The effect of Túpac Amaru's gruesome death was to strengthen his surviving commanders in their desire for revenge, and intensify the savagery of a war which raged over a vast mountainous region for a further two years. The centre of gravity of the rebellion moved to the Lake Titicaca region and Upper Peru, where the Aymarás, who had recently seen their messianic leader, Tomás Katari, assassinated, joined forces with the Quechua-speaking rebels from the Cuzco region to lay siege to La Paz in the summer of 1781. But the traditional antagonisms between Quechuas and Aymarás made this an uneasy alliance, and royalist troops succeeded in raising the siege of La Paz, as they had raised that of Cuzco a few months earlier. By the time the war ended in 1783 with the victory of the royalist forces, as many as 100,000 Indians and 10,000 Spaniards are alleged to have lost their lives, out of a total population in the rebel territories of some 1,200,000.[162]

The attempt to restore a lost order had failed, leaving behind a traumatized people with memories, dreams and expectations which would permeate all the subsequent history of colonial, and post-colonial, Peru. The failure had as much to do with internal divisions – between Indian and creole, and Indian and Indian – as with the military force which the viceregal regime was eventually able to put into the field. Those divisions in turn reflected contradictions over the nature of the order that was to be restored. Was this once again to be a world without Spaniards, as many of the insurgents demanded, or was it to be one – as Túpac Amaru himself may initially have intended – in which the restored Incas headed a united nation of Indians, mestizos and creoles, and ushered in a new era of justice and harmony, in which Andean and Hispanic religion and culture were somehow fused? This was the kind of vision, at once uplifting and diffuse, that the intoxicating brew of Garcilaso's *Royal Commentaries* could so easily inspire.

Significantly, one of Areche's first actions after the trial and execution of Túpac Amaru was to ban the *Royal Commentaries*. He also prohibited the wearing of Inca royal dress, abolished the hereditary position of cacique, placed restrictions on the use of the Quechua language, and forbade the depiction of

Inca rulers, whether in paintings or on the stage.[163] This amounted to a systematic attempt to eradicate the Inca revivalism always latent in the collective consciousness of the Andean world – a revivalism that had given at least a momentary cohesion to a vast movement of protest against the iniquities of the viceregal regime. But the contrast between Areche's savage punishment of Indian rebels and the relative leniency accorded to rebellious creoles suggests a policy designed to minimize the degree of creole complicity, and place the burden of responsibility for the rebellion squarely on the backs of the indigenous population and a number of mestizos, in an effort to play on ethnic divisions and win back the loyalty of creoles alienated from the crown by the recent reforms.[164]

In any comparison with the revolt of the white population of the British colonies, the multi-ethnic character of the Túpac Amaru rebellion in its opening stages would appear to have been a fatal obstacle to success because of the inherent tendency to racial tension. But that it need not necessarily have been so is suggested by the simultaneous development of regional rebellion in the neighbouring viceroyalty of New Granada.[165] The visitor-general Gutiérrez de Piñeres, like his opposite number Antonio de Areche in Peru, had introduced a number of deeply unpopular administrative and fiscal changes. These were intended to curb the massive contraband trade along New Granada's northern coastline and thus to increase viceregal revenues. The reforms included the elimination of creole judges from the Audiencia of Santa Fe de Bogotá, the reorganization of the monopolies on brandy and tobacco, and a revised system for the more effective collection of sales taxes. In addition, in 1780 a 'voluntary' donation was demanded of every adult male to pay for the war with England.[166]

The first major disturbances provoked by these reforms broke out in March 1781 in Socorro, a town 200 kilometres north of Santa Fe, which had only secured municipal status a decade earlier, and was located in a tobacco- and cotton-growing region particularly affected by the new fiscal measures. Following a succession of riots, a group of prominent citizens were persuaded to take over the leadership of a movement of popular protest with which they more or less actively sympathized. One of their number, Juan Francisco Berbeo, a middling landowner of good family and connections, emerged as the leader of what was rapidly to become a large-scale regional rebellion.

Berbeo and his colleagues succeeded in forging a coalition between patricians and plebeians in their native town, and subsequently in keeping control of an insurrection that soon spread beyond Socorro and its immediate hinterland, a countryside settled by small-scale peasant farmers. New Granada was a land of numerous small communities living in geographical isolation, but other towns adhered to the uprising in Socorro, and new recruits, including Indian villagers distressed by recent resettlement policies, flocked to join the rebellion after the rebels roundly defeated a small government force belatedly sent to crush them. Encouraged by its victory and by the news of the great revolt in Peru,[167] the Comunero army led by Berbeo, who, like George Washington, had learnt the art of soldiering in Indian frontier warfare, prepared to march on Bogotá. Its rallying call was the traditional Hispanic cry of 'Long live the king and down with bad government', while the central demand of what had now become a combined uprising of creoles, mestizos and Indians was for a return to the old ways in the name of *el común*, 'the common good'.[168]

In Peru the authorities had been able to produce an effective military response after a hesitant start, but the viceregal administration in Bogotá was ill-prepared to move against the rebels. When the revolt broke out there were only 75 professional soldiers in the capital, and the viceroy himself was in Cartagena, six weeks' travelling time from Bogotá,[169] preparing the port's defences against a possible English attack.[170] With a rebel army 20,000 strong assembled at Zipaquirá, the administration had no choice but to negotiate.

The peace commissioners headed by the Archbishop of Santa Fe de Bogotá, Antonio de Caballero y Góngora, found themselves presented by the rebels with a set of 35 demands designed to deal with a range of abuses.[171] These included the abolition of the new taxes and monopolies and the expulsion of the visitor-general, Gutiérrez de Piñeres. The articles addressed, too, the complaints of the Indians about the tribute tax, clerical exactions and the resettlement policy. The rebels, however, were interested in more than the remedy of current fiscal grievances, of whatever ethnic group. In demanding what would effectively be a creole monopoly of offices, the elimination of the office of visitor-general, and the almost complete removal of peninsular Spaniards from the viceroyalty, they were insisting on a general reordering of government which would have made New Granada virtually autonomous under the rule of a distant crown.

However unpalatable these demands to the viceregal administration, in the circumstances it was in no position to reject them. On 8 June 1781 the peace commissioners accepted the Pact of Zipaquirá, although the authorities in Bogotá had secretly decided in advance that they were not bound to abide by the conditions of an agreement reached under duress. The terms still had to be approved by the crown, but most of the Comunero rebels dispersed after the commissioners swore an oath to accept the Pact. Sporadic resistance persisted, however, and one of Berbeo's commanders who refused to lay down his arms was later tried and sentenced, like Túpac Amaru, to death by dismemberment. The viceroy, however, issued a general pardon on Caballero y Góngora's advice, and confirmed the principal fiscal concessions made by the commissioners.

When the archbishop himself succeeded to the post of viceroy in the summer of 1782, he embarked on a policy of reconciliation with the creoles, in which he encouraged them to turn their attention to the promotion of economic improvement under the benevolent leadership of the crown. Yet this was a crown as insistent as ever on the unconditional acceptance of its authority by its loyal subjects, and great care was taken by Caballero and his successors to ensure that, in the military reorganization that followed in the wake of the revolt, the principal positions of command should all be held by peninsular Spaniards.[172]

The rebellion of the Comuneros, like that of Túpac Amaru, was a revolt aimed at restoring a political order overturned by ill-advised and intrusive Bourbon reforms. In this sense, the aims of the rebels were similar to those of the rebels in the British colonies who wished to return to the world of 1763. The Comuneros at least, and probably also the Tupamaristas, for all the opacity of their leader's intentions, had no desire for a rupture with the crown, any more than the North American Patriots at the start of their rebellion. Exasperated by the activities and exactions of officials sent out to govern them from the metropolis, they did, how-ever, want to secure a degree of control over their own affairs that would effec-tively ensure equality of status with peninsular Spain. For the British colonies, shaped by parliamentary tradition, equality of status with the mother country was conceived in terms of legislative autonomy in all matters of internal govern-ment. For the creoles of the bureaucratized world of Spanish America it was essentially administrative, and would be ensured by the appointment of locals, rather than peninsular Spaniards, to administrative and judicial posts.[173]

In both instances, however, what seemed to colonial elites like the realignment of a disturbed balance in the name of justice and equity appeared to the metro-politan centre to be a demand at pistol point for unacceptable change. To accede to such a demand would be to surrender imperial authority, and turn colonial subjects into the masters of their lands. At all costs, authority had to be upheld, and by force if need be. But where the British crown failed to reimpose its author-ity, in spite of the deployment of an army that at one moment was 50,000 strong,[174] the Spanish crown succeeded in containing the crisis, even in New Granada where it lacked the military capability to take on the rebels.

Part of the explanation for the different outcomes is to be found in contingent circumstances. Of these the most important was the success of the North American rebels in securing the military and naval participation of France and Spain in their struggle. Although prophecies might circulate in the Andes about the restoration of Inca rule with the help of the English, there was not the remotest possibility at this juncture of English, or any other external support. Even if foreign powers had been willing and ready to help, logistics would have constituted an insuperable deterrent. The Spanish American rebellions occurred in regions remote from the seaboard, and isolated from each other by an implaca-ble geography. North America itself was a world away and the English colonists were otherwise engaged. Even if the Comuneros drew inspiration from Túpac Amaru's uprising, that too was of no practical consequence for their own strug-gle. The viceroyalty of New Granada by itself was so fractured by geography that it took all Berbeo's political skills to prevent the resulting inter-regional and municipal rivalries from wrecking his coalition as he faced the decision as to whether to march on Bogotá.[175]

Disunity, however, also haunted the leaders of rebellion in British America. They were confronted, like the Comunero leadership, with inter-regional rival-ries, which were bridged but far from eradicated when the oligarchs of Virginian society decided to throw in their lot with the Massachusetts Patriots. They were faced, too, with the consequences of social divisions that may have been tem-porarily set aside in the wave of popular enthusiasm generated by the initial resistance to British demands, but which, like the regional divisions, inevitably resurfaced as the war went on. From 1777 onwards, it was the poor – landless labourers, the down-and-outs and blacks – who manned the Continental Army, and did so for the money rather than out of enthusiasm for the cause. Given the divisions both between and within the colonies, and the size of the Loyalist minority, a successful outcome to the Revolution was far from assured, and the part played by British political and strategic misjudgments may in the end have tipped the balance.[176]

Ethnic divisions proved fatal to Túpac Amaru's rebellion. In this respect the North American rebel leaders had an easier task, since they did not have to hold together coalitions of whites, mestizos and Indians, each of these groups with an agenda of its own. By taking matters into their own hands, and attacking whites and their properties indiscriminately, the Andean Indians soon alienated creoles who had initially shown themselves sympathetic to Túpac Amaru's revolt. But in New Granada the Indians were less radical in their demands, and the savagery that accompanied the Peruvian rebellion was absent.[177] To some extent this may have been the consequence of more capable leadership, although the rapidity with which the Comuneros achieved their aims saved New Granada from the kind of protracted civil war which inevitably leads to the escalation of hatreds and the perpetration of atrocities – something that occurred in North America as well as the Andes.[178]

Quality of leadership in any revolution is difficult to assess by any criterion other than the eventual outcome. From this perspective, the leaders of the North American rebellion appear to posterity to have been cast in a heroic mould. This makes it difficult to recapture the ambiguities, the hypocrisy and the personal tensions that lay behind the achievements of the North American Founding Fathers.[179] These, however, were men of experience in local life and politics, and the willingness of the colonial population to place its trust in men of experience to guide them through the turmoil of war and revolution gave them the space in which to develop their talents and justify that trust. In this sense, the degree of political participation to be found in pre-revolutionary North America was a vital element, both in forming a generation of leaders, and in providing them with the popular support which they needed to see their task through to the end.

The character of Spanish American society did not allow for this kind of popular participation in government, or create the accountability to an electorate which compelled the holders of public office to hone their political skills. A cacique like Túpac Amaru acquired his post through a combination of inheritance and appointment. Berbeo, although he possessed military experience and proved himself an outstanding leader, was not in fact a holder of municipal office – the usual and most obvious training ground for members of the creole elite.[180]

Yet if, as seems plausible, the majority of the North American Patriots initially hoped to preserve their liberties within the British Empire rather than press forward to independence, they failed to achieve their ends. From this point of view the Comunero Revolution came closer to the mark. The rebels secured major tax concessions from the royal authorities, and compelled them to act within the spirit of the unwritten constitution that in pre-Bourbon times had regulated the crown's relations with its American subjects. The visitor-general, Gutiérrez de Piñeres, was recalled to Madrid, and the plan to extend to New Granada the system of local intendancies was dropped.[181] Even in Peru, where a pall of fear hung over the Andes after the savage repression of Túpac Amaru's rebellion, a crown now more than ever insistent on the divine nature of monarchy[182] was still prepared to manoeuvre and make concessions, partly in order to ward off the danger of more uprisings, but also as part of a genuine attempt to redress grievances. Unpopular officials, starting with the visitor-general Areche himself, were removed from their posts. The system of forced purchase of goods by Indians was abolished, labour services were modified, and, as Túpac Amaru had demanded, an Audiencia was established in Cuzco. In the end, many of the Indian caciques due to be deprived of their positions managed to retain them by having recourse to the courts.[183]

The ability of the Spanish crown to contain the crisis indicates the continuing strength and resilience of the imperial structure, in spite of all the strains imposed upon it by the Bourbon reforms. The institutions of imperial government had become deeply embedded in the Hispanic American world, as they had not in British America. Although colonial elites in the Spanish Indies might often ignore and sometimes actively defy royal commands, they themselves formed part of a complex system of institutional structures and patronage networks stretching downwards from the king.

Traditionally, this system also possessed a self-correcting mechanism in the form of checks and balances. Petition and protest by the aggrieved, followed by intense bargaining and mutual concessions within an accepted legal and constitutional framework, was the accepted way of proceeding. When this failed, armed revolt could be represented as a legitimate last resort. This in turn, however, was expected to trigger a fresh round of bargaining. Both the rebellion of the Comuneros and the authorities' response conformed perfectly to this traditional pattern. This was a rebellion imbued with traditional notions of contract and the common good, and the authorities reverted to traditional Habsburg methods when they took steps to reaffirm the common good once the rebellion was at an end.

How little the Comunero uprising was touched by Enlightenment ideology is suggested by a pasquinade posted in Bogotá in April 1781: '. . . these days, books destructive of the whole spirit of ecclesiastical immunity are permitted . . . In former times Spaniards coming to the Indies used to teach good, civil customs, but those who arrive today simply teach new sins, heretical maxims and bad habits . . .' The pasquinade then went on to denounce the schemes put forward by royal officials for the reform of higher education and the foundation of a university offering a modern curriculum.[184] It was the authorities who wished to promote the cause of the Enlightenment in the face of resistance from society. Once the Comunero rebellion was over, it was again authority, in the person of Archbishop

Caballero y Góngora as viceroy, which pressed ahead with educational reform. Later the administration was to reap the reward of its educational efforts when it found itself confronted by a new generation all too willing to embrace foreign and revolutionary ideas.[185]

These inflammatory foreign doctrines found their realization in the American and French revolutions, which aspired to put into practice political ideas that had long formed the subject of passionate European debate. Their exposure to that debate gave the leaders of the North American rebellion access to a wider set of political and cultural traditions than those enjoyed by their Spanish American counterparts in the 1770s. This in turn is likely to have enhanced their capacity to adjust their positions in the light of evolving events and to come up with new solutions when obstacles blocked their path. The eventual outcome was a genuinely new political creation – an independent federal republic on a potentially continental scale.

The intellectual resourcefulness displayed by the American Patriots once they had taken the decision to break with the British crown made them a difficult enemy to defeat. Even in the worst moments of the war they could sustain morale by holding before the people the vision of independence, and with it the hope of ushering in 'a New Order of the Ages'. In reply to this Britain had little to offer but the commercial and practical benefits that would flow from a return to loyalty and the ending of the war.

Although the British entered that war determined to uphold imperial authority, even at the price of fighting their own kith and kin, the suppression of the rebellion moved to second place in their list of priorities following France's entry into the conflict in 1778. The immediate priority was now the protection of the West Indies from French attack. In the changed circumstances even George III began to weaken in his obstinate determination to bring the Americans to heel. It was, he felt, 'so desirable to end the war with that country, to be enabled with redoubled ardour to avenge the faithless and insolent conduct of France . . .'[186]

Although it now became possible to contemplate the eventual granting of independence to the Americans, Lord North's ministry, in spite of internal opposition and the rise of domestic discontents, successfully kept the country at war with the nascent republic right up to the time of his fall from power in February 1782.[187] The surrender at Yorktown, however, in October 1781 destroyed any realistic prospect of recovering the colonies, and when the Rockingham administration came to office it was determined to wind up the American war. The loss of the thirteen colonies was a bitter pill to swallow, but its effects were tempered by the retention of Canada and the West Indies, and still more by the emerging prospects of a new and greater empire in India and the East.

For Spain, on the other hand, there was no alternative empire in prospect if its American possessions should be lost. Deprived of the silver of Mexico and Peru, what kind of future awaited it? The crown therefore remained totally committed to the retention of its American empire and to the continuing development of American resources for the benefit of the mother country. At the same time, the revolts in New Granada and Peru administered a drastic shock to the system. Manuel Godoy, the future first minister of Charles IV of Spain, was later to write in his memoirs: 'Nobody is unaware how close we were to losing in the years 1781–2 the whole viceroyalty of Peru and part of La Plata, when the famous Condorcanqui raised the standard of rebellion . . . The swell from this storm was felt with more or less strength in New Granada, and even reached New Spain.'[188]

The shock of the storm was made all the worse by the coincidence of the rebellions in Spain's empire with the winning of independence by Britain's American colonies. The implications of the American Revolution for the Spanish viceroyalties frightened the Spanish ministers. It also frightened the Count of Aranda, who, after losing ministerial office, had watched the development of events from a ringside seat as ambassador to France. In a secret memorandum of 1783, following the signing of the Peace of Versailles, he warned Charles III that 'it has never been possible to retain for long such large possessions at such enormous distances from the metropolis.' Presciently he argued that the new United States, although for the present a pygmy, would grow into a giant which would first want to absorb Florida and then would cast covetous eyes on New Spain. In order to save what could be saved of Spain's Atlantic empire he therefore proposed that mainland America should be divided into three independent kingdoms – Mexico, Peru and the remaining mainland territories – each to be ruled by a prince of the Spanish royal house, while the King of Spain himself assumed the title of Emperor. Each kingdom would make an annual contribution to the Spanish crown in the form of precious metals or colonial produce, and the Spanish and American royal houses would intermarry in perpetuity.[189]

Nothing came of Aranda's proposal, which had as little chance of implementation as Lord Shelburne's despairing attempt in the preceding year to save Britain's North American empire by reconstituting it as a consortium of independent states, each with its own assembly but still subject to the crown – a proposal that earned from Franklin the scathing retort that 'surely there was never a more preposterous chimera conceived in the brain of a minister.'[190] Madrid was in no mood to retreat from empire. A strong military establishment and a continued but judiciously applied programme of reforms seemed to be the best way of avoiding the fate that had overtaken Britain's American possessions. This remained Charles III's chosen policy up to the time of his death in 1788 on the eve of the French Revolution.

Yet it remained an open question how long the ministers in Madrid could hope to hold the line in a world swept by revolutionary winds. By now, as Madrid feared, a handful of Spanish American creoles were beginning to think the previously unthinkable. Among them was Francisco de Miranda, a Venezuelan who had joined the Spanish army as an infantry captain. Appointed aide to the Spanish commander in Cuba, he fought against the British in Pensacola and helped the French fleet to reach the Chesapeake Bay and provide the support which would enable Washington to secure the surrender of Cornwallis at Yorktown. Miranda later described his reactions to the settlement negotiated between the Comuneros and the royal authorities: 'When I realized on receiving the Pact of Zipaquirá how simple and inexperienced the Americans were, and on the other hand how astute and perfidious the Spanish agents had proved, I thought it best to suffer for a time in patience until the Anglo-American colonies achieved their independence, which was bound to be . . . the infallible preliminary to our own.'[191] If Miranda's was the voice of the future, the curtain was finally descending on a repetitive and long-running drama – the drama of confrontation followed by accommodation that had enabled Spain to retain its empire of the Indies for nearly 300 years.

CHAPTER 12

A New World in the Making

The search for legitimacy

The Articles of Confederation which bound the rebellious North American colonies together into a precarious Union were agreed by Congress, after intense debate, in November 1777. Union did not come easily. The intensity of local loyalties had traditionally militated against inter-colonial collaboration, and numerous boundary disputes, like those which pitted Virginia against its neighbours for control of Indian territory west of the Alleghenies, fanned the flames of rivalry. There were, too, deep social, political and ideological divisions within each of the newly united states over the character of the republic that was now to be established.

Resistance and revolution had both encouraged and brought into positions of prominence radical elements in the various colonies, motivated not only by hostility to continuing British rule but also by resentment at the dominance of traditional elites. These radicals, deeply engaged in framing their own state constitutions, had no intention of replacing one centralizing authority – that of the King of England – by another, the Congress of the United States. The new Confederation must be firmly grounded on the rights of individual states and the principle of popular sovereignty, and, for some at least, this sovereignty had to be 'popular' in the most democratic sense of the word. Against these populist radicals were ranged those more conservative elements in society, not least from among the mercantile and planter elites, who were horrified by the outbreaks of mob violence that had accompanied the Revolution, viewed with deep concern the prospect of 'democratic' rule in the new republic, and were convinced of the need for a strong executive, both to prosecute the war of independence to a successful conclusion, and to maintain political and social stability once the war was won.[1]

Given these deep differences, it is not surprising that it took until March 1781 for the Articles of Confederation to be ratified by all thirteen states. The western land question in particular proved enormously contentious, with states that had no western land claims anxious to ensure that newly settled territories should form part of a genuinely national domain. A combination of hard bargaining and the pressures of war eventually brought the recalcitrant states to heel, with Maryland taking up the rear. The approval of the Articles formally endowed the new republic with a national government. Reflecting the balance of political forces during the revolutionary years, however, the 'national' element in the Confederation set up by the Articles was weak in relation to the federal element. As the new republic found itself confronted by the enormous problems of the post-war era – a heavy burden of debt, a depreciated currency, widespread social unrest, and the unresolved question of expansion to the west – there were growing doubts about its long-term prospects for survival. The states were drawing in again on themselves, and Congress, its reputation in decline, was proving increasingly powerless to mediate disputes and halt the general process of drift. Each new problem that emerged in these immediate post-war years appeared to strengthen the force of the conventional argument that a republic could only be viable so long as it was small.[2]

Those Americans who gave thought to the future of their country as one in which a kingless people would live together in harmony on a continental scale were driven by the logic of events to realize that they were faced by a challenge of even greater magnitude than that of overthrowing British rule. Their revolution would not be complete until they had succeeded in devising a new political order in which the claims of the component states to sovereign rights and of individuals to their fundamental liberties would be balanced by the creation of a central executive strong enough to regulate matters of mutual concern and to defend American interests on the international stage. In the years after the winning of independence this challenge was to exercise the most creative minds in the new republic, and not least that of James Madison, who had become keenly aware, while representing his home state of Virginia in the Congress, of the weaknesses and inadequacy of the Articles of Confederation.

The balance of forces in the Congress had favoured those elements in the society of revolutionary America determined to secure in perpetuity the rights of the states by granting a bare minimum of powers to the central executive. The 55 delegates to the Constitutional Convention which met in Philadelphia in May 1787, on the other hand, were of a background and temperament that tended to predispose them towards a strengthening of the national government. For Thomas Jefferson, scrutinizing the list of names in Paris, where he had been posted as the minister of the new republic, the Convention was 'an assembly of demigods'.[3] Largely drawn from the political elite of their states, most of the delegates had been associated with the Revolution in one way or another, and between them they had accumulated an impressive range of political experience at both the local and the national level. Of the 55, 42 had served at one time or another in Congress,[4] and in spite of their intense loyalty to their own state, many of them, like Madison, had come to see the overriding need for a more effective system of government.

The task that Madison set himself was to replace the Articles of Confederation with a constitution that would establish a strong national government, but one that was firmly based on the foundation of genuine popular sovereignty. The task inevitably required much squaring of the circle. Hard and often acrimonious bargaining was required to hammer out often painful compromises between competing interests. The most successful of these compromises was the provision whereby representation in the lower house of the legislature would be apportioned on the basis of population, while in the upper house the states would enjoy equal votes. The least successful was on the hopelessly divisive issues of slavery and the slave trade. Any attempt to abolish slavery would effectively strangle the union at birth, and the overriding concern at this moment was to keep the republic alive and ensure that its vital organs were strong enough to let it breathe and grow. This could only be achieved by a series of deals in which the continuation of slavery was obliquely confirmed by a number of sections in the articles of the new constitution. For purposes of representation in the House of Representatives, slaves were to be counted as three-fifths of a person, and a further period of twenty years' grace was allowed before Congress would return to the issue of the slave trade.[5] Evasiveness in this instance was the prerequisite for survival.

Having appropriated the name of 'Federalists' for themselves, those who favoured a strong national executive took their case to the people in the great national debate over the ratification of the proposed new constitution in 1787–8. In the hard-fought struggle between Federalists and anti-Federalists, it was the Federalists who prevailed. With its ratification by the ninth of the thirteen states, New Hampshire, in June 1788, the new constitution officially became the law of the land, although four states, including Virginia and New York, were still holding out. But when both these major states agreed to ratification a few weeks later, although by narrow majorities, the battle was won.

When it came to choosing the first president of the new republic, the choice was foreordained. One figure, the hero of the war of independence, towered above the rest. The election of George Washington in March 1789 conferred dignity on the institution of the presidency while guaranteeing moderation and common sense in the exercise of its powers. Above all it linked, in the person of a renowned and universally respected individual, the revolutionary struggle against the British to the great constitutional experiment on which the newly established United States of America was now well and truly embarked.

In 1787, while the Federalists and anti-Federalists in North America were fighting each other for the soul of the new republic, Thomas Jefferson wrote from Paris to the secretary of the American delegation in London: 'You ask me if any thing transpires here on the subject of S. America? Not a word. I know that there are combustible materials there, and that they wait the torch only.'[6] His assessment, however, proved premature. In New Granada and Peru the fires had been effectively extinguished, and in the central regions of the viceroyalty of New Spain no figure emerged to light the torch of rebellion when harvest failure and a devastating shortage of food provoked widespread social disruption in 1785–6.[7]

Although the North American example encouraged a few radicals like Francisco de Miranda to dream and conspire, the Spanish crown seemed to have succeeded in damping down the combustible materials, and had emerged from the conflagrations of the early 1780s with its authority reaffirmed.

With the confidence given them by the sense of a crisis overcome, José de Gálvez and his colleagues in Madrid pressed ahead with their restructuring of the old administrative system, extending administration by intendants to Peru in 1784 and to New Spain in 1786. Gálvez himself died in 1787 but ministers continued to pursue the programme of reform, and most notably the reform of the transatlantic trading system which had been inaugurated by the proclamation of 'free trade' in 1778. In this they were responding to continuing pressures from the peripheral regions of the Iberian peninsula for a foothold in a commercial system long dominated by the Consulado of Cadiz. Statistics suggesting that the ten years since the promulgation of the decree had seen a threefold expansion in colonial trade were sufficiently encouraging to persuade them to extend the system to Venezuela in 1788, and then in the following year to New Spain.

In reality the trading system remained heavily protectionist, in spite of its gestures towards the now fashionable economic liberalism. Yet for all its limitations it did afford greater latitude to Iberian and Spanish American merchants conducting business outside the old monopolistic structure. It also helped to stimulate economic activity in hitherto marginalized regions of the Indies, although simultaneously generating new inter-colonial rivalries as different provinces competed for a share of the expanding opportunities.[8]

The fiscal and economic rewards which Madrid anticipated from the latest phase of the reform programme were, however, soon offset by the impact of war. Spain would pay a high price for its intervention in the American War of Independence. Trade was disrupted by the English naval blockade, ships were lost and businesses paralysed. New wars brought further disruption in the 1790s. Charles III died at the end of 1788, and the new reign of Charles IV was overshadowed almost from the start by the outbreak of revolution in France. In the spring of 1793 revolutionary France declared war on Spain, shortly after Charles IV had dispensed with the services of the last of his father's team of ministers, the Count of Aranda. The royal favourite, the young and politically inexperienced guards officer Manuel Godoy, now became first secretary of state. The new war brought Spain into uneasy partnership with Great Britain, whose maritime supremacy was resented and feared by Madrid. It also had the effect of cutting off the supply of French products traditionally re-exported by Spanish merchants to the Indies, opening the lucrative Spanish American market to penetration not only by British merchants but also by those of the United States.

Godoy's anxieties over the threat to Spain's American empire from British naval and commercial power persuaded him of the need to change tack. In October 1796 Spain joined regicide France in an offensive and defensive alliance against Great Britain. French support was to come at a price. In 1800, at the treaty of San Ildefonso, Spain agreed under pressure from Napoleon to restore Louisiana to the

French, although Charles IV, anxious about the growing power of the United States and its implication for the future of the Floridas, only accepted the transfer on condition that Louisiana was not subsequently relinquished to a third party. In 1802 Spain duly transferred Louisiana to French rule, but in the following year Napoleon reneged on his promise and sold it to the United States. Thanks to President Jefferson's opportune negotiation of the Louisiana purchase the new republic had doubled its territory at a stroke, weakening in the process Spain's already precarious hold on the Floridas, which would eventually be ceded to the United States in 1819, and opening the road to the colonization of the American interior.[9]

The concessions forced upon Charles IV to secure the support of the French failed to yield the expected results. The war with Great Britain, which continued until 1802 and was then renewed in 1804, proved a disaster for Spain. In February 1797 its fleet was defeated at the battle of Cape St Vincent, and the British seized the island of Trinidad, off the Venezuelan coast. The blockade of Cadiz by the British fleet made it impossible for Spain to keep the American market supplied, and Madrid was compelled to open Spanish American ports to neutral carriers. Again United States traders were the great beneficiaries, supplying wheat, flour and other commodities to the Spanish Antilles, Venezuela and New Granada. The new protectionist system launched by Madrid under the deceptive flag of 'free trade', and intended to make the peninsula the metropolis of a great commercial empire on the British model, had effectively collapsed.[10]

While economic control of the Indies was slipping irrevocably out of Spanish hands, more than a decade of almost continuous warfare placed the finances of the Spanish crown under intolerable strain. Both in Spain and in the Indies the wealth of the church and of religious and charitable institutions proved an irresistible attraction to a near-bankrupt state. An encouraging precedent existed in the seizure of Jesuit property on both sides of the Atlantic in 1767. In 1798 the crown decreed the disentailment and auction of church property in peninsular Spain, the resulting funds being used to consolidate loans to meet the costs of war. In 1804, following the renewal of war with England, this Law of Consolidation was extended to charitable funds in Spanish America. The measure aroused intense anger. Over large parts of America, church assets were integral to the working of the credit system, and the new law meant in effect the forced sale of large numbers of private estates and businesses as proprietors were compelled by the withdrawal of credit to redeem the capital value of their loans. Not all regions were equally affected, but New Spain, where mining and other enterprises were heavily reliant on credit and where the viceroy José de Iturrigaray energetically enforced the royal order, was especially hard hit. By the time the decree was revoked five years later enormous damage had been done. Mining, agriculture and trade had all been drastically affected, and parish priests and clergy living on interest from loans saw their livelihood gone. Already undermined by the regalist policies of Charles III, the church–state alliance, the central pillar of the elaborate edifice of Spain's empire of the Indies, was beginning to totter.[11]

In spite of increased revenues from the Indies, which constituted a fifth of the Spanish treasury's receipts in the period between 1784 and 1805,[12] the Spanish state was now struggling to keep afloat. Its finances were heavily mortgaged; the combination of harvest failures and depression in Spain's war-damaged economy was generating fresh social tensions; and Godoy's government was in disarray. In March 1808 he was overthrown in a palace coup and Charles IV was forced to abdicate in favour of his son and heir, Ferdinand, Prince of Asturias. But Napoleon had had enough of his unreliable Spanish ally. As French forces moved on Madrid, the new king, Ferdinand VII, was lured to France, where he joined his parents and Godoy in exile at Bayonne. On 10 May he too was forced to abdicate. When Napoleon subsequently transferred the crown to Joseph Bonaparte, there was no longer an uncontested source of legitimate authority in Spain and its empire of the Indies.

The overthrow of the Bourbons and the French occupation unleashed a popular uprising which plunged the peninsula into years of chaos and war that would only end with the defeat of the French and the restoration of the Bourbons in 1814. Not only metropolitan Spain but also its overseas empire were confronted with a crisis of unprecedented proportions. With a power vacuum at the very centre of the imperial government in Madrid, where did legitimate authority lie? To some extent, Spain's American empire had been faced with a comparable problem on the death of Carlos II in 1700, but the problem had been quickly transcended as the overseas viceroyalties fell into line behind Carlos's legally designated successor, Philip V. But the situation this time was very different. Joseph Bonaparte was a usurper; Ferdinand VII was in exile; and, as Jefferson had written in 1787, 'there are combustible materials there and they wait the torch only.' Would the overthrow of the dynasty prove to be the torch?

The collapse of royal power in the Hispanic world precipitated a very different kind of crisis from that which faced Britain's American colonies in the 1770s. The Spanish American crisis of 1808 was brought about by the absence, not the exercise, of imperial authority. In this sense it was closer to the situation created in the English Atlantic world by the execution of Charles I. But although the regicide of 1649 and the subsequent transfer of imperial authority to the people in parliament posed serious constitutional and practical problems for colonies that owed their existence to royal charters, the policies pursued by the imperial government under the Commonwealth and Protectorate were sufficiently respectful of established institutions and interests to prevent violent confrontation, even with those colonies which had proclaimed their loyalty to the dead king's son.[13] The transition was further eased by the willingness of the new regime to abide by the largely non-interventionist approach of its predecessor to the internal affairs of the colonial societies. Moreover, the Cromwellian government spoke a language of national power which they could both understand and respect.

The peoples of Spanish America, on the other hand, had lived for centuries under a royal government which was traditionally interventionist in principle, if not always in practice. They had grown accustomed to conducting their lives by reference to the royal authority, however ineffectual it might often have been. Now suddenly that authority was gone, and they found themselves drifting rudderless on an ocean of uncertainty. Nor could they expect metropolitan Spain to come to their rescue. The country was in chaos, and the ships that arrived from Spanish ports at irregular intervals brought conflicting messages and tardy news of a war that was going from bad to worse.

As the people of Spain took up arms, a number of regional and local juntas sprang to life in the peninsula to organize popular resistance against the French. In September 1808 these juntas were co-ordinated with some difficulty into a Junta Central, which took refuge in Seville after the French capture of Madrid. As French forces moved southwards into Andalusia in January 1810, the Junta again fled, this time to Cadiz, which was sheltered by the protective power of the British fleet. Here the Junta dissolved itself in favour of a Regency Council acting on behalf of the exiled Ferdinand VII, the *deseado*, the longed-for king.

Although the Regency Council was a conservative body, it was dependent on the mercantile oligarchy of Cadiz, which was politically liberal, although tenacious in its determination to cling to what remained of its privileged position in the American trade. Under pressure from the Cadiz elite, the Regency Council went ahead with plans already set in train by the Junta Central for the convocation of a great national assembly, or Cortes, in which deputies from Spanish America were also invited to participate. The Cortes assembled in Cadiz on 14 September 1810 and were to remain in session until the restoration of Ferdinand VII in 1814.[14]

With the king in exile, and metropolitan Spain apparently on the point of being engulfed by the tide of the French advance, the four viceroyalties and nine presidencies and captaincies-general which constituted Spain's American empire were thrown back on their own devices. In contrast to the British American colonies, these diverse territories had no colonial assemblies to act as potential alternative sources of leadership if royal authority were challenged or collapsed. The cabildos of major cities, like Mexico City, Lima and Bogotá, traditionally put forward claims to speak on behalf of the wider community, but these claims were liable to be contested by rival town councils, and there was no generally accepted forum for the discussion and resolution of problems of common concern to the territory as a whole. Not surprisingly, therefore, in 1808 different territories adopted different *ad hoc* solutions to the problem of legitimacy – solutions which reflected the balance of local forces in societies already under strain from the tensions created by ethnic diversity and by the antagonism between creoles and *peninsulares*.

Yet it was the search for legitimacy rather than aspirations after independence that initially dictated the course of events. The instinctive reaction, in Spanish America as in metropolitan Spain, was to resort to the principle that, in the absence of the legitimate monarch, sovereignty reverted to the people. This was the principle that legitimized the juntas that had sprung into life in the peninsula when the monarchy was overthrown. When 'the kingdom found itself suddenly without a king or a government', declared the supreme junta of Seville in 1808,

'. . . the people legally resumed the power to create a government.'[15] As news of events in Spain trickled across the Atlantic, the Americans followed the Spanish example. Following the arrival of letters in Caracas in July 1808 ordering the authorities to take the oath of allegiance to Joseph Bonaparte, the city council urged the captain-general to set up a junta to decide on the course of action to be taken.[16] Similarly, the councils of Mexico City, Bogotá, Quito and Buenos Aires would all see in the formation of provisional juntas acting in the name of Ferdinand VII an appropriate mechanism for ensuring the legitimation of authority through the assertion of the popular will.[17]

There was, however, in America as in Spain, an inherent tension between the absolutist traditions of Bourbon monarchy as legitimately represented by the exiled Ferdinand VII and a doctrine of popular sovereignty which, although rooted in medieval Hispanic constitutionalism, was in the process of acquiring the colouring and characteristics of a new and very different age. The reforming ministers of Charles III had persistently sought to remould the aggregated territories of the old Habsburg monarchy and their privileged corporations into a unitary nation-state subordinate to a benevolent but all-powerful monarch.[18] In the peninsula the incipient sense of Spanish nationhood that ministers had tried so hard to inculcate was dramatically transmuted by the French invasion into the full-blooded nationalist response of a mass uprising. But at the same time the crisis of legitimacy created by the events of 1808 gave those sections of Spanish opinion which had assimilated revolutionary French and American notions of popular sovereignty an unparalleled opportunity to reconstruct on liberal foundations the antiquated edifice of old regime Spain. Their instrument for the process of reconstruction would be the Cortes of Cadiz, which enthusiastically set about endowing Spain with a written constitution that would hold monarchical power in check. Ferdinand in his exile might still be an unknown quantity, but a liberal Cortes and an absolutist dynasty were infallibly set on a collision course.

In America, the attempts of Charles III's ministers to encompass his New World subjects within the framework of the unitary nation-state had proved counter-productive. The imposition of unpopular fiscal measures and the replacement of creoles by *peninsulares* in offices which they believed belonged to them of right had merely heightened traditional resentments against the mother country. Denied participation in the Bourbon nation-state on an equal basis with the peoples of metropolitan Spain, the creoles were confirmed in their belief that they had been rejected by the community to which they had always thought they belonged. In British America the colonial elites had felt a similar sense of rejection when confronted by the assertive nationalism emanating from the metropolitan centre in the triumphalist years of Britain's victory over France. For reasons they failed to understand they had been excluded from the victory feast.[19]

The British colonists, however, had not gone as far as their Spanish American counterparts in developing a historically based creole patriotic mythology into which their sense of injustice could be incorporated. Unable to win redress for their grievances by asserting their claims to their hereditary English privileges, they turned in exasperation to the invocation of their natural rather than their historic rights. The consciousness of a distinctively American identity that eventually emerged in the thirteen colonies was less a cause than a consequence of revolution, the outcome of their shared experience of war and nation-building as they sought to establish a republic dedicated to the consecration and diffusion of those natural rights.

By contrast, renewed metropolitan pressure since the mid-century on the creoles of Spanish America had reinforced an existing sense of distinctive identities already well rooted in time and place. By 1808 a new generation of Spanish Americans had begun to pick up the new international language of universal natural rights, but the predominant language remained that of a plurality of creole patriotisms, operating within the traditional framework of the Spanish imperial monarchy. These local patriotisms, however, were too circumscribed, both socially and geographically, to have created by 1808 genuinely 'national' movements aspiring to independence from Spain.[20] Socially they hardly extended beyond the creole elite, leaving only the most notional space for the other ethnic groups. Geographically they tended to be confined to the leading cities and their hinterlands. Even within the larger-sized administrative units created by Spanish imperialism, local patriotism proved dangerously divisive.

The question posed by the catastrophe of 1808 was whether creole patriotism could still be contained within the framework of the imperial monarchy once legitimate authority had collapsed. Spurred by hostility to France and to Godoy, who had appointed several of the peninsular officials currently in office,[21] creole elites across America responded initially to the news from Spain by rallying to the cause of Ferdinand VII. At the same time, however, they saw in the crisis their chance to reverse the unpopular royal policies of recent years, like the Law of Consolidation, and secure a degree of control over their own affairs which would effectively amount to self-government. As they began to talk of sovereignty reverting to the people in the absence of the king, and organized town meetings and juntas to chart the way forward, their behaviour inevitably provoked confrontations with royal officials and *peninsulares*, who feared that Spain's American empire would soon go the way of Britain's, and who were desperate to cling to the remnants of metropolitan authority.

Normality, or at least the appearance of it, was best maintained in Peru, where memories of the Túpac Amaru revolt were still raw, and where the viceroy, José Fernando de Abascal, played his cards with skill.[22] Elsewhere, 1808 and 1809 were years of conspiracies and coups. The situation was especially acute in New Spain, where the viceroy, José de Iturrigaray, was regarded by *peninsular* officials as too sympathetic to creole aspirations, and was deposed in October 1808 by a group of *peninsulares,* acting with the connivance of Spanish merchants, landlords and high-ranking clerics. The conspirators, supported by a privately recruited militia, known as the Volunteers of Ferdinand VII, followed up their success by imposing a repressive and reactionary regime which would only serve to stoke the fires of resentment against Spanish domination.[23]

In 1809 a British observer, possibly James Mill writing under the pseudonym of 'William Burke', wrote that 'Spanish America is, virtually, independent at this moment.'[24] Whether creole hopes for autonomy, however, would tip over into full-blown demands for independence was very much an open question in 1809–10. The situation was changing in both Spain and America with extreme rapidity, and what was unthinkable one day became thinkable the next. On the one hand there were indications of a new receptiveness to creole aspirations in Spain itself, while inside America, on the other hand, there was growing disaffection over the opposition of Spanish officials and Spanish interest groups to those aspirations. At the same time, the loosening of imperial control created opportunities for radicals, especially on the fringes of empire, to spread, and act upon, revolutionary ideas which were now emerging into the open after years of twilight circulation.

In January 1809 the Spanish Junta Central issued a decree which suggested that metropolitan Spain was at last prepared to listen to long-standing American complaints. In the name of Ferdinand VII it affirmed that 'the vast and precious dominions which Spain possesses in the Indies are not properly colonies, or *factorías*, like those of other nations, but an essential and integral part of the Spanish Monarchy.' In order to tighten 'the sacred bonds uniting the various dominions', the overseas territories were now to enjoy 'national representation', and were asked to send deputies to join the Junta Central.[25] There was a clear inequality of numbers – nine Americans to thirty-six deputies from metropolitan Spain – but for the first time American representatives had been asked to take their place in a central organ of Spanish government. These were, moreover, to be elected representatives, one for each kingdom. This, too, was a novelty. The elections were to fall to the city councils, and there were lengthy and complicated debates over electoral procedures and over how important a city must be to qualify for the franchise.[26]

The elections in America were overtaken by the decision of the Junta Central to summon a national assembly, and the American territories were duly invited to send deputies to the Cortes that eventually met in Cadiz in the autumn of 1810. These Cortes, entrusted with the task of restructuring the government of Spain, were to embark on an unprecedented exercise – the drafting of a constitution for a nation-state of which an overseas empire formed an integral part.[27] The House of Commons had shown no interest when Franklin argued in 1767 that 'a fair and equal representation of all parts of this Empire in Parliament, is the only firm Basis on which its political Grandeur and Stability can be founded.'[28] Instead it was happy to assume, as Thomas Whately assumed in 1767, that the colonists were 'virtually represented' in parliament, and that this was sufficient.[29] Now the Regency Council and the Cortes of Cadiz were taking the road that Britain had failed to take, although they were doing so with very little knowledge of the true situation in Spain's American territories. In its place they cherished a blind faith that Spain and America were afflicted by the same ills, and that a 'common cure' would do for both.[30]

The number of deputies allocated to the American territories was in fact very far from allowing for that 'fair and equal representation' that Franklin had demanded for the American colonists in the British imperial parliament. This inequality in their representation was to be a major source of grievance to the Americans even before the Cortes assembled. The Junta of Caracas complained in May 1810 of the 'disproportion in the number of deputies to the population of America', and the question of proportionality was promptly taken up, although unsuccessfully, by the American representatives when the Cortes convened. This was a point on which the Spanish deputies were afraid to give ground. Contemporary estimates put the population of Spanish America at between 15 and 16 million, as against a Spanish population of 10 million, and metropolitan Spain could not afford to let itself be outvoted by its imperial possessions.[31]

Beyond the question of numbers lay the even more intractable question of how to integrate into a nation-state established on the principle of popular sovereignty a number of erstwhile colonies that were now to enjoy juridical parity with the metropolis. The British colonies after winning their independence solved a comparable problem by transforming themselves into a federal republic in which central authority and local autonomy were carefully balanced. Spanish liberals, however, rejected the notion of a republic, which was too closely associated with revolutionary France and its invading armies to be an acceptable solution, and hoped instead to turn their country into a British-style constitutional monarchy. But their instincts were to centralize, and it was not easy to see how centralizing tendencies could be reconciled with American demands for local autonomy, or how the resulting structure could be convincingly articulated into a unitary nation-state in the form of a constitutional monarchy spanning the Atlantic.[32]

The times, in any event, could scarcely have been less propitious for a novel constitutional experiment of this kind. From early 1810, when it seemed that the entire peninsula was about to fall into French hands, the American territories independently began taking emergency measures to ensure their own survival. The city council of Caracas was the first to act. The captain-general, Vicente Emparán, was looked upon as a francophile who might well deliver Venezuela into the hands of Joseph Bonaparte. The new Regency Council in Spain, for its part, was seen as the instrument of the Consulado of Cadiz merchants, and therefore as a threat to the freedom of trade essential to the survival of Venezuela's export economy. In April 1810 the Caracas council transformed itself into a Supreme Junta, and voted Emparán out of office, while simultaneously rejecting the authority of the Regency Council in Spain. It was careful, however, to explain that it was not declaring its independence of the mother country, but was acting to preserve the rights of Ferdinand VII.[33]

A month later the mercantile and landowning elite of Buenos Aires reacted in much the same way as that of Caracas to the news from Spain, and for much the same reasons, although here the city council was dominated by *peninsulares*, and the pressure for action in May 1810 came from outside the council. Since the creation of the viceroyalty of La Plata in 1776 and its release from its old dependency on Lima, Buenos Aires had prospered.[34] The liberalization of trade had brought growth in the export trade in hides and agricultural produce, although the silver of Upper Peru remained the viceroyalty's principal export. It was with this silver that Buenos Aires merchants paid for the European manu-factured goods which they made it their business to distribute through the continent.[35]

The French occupation of Spain and the establishment of a Regency Council suspected of wanting to promote the restrictive interests of the Cadiz merchants made the creole elite of Buenos Aires, like that of Caracas, fearful for the future. But the successful repulse by the militia regiments of two attempted invasions by British expeditionary forces in 1806 and 1807 had generated a new sense of local pride and self-reliance, while leaving the inadequacy of the viceregal administra-tion painfully exposed. The creole elite, therefore, with the support of the local militia, felt confident enough to bypass the peninsula-controlled city council, establish a junta and overthrow the viceroy.[36]

Over the summer and autumn of 1810 similar moves for the removal of local governors and officials and the establishment of juntas occurred in Santiago de Chile, Cartagena and Santa Fe de Bogotá, as a chain reaction developed across the continent. The juntas all claimed, like that of Caracas, to be acting in the name of the people to preserve the rights of their legitimate ruler, Ferdinand VII. The next step, intended to broaden the basis of support for further action, was likely to be the calling of a national congress, as in Buenos Aires in the 'May Revolution' of 1810, and in Caracas and Santiago de Chile in March and July of 1811 respectively.[37] The Cortes of Cadiz, at least as much as the French and American models, were the inspiration behind the calling of these assemblies.[38] Based on a narrow electorate of property-holders, their convocation would allow the creole elites to consolidate their still precarious hold on power while simultaneously speaking the language of popular sovereignty.

Beneath a veneer of legality, therefore, one after another the creole elites of Spanish America were exploiting the weakness of the metropolitan government to grasp at local autonomy. This was still autonomy within the framework of the monarchy and empire, but the framework was now so weak that autonomous provinces would in practice be more or less free to do as they pleased. These years, however, had seen the emergence of constellations of radicals who would be con-tent with nothing less than separation from the Spanish crown and total inde-pendence. This was particularly true of Venezuela, where the gilded youth of Caracas responded with enthusiasm to the ideas of liberty enshrined in the French and American revolutions. A minority among the members of the newly founded Patriotic Society, influenced by that veteran revolutionary Francisco de Miranda and the visionary young Simón Bolivar, was now actively working for a free and independent republic. It was under the inspiration of Bolívar's oratory in the national congress that the old creole elite joined forces with the young Patriots on 5 July 1811 to proclaim the independence of Venezuela – the first such decla-ration in the territories of Spain's American empire. They proceeded to draft a new and nominally democratic constitution on the model of the federal constitution of the United States. Its life, however, was short. The decision taken by the national congress plunged the country into civil war, and within a year the first Venezuelan republic had collapsed.[39]

The failure of the Venezuelan republic was an early indication of the obstacles on the road that led to genuine independence. From the beginning, strong forces were ranged against movements for autonomy, which looked to many people like mere preliminaries to total separation from Spain. The coup that had been launched in New Spain in 1808 by peninsular Spaniards and creoles closely identified with Spanish interests revealed the strength of these forces. Their subsequent dominance provoked a backlash in October 1810, when Miguel Hidalgo, the parish priest of the town of Dolores in the Bajío, tolled the church bell to launch what he hoped would become a national insurrection. As massed bands of peasants – Indians and castas – rallied behind the image of the Virgin of Guadalupe on Hidalgo's southward march, it looked for a moment as if the entire viceroyalty would be swept up in a general rebellion which would put an end to the dominance of the hated *peninsulares*. But Hidalgo's inability to restrain the indiscriminate violence of his followers, and a programme of social reforms that included the abolition of Indian tribute and of ethnic distinctions, rapidly alienated the creole elite which had at first seen the rebellion as favouring their bid for autonomy. Their fear of social upheaval, as in Peru after the revolt of Túpac Amaru, proved stronger than their dislike of *peninsulares*, with whom they now made common cause to stem the tide of violence. With the great mass of provincial as well as regular troops remaining loyal to the authorities, Hidalgo's revolt was crushed.[40]

If alarm at the prospect of ethnic and class warfare held back even those creoles most anxious to free themselves from metropolitan shackles, local and provincial rivalries also obstructed their moves to seize autonomy. The town councils of Coro and Maracaibo, for instance, refused to follow Caracas in 1810 and instead declared their support for the Regency Council in Spain.[41] Similarly, the revolution of May 1810 in Buenos Aires was opposed by the rival city of Montevideo in the so-called Banda Oriental – the future Uruguay – and also by the interior provinces of the viceroyalty of La Plata, Paraguay and Upper Peru.[42] These regions had their own agendas and their own economic concerns, and were more inclined to rally to the Spanish authorities than to follow a Buenos Aires whose dominance they resented.

Loyalism in Spanish America, as in the rebel British colonies a generation earlier, had many different faces.[43] As the reactions of Maracaibo or Montevideo indicated, it contained, as in British America, a strong economic and geographical determinant. In Venezuela the fault-line ran between the mercantile and landowning elite of Caracas and the Indian peasants and *pardos* (people with some degree of African ancestry) who ranged freely with their animals over the *llanos* – the grasslands of the interior – and saw the crown as their protector against the growing menace of encroachment by the Caracas landowners.[44]

In British America the loyalist regions similarly tended to be those regions facing, or already suffering from, the economic and political dominance of richer adjoining areas. Such regions included the Appalachian frontier territories whose thinly settled inhabitants looked to the crown to protect their way of life as hunters, trappers and traders against the advance of close agricultural settlement.[45]

Geography was far from being the sole determinant of loyalty. As events in the viceroyalties of Peru and New Spain suggested, the extent of the ethnic division in Spain's American territories was liable to make loyalists of creoles who might otherwise have been inclined to favour the struggle for autonomy. The fear of social and racial upheaval in a Venezuela where over 50 per cent of the population was of mixed blood and where there were repeated slave rebellions was to act as a similar restraining influence on the Caracas elite in 1812 and 1814.[46] But in Spanish as in British America there were many whose loyalism was instinctive, rather than merely opportunistic. Creole patriotism had always been compatible with a deep reverence for monarchy, and, as the British North American experience showed, traditional instincts of loyalty died hard even after the king himself came to be seen as the direct source of the people's ills. When, as in Spanish America, the monarch was not the oppressor but the oppressed, an extra emotional element was added to the fervour of loyalty.

Whereas native British officials were relatively few and far between in the pre-revolutionary colonies, there was a hard loyalist core of Spanish officials in Spain's American territories. There were also many Spanish troops and officers in the military establishment in the Indies, although by 1800 European wars and the problem of sending troop reinforcements through British-controlled waters had drastically reduced their number. By the beginning of the new century, Spanish officers, who until 1770 had been in the majority, constituted no more than 36.4 per cent of the total officer corps, with creole officers now predominating. Only 5,500 of the 35,000 men in the army of America were natives of Spain.[47] The church hierarchy had experienced a similar process of Americanization over recent decades, but just over half of the American prelates in the second half of the eighteenth century were still Spanish-born, and these occupied the richest and most influential dioceses.[48]

Alongside Spaniards holding high positions in church and state in the Indies, there were many recent immigrants from Spain, especially in the mercantile community, whose prime affiliation was still likely to be to the country of their birth. Lima alone, with a total population of some 55,000, had 10,000 Spanish residents in 1820.[49] The prominence and wealth of many of these *peninsulares*, and the influence which some of them enjoyed with their fellow Spaniards in the royal administration, made them an exposed and vulnerable group. Yet the widespread antipathy to the *gachupines* did not necessarily rule out an alliance of convenience between them and sections of the creole elite in troubled times. The terror provoked by Hidalgo's insurrection inspired the formation of just such an alliance in New Spain. When the Cortes of Cadiz convened in September 1810 there was still a chance that the shaky edifice of Spain's empire of the Indies might yet be sustained, as Britain's American empire could not be sustained, by a mixture of loyalty and fear.

The end of empire

The most effective grave-diggers of empire are usually the imperialists themselves. The Cortes of Cadiz proved as incapable as the British House of Commons of finding an adequate response to the concerns of the Americans. They could, however, claim a greater justification for their failure. With Spain engaged in a desperate struggle for national survival, the Spanish deputies could not afford to run the risk of losing essential American revenues with which to fight the war. This inevitably limited their room for manoeuvre when confronted with American demands. In particular it meant that American requests for the extension of free trade were consistently rejected. 'No disposition exists here', the British ambassador to the Cortes, Henry Wellesley, wrote from Cadiz in July 1812, 'to make any commercial concessions, even for the important object of tranquillizing America.'[50] Concessions on this front would have further reduced revenues that were already shrinking as a result of troubled conditions in America, although the dominance of the Consulado of Cadiz over the Cortes meant that the lack of any 'disposition' to make commercial concessions was persistently reinforced by the strength of vested interests.[51]

For all the expressions of sympathy coming from liberal Spanish deputies, the American question proved a continuous source of conflict in the debates that eventually culminated in the approval of the new Spanish constitution of 1812. The American representatives naturally saw the Cortes as an opportunity to right long-standing wrongs. Here was the chance to secure for themselves not only control over their own economic activities, but also the equitable share of appointments to offices in church and state which, as the creoles constantly claimed, had been denied them since the earliest years of colonization.[52] They were members of a generation that had felt the full impact of the Bourbon reforms. As a result, they instinctively tended to see the history of Spain's record in America through the distorting lens of their own experience. For them it was a history of 300 years of oppression by an imperial power that had consistently sought to deprive of their proper rights and rewards the descendants of Spaniards who had conquered and settled the land through blood and toil. Theirs was an interpretation of the past that ignored the considerable degree of control acquired by the creoles over their own societies during a long stretch of Spanish rule – a control that had only been seriously challenged in the last decades of the eighteenth century. Now, in the Cortes of Cadiz, they saw their opportunity to redress the balance of an alleged three centuries of tyranny, misunderstanding and contempt.

Liberal-minded Spanish deputies, on the other hand, came to Cadiz with a different agenda, which had little place for, or interest in, American concerns. For them, misgovernment began at home. They looked on the Cortes not, as the Americans looked on them, as a traditional forum for the discussion of grievances and the redress of wrongs, but as a genuinely revolutionary assembly that would set about the task of reconstructing the Spanish nation on the firm constitutional foundation of the sovereignty of the people.[53]

This Spanish nation spanned the Atlantic, but the presence of the American deputies in the Cortes of Cadiz immediately raised the awkward question of who exactly constituted the 'people' of America. No census existed for the overseas territories, and deputies were therefore forced to rely on the estimates contained in the work of Alexander von Humboldt, partially published in French and Spanish between 1806 and 1811.[54] It was thought that of the 15 or 16 million inhabitants of the American territories, some 6 million were Indians, 6 million were castas, and the remainder creoles or Spanish residents.[55] This demographic pattern inevitably propelled the racial question to centre stage. It was in the interest of the American deputies to swell the numbers of those entitled to enjoy full political rights in order to give America parity of representation with Spain in the Cortes. Yet as creoles they were not about to jettison their own predominance over other ethnic groups in the name of a factitious equality. For their part, liberal Spanish deputies spoke with enthusiasm the language of equality, but would not contemplate a system of representation that gave the American deputies a majority in the Cortes over metropolitan Spaniards. Each side therefore had its own strong sectional interests to uphold.

The issue was eventually resolved by compromise and dishonourable deceit. The first article of the 1812 constitution proclaimed the fundamental principle that 'the Spanish nation is the union of all Spaniards of both hemispheres'. The definition of 'Spaniards' in article five was drawn so widely as to include Indians, mestizos, castas or *castas pardas* (defined as those with some element of African ancestry) and free blacks.[56] Slaves were excluded. It turned out, however, that not all 'Spaniards' were deemed to be equally Spanish. Creoles, Indians and mestizos were to have, at least in principle, the same entitlement to representation and participation as metropolitan Spaniards, but members of the *castas pardas*, whose black ancestry carried with it the taint of servility, saw their rights whittled away as the constitution proceeded. Even if deemed 'Spaniards' they were not to be classed as 'citizens', although it was open to individuals to apply to the Cortes for letters of citizenship if they satisfied certain criteria, like good conduct and meritorious service.

Nobody in fact knew what proportion of the population of Spanish America fell under the heading of *castas pardas*. They formed a substantial part of the population of the Antilles, Venezuela and the coastal regions of Peru, and a still appreciable one in Chile, the La Plata provinces and New Spain, where the 1812 census, carried out in accordance with the new constitution, registered some 214,000 persons of African blood out of a total population of 3,100,000.[57] Here, as elsewhere, so many of them had by now been assimilated into the increasingly mixed Indian and white population that one American deputy felt able to assert that no fewer than 10 million of the 16 million inhabitants of Spain's empire of the Indies possessed some element of African ancestry. It was assumed, however, that the effect of their exclusion would be roughly to equalize the participating populations on the two sides of the Atlantic, thus opening the way to the acceptance of parity of representation for Spain and America in future meetings of the Cortes.[58]

The discrimination against people of African ancestry was reinforced by the failure of attempts in the Cortes to abolish either slavery or the slave trade. The constitution of the United States had notoriously side-stepped the issue of slavery, although Section 9 of Article 1 opened the way to the abolition of the slave trade in 1808, after a twenty-year interval.[59] Under the influence of British pressure and the British example, the slavery question was discussed in the Cortes of Cadiz in 1811, but the Cuban representatives played the same role as the southern delegates to the American Constitutional Convention and succeeded in closing off the issue.[60]

If the new Spanish constitution, like that of the United States, was silent or equivocal on matters relating to the black population, it was, at least in principle, far more generous where the Indians were concerned. It was only in 1924 that the United States extended citizenship to the entire North American Indian population.[61] But in their approach to the Indians, as elsewhere, the Cortes, through ignorance or a refusal to face unpleasant facts, were remote from American realities. The nominal concession of full citizenship rights did nothing to alleviate the lot of the Indians, and, if anything, worsened it. Equality meant an end to the system of legal protection they had hitherto enjoyed, leaving them still more exposed to creole exploitation.[62] At the same time, the abolition of the traditional Indian tribute payments, on which the viceregal administrations of New Spain and Peru were dependent for a substantial portion of their annual revenues, threatened to paralyse their operations and drove them to look for alternative forms of contribution that could well bear more heavily on Indian communities than the tribute they replaced.[63]

The gulf between the high-minded intentions of the Cortes of Cadiz and the practical results of its deliberations only served to intensify the disillusionment of American populations which already by 1810 had begun to despair of the mother country. In proclaiming the peoples of Spain and America a single nation with a common constitution, the Cortes had, at least in principle, moved – in ways that the British parliament was never prepared to move – in a direction that would logically end in the creation of a federal structure. As a body in which two-thirds of the members were Spanish, however, the Cortes showed no inclination to accept the implications of their own actions. From the beginning they displayed an arrogance in their attitude to America which alienated those they had hoped to attract. In Chile a leading patriot, Juan Martínez de Rosas, told the opening session of the national congress of 1811 that the Americans had been summoned to attend the Cortes in an insulting manner and would therefore not attend.[64] Similarly, the unwillingness to make concessions over trade or appointment to offices made it painfully obvious that some members of the new and egalitarian Hispanic nation considered themselves more equal than others.

Even where the reforms instituted by the Cortes were acceptable to many Americans, there was a strong possibility that the royal authorities in the Indies would be unwilling to implement them. José Fernando de Abascal, as viceroy of Peru, did everything in his power to obstruct those reforms of which he disapproved, winning in the process the support of creoles and *peninsulares* who disliked the new liberal policies emerging from Cadiz and feared the social and political upheaval that they were likely to provoke. The natural result was to polarize opinion in the viceroyalty, reinforcing conservative attitudes on the one hand and liberal attitudes on the other.[65]

Yet for all the deficiencies of the Cortes and the attempts of local officials to obstruct or delay the implementation of reform, the constitution of 1812 – proclaimed and accepted throughout America – opened the way to major political and constitutional change, peacefully achieved. Effectively it transformed Spain and its American possessions into a single nation–state, based on a much wider franchise than that of the Anglo-American world, since it included no literacy or property requirements. All adult males were given the vote, other than those of African descent, together with members of the religious orders, domestic servants, public debtors and convicted criminals.[66] The effect of this was to place 93 per cent of the adult male population of Mexico City on the electoral register for 1813.[67]

A massive process of decentralization now began, under a new system of representative government, which, given time and good will, might have accommodated creole aspirations for home rule without destroying the structure of Spain's monarchy and empire. All cities and towns with more than a thousand inhabitants were given their own *ayuntamientos*, and America was divided into twenty provincial deputations, or governments – six, for instance, for New Spain – which effectively meant the end of the system of omnicompetent viceregal administration. These *ayuntamientos* and deputations were to be representative bodies, voted into office by a much expanded electorate, although there was widespread confusion as to who was actually entitled to vote. While Indians and mestizos, as 'Spanish' citizens, were at least nominally included in the franchise, the exclusion of blacks and mulattoes, on whom the militia regiments were heavily dependent, led to ugly incidents.[68] Women, too, who had traditionally been able to vote if they headed a household, found themselves disenfranchised under a system in which men voted not as heads of households but as individuals.[69]

During 1813 and 1814, large parts of Spanish America – although primarily those that were still under the control of royalist authorities – embarked on a vast electoral exercise, which was conducted amidst considerable confusion, and with varying degrees of impartiality.[70] Inevitably, the creole elites tended to dominate the electoral process. Yet now, for the first time, large numbers of Spain's American subjects found themselves pitchforked into some form of political participation. While Indian communities had continued all through the colonial period to engage in often vigorous elections for their local officials,[71] creole town councils were essentially self-perpetuating oligarchies, offering little or no scope for wider citizen involvement. Some modification of this occurred in the course of the Bourbon reforms, at least in New Spain, where in the 1770s a form of municipal election was introduced into a number of towns in an attempt to limit the power of the oligarchies and reduce corruption.[72] It was also true that Spanish Americans were used to elections for confraternities and other corporate bodies, but the contrast with the North American colonies, with their relatively wide franchises and their long tradition of elections for representative assemblies, remains striking. The fledgling United States were considerably better prepared for popular politics than the new provincial units into which the Cortes of Cadiz had divided Spain's American territories.

Yet while there was no substantial tradition of popular participation in the political process, the dramatic events of the past two decades had the effect of politicizing growing numbers of people, especially in the cities. This was particularly true of New Spain, where the educational reforms promoted by church and crown during the second half of the eighteenth century had produced a society sufficiently literate for the written word to shape and sway opinion, even in relatively remote communities.[73] With freedom of the press decreed by the Cortes of Cadiz, reports of the Cortes debates were widely followed, both inside and outside the peninsula, and Havana became a major centre for the publication and distribution of Spanish political news. In America there was an upsurge in the regional printing of pamphlets and newspapers, with a single day's issue of the *Diario de México* in 1811 enjoying a print run of 7,000 copies. Yet even following the publication of the Cadiz constitution in the New World, freedom of the press remained precarious. It was not difficult for the authorities, as in New Spain, to suspend the operation of the decree, although printed matter originating in Spain, Britain and the United States still continued to keep Spanish American populations abreast of new developments both in Europe and in their own hemisphere.[74]

The more informed people became about events in Spain, however, the greater was their disillusionment with the response of the Cadiz Cortes to American complaints. At the same time, conditions in America itself were proving unfavourable to effective American representation in the new, regular, Cortes that were due to be inaugurated in October 1813. Venezuela, Buenos Aires, Chile and New Granada all declined to participate in the elections for deputies.[75] Even if other parts of the continent hesitated to follow the Venezuelan example in proclaiming independence, disaffection and insurgency were spreading. In New Spain, where Hidalgo's rebellion had been crushed in January 1811, another priest, José María Morelos, took over the leadership of the defeated rebellion, and – exercising greater control than Hidalgo over his troops – launched highly effective guerrilla operations into the Mexican heartland. Under such conditions, it was often difficult to proceed with the elections to the Cortes under the new constitution, and even where deputies were elected, the authorities in some instances intervened to prevent them from travelling to Spain. Only 65 Americans – of whom a mere 23 had been elected under the new constitutional system –

therefore took part in the sessions of the new Cortes, which were abruptly terminated in May 1814, following the return of Ferdinand VII to a peninsula now liberated from the occupying armies of the French.[76]

No event had been more eagerly anticipated than the restoration of Ferdinand VII to his throne, and no event was to be more cruelly disillusioning for those already disillusioned by the failure of the Cortes to satisfy American demands. The new regime annulled all the acts of the Cortes of Cadiz, and abolished the liberal constitution of 1812. The reaction was soon to extend from Spain to America, where the large majority had shown themselves initially happy to welcome the return of the king. Although a determined minority would by now be content with nothing less than full independence from Spain, the difficulties faced by insurgents across the continent suggest that a broad mass of opinion would have been satisfied with some form of autonomy within the structure of the empire. Veneration for the person of the monarch ran deep, not least among the Indian population of New Spain, where, during the years of his captivity in France, Ferdinand had allegedly been glimpsed in a black coach travelling across the Mexican countryside and urging the people to follow Hidalgo in revolt. Such was the mystical faith in a messianic king that some of the insurgent leaders understandably feared that the news of his return to the throne would undermine Indian support for their rebellion.[77]

Following his restoration, the king was bombarded by representations from his American subjects, still hopeful for the reforms that the Cortes had denied them. But, as so often had happened in the past, the representations received careful consideration only to be shelved.[78] With the Spanish state bankrupt, the crown was desperately in need of its American revenues, and it was counting on the effectiveness of its local representatives and the innate loyalty of the Americans to restore the status quo that had existed before 1808. Now that Morelos had been driven on to the defensive in New Spain, and Viceroy Abascal had stamped out rebellion in Chile, Quito and Upper Peru, Madrid assumed that the old order in the New World would rapidly be restored. Ferdinand's advisers showed little or no awareness of how profoundly times had changed. Six years of turmoil and constitutional upheaval in Spain itself, the breakdown of authority over large parts of America, the rise of a more informed public opinion with a new taste for liberty, and heavy pressure from Great Britain and the United States, eager to capture valuable American markets – all this made a return to the past impossible.

Madrid's expectations of a rapid return to normality were belied by continuing revolt in Buenos Aires and New Granada, and by the persistence of bloody civil conflict in Venezuela, in spite of – and in part because of – the harshly repressive activities of royalist forces under the command of Captain Juan Domingo Monteverde. In the autumn of 1814 the newly restored Council of the Indies recommended the despatch of an expeditionary force from Spain to restore order and crush the rebellions. In February 1815 an army of 10,500 men under the command of a Peninsular War veteran, Field Marshal Pablo Morillo, set sail from

Cadiz. His arrival in Venezuela and his counter-revolutionary campaign, which included the confiscation of the estates of creoles associated with the patriot cause, among them Bolívar, wrecked the chances of a negotiated solution to the problem of America.[79]

The restoration of the monarchy in Spain, therefore, which might have paved the way for reconciliation between the American territories and Madrid, proved to be the catalyst for movements aimed at winning outright independence. Ferdinand VII's American army, like that of George III, only succeeded in exacerbating the problem that it was sent to cure. It was now a question of which party could persist longer on its chosen course – a bankrupt Spanish monarchy which had opted for repression, or groups of insurgents determined to fight to the end for the cause of independence.

By 1816 the royalist cause, backed by military power, appeared in the ascendant. In Chile, the Patriot army was decisively defeated in October 1814 by royalist forces descending from Peru; in New Spain, a year later, Morelos was caught, defrocked and executed; and by the end of 1816 Morillo's army had recovered control over most of Venezuela and New Granada. The remoteness of the La Plata region offered at least temporary protection from royalist attempts to recover it, but even here by 1816 the cause of independence was in serious trouble. The newly instituted regime in Buenos Aires proved incapable of asserting its authority over Paraguay, which had declared its own independence in 1811, or over the Banda Oriental, which was later to evolve into an independent Uruguay. One after another the military expeditions that it despatched to Upper Peru were driven back; and although a congress in Buenos Aires proclaimed the 'independence of the United Provinces of South America' in July 1816, the provinces of the Argentine interior, resolutely opposed to domination by the *porteños* of Buenos Aires, proved to be very far from participating in the unity. By this time, Spain was planning to send a military expedition to the River Plate, and the movement for independence threatened to unravel.[80]

The subsequent five years, however, were to see a spectacular reversal of fortunes, brought about in large measure by the courage, skill and persistence of a handful of revolutionary leaders who were not prepared to abandon their struggle for independence. In the southern half of the continent the breakthrough for the independence movement came with José de San Martín's creation of an army of the Andes. In 1817 his forces struck westwards from Mendoza, hazardously making their way across the mountains in a bold attempt to break the power of the royalists and their hold over Lima. With his victory at Maipó, outside Santiago, on 5 April 1818 San Martín effectively freed Chile, only to find on entering Peru that its creole population showed no enthusiasm for liberation from Spain.[81]

Away to the north, Simón Bolívar, having fled with other patriot leaders to Jamaica from New Granada in the spring of 1815, sought to rally support for the cause of independence in his famous 'Jamaica letter' of 6 September. Defeated once again by royalist forces in his attempt to raise rebellion in his native

Venezuela in the summer of 1816, he embarked at the end of the year on yet another, and this time successful, bid to liberate the continent. Forging an army of creoles, mulattoes, and slaves to whom he offered emancipation in return for conscription, he was gradually able to move over to the offensive. A brilliant campaign for the liberation of New Granada culminated in victory over the royalist army at the battle of Boyacá, north-east of Bogotá, in May 1819. Bolívar then turned on Morillo's forces in western Venezuela, and entered Caracas in triumph in June 1821.

Now that the liberation of his homeland had been achieved, he could turn his attention to winning independence for Quito and the viceroyalty of Peru. In the struggle for Quito, his most faithful commander, Antonio José de Sucre, was victorious in May 1822. Peru, the greatest prize of all, still awaited Bolívar. Effectively marginalizing San Martín, he defeated the royalist army at Junín in the summer of 1824. The creoles of Peru, ambivalent to the end, were at last brought face to face with the challenge of independence when Sucre decisively defeated the one remaining Spanish army on the continent at the battle of Ayacucho on 9 December.[82]

For all the skill and daring of San Martín, Bolívar and other insurgent leaders, their eventual triumph also owed much to Spanish weakness and ineptitude. The royalist forces in America were heavily over-extended, and financial problems in Spain made it difficult, or impossible, to send reinforcements when they were needed. When an expeditionary force of 14,000 men was finally ready to embark at Cadiz for the recovery of Buenos Aires, a section of the troops under the command of Major Rafael Riego mutinied early in 1820, and demanded a return to the 1812 constitution. The revolt turned into a revolution, the constitution was restored, and for the next three years, before a French invading force restored the status quo, Ferdinand VII found himself acting in the unaccustomed and uncongenial role of a constitutional monarch.[83]

Ironically, the restoration of a liberal regime in Spain was to prove the prelude to the independence of those regions of the American mainland that had not yet been lost. In its early stages the new administration in Madrid, deeply absorbed in domestic problems, was unable to pay more than fitful attention to the American question, and when it did so it showed no greater understanding of American realities than its 1810 predecessor. The Cortes approved a law in September 1820 depriving the officers of colonial militias of the privilege they had enjoyed since 1786 of trial by court-martial for non-military offences. Simultaneously, news crossed the Atlantic that the Cortes were also planning to curtail the privileges and property rights of the church. In the face of these threats to their corporate rights, creoles and *peninsulares* in New Spain sank their differences and joined in a fragile coalition to make common cause against Madrid. A group of army officers and clerics began to lay plans for independence from Spain.[84]

The independence of Mexico was achieved by conspiracy, and not by revolution or a prolonged war of liberation. The social and ethnic violence unleashed by the unsuccessful rebellions of Hidalgo and Morelos in the preceding decade stood as a dreadful warning to the elite of New Spain. Although willing to contemplate the nominal abolition of caste barriers in order to neutralize the dangers of social conflict, its aim, like that of the leaders of the British American Revolution, was to achieve home rule with a minimum of social upheaval. This was to be a counter-revolution designed to defend an established order in church and state no longer guaranteed by its traditional protector, the Spanish monarchy.

The forces of political and social conservatism found their champion, or their instrument, in Agustín de Iturbide, a creole officer in the royalist army who had been ruthless in repressing the earlier revolts. Iturbide and his fellow conspirators prepared the ground well. Under the Plan of Iguala of February 1821 – a constitutional scheme carefully crafted to appeal to different sections of the society of New Spain – Mexico was proclaimed a self-governing Catholic and constitutional monarchy. In those instances where royalist forces did not defect to the rebels, they showed little inclination to resist. Independence in Mexico therefore rode to an almost bloodless triumph on the back of counter-revolution. Iturbide, as the hero of the hour, possessed the prestige and military authority to assume the leadership of the newly independent state. In quick succession he was proclaimed president of the Regency, and then – evoking an Aztec past which the creoles had appropriated as their own – the first emperor of a Mexico now metamorphosed into a 'constitutional' empire. If he was no Bolívar, he was also no Washington.

In the meantime, what remained of Spanish government in America was disintegrating, and even Santo Domingo, Spain's first island possession in the New World, declared its independence in December 1821.[85] Mexico's break from Spain was followed by that of Guatemala and the other central American territories. By the end of the decade, of the once proud transatlantic empire of Spain only Cuba and Puerto Rico remained. Like the planter elite of the British West Indies in the later eighteenth century the Cuban elite calculated that it would lose more than it stood to gain by independence. Not only had it been shaken by the savagery and the success of the slave revolt of 1791 in Saint Domingue (Haiti), but it had prospered in the years after 1790 from the opening of the island to international trade and its growing sugar exports to the United States.[86] The experience of Virginia to the contrary, plantation economies based on slave labour were not the natural breeding-grounds of elite revolt.

The emancipation of America: contrasting experiences

Independence came to Spanish America some forty to fifty years after it came to British America, and in very different circumstances. It would not have come, or come in the form that it did, without the American Revolution to the north. As George Canning observed when looking back in 1825 on the events of the preceding forty years, 'the operation of that example sooner or later was inevitable', although in his opinion the mistaken policies of the metropolis helped to make it so. 'Spain,' he continued 'untaught by the lesson of the British American war, has postponed all attempt at accommodation with her Colonies until their separation is now irretrievably established.'[87] But Spain found itself in a much less favourable position than Britain at the outbreak of the struggle for independence, and independence, when it came, was the consequence less of metropolitan pressure on the periphery of empire than of collapse at its centre. Not the Declaration of Independence but the armies of Napoleon set in motion the process that would culminate in the emancipation of Spain's empire of the Indies.

It was a process that proved to be devastatingly costly in terms of societies disrupted and lives destroyed, and the new Iberian America that arose from the ashes of the old Spanish Empire was to live with the consequences of this for generations to come. In the North American War of Independence acts of brutality had been perpetrated by both sides, with soldiers in the British armies engaging in wide-scale rapine and plunder, some of it the result of deliberate policy. Lord Rawdon, a young British officer, wrote in 1776: 'I think we should (whenever we get further into the country) give free liberty to the soldiers to ravage it at will, that these infatuated creatures may feel what a calamity war is.'[88] The rebels, for their part, gave short shrift to the loyalists.[89] But British America was never subjected to the kind of massive campaign of terror and destruction conducted in Venezuela by the royalist commander Juan Domingo Monteverde. Nor did the hostility between rebels and loyalists in the British colonies lead, as it did in Venezuela, to full-scale civil war between the colonists themselves. British commanders like General Sir Henry Clinton hesitated to unleash loyalist forces to wage campaigns of terror that could only serve to alienate those sections of the population whose hearts and minds they needed to win.[90]

In Spanish America, and notably in Venezuela, the savagery of civil war was enhanced by the extent of the ethnic divisions, which all too easily came to overshadow what had begun as a domestic dispute within the Hispanic community. While the ethnic question was always present in North America, it played a less prominent part in the British-American War of Independence than in the conflicts in Spain's colonies, where non-white or mixed populations predominated. In Peru, for instance, of the 1,115,000 inhabitants in 1795, only 140,000 were whites. The remainder consisted of 674,000 Indians, 244,000 mestizos and 81,000 blacks of whom half were slaves.[91] While many of the non-whites sought to steer clear of commitment in these internal Hispanic disputes, it was difficult to avoid being sucked into the conflict, given the extent of drafting and recruitment by both sides. With many militia regiments made up of blacks and mulattoes, the loyalties of their creole commanders could be decisive in determining whether they fought as rebels or royalists. Both sides armed the slaves, and Indians formed the majority of the soldiers in the royalist army in Peru.[92]

The British crown made no concerted effort to mobilize Indians or blacks, in part at least out of a justifiable fear that this would alienate the white population whose loyalty it hoped to recover or preserve. When defending the ruthlessness of Bolívar's 'war to the death' in the United States Congress, Henry Clay would ask rhetorically: 'Could it be believed, if the slaves had been let loose upon us in the south, as they had been let loose in Venezuela; if quarters had been refused; capitulations violated; that General Washington, at the head of the armies of the United States, would not have resorted to retribution?'[93] Shortage of manpower did, however, compel an initially reluctant Congress and General Washington to accept slaves into the ranks of the Continental Army, with the offer of freedom in return. But when the British moved their war effort to the south in 1779, the southern colonies were understandably resistant to the idea of defending themselves against attack by arming their slaves.[94]

Apart from any risk involved in supplying arms to slaves, their diversion into military service meant an inevitable loss of labour on plantations and estates. As a result of the recruitment or the flight of slaves, production on many haciendas in Peru was abandoned as the conflict reached a climax, adding one further element of disruption to an economy already disrupted by naval blockade and the shortage of mercury supplies for the refinement of silver from the mines.[95] Although seven years of war in North America brought widespread economic dislocation and social distress, with levels of income and wealth at the outbreak of the war possibly not reached again until the early nineteenth century,[96] it is hard to believe that the British colonies suffered anything like the level of destruction reached in Spanish America, where the conflict was frequently not only more savage, but also much more prolonged. Even if some parts of the Spanish American world, like the cities of central Mexico, managed to remain 'islands in the storm',[97] others were subjected to almost continuous battering over a decade or more.

It is not only the intensity of the internal divisions and the obstinacy of metropolitan Spain in refusing to relinquish its tight grasp on its empire which explain the length and ferocity of the wars of independence. When the British colonies revolted, active involvement by the European powers in the form of French and Spanish intervention against Britain notably shortened the length of the struggle the rebels would otherwise have faced. The international conjuncture a generation later proved less favourable to the winning of independence by the Spanish American rebels. Although Francisco de Miranda, Bolívar and other rebel leaders met with a warm reception on their arrival in London, there was no question of Britain coming forward with military or naval help for their independence movements once Britain and Spain had become allies in the struggle against Napoleon. Trade – those lucrative Spanish American markets on which British eyes had been fixed for so long – was, and remained, the overriding concern of British foreign policy. While London was happy, and indeed anxious, to mediate between Spain and the rebels in the hope of restoring the peace and stability essential for trade, this was officially as far as it would go.[98] It was therefore left to mercenaries and adventurers, like Admiral Cochrane and his captains, or the officers and men who took service under Bolívar after the ending of the Napoleonic wars, to provide the vital British contribution to the independence of Venezuela and New Granada, Chile and Peru.

For its part, the young republic of the United States might have been expected to lend support and encouragement to movements for the establishment of fellow republics in its own hemisphere. Yet while political circles did indeed engage in lively discussion about the potential advantages of Spanish American independence to the United States, generalized sympathy – tempered by characteristic Anglo-American scepticism about the capacity of Spanish Americans to govern themselves – was no more translated into decisive assistance than it was in Great Britain. Not only did the new republic lack the military strength to intervene in support of the insurgents, but the overriding preoccupation of the administration during the period of the Napoleonic Wars was to steer clear of actions liable to provoke military and naval confrontation with a Britain that was now allied to Spain. Although after 1810 it was sending consular agents to South America to protect its growing commercial interests, the United States therefore held back from giving official recognition to the new republics. National self-interest remained here, as in Great Britain, the order of the day.[99]

Lacking the active assistance of foreign powers, Bolívar, San Martín and their fellow insurgents were consequently compelled to mount and sustain campaigns which depended heavily on their own inner resources and powers of leadership. Since their invading armies were faced with strong resistance and could count on only limited local support, they were perpetually struggling to mobilize reluctant populations that were deeply divided by ethnic and social antagonisms. As a result, the process of liberation became a grinding struggle, which inevitably gave victorious military leaders a commanding influence in the task of nation-building that followed emancipation. In this respect, the winning of independence by Spanish South America contrasted sharply with the winning of independence by the British colonies. Here a Congress reasonably representative of different sectional interests retained general control, however inefficiently exercised, over the colonial war machine. At the same time it had chosen in General Washington a supreme commander who displayed a rocklike adherence to the tenets of the political culture in which he had been educated – a culture that looked on standing armies as instruments of tyranny, and insisted on the subordination of the military to the civil authority (fig. 42).

During the colonial period, authority in Spanish America was and remained pre-eminently a civil authority, although the Bourbon reforms, in extending the *fuero militar* to members of the colonial militias, had to some extent made the military a corporation apart. Along with military titles and uniforms, exemption from civilian jurisdiction had become one of the great attractions of service in the colonial militias for the sons of the creole elite.[100] The militias themselves may not have provided much more than a rudimentary military experience, but they constituted a natural breeding-ground for future leaders of the independence movements, in part because they brought young creoles into contact with Spanish officers who had imbibed some of the spirit and attitudes of the European Enlightenment. They fostered, too, a corporate spirit nurtured by resentment at the way in which creoles found themselves excluded from positions of command in the regular regiments, in spite of the changes that occurred during the 1790s as Spain's European wars reduced the number of native Spanish officers who could be spared for service in America. By the time the wars of liberation began, creole officers were well placed, through their local influence and their command of the colonial militia regiments, to exercise considerable influence over the course of events. The collapse of the civil authority and the breakdown of law and order gave ambitious officers an opportunity to seize the initiative on behalf of either the insurgents or the royalists, and provided the occasion, and the pretext, for an Iturbide to irrupt on to the stage.

The liberators of Spanish America, however, were far from being the products of a narrow military culture, and several had received an extensive and wide-ranging education. Simón Bolívar, who joined the militia at the age of fourteen, came from one of the wealthiest creole families in Caracas and received a private education which made him an enthusiast for the works of the *philosophes*, and above all of Rousseau (fig. 43). Manuel Belgrano, the son of a rich Buenos Aires merchant, was given the best education to be had in his native city before being sent to Spain to study law at Salamanca, Valladolid and Madrid.[101] While Iturbide, like Washington, had never crossed the Atlantic, not only Belgrano, but also Miranda, Bolívar, San Martín and Bernardo O'Higgins all spent at least some of their formative years in Spain, either to pursue their education or to receive professional training in a military academy.

Once in Europe they were exposed, like Belgrano, to the ferment of ideas brought about by the impact of the French Revolution. 'Since I was in Spain in 1789', he wrote in his autobiography, 'at a time when the French Revolution was causing a change in ideas, particularly among the men of letters with whom I associated, the ideas of liberty, equality, security and property, took a firm hold on me, and I saw only tyrants in those who would prevent a man, wherever he might be, from enjoying the rights with which God and nature had endowed him.'[102] Enthused by the ideals of liberty and equality, and impressed by the potential of a now fashionable political economy, they would set the world to rights. In Spain they experienced, like North Americans in England, the arrogance with which an imperial power treated mere colonials. They also saw for themselves the defects of a society condemned by the *philosophes* for its superstition and its backwardness. Those of them who, like Miranda, Bolívar and O'Higgins, also travelled to England can only have been struck by the sharpness of the contrast between the sluggishness of their own mother country and the dynamism of a society in which industry and commerce flourished, and freedom was the norm.[103]

The extent of their European experience distinguishes the liberators of Spanish America from the leading actors in the American Revolution, with the notable exception of Benjamin Franklin. George Washington had never travelled further abroad than to the West Indies, and was later described by John Adams as having seen too little of the world for someone in his 'station'.[104] These, however, were the words of a man who himself had seen nothing beyond North America before 1778, the year in which, at the age of 42, he was sent by Congress on a mission to Paris to secure French support. This would later enable him to look back on the revolutionary period with the superiority of a man who, in contrast to Washington, had indeed by that time seen something of the world. Of the 55 signers of the Declaration of Independence, six had been born in the British Isles, and five of the six were still young when they or their families moved to America.[105] Twelve of the remaining 49 spent some time in the British Isles. Most of these, like three of South Carolina's four representatives, were sent to England for their schooling or for study at the Inns of Court. The most travelled among them, apart perhaps from Robert Treat Paine, a Massachusetts merchant whose voyages included a trip to Spain in 1751, appears to have been the one Roman Catholic signer of the Declaration, Charles Carroll of Carrollton in Maryland, who was educated at the Jesuit College of St Omer, and spent sixteen years in England and continental Europe before returning home.[106]

By the time the Philadelphia Convention met in 1787, the situation had changed. At least 18 of the 55 delegates to the Convention had spent a year or more of their lives abroad as grown men.[107] If, however, the Spanish American leaders had seen more of the world before launching their revolutions than their North American counterparts, it is not easy to assess the impact on them of their foreign experience. In so far as it confirmed their impressions of the archaic character of the imperial power to which they owed allegiance, it is likely to have encouraged them to turn their backs on their inherited political culture and seek to build anew. Where British Americans, proud of their British constitutional traditions, sought to purge their inherited political culture of the corrupting elements introduced by power and privilege, and adapt it to new purposes within the broad context of universal rights, Bolívar turned first to universal principles to construct on the ruins of a collapsing Spanish empire a new nation of new men.[108]

Yet as Bolívar and his fellow liberators soon came to discover, this ambition was not easily realized in the inhospitable landscape of Spanish America. First, they had to liberate an entire continent, and not merely, as in British America, the corner of a continent. Having accomplished this in the face of ferocious resistance and almost impossible geographical odds, they then had to build a new political order on the slenderest of foundations. Although the Spanish empire possessed the superficial unity given it by a common culture, there was no way in which its territorial integrity could be conserved in the wake of emancipation. Even in Britain's more compact American empire, the rebels had failed to carry with them the West Indies and Canada, and only an ingenious constitution, together with a tacit agreement to ignore the fundamental question of slavery, had prevented further fragmentation.

The difficulty of preserving any semblance of unity in Spain's liberated empire was compounded not only by its vast scale and extreme physical and climatic diversity, but also by the strength of the local and regional traditions that had developed over three centuries of imperial rule. The administrative and juridical boundaries delimiting viceroyalties, Audiencias and lesser territorial units had hardened sufficiently to provide a focus for the development of loyalties to a host of *patrias* more sharply defined than the generalized American *patria* which the rebels sought to liberate. Bolívar dreamt of replacing the old and discredited Spanish Monarchy with a pan-American continental union, or – failing this – an Andean confederation comprising Venezuela, New Granada, Quito and Peru. But he discovered to his disillusionment that no amount of constitutional tinkering could hold together a union of territories so historically and geographically diverse. Once the danger from Spain was removed, his Greater Colombia of Venezuela, New Granada and Quito was torn apart by local loyalties. The same fate befell the Federation of United Provinces of Central America, created in 1824.

The thirteen British colonies, although widely diverse in character, had joined together in 1776 in a common act of defiance against the British crown. Their battle for independence, conducted under the aegis of a shared constitutional body, the Congress, and waged by a shared Continental Army, had accustomed them to working together, and had created a network of personal acquaintance and friendships that transcended state and local boundaries. By the time the battle had been won, the transition to a more lasting union, although still difficult to achieve, was at least within the bounds of practical politics. The Spanish American colonies emerged into independence without having gone through a comparable educational experience of close and continuing collaboration in a common cause. Not only did independence come to them at different times and in different ways, but the liberators – Bolívar, San Martín, Santander, O'Higgins – working on a vast continental canvas, found it difficult to co-ordinate their efforts, or set aside their rivalries.

As the transcontinental Spanish imperial system foundered, and attempts to replace it with a number of federal unions broke down, the challenge confronting Spain's former colonies was to transform themselves into viable nation-states. But a sense of nationhood was an elusive concept, more prone to generate rhetoric than encourage an engagement with reality. The pronouncement in Mexico's Act of Independence that 'the Mexican nation, which for three hundred years has had no will of its own, nor free expression, emerges today from the oppression under which it has lived', was no doubt intended to resonate down the ages.[109] Yet what continuities linked the empire of Montezuma to that of Iturbide, and were they strong enough to give cohesion and direction to an ethnically diverse society now suddenly cut loose from its traditional moorings?

Creole patriotism was woven out of religion and history – or, more specifically, a selective interpretation of the past – and provided at least some of the elements that could be used to create a new sense of national identity. Mexico, with its strong historiographical tradition and a religious symbol, in the figure of the Virgin of Guadalupe, who commanded the loyalties of wide sections of the population, was better placed than the majority of the new states to fashion itself as a nation. Everywhere, however, there were tensions between centralizing aspirations and local patriotisms. These were especially acute in regions, such as the viceroyalty of La Plata, where Bourbon reformers had redrawn the boundary lines, incorporating older jurisdictional units like the Audiencia of Las Charcas, or Upper Peru, which in 1825 broke free from the grasp of Buenos Aires to proclaim itself the independent republic of Bolivia. Old loyalties ran deeper than new political geography. Everywhere, too, creole patriotism was closely identified with the interests of privileged elites bent on exploiting the break with Spain to tighten their grip on power. This limited its ability to generate a genuinely national consciousness in new states whose republican constitutions, by contrast, spoke the contemporary language of universal rights and gave at least nominal representation to social and ethnic groups traditionally regarded as inferior.[110]

State-building itself proved a difficult, elusive and time-consuming task. The wars of independence had destroyed political institutions elaborated over 300 years of imperial rule. For all its failings, the Spanish imperial state had created an indispensable framework for colonial life, as the British imperial state in North America had not. Royal decrees emanating from Madrid might be ignored or subverted, but the imperial administrative apparatus was an overshadowing presence, which could not be indefinitely ignored. Where the disappearance of the imperial state from British America left individual colonies to manage their own lives much as they had before, the disappearance of the Spanish imperial state therefore left a vacuum that the successor states were ill prepared to fill.

Although the creole societies of Spanish America had enjoyed a substantial degree of effective autonomy, at least before the advent of the Bourbon reforms, this was exercised in particular by city councils dominated by small, self-perpetuating oligarchies, and had constantly to be mediated through negotiation with the agents and institutions of the crown. The absence of representative bodies like the assemblies in the British colonies meant that there was no provincial legislative tradition, and little practical experience of local representatives gathering to discuss and frame policies in response to common needs. The summoning of deputies to the Cortes of Cadiz and the convoking of elections over wide areas of territory in 1813 and 1814, however, marked the beginnings of an important change in the political culture of Spanish America. Not only did the new electoral arrangements enable a newly enfranchised populace to participate for the first time in the political process, but they also meant that those chosen to represent the American territories in the Spanish Cortes gained valuable experience of parliamentary procedure and debate. This could later be turned to account, as it was in Mexico, where former representatives to the Cortes of 1810–14 and 1820–2 returned from Europe to play an important part in the building of the new Mexican state.[111]

The experience of active political representation, however, came very late in the day, and the pool of experienced legislative talent on which the new states could draw would seem to have been substantially smaller than that available for the construction of the United States. This is likely to have reduced the chances of constructing governmental systems capable, as in the United States, of turning to creative purpose the tension between the centralizing and separatist tendencies inherent in the colonial tradition. Instead, a series of federalist movements in the 1820s – in Mexico and central America, Gran Colombia and Peru – mounted a challenge to potentially authoritarian regimes which laid claim to the centralizing traditions of the old imperial state. Under the banners of either centralism or federalism, the old creole family networks fought among themselves over the division of the spoils. As they did so, the new states descended into anarchy, and all too often the only escape from anarchy appeared to be the surrender of legitimacy to a strong-armed *caudillo*. Only Chile, with a closely interlocking creole elite, was able to achieve reasonable stability, on the basis of a strongly centralized government and the perpetuation of the hierarchical social order of colonial times.[112]

If British America enjoyed a smoother transition to independence than Spanish America, fortuitous as well as structural elements would seem to have played their part. While federalists and anti-federalists were still bitterly disputing the character and extent of the powers to be exercised by the central government of the new republic of the United States, the energies and attention of Europe were diverted by the French Revolutionary and Napoleonic wars. These brought unexpected bonanzas to the United States.

At the time of its birth, the security and prosperity of the republic depended heavily on decisions being taken in London, Paris and Madrid. Ignoring the terms of the peace settlement, Britain showed no inclination to evacuate its military positions along the lakes in the Northwest. As long as it retained them, there was a danger that it might reconstitute its alliances with the Indian peoples, who stood in the way of American expansion beyond the Appalachians. Similarly, Spain's closure of navigation of the Mississippi to citizens of the United States in 1784 reduced the viability of the Mississippi and Ohio valley settlements by depriving them of access to the sea.

The descent of Europe into war, however, provided a welcome opening for American diplomacy. The Jay treaty of 1794 secured the evacuation of Britain's Northwestern forts, and in the following year Spain agreed, under the Pinckney treaty, to accept the 31st parallel as the boundary between the United States and Spanish Florida, and open the Mississippi to American shipping.[113] Spain itself inspired little respect among the leading figures in American political life, but behind Spain there loomed the shadow of post-revolutionary France. Napoleon's ambitions seemed limitless, and there was a growing apprehension that he planned to use Louisiana, once Spain restored it to French sovereignty, as a launching-pad for the reconstitution of France's former American empire. The situation was saved by the failure of a large French expeditionary force to suppress the slave revolt on Saint Domingue, and the resumption of war with England after a brief interlude of peace. Any plans for the restoration of French America now had to be abandoned, and Jefferson's purchase of Louisiana from France in 1803 delivered into the hands of the United States almost half a continent. However tenacious the resistance put up by the Indian peoples of the interior, nothing could now thwart the national enterprise on which the peoples of the new republic were embarking – the building of a continental empire, an 'empire of liberty'.

The Napoleonic wars brought not only new prospects for westwards expansion, but also new prospects for the expansion of America's international trade.

Although the Jay treaty was fiercely denounced by Republicans as once again subordinating the United States to British commercial and maritime dominance, the European demand for American grain to feed its hungry peoples and the British demand for the cotton of the southern states combined to open up new opportunities for American merchants, farmers and planters. The commercial infrastructure inherited by the republic from the colonial period was strong enough to allow United States merchants and shippers to capitalize on American neutrality to become the carriers to the belligerent powers of Europe. A dramatically expanding Atlantic trade in exports and re-exports brought a new prosperity to the mainland, revitalizing the eastern seaboard and providing employment for a growing population.[114]

The international conjuncture proved considerably less favourable to the Spanish American republics at the moment of their birth. Napoleon had now been defeated and peace had returned to Europe. In the intervening period, the Spanish Atlantic trading system had collapsed, and the Peninsular War had ravaged the economy of metropolitan Spain. In the aftermath of emancipation, trade between Spain and the new Spanish American republics almost disappeared, whereas Britain rapidly resumed trading relations with its former colonies after they won their independence.[115] Instead, with their economies shattered by years of war and civil disorder, the new states, still groping for political stability, found themselves on the fringes of an international trading community that wanted their markets but did not want their produce. They also found themselves overshadowed by an increasingly confident and assertive United States, to which Mexico would lose half its territory between 1845 and 1854.[116]

The new republics, too, found themselves saddled with a colonial legacy, both political and psychological, that made it difficult for them to adjust to their new situation. Governed for three centuries by a bureaucratic and interventionist state, they instinctively sought to re-create after independence the system of government with which they were familiar. Strong central control seemed in any event necessary to prevent the spread of anarchy. Liberal elements in the new societies might aspire to throw off the shackles of the past, but they too needed an administrative apparatus that would enable them to realize their dreams.

The consequence was the survival into the era of independence of long-established attitudes and practices inherited from the old political order which tended to reduce the capacity of the new republics to respond to the economic challenges of a new age: government interventionism that was either arbitrary or inclined to favour the sectional interests of one group in society at the expense of another; a plethora of overlapping laws and an excess of regulation; continuing discrimination against the castas, in spite of all the egalitarian rhetoric; and old-style reliance on patronage, kinship networks and corruption to secure economic advantages and influence the decisions taken by a state that was too closely modelled on the pattern of the old. The effect was to inhibit innovation and entrepreneurial enterprise, with results that became all too apparent as the nineteenth century advanced. Around 1800 Mexico produced more than half as many goods and services as the United States. By the 1870s the figure was down to 2 per cent.[117]

Unlike the former American dependencies of Spain, the United States had favourable winds behind them as they set out on their voyage into uncharted seas. Their population was growing by leaps and bounds – from 3.9 million in 1790 to 9.6 million in 1820[118] – their economy was buoyant, and westwards expansion offered unlimited possibilities for the investment of energies, resources and national enterprise. Deep divisions over the scope, character and direction of the new federal republic may at moments in the 1790s have raised the spectre of civil war, but the curtain on the Federalist era was rung down peacefully in 1800 with the election of Jefferson to the presidency and a formal transfer of power which showed how firmly the new republic had been grounded on the principle that the will of the people must prevail. In the new Spanish American republics it would take much more than a single election to dispel the notion that membership of the social elite carried with it automatic entitlement to the exercise of political power.

The upsurge of prosperity, the opportunities for westwards expansion and the democratization of America in the age of Jefferson all helped to release individual energies for participation in the great collective enterprise of constructing a new nation. The first post-revolutionary generation was coming into its own, innovative, entrepreneurial, and infused with optimism over the prospects of its country.[119] The society in process of creation would not, as the Federalists had feared, descend into chaos under the impact of mob rule. But neither, as Jefferson and his Republican friends hoped and expected, would it transform itself into the virtuous agrarian republic of their dreams.

With the consolidation of the Union and the building of a new society came a developing sense of national identity. This was reinforced by the war of 1812–14 with Great Britain over neutrality and trade – a war which vindicated the conception of the United States as God's Republic, and gave it a new set of heroes and a future national anthem in 'The Star Spangled Banner'. In holding off the British the Americans saved their Revolution, and the spectre of imperial reconquest was finally removed.[120]

Yet the sense of national identity coalescing around the young republic was neither all-inclusive nor universally shared. For all its successes this was, and remained, a partisan and faction-ridden society. While foreign observers were impressed by the character and extent of its democracy, its egalitarian spirit and the totality of its rejection of secular and ecclesiastical controls, it still excluded many who lived within its borders. Suffrage, although in process of extension in state constitutions, remained largely the preserve of a white male population, to the exclusion not only of women and slaves, but also of American Indians and many free blacks.[121] Above all, the old fault-line between North and South was becoming more pronounced as the boom in cotton exports clamped slavery more tightly on the southern states.[122] In turn, an increasingly strident abolitionist response drove the South back on itself, leaving the field open for northern society to dictate the values and aspirations that would shape the self-image of the new republic, and with it the image that it would offer to the world.

Those values and aspirations – a spirit of enterprise and innovation, the pursuit of individual and collective improvement, the restless search for opportunity – would come to constitute the defining characteristics of an American national identity. They were values which conflicted at least in part with those of the traditional honour culture of the South.[123] They were alien, too, to the inherited culture of the newly independent states of Spanish-speaking America, where constitutions articulated in terms of universal rights sat uneasily with societies in which the old hierarchies had not lost their hold. But it was the possession of those values that would allow the new American republic to make its way, with growing confidence, in the ruthlessly competitive environment of an industrializing western world.

Epilogue

In the early 1770s, J. Hector St John de Crèvecoeur, who won fame a few years later with his *Letters of an American Farmer*, wrote an unpublished 'Sketch of a Contrast Between the Spanish and the English Colonies'. 'Could we have a perfect representation', it began, 'of the customs and manners of the Spanish Colonies, it would, I believe, exhibit a most astonishing contrast, when viewed in opposite to those of these Provinces. But they have kept their country so invariably shut against all strangers, that it is impossible to obtain any certain and particular knowledge of them.'[1] Yet Spanish obfuscation and his own ignorance did not inhibit Crèvecoeur from delivering a series of summary judgments, which cast an unflattering light on Spanish America when contrasted with the British colonies to the north.

Crèvecoeur's comparison, such as it was, paraded a cluster of stereotypes, with religion given pride of place. It was sufficient to compare a Quaker congregation with 'the more gaudy, more gorgeous Spanish one of Lima, coming out of their superb churches glittering with gold, irradiated with the combined effects of diamonds, rubies and topazes, ornamented with everything which the art of man can execute and the delirious imagination of a voluptuous devotee can devise or furnish'. Instead of reading the biographies of so many saints 'whose virtues are useless to mankind', the inhabitants of Lima and Cuzco should study the life of William Penn, who 'treated the savages as his brethren and friends' when he arrived in Pennsylvania, 'the Peru of North America'.

Writing more generally of British America, Crèvecoeur found that 'from the mildness and justice of their laws, from their religious toleration, from the ease with which foreigners can transport themselves here, they have derived that ardour, that spirit of constancy and perseverance' which had enabled them to 'raise so many sumptuous cities', display so much 'ingenuity in trade and arts', and ensure 'a perpetual circulation of books, newspapers, useful discoveries from all parts of the world'. 'This great continent', he concluded, 'wants nothing but time and hands to become the great fifth monarchy which will change the present political system of the world.'

What, then, of Spain's American possessions? 'The mass of their society is composed of the descendants of the ancient conquerors and conquered, of slaves and of such a variety of castes and shades, as never before were exhibited on any part of the earth, which it appears never can live in a sufficient degree of harmony, so as to carry on with success extensive schemes of industry . . . In South America this oppressive government is not at all calculated to raise; 'tis more immediately adapted to pull down. It looks on the obedience of few as much more useful than the ingenuity of the many . . . In short, that languor which corrodes and enervates the mother country, enfeebles also those beautiful provinces . . .'

Crèvecoeur's indictment of Spain and its American territories, which itself was no more than a banal encapsulation of the prejudices and assumptions of eighteenth-century Europe, still resonates today. The nineteenth- and twentieth-century history of the republics constructed on the ruins of Spain's American empire only served to underline the flaws and deficiencies mercilessly singled out by Crèvecoeur. The history of independent Latin America came to be seen as a chronicle of economic backwardness and political failure, while any achievements were underplayed or dismissed.

Some of the economic and political deficiencies identified by both foreign and Latin American commentators were a consequence of the international conjuncture and the balance of global forces in the two centuries that followed the winning of independence from Spain. Some were the consequence of the struggle for independence itself, a struggle so much more bloody and prolonged than that waged by North Americans against their British 'oppressors'. Others derived from the distinctive geographical and environmental features of a vast and infinitely variegated land-mass, while still others can properly be traced back to the particular cultural, social and institutional characteristics of the colonial societies and their imperial ruler.[2]

It is one thing, however, to single out specific features of Spanish American colonial society, like endemic corruption, as casting a baleful shadow over the history of the post-colonial republics, and another to issue a blanket indictment of 'the Spanish inheritance' as the root cause of their tribulations and failures. In many respects the indictment is no more than a perpetuation into the post-colonial era of the grand narrative of 'the Black Legend', whose origins can be traced back to the early years of overseas conquest and colonization.[3] Constructed out of the atrocity stories that accumulated around the behaviour of Spain's armies in Europe and of the conquistadores in America, it subsequently received a powerful injection of anti-Catholic sentiment as Protestant Europe struggled to hold Spanish power at bay. During the course of the seventeenth century, as the image of a global power aspiring to universal monarchy was replaced by that of a vulnerable colossus, Spain acquired those connotations of backwardness, superstition and sloth that Enlightenment Europe took such delight in condemning. These were the images that impressed themselves on the minds of the leaders of the independence movements, who took solace in blaming the Spanish legacy for their failure to realize their own exalted ideals.

For Bolívar, Spain had created societies that were constitutionally incapable of benefiting from the fruits of liberty.[4]

The infant United States, on the other hand, seemed destined to success from birth. Even before the British colonies broke free, Crèvecoeur and his contemporaries were prophesying a glowing future for societies that appeared to meet all the criteria of the Enlightenment for the achievement of individual happiness and collective prosperity. Writing five years after the Declaration of Independence, Thomas Pownall, a former governor of Massachusetts who at first supported Lord North's policy in the House of Commons but subsequently became an enthusiastic advocate of the new United States, spelled out in his typically convoluted phraseology the characteristics of the new republic and its citizens:

> In America, all the inhabitants are free, and allow universal naturalization to all that wish to be so, and a perfect liberty of using any mode of life they choose, or any means of getting a livelihood that their talents lead them to . . . Where every man has the free and full exertion of his powers, and may acquire any share either of profit or of power that his spirit can work him up to, there is an unabated application; and a perpetual struggle of spirits sharpens the wit and trains the mind . . . They are animated with the spirit of the New Philosophy. Their life is a course of experiments; and standing on as high ground of improvement as the most enlightened parts of Europe, they have advanced like Eagles, they commencing the first efforts of their pinions from a towering advantage.[5]

As the eagle began to soar in the nineteenth century, so the qualities identified by contemporaries as promising a spectacular flight for the fledgling republic were validated and reinforced. An idealized British America, whose indigenous and African peoples were too easily air-brushed out of the picture, presented a striking contrast to its earthbound Iberian counterpart. A relatively benign colonial legacy in one instance, and a predominantly malign one in the other, appeared the key to an understanding of their very different destinies.

The retrospective reading of the histories of colonial societies inevitably conceals or distorts aspects of a past that needs to be understood on its own terms, rather than in the light of later preconceptions and preoccupations. To see societies in the context of their own times rather than from the privileged vantage-point afforded by hindsight is not to excuse or mitigate their crimes and follies. As the fate of the indigenous peoples and imported Africans makes all too clear, the records of New World colonization by both Britons and Spaniards are stained by innumerable horrors.

A scrutiny of the record of the two imperial powers in the light of contemporary, rather than later, assumptions, attitudes and capabilities suggests that Spain possessed both the advantages and the disadvantages commonly associated with the role of the pioneer. As first comers to America, Spaniards enjoyed more room for manoeuvre than their rivals and successors, who had to content themselves with territories not already occupied by the subjects of the Spanish crown. Since the lands seized by Spain included large settled indigenous populations and rich mineral deposits, this dictated an imperial strategy that had as its aim the bringing of Christianity and European-style 'civility' to these populations, and the exploitation of their mineral resources, in line with the not unreasonable contemporary equation of precious metals with wealth.

As first comers, however, the Spaniards were faced with enormous problems, and had few precedents to guide their responses. They had to confront, subdue and convert large populations of whose very existence Europe had hitherto been unaware. They had to exploit the human and natural resources of the conquered territories in ways that would ensure the viability of the new colonial societies they were in process of establishing, while simultaneously ensuring a steady flow of benefits to the metropolitan centre; and they had to institute a system of government that would enable them to pursue their imperial strategy in lands that were spread over an immense geographical area, and were separated from the home country by a sea voyage of eight weeks or more.

Not surprisingly, the Spanish crown and its agents made massive mistakes as they set about their task. They first over-estimated, and then under-estimated, the readiness of indigenous peoples to assimilate the religious and cultural gifts they believed themselves to be bringing. The church compounded the error by rejecting the idea of a native priesthood, which might have facilitated the work of conversion. In matters of government, the crown's determination to create an institutional framework designed to ensure compliance by its officials and the obedience of its overseas subjects encouraged the creation of excessively elaborate bureaucratic mechanisms that tended to subvert the very purposes for which they had been devised. In its pursuit of financial benefits from its overseas possessions, the accordance by the crown of priority to the exploitation of the astonishing mineral wealth of its American territories introduced distortions into the development of local and regional economies, and locked Spain and its empire into a commercial system so heavily regulated as to prove counter-productive.

Spanish policies were in line with early sixteenth-century European assumptions about the nature of non-European peoples, the nature and sources of wealth, and the promotion of the civil and religious values of Christendom. Once adopted, however, they were not easily changed. Too much work went into the initial setting of the course to allow for major changes of tack, as the Bourbon reformers would in due course find to their cost. Consequently, like one of the great galleons sailing on the *carrera de Indias,* the Spanish Monarchy and empire sailed majestically on its way, while foreign predators closed in for the kill.

Among those predators, although not initially in the forefront, were the English. Through a combination of choice and necessity, theirs was a smaller vessel, and easier to manoeuvre. Elizabethan and Stuart Englishmen also possessed the incalculable advantage of being able to take Spain first as a model, and then as a warning. If they sought initially to replicate Spanish methods and achievements, the very different nature of the American environment in which they found themselves, together with the transformations in English society and the English polity brought about by the Protestant Reformation and by changes in contemporary conceptions of national power and wealth, set them on their own distinctive course.

That course, which was the result of a multitude of individual and local decisions rather than of a centrally directed imperial strategy, led to the creation of a number of colonial societies that differed markedly from each other, although they came to share certain fundamental features. Among the most important of these were representative assemblies, and the acceptance, often grudging, of a plurality of faiths and creeds. As the Dutch Republic had already shown, and as seventeenth-century England came to discover, the combination of political consent and religious tolerance proved to be a successful formula for unlocking the door to economic growth. Shielded by Britain's growing military and naval power, the mainland American colonies confirmed once again the effectiveness of the formula as they moved in the eighteenth century at an accelerating pace towards demographic and territorial expansion, and rising productivity.

The visibly increasing prosperity of its colonies offered an obvious inducement to eighteenth-century Britain to capitalize more effectively on the expected benefits of empire. While the mother country had always looked on the American colonies as a potentially valuable source of products that could not be grown at home, it became increasingly apparent that Britain was spending more money on colonial administration and defence than it obtained in return. Adam Smith expressed the dilemma nicely when he wrote in 1776:

> The rulers of Great Britain have, for more than a century past, amused the people with the imagination that they possessed a great empire on the west side of the Atlantic. This empire, however, has existed in imagination only. It has hitherto been, not an empire, but the project of an empire . . . If the project cannot be completed, it ought to be given up. If any of the provinces of the British empire cannot be made to contribute towards the support of the whole empire, it is surely time that Great Britain should free herself from the expence of defending those provinces in time of war, and of supporting any part of their civil or military establishments in time of peace, and endeavour to accommodate her future views and designs to the real mediocrity of her circumstances.[6]

Modern attempts at cost–benefit analysis tend to bear out Smith's perception. Although the colonies provided a rapidly expanding market for eighteenth-century Britain's industrial output, and the ratio of costs to benefits fluctuated over time, current estimates suggest that in the period just before the American Revolution, the thirteen mainland colonies, and possibly also the British West Indies, brought 'no significant, if any, positive benefits to Britain'.[7] The calculation, restricted purely to what can be measured and quantified, naturally leaves out of account such imponderables as the contribution of its American colonies to Great Britain's international power and prestige, and the range of alternative possibilities open to the British economy if there had been no American empire.

To appearances, at least, the ratio of costs to benefits for Spain was substantially more favourable. The massive silver resources of New Spain and Peru enabled it over the course of three centuries not only to cover the expenses of American administration and defence, but also to ship regular remittances to Seville or Cadiz that amounted to some 15–20 per cent of the crown's annual revenues in the reign of Charles III, just as in the reign of Philip II two centuries before. Spanish America, therefore, unlike British America, was self-sustaining, and did not of itself constitute a drain on the Castilian tax-payer.[8]

This, however, should not obscure the enormous costs and consequences to metropolitan Spain arising from its possession of a silver-rich American empire.[9] While bullion from the Indies sustained the international position of the Spanish Monarchy between the mid-sixteenth and mid-seventeenth centuries as the dominant power in the western world, it also encouraged the Spanish crown and Castilian society to live consistently beyond their means. Imperial ambition consistently outran imperial resources, and it was this situation that the Bourbons hoped to correct when they embarked on their programme of reforms. These were at least partially successful in that the increased income from America allowed the Spanish treasury to keep pace over some three decades with the escalating costs of maintaining the country's great power status. At a time when France and Britain were faced with a rapidly mounting public debt, Spanish public finances avoided running serious deficits during the reign of Charles III (1759–88), thanks to the enormous contributions made by the treasuries of New Spain and Peru. Even these, however, proved insufficient in the end. Solvency dwindled and disappeared under the pressures of almost constant warfare in the years after 1790.[10]

While regular injections of American silver served to keep Spanish royal finances afloat, over the long term the benefits of Spain's empire of the Indies accrued more to Europe in general than to the mother country. The initial stimulus given to the Castilian economy by the conquest and colonization of America tended to diminish as Castilian products lost their competitiveness in international markets as a consequence of inflationary pressures which can be at least partially attributed to the influx of American silver.[11] Although America continued to generate some incentives to Spanish economic growth, it failed to propel the metropolitan economy forward, partly because so many of the profits of empire were devoted to sustaining foreign and dynastic policies that were inimical, or largely unfavourable, to development of the domestic economy. These policies in turn reinforced traditional social and political institutions and structures, thus reducing Spain's capacity for innovating change.

Unable to make effective use of the rewards of empire in ways that would enhance national productivity, Spain also saw those rewards slip from its grasp. 'There is nothing more common', wrote a British historian of Spain's American empire in 1741, 'than to hear Spain compared to a sieve, which, whatever it receives, is never the fuller.'[12] The silver of the Indies poured through the sieve as Spanish consumers used it to finance their purchase of foreign luxuries, and the crown deployed it to fund its foreign wars. With Spain's domestic economy incapable of supplying the goods required by an expanding colonial market, the shortfall was made up by foreign manufactures that were either shipped in the fleets departing annually from Seville or Cadiz, or were smuggled directly into Spain's American territories in a massive international contraband operation that no amount of mercantilist legislation could prevent or control. The silver that, in consequence, fell through the meshes of the Spanish sieve flowed into the economies of Europe and Asia, generating in the process an international monetary system whose development did much to facilitate the global expansion of trade.[13]

Spain's American empire, however, was much more than simply a mechanism for extracting and exporting the precious metals that would replenish royal coffers and sustain global commerce. It also represented a conscious, coherent and – at least in theory – centrally controlled attempt to incorporate and integrate the newly discovered lands into the King of Spain's dominions. This involved Christianizing and reducing to European norms their indigenous peoples, harnessing their labour and skills to meet imperial requirements, and establishing on the farther side of the Atlantic new societies made up of conquerors and conquered that would be authentic extensions of the mother country and replicate its values and ideals.

Inevitably, this grand imperial design could only be realized in part. There were too many differences between the American environment and the more familiar environment of Europe; too many conflicting interests were involved in the enterprise to ensure the coherent application of a unified policy; and the presence of so many indigenous survivors of the pre-conquest societies inevitably shaped the character of the successor societies in ways that proved disconcerting to peninsular Spaniards, who were alarmed by the rise of racially and culturally mixed populations through the mingling of the blood of the conquerors with that of the conquered. Added to this was the importation of large numbers of Africans. The outcome of all this mingling was the creation of societies composed, as Crèvecoeur disparagingly noted, 'of such a variety of castes and shades, as never before were exhibited on any part of the earth'.

Given the scale and complexity of the challenges that faced them, it is surprising that the Spaniards realized as much of their imperial dream as they did. By violence and example they managed to Christianize and hispanicize large sections of the indigenous population to a degree that may not have satisfied their own expectations, but left a decisive and lasting imprint on indigenous beliefs and practices. They established the institutions of an American empire that lasted for 300 years, and – at enormous cost to their indigenous subjects and an imported African labour force – they reshaped the economies of the subjugated lands into patterns tailored to meet European requirements. This won for them a regular surplus for export to Europe while simultaneously creating the conditions that permitted the development of a distinctive and culturally creative urban-based civilization in their American possessions.

This civilization, of increasing ethnic complexity with each passing generation, was given coherence by the common institutions of church and state, a common religion and language, the presence of an elite of Spanish descent, and a set of underlying assumptions about the working of the political and social order that had been reformulated and articulated in the sixteenth century by Spanish neo-scholastics.[14] Their organic conception of a divinely ordained society dedicated to the achievement of the common good was inclusive rather than exclusive in approach. As a result, the indigenous peoples of Spanish America were given at least a limited space of their own in the new political and social order. By seizing such religious, legal and institutional opportunities as were afforded them, individuals and communities succeeded in establishing rights, affirming identities, and fashioning for themselves a new cultural universe on the ruins of the universe that had been shattered beyond recall in the trauma of European conquest and occupation.

After an uneasy period of cohabitation, the English settlers, faced with sparser indigenous populations which did not lend themselves so readily to mobilization as a labour force, chose instead to adopt an exclusionary rather than an inclusive approach, along the lines already established in Ireland. Their Indians, unlike those of the Spaniards, were shunted to the margins of the new colonial societies, or were expelled beyond their borders. When the colonists followed the Iberian example and turned to imported Africans to meet their labour needs, the space accorded their slaves by law and religion was even more limited than it was in Spanish America.

Although their refusal to include Indians and Africans within the boundaries of their imagined communities would store up a terrible legacy for future generations, it also gave the English colonists more freedom of manoeuvre to make reality conform to the constructs of their imagination. Without the impulsion to integrate the indigenous population into the new colonial societies, there was less need for the compromises that their Spanish American counterparts found themselves compelled to accept. Similarly, there was less need for the external mechanisms of control through imperial government adopted by the Spaniards in order to bring stability and social cohesion to racially mixed societies.

The latitude allowed by the British crown to the transatlantic communities to live their lives largely free of external restraints reflected the absence on the northern American mainland of the imperatives provided by the existence of mineral wealth and large indigenous populations that prompted the Spanish crown to adopt its interventionist policies. It also reflected the changing balance of political and social forces in Stuart England. The comparative weakness of the Stuarts gave free rein to groups of English men and women to establish themselves more or less as they wished on the farther shores of the Atlantic, with only sporadic and relatively ineffectual interference by the imperial government. As a result, eighteenth-century Britain woke up belatedly to discover that, in Adam Smith's words, its American empire had 'existed in imagination only'.

Imperial weakness, if measured by the failure of the British state to appropriate more of the wealth generated by the colonial societies and to intervene more effectively in the management of their domestic affairs, proved to be a source of long-term strength for those societies themselves. They were left to make their own way in the world, and to develop their own mechanisms for survival. This gave them resilience in the face of adversity, and a growing confidence in their capacity to shape their own institutions and cultural patterns in the ways best suited to their own particular needs. Since the motives for the foundation of distinctive colonies varied, and since they were created at different times and in different environments over the span of more than a century, there were wide variations in the responses they adopted and in the character their societies assumed. This diversity enriched them all.

Yet, for all their diversity, the colonies also had many features in common. These did not, however, derive, as in Spain's American empire, from the imposition by the imperial government of uniform administrative and judicial structures and a uniform religion, but from a shared political and legal culture which gave a high priority to the right of political representation and to a set of liberties protected by the Common Law. The possession of this culture set them on the path that led to the development of societies based on the principles of consent and the sanctity of individual rights. In the crisis years of the 1760s and 1770s this shared libertarian political culture proved sufficiently strong to rally them in defence of a common cause. In uniting to defend their English liberties, the colonies ensured the continuation of the creative pluralism that had characterized their existence from the start.

Yet the story could have been very different. If Henry VII had been willing to sponsor Columbus's first voyage, and if an expeditionary force of West Countrymen had conquered Mexico for Henry VIII, it is possible to imagine an alternative, and by no means implausible, script: a massive increase in the wealth of the English crown as growing quantities of American silver flowed into the royal coffers; the development of a coherent imperial strategy to exploit the resources of the New World; the creation of an imperial bureaucracy to govern the settler societies and their subjugated populations; the declining influence of parliament in national life, and the establishment of an absolutist English monarchy financed by the silver of America.[15]

As it happened, matters turned out otherwise. The conqueror of Mexico showed himself to be a loyal servant of the King of Castile, not the King of England, and it was an English, not a Spanish, trading company that commissioned an ex-privateer to found his country's first colony on the North American mainland. Behind the cultural values and the economic and social imperatives that shaped the British and Spanish empires of the Atlantic world lay a host of personal choices and the unpredictable consequences of unforeseen events.

Abbreviations

AHR	*The American Historical Review*
BAE	*Biblioteca de Autores Españoles*
CHLA	*The Cambridge History of Latin America*, ed. Leslie Bethell (11 vols, Cambridge, 1984–95)
HAHR	*The Hispanic American Historical Review*
OHBE	*The Oxford History of the British Empire*, ed. Wm. Roger Louis *et al.* (5 vols, Oxford, 1998)
TRHS	*Transactions of the Royal Historical Society*
WMQ	*The William and Mary Quarterly*

Notes

Introduction. Worlds Overseas

1. Cited by Carla Rahn Phillips, *Life at Sea in the Sixteenth Century. The Landlubber's Lament of Eugenio de Salazar* (The James Ford Bell Lectures, no. 24, University of Minnesota, 1987), p. 21.
2. For numbers of emigrants, see Ida Altman and James Horn (eds.), *'To Make America'. European Emigration in the Early Modern Period* (Berkeley, Los Angeles, Oxford, 1991), p. 3.
3. Enrique Otte, *Cartas privadas de emigrantes a Indias, 1540–1616* (Seville, 1988), letter 73. For life at sea on the Spanish Atlantic see Pablo E. Pérez-Mallaína, *Spain's Men of the Sea. Daily Life on the Indies Fleets in the Sixteenth Century* (Baltimore and London, 1998).
4. Cited in David Cressy, *Coming Over. Migration and Communication between England and New England in the Seventeenth Century* (Cambridge, 1987), p. 157.
5. See Daniel Vickers, 'Competency and Competition: Economic Culture in Early America', *WMQ*, 3rd ser., 47 (1990), pp. 3–29.
6. For the cognitive problems facing Early Modern Europeans in America, see Anthony Pagden, *The Fall of Natural Man* (revised edn, Cambridge, 1986), especially the Introduction and ch. 1.
7. David Hume, *Essays. Moral, Political and Literary* (Oxford, 1963), p. 210.
8. See Antonello Gerbi, *The Dispute of the New World. The History of a Polemic, 1750–1900*, trans. Jeremy Moyle (Pittsburgh, 1973).
9. Louis Hartz, *The Founding of New Societies* (New York, 1964), p. 3.
10. Turner first advanced his hypothesis in his 1893 lecture to the American Historical Association on 'The Significance of the Frontier in American History' (reprinted in *Frontier and Section. Selected Essays of Frederick Jackson Turner* (Englewood Cliffs, NJ, 1961)).
11. For a summary of the criticisms, see Ray Allen Billington, 'The American Frontier', in Paul Bohannen and Fred Plog (eds), *Beyond the Frontier. Social Process and Cultural Change* (Garden City, NY, 1967), pp. 3–24.
12. See, for Latin America, Alistair Hennessy, *The Frontier in Latin American History* (Albuquerque, NM, 1978), and Francisco de Solano and Salvador Bernabeu (eds), *Estudios (nuevos y viejos) sobre la frontera* (Madrid, 1991).
13. Herbert E. Bolton, 'The Epic of Greater America', reprinted in his *Wider Horizons of American History* (New York, 1939; repr. Notre Dame, IL, 1967). See also Lewis Hanke (ed.), *Do the Americas Have a Common History?* (New York, 1964), and J. H. Elliott, *Do the Americas Have a Common History? An Address* (The John Carter Brown Library, Providence, RI, 1998).
14. Although, for a recent bold attempt to grapple with the question in short compass, see Felipe Fernández-Armesto, *The Americas. A Hemispheric History* (New York, 2003).

15. Beginning with Frank Tannenbaum's seminal and provocative book, *Slave and Citizen. The Negro in the Americas* (New York, 1964).

16. See in particular Altman and Horn (eds), '*To Make America*', and Nicholas Canny (ed.), *Europeans on the Move. Studies on European Migration, 1500–1800* (Oxford, 1994). For the now fashionable concept of 'Atlantic History', in which slavery and emigration are important players, see Bernard Bailyn, *Atlantic History. Concept and Contours* (Cambridge, MA and London, 2005), David Armitage and Michael J. Braddick (eds), *The British Atlantic World, 1500–1800* (New York, 2002), and Horst Pietschmann (ed.), *Atlantic History and the Atlantic System* (Göttingen, 2002).

17. Ronald Syme, *Colonial Elites. Rome, Spain and the Americas* (Oxford, 1958), p. 42.

18. James Lang, *Conquest and Commerce. Spain and England in the Americas* (New York, San Francisco, London, 1975).

19. Claudio Véliz, *The New World of the Gothic Fox. Culture and Economy in British and Spanish America* (Berkeley, Los Angeles, London, 1994). See my review, 'Going Baroque', *New York Review of Books*, 20 October 1994.

20. For discussions of the problems of comparative history see George M. Frederickson, 'Comparative History', in Michael Kammen (ed.), *The Past Before Us* (New York, 1980), ch. 19, and John H. Elliott, 'Comparative History', in Carlos Barra (ed.), *Historia a debate* (3 vols, Santiago de Compostela, 1995), 3, pp. 9–19, and the references there given.

Chapter 1. Intrusion and Empire

1. England and its overseas possessions finally switched to the Gregorian calendar in 1752. The transition in the American colonies went smoothly, partly because the presence of so many immigrants from continental Europe meant that many colonial Americans had become used to operating the Julian and Gregorian calendars simultaneously. See Mark M. Smith, 'Culture, Commerce and Calendar Reform in Colonial America', *WMQ*, 3rd ser., 55 (1998), pp. 557–84.

2. For the total figure of about 530 Europeans on Cortés's expedition see Hugh Thomas, *The Conquest of Mexico* (London, 1993), p. 151, n. 36.

3. Francisco López de Gómara, *Cortés. The Life of the Conqueror by his Secretary*, trans. and ed. Lesley Byrd Simpson (Berkeley and Los Angeles, 1964), p. 66. For the events of the conquest, see Thomas, *The Conquest*, and Hernán Cortés, *Letters from Mexico*, trans. and ed. Anthony Pagden (New Haven and London, 1986).

4. José Luis Martínez (ed.), *Documentos cortesianos* (4 vols, Mexico City, 1990–2), 1, p. 55 (Doc. 1, 'Instrucciones de Diego Velázquez a Hernán Cortés', clause 55). See also Francisco Morales Padrón, 'Descubrimiento y toma de posesión', *Anuario de Estudios Americanos*, 12 (1955), pp. 321–80 for the ceremonial acts by which Spaniards took possession.

5. See Martínez (ed.), *Documentos*, 1, and José Luis Martínez, *Hernán Cortés* (Mexico City, 1990), pp. 141–3.

6. See John H. Elliott, 'Cortés, Velázquez and Charles V', in Cortés, *Letters from Mexico*, pp. xi-xxxvii, for this and Cortés's further manoeuvres.

7. Gómara, *Cortés*, pp. 138–9.

8. Cortés, *Letters from Mexico*, pp. 85–6 and 98–9.

9. Anthony Pagden, *Lords of All the World. Ideologies of Empire in Spain, Britain and France c.1500–c.1800* (New Haven and London, 1995), p. 64.

10. John Parker, *Books to Build an Empire* (Amsterdam, 1965), pp. 45, 94.

11. Francisco López de Gómara, *The Pleasant Historie of the Conquest of the Weast India, now called New Spayne* (London, 1578). The book was republished in 1596. See the introduction by L. B. Simpson to his translation of Gómara, *Cortés*, p. xvii, and Parker, *Books to Build an Empire*, pp. 87–8.

12. Gómara, *Cortés*, p. 184; *The Pleasant Historie*, pp. 230 and 232.

13. Richard Hakluyt, *The Principall Navigations Voiages and Discoveries of the English Nation*, facsimile edn (2 vols, Hakluyt Society, Cambridge, 1965), 2, p. 715 (here, as elsewhere in the book, I have modernized the spelling).

14. Parker, *Books to Build*, p. 105.

15. E. G. R. Taylor, *The Original Writings and Correspondence of the Two Richard Hakluyts* (2 vols, Hakluyt Society, 2nd ser., 76–7, London, 1935), 2, p. 275.

16. D. B. Quinn (ed.), *The Roanoke Voyages* (2 vols, Hakluyt Society, 2nd ser., 104–5, London, 1955), 1, p. 6, and see for the Roanoke enterprise David Beers Quinn, *Set Fair for Roanoke. Voyages and Colonies, 1584–1606* (Chapel Hill, NC and London, 1985).

17. Henry R. Wagner, *The Rise of Fernando Cortés* (Los Angeles, 1944), pp. 27–8; Martínez, *Hernán Cortés*, pp. 128–9.

18. Charles M. Andrews, *The Colonial Period of American History* (4 vols, New Haven, 1934–8; repr. 1964), 1, ch. 4; David Beers Quinn, *England and the Discovery of America, 1481–1620* (London, 1974), ch. 18; and see Theodore K. Rabb, *Enterprise and Empire* (Cambridge, MA, 1967), for merchant and gentry investment.

19. Hugh Thomas, in his *Conquest of Mexico*, pp. 129–30, seems to have established that he sailed in 1506 and not, as is normally stated, in 1504.

20. The story is recounted by the sixteenth-century chronicler, Cervantes de Salazar. See J. H. Elliott, *Spain and its World, 1500–1700* (New Haven and London, 1989), ch. 2 ('The Mental World of Hernán Cortés'), pp. 33–4.

21. For Newport's life, about which relatively little is known, see Kenneth R. Andrews, 'Christopher Newport of Limehouse, Mariner', *WMQ*, 3rd ser., 11 (1954), pp. 28–41, and his *Elizabethan Privateering* (Cambridge, 1964), pp. 84–6.

22. No complete list is available, but a partial list is provided by Captain John Smith in *The Complete Works of Captain John Smith*, ed. Philip L. Barbour (3 vols, Chapel Hill, NC and London, 1986), 1, pp. 207–9.

23. Edmund S. Morgan, *American Slavery, American Freedom* (New York, 1975), p. 84.

24. Robert Himmerich y Valencia, *The Encomenderos of New Spain, 1521–1555* (Austin, TX, 1991), p. 29.

25. Bernal Díaz del Castillo, *Historia verdadera de la conquista de la Nueva España*, ed. Joaquín Ramírez Cabañas (3 vols, Mexico City, 1944), 3, p. 239.

26. Himmerich, *Encomenderos*, p. 10.

27. Alden Vaughan, *American Genesis. Captain John Smith and the Founding of Virginia* (Boston and Toronto, 1975), p. 31.

28. M. I. Finley, 'Colonies – an Attempt at a Typology', *TRHS*, 5th ser., 26 (1976), pp. 167–88.

29. Nicholas Canny, *Kingdom and Colony. Ireland in the Atlantic World, 1560–1800* (Baltimore, 1988), p. 13.

30. A possible distinction between a *plantation* and a *colony*, meaning the people who settled and worked the land, appears in a letter written by Emmanuel Downing in 1633, when he writes that Sir Ferdinando Gorges and his co-partners 'have these many years laboured to make a plantation in New England', and 'have of late made claim to the very ground where Mr. Winthrop, with a colony, hath built and planted . . .' (cited by Francis J. Bremer, *John Winthrop. America's Forgotten Founding Father* (Oxford, 2003), p. 233).

31. From *The Planter's Plea* (Anon., 1630), in Myra Jehlen and Michael Warner (eds), *The English Literatures of America, 1500–1800* (New York and London, 1997), p. 100. 'Settler', as a word interchangeable with 'planter', first appeared at the end of the seventeenth century.

32. Jaime Eyzaguirre, *Ideario y ruta de la emancipación chilena* (Santiago de Chile, 1957), p. 27.

33. Philip L. Barbour (ed.), *The Jamestown Voyages under the First Charter, 1606–1609* (2 vols, Hakluyt Society, 2nd ser., 136–7, Cambridge, 1969), 1, doc. 1, p. 24 (Letters Patent to Sir Thomas Gates and Others, 10 April 1606).

34. Milagros del Vas Mingo, *Las capitulaciones de Indias en el siglo XVI* (Madrid, 1986), doc. 10.

35. Taylor, *Writings of the Two Hakluyts*, 2, doc. 47, p. 330.

36. Smith, *Works*, 1, p. 205; Vaughan, *American Genesis*, p. 27.

37. For the early Spanish interest in this region, see Paul E. Hoffman, *A New Andalucia and a Way to the Orient. The American Southeast During the Sixteenth Century* (Baton Rouge, LA and London, 1990).

38. For Ajacán see Clifford M. Lewis and Albert J. Loomie (eds), *The Spanish Jesuit Mission in Virginia, 1570–1572* (Chapel Hill, NC, 1953), and Charlotte M. Gradie, 'Spanish Jesuits

in Virginia. The Mission that Failed', *The Virginia Magazine of History and Biography*, 96 (1988), pp. 131–56. Also David J. Weber, *The Spanish Frontier in North America* (New Haven and London, 1992), pp. 71–3. For 'Don Luis de Velasco' and his identification with Opechancanough, Carl Bridenbaugh, *Jamestown, 1544–1699* (New York and Oxford, 1989), pp. 14–20. The identification is much contested. See Helen C. Rountree, *Pocahontas's People. The Powhatan Indians of Virginia through Four Centuries* (Norman, OK and London, 1990), pp. 18–19.

39. Smith, *Works*, 1, p. 206. For relations between the settlers and the Powhatan in the first years of Jamestown, see Martin H. Quitt, 'Trade and Acculturation at Jamestown, 1607–1609: the Limits of Understanding', *WMQ*, 3rd ser., 52 (1995), pp. 227–58.

40. Barbour, *Jamestown Voyages*, 1, doc. 13, p. 88 ('A Relation . . . 21 May–21 June 1607').

41. Alexander Brown, *The Genesis of the United States* (2 vols, London, 1890), 1, doc. lxxxix, p. 299; Wesley Frank Craven, 'Indian Policy in Early Virginia', *WMQ*, 3rd ser., 1 (1944), pp. 65–82, at p. 65.

42. Charles Verlinden, *The Beginnings of Modern Colonization* (Ithaca, NY and London, 1970), pp. 230–1. For a recent brief survey of interpretations of the Alexandrine bulls, see Guy Bédouelle, 'La Donation alexandrine et le traité de Tordesillas', in *1492. Le choc des deux mondes* (Actes du Colloque international organisé par la Commission Nationale Suisse pour l'UNESCO, Geneva, 1992), pp. 193–209.

43. See Juan López de Palacios Rubios, *De las islas del mar océano*, ed. S. Zavala and A. Millares Carlo (Mexico and Buenos Aires, 1954), pp. cxxiv–cxxvi; James Muldoon, *The Americas in the Spanish World Order. The Justification for Conquest in the Seventeenth Century* (Philadelphia, 1994), pp. 136–9; Patricia Seed, *Ceremonies of Possession in Europe's Conquest of the New World, 1492–1640* (Cambridge, 1995), ch. 3.

44. Richard Hakluyt, 'Discourse of Western Planting' (1584) in Taylor, *Writings of the Two Hakluyts*, 2, p. 215.

45. D. B. Quinn (ed.), *The Voyages and Colonizing Enterprises of Sir Humphrey Gilbert* (Hakluyt Society, 2nd ser., vols 83–4, London, 1940), 2, p. 361.

46. William Strachey, *The Historie of Travell into Virginia Britania* (1612), ed. Louis B. Wright and Virginia Freund (Hakluyt Society, 2nd ser., vol. 103, London, 1953), pp. 9–10.

47. Pagden, *Lords of All the World*, pp. 76–7.

48. Francisco de Vitoria, *Political Writings*, ed. Anthony Pagden and Jeremy Lawrance (Cambridge, 1991), pp. 278–80 ('On the American Indians', 3.1).

49. William Crashaw's Sermon of 21 February 1609 (i.e. 1610 New Style) in Brown, *Genesis of the United States*, 1, doc. cxx, p. 363.

50. Barbour, *Jamestown Voyages*, 1, doc. 4, p. 51.

51. *Ibid.*, p. 52.

52. Ian K. Steele, *Warpaths. Invasions of North America* (Oxford, 1994), p. 41.

53. James Axtell, *After Columbus. Essays in the Ethnohistory of Colonial North America* (Oxford, 1988), ch. 10 ('The Rise and Fall of the Powhatan Empire').

54. Francis Jennings, *The Invasion of America* (Chapel Hill, NC, 1975), pp. 23–4; Axtell, *After Columbus*, p. 186.

55. For a review of the debate on the population of pre-conquest Mexico see Thomas, *The Conquest of Mexico*, appendix 1; Frederic W. Gleach, *Powhatan's World and Colonial Virginia. A Conflict of Cultures* (Lincoln, NE and London, 1997), p. 26, for Powhatan.

56. Smith, *Works*, 1, p. 173.

57. For early relations between Powhatan and the English, in addition to Rountree, *Pocahontas's People*, Gleach, *Powhatan's World*, and Axtell, *After Columbus*, ch. 10, see April Lee Hatfield, *Atlantic Virginia. Intercolonial Relations in the Seventeenth Century* (Philadelphia, 2004), ch. 1.

58. Strachey, *Travell into Virginia*, p. 106.

59. See the interpretation in Gleach, *Powhatan's World*, pp. 109–22.

60. Smith, *Works*, 1, p. 55.

61. Axtell, *After Columbus*, p. 129.

62. Elliott, *Spain and its World*, pp. 36–8; James Lockhart (ed.), *We People Here. Nahuatl Accounts of the Conquest of Mexico* (Repertorium Columbianum, 1, Berkeley, Los

Angeles, and London, 1993), p. 17; Susan D. Gillespie, *The Aztec Kings* (Tucson, AZ, 1989), pp. 226–30.

63. Smith, *Works*, 1, pp. 236–7.
64. Barbour, *Jamestown Voyages*, 1, doc. 1, p. 28.
65. *Ibid.*, 1, doc. 17, p. 107 (letter from William Brewster, 1607).
66. *Ibid.*, 1, doc. 21, p. 113.
67. *Ibid.*, 1, doc. 14, p. 101.
68. Morgan, *American Slavery, American Freedom*, pp. 76–7.
69. Smith, *Works*, 1, p. 327.
70. For a recent account of 'the Great Massacre of 1622' in the context of Powhatan culture, see Gleach, *Powhatan's World*, ch. 6. Gleach prefers the word *coup* to *massacre*. Other historians speak of an *uprising* (see his Introduction, pp. 4–5). No single word can be found to cover all interpretations.
71. As in James Lang's *Conquest and Commerce*.
72. See R. R. Davies, *The First English Empire. Power and Identities in the British Isles, 1093–1343* (Oxford, 2000), for an acute analysis of English expansion into medieval Wales and Ireland as a colonizing and annexing process.
73. Nicholas Canny, *The Elizabethan Conquest of Ireland. A Pattern Established, 1565–1576* (New York, 1976), p. 118.
74. For a brief account in English of the Reconquista, see D. W. Lomax, *The Reconquest of Spain* (London and New York, 1978).
75. For European voyages of exploration before Columbus, see the surveys by J. R. S. Phillips, *The Medieval Expansion of Europe* (Oxford, 1988), and Felipe Fernández-Armesto, *Before Columbus. Exploration and Colonisation from the Mediterranean to the Atlantic, 1229–1492* (London, 1987).
76. See in particular Vitorino De Maghalaes Godinho, *A economia dos descobrimentos henriquinos* (Lisbon, 1962), ch. 5, and Peter Russell, *Prince Henry 'the Navigator'. A Life* (New Haven and London, 2000).
77. For the Canary Islands, see Felipe Fernández-Armesto, *The Canary Islands after the Conquest* (Oxford, 1982).
78. See Verlinden, *Beginnings of Modern Colonization*, ch. 1.
79. Christopher Columbus, *Journal of the First Voyage*, ed. and trans. B. W. Ife (Warminster, 1990), pp. 133–5.
80. Juan Pérez de Tudela, *Las armadas de Indias y los orígenes de la política de colonización, 1492–1505* (Madrid, 1956), pp. 82–5.
81. Carl Ortwin Sauer, *The Early Spanish Main* (Cambridge, 1966), remains fundamental for Hispaniola and its fate. For a more recent survey, based on the results of archaeological investigation, see Kathleen Deagan and José María Cruxent, *Columbus's Outpost among the Taínos. Spain and America at La Isabela, 1492–1498* (New Haven and London, 2002). Hugh Thomas, *Rivers of Gold. The Rise of the Spanish Empire* (London, 2003), provides a comprehensive survey of early Spanish activities in the Caribbean and on the central American mainland.
82. See Mario Góngora, *Studies in the Colonial History of Spanish America* (Cambridge, 1975), ch. 1.
83. For example, when describing the city of Cholula in his second letter: 'I counted from a mosque more than 430 towers in this city, and they were all of mosques' (Hernán Cortés, *Cartas y documentos* (ed. Mario Sánchez-Barba (Mexico City, 1963), p. 51).
84. Góngora, *Studies*, p. 2; Cortés, *Letters from Mexico*, p. 40.
85. Ursula Lamb, *Frey Nicolás de Ovando. Gobernador de las Indias, 1501–1509* (Madrid, 1956).
86. Francisco López de Gómara, *Primera parte de la historia general de las Indias* (BAE, vol. 22, Madrid, 1852), p. 181. For Cortés and his philosophy of settlement, see Richard Konetzke, 'Hernán Cortés como poblador de la Nueva España', *Estudios Cortesianos* (Madrid, 1948), pp. 341–81.
87. For Cortés's entrepreneurial activities, see France V. Scholes, 'The Spanish Conqueror as a Business Man: a Chapter in the History of Fernando Cortés', *New Mexico Quarterly*, 28 (1958), pp. 5–29.

88. Murdo J. MacLeod, *Spanish Central America. A Socioeconomic History, 1520–1720* (Berkeley, 1973), ch. 6.

89. Cited by J. H. Elliott, *The Old World and the New, 1492–1650* (Cambridge, 1970; repr. 1992), p. 78, from Gonzalo Fernández de Oviedo, *Historia general y natural de las Indias* (5 vols, BAE, vols 117–21, Madrid, 1959), 1, p. 110.

90. Gómara, *Historia general*, BAE, vol. 22, pp. 177 and 184. Gómara uses the word *mejorar* for *improve*. For the language of improvement in British America, see Nicholas Canny and Anthony Pagden (eds), *Colonial Identity in the Atlantic World, 1500–1800* (Princeton, 1987), pp. 10–11, 228–9, and David Hancock, *Citizens of the World. London Merchants and the Integration of the British Atlantic Community, 1735–1785* (Cambridge, 1995), pp. 281–2.

91. The Pedrarias Dávila expedition of 1513 is another. See María del Carmen Mena García, *Pedrarias Dávila o 'la Ira de Dios'. Una historia olvidada* (Seville, 1992), p. 32, for Ferdinand's close personal interest in the details of the expedition.

92. Cortés, *Letters from Mexico*, p. 48.

93. Roy Strong, *Gloriana. The Portraits of Queen Elizabeth I* (London, 1987), pp. 131–3. I am grateful to Professor David Armitage for drawing my attention to this reference.

94. e.g. by Edmund Spenser in his dedication of *The Faerie Queene* to Elizabeth as the 'Magnificent Empresse Elizabeth by the Grace of God Queen of England Fraunce and Ireland and of Virginia'. David Armitage, *The Ideological Origins of the British Empire* (Cambridge, 2000), pp. 52–3, and see pp. 45–7 for the sixteenth-century emergence of an 'Empire of Great Britain'.

95. Strachey, *Travell into Virginia*, p. 9.

96. David Quinn's pioneering work in finding connections between the colonization of Ireland and North America, for instance in *The Elizabethans and the Irish* (Ithaca, NY, 1966), has been followed up by Nicholas Canny, especially in his *Kingdom and Colony*.

97. *Voyages of Gilbert*, 1, p. 9.

98. For a convenient summary of the arguments, see Kenneth R. Andrews, *Trade, Plunder and Settlement. Maritime Enterprise and the Genesis of the British Empire, 1480–1630* (Cambridge, 1984), pp. 187–90.

99. For Norumbega, see Emerson W. Baker *et al.* (eds), *American Beginnings. Exploration, Culture and Cartography in the Land of Norumbega* (Lincoln, NE and London, 1994).

100. For Extremadura, see Ida Altman, *Emigrants and Society. Extremadura and Spanish America in the Sixteenth Century* (Berkeley, Los Angeles, London, 1989), ch. 6. For the West Country connection, Joyce Youings, 'Raleigh's Country and the Sea', *Proceedings of the British Academy*, 75 (1989), pp. 267–90.

101. Morgan, *American Slavery, American Freedom*, pp. 83–4.

102. *Voyages of Gilbert*, 1, p. 71.

103. See Juan Friede, *Los Welser en la conquista de Venezuela* (Caracas, 1961), for the failure of the Welsers, and Wesley Frank Craven, *Dissolution of the Virginia Company. The Failure of a Colonial Experiment* (New York, 1932), for that of the Virginia Company.

104. See John H. Elliott, *Illusion and Disillusionment. Spain and the Indies* (The Creighton Lecture for 1991, University of London, 1992).

105. Richard Helgerson, *Forms of Nationhood. The Elizabethan Writing of England* (Chicago and London, 1992), p. 168.

106. Taylor, *Writings of the Two Hakluyts*, 1, p. 143.

107. *Ibid.*, 2, pp. 233–4.

108. Cited by Elliott, *Illusion and Disillusionment*, p. 14.

109. For an introduction to this debate, see Elliott, *Spain and its World*, ch. 11 ('Self-Perception and Decline in Early Seventeenth-Century Spain').

110. Cited from his *Memorial de la política necesaria y útil restauración a la república de España* (Valladolid, 1600), fo. 15v, in Elliott, *Illusion and Disillusionment*, pp. 12–13.

111. See Michel Cavillac, *Gueux et marchands dans le 'Guzmán de Alfarache', 1599–1604* (Bordeaux, 1993), especially ch. 5, for insights into this struggle in Castile at the turn of the century.

112. See Carole Shammas, 'English Commercial Development and American Colonization 1560–1620', in K. R. Andrews *et al.*, *The Westward Enterprise* (Liverpool, 1978), ch. 8. Also Charles Wilson, *Profit and Power* (London, 1957), and Barry Supple, *Commercial Crisis and Change in England, 1600–1642* (Cambridge, 1959).

113. Andrews, *Trade, Plunder and Settlement*, pp. 312–13.

114. Cited by Richard S. Dunn, *Puritan and Yankee. The Winthrop Dynasty of New England, 1630–1717* (Princeton, 1962), p. 36.

Chapter 2. Occupying American Space

1. William Burke, *An Account of the European Settlements in America* (6th edn., London, 1777), pp. 203–4. I am grateful to Dr Ian Harris of the University of Leicester for making available to me a copy of this book.

2. For a brilliant account by a modern geographer of the varieties of settlement of 'Atlantic America', see vol. 1 ('Atlantic America, 1492–1800') of D. W. Meinig, *The Shaping of America* (New Haven and London, 1986).

3. Everett Emerson (ed.), *Letters from New England. The Massachusetts Bay Colony, 1629–1638* (Amherst, MA, 1976), p. 21.

4. Smith, *Works*, 1, p. 143 ('A Map of Virginia').

5. José de Acosta, *Historia natural y moral de las Indias*, ed. Edmundo O'Gorman (2nd edn, Mexico City and Buenos Aires, 1962), p. 127.

6. Thomas Gomez, *L'Envers de l'Eldorado. Économie coloniale et travail indigène dans la Colombie du XVIème siècle* (Toulouse, 1984), p. 143.

7. The suggestive work of Patricia Seed, *Ceremonies of Possession*, and 'Taking Possession and Reading Texts: Establishing the Authority of Overseas Empires', *WMQ*, 3rd ser., 49 (1992), pp. 183–209, seems too keen to emphasize differences based on national stereotypes.

8. Above, p. 12; Pagden, *Lords of All the World*, p. 76.

9. Cited from *Partida* III, tit. 28, ley 29, by Morales Padrón, 'Descubrimiento y toma de posesión', p. 332.

10. Introduction by Eduardo Arcila Farias to Joseph del Campillo y Cosío, *Nuevo sistema de gobierno económico para la América* (2nd edn, Mérida, Venezuela, 1971), p. 50.

11. Pagden, *Lords of All the World*, pp. 91–2.

12. Cited by Morales Padrón, 'Descubrimiento y toma de posesión', p. 334.

13. *Journal of the First Voyage*, pp. 29 and 36.

14. Cristóbal Colón, *Textos y documentos completos*, ed. Consuelo Varela (2nd edn, Madrid, 1992), p. 272.

15. Morales Padrón, 'Descubrimiento y toma de posesión', pp. 331 and 342. For Cortés, see above, p. 4.

16. Hakluyt, *Navigations*, 2, pp. 687 and 702; Seed, 'Taking Possession', pp. 183–4.

17. Hakluyt, *Navigations*, 2, p. 677.

18. Gradie, 'Spanish Jesuits in Virginia', p. 133.

19. Pagden, *Lords of All the World*, pp. 76–9; and above p. 12.

20. Hakluyt, *Navigations*, 2, p. 687.

21. D. B. Quinn and Alison M. Quinn (eds.), *The New England Voyages 1602–1608* (Hakluyt Society, 2nd ser., vol. 161, London, 1983), p. 267.

22. Seed, 'Taking Possession', pp. 190–1.

23. Carmen Val Julián, 'Entre la realidad y el deseo. La toponomía del descubrimiento en Colón y Cortés', in Oscar Mazín Gómez (ed.), *México y el mundo hispánico* (2 vols, Zamora, Michoacán, 2000), 1, pp. 265–79; Stephen Greenblatt, *Marvelous Possessions. The Wonder of the New World* (Chicago, 1991), pp. 82–3; and, for the wider context of Columbus's choice of names, Valerie I. J. Flint, *The Imaginative Landscape of Christopher Columbus* (Princeton, 1992).

24. Helen Nader (trans. and ed.), *The Book of Privileges Issued to Christopher Columbus by King Fernando and Queen Isabel 1492–1502* (Repertorium Columbianum, 3, Berkeley, Los Angeles, Oxford, 1996), p. 99 (Letter of 16 August 1494).

25. Greenblatt, *Marvelous Possessions*, p. 82.

26. Barbara E. Mundy, *The Mapping of New Spain* (Chicago and London, 1996), p. 144.

27. Cortés, *Letters from Mexico*, p. 158. For naming practices by Cortés and other conquistadores, see Carmen Val Julián, 'La toponomía conquistadora', *Relaciones* (El Colegio de Michoacán), 70 (1997), pp. 41–61.

28. Baker, *American Beginnings*, ch. 3.

29. Smith, *Works*, 1, p. 324; Quinn, *New England Voyages*, p. 3.

30. Smith, *Works*, 3, p. 278.

31. Smith, *Works*, 1, pp. 309 and 319.

32. George R. Stewart, *Names on the Land. A Historical Account of Place-Naming in the United States* (New York, 1945; repr. 1954), p. 64.

33. *Ibid.*, p. 59.

34. Fernández de Oviedo, *Historia general y natural*, 2, p. 334. See also Seed, *Ceremonies of Possession*, p. 175.

35. *Iconoclastes*, p. 1, cited by Alicia Mayer, *Dos americanos, dos pensamientos. Carlos de Sigüenza y Góngora y Cotton Mather* (Mexico City, 1998), p. 161.

36. Cited by Stewart, *Names on the Land*, p. 53.

37. See Geoffrey Parker, *Empire, War and Faith in Early Modern Europe* (London, 2002), ch. 4 ('Philip II, Maps and Power'), and, more generally, for Iberian cartography in this period, Ricardo Padrón, *The Spacious World. Cartography, Literature, and Empire* (Chicago, 2004).

38. Mundy, *The Mapping of New Spain*; Richard L. Kagan, *Urban Images of the Hispanic World, 1493–1793* (New Haven and London, 2000), ch. 3; Francisco de Solano (ed.), *Cuestionarios para la formación de las Relaciones Geográficas de Indias, siglos XVI/XIX* (Madrid, 1988); Howard F. Cline, 'The Relaciones Geográficas of the Spanish Indies, 1577–1586', *HAHR*, 44 (1964), pp. 341–74.

39. Quoted by I. K. Steele, *Politics of Colonial Policy. The Board of Trade in Colonial Administration, 1696–1720* (Oxford, 1968), p. 154.

40. Benjamin Schmidt, 'Mapping an Empire: Cartographic and Colonial Rivalry in Seventeenth-Century Dutch and English North America', *WMQ*, 3rd ser., 54 (1997), pp. 549–78.

41. Baker, *American Beginnings*, p. 304.

42. Vas Mingo, *Las capitulaciones de Indias*, pp. 81 and 196.

43. Hakluyt, *Navigations*, 2, p. 687.

44. Friede, *Los Welser*, pp. 135–46; and see above, p. 25.

45. Andrews, *The Colonial Period*, 2, p. 282.

46. William Cronon, *Changes in the Land. Indians, Colonists, and the Ecology of New England* (New York, 1983), p. 69.

47. Gómara, *Cortés*, p. 67.

48. William Bradford, *Of Plymouth Plantation, 1620–1647*, ed. Samuel Eliot Morison (New York, 1952), p. 76; George D. Langdon Jr., 'The Franchise and Political Democracy in Plymouth Colony', *WMQ*, 3rd ser., 20 (1963), pp. 513–26.

49. Bradford, *Plymouth Plantation*, p. 62.

50. Patricia U. Bonomi, *A Factious People. Politics and Society in Colonial New York* (New York and London, 1971), p. 22.

51. Kenneth A. Lockridge, *A New England Town. The First Hundred Years. Dedham, Massachusetts, 1636–1736* (New York, 1970), p. 12.

52. Smith, *Works*, 3, p. 277.

53. William Wood, *New England's Prospect*, ed. Alden T. Vaughan (Amherst, MA, 1977), p. 68; and see Vickers, 'Competency and Competition'.

54. Otte, *Cartas privadas*, pp. 169 (*pasar mejor*) and 113 (Francisco Palacio to Antonio de Robles, 10 June 1586). Translations of some of this correspondence can be found in James Lockhart and Enrique Otte (eds), *Letters and People of the Spanish Indies. The Sixteenth Century* (Cambridge, 1976).

55. See Pedro Corominas, *El sentimiento de la riqueza en Castilla* (Madrid, 1917).

56. Charles Gibson, *The Aztecs under Spanish Rule* (Stanford, CA, 1964), p. 406.

57. Richard Konetzke, *América Latina. II. La época colonial* (Madrid, 1971), p. 38.

58. Francisco de Solano, *Ciudades hispanoamericanas y pueblos de indios* (Madrid, 1990), p. 18.
59. Cortés, *Letters from Mexico*, pp. 102–3.
60. For Spanish urban traditions and their transfer to the New World, see in particular Richard M. Morse, 'A Prologomenon to Latin American Urban History', *HAHR*, 52 (1972), pp. 359–94, and 'The Urban Development of Colonial Spanish America', *CHLA*, 2, ch. 3. Also Kagan, *Urban Images of the Hispanic World*, ch. 2, and Solano, *Ciudades hispanoamericanas*.
61. Martínez, *Documentos cortesianos*, 1, doc. 34, especially p. 281.
62. Gómara, *Cortés*, p. 10.
63. Konetzke, *La época colonial*, p. 41.
64. Above, p. 21.
65. Himmerich y Valencia, *The Encomenderos of New Spain*, p. 12.
66. José de la Puente Brunke, *Encomienda y encomenderos en el Perú* (Seville, 1992), p. 18.
67. Silvio Zavala, *Ensayos sobre la colonización española en América* (Buenos Aires, 1944), pp. 153–4; James Lockhart, *Spanish Peru, 1532–1560* (Madison, WI, Milwaukee, WI, London, 1968), p. 12.
68. For the encomienda, the fundamental works remain Silvio Zavala, *La encomienda mexicana* (1935; 2nd edn, Mexico City, 1973), and Lesley Byrd Simpson, *The Encomienda in New Spain* (Berkeley and Los Angeles, 1950).
69. Silvio Zavala, *Estudios indianos* (Mexico City, 1948), p. 298.
70. In England, on the other hand, the crown's rights to ownership of mineral deposits were transferable. For the different approaches in Castile and England to possession of the subsoil, see Patricia Seed, *American Pentimento. The Invention of Indians and the Pursuit of Riches* (Minneapolis and London, 2001), ch. 4. The failure of the British to discover precious metals in the territories under their control reduces the importance in the American context of any difference between English and Spanish practice in regard to mineral rights. For the development of mining in Spanish America through private enterprise, see below, p. 93.
71. Cronon, *Changes in the Land*, p. 130.
72. Campillo, *Nuevo sistema*, introduction, pp. 50–2.
73. Guillermo Céspedes del Castillo, *América hispánica, 1492–1898* (Manuel Tuñón de Lara (ed.), *Historia de España*, 6 (Barcelona, 1983), pp. 217–18); James Lockhart and Stuart B. Schwartz, *Early Latin America. A History of Colonial Spanish America and Brazil* (Cambridge, 1983), p. 137.
74. Himmerich y Valencia, *The Encomenderos of New Spain*, pp. 41, 50–1.
75. Nicolás Sánchez-Albornoz, 'The Population of Colonial Spanish America', *CHLA*, 2, p. 18.
76. Céspedes del Castillo, *América hispánica*, p. 149.
77. See Solano, *Ciudades hispanoamericanas*, ch. 3.
78. See Erwin Walter Palm, *Los monumentos arquitectónicos de la Española* (2 vols, Ciudad Trujillo, 1955), 1, ch. 2; Valerie Fraser, *The Architecture of Conquest. Building in the Viceroyalty of Peru 1535–1635* (Cambridge, 1990); Kagan, *Urban Images*, pp. 31–4.
79. Richard Kagan, 'A World Without Walls: City and Town in Colonial Spanish America', in James D. Tracy (ed.), *City Walls. The Urban Enceinte in Global Perspective* (Cambridge, 2000), ch. 5.
80. Quinn, *New England Voyages*, pp. 236–41; Fraser, *Architecture of Conquest*, p. 176, n. 31.
81. Susan Myra Kingsbury (ed.), *The Records of the Virginia Company of London* (4 vols, Washington, 1906–35), 3, pp. 669–70; and see John W. Reps, *Tidewater Towns. City Planning in Colonial Virginia and Maryland* (Williamsburg, VA, 1972), p. 46.
82. Craven, 'Indian Policy', p. 70.
83. *Ibid.*, pp. 74–5.
84. Kevin P. Kelly, ' "In dispers'd Country Plantations": Settlement Patterns in Seventeenth-Century Surry County, Virginia', in Thad W. Tate and David L. Ammerman (eds), *The Chesapeake in the Seventeenth Century* (New York and London, 1979), essay 6.
85. Meinig, *The Shaping of America*, 1, p. 148; T. H. Breen, 'The Culture of Agriculture: the Symbolic World of the Tidewater Planter, 1760–1790', in David D. Hall, John M. Murrin, Thad W. Tate (eds), *Saints and Revolutionaries. Essays on Early American History* (New

York and London, 1984), pp. 247–84; Rhys Isaac, *The Transformation of Virginia, 1740–1790* (Chapel Hill, NC, 1982), pp. 15–17, and chs 1–3 for the Virginia landscape in general.

86. Reps, *Tidewater Towns*, p. 197; Richard R. Beeman and Rhys Isaac, 'Cultural Conflict and Social Change in the Revolutionary South: Lunenburg County, Virginia', *The Journal of Southern History*, 46 (1980), pp. 525–50, at p. 528.

87. W. W. Abbot, *The Colonial Origins of the United States, 1607–1763* (New York, London, Sydney, Toronto, 1975), p. 44.

88. John Frederick Martin, *Profits in the Wilderness* (Chapel Hill, NC and London, 1991), p. 319.

89. Meinig, *Shaping of America*, 1, p. 104; Martin, *Profits in the Wilderness*, pp. 37–8.

90. See Carl Bridenbaugh, *Cities in the Wilderness. The First Century of Urban Life in America, 1625–1742* (1939; repr. Oxford, London, New York, 1971).

91. Richard Bushman, *The Refinement of America* (New York, 1992), p. 142.

92. James D. Kornwolf, *Architecture and Town Planning in Colonial North America* (3 vols, Baltimore and London, 2002), 2, p. 1174; John Nicholas Brown, *Urbanism in the American Colonies* (Providence, RI, 1976), p. 5.

93. Cited by Bushman, *Refinement of America*, p. 142.

94. Reps, *Tidewater Towns*, p. 296; Kornwolf, *Architecture and Town Planning*, 2, pp. 1175–6.

95. John J. McCusker and Russell R. Menard, *The Economy of British America, 1607–1789* (Chapel Hill, NC and London, 1985), p. 254.

96. Abbot, *Colonial Origins*, p. 45. For the headright system, see below, p. 55.

97. Alison Games, *Migration and the Origins of the English Atlantic World* (Cambridge, MA and London, 1999), pp. 52–3, and Virginia DeJohn Anderson, *New England's Generation* (Cambridge, 1991), p. 21, for the preponderance of family groups.

98. John Demos, *A Little Commonwealth. Family Life in Plymouth Colony* (London, Oxford, New York, 1970), p. 6.

99. *The Journal of John Winthrop 1630–1649*, ed. Richard S. Dunn, James Savage and Laetitia Yeandle (Cambridge, MA and London, 1996), p. 433.

100. See Karen Ordahl Kupperman, *Providence Island, 1630–1641* (Cambridge, 1993).

101. *Ibid.*, pp. 110–16.

102. Cited Anderson, *New England's Generation*, p. 38.

103. See Martin, *Profits in the Wilderness*.

104. *Ibid.*, pp. 235 and 217–18. For the status and rights of *vecinos* in the Hispanic world, see Tamar Herzog, *Defining Nations. Immigrants and Citizens in Early Modern Spain and Spanish America* (New Haven and London, 2003), ch. 2. Also María Inés Carzolio, 'En los orígenes de la ciudadanía en Castilla. La identidad política del vecino durante los siglos XVI y XVII', *Hispania*, 62 (2002), pp. 637–91.

105. Martin, *Profits in the Wilderness* p. 79.

106. Cited *ibid.*, p. 118.

107. Oliver A. Rink, *Holland on the Hudson. An Economic and Social History of Dutch New York* (Ithaca, NY and London, 1986); Meinig, *Shaping of America*, pp. 122–3.

108. See Douglas Greenberg, 'The Middle Colonies in Recent American Historiography', *WMQ*, 3rd ser., 36 (1979), pp. 396–427.

109. James T. Lemon, *The Best Poor Man's Country. A Geographical Study of Early Southeastern Pennsylvania* (Baltimore and London, 1972), ch. 2; Gary B. Nash, *Race, Class and Politics. Essays on American Colonial and Revolutionary Society* (Urbana, IL and Chicago, 1986), pp. 8–11.

110. Cited by Gordon S. Wood, *The Radicalism of the American Revolution* (New York, 1992; repr. 1993), p. 128.

111. Magnus Mörner, *La corona española y los foraneos en los pueblos de indios de América* (Stockholm, 1979), pp. 75–80.

112. For initial attitudes to the Indians, and English policy to the Indians in the first stages of colonization, see especially Karen Ordahl Kupperman, *Settling with the Indians. The Meeting of English and Indian Cultures in America, 1580–1640* (Totowa, NJ, 1980), and *Indians and English. Facing Off in Early America* (Ithaca, NY, and London, 2000); Alden T. Vaughan, *New England Frontier. Puritans and Indians 1620–1675* (1965; 3rd edn, Norman, OK and London, 1995); James Axtell, *The Invasion Within. The Contest of*

Cultures in Colonial North America (New York and Oxford, 1985); Wesley Frank Craven, 'Indian Policy in Early Virginia', and *White, Red and Black. The Seventeenth-Century Virginian* (Charlottesville, VA, 1971).

113. Craven, 'Indian Policy'.
114. Vaughan, *New England Frontier*, pp. 107–9.
115. Bradford, *Plymouth Plantation*, p. 62.
116. Winthrop, *Journal*, p. 416 (22 September 1642).
117. James Horn, *Adapting to a New World* (Chapel Hill, NC and London, 1994), p. 128.
118. See Perry Miller, *Errand into the Wilderness* (Cambridge, MA, 1956); Peter N. Carroll, *Puritanism and the Wilderness* (New York and London, 1969); John Canup, *Out of the Wilderness. The Emergence of an American Identity in Colonial New England* (Middletown, CT, 1990).
119. See under *despoblado* in Peter Boyd-Bowman, *Léxico hispanoamericano del siglo XVI* (London, 1971).
120. Fernando R. de la Flor, *La península metafísica. Arte, literatura y pensamiento en la España de la Contrarreforma* (Madrid, 1999), pp. 130–54; D. A. Brading, *Church and State in Bourbon Mexico. The Diocese of Michoacán* (Cambridge, 1994), p. 29.
121. Canup, *Out of the Wilderness*, p. 50.
122. For a general survey of Spanish American frontiers, see Hennessy, *The Frontier in Latin American History*.
123. Noble David Cook, *Born to Die. Disease and New World Conquest, 1492–1650* (Cambridge, 1998), p. 44.
124. *OHBE*, 1, p. 197.
125. For overseas European migration, especially to the Americas, in the Early Modern period, see in particular the essays assembled in Altman and Horn (eds), '*To Make America*', and Nicholas Canny (ed.), *Europeans on the Move*. For Spanish New World emigration, in addition to Altman, *Emigrants and Society*, previously cited, see Peter Boyd-Bowman, *Índice geobiográfico de cuarenta mil pobladores españoles de América en el siglo XVI* (2 vols, Bogotá, 1964; Mexico City, 1968); Antonio Eiras Roel (ed.), *La emigración española a Ultramar, 1492–1914* (Madrid, 1991); Auke P. Jacobs, *Los movimientos entre Castilla e Hispanoamérica durante el reinado de Felipe III, 1598–1621* (Amsterdam, 1995). For British emigration, in addition to Anderson, *New England's Generation*, and Games, *Migration and the Origins*, previously cited, see Cressy, *Coming Over*, and Bernard Bailyn, *The Peopling of British America. An Introduction* (New York, 1986) and *Voyagers to the West* (New York, 1986).
126. Fredi Chiappelli (ed.), *First Images of America* (2 vols, Berkeley, Los Angeles, London, 1976), 2, p. 753; Altman, *Emigrants and Society;* and, for seigneurial arrangements in the lands owned by the Order of Santiago in Extremadura, the pioneering article by Mario Góngora, 'Régimen señorial y rural en la Extremadura de la Orden de Santiago en el momento de la emigración a Indias', *Jahrbuch für Geschichte von Staat, Wirtschaft und Gesellschaft Lateinamerikas*, 2 (1965), pp. 1–29.
127. Richard Konetzke, 'La legislación sobre inmigración de extranjeros en América durante el reinado de Carlos V', in *Charles-Quint et son Temps* (Colloques Internationaux du Centre National de la Recherche Scientifique, Paris, 1959), pp. 93–108.
128. Jacobs, *Los movimientos*, p. 33.
129. Games, *Migration and the Origins*, pp. 18–20; Cressy, *Coming Over*, ch. 5.
130. Jacobs, *Los movimientos*, pp. 111–20.
131. Konetzke, *La época colonial*, pp. 37 and 54.
132. *Ibid.*, p. 56.
133. Annie Molinié-Bertrand, *Au siècle d'or. L'Espagne et ses hommes* (Paris, 1985), p. 307.
134. Altman, *Emigrants and Society*, pp. 189–91; Altman and Horn, '*To Make America*', pp. 65–9. Of the emigrants from Andalusia in the seventeenth century, 36.8 per cent registered as 'servants' (*criados*), but the figure needs to be treated with caution since registration as a servant was an easy way of obtaining a licence, and family members and friends may often have used this device. See Lourdes Díaz-Trechuelo, 'La emigración familiar andaluza a América en el siglo XVII', in Eiras Roel (ed.), *La emigración española*, pp. 189–97.

135. Nicolás Sánchez-Albornoz, 'The Population of Colonial Spanish America', *CHLA*, 1, pp. 15–16. But Jacobs, *Los movimientos migratorios*, pp. 5–9, argues that the figure should be reduced to 105,000, giving an annual average of 1,000 emigrants.

136. Céspedes del Castillo, *América hispánica*, p. 182.

137. Díaz-Trechuelo, 'La emigración familiar', p. 192.

138. Canny, *Europeans on the Move*, pp. 29–30.

139. cf. Otte, *Cartas privadas*, and Lockhart and Otte (eds), *Letters and People*.

140. Jacobs, *Los movimientos*, p. 170.

141. Altman, *Emigrants and Society*, p. 248.

142. E. A. Wrigley, *People, Cities and Wealth* (Oxford, 1987), pp. 215 and 179.

143. J. H. Elliott, *Imperial Spain, 1469–1716* (1963; repr., London, 2002), p. 25, for land area (378,000 sq. kilometres); Bartolomé Bennassar, *Recherches sur les grandes épidémies dans le nord de l'Espagne à la fin du XVIe siècle* (Paris, 1969), p. 62.

144. Canny, *Europeans on the Move*, p. 62.

145. *New England's Plantation*, in Peter Force, *Tracts and other Papers Relating Principally to the Origin, Settlement and Progress of the Colonies in North America* (4 vols, Washington, 1836–46), 1, no. 12, pp. 12–13.

146. Loren E. Pennington, 'The Amerindian in English Promotional Literature 1575–1625', in Andrews *et al.*, *The Westward Enterprise*, ch. 9.

147. Emerson (ed.), *Letters from New England*, p. 96.

148. Horn, *Adapting to a New World*, pp. 55–6.

149. See Cressy, *Coming Over*, ch. 3, for Puritan foundation myths and their relation to reality.

150. *Ibid.*, p. 68. Games, *Migration and the Origins*, p. 243, n. 5, estimates an appreciably higher figure, of 80,000 to 90,000, for the total number of migrants in the Great Migration.

151. Cressy, *Coming Over*, p. 109.

152. Abbot, *Colonial Origins*, p. 28.

153. For indentured service, see especially David Galenson, *White Servitude in Colonial America* (Cambridge, 1981).

154. Horn, *Adapting to a New World*, p. 66.

155. Altman and Horn, '*To Make America*', p. 7.

156. Christine Daniels, '"Liberty to Complaine": Servant Petitions in Maryland, 1652–1797', in Christopher L. Tomlins and Bruce M. Mann (eds), *The Many Legalities of Early America* (Chapel Hill, NC and London, 2001), pp. 219–49.

157. Altman and Horn, '*To Make America*', pp. 7–8.

158. Galenson, *White Servitude*, p. 24.

159. Richard Archer, 'A New England Mosaic: a Demographic Analysis for the Seventeenth Century', *WMQ*, 3rd ser., 47 (1990), pp. 477–502. See Table III for gender and family status.

160. For these figures and their social consequences, see Lorena S. Walsh, '"Till Death Us Do Part": Marriage and Family in Seventeenth-Century Maryland', and Lois Green Carr and Russell R. Menard, 'Immigration and Opportunity: The Freedman in Early Colonial Maryland', in Tate and Ammerman (eds), *The Chesapeake*, essays 4 and 7.

161. Horn, *Adapting to a New World*, pp. 137–8.

162. Carr and Menard 'Immigration and Opportunity', in Tate and Ammerman (eds), *The Chesapeake*, p. 209.

163. *CHLA*, 2, p. 17; Cressy, *Coming Over*, p. 70.

Chapter 3. Confronting American Peoples

1. Samuel M. Wilson, 'The Cultural Mosaic of the Indigenous Caribbean', in Warwick Bray (ed.), *The Meeting of Two Worlds. Europe and the Americas 1492–1650* (Proceedings of the British Academy, 81, Oxford, 1993), pp. 37–66.

2. Columbus, *Journal*, p. 135 (17 December 1492).

3. Fernández de Oviedo, *Historia general y natural*, 1, p. 111.

4. Cortés, *Letters from Mexico*, p. 36.

5. Thomas, *Conquest of Mexico*, p. 172.

6. Smith, *Works*, 1, p. 150.
7. Smith, *Works*, 1, p. 216; James Axtell, *Natives and Newcomers. The Cultural Origins of North America* (Oxford, 2001), p. 71.
8. Díaz del Castillo, *Historia verdadera*, 2, p. 27 (chapter cxv).
9. For European reactions to human diversity, see especially Margaret T. Hodgen, *Early Anthropology in the Sixteenth and Seventeenth Centuries* (Philadelphia, 1964; repr., 1971), chs 6 and 7.
10. Cortés, *Letters from Mexico*, p. 108.
11. Agustín de Zárate, *The Discovery and Conquest of Peru*, trans. and ed. J. M. Cohen (Harmondsworth, 1968), p. 54.
12. Elliott, *The Old World and the New*, pp. 41–50; Pagden, *Fall of Natural Man*, ch. 2.
13. Ralph Roys, *The Indian Background of Colonial Yucatán* (1943; repr. Norman, OK, 1972); Robert S. Chamberlain, *The Conquest and Colonization of Yucatán, 1517–1550* (Washington, 1948); Nancy M. Farriss, *Maya Society under Colonial Rule* (Princeton, 1984).
14. Gomez, *L'Envers de l'Eldorado*, pp. 56–61.
15. Juan de Cárdenas, *Problemas y secretos maravillosos de las Indias* (facsimile of 1591 edition, Madrid, 1945), fo. 188.
16. Steele, *Warpaths*, p. 3.
17. Wilcomb E. Washburn, *The Indian in America* (New York, 1975), p. 46.
18. Smith, *Works*, 2, pp. 315–16.
19. For the superiority of European weaponry, see Alberto Mario Salas, *Las armas de la conquista* (Buenos Aires, 1950); John F. Guilmartin, 'The Cutting Edge: an Analysis of the Spanish Invasion and Overthrow of the Inca Empire, 1532–1539', in Kenneth J. Andrien and Rolena Adorno (eds), *Transatlantic Encounters. Europeans and Andeans in the Sixteenth Century* (Berkeley, Los Angeles, Oxford, 1991), ch. 2; Geoffrey Parker, *The Military Revolution* (Cambridge, 1988), ch. 4. For a historiographical survey, Wayne E. Lee, 'Early American Warfare: a New Reconnaissance, 1600–1815', *Historical Journal*, 44 (2001), pp. 269–89.
20. Lockhart, *We People Here*, p. 80.
21. Weber, *The Spanish Frontier*, ch. 1.
22. See Philip Wayne Powell, *Soldiers, Indians and Silver. The Northwest Advance of New Spain, 1550–1600* (Berkeley, 1952).
23. Craven, 'Indian Policy', p. 75.
24. Powell, *Soldiers*, p. 5.
25. *Ibid.*, p. 134.
26. *Ibid.*, pp. 186–7; Alvaro Jara, *Guerre et société au Chili. Essai de sociologie coloniale* (Paris, 1961), p. 138; Sergio Villalobos R., 'Tres siglos y medio de vida fronteriza chilena', in Solano and Bernabeu (eds.), *Estudios sobre la frontera*, pp. 289–359.
27. John Shy, *A People Numerous and Armed* (revised edn., Ann Arbor, 1990), ch. 2 ('A New Look at the Colonial Militia'); T. H. Breen, 'English Origins and New World Development: the Case of the Covenanted Militia in Seventeenth-Century Massachusetts', *Past and Present*, 57 (1972), pp. 74–96.
28. Shy, *A People Numerous*, p. 33.
29. Craven, *White, Red and Black*, pp. 55–8, 66–7; Gleach, *Powhatan's World*, pp. 176–83; Warren M. Billings, *Sir William Berkeley and the Forging of Colonial Virginia* (Baton Rouge, LA, 2004), pp. 96–9; Hatfield, *Atlantic Virginia*, pp. 24 and 34.
30. See Jill Lepore, *The Name of War. King Philip's War and the Origins of American Identity* (New York, 1998), for 'King Philip's War' and its character.
31. Bradford, *Plymouth Plantation*, pp. 206–7.
32. Richard Konetzke, *Colección de documentos para la historia de la formación social de Hispanoamérica 1493–1810* (vol. 1, Madrid, 1953), doc. 7 (16 September 1501); Magnus Mörner, *Race Mixture in the History of Latin America* (Boston, 1967), p. 41.
33. Vaughan, *New England Frontier*, pp. 100–1; Axtell, *Invasion Within*, p. 148.
34. Jara, *Guerre et société*, p. 63; Edward H. Spicer, *Cycles of Conquest* (Tucson, AZ, 1962), p. 243.
35. Adam J. Hirsch, 'The Collision of Military Cultures in Seventeenth-Century New England', *The Journal of American History*, 74 (1988), pp. 1187–212; Vaughan, *New England Frontier*, pp. 153–4.

36. Powell, *Soldiers*, pp. 170–1; Shy, *A People Numerous*, p. 33; Vaughan, *New England Frontier*, p. 314.
37. For valuable guidance to a vast and polemical literature, see J. N. Biraben, 'La Population de l'Amérique précolombienne. Essai sur les méthodes', *Conferencia Internationale. El poblamiento de las Américas,* Vera Cruz, 18–23 May 1992 (Institut National d'Études Démographiques, Paris, 1992); John D. Daniels, 'The Indian Population of North America in 1492', *WMQ*, 3rd ser., 49 (1992), pp. 298–320; Linda A. Newson, 'The Demographic Collapse of Native Peoples of the Americas, 1492–1650', in Bray (ed.), *The Meeting of Two Worlds*, pp. 247–88; Cook, *Born to Die.*
38. Cook, *Born to Die*, p. 206.
39. Alonso de Zorita, *The Lords of New Spain*, trans. and ed. Benjamin Keen (London, 1963), p. 202.
40. Bernardo Vargas Machuca, *Refutación de Las Casas* (edn, Paris, 1913), p. 173.
41. Zorita, *Lords of New Spain*, p. 212.
42. Gibson, *The Aztecs Under Spanish Rule*, p. 150; Inga Clendinnen, 'Ways to the Sacred: Reconstructing "Religion" in Sixteenth-Century Mexico', *History and Anthropology*, 5 (1990), pp. 105–41; Washburn, *The Indian in America*, pp. 107–10.
43. See Table 3.2 (p. 132) of Cook, *Born to Die.*
44. Newson, 'Demographic Collapse', pp. 254–62.
45. Steele, *Warpaths*, p. 37. For Velasco, see above, p. 10.
46. Jennings, *The Invasion of America*, p. 24; Cook, *Born to Die*, pp. 170–1; James H. Merrell, '"The Customs of Our Country". Indians and Colonists in Early America', in Bernard Bailyn and Philip D. Morgan (eds), *Strangers Within the Realm. Cultural Margins of the First British Empire* (Chapel Hill, NC and London, 1991), pp. 117–56, at p. 123; Daniel K. Richter, *Facing East from Indian Country. A Native History of Early America* (Cambridge, MA, and London, 2001), pp. 60–7.
47. Smith, *Works*, 3, pp. 293–4.
48. Emerson, *Letters from New England*, p. 116.
49. See above, p. 11.
50. cf. Axtell, *The Invasion Within*, p. 135.
51. Sebastián de Covarrubias, *Tesoro de la lengua castellana o española* (facsimile edn., ed. Martín de Riquer, Barcelona, 1987).
52. Luke 14: 23. Juan Ginés de Sepúlveda, *Democrates segundo o de las justas causas de la guerra contra los indios*, ed. Angel Losada (Madrid, 1951), p. 70.
53. See above, p. 60.
54. See Lewis Hanke, *Aristotle and the American Indians* (London, 1959); Elliott, *Spain and its World*, ch. 3; Pagden, *The Fall of Natural Man.*
55. Alain Milhou, *Colón y su mentalidad mesiánica en el ambiente franciscanista español* (Valladolid, 1983), especially pp. 350–7, and part 2, ch. 4.
56. Fray Ramón Pané, '*Relación acerca de las Antigüedades de los Indios'. El primer tratado escrito en América*, ed. José Juan Arrom (Mexico City, 1974); English translation by Susan C. Griswold, *An Account of the Antiquities of the Indians* (Durham, NC, 1999).
57. Lewis Hanke, *The Spanish Struggle for Justice in the Conquest of America* (Philadelphia, 1949). For the Laws of Burgos, Konetzke, *Colección de documentos*, 1, doc. 25, and Lesley Byrd Simpson (trans. and ed.), *The Laws of Burgos of 1512–1513* (San Francisco, 1960). See also Simpson, *The Encomienda in New Spain*, ch. 3.
58. Angel Losada, *Fray Bartolomé de las Casas a la luz de la moderna crítica histórica* (Madrid, 1970), ch. 4.
59. Pedro de Leturia S.I., *Relaciones entre la Santa Sede e Hispanoamérica. 1. Época del Real Patronato, 1493–1800* (Caracas, 1959), ch. 1; Ismael Sánchez Bella, *Iglesia y estado en la América española* (Pamplona, 1990), pp. 22–3.
60. Cortés, *Letters from Mexico*, pp. 332–3.
61. Robert Ricard, *La 'Conquête spirituelle' du Mexique* (Paris, 1933), p. 35; Fernando de Armas Medina, *Cristianización del Perú, 1532–1600* (Seville, 1953), pp. 21–36.
62. See below, p. 185.

63. Jacobs, *Los movimientos*, pp. 92–5.
64. Lockhart and Schwartz, *Early Latin America*, p. 109.
65. Ricard, *La 'Conquête spirituelle'*, pp. 320–2.
66. Pierre Duviols, *La Lutte contre les religions autochtones dans le Pérou colonial* (Lima, 1971), pp. 82–3.
67. Inga Clendinnen, *Ambivalent Conquests. Maya and Spaniard in Yucatan, 1517–1570* (Cambridge, 1987), p. 70.
68. Cited by Elliott, *The Old World and the New*, p. 33.
69. José Luis Suárez Roca, *Lingüística misionera española* (Oviedo, 1992), p. 42.
70. For the mendicant chroniclers of New Spain, see Georges Baudot, *Utopía e historia en México. Los primeros cronistas de la civilización mexicana (1520–1569)* (Madrid, 1983). For Sahagún, see J. Jorge Klor de Alva, H. B. Nicholson and Elise Quiñones Keber (eds), *The Work of Bernardino de Sahagún. Pioneer Ethnographer of Sixteenth-Century Mexico* (Institute for Mesoamerican Studies, Albany, NY, 1988).
71. Fernando Cervantes, *The Devil in the New World. The Impact of Diabolism in New Spain* (New Haven and London, 1994), ch. 1.
72. See Clendinnen, 'Ways to the Sacred'.
73. Gibson, *The Aztecs under Spanish Rule*, p. 151.
74. *Ibid.*, pp. 336–7; James Lockhart, *The Nahuas After the Conquest* (Stanford, CA, 1992), pp. 198–200.
75. Elliott, *Spain and its World*, pp. 61 and 52.
76. For problems of religious change and 'syncretism', see William B. Taylor, *Magistrates of the Sacred. Priests and Parishioners in Eighteenth-Century Mexico* (Stanford, CA, 1996), pp. 51–62. For the general problem of acculturation in a conquest culture, George M. Foster, *Culture and Conquest. America's Spanish Heritage* (Chicago, 1960), although this is more concerned with the culture of the conquerors than the conquered. See also James Lockhart, *Of Things of the Indies. Essays Old and New in Early Latin American History* (Stanford, CA, 1999), ch. 11 ('Receptivity and Resistance').
77. Ricard, *La 'Conquête spirituelle'*, pp. 275–6.
78. Fray Bartolomé de Las Casas, *Apologética historia sumaria*, ed. Edmundo O'Gorman (2 vols, Mexico City, 1967), 2, p. 262.
79. See Pagden, *The Fall of Natural Man*, chs 3 and 5.
80. Cited Elliott, *Spain and its World*, p. 51.
81. Strachey, *Travell into Virginia Britania*, pp. 20 and 18.
82. William H. Seiler, 'The Anglican Parish in Virginia', in James Morton Smith (ed.), *Seventeenth-Century America. Essays in Colonial History* (Chapel Hill, NC, 1959), p. 122.
83. Patricia U. Bonomi, *Under the Cope of Heaven. Religion, Society and Politics in Colonial America* (New York, 1986), p. 16.
84. Jon Butler, *Awash in a Sea of Faith* (Cambridge, MA and London, 1990), pp. 127–8.
85. Axtell, *The Invasion Within*, p. 180.
86. Bonomi, *Cope of Heaven*, pp. 21–2; Horn, *Adapting to a New World*, pp. 386–8.
87. See Edmund S. Morgan, *Visible Saints. The History of a Puritan Idea* (1963; repr. Ithaca, NY, 1971).
88. Lepore, *The Name of War*, p. xv; Axtell, *The Invasion Within*, pp. 133–4; Vaughan, *New England Frontier*, p. 240.
89. Edmund S. Morgan, *Roger Williams. The Church and the State* (1967; repr. New York, 1987), pp. 43–4.
90. Winthrop, *Journal*, p. 682.
91. See Vaughan, *New England Frontier*, chs 9–11.
92. *Ibid.*, pp. 254–5; Joyce E. Chaplin, *Subject Matter. Technology, the Body, and Science on the Anglo-American Frontier, 1500–1676* (Cambridge, MA, and London, 2001), pp. 289–90.
93. See the list of publications in Eliot's 'Indian Library', as given in Lepore, *The Name of War*, p. 35.
94. Axtell, *The Invasion Within*, ch. 8.
95. See, most recently, Richard W. Cogley, *John Eliot's Mission to the Indians before King Philip's War* (Cambridge, MA and London, 1999).

96. See, for instance, for Peru, Duviols, *La Lutte*, pp. 248–63.
97. *Ibid.*, pp. 257–8; Merrell, 'Indians and Colonists', in Bailyn and Morgan, *Strangers Within the Realm*, p. 150.
98. Axtell, *The Invasion Within*, pp. 225–7.
99. Vaughan, *New England Frontier*, p. 303.
100. Ricard, *La 'Conquête spirituelle'*, pp. 266–9; Vaughan, *New England Frontier*, pp. 281–4.
101. Cited by Cogley, *John Eliot's Mission*, p. 18.
102. Vaughan, *New England Frontier*, pp. 303–8; Axtell, *The Invasion Within*, p. 278. See also, for an examination in a comparative context of the challenges facing the New England colonists in converting Indians, Axtell, *After Columbus*, chs 3–7.
103. Cited by Vaughan, *New England Frontier*, p. 260.
104. Axtell, *The Invasion Within*, p. 141.
105. Cited in Roger Williams, *The Complete Writings of Roger Williams* (Providence, RI, 1866), 1, p. 136, n. 97, from John Wilson (?), *The Day-Breaking of the Gospell with the Indians* (1647). See also Axtell, *The Invasion Within*, pp. 175–8.
106. Juan de Matienzo, *Gobierno del Perú (1567)*, ed. Guillermo Lohmann Villena (Paris and Lima, 1967), p. 80.
107. Axtell, *The Invasion Within*, pp. 285–6. For an example of the ways in which Puritan teaching could successfully be blended with Indian beliefs and traditions, see David J. Silverman, 'Indians, Missionaries, and Religious Translation: Creating Wampanoag Christianity in Seventeenth-Century Martha's Vineyard', *WMQ*, 3rd ser., 62 (2005), pp. 141–74.
108. Cited by Canup, *Out of the Wilderness*, p. 167.
109. Thomas Morton, *New English Canaan* (1632), in Force, *Tracts*, 2, no. 11, p. 77.
110. Vaughan, *New England Frontier*, p. 245.
111. For the Valladolid debate, see Lewis Hanke, *All Mankind is One* (DeKalb, IL, 1974), and his *Spanish Struggle for Justice*, ch. 8. Also Losada, *Fray Bartolomé de Las Casas*, ch. 13. The literature on Las Casas is now vast, but see in particular Pagden, *Fall of Natural Man*, for his views and those of Sepúlveda in the general context of the sixteenth-century Spanish debate on the nature of the Indian.
112. Woodrow Borah, *Justice by Insurance. The General Indian Court of Colonial Mexico and the Legal Aides of the Half-Real* (Berkeley, Los Angeles, London, 1983), pp. 80–2.
113. Stafford Poole, *Juan de Ovando. Governing the Spanish Empire in the Reign of Philip II* (Norman, OK, 2004), pp. 154–6.
114. Bartolomé de Las Casas, *Tears of the Indians* (repr. Williamstown, MA, 1970). For a modern translation, see Bartolomé de Las Casas, *A Short Account of the Destruction of the Indies*, trans. and ed. Nigel Griffin (Harmondsworth, 1992).
115. Borah, *Justice by Insurance*, p. 64.
116. Vaughan, *New England Frontier*, pp. 190–5; Katherine Hermes, '"Justice Will be Done Us." Algonquian Demands for Reciprocity in the Courts of European Settlers', in Tomlins and Mann (eds), *The Many Legalities of Early America*, pp. 123–49.
117. Merrell, 'Indians and Colonists', pp. 144–6.
118. William B. Taylor, *Drinking, Homicide and Rebellion in Colonial Mexican Villages* (Stanford, CA, 1979), pp. 105–6.
119. See Lepore, *The Name of War*, pp. 158–67.
120. Cited from William Hubbard, *General History of New England* (1680), by Canup, *Out of the Wilderness*, p. 74.
121. Columbus, *Journal*, p. 31(3 October 1492).
122. Winthrop D. Jordan, *White Over Black* (1968; repr. Baltimore, 1969), pp. 6–9.
123. Juan López de Velasco, *Geografía y descripción universal de las Indias*, ed. Justo Zaragoza (Madrid, 1894) p. 27; Strachey, *The Historie of Travell into Virginia*, p. 70.
124. Gómara, *Historia general*, BAE, 22, p. 289.
125. See Karen Ordahl Kupperman, 'The Puzzle of the American Climate in the Early Colonial Period', *AHR*, 87 (1982), pp. 1262–89. For climatic determinism in Spanish America see Jorge Cañizares-Esguerra, 'New World, New Stars: Patriotic Astrology and the Invention of Indian and Creole Bodies in Colonial Spanish America, 1600–1650', *AHR*, 104 (1999), pp. 33–68.

126. Richard Eburne, *A Plain Pathway to Plantations* (1624), ed. Louis B. Wright (Ithaca, NY, 1962), p. 56.

127. Joseph Pérez, *Histoire de l'Espagne* (Paris, 1996), p. 79.

128. Miguel Angel de Bunes Ibarra, *La imagen de los musulmanes y del norte de Africa en la España de los siglos XVI y XVII* (Madrid, 1989), p. 113.

129. Quoted from Sir John Davies, *Discovery of the True Causes why Ireland was never Entirely Subdued* (1612), by James Muldoon, 'The Indian as Irishman', *Essex Institute Historical Collections*, 111 (1975), pp. 267–89, at p. 269 (spelling modernized).

130. For the Statutes of Kilkenny and Anglo-Irish intermarriage, Muldoon, 'The Indian as Irishman', p. 284; A. Cosgrove, 'Marriage in Medieval Ireland', in A. Cosgrove (ed.), *Marriage in Ireland* (Dublin, 1985), p. 35; John Darwin, 'Civility and Empire', in Peter Burke, Brian Harrison and Paul Slack (eds), *Civil Histories. Essays Presented to Sir Keith Thomas* (Oxford, 2000), p. 322.

131. For the degree of 'gaelicization' of English settlers in Ireland, see James Lydon, 'The Middle Nation', in James Lydon (ed.), *The English in Medieval Ireland* (Dublin, 1984), pp. 1–26.

132. For the general question of the fear of degeneration among English settlers in America, see Canup, *Out of the Wilderness*, especially ch. 1, and his 'Cotton Mather and "Creolian Degeneracy"', *Early American Literature*, 24 (1989), pp. 20–34.

133. Morton, *New English Canaan* (Force, *Tracts*, 2, no. 11, p. 19).

134. Cited by H. C. Porter, *The Inconstant Savage* (London, 1979), p. 203. I am grateful to Alden Vaughan for pointing out to me in a private communication that Hugh Peter, who had lived through the Pequot War in New England, made the transposition in the context of his recommendations for the conquest of Ireland. The interchangeability between Irish and Indians clearly worked both ways.

135. Spenser, *Works*, 9, p. 96, cited by Muldoon, 'The Indian as Irishman', pp. 275–6 (spelling modernized).

136. William Symonds, *Virginia Britannia*, in Brown, *Genesis of the United States*, 1, pp. 287 and 290.

137. Cited by David D. Smits, '"We are not to Grow Wild": Seventeenth-Century New England's Repudiation of Anglo-Indian Intermarriage', *American Indian Culture and Research Journal*, 11 (1987), pp. 1–32, at p. 6 (spelling modernized).

138. For the distinction between the Genesis and Exodus types of emigration, see Avihu Zakai, *Exile and Kingdom. History and Apocalypse in the Puritan Migration to America* (Cambridge, 1992), pp. 9–10.

139. Canup, *Out of the Wilderness*, pp. 79–80. As Conrad Russell kindly pointed out to me, colonists would also have been well aware of the dreadful warning against marriage between the Israelites and the Midianites in the story of Phinehas (Numbers: 25).

140. David D. Smits, '"We are not to Grow Wild"', pp. 3 and 6, and '"Abominable Mixture": Toward the Repudiation of Anglo-Indian Intermarriage in Seventeenth-Century Virginia', *The Virginia Magazine of History and Biography*, 95 (1987), pp. 157–92.

141. Robert Beverley, *The History and Present State of Virginia*, ed. Louis B. Wright (Chapel Hill, NC, 1947), p. 38.

142. Konetzke, *Colección de documentos*, 1, pp. 12–13.

143. Magnus Mörner, *Race Mixture in the History of Latin America* (Boston, 1967), p. 26.

144. Konetzke, *Colección de documentos*, 1, doc. 28 (15 October 1514). See also Alberto M. Salas, *Crónica florida del mestizaje de las Indias* (Buenos Aires, 1960), pp. 54–5.

145. 'Carta colectiva de los franciscanos de México al Emperador', 1 Sept. 1526, in Fray Toribio de Benavente o Motolinía, *Memoriales o libro de las cosas de la Nueva España y de los naturales de ella*, ed. Edmundo O'Gorman (Mexico City, 1971), p. 429.

146. Cited by Salas, *Crónica florida*, p. 56.

147. See Donald Chipman, 'Isabel Moctezuma: Pioneer of *Mestizaje*', in David G. Sweet and Gary B. Nash (eds), *Struggle and Survival in Colonial America* (Berkeley, Los Angeles, London, 1981), ch. 11.

148. Angel Rosenblat, *La población indígena y el mestizaje en América* (2 vols, Buenos Aires, 1954), 2, pp. 60–2.

149. Otte, *Cartas privadas*, p. 61.

150. Mörner, *Race Mixture*, p. 55.
151. Ann Marie Plane, *Colonial Intimacies. Indian Marriage in Early New England* (Ithaca, NY and London, 2000), p. 36.
152. Gary B. Nash, 'The Hidden History of Mestizo America', *The Journal of American History*, 82 (1995), pp. 941–62.
153. Canny and Pagden (eds), *Colonial Identity*, pp. 145–6.
154. Elman R. Service, *Spanish-Guaraní Relations in Early Colonial Paraguay* (1954; repr. Westport, CT, 1971), pp. 19–20; and see a Jesuit's report of 1620, cited in *CHLA*, 2, p. 76.
155. See Solange Alberro, *Les Espagnols dans le Mexique colonial. Histoire d'une acculturation* (Paris, 1992) for Spanish-Indian interaction.
156. For segregation policies, Konetzke, *La época colonial*, pp. 196–7. For an excellent general survey of cultural *mestizaje*, see Carmen Bernand and Serge Gruzinski, *Histoire du nouveau monde* (2 vols, Paris, 1991–3), vol. 2 (*Les Métissages*).
157. Konetzke, *Colección de documentos*, 1, doc. 183.
158. Lockhart, *The Nahuas*, ch. 7.
159. Farriss, *Maya Society*, pp. 111–12.
160. Konetzke, *La época colonial*, pp. 200–4; Emma Martinell Gifre, *La comunicación entre españoles e indios. Palabras y gestos* (Madrid, 1992), pp. 188–93.
161. Bailyn and Morgan (eds.), *Strangers within the Realm*, pp. 128–30.
162. See Richard Morse, 'Towards a Theory of Spanish American Government', *Journal of the History of Ideas*, 15 (1954), pp. 71–93.
163. 'Letter of Sir Francis Wyatt, Governor of Virginia, 1621–1626', *WMQ*, 2nd ser., 6 (1926), pp. 114–21.
164. See Kupperman, *Settling with the Indians*, pp. 175–80.
165. Thomas, *Conquest of Mexico*, pp. 163–4.
166. Nicholas Canny, 'The Permissive Frontier: the Problem of Social Control in English Settlements in Ireland and Virginia 1550–1650', in Andrews, *et al.* (eds), *The Westward Enterprise*, pp. 30–5.
167. Powell, *Soldiers, Indians*, ch. 11.
168. Weber, *Spanish Frontier*, p. 107.
169. Ramón A. Gutiérrez, *When Jesus Came, the Corn Mothers Went Away. Marriage, Sexuality and Power in New Mexico, 1500–1800* (Stanford, CA, 1991), p. 103; Spicer, *Cycles of Conquest*, p. 301.

Chapter 4. Exploiting American Resources

1. See Columbus's description of Cuba on his first voyage, in Columbus, *Journal*, p. 59; and, for a general overview, Hugh Honour, *The New Golden Land. European Images of America from the Discoveries to the Present Time* (New York, 1975).
2. For Columbus's 'rivers of gold' see Thomas, *Rivers of Gold*, p. 122.
3. Antonello Gerbi, *Il mito del Perù* (Milan, 1988), p. 29.
4. Cited Honour, *The New Golden Land*, p. 18.
5. *The Cambridge Economic History of the United States*, ed. Stanley L. Engerman and Robert E. Gallman, 1, *The Colonial Era* (Cambridge, 1996), p. 95; and, for Indian land-use in general, Cronon, *Changes in the Land*.
6. For initial English expectations of the new American environment and gradual adaptation to its realities, see Kupperman, 'The Puzzle of the American Climate'.
7. For the 'archipelago' pattern of Andean settlement and the system of vertical control, see especially John V. Murra, *Formaciones económicas y políticas del mundo andino* (Lima, 1975), and his 'Andean Societies Before 1532', *CHLA*, 1, ch. 3.
8. For the 'plunder economy' of the 1530s–1560s in Peru, see Karen Spalding, *Huarochirí. An Andean Society under Inca and Spanish Rule* (Stanford, CA, 1984), p. 109.
9. Cited in José Durand, *La transformación social del conquistador* (2 vols, Mexico City, 1953), 1, pp. 41–2.
10. Arturo Warman, *La historia de un bastardo. Maíz y capitalismo* (Mexico City, 1988), p. 27; MacLeod, *Spanish Central America*, p. 18.

11. Alberro, *Les Espagnols dans le Mexique colonial*, pp. 46–9.
12. John C. Super, *Food, Conquest, and Colonization in Sixteenth-Century Spanish America* (Albuquerque, NM, 1988), pp. 32–7; Arnold J. Bauer, *Goods, Power, History. Latin America's Material Culture* (Cambridge, 2001), pp. 86–90.
13. Cronon, *Changes in the Land*, pp. 154–5; Jack P. Greene, *Pursuits of Happiness. The Social Development of Early Modern British Colonies and the Formation of American Culture* (Chapel Hill, NC and London, 1988), p. 86; Horn, *Adapting to a New World*, p. 144 and, for 'chiefest Diett', 278.
14. Super, *Food, Conquest, and Colonization*, p. 19.
15. François Chevalier, *La Formation des grands domaines au Mexique* (Paris, 1952), p. 66.
16. William H. Dusenberry, *The Mexican Mesta* (Urbana, IL, 1963).
17. Charles Julian Bishko, 'The Peninsular Background of Latin American Cattle Ranching', *HAHR*, 32 (1952), pp. 491–515; Chevalier, *La Formation*, part 1, ch. 3; Robert G. Keith, *Conquest and Agrarian Change. The Emergence of the Hacienda System on the Peruvian Coast* (Cambridge, MA and London, 1976), p. 60.
18. Keith, *Conquest and Agrarian Change*, pp. 92–105.
19. Pierre Chaunu, *L'Amérique et les Amériques* (Paris, 1964), p. 92.
20. Wood, *New England's Prospect*, pp. 35, 37, 38.
21. Enrique Otte, *Las perlas del Caribe. Nueva Cádiz de Cubagua* (Caracas, 1977).
22. Richard L. Lee, 'American Cochineal in European Commerce, 1526–1635', *Journal of Modern History*, 23 (1951), pp. 205–24. For the history of cochineal see Amy Butler Greenfield, *A Perfect Red. Empire, Espionage, and the Quest for the Color of Desire* (New York, 2005).
23. MacLeod, *Spanish Central America*, ch. 10; Chevalier, *La Formation*, pp. 87–9.
24. MacLeod, *Spanish Central America*, ch. 5.
25. Antonio de León Pinelo, *Questión moral si el chocolate quebranta el ayuno eclesiástico* (Madrid, 1636; facsimile edn, Mexico City, 1994).
26. David Watts, *The West Indies. Patterns of Development, Culture and Environmental Change since 1492* (Cambridge, 1987), pp. 125–6; Frank Moya Pons, *La Española en el siglo XVI, 1493–1520* (Santiago, Dominican Republic, 1978), pp. 256–68; Sauer, *The Spanish Main*, pp. 209–12; Robin Blackburn, *The Making of New World Slavery. From the Baroque to the Modern, 1492–1800* (London, 1997), p. 137.
27. Ward Barrett, *The Sugar Hacienda of the Marqueses del Valle* (Minneapolis, 1970).
28. Wood, *New England's Prospect*, p. 68, and see above, p. 37.
29. Stephen Innes, *Labor in a New Land. Economy and Society in Seventeenth-Century Springfield* (Princeton, 1983).
30. See Richard J. Salvucci, *Textiles and Capitalism in Mexico. An Economic History of the Obrajes, 1539–1840* (Princeton, 1987).
31. P. J. Bakewell, *Silver Mining and Society in Colonial Mexico, Zacatecas 1546–1700* (Cambridge, 1971).
32. Peter Bakewell, *A History of Latin America* (Oxford, 1997), p. 180; and see Richard L. Garner, 'Long-Term Silver Mining Trends in Spanish America. A Comparative Analysis of Peru and Mexico', *AHR*, 93 (1988), pp. 898–935.
33. See above, pp. 40 and 421 n. 70.
34. Bakewell, *Silver Mining*, pp. 181–2.
35. Peter Bakewell, *Miners of the Red Mountain. Indian Labor in Potosí 1545–1650* (Albuquerque, NM, 1984), p. 18.
36. G. Lohmann Villena, *Las minas de Huancavelica en los siglos XVI y XVII* (Seville, 1949); Bakewell, *Silver Mining*, ch. 7.
37. Peter Bakewell, *Silver and Entrepreneurship in Seventeenth-Century Potosí. The Life and Times of Antonio López de Quiroga* (Albuquerque, NM, 1988), p. 23.
38. Gwendolin B. Cobb, 'Supply and Transportation for the Potosí Mines, 1545–1640', *HAHR*, 29 (1949), pp. 25–45. Zacarias Moutoukias, *Contrabando y control colonial en el siglo XVII. Buenos Aires, el Atlántico y el espacio peruano* (Buenos Aires, 1988), provides a detailed and valuable account of how the system worked.
39. Wilbur T. Meek, *The Exchange Media of Colonial Mexico* (New York, 1948), pp. 42 and 69–79; John Porteous, *Coins in History* (London, 1969), p. 170.

40. Bakewell, *History of Latin America*, p. 203.
41. Lockhart, *The Nahuas After the Conquest*, pp. 177–80.
42. Matienzo, *Gobierno del Perú*, p. 20.
43. Darrett B. and Anita H. Rutman, *A Place in Time. Middlesex County, Virginia 1650–1750* (New York and London, 1984), p. 42.
44. Richard L. Bushman, *King and People in Provincial Massachusetts* (Chapel Hill, NC and London, 1965), pp. 143–4.
45. John J. McCusker and Russell R. Menard, *The Economy of British America, 1607–1789* (Chapel Hill, NC and London, 1985), p. 339.
46. Richard B. Sheridan, 'The Domestic Economy', in Jack P. Greene and J. R. Pole (eds), *Colonial British America. Essays in the New History of the Early Modern Era* (Baltimore and London, 1984), pp. 72–3; John J. McCusker, *Money and Exchange in Europe and America, 1600–1771. A Handbook* (London, 1978), ch. 3; and for late seventeenth-century New England, Bernard Bailyn, *The New England Merchants in the Seventeenth Century* (1955; New York, 1964), pp. 182–9.
47. Meek, *Exchange Media*, p. 57.
48. Daviken Studnicki-Gizbert, 'From Agents to Consulado: Commercial Networks in Colonial Mexico, 1520–1590 and Beyond', *Anuario de Estudios Americanos*, 57 (2000), pp. 41–68; Bakewell, *History of Latin America*, pp. 203–4.
49. Céspedes del Castillo, *América hispánica*, p. 128; Garner, 'Long-Term Silver Mining Trends', p. 902.
50. For a succinct survey, summarizing much recent work, see Ward Barrett, 'World Bullion Flows, 1450–1800', in James D. Tracy (ed.), *The Rise of Merchant Empires. Long-Distance Trade in the Early Modern World, 1350–1750* (Cambridge, 1990), ch. 7.
51. Chaunu, *L'Amérique et les Amériques*, p. 92; John R. Fisher, *The Economic Aspects of Spanish Imperialism in America, 1492–1810* (Liverpool, 1997), p. 38.
52. Robert J. Ferry, *The Colonial Elite of Early Caracas. Formation and Crisis, 1567–1767* (Berkeley, Los Angeles, London, 1989), chs 1 and 2.
53. Gloria L. Main, *Tobacco Colony. Life in Early Maryland 1650–1720* (Princeton, 1982), pp. 18–19.
54. Richard S. Dunn, *Sugar and Slaves. The Rise of the Planter Class in the English West Indies, 1624–1713* (New York, 1972), p. 49; Andrews, *The Colonial Period*, vol. 2, ch. 7.
55. Watts, *The West Indies*, pp. 182–3; Dunn, *Sugar and Slaves*, pp. 59–67.
56. Watts, *The West Indies*, p. 230; Blackburn, *Making of New World Slavery*, p. 267.
57. Main, *Tobacco Colony*, pp. 239 and 254.
58. Cited from Bartolomé de Las Casas by Hugh Thomas, *Rivers of Gold*, pp. 157–8. For a summary of the development of the crown's policy on Indian enslavement, see Konetzke, *La época colonial*, pp. 153–9. For a close study of policy and practice on Hispaniola, Carlos Esteban Deive, *La Española en la esclavitud del indio* (Santo Domingo, 1995).
59. Konetzke, *Colección de documentos*, 1, doc. 10.
60. For the *requerimiento* see above, p. 11.
61. Hanke, *The Spanish Struggle for Justice*, pp. 33–5.
62. O. Nigel Bolland, 'Colonization and Slavery in Central America', in Paul E. Lovejoy and Nicholas Rogers (eds), *Unfree Labour in the Development of the Atlantic World* (Ilford, 1994), pp. 11–25.
63. Konetzke, *Colección de documentos*, 1, docs 143 and 144.
64. Gutiérrez, *When Jesus Came, the Corn Mothers Went Away*, pp. 150–1; and see below, p. 275.
65. Juan A. and Judith E. Villamarín, *Indian Labor in Mainland Colonial Spanish America* (Newark, DE, 1975), pp. 16–18.
66. The Conde de Nieva (1563), quoted in Bakewell, *Miners of the Red Mountain*, p. 56, n. 51.
67. For the *mingas* see Bakewell, *Miners of the Red Mountain*, especially ch. 4.
68. The literature on black slavery in the Americas is now enormous. Frank Tannenbaum's *Slave and Citizen* (1946) retains its importance as a pioneering comparative study of slavery in British and Spanish America. A comparative approach is also adopted by Herbert S. Klein, *Slavery in the Americas. A Comparative Study of Virginia and Cuba* (Chicago, 1967). Hugh Thomas, *The Slave Trade. The History of the Atlantic Slave Trade 1440–1870*

(New York and London, 1997) is a comprehensive synthesis, which pays due attention to the Iberian contribution, for which see also Enriqueta Vila Vilar, *Hispano-America y el comercio de esclavos* (Seville, 1977). For Mexico, see Colin A. Palmer, *Slaves of the White God. Blacks in Mexico, 1570–1650* (Cambridge, MA and London, 1976), Herman L. Bennett, *Africans in Colonial Mexico. Absolutism, Christianity, and Afro-Creole Consciousness, 1570–1640* (Bloomington, IN and Indianapolis, 2003). For Peru, Lockhart, *Spanish Peru*, ch. 10; Federick P. Bowser, *The African Slave in Colonial Peru, 1524–1650* (Stanford, CA, 1974). For British America, most recently, Ira Berlin, *Many Thousands Gone. The First Two Centuries of Slavery in North America* (Cambridge, MA, 1998). Valuable general studies covering the Atlantic world as a whole include, in addition to Robin Blackburn, *The Making of New World Slavery* (previously cited), Barbara L. Solow (ed.), *Slavery and the Rise of the Atlantic System* (Cambridge, 1991), and David Eltis, *The Rise of African Slavery in the Americas* (Cambridge, 2000).

69. Hayward Keniston, *Francisco de Los Cobos. Secretary of the Emperor Charles V* (Pittsburgh, PA, 1960), p. 64; Thomas, *Rivers of Gold*, pp. 361–3.
70. Lockhart, *Spanish Peru*, p. 171.
71. Bowser, *The African Slave*, p. 28.
72. Blackburn, *The Making of New World Slavery*, pp. 135 and 140.
73. For the figures, see David Eltis, 'The Volume and Structure of the Transatlantic Slave Trade: a Reassessment', *WMQ*, 3rd ser., 58 (2001), pp. 17–46, modifying the statistics given in Philip D. Curtin's standard work, *The Atlantic Slave Trade. A Census* (Madison, WI, 1969). For the Gomes Reinel contract, Vila Vilar, *Hispano-América y el comercio de esclavos*, pp. 23–8; Thomas, *The Slave Trade*, pp. 141–3.
74. Luiz Felipe de Alencastro, *O trato dos viventes. Formação de Brasil no Atlântico Sul. Séculos XVI e XVII* (São Paulo, 2000), ch. 3.
75. Vila Vilar, *El comercio de esclavos*, p. 209.
76. Carmen Bernand, *Negros esclavos y libres en las ciudades hispanoamericanas* (2nd edn, Madrid, 2001), p. 60.
77. William Alexander, *An Encouragement to Colonies* (London, 1624), p. 7.
78. For the importance of the African population in Spanish American cities, for long a neglected subject, Bernand, *Negros esclavos y libres*, and, for New Spain, Bennett, *Africans in Colonial Mexico*. For slaves as a percentage of city populations, Bernand, p. 11.
79. Bowser, *The African Slave*, ch. 6; Lockhart, *Spanish Peru*, pp. 182–4.
80. Bowser, *The African Slave*, pp. 272–3.
81. *Thomas Gage's Travels in the New World*, ed. J. Eric S. Thompson (Norman, OK, 1958), p. 73. This is a modernized edition of Thomas Gage, *The English-American his Travail by Sea and Land* (London, 1648).
82. Palmer, *Slaves of the White God*, p. 67.
83. Blackburn, *Making of New World Slavery*, p. 147; Lockhart and Schwartz, *Early Latin America*, p. 179.
84. Bakewell, *Silver Mining and Society*, p. 122.
85. Bowser, *The African Slave*, p. 13.
86. *Ibid.*, chs. 3 and 6.
87. Vila Vilar, *El comercio de esclavos*, p. 228.
88. Bennett, *Africans in Colonial Mexico*, p. 19; Bowser, *The African Slave*, p. 75.
89. Main, *Tobacco Colony*, p. 100.
90. Craven, *White, Red and Black*, p. 73.
91. For South Carolina and its slave trade, see Alan Gallay, *The Indian Slave Trade. The Rise of the English Empire in the American South, 1670–1717* (New Haven and London, 2002). Statistics on pp. 298–9 and 346.
92. *Ibid.*, pp. 302–3; Margaret Ellen Newell, 'The Changing Nature of Indian Slavery in New England, 1670–1720', in Colin G. Calloway and Neal Salisbury (eds), *Reinterpreting New England Indians and the Colonial Experience* (Boston, 2003), pp. 106–36; and, for a good general survey, Joyce E. Chaplin, 'Enslavement of Indians in Early America. Captivity Without the Narrative', in Mancke and Shammas (eds), *Creation of the British Atlantic World*, pp. 45–70.

93. Oscar and Mary Handlin, 'Origins of the Southern Labor System', *WMQ*, 3rd ser., 7 (1950), pp. 199–222, at p. 103. For the Vagrancy Act, C. S. L. Davies, 'Slavery and Protector Somerset: the Vagrancy Act of 1547', *Economic History Review*, 2nd ser., 19 (1966), pp. 533–49.
94. See above, p. 55.
95. Dunn, *Sugar and Slaves*, p. 120.
96. Philip D. Morgan, 'British Encounters with Africans and African-Americans circa 1600–1780', in Bailyn and Morgan (eds.), *Strangers within the Realm*, pp. 169–70.
97. Kupperman, *Providence Island*, pp. 165–75.
98. *Ibid.*, p. 177.
99. Alden T. Vaughan, 'Blacks in Virginia: a Note on the First Decade', *WMQ*, 3rd ser., 29 (1972), pp. 469–78.
100. Philip D. Morgan, *Slave Counterpoint. Black Culture in the Eighteenth-Century Chesapeake and Low Country* (Chapel Hill, NC and London, 1998), p. 58; Morgan, 'British Encounters with Africans', p. 171; Kupperman, *Providence Island*, p. 176; Galenson, *White Servitude*, p. 153.
101. Dunn, *Sugar and Slaves*, pp. 71–3.
102. *Ibid.*, pp. 75–6 and 224.
103. Blackburn, *The Making of New World Slavery*, p. 258.
104. See Richard R. Beeman, 'Labor Forces and Race Relations: a Comparative View of the Colonization of Brazil and Virginia', *Political Science Quarterly*, 86 (1971), pp. 609–36.
105. Watts, *The West Indies*, pp. 123–6; Blackburn, *The Making of New World Slavery*, pp. 138–9; Kenneth R. Andrews, *The Spanish Caribbean. Trade and Plunder 1530–1630* (New Haven and London, 1978), pp. 76–9.
106. Stuart B. Schwartz, *Sugar Plantations in the Formation of Brazilian Society. Bahia, 1550–1835* (Cambridge, 1985), chs 2 and 3.
107. Watts, *The West Indies*, p. 183.
108. Blackburn, *The Making of New World Slavery*, p. 309; and above, p. 9.
109. Canup, *Out of the Wilderness*, p. 9.
110. Blair Worden, *The Sound of Virtue* (New Haven and London, 1996), p. 55.
111. Thomas, *The Slave Trade*, pp. 433–4.
112. Alonso de Sandoval, *Un tratado sobre la esclavitud,* ed. Enriqueta Vila Vilar (Madrid, 1987), pp. 236–7.
113. Lockhart and Schwartz, *Early Latin America*, p. 91.
114. Blackburn, *The Making of New World Slavery*, p. 139; Bowser, *The African Slave*, ch. 8.
115. *Las Siete Partidas del Sabio Rey Don Alonso el nono* (Salamanca, 1555), partida 3, tit. 5, ley iv. See also Palmer, *Slaves of the White God*, p. 86.
116. For laws and ordinances relating to slavery in Spanish America, see Manuel Lucena Salmoral, *La esclavitud en la América española* (Centro de Estudios Latinoamericanos, University of Warsaw, *Estudios y materiales*, 22, Warsaw, 2002).
117. See the numerous examples provided by Bennett in *Africans in Colonial Mexico*.
118. Palmer, *Slaves of the White God*, pp. 62–3.
119. David Brion Davis, *The Problem of Slavery in Western Culture* (London, 1970), pp. 290–1.
120. Magnus Mörner, *Race Mixture in the History of Latin America* (Boston, 1967), p. 117.
121. Davis, *The Problem of Slavery*, p. 297; Morgan, 'British Encounters with Africans', pp. 167–8.
122. Mörner, *Race Mixture*, pp. 116–17; Palmer, *Slaves of the White God*, pp. 172–8.
123. Bennett, *Africans in Colonial Mexico*, p. 19.
124. Bernand, *Negros esclavos y libres*, p. 46.
125. Berlin, *Many Thousands Gone*, p. 96; Blackburn, *The Making of New World Slavery*, p. 258.
126. Pierre Chaunu, *Conquête et exploitation des nouveaux mondes* (Paris, 1969), p. 286.
127. *Eastward Ho* (1605), Act III, Scene 3, in *The Plays and Poems of George Chapman. The Comedies,* ed. Thomas Marc Parrott (London, 1914), p. 499; Chaunu, *L'Amérique et les Amériques*, p. 88, and map 6.
128. Antonio García-Baquero González, *Andalucía y la carrera de Indias, 1492–1824* (Seville, 1986), p. 28.

129. José María Oliva Melgar, 'Puerto y puerta de las Indias', in Carlos Martínez Shaw (ed.), *Sevilla siglo XVI. El corazón de las riquezas del mundo* (Madrid, 1993), p. 99.

130. For the Consulado, R. S. Smith, *The Spanish Guild Merchant* (Durham, NC, 1940), ch. 6; Guillermo Céspedes del Castillo, *La avería en el comercio de Indias* (Seville, 1945); Antonio-Miguel Bernal, *La financiación de la Carrera de Indias, 1492–1824* (Seville and Madrid, 1992), especially pp. 209–22; Enriqueta Vila Vilar, 'El poder del Consulado y los hombres del comercio en el siglo XVII', in Enriqueta Vila Vilar and Allan J. Kuethe (eds), *Relaciones del poder y comercio colonial. Nuevas perspectivas* (Seville, 1999), pp. 3–34.

131. For the Portuguese, see above, p. 100; for the Genoese, Ruth Pike, *Enterprise and Adventure. The Genoese in Seville and the Opening of the New World* (Ithaca, NY, 1966); for Corsicans, Enriqueta Vila Vilar, *Los Corzo y los Mañara. Tipos y arquetipos del mercader con América* (Seville, 1991); for the community of foreign merchants in Seville, Michèle Moret, *Aspects de la société marchande de Séville au début du XVIIe siècle* (Paris, 1967), pp. 34–58; and for foreign participation in Spanish commercial life in general, Antonio Domínguez Ortiz, *Los extranjeros en la vida española durante el siglo XVII y otros artículos* (Seville, 1996).

132. Enriqueta Vila Vilar and Guillermo Lohmann Villena, *Familia, linajes y negocios entre Sevilla y las Indias. Los Almonte* (Madrid, 2003).

133. Studnicki-Gizbert, 'From Agents to Consulado'; Margarita Suárez, *Comercio y fraude en el Perú colonial. Las estrategias mercantiles de un banquero* (Lima, 1995), and *Desafíos transatlánticos. Mercaderes, banqueros y el estado en el Perú virreinal, 1600–1700* (Lima, 2001).

134. Eduardo Arcila Farías, *Comercio entre Venezuela y México en los siglos XVII y XVIII* (Mexico City, 1950), pp. 52–3.

135. Woodrow Borah, *Early Colonial Trade and Navigation between Mexico and Peru* (Berkeley and Los Angeles, 1954). Inter-colonial trade in Spanish America needs further investigation. See Fisher, *Economic Aspects of Spanish Imperialism*, ch. 5.

136. Ian K. Steele, *The English Atlantic, 1675–1740* (Oxford, 1986), pp. 78–9.

137. Cressy, *Coming Over*, p. 156; Steele, *English Atlantic*, pp. 90–1 and 45.

138. Steele, *English Atlantic*, pp. 42–3.

139. Below, pp. 117–18.

140. Robert M. Bliss, *Revolution and Empire. English Politics and the American Colonies in the Seventeenth Century* (Manchester and New York, 1990), p. 20.

141. *OHBE*, 1, pp. 20–1.

142. R. W. Hinton, *The Eastland Trade and the Common Weal in the Seventeenth Century* (Cambridge, 1959), p. 95.

143. *OHBE*, 1, p. 423.

144. George Gardyner, *A Description of the New World* (London, 1651), pp. 7–8.

Chapter 5. Crown and Colonists

1. Cited in Bliss, *Revolution and Empire*, pp. 19–20, from Clarence S. Brigham (ed.), *British Royal Proclamations Relating to America, 1603–1763* (American Antiquarian Society, Transactions and Collections, XII, Worcester, MA, 1911), pp. 52–5. See also Craven, *Dissolution of the Virginia Company*, p. 330, for the move to royal rule.

2. John Robertson, 'Empire and Union', in David Armitage (ed.), *Theories of Empire, 1450–1800* (Aldershot, 1998), pp. 18–20.

3. David Armitage, 'Literature and Empire', *OHBE*, 1, pp. 114–15.

4. See John H. Elliott, 'A Europe of Composite Monarchies', *Past and Present*, 137 (1992), pp. 48–71.

5. Andrews, *The Colonial Period*, 2, p. 250.

6. *Ibid.*, 2, pp. 197 and 282.

7. Kupperman, *Providence Island*, p. 327.

8. *OHBE*, 1, pp. 22–3, 25–6, and 113. Nathaniel Crouch published in 1685, under the pseudonym 'R. B.', a tract entitled *The English Empire in America*. The figures for

publications containing the term 'British Empire' are given in John E. Crowley, 'A Visual Empire. Seeing the Atlantic World from a Global British Perspective', in Mancke and Shammas (eds), *Creation of the Atlantic World*, pp. 283–303. Against the 124 references to 'British Empire' in titles published before 1800, he finds over 4,000 containing the words 'colony' or 'plantation', or their cognates.

9. John M. Headley, 'The Habsburg World Empire and the Revival of Ghibellinism', in Armitage (ed.), *Theories of Empire*, p. 51.

10. María José Rodríguez Salgado, 'Patriotismo y política exterior en la España de Carlos V y Felipe II', in Felipe Ruiz Martín (ed.), *La proyección europea de la monarquía española* (Madrid, 1996), p. 88.

11. Above, p. 23.

12. Gonzalo Fernández de Oviedo, *Sumario de la natural historia de las Indias*, ed. José Miranda (Mexico City and Buenos Aires, 1950), p. 272; Góngora, *Studies*, pp. 45–6.

13. Pagden, *Lords of All the World*, p. 32, and n. 12 for examples, to which others could be added.

14. Elliott, 'A Europe of Composite Monarchies', pp. 52–3, citing Solórzano Pereira.

15. Juan de Solórzano Pereira, *Obras varias posthumas* (Madrid, 1776), pp. 186–7. For Solórzano and his views on Alexander VI and the papal bulls, see Muldoon, *The Americas in the Spanish World Order*, ch. 7.

16. José Manuel Pérez Prendes, *La monarquía indiana y el estado de derecho* (Valencia, 1989), pp. 85–6.

17. *Recopilación de leyes de los reynos de las Indias* (facsimile of 1791 edition, 3 vols, Madrid, 1998), lib. III, tit. 1, ley 1.

18. See Manuel Serrano y Sanz, *Orígenes de la dominación española en América* (Madrid, 1918).

19. For this much debated question, see R. Konetzke, 'La legislación sobre inmigración de extranjeros en América durante el reinado de Carlos V', in *Charles-Quint et son temps*, pp. 93–111, and, more recently, Romà Pinya i Homs, *La debatuda exclusió catalano-aragonesa de la conquesta d'Amèrica* (Barcelona, 1992), for a close discussion of the relevant legislation.

20. See Alfonso García-Gallo, *Los orígenes españoles de las instituciones americanas* (Madrid, 1987), pp. 715–41 ('El pactismo en el reino de Castilla y su proyección en América').

21. Luis Sánchez-Agesta, 'El "poderío real absoluto" en el testamento de 1554', in *Carlos V: Homenaje de la Universidad de Granada* (Granada, 1958), pp. 439–60.

22. Guillermo Lohmann Villena, 'Las Cortes en Indias', *Anuario de Historia del Derecho Español*, 17 (1947), pp. 655–62; Woodrow Borah, 'Representative Institutions in the Spanish Empire in the Sixteenth Century', *The Americas*, 12 (1956), pp. 246–57.

23. Góngora, *Studies*, p. 79.

24. For a hostile account of Fonseca and his activities, see Manuel Giménez Fernández, *Bartolomé de Las Casas* (2 vols, Seville, 1953–60). A more sympathetic treatment can be found in Thomas, *Rivers of Gold*.

25. Giménez Fernández, *Las Casas*, 2, p. 369.

26. Demetrio Ramos, 'El problema de la fundación del Real Consejo de las Indias y la fecha de su creación', in *El Consejo de las Indias en el siglo XVI* (Valladolid, 1970), p. 37, supplementing the information given in the standard work on the Council, Ernesto Schäfer, *El Consejo real y supremo de las Indias* (2 vols, Seville, 1935–47), 1, p. 44, who considered 1524 as the date of its foundation.

27. Martínez, *Hernán Cortés*, chs 18–20; Rafael Varón Gabai, *Francisco Pizarro and his Brothers* (Norman, OK and London, 1997), pp. 47–51.

28. Bakewell, *History of Latin America*, pp. 113–16; Pérez Prendes, *La monarquía indiana*, pp. 206–19; J. M. Ots Capdequi, *El estado español en las Indias* (3rd edn, Mexico City, 1957), pp. 64–5.

29. *CHLA*, 1, p. 293.

30. José Ignacio Rubio Mañé, *Introducción al estudio de los virreyes de la Nueva España, 1535–1746* (3 vols, Mexico City, 1955), 1, p. 13.

31. *Recopilación*, lib. III, tit. 3, ley 1.

32. Octavio Paz, *Sor Juana Inés de la Cruz* (3rd edn, Mexico City, 1985), pp. 195–201. A vivid contemporary account of a viceregal progress through New Spain in 1640 is to be found in

Cristóbal Gutiérrez de Medina, *Viaje del Virrey Marqués de Villena*, ed. Manuel Romero de Terreros (Mexico City, 1947). For comparable, if smaller-scale, ceremonies, on the arrival of a new governor of Chile, see Jaime Valenzuela Márquez, 'La recepción pública de una autoridad colonial: modelo peninsular, referente virreinal y reproducción periférica (Santiago de Chile, siglo XVII)', in Oscar Mazín Gómez (ed.), *México en el mundo hispánico* (2 vols, Zamora, Michoacán, 2000), pp. 495–516.

33. Konetzke, *La época colonial*, p. 121.
34. For royal symbolism and viceregal rituals, see Víctor Mínguez Cornelles, *Los reyes distantes. Imágenes del poder en el México virreinal* (Castelló de la Plana, 1995); Inmaculada Rodríguez Moya, *La mirada del virrey. Iconografía del poder en la Nueva España* (Castelló de la Plana, 2003); Alejandro Cañeque, *The King's Living Image. The Culture and Politics of Viceregal Power in Colonial Mexico* (New York and London, 2004).
35. Pérez Prendes, *La monarquía indiana*, pp. 232–7.
36. Peter Marzahl, *Town in the Empire. Government, Politics and Society in Seventeenth Century Popayán* (Austin, TX, 1978), pp. 123 and 165.
37. Góngora, *Studies*, pp. 68–9.
38. Borah, *Justice by Insurance*, pp. 253–5.
39. Cited by Juan Manzano, 'La visita de Ovando al Real Consejo de las Indias y el código ovandino', in *El Consejo de las Indias*, p. 116. For Ovando's career see Poole, *Juan de Ovando*.
40. Javier Malagón and José M. Ots Capdequi, *Solórzano y la política indiana* (2nd edn, Mexico City, 1983), ch. 1; Antonio de León Pinelo, *El Gran Canciller de Indias*, ed. Guillermo Lohmann Villena (Seville, 1953), introduction.
41. Ruggiero Romano, *Conjonctures opposées. La 'Crise' du XVIIe siècle en Europe et en Amérique ibérique* (Geneva, 1992), p. 187.
42. Above, p. 68.
43. *CHLA*, 1, p. 518; Konetzke, *La época colonial*, p. 207.
44. Bakewell, *History of Latin America*, p. 138; Konetzke, *La época colonial*, p. 217; and see below, pp. 198–9.
45. Sánchez Bella, *Iglesia y estado*, pp. 71–4.
46. Konetzke, *La época colonial*, p. 223.
47. Cited in Góngora, *Studies*, p. 71, from Juan de Ovando's *Gobernación espiritual*.
48. *The Works of Francis Bacon*, ed. J. Spedding (14 vols, London 1857–74), 7, pp. 130–1. Antonio de Mendoza moved in 1551 from the viceroyalty of New Spain to that of Peru, where he died in the following year. I have not found the source for Bacon's story.
49. Cortés, *Letters from Mexico*, p. 146 (second letter, 30 October 1520).
50. For the coincidence, see Manuel Giménez Fernández, *Hernán Cortés y la revolución comunera en la Nueva España* (Seville, 1948).
51. Víctor Frankl, 'Hernán Cortés y la tradición de las Siete Partidas', *Revista de Historia de América*, 53–4 (1962), pp. 9–74 (reprinted in Armitage (ed.), *Theories of Empire*, ch. 5).
52. Luciano Pereña Vicente, *La Universidad de Salamanca, forja del pensamiento político español en el siglo XVI* (Salamanca, 1954). For a general survey of Spanish political thinking in this period, see J. A. Fernández-Santamaría, *The State, War and Peace. Spanish Political Thought in the Renaissance, 1516–1559* (Cambridge, 1977), and for an exposition of ideas and practice in Spain's American possessions, Colin M. MacLachlan, *Spain's Empire in the New World. The Role of Ideas in Institutional and Social Change* (Berkeley, Los Angeles, London, 1988).
53. See Góngora, *Studies*, pp. 68–79. Also Richard M. Morse, 'Towards a Theory of Spanish American Government', *Journal of the History of Ideas*, 15 (1954), pp. 71–93; 'The Heritage of Latin America' in Hartz, *The Founding of New Societies*, pp. 123–77; and his ideas as reformulated in the context of the development of western civilization, in Richard M. Morse, *El espejo de Próspero. Un estudio de la dialéctica del Nuevo Mundo* (Mexico City, 1982), pp. 66ff.
54. For the formula as part of Basque law, Bartolomé Clavero, *Derecho de los reinos* (Seville, 1977), pp. 125–30. See also Pérez Prendes, *La monarquía indiana*, pp. 167–8, and *Recopilación de Indias*, lib. II, tit. 1, ley 22.
55. Above, p. 4.

56. Simpson, *The Encomienda in New Spain*, pp. 132–3.
57. For the rebellion and its justification, Guillermo Lohmann Villena, *Las ideas jurídicas-políticas en la rebelión de Gonzalo Pizarro* (Valladolid, 1977); Góngora, *Studies*, pp. 27–30 and 75. For La Gasca, Teodoro Hampe Martínez, *Don Pedro de la Gasca. Su obra política en España y América* (Lima, 1989)
58. Andrews, *Colonial Period*, 1, p. 86.
59. Craven, *Dissolution of the Virginia Company*, ch. 3; and see the documents in chapter 1 of Warren M. Billings, *The Old Dominion in the Seventeenth Century. A Documentary History of Virginia, 1606–1689* (Chapel Hill, NC, 1975), for the beginnings of government in Virginia.
60. Michael Kammen, *Deputyes and Libertyes. The Origins of Representative Government in Colonial America* (New York, 1969), p. 17.
61. Langdon, 'The Franchise and Political Democracy', p. 515.
62. *Ibid.*, p. 514.
63. Kammen, *Deputyes and Libertyes*, p. 54; and see the table of colonies (pp. 11–2) with the date of their first assemblies.
64. *Ibid.*, p. 19.
65. Michael Kammen, *Colonial New York. A History* (New York, 1975), p. 102.
66. Robert C. Ritchie, *The Duke's Province. A Study of New York Politics and Society, 1664–1691* (Chapel Hill, NC, 1977), pp. 159 and 166.
67. Jack P. Greene, *Peripheries and Center. Constitutional Development in the Extended Polities of the British Empire and the United States, 1607–1788* (Athens, GA, London, 1986), pp. 23–4; John Phillip Reid, *In a Defiant Stance* (University Park, PA, London, 1977), p. 12.
68. Leonard Woods Labaree, *Royal Government in America* (New Haven, 1930), pp. 32–3.
69. For the powers of governors, see *ibid.*, especially ch. 3.
70. *Ibid.*, p. 102.
71. Cited by Bernard Bailyn, *The Origins of American Politics* (New York, 1970), p. 113. Labaree's comparison of Osborn's instructions with those of Governor Clinton in 1741 in fact shows that 67 of the original 97 articles were repeated verbatim, four showed changes in phraseology, sixteen were modified in content, ten were omitted, and twelve new paragraphs were added (*Royal Government*, p. 64). For British royal instructions see Leonard Woods Labaree (ed.), *Royal Instructions to British Colonial Governors, 1670–1776* (New York, 1935). Instructions, both standard and secret, for the viceroys of Habsburg Spanish America may be found in Lewis Hanke (ed.), *Los virreyes españoles en América durante el gobierno de la Casa de Austria* (BAE, vols 233–7, Madrid, 1967–8 for Mexico, and vols 280–5 for Peru, Madrid, 1978–80).
72. Labaree, *Royal Government*, p. 83.
73. *Ibid.*, pp. 85–9.
74. Patricia U. Bonomi, *The Lord Cornbury Scandal. The Politics of Reputation in British America* (Chapel Hill, NC and London, 1988).
75. *Ibid.*, pp. 92–7.
76. Labaree, *Royal Government*, p. 43.
77. Richard R. Johnson, *Adjustment to Empire. The New England Colonies 1675–1715* (Leicester, 1981), p. 332.
78. Cited in Alan Tully, *Forming American Politics. Ideals, Interests and Institutions in Colonial New York and Pennsylvania* (Baltimore and London, 1994), p. 95.
79. Labaree, *Royal Government*, p. 126; Konetzke, *La época colonial*, pp. 120–1. The three-year rule was introduced in 1629.
80. Konetzke, *La época colonial*, p. 121.
81. Labaree, *Royal Government*, p. 38. The Jamaican-born Moore was governor of New York 1765–9.
82. Konetzke, *Colección de documentos*, 1, doc. 350; John Leddy Phelan, *The Kingdom of Quito in the Seventeenth Century* (Madison, WI, Milwaukee, WI, London, 1967), pp. 151–3.
83. Jonathan Israel, *Race, Class and Politics in Colonial Mexico, 1610–1670* (Oxford, 1975), ch. 5.
84. C. H. Haring, *The Spanish Empire in America* (New York, 1947), pp. 148–57. Haring's survey remains a useful guide to governmental organization and practice in colonial America.

85. Labaree, *Royal Government*, ch. 5; Jack P. Greene, *Negotiated Authorities. Essays in Colonial Political and Constitutional History* (Charlottesville, VA and London, 1994), p. 173.

86. Ismael Sánchez-Bella, *La organización financiera de las Indias. Siglo XVI* (Seville, 1968), pp. 21–3.

87. *Ibid.*, pp. 52–3; Robert Sidney Smith, 'Sales Taxes in New Spain, 1575–1770', *HAHR*, 28 (1948), pp. 2–37.

88. For the working of this system, see Herbert S. Klein, *The American Finances of the Spanish Empire. Royal Income and Expenditures in Colonial Mexico, Peru, and Bolivia, 1680–1809* (Albuquerque, NM, 1998).

89. Anthony McFarlane, *The British in the Americas, 1480–1815* (London and New York, 1994), pp. 207–8.

90. Labaree, *Royal Government*, p. 271.

91. Jack P. Greene, *The Quest for Power. The Lower Houses of Assembly in the Southern Royal Colonies, 1689–1776* (Chapel Hill, NC, 1963), p. 3.

92. Cited in David Hackett Fischer, *Albion's Seed. Four British Folkways in America* (New York and Oxford, 1989), p. 407.

93. Labaree, *Royal Government*, pp. 170 and 274–5; Greene, *The Quest for Power*, part 2.

94. Bernard Bailyn, 'Politics and Social Structure in Virginia', in Stanley N. Katz and John M. Murrin (eds), *Colonial America. Essays in Politics and Social Development* (New York, 1983), pp. 207–30, at pp. 210–15.

95. Billings, *The Old Dominion*, p. 68.

96. Warren M. Billings, 'The Growth of Political Institutions in Virginia, 1634–1676', *WMQ*, 3rd ser., 31 (1974), pp. 225–42; Billings, *The Old Dominion*, p. 70.

97. Horn, *Adapting to a New World*, p. 190.

98. *Ibid.*, pp. 195–7.

99. Billings, 'The Growth of Political Institutions', p. 232.

100. For legal pluralism in colonial societies, see Lauren Benton, *Law and Colonial Cultures. Legal Regimes in World History, 1400–1900* (Cambridge, 2002), and especially ch. 2, which discusses legal regimes in the Atlantic world. See also for varieties of jurisdiction in Renaissance Spain, Richard L. Kagan, *Lawsuits and Litigants in Castile, 1500–1700* (Chapel Hill, NC, 1981), pp. 22–32. For the English Atlantic world, see especially William M. Offutt, 'The Atlantic Rules: the Legalistic Turn in Colonial British America', in Mancke and Shammas (eds), *The Creation of the Atlantic World*, pp. 160–81, and Tomlins and Mann (eds), *The Many Legalities of Early America*, together with the review of this important collection of essays by Jack P. Greene, ' "By Their Laws Shall Ye Know Them": Law and Identity in Colonial British America', *Journal of Interdisciplinary History*, 33 (2002), pp. 247–60.

101. Offutt, 'The Atlantic Rules', p. 161.

102. See Warren M. Billings, 'The Transfer of English Law to Virginia, 1606–1650', in Andrews *et al.* (eds), *The Westward Enterprise*, ch. 11.

103. Offutt, 'The Atlantic Rules', p. 166.

104. *Ibid.*, p. 178.

105. See the essays by John M. Murrin and G. B. Warden in David D. Hall, John M. Murrin and Thad W. Tate (eds), *Saints and Revolutionaries. Essays in Early American History* (New York and London, 1984). Also Peter Charles Hoffer, *Law and People in Colonial America* (Baltimore and London, 1992), pp. 87–9.

106. 'Shipwrecked Spaniards 1639. Grievances against Bermudans', trans. from the Spanish by L. D. Gurrin, *The Bermuda Historical Quarterly*, 18 (1961), pp. 13–28, at pp. 27–8.

107. Below, pp. 228–9.

108. See Peter Marzahl, *Town in the Empire. Government, Politics and Society in Seventeenth-Century Popayán* (Austin, TX, 1978).

109. See the description of Easthampton in John Putnam Demos, *Entertaining Satan. Witchcraft and the Culture of Early New England* (New York and Oxford, 1982), pp. 220–33. The history of East Hampton, as it now styles itself, is explored in T. H. Breen, *Imagining the Past. East Hampton Histories* (Reading, MA, 1989).

110. See Demos, *A Little Commonwealth*, pp. 7–8; Lockridge, *A New England Town*, ch. 3.

111. Gary B. Nash, *The Urban Crucible. Social Change, Political Consciousness and the Origins of the American Revolution* (Cambridge, MA, and London, 1979), pp. 31–2.
112. Demos, *Entertaining Satan*, p. 228.
113. Langdon, 'The Franchise and Political Democracy', pp. 522–5.
114. Winthrop, *Journal*, p. 145.
115. Dunn, *Puritans and Yankees*, p. 29; Howard Millar Chapin, *Roger Williams and the King's Colors* (Providence, RI, 1928).
116. Enrique Florescano, *La bandera mexicana. Breve historia de su formación y simbolismo* (Mexico City, 1998).
117. Cited in Bliss, *Revolution and Empire*, p. 42 (spelling modernized).
118. Dunn, *Puritans and Yankees*, p. 37.
119. Below, p. 229.
120. Craven, *The Southern Colonies*, ch. 7; Bliss, *Revolution and Empire*, pp. 51–2 and ch. 4; and, for a general survey of the Civil War period, see Carla Gardina Pestana, *The English Atlantic in an Age of Revolution, 1640–1661* (Cambridge, MA, 2004).
121. Mary Beth Norton, *Founding Mothers and Fathers. Gendered Power and the Forming of American Society* (New York, 1997), p. 282.
122. Dunn, *Puritans and Yankees*, p. 37.
123. *Ibid.*, p. 42; Bremer, *John Winthrop*, pp. 325–7.
124. Bliss, *Revolution and Empire*, p. 46.
125. *Ibid.*, pp. 60–1.
126. Andrews, *The Colonial Period*, vol. 4, pp. 54–5.
127. J. M. Sosin, *English America and the Restoration Monarchy of Charles II* (Lincoln, NE, and London, 1980), pp. 39–41. This unwieldy structure was replaced, after Clarendon's fall in 1667, by a Privy Council Committee for Trade and Plantations. A further reorganization occurred in 1672, with the establishment of a Council of Trade and Foreign Plantations.
128. *OHBE*, 1, p. 452.
129. F. R. Harris, *The Life of Edward Mountague, K.G., First Earl of Sandwich, 1625–1672*, 2 vols (London, 1912), Appendix K (spelling modernized).
130. See Johnson, *Adjustment to Empire*; Bernard Bailyn, *The New England Merchants in the Seventeenth Century* (1955; edn New York, 1964).
131. Stephen Saunders Webb, *The Governors-General. The English Army and the Definition of the Empire, 1569–1681* (Chapel Hill, NC, 1979), p. 194.
132. Cited by Greene, *Peripheries and Center*, pp. 39–40.
133. For the idea of 'garrison government', as expounded by Stephen Saunders Webb, see his *Governors-General*, and *1676. The End of American Independence* (New York, 1984). For a critique, see Richard R. Johnson, 'The Imperial Webb', and Webb's reply, in *WMQ*, 3rd ser., 43 (1986), pp. 408–59.
134. Labaree, *Royal Government*, p. 275.
135. W. A. Speck, 'The International and Imperial Context', in Greene and Pole, *Colonial British America*, p. 390.
136. Michael Garibaldi Hall, *Edward Randolph and the American Colonies, 1676–1703* (1960; New York, 1969), p. 22. For Randolph see also Dunn, *Puritans and Yankees*, pp. 212–28.
137. For the career of Andros, Mary Lou Lustig, *The Imperial Executive in America. Sir Edmund Andros, 1637–1714* (Madison, NJ, 2002).
138. See Viola Florence Barnes, *The Dominion of New England* (New Haven, 1923).
139. Alison Gilbert Olson, *Anglo-American Politics, 1660–1775* (New York and Oxford, 1973), p. 66.
140. Ritchie, *The Duke's Province*, pp. 168–73; Michael Kammen, *Colonial New York. A History* (New York, 1975), p. 102.
141. Barnes, *Dominion of New England*, p. 87.
142. Cited by Lustig, *The Imperial Executive*, p. 151.
143. For 1688 see David S. Lovejoy, *The Glorious Revolution in America* (New York, 1972); J. M. Sosin, *English America and the Revolution of 1688* (Lincoln, NE, and London, 1982). Also Richard Dunn, 'The Glorious Revolution and America', *OHBE*, 1, ch. 20.
144. Hall, *Edward Randolph*, p. 32.

Chapter 6. The Ordering of Society

1. Cited by Perry Miller, 'Errand into the Wilderness', in *In Search of Early America. The William and Mary Quarterly 1943–1993* (Richmond, VA, 1993), p. 3. For the date and place of the sermon's delivery, see Bremer, *John Winthrop*, pp. 431–2 (spelling modernized).

2. Cited by Salas, *Las armas de la conquista*, pp. 140–1, from the *Relación del sitio de Cuzco*.

3. Cited in Perry Miller, *The New England Mind in the Seventeenth Century* (Cambridge, MA, and London, 1939), p. 428.

4. Cited in Guillaume Boccara and Sylvia Galindo (eds), *Lógica mestiza en América* (Temuco, Chile, 1999), p. 61.

5. See Dietrich Gerhard, *Old Europe. A Study of Continuity, 1000–1800* (New York, 1981).

6. See Aldo Stella, *La rivoluzione contadina del 1525 e l'Utopia di Michael Gaismayr* (Padua, 1975).

7. For a comprehensive study of these religious movements see G. H. Williams, *The Radical Reformation* (London, 1962).

8. Below, p. 185.

9. Durand, *La transformación social del conquistador*, vol. 1, ch. 3 ('El valer más').

10. James Lockhart, *The Men of Cajamarca. A Social and Economic History of the First Conquerors of Peru* (Austin, TX and London 1972), p. 32.

11. Baltasar Dorantes de Carranza, *Sumaria relación de las cosas de la Nueva España* (1604; ed. Ernesto de la Torre Villar, Mexico City, 1987), p. 201.

12. Thomas N. Ingersoll, 'The Fear of Levelling in New England', in Carla Gardina Pestana and Sharon V. Salinger (eds), *Inequality in Early America* (Hanover, NH, and London, 1999), pp. 46–66.

13. Norton, *Founding Mothers and Fathers*, ch. 8.

14. *OHBE*, 1, p. 203.

15. Winthrop, *Journal*, p. 612 (spelling modernized).

16. Barry Levy, *Quakers and the American Family* (New York and Oxford, 1988), pp. 76–9; Gary Nash, *Quakers and Politics in Pennsylvania, 1681–1726* (Princeton, 1968), p. 43.

17. Above, pp. 44 and 55.

18. Bernard Bailyn, *Education in the Forming of American Society* (New York and London, 1960), p. 28.

19. Above, p. 55.

20. Konetzke, *Colección de documentos*, 1, doc. 112 (royal cédula to Viceroy Mendoza, 23 August 1538).

21. The voluminous correspondence collected in Rocío Sánchez Rubio and Isabel Testón Núñez, *El hilo que une: Las relaciones epistolares en el viejo y el nuevo mundo, siglos XVI–XVIII* (Mérida, 1999), derives from bigamy prosecutions. For an individual case in sixteenth-century Peru, see Alexandra Parma Cook and Noble David Cook, *Good Faith and Truthful Ignorance. A Case of Transatlantic Bigamy* (Durham, NC, and London, 1991).

22. See in particular Demos, *A Little Commonwealth*, part 2, and Philip J. Greven, *Four Generations. Population, Land and Family in Colonial Andover, Massachusetts* (Ithaca, NY, and London, 1970), part 1.

23. Norton, *Founding Mothers and Fathers*, pp. 83–9; Demos, *A Little Commonwealth*, pp. 84–7.

24. Tate and Ammerman (eds), *The Chesapeake in the Seventeenth Century*, p. 127; Horn, *Adapting to a New World*, p. 206.

25. Horn, *Adapting to a New World*, p. 216.

26. Tate and Ammerman (eds), *The Chesapeake in the Seventeenth Century*, p. 173.

27. Mörner, *Race Mixture*, p. 55.

28. Above, p. 82.

29. Dunn, *Sugar and Slaves*, pp. 252–5. I am grateful to Professor Philip Morgan for his advice on this point.

30. Foster, *Culture and Conquest*, pp. 122–3; *CHLA*, vol. 2, p. 290. It may not, however, always have worked to this effect. In Santiago de Chile in the seventeenth century, for instance, godparents seem to have been chosen from within the same social or racial milieu as that of the parents. See Jean-Paul Zúñiga, *Espagnols d'outre-mer. Émigration,*

métissage et reproduction sociale à Santiago du Chili, au 17ᵉ siècle (Paris, 2002), pp. 287–301. There is a need for a systematic study of the workings and importance of *compadrazgo* in Spanish-American societies.

31. Horn, *Adapting to a New World*, p. 218.
32. Norton, *Founding Mothers and Fathers*, pp. 111–12, and 145; and see Carole Shammas, 'Anglo-American Household Government in Comparative Perspective', *WMQ*, 3rd ser., 52 (1995), pp. 104–44, and the debate that follows it. See also the subsequent book by Carole Shammas, *A History of Household Government in America* (Charlottesville, VA and London, 2002).
33. *Siete Partidas*, partida 4, títulos 17 and 18; Shammas, 'Anglo-American Household Government', p. 137; Patricia Seed, *To Love, Honor, and Obey in Colonial Mexico* (Stanford, CA, 1988), p. 235.
34. James Casey, *Early Modern Spain. A Social History* (London and New York, 1999), pp. 28–9.
35. Adam Smith, *The Wealth of Nations*, ed. Edwin Cannan (2 vols, 6th edn, London, 1950), vol. 2, pp. 84–5 (Book 4, ch. 7, part 2).
36. José F. de la Peña, *Oligarquía y propiedad en Nueva España 1550–1624* (Mexico City, 1983), p. 220.
37. Magnus Mörner, 'Economic Factors and Stratification in Colonial Spanish America with Special Regard to Elites', *HAHR*, 63 (1983), pp. 335–69. For León, D. A. Brading, *Haciendas and Ranchos in the Mexican Bajío. León 1700–1860* (Cambridge, 1978), pp. 118–19.
38. Louisa Schell Hoberman, *Mexico's Merchant Elite, 1590–1660. Silver, State and Society* (Durham, NC, and London, 1991), pp. 231–2.
39. Horn, *Adapting to a New World*, pp. 230–1.
40. Bertram Wyatt-Brown, *Southern Honor. Ethics and Behavior in the Old South* (New York, 1982), pp. 5–6; Fischer, *Albion's Seed*, pp. 380–1; and for important new light on the prevalence of entail in Virginia, see Holly Brewer, 'Entailing Aristocracy in Colonial Virginia: "Ancient Feudal Restraints" and Revolutionary Reform', *WMQ.*, 3rd ser., 54 (1997), pp. 307–46.
41. Louis B. Wright, *The First Gentlemen of Virginia. Intellectual Qualities of the Early Colonial Ruling Class* (San Marino, CA, 1940), p. 57.
42. Norton, *Founding Mothers and Fathers*, pp. 144–7; Horn, *Adapting to a New World*, pp. 230–1.
43. Patricia Seed, 'American Law, Hispanic Traces: Some Contemporary Entanglements of Community Property', *WMQ*, 3rd ser., 52 (1995), pp. 157–62. For the age of majority, Lockhart, *Spanish Peru*, pp. 164–5.
44. Luis Martín, *Daughters of the Conquistadores. Women of the Viceroyalty of Peru* (Dallas, TX, 1983), pp. 46 and 50; Lockhart, *Spanish Peru*, ch. 9.
45. Shammas, 'Anglo-American Household Government', p. 111.
46. Seed, *To Love, Honor, and Obey*, pp. 34–40; Casey, *Early Modern Spain*, pp. 208–9.
47. Martin Ingram, *Church Courts, Sex and Marriage in England, 1570–1640* (Cambridge, 1987), p. 132.
48. Norton, *Founding Mothers and Fathers*, p. 64; Horn, *Adapting to a New World*, p. 211.
49. Horn, *Adapting to a New World*, p. 210.
50. Fischer, *Albion's Seed*, pp. 88–91.
51. Seed, *To Love, Honor, and Obey*, pp. 63 and 266–7; Zúñiga, *Espagnols d'outre-mer*, pp. 177–86. For the eighteenth century see Ann Twinam, *Public Lives, Private Secrets. Gender, Honor, Sexuality, and Illegitimacy in Colonial Spanish America* (Stanford, CA, 1999).
52. Ann Twinam, 'Honor, Sexuality and Illegitimacy in Colonial Spanish America', in Asunción Lavrín (ed.), *Sexuality and Marriage in Colonial Latin America* (Lincoln, NE, and London, 1989), pp. 136 and 125.
53. Seed, *To Love, Honor, and Obey*, pp. 69–74.
54. *Ibid.*, p. 80.
55. Thomas Calvo, 'The Warmth of the Hearth: Seventeenth-Century Guadalajara Families', in Lavrín, *Sexuality and Marriage*, p. 299.
56. Susan M. Socolow, 'Acceptable Partners: Marriage Choice in Colonial Argentina, 1778–1810', in Lavrín, *Sexuality and Marriage*, pp. 210–13; Seed, *To Love, Honor, and Obey*, pp. 200–4.

57. Lavrín, *Sexuality and Marriage*, p. 6.

58. Seed, 'American Law, Hispanic Traces', p. 159.

59. De la Peña, *Oligarquía y propiedad*, pp. 191–3.

60. Jack P. Greene, *Imperatives, Behaviors and Identities. Essays in Early American Cultural History* (Charlottesville, VA and London, 1992), pp. 191–3.

61. Above, p. 8.

62. Otte, *Cartas privadas*, no. 127.

63. *Descripción del virreinato del Perú*, ed. Boleslao Lewin (Rosario, 1958), p. 39.

64. Konetzke, *Colección de documentos*, 1, doc. 145.

65. Himmerich y Valencia, *Encomenderos of New Spain*, p. 57.

66. Norman H. Dawes, 'Titles as Symbols of Prestige in Seventeenth-Century New England', *WMQ*, 3rd ser., 6 (1949), pp. 69–83.

67. Cotton Mather, *A Christian at his Calling* (Boston, 1701), p. 42.

68. Dawes, 'Titles as Symbols', p. 78; Michael Craton, 'Reluctant Creoles. The Planters' World in the British West Indies', in Bailyn and Morgan (eds), *Strangers Within the Realm*, pp. 314–62, at p. 326; Christon I. Archer, *The Army in Bourbon Mexico, 1760–1810* (Albuquerque, NM, 1977), p. 165, citing Humboldt.

69. Cited in Isaac, *The Transformation of Virginia*, p. 161.

70. Wilcomb E. Washburn, *The Governor and the Rebel. A History of Bacon's Rebellion in Virginia* (Chapel Hill, NC, 1957), p. 35. For Berkeley, see Warren M. Billings, *Sir William Berkeley and the Forging of Colonial Virginia* (Baton Rouge, LA, 2004).

71. Bacon's rebellion has been the subject of much debate since the publication of Thomas J. Wertenbaker's *Torchbearer of the Revolution. The Story of Bacon's Rebellion and its Leader* (Princeton, 1940). The arguments of Wertenbaker in favour of Bacon's 'democratic' credentials were contested by Wilcomb Washburn in *The Governor and the Rebel*, which makes the case for Governor Berkeley. More recently, Stephen Saunders Webb has retold the story in the spirit of Wertenbaker in Book 1 of his *1676*. See also for the background and motivations of Bacon and his followers Wesley Frank Craven, *The Southern Colonies in the Seventeenth Century* (Baton Rouge, LA, 1949), ch. 10, which rightly emphasizes the complexity of the story; Bernard Bailyn, 'Politics and Social Structure in Virginia', in James Morton Smith, *Seventeenth-Century America. Essays in Colonial History* (Chapel Hill, NC, 1959), ch. 5; Morgan, *American Slavery, American Freedom*, ch. 13; Kathleen M. Brown, *Good Wives, Nasty Wenches, and Anxious Patriarchs* (Chapel Hill, NC and London, 1996), ch. 5; Horn, *Adapting to a New World*, pp. 372–9.

72. Bacon's 'manifesto', in Billings, *The Old Dominion*, p. 278. I have corrected an obvious misprint, substituting 'compared' for 'composed', and have inserted the word 'enter' to make sense of the sentence.

73. Fischer, *Albion's Seed*, pp. 207–32; Bailyn, 'Politics and Social Structure'.

74. Horn, *Adapting to a New World*, pp. 151–6.

75. Cited in T. H. Breen, *Puritans and Adventurers. Change and Persistence in Early America* (New York and Oxford, 1980), p. 132.

76. Horn, *Adapting to a New World*, p. 378.

77. Morgan, *American Slavery, American Freedom*, p. 283.

78. Brown, *Good Wives, Nasty Wenches*, p. 178.

79. *Ibid.*, p. 179.

80. Breen, *Puritans and Adventurers*, p. 141.

81. Above, p. 104.

82. Hatfield, *Atlantic Virginia*, p. 228.

83. E. Morgan, *American Slavery, American Freedom*, p. 329.

84. P. Morgan, *Slave Counterpoint*, p. 58.

85. *Ibid.*, pp. 422–3.

86. *Ibid.*, pp. 15–16.

87. See Brown, *Good Wives, Nasty Wenches*, especially pp. 184–5.

88. Breen, *Puritans and Adventurers*, p. 162.

89. E. Morgan, *American Slavery, American Freedom*, p. 344.

90. Dunn, *Sugar and Slaves*, pp. 98, 131, 162–5; and, for a useful survey of planter society, see Craton, 'Reluctant Creoles'.

91. Fischer, *Albion's Seed*, p. 385.
92. See Wyatt-Brown, *Southern Honor*.
93. Wright, *The First Gentlemen of Virginia*, p. 60.
94. For social structure in the Indies, see especially Lyle C. McAlister, 'Social Structure and Social Change in New Spain', *HAHR*, 43 (1963), pp. 349–70, and Magnus Mörner, 'Economic Factors and Stratification in Colonial Spanish America with Special Regard to Elites', *HAHR*, 63 (1983), pp. 335–69.
95. Below, p. 234.
96. Humboldt, *Ensayo político*, II, p. 141 (lib. 2. cap. 7).
97. See under *casta* in the *Diccionario de autoridades* (Madrid, 1726; facsimile edn, 3 vols, Real Academia Española, Madrid, 1969). Also Mörner, *Race Mixture*, p. 53.
98. R. Douglas Cope, *The Limits of Racial Domination. Plebeian Society in Colonial Mexico City, 1660–1720* (Madison, WI, 1994), p. 24.
99. See the exhibition catalogue, Ilona Katzew (ed.), *New World Orders. Casta Painting and Colonial Latin America* (Americas Society Art Gallery, New York, 1996), and her comprehensive study, *Casta Painting. Images of Race in Eighteenth-Century Mexico* (New Haven and London, 2004). For the number of sets so far located, Katzew, *Casta Painting*, p. 63. The earliest known set dates from 1711 (p. 10).
100. Magnus Mörner, 'Labour Systems and Patterns of Social Stratification', in Wolfgang Reinhard and Peter Waldmann (eds), *Nord und Süd in Amerika: Gegensätze-Gemeinsamkeiten-Europäischer Hintergrund* (Freiburg, 1992), I, pp. 347–63.
101. Twinam, 'Honor, Sexuality', in Lavrín, *Sexuality and Marriage*, pp. 123–4.
102. Carmen Castañeda, *Círculos de poder en la Nueva España* (Mexico City, 1998), pp. 112–14; Bernand, *Negros esclavos y libres*, pp. 130–1; María Elena Martínez, 'The Black Blood of New Spain: *Limpieza de Sangre*, Racial Violence, and Gendered Power in Early Colonial Mexico', *WMQ*, 3rd ser., 61 (2004), pp. 479–520.
103. Castañeda, *Círculos de poder*, p. 113.
104. Cited by Katzew, *New World Orders*, p. 11, from a 1774 treatise by Pedro Alonso O'Crouley.
105. Twinam, 'Honor, Sexuality and Illegitimacy', p. 125.
106. Cited by Bernard Lavallé, *Las promesas ambiguas. Ensayos sobre el criollismo colonial en los Andes* (Lima, 1993), p. 47.
107. Cope, *Limits of Racial Domination*, p. 121.
108. Lavallé, *Las promesas ambiguas*, p. 47; Katzew, *New World Orders*, p. 12.
109. Cited by Winthrop D. Jordan, *White Over Black. American Attitudes toward the Negro 1550–1812* (1968; Baltimore 1969), p. 176.
110. Lockhart and Schwartz, *Early Latin America*, pp. 129–30; Mörner, *Race Mixture*, pp. 60–1.
111. Solange Alberro, *Del gachupín al criollo. O de cómo los españoles de México dejaron de serlo* (El Colegio de México, Jornadas, 122, 1992), p. 170, n. 13.
112. Humboldt, *Ensayo político*, II, p. 141 (lib. 2, cap. 7).
113. See Israel, *Race, Class and Politics*, ch. 5.
114. Cope, *Limits of Racial Domination*, pp. 22–3; Wyatt-Brown, *Southern Honor*, ch. 4.
115. See the graph of seventeenth-century maize prices in Mexico City in Enrique Florescano, *Etnia, estado y nación. Ensayo sobre las identidades colectivas en México* (Mexico City, 1997), p. 259.
116. Cope, *Limits of Racial Domination*, ch. 7; Natalia Silva Prada, 'Estrategias culturales en el tumulto de 1692 en la ciudad de México: aportes para la reconstrucción de la historia de la cultura política antigua', *Historia Mexicana*, 209 (2003), pp. 5–63. For a contemporary account, Carlos de Sigüenza y Góngora, 'Alboroto y Motín de México del 8 de junio de 1692', in a selection of his *Relaciones históricas* (4th edn, Mexico City, 1987), pp. 97–174.
117. Juan A. and Judith E. Villamarín, 'The Concept of Nobility in Colonial Santa Fe de Bogotá', in Karen Spalding (ed.), *Essays in the Political, Economic and Social History of Colonial Latin America* (Newark, DE, 1982), pp. 125–53.
118. Marzahl, *Town in the Empire*, p. 40.
119. De la Peña, *Oligarquía y propiedad*, pp. 200–6; Ma. Justina Sarabia Viejo, *Don Luis de Velasco, virrey de Nueva España, 1550–1564* (Seville, 1978), pp. 474–5.

120. Mark A. Burkholder and D. S. Chandler, *From Impotence to Authority. The Spanish Crown and the American Audiencias, 1687–1808* (Columbia, MO, 1977), p. 2.
121. Konetzke, *La época colonial*, p. 138; De la Peña, *Oligarquía y propiedad*, p. 195.
122. J. H. Parry, *The Sale of Public Office in the Spanish Indies under the Hapsburgs* (Berkeley and Los Angeles, 1953); Mark A. Burkholder, 'Bureaucrats', in Louisa Schell Hoberman and Susan Migden Socolow (eds), *Cities and Society in Colonial Latin America* (Albuquerque, NM, 1986), ch. 4.
123. Hoberman, *Mexico's Merchant Elite*, p. 55 and table 8; Suárez, *Comercio y fraude*, p. 124.
124. Hanke, *Los virreyes españoles. México*, 5, p. 12.
125. Hoberman, *Mexico's Merchant Elite*, pp. 223–4.
126. Guillermo Lohmann Villena, *Los americanos en las ordenes nobiliarias*, 2 vols (Madrid, 1947). Also Romano, *Conjonctures opposées*, p. 188.
127. Stuart B. Schwartz, 'New World Nobility: Social Aspirations and Mobility in the Conquest and Colonization of Spanish America', in Miriam Usher Chrisman (ed.), *Social Groups and Religious Ideas in the Sixteenth Century* (Studies in Medieval Culture, XIII, The Medieval Institute, Western Michigan University, Kalamazoo, MI, 1978), pp. 23–37.
128. Zúñiga, *Espagnols d'outre-mer*, pp. 305–11.
129. Hatfield, *Atlantic Virginia*, pp. 86–9.
130. Tully, *Forming American Politics*, p. 4.
131. For 'conquest culture', see Foster, *Culture and Conquest*.
132. Breen, *Puritans and Adventurers*, pp. 68–9 and ch. 8.
133. Innes, *Labor in a New Land*, pp. 17–18; and above, p. 92, for the Pynchons.
134. Sacvan Bercovitch, *The American Jeremiad* (Madison, WI, 1978). For the second New England generation, Robert Middlekauff, *The Mathers. Three Generations of Puritan Intellectuals, 1596–1728* (London, Oxford, New York, 1971), pp. 97–9.
135. Bailyn, *New England Merchants*, chs 5 and 6.
136. See, for the mercantile elites of the two viceroyalties, Hoberman, *Mexico's Merchant Elite*, and Suárez, *Desafíos transatlánticos*.
137. Sosin, *English America*, p. 64.
138. Middlekauff, *The Mathers*, pp. 263–8.
139. Gary B. Nash, *The Urban Crucible. Social Change, Political Consciousness and the Origins of the American Revolution* (Cambridge, MA and London, 1979), p. 31.
140. Dunn, *Puritans and Yankees*, pp. 251–57; Sosin, *English America and the Revolution of 1688*, ch. 6; Nash, *Urban Crucible*, pp. 38–44; and see above, pp. 151–2.
141. T. H. Breen, *The Character of the Good Ruler. Puritan Political Ideas in New England, 1630–1730* (New Haven, 1970), p. 177.
142. For city politics in later seventeenth-century New York, see, in addition to Ritchie, *The Duke's Province*, the relevant sections in Kammen, *Colonial New York*, Nash, *The Urban Crucible*, and Tully, *Forming American Politics*. For the part played by religion and ethnicity in Leisler's rebellion, see David William Vorhees, 'The "Fervent Zeale" of Jacob Leisler', *WMQ*, 3rd ser., 51 (1994), pp. 447–72, and John M. Murrin, 'English Rights as Ethnic Aggression: the English Conquest, the Charter of Liberties of 1683, and Leisler's Rebellion', in William Pencak and Conrad Edick Wright (eds), *Authority and Resistance in Early New York* (New York, 1988), pp. 56–94.
143. Hoberman and Socolow, *Cities and Society*, p. 5.
144. Nash, *The Urban Crucible*, p. 4.
145. *Ibid.*, p. 21.
146. *Ibid.*, pp. 29–30.
147. Cited by Breen, *The Character of the Good Ruler*, p. 178.
148. For political debate and social disruption in Boston in these decades, see Nash, *The Urban Crucible*, pp. 76–88.
149. Douglas Adair, 'Rumbold's Dying Speech, 1685, and Jefferson's Last Words on Democracy, 1826', *WMQ*, 3rd ser., 9 (1952), pp. 521–31.

Chapter 7. America as Sacred Space

1. Cotton Mather, *Magnalia Christi Americana* (1702), 2 vols (repr. Edinburgh, 1979), vol. 1, pp. 41–2.
2. Giovanni Botero, *Relationi universali* (Brescia, 1599), part IV, lib. 2, p. 45 (facsimile reprint of selected passages on the New World in Aldo Albònico, *Il mondo americano di Giovanni Botero* (Rome, 1990), p. 216).
3. John Leddy Phelan, *The Millennial Kingdom of the Franciscans in the New World* (2nd edn, Berkeley and Los Angeles, 1970), p. 32.
4. See Sacvan Bercovitch, *The Puritan Origins of the American Self* (New Haven and London, 1975), pp. 140–1.
5. For the millennial and apocalyptic tradition, see Marjorie Reeves, *The Influence of Prophecy in the Later Middle Ages. A Study in Joachimism* (Oxford, 1969); and for its transfer to Spanish America, Phelan, *The Millennial Kingdom of the Franciscans*; José Antonio Maravall, *Utopía y reformismo en la España de los Austrias* (Madrid, 1982), ch. 2; D. A. Brading, *The First America. The Spanish Monarchy and the Liberal State, 1492–1867* (Cambridge, 1991), ch. 5; Baudot, *Utopía e historia en México*, pp. 85–98.
6. Benavente (Motolinía), *Memoriales*, pp. 20–1.
7. Brading, *First America*, p. 126.
8. Benno M. Biermann, 'Bartolomé de las Casas and Verapaz', in Juan Friede and Benjamin Keen (ed.), *Bartolomé de Las Casas in History* (DeKalb, IL, 1971), pp. 443–84; Marcel Bataillon, *Études sur Bartolomé de Las Casas* (Paris, 1965), pp. 137–202.
9. Fintan B. Warren, *Vasco de Quiroga and his Pueblo-Hospitals of Santa Fe* (Washington, 1963); Silvio Zavala, *Sir Thomas More in New Spain. A Utopian Adventure of the Renaissance* (*Diamante* III, The Hispanic and Luso-Brazilian Councils, London, 1955); Phelan, *Millennial Kingdom*, p. 47, and p. 150, n. 10.
10. Brading, *First America*, p. 110.
11. For the Jesuit communities in Paraguay, see especially Alberto Armani, *Ciudad de Dios y Ciudad del Sol. El 'Estado' jesuita de los guaraníes, 1609–1768* (Mexico City, 1982; repr. 1987); Girolamo Imbruglia, *L'invenzione del Paraguay* (Naples, 1983); Magnus Mörner, *The Political and Economic Activities of the Jesuits in the La Plata Region. The Hapsburg Era* (Stockholm, 1953).
12. Armani, *Ciudad de Dios*, p. 96.
13. Force, *Tracts*, 1, no. 6, p. 14.
14. Above, p. 74.
15. Mather, *Magnalia*, 2, p. 442.
16. Cited by Phelan, *Millennial Kingdom*, p. 50. See also Brading, *First America*, p. 348.
17. See David D. Hall, *Worlds of Wonder, Days of Judgment. Popular Religious Beliefs in Early New England* (New York, 1989), pp. 91–3.
18. Cited by Perry Miller, *Errand into the Wilderness* (Cambridge, MA, 1956), p. 119.
19. Richard Crakanthorpe (1608), cited by Avihu Zakai, *Exile and Kingdom. History and Apocalypse in the Puritan Migration to America* (Cambridge, 1992), p. 62.
20. Mather, *Magnalia*, 1, pp. 44 and 46.
21. Morgan, *Roger Williams*, pp. 99–103.
22. Mather, *Magnalia*, 1, p. 66.
23. *Ibid.*, p. 50.
24. Above, p. 48.
25. Sacvan Bercovitch, 'The Winthrop Variation: a Model of American Identity', *Proceedings of the British Academy*, 97 (1997), pp. 75–94.
26. Cited by Bercovitch, *Puritan Origins of the American Self*, p. 102.
27. See the introduction to Fray Diego Durán, *Book of the Gods and Rites, and the Ancient Calendar*, trans. and ed. by Fernando Horcasitas and Doris Heyden (Norman, OK, 1971), pp. 23–5, and Lee Eldridge Huddleston, *Origins of the American Indians. European Concepts, 1492–1729* (Austin, TX, and London, 1967), ch. 1.
28. Huddleston, *Origins*, pp. 131–2. See also the contributions to part 1 of Paolo Bernardini and Norman Fiering (eds), *The Jews and the Expansion of Europe to the West, 1450 to 1800* (New York and Oxford, 2001), and Richard H. Popkin, 'The Rise and Fall of the

Jewish Indian Theory', in Y. Kaplan, H. Méchoulan and R. H. Popkin (eds), *Menasseh ben Israel and his World* (Leiden, 1989), pp. 63–82. I am indebted to Professor David Katz for drawing my attention to this essay.

29. See Cogley, *John Eliot's Mission*, chs 1 and 4.
30. *Ibid.*, p. 92; and see above, p. 74.
31. Cited by Canup, *Out of the Wilderness*, p. 74.
32. Mather, *Magnalia*, 1, p. 556.
33. Stuart Clark, *Thinking with Demons. The Idea of Witchcraft in Early Modern Europe* (Oxford, 1997), p. 80.
34. Fernando Cervantes, *The Devil in the New World. The Impact of Diabolism in New Spain* (New Haven and London, 1994), pp. 14–16.
35. See Kenneth Mills, *Idolatry and its Enemies. Colonial Andean Religion and Extirpation, 1640–1750* (Princeton, 1997), and Nicholas Griffiths, *The Cross and the Serpent. Religious Repression and Resurgence in Colonial Peru* (Norman, OK, and London, 1995).
36. Mather, *Magnalia*, 1, p. 55.
37. Hall, *Worlds of Wonder*, p. 167.
38. *Ibid.*, p. 118.
39. Richard Godber, *The Devil's Dominion. Magic and Religion in Early New England* (Cambridge, 1992), pp. 5–6; Hall, *Worlds of Wonder*, p. 100. For magic in colonial British America as a whole, see Butler, *Awash in a Sea of Faith*, ch. 3.
40. Bernand and Gruzinski, *Les Métissages,* p. 301.
41. Alberro, *Inquisition et société au Mexique*, pp. 93–4.
42. Irene Silverblatt, 'The Inca's Witches', in Robert Blair St George (ed.), *Possible Pasts. Becoming Colonial in Early America* (Ithaca, NY and London, 2000), pp. 109–30; Sabine MacCormack, *Religion in the Andes. Vision and Imagination in Early Colonial Peru* (Princeton, 1991), p. 415.
43. Godber, *The Devil's Dominion*, p. 69.
44. *Ibid.*, pp. 73–7.
45. Cited by Demos, *Entertaining Satan*, p. 173, and see also Godber, *The Devil's Dominion*, p. 63.
46. For witchcraft in New England and the Salem trials, see especially Godber, *The Devil's Dominion*, Demos, *Entertaining Satan*, and Mary Beth Norton, *In the Devil's Snare. The Salem Witchcraft Crisis of 1692* (New York, 2002), which makes the frontier war with the Indians central to the story.
47. Tituba's Indian origins are discussed in Norton, *In the Devil's Snare*, pp. 20–1. An alternative suggestion is that she was an Arawak from the Orinoco region, and was shipped to Barbados as a child by a slave-trader. See Elaine Breslaw, *Tituba, Reluctant Witch of Salem* (New York and London, 1996), pp. 12–13.
48. Norton, *In the Devil's Snare*, pp. 3–4.
49. Demos, *Entertaining Satan*, p. 373.
50. Norton, *In the Devil's Snare*, p. 299.
51. See Fernando Cervantes, 'The Devils of Querétaro: Scepticism and Credulity in Late Seventeenth-Century Mexico', *Past and Present*, 130 (1991), pp. 51–69, and his *The Devil in the New World*, for detailed discussion and analysis of this episode.
52. Cervantes, *The Devil in the New World*, p. 114.
53. Alberro, *Inquisition et société*, pp. 253–4.
54. Cervantes, *The Devil in the New World*, pp. 119–20.
55. Clark, *Thinking with Demons*, pp. 452–4; Cervantes, *The Devil in the New World*, pp. 133–6.
56. Godber, *The Devil's Dominion*, pp. 216–22.
57. Mayer, *Dos Americanos*, pp. 195–212.
58. Godber, *The Devil's Dominion*, pp. 27–8.
59. For confession in New England, see Hall, *Worlds of Wonder*, pp. 172–86, 189–90.
60. Cited by Clark, *Thinking with Demons*, p. 346.
61. See the brilliant account of the development of this tradition and its transmission to Peru in Ramón Mujica Pinilla, *Ángeles apócrifos en la América virreinal* (2nd edn, Lima, 1996).
62. See William A. Christian, Jr., *Local Religion in Sixteenth-Century Spain* (Princeton, 1981).
63. Luis Millones, *Dioses familiares* (Lima, 1999), pp. 23–6.

64. D. A. Brading, *Mexican Phoenix. Our Lady of Guadalupe. Image and Tradition Across Five Centuries* (Cambridge, 2001), p. 4.
65. Bernand and Gruzinski, *Les Métissages*, pp. 319–20; Brading, *First America*, pp. 332–3.
66. For the Virgin of Guadalupe and her cult, see Brading, *Mexican Phoenix*; Francisco de la Maza, *El guadalupanismo* (Mexico City, 1953); Jacques Lafaye, *Quetzalcoatl and Guadalupe. The Formation of Mexican National Consciousness, 1531–1813* (Chicago, 1976); Enrique Florescano, *Memoria mexicana* (2nd edn, Mexico City, 1995), pp. 392–411.
67. Brading, *First America*, pp. 337–40; Luis Millones, *Una partecita del cielo* (Lima, 1993). It is possible that Santa Rosa was in fact not a creole but of mixed blood, and that her racial origins were concealed. See the contribution by Ramón Mujica Pinilla, 'Santa Rosa de Lima y la política de la santidad americana', in the exhibition catalogue, *Perú indígena y virreinal* (Sociedad Estatal para la Acción Cultural Exterior, Madrid, 2004), pp. 96–101.
68. See Clara Bargellini, 'El barroco en Latinoamérica', in John H. Elliott (ed.), *Europa/América* (El País, Madrid, 1992), pp. 101–3.
69. Luis Millones, *Perú colonial. De Pizarro a Tupac Amaru II* (Lima, 1995), p. 172.
70. James P. Walsh, 'Holy Time and Sacred Space in Puritan New England', *American Quarterly*, 32 (1980), pp. 79–95.
71. Cotton Mather, *Ratio Disciplinae Fratrum* (Boston, 1726), p. 5.
72. Walsh, 'Holy Time', pp. 85–8; Hall, *Worlds of Wonder*, pp. 166–7.
73. Mark A. Peterson, 'Puritanism and Refinement in Early New England: Reflections on Communion Silver', *WMQ*, 3rd ser., 58 (2001), pp. 307–46.
74. Isaac, *Transformation of Virginia*, pp. 58–65.
75. Above, pp. 128–9.
76. Enrique Dussel, *Les Évêques hispano-américains. Défenseurs et évangélisateurs de l'Indien, 1504–1620* (Wiesbaden, 1970), p. 29 (table IV).
77. Konetzke, *La época colonial*, pp. 216–17.
78. Israel, *Race, Class and Politics*, p. 48.
79. Taylor, *Magistrates of the Sacred*, pp. 83–8; Oscar Mazín, *Entre dos majestades* (Zamora, Michoacán, 1987), pp. 37–45.
80. For the intricacies of this tangled affair, see Israel, *Race, Class and Politics*, ch. 5.
81. Gage, *Travels*, pp. 80–1.
82. *CHLA*, 1, p. 523.
83. Dussel, *Les Évêques hispano-américains*, p. 40.
84. Above, p. 162; and see Kathryn Burns, *Colonial Habits. Convents and the Spiritual Economy of Cuzco, Peru* (Durham, NC, and London, 1999).
85. *CHLA*, 1, p. 521; Jacobs, *Los movimientos migratorios*, pp. 92–5.
86. Armas Medina, *Cristianización del Perú*, pp. 362–3.
87. Gage, *Travels*, p. 105.
88. *Ibid.*, pp. 71–2.
89. Antonine Tibesar, 'The Alternative: A Study in Spanish-Creole Relations in Seventeenth-Century Peru', *The Americas*, 11 (1955), pp. 229–83; Lavallé, *Las promesas ambiguas*, pp. 157–72; Céspedes del Castillo, *América hispánica*, pp. 299–300.
90. See Cayetana Alvarez de Toledo, *Politics and Reform in Spain and Viceregal Mexico. The Life and Thought of Juan de Palafox, 1600–1659* (Oxford, 2004), and Israel, *Race, Class and Politics*, pp. 199–247.
91. Bartolomé Escandell Bonet, 'La inquisición española en Indias y las condiciones americanas de su funcionamiento', in *La Inquisición* (Ministerio de Cultura, Madrid, 1982), pp. 81–92.
92. Alvarez de Toledo, *Politics and Reform*, pp. 257–8; Montserrat Galí Boadella (ed.), *La catedral de Puebla en el arte y en la historia* (Mexico City, 1999).
93. Gage, *Travels*, p. 71.
94. Antonio Vázquez de Espinosa, *Compendio y descripción de las Indias Occidentales*, transcribed by Charles Upson Clark (Washington, DC, 1948), p. 403.
95. See Millones, *Perú colonial*, ch. 16 ('La ciudad ceremonial').
96. Above, p. 129.
97. Konetzke, *La época colonial*, p. 224.
98. Burns, *Colonial Habits*, p. 62.

99. The point is well made by Arnold J. Bauer, 'Iglesia, economía y estado en la historia de América Latina', in Ma. del Pilar Martínez López-Cano (ed.), *Iglesia, estado y economía. Siglos XVI y XVII* (Mexico City, 1995), pp. 30–1.

100. *Ibid.*, p. 21.

101. Chevalier, *La Formation des grands domaines*, pp. 301–44.

102. Bauer, 'Iglesia, economia', in *Iglesia, estado*, ed. Martínez López-Cano, p. 18.

103. Suárez, *Desafíos transatlánticos*, pp. 389–40. For New Spain, see John F. Schwaller, 'La iglesia y el crédito comercial en la Nueva España en el siglo XVI', in *Iglesia, estado*, ed. Martínez López-Cano, pp. 81–93.

104. There were no monks in Spanish America, as it was the crown's policy to keep out the contemplative orders in favour of the missionary orders (Konetzke, *La época colonial*, p. 239).

105. For a lucid account of the system as operated by convents in Cuzco, see Burns, *Colonial Habits*, pp. 63–7.

106. Bauer, 'Iglesia, economia', in *Iglesia, estado*, ed. Martínez López-Cano, p. 30.

107. Paul Ganster, 'Churchmen', in Hoberman and Socolow, *Cities and Society*, p. 146.

108. Chevalier, *La Formation des grands domaines*, pp. 307–8.

109. Bauer, 'Iglesia, economia', in *Iglesia, estado*, ed. Martínez López-Cano, p. 22.

110. Chevalier, *La Formation des grands domaines*, pp. 323–7; Mörner, *Political and Economic Activities of the Jesuits*.

111. A university by university account in Águeda Ma. Rodríguez Cruz, *La universidad en la América hispánica* (Madrid, 1992).

112. Pilar Gonzalbo Aizpuru, *Historia de la educación en la época colonial. El mundo indígena* (Mexico City, 1990); José María Kobayashi, *La educación como conquista (empresa franciscana en México)* (Mexico City, 1974).

113. Pilar Gonzalbo Aizpuru, *Historia de la educación en la época colonial. La educación de los criollos y la vida urbana* (Mexico City, 1990). For women's education, see her ch. 12.

114. Euan Cameron in Burke (ed.), *Civil Histories*, pp. 57–8. For the Jesuit colleges, see Gonzalbo Aizpuru, *La educación de los criollos*, chs. 6–9.

115. Clive Griffin, *The Crombergers of Seville. The History of a Printing and Merchant Dynasty* (Oxford, 1988), pp. 82–97.

116. Francisco Morales Padrón, *Historia general de América* (*Manual de historia universal*, vol. VI, Madrid, 1975), p. 664.

117. Bridenbaugh, *Cities in the Wilderness*, p. 130.

118. Irving A. Leonard, *Books of the Brave* (1949; repr. Berkeley, Los Angeles, Oxford, 1992), pp. 79–85; Antonio Castillo Gómez (ed.), *Libro y lectura en la península ibérica y América* (Junta de Castilla y León, Salamanca, 2003), pp. 85–6.

119. Carlos Alberto González Sánchez, *Los mundos del libro. Medios de difusión de la cultura occidental en las Indias de los siglos XVI y XVII* (Seville, 1999), pp. 52–6; Leonard, *Books of the Brave*, ch. 10; Teodoro Hampe Martínez, *Bibliotecas privadas en el mundo colonial* (Madrid, 1996).

120. González Sánchez, *Los mundos del libro*, p. 89.

121. See letters 74–6 in Sánchez Rubio and Testón Núñez, *El hilo que une*. I am grateful to Dr Pedro Rueda Ramírez for information and clarification on the Vatable Bible.

122. González Sánchez, *Los mundos del libro*, p. 89.

123. For a succinct account of the sixteenth-century revival of Thomism, see Quentin Skinner, *The Foundations of Modern Political Thought* (2 vols, Cambridge, 1978), 2, ch. 5. For neo-Thomism in the Hispanic world, see Anthony Pagden, *The Uncertainties of Empire* (Aldershot, 1994), ch. 3 ('The Search for Order: the "School of Salamanca"') and Morse, 'Toward a Theory of Spanish American Government'. I am grateful to Professor Shmuel Eisenstadt for placing at my disposal a typescript (1990) of S. N. Eisenstadt, Adam B. Seligman and Batia Siebzehner, 'The Classic Tradition in the Americas. The Reception of Natural Law Theory and the Establishment of New Societies in the New World', which contains a suggestive comparison of the approaches of British and Spanish America to the natural law tradition.

124. For trends in historical writing on religion in colonial America, see the helpful survey by David Hall in Greene and Pole, *Colonial British America*, ch. 11, and, more recently,

Charles L. Cohen, 'The Post-Puritan Paradigm of Early American Religious History', *WMQ*, 3rd ser., 54 (1997), pp. 695–722.

125. Above, pp. 72–3.
126. Butler, *Awash in a Sea of Faith*, pp. 98–116.
127. Bonomi, *Under the Cope of Heaven*, p. 48.
128. Isaac, *Transformation of Virginia*, pp. 144–5.
129. Cited by Wright, *First Gentlemen of Virginia*, p. 96.
130. Beverley, *History and Present State of Virginia*, pp. 99–100.
131. Wright, *First Gentlemen of Virginia*, pp. 95–6 and 111–13; Isaac, *Transformation of Virginia*, p. 130; Richard L. Morton, *Colonial Virginia* (2 vols, Chapel Hill, NC, 1960), 2, pp. 767 and 782.
132. Morgan, *Roger Williams*, pp. 65–79. For a general introduction to Calvinism in North America, see Menna Prestwich (ed.), *International Calvinism, 1541–1715* (Oxford, 1985), ch. 9. For a subtle account of the changing interaction between ministers and laity, see Stephen Foster. *The Long Argument. English Puritanism and the Shaping of New England Culture, 1570–1700* (Chapel Hill, NC, and London, 1991).
133. Paul Lucas, *Valley of Discord. Church and Society along the Connecticut River, 1636–1725* (Hanover, NH, 1976), pp. 19–20.
134. David D. Hall, *The Faithful Shepherd. A History of the New England Ministry in the Seventeenth Century* (Chapel Hill, NC, 1972), p. 4.
135. Lucas, *Valley of Discord*, p. 31.
136. For Presbyterians and synods, in addition to Hall, *The Faithful Shepherd*, see Prestwich, *International Calvinism*, pp. 264–5 and 280–1.
137. Darrett B. Rutman, *Winthrop's Boston. Portrait of a Puritan Town, 1630–1649* (Chapel Hill, NC, 1965), pp. 146–7.
138. Morgan, *Visible Saints*, ch. 4; Hall, *TheFaithful Shepherd*, ch. 8; Foster, *The Long Argument*, ch. 5.
139. Lucas, *Valley of Discord*, pp. 25–6.
140. Prestwich, *International Calvinism*, pp. 280–1.
141. For Penn and early Pennsylvania, see especially Mary Maples Dunn, *William Penn, Politics and Conscience* (Princeton, 1967); Richard S. and Mary Maples Dunn (eds), *The World of William Penn* (Philadelphia, 1986); Nash, *Quakers and Politics*; Lemon, *The Best Poor Man's Country*; Tully, *Forming American Politics*. For a summary account of other holy experiments, see Bailyn, *Peopling of North America*, pp. 123–7, and his *Atlantic History*, pp. 76–81.
142. Dunn and Dunn, *The World of William Penn*, p. 37.
143. Nash, *Quakers and Politics*, pp. 13–14.
144. Richard S. and Mary Maples Dunn (eds), *The Papers of William Penn* (5 vols, Philadelphia, 1981–6), 2, pp. 414–15 (letter to Lord North, 24 July 1683); Lemon, *The Best Poor Man's Country*, p. 60.
145. For the causes of instability in early Pennsylvania, see Nash, *Quakers and Politics*, pp. 161–80.
146. Jon Butler, '"Gospel Order Improved": the Keithian Schism and the Exercise of Quaker Ministerial Authority in Pennsylvania', *WMQ*, 3rd ser., 31 (1974), pp. 431–52.
147. Marianne S. Wokeck, 'Promoters and Passengers: the German Immigrant Trade, 1683–1775', in Dunn and Dunn, *The World of William Penn*, pp. 259–78.
148. Ronald Hoffman, *Princes of Ireland, Planters of Maryland. A Carroll Saga, 1500–1782* (Chapel Hill, NC and London, 2000), pp. 81 and 94; Bonomi, *Under the Cope of Heaven*, p. 36.
149. Jon Butler, *Becoming America. The Revolution before 1776* (Cambridge, MA and London, 2000), pp. 26–7. For the Jewish diaspora in the New World, see Bernardini and Fiering (eds), *The Jews and the Expansion of Europe*, and the relevant essays in Jonathan Israel, *Diasporas within a Diaspora. Jews, Crypto-Jews and the World Maritime Empires, 1540–1740* (Leiden, Boston, Cologne, 2002).
150. Seymour B. Liebman, *The Jews in New Spain* (Coral Gables, FL, 1970), p. 46.

151. Efrén de la Madre de Dios and O. Steggink, *Tiempo y vida de Santa Teresa* (Madrid, 1968), pp. 36–40; Valentín de Pedro, *América en las letras españolas del siglo de oro* (Buenos Aires, 1954), ch. 18.

152. Vila Vilar, *Hispano-américa y el comercio de esclavos*, pp. 94 and 99–103; and see above, p. 100.

153. James C. Boyajian, *Portuguese Bankers at the Court of Spain, 1626–1650* (New Brunswick, NJ, 1983), pp. 121–8; Israel, *Race, Class and Politics*, pp. 124–30; Liebman, *The Jews in New Spain*, pp. 259–66.

154. See Fischer, *Albion's Seed*, pp. 199–205 and 410–18.

155. For instability in the Middle Colonies, see in particular Nash, *Quakers and Politics*, and Tully, *Forming American Politics*. The historiography of the Middle Colonies was surveyed in 1979 by Greenberg, 'The Middle Colonies in Recent American Historiography', and, more recently, by Wayne Bodle, 'Themes and Directions in Middle Colonies Historiography, 1980–1994', *WMQ*, 3rd ser., 51 (1994), pp. 355–88.

156. See Lucas, *Valley of Discord*.

157. Fischer, *Albion's Seed*, p. 334; Isaac, *Transformation of Virginia*, p. 65; Hall, *Worlds of Wonder*, p. 51.

158. Hall, *Worlds of Wonder*, pp. 23–4.

159. Wright, *First Gentlemen of Virginia*, p. 117.

160. Isaac, *Transformation of Virginia*, pp. 124–5.

161. Bailyn, *Education in the Forming of American Society*, pp. 27–8; and for biblical culture, schooling, and the availability of the book in New England, see Hugh Amory and David D. Hall (eds), *The Colonial Book in the Atlantic World* (Cambridge, 2000), ch. 4.

162. John Eliot to Sir Simonds D'Ewes, 18 September 1633, in Emerson, *Letters from New England*, p. 107.

163. Hall, *Worlds of Wonder*, pp. 34–5.

164. Bailyn, *Education in the Forming of American Society*, pp. 27–9.

165. Isaac, *Transformation of Virginia*, p. 122.

166. Kenneth A. Lockridge, *Literacy in Colonial New England* (New York, 1974), pp. 13–14.

167. Butler, *Becoming America*, p. 111.

168. González-Sánchez, *Los mundos del libro*, p. 155, where it is suggested that 20 per cent of male settlers in the sixteenth century could read and write with ease.

169. Gurrin, 'Shipwrecked Spaniards', pp. 26–7. See above, p. 144.

170. Cited by Verner W. Crane, *The Southern Frontier 1670–1732* (Durham, NC, 1928; repr. New York, 1978), p. 3.

171. For the development of the English image of Spain, see J. N. Hillgarth, *The Mirror of Spain, 1500–1799. The Formation of a Myth* (Ann Arbor, MI, 2003), chs 10–12.

172. Colin Steele, *English Interpreters of the Iberian New World from Purchas to Stevens, 1603–1726* (Oxford, 1975), p. 59; and see J. Eric S. Thompson's introduction to his edition of Gage, *Travels in the New World*.

173. Mayer, *Dos americanos*, p. 298, n. 116.

174. Gage, *Travels*, p. 51.

175. Cotton Mather, *The Diary of Cotton Mather*, 2 vols (Boston, 1911–12), 1, p. 206.

176. Mather, *Diary*, 1, pp. 284–5.

177. *Ibid.*, 1, p. 420; and see also for the evangelizing hopes of Bostonian ministers and early contacts with the Spanish American world, Harry Bernstein, *Origins of Inter-American Interest, 1700–1812* (Philadelphia, 1945), pp. 66–71.

Chapter 8. Empire and Identity

1. Samuel Sewall, *The Diary of Samuel Sewall, 1674–1729*, ed. M. Halsey (2 vols, New York, 1973), 1, p. 380.

2. Slingsby Bethel, *The Interest of Princes and States* (London, 1680), preface (no page numbers).

3. A. P. Newton, *The European Nations in the West Indies, 1493–1688* (London, 1933; repr., 1966), pp. 269–71.

4. Bethel, *The Interest of Princes*, p. 75.

5. *Ibid.*, pp. 76–7.

6. Roger Coke, *A Discourse of Trade* (London, 1670), Part 1, p. 46. For Coke and other later seventeenth-century pamphleteers and economic theorists, see Joyce Oldham Appleby, *Economic Thought and Ideology in Seventeenth-Century England* (Princeton, 1978). In this, as in other accounts of British economic thought in the seventeenth century, more attention tends to be paid to the example of the Dutch than to the counter-example of Spain.

7. Sir Josiah Child, *A New Discourse of Trade* (London, 1693), pp. 164–5; and see Armitage, *Ideological Origins of Empire*, pp. 166–7. Child's ideas, first elaborated in the 1660s, found their final form in his *New Discourse* of 1693. See Joseph A. Schumpeter, *History of Economic Analysis* (1954; 6th printing, London, 1967), p. 195, n. 3.

8. For a recent summary of the growth of the colonial trade and its impact, see Nuala Zahedieh, 'Overseas Expansion and Trade in the Seventeenth Century', *OHBE*, 1, ch. 18.

9. Above, p. 113.

10. For this eighteenth-century ideology, see especially Armitage, *Ideological Origins of Empire*, Linda Colley, *Britons. Forging the Nation 1707–1837* (New Haven and London, 1992), and Peter N. Miller, *Defining the Common Good. Empire, Religion and Philosophy in Eighteenth-Century Britain* (Cambridge, 1994).

11. See especially Richard S. Dunn, 'The Glorious Revolution and America', *OHBE*, 1, ch. 20, and J. M. Sosin, *English America and the Revolution of 1688* (Lincoln, NE, and London, 1982).

12. As chronicled by Greene, *The Quest for Power*.

13. Dunn, 'The Glorious Revolution', p. 463.

14. Johnson, *Adjustment to Empire*, pp. 229–30.

15. Sosin, *English America and the Revolution of 1688*, p. 231.

16. Thomas C. Barrow, *Trade and Empire. The British Customs Service in Colonial America, 1660–1775* (Cambridge, MA, 1967), p. 74 and Appendix A. Also Alison Gilbert Olson, *Making the Empire Work. London and American Interest Groups, 1690–1790* (Cambridge, Mass., 1992), p. 58, where the total number of English officials in the American colonies at the end of Queen Anne's reign is put at around 240.

17. Olson, *Making the Empire Work*, p. 61.

18. *Ibid.*, p. 52; Steele, *The English Atlantic*, p. 92; and see also Hancock, *Citizens of the World*, for the accelerating integration of the British Atlantic economy in the eighteenth century.

19. For the improvement of transatlantic postal services and its impact, see Steele, *The English Atlantic*, chs 7–9.

20. Above, p. 193.

21. Cited by Johnson, *Adjustment to Empire*, p. 364.

22. Coke, *A Discourse of Trade*, part 1, p. 10.

23. Newton, *European Nations in the West Indies*, pp. 271–6.

24. Bernstein, *Origins of Inter-American Interest*, pp. 15–19.

25. Nuala Zahedieh, 'The Merchants of Port Royal, Jamaica, and the Spanish Contraband Trade, 1655–1692', *WMQ*, 3rd ser., 43 (1986), pp. 570–93; Curtis Putnam Nettels, *The Money Supply of the American Colonies before 1720* (University of Wisconsin Studies in the Social Sciences and History, no. 20, Madison, WI, 1934), pp. 15–21; Fisher, *Economic Aspects of Spanish Imperialism*, pp. 81–2.

26. Lutgardo García Fuentes, *El comercio español con América, 1650–1700* (Seville, 1980), pp. 55–66; Antonio García-Baquero, *Cádiz y el Atlántico, 1717–1778* (2 vols, Seville, 1976), 1, p. 104.

27. For a recent account of the process, see Stanley J. Stein and Barbara H. Stein, *Silver, Trade and War. Spain and America in the Making of Early Modern Europe* (Baltimore and London, 2000), ch. 3.

28. William Lytle Schurz, *The Manila Galleon* (1939; repr. New York, 1959); *El galeón de Acapulco* (Exhibition catalogue, Museo Nacional de Historia, Mexico City, 1988); *Los galeones de la plata* (Exhibition catalogue, Consejo Nacional para la Cultura y las Artes, Mexico City, 1998).

29. For the participation of American merchants in the Atlantic trade, see Studnicki-Gizbert, 'From Agents to Consulado', and Suárez, *Comercio y fraude*, and *Desafíos transatlánticos*.

30. Above, p. 111.

31. Moutoukias, *Contrabando y control colonial*, p. 31.

32. For the seventeenth-century growth of inter-regional trade, see, in addition to the important study of the La Plata region by Moutoukias, *Contrabando y control colonial*, Fisher, *Economic Aspects of Spanish Imperialism*, pp. 65–71.

33. Woodrow Borah, *New Spain's Century of Depression* (Berkeley and Los Angeles, 1951), is the classic exposition of depression in the seventeenth-century economy of New Spain. For a useful discussion of the 'depression' thesis, see John J. TePaske and Herbert S. Klein, 'The Seventeenth-Century Crisis in New Spain: Myth or Reality?', *Past and Present*, 90 (1981), pp. 116–35. The case for seeing the seventeenth century as a period of economic transition, rather than of depression, for the Spanish American economies, has been effectively argued by John Lynch, *The Hispanic World in Crisis and Change, 1598–1700* (Oxford, 1992), ch. 8.

34. See Bakewell, *Silver Mining and Society*, especially ch. 9, for these trends, and suggested explanations for them.

35. Garner, 'Long-Term Silver Mining Trends'; Kenneth J. Andrien, *Crisis and Decline. The Viceroyalty of Peru in the Seventeenth Century* (Albuquerque, NM, 1985), p. 200; Fisher, *Economic Aspects of Spanish Imperialism*, pp. 100–1.

36. TePaske and Klein, 'The Seventeenth-Century Crisis', pp. 120–1.

37. On the basis of information provided by European flysheets and Dutch gazettes Morineau, *Incroyables gazettes*, has introduced major modifications into the figures for bullion imports into Spain given by Earl J. Hamilton in his *American Treasure and the Price Revolution in Spain, 1501–1650* (Cambridge, MA, 1934) and *War and Prices in Spain, 1651–1800* (Cambridge, MA, 1947). Morineau's figures have themselves subsequently been revised by Antonio García-Baquero González, 'Las remesas de metales preciosos americanos en el siglo XVIII: una aritmética controvertida', *Hispania*, 192 (1996), pp. 203–66. See also Table 1 in Stein and Stein, *Silver, Trade and War*, p. 24, for the disparity between registered and unofficial receipts.

38. This argument is developed by Ruggiero Romano in his *Conjonctures opposées*.

39. Andrien, *Crisis and Decline*, ch. 5; Peter T. Bradley, *Society, Economy and Defence in Seventeenth-Century Peru. The Administration of the Count Alba de Liste, 1655–61* (Liverpool, 1992), pp. 111–14.

40. Burkholder and Chandler, *From Impotence to Authority*, p. 23. For the general question of the sale of offices in Spanish America, see Parry, *The Sale of Public Office*.

41. For corruption and its impact in Spanish America, see Horst Pietschmann, *El estado y su evolución al principio de la colonización española de América* (Mexico City, 1989), pp. 163–82.

42. Carlos Martínez Shaw and Marina Alfonso Mola, *Felipe V* (Madrid, 2001), p. 206; John Lynch, *Bourbon Spain, 1700–1808* (Oxford, 1989), pp. 52–4.

43. For the transition from a 'horizontal' Habsburg Spain to a 'vertical' Bourbon Spain, and a brief discussion of the character and extent of the changes introduced by Philip V, see Ricardo García Cárcel, *Felipe V y los españoles. Una visión periférica del problema de España* (Barcelona, 2002), pp. 114–24.

44. Armitage, *Ideological Origins*, p. 149; and see, for the international context of the Union and the debate over the form it should take, John Robertson, 'Union, State and Empire: the Union of 1707 in its European Setting', in Lawrence Stone (ed.), *An Imperial State at War. Britain from 1689 to 1815* (London, 1994), pp. 224–57.

45. Lynch, *Bourbon Spain*, pp. 99–100; Stein and Stein, *Silver, Trade and War*, p. 160.

46. Céspedes del Castillo, *América hispánica*, p. 279.

47. Burkholder and Chandler, *From Impotence to Authority*, p. 17.

48. See Geoffrey J. Walker, *Spanish Politics and Imperial Trade, 1700–1789* (London, 1979), ch. 4, and pp. 111–13.

49. Patricia R. Wickman, 'The Spanish Colonial Floridas', in Robert H. Jackson (ed.), *New Views of Borderland History* (Albuquerque, NM, 1998), ch. 7, p. 211.

50. Stein and Stein, *Silver, Trade and War*, p. 148.
51. Gerónimo de Uztáriz, *Theorica y práctica de comercio y de marina* (Madrid, 1724). The book was translated into English in 1751 under the title of *The Theory and Practice of Maritime Affairs*. For Uztáriz and his ideas, see Stein and Stein, *Silver, Trade and War*, pp. 164–79, and Reyes Fernández Durán, *Gerónimo de Uztáriz (1670–1732). Una política económica para Felipe V* (Madrid, 1999).
52. Stein and Stein, *Silver, Trade and War*, p. 202; Céspedes del Castillo, *América hispánica*, p. 162.
53. Although the authorship of the *Nuevo sistema de gobierno económico de América* is generally attributed to José del Campillo y Cosío, who died in 1743, the attribution remains a subject of debate. The book was not published until 1789, but manuscript copies circulated widely in governmental circles. Citations are taken from the edition published in Mérida, Venezuela, in 1971.
54. Campillo, *Nuevo sistema*, pp. 67 and 76–7.
55. Kathleen Wilson, *The Sense of the People. Politics, Culture and Imperialism in England, 1715–1785* (Cambridge, 1995), pp. 140–65.
56. Armitage, *Ideological Origins of Empire*, pp. 182–8.
57. Fisher, *Economic Aspects of Spanish Imperialism*, pp. 128–30.
58. See James Henretta, *'Salutary Neglect'. Colonial Administration Under the Duke of Newcastle* (Princeton, 1972).
59. Cited by Lavallé, *Promesas ambiguas*, p. 17.
60. *Ibid.*, p. 19.
61. Strachey, *Historie of Travell into Virginia Britania*, p. 12.
62. Above, p. 201.
63. Carole Shammas, 'English-Born and Creole Elites in Turn-of-the-Century Virginia', in Tate and Ammerman (eds), *The Chesapeake in the Seventeenth Century*, pp. 284–5.
64. James Otis, 'The Rights of the British Colonies Asserted and Proved', in Bernard Bailyn (ed.), *Pamphlets of the American Revolution, 1750–1776*, vol. 1, *1750–1765* (Cambridge, Mass., 1965), pamphlet 7, p. 440.
65. Solórzano y Pereyra, *Política indiana*, 1, p. 442 (lib. II, cap. 30).
66. A. W. Plumstead (ed.), *The Wall and the Garden. Selected Massachusetts Election Sermons, 1670–1775* (Minneapolis, 1968), p. 137.
67. See Kupperman, 'The Puzzle of the American Climate'.
68. Letter of 23 July 1630 in Emerson (ed.), *Letters from New England*, p. 51.
69. For discussions of this question, see in particular John Canup, 'Cotton Mather and "Criolian Degeneracy"', *Early American Literature*, 24 (1989), pp. 20–34, and Cañizares-Esguerra, 'New World, New Stars', to both of which I am indebted for the discussion that follows. Also John H. Elliott, 'Mundos parecidos, mundos distintos', *Mélanges de la Casa de Velázquez,* 34 (2004), pp. 293–311.
70. Above, p. 80.
71. Reginaldo de Lizárraga, cited by Lavallé, *Promesas ambiguas*, p. 48.
72. Fray Bernardino de Sahagún, *Historia general de las cosas de Nueva España*, ed. Angel María Garibay K. (2nd edn, 4 vols, Mexico City, 1969), 3, p. 160.
73. Marian J. Tooley, 'Bodin and the Medieval Theory of Climate', *Speculum*, 28 (1983), pp. 64–83.
74. Cited by Pilar Ponce Leiva, *Certezas ante la incertidumbre. Élite y cabildo de Quito en el siglo XVII* (Quito, 1998), p. 201. A brief account of Villarroel's life, and a selection from his published writings, some of them difficult to locate, may be found in Gonzalo Zaldumbide, *Fray Gaspar de Villarroel. Siglo XVII* (Puebla, 1960). The family history of Fray Gaspar, born in Quito, perhaps in 1592, of a father who was a *licenciado* from Guatemala and a mother from Venezuela, and then taken as a child by his parents to live in Lima, offers a vivid example of personal and family mobility across the vast distances of Spanish America.
75. Gregoria García, *Orígen de los indios del nuevo mundo, e Yndias Occidentales* (Valencia, 1607), lib. II, cap. v, pp. 149–54.
76. See Cañizares-Esguerra, 'New World, New Stars'.
77. Chaplin, *Subject Matter*, p. 174–7. For the general question of identity in British America, see especially Jack P. Greene, 'Search for Identity: an Intepretation of Selected Patterns of

Social Response in Eighteenth-Century America', in his *Imperatives, Behaviors and Identities*, ch. 6.

78. The lexical history of *American* in both English and Spanish deserves more systematic study. For New England, see Canup, 'Cotton Mather and "Criolian Degeneracy"', pp. 25–6. The Virginian author of a tract composed in 1699 identifies himself as 'An American' (Shammas, 'English-Born and Creole Elites', p. 290). In 1725, the Mexican-born lawyer, Juan Antonio de Ahumada, wrote that 'the Indies were conquered, settled and established as provinces with the sweat and toil of the ancestors of the Americans' (Brading, *The First America*, p. 380), but Villarroel's reference to an *americano* suggests that other instances of its use in Spanish America may be found, both before 1661, and between the time of Villarroel and that of Ahumada.
79. Horn, *Adapting to a New World*, pp. 436–7.
80. Ponce Leiva, *Certezas*, p. 207.
81. Giovanni Francesco Gemelli Careri, *Viaje a la Nueva España*, ed. Francisca Perujo (Mexico City, 1976), p. 22.
82. Child, *A New Discourse*, pp. 170–1.
83. Cited by Dunn, *Sugar and Slaves*, p. 340.
84. Ned Ward, *A Trip to New England* (1699), in Jehlen and Warner (eds), *The English Literatures of America*, p. 401. For further examples of negative stereotypes, see Michael Zuckerman, 'Identity in British America: Unease in Eden', in Canny and Pagden (eds), *Colonial Identity in the Atlantic World*, pp. 120–1.
85. Beverley, *History of Virginia*, p. 9.
86. Cited by Jack P. Greene, 'Changing Identity in the British Caribbean: Barbados as a Case Study', in Canny and Pagden (eds), *Colonial Identity in the Atlantic World*, pp. 120–1.
87. Dorantes de Carranza, *Sumaria relación*, p. 203.
88. Craton, 'The Planters' World', in Bailyn and Morgan (eds), *Strangers Within the Realm*, p. 325.
89. Wright, *The First Gentlemen of Virginia*, ch. 3.
90. For comparative figures of West Indians and North Americans receiving at least part of their education in Britain, see Andrew J. O'Shaughnessy, *An Empire Divided. The American Revolution and the British Caribbean* (Philadelphia, 2000), pp. 19–27.
91. Kenneth A. Lockridge, *The Diary and Life of William Byrd II of Virginia, 1674–1744* (Chapel Hill, NC and London, 1987), pp. 12–31.
92. Cited by Wright, *The First Gentlemen of Virginia*, p. 294.
93. Otte, *Cartas*, letter 571 (Juan de Esquivel to Cristóbal de Aldana, 20 January 1584).
94. Fray Bonaventura de Salinas y Córdova, *Memoria de las historias del nuevo mundo Piru* (1630; ed. Luis E. Valcárcel, Lima, 1957), pp. 99 and 246.
95. For the development of 'creole patriotism', see especially Brading, *The First America*, ch. 14.
96. See Serge Gruzinski, *Les Quatre Parties du monde. Histoire d'une mondialisation* (Paris, 2004), ch. 5.
97. For the Saint Thomas legend, see Lafaye, *Quetzalcóatl and Guadalupe*, ch. 10.
98. Above, p. 196, and see Brading, *The First America*, pp. 343–8.
99. Anthony Pagden, 'Identity Formation in Spanish America', in Canny and Pagden (eds), *Colonial Identity in the Atlantic World*, p. 66.
100. Above, pp. 146–7.
101. Carlos de Sigüenza y Góngora, *Theatro de virtudes políticas* (1680; repr. in his *Obras históricas*, ed. José Rojas Garcidueñas, Mexico City, 1983).
102. Garcilaso de la Vega, *Comentarios reales de los Incas*, ed. Angel Rosenblat (2 vols, Buenos Aires, 1943; English trans. by H. V. Livermore, 2 vols, Austin, TX, 1966); Carlos Daniel Valcárcel, 'Concepto de la historia en los "Comentarios reales" y en la "Historia general del Perú"', in *Nuevos estudios sobre el Inca Garcilaso de la Vega* (Lima, 1955), pp. 123–36; Brading, *The First America*, ch. 12.
103. Karine Perissat, 'Los incas representados (Lima – siglo XVIII): ¿supervivencia o renacimiento?', *Revista de Indias*, 60 (2000), pp. 623–49; Peter T. Bradley and David Cahill, *Habsburg Peru. Images, Imagination and Memory* (Liverpool, 2000), Part II.
104. Beverley, *History of Virginia*, p. 232.

105. Richard Slotkin, *Regeneration Through Violence. The Mythology of the American Frontier, 1600–1860* (Middletown, CT, 1973), pp. 56 and 116.
106. Mary Rowlandson, *The Sovereignty and Goodness of God* (1682), in Jehlen and Warner (eds), *The English Literatures of America*, p. 359.
107. See Slotkin, *Regeneration Through Violence*, ch. 7.
108. Beverley, *History of Virginia*, pp. 118–19.
109. Richard Ligon, *A True and Exact History of the Island of Barbadoes* (2nd edn, London, 1673), p. 108.
110. Jack P. Greene in Canny and Pagden (eds), *Colonial Identity*, pp. 228–9, and *Imperatives, Behaviors*, pp. 190–3; Hancock, *Citizens of the World*, ch. 9, and especially pp. 282–3. For the ideology of agrarian improvement in the Anglo-American world, see Richard Drayton, *Nature's Government. Science, Imperial Britain, and the 'Improvement' of the World* (New Haven and London, 2000), ch. 3.
111. Sir Dalby Thomas, *An Historical Account of the Rise and Growth of the West-India Collonies* (London, 1690), p. 53.
112. For the consumer movement and aspirations to gentility in eighteenth-century Britain, see Neil McKendrick, John Brewer and J. H. Plumb, *The Birth of a Consumer Society: the Commercialization of Eighteenth-Century England* (Bloomington, IN, 1982); John Brewer and Roy Porter (eds), *Consumption and the World of Goods* (London, 1993); and Paul Langford, *A Polite and Commercial People. England, 1727–1783* (Oxford, 1989). For British America, Richard L. Bushman, *The Refinement of America. Persons, Houses, Cities* (New York, 1992); T. H. Breen, '"Baubles of Britain": The American and Consumer Revolutions of the Eighteenth Century', *Past and Present*, 119 (1988), pp. 73–104, and *The Marketplace of Revolution. How Consumer Politics Shaped American Independence* (Oxford and New York, 2004); Cary Carson, Ronald Hoffman and Peter J. Albert (eds), *Of Consuming Interests. The Style of Life in the Eighteenth Century* (Charlottesville, VA, 1994); Maxine Berg, *Luxury and Pleasure in Eighteenth-Century Britain* (Oxford, 2005), ch. 8.
113. Bushman, *Refinement*, ch. 4.
114. Cited by Dunn, *Sugar and Slaves*, p. 291.
115. Main, *Tobacco Colony*, ch. 4.
116. Bushman, *Refinement*, pp. 74–8.
117. Cited by Main, *Tobacco Colony*, p. 239; and, for ambivalence over luxuries, see Bushman, *Refinement*, ch. 6, and Greene, *Imperatives, Behaviors*, pp. 150–9.
118. Gage, *Travels*, p. 68. For conspicuous consumption in Spanish America see Bauer, *Goods, Power, History*, pp. 110–13; and see also Bauer, 'Iglesia, economia', in *Iglesia, estado*, ed. Martínez López-Cano, pp. 30–1.
119. For both the supply and the demand, with the take-off occurring in the 1740s, see Breen's impressively documented *Marketplace of Revolution*.
120. Francisco Cervantes de Salazar, *México en 1554 y el túmulo imperial*, ed. Edmundo O'Gorman (Mexico City, 1963), Diálogo 2, p. 63.
121. For a list of universities in Spanish America, with dates of foundation, see Rodríguez Cruz, *La universidad*, appendix I.
122. See, for example, Salinas y Córdova, *Memorial*, Discurso II cap. 4, on Lima's University of San Marcos.
123. Villarroel, cited in Ponce Leiva, *Certezas ante la incertidumbre*, p. 237.
124. For this argument in relation to Spanish American cultural production, see, for example, the exhibition catalogue, Donna Pierce (ed.), *Painting a New World. Mexican Art and Life, 1521–1821* (Denver Art Museum, 2004), and in particular the Introduction by Jonathan Brown, to whom I am grateful for advice on this section. For British America, Richard L. Bushman, 'American High Style and Vernacular Cultures', in Greene and Pole (eds), *Colonial British America*, ch. 12, and Bernard Bailyn, *To Begin the World Anew. The Genius and Ambiguities of the American Founders* (New York, 2003), ch. 1, which takes as its starting-point Kenneth Clark's essay on 'Provincialism', reprinted in his *Moments of Vision* (London, 1981). A general survey of Iberian American colonial art and architecture is provided by Gauvin Alexander Bailey, *Art of Colonial Latin America* (London, 2005).

125. For Flemish and Castilian artists in New Spain, see Gruzinski, *Les Quatre Parties du monde*, ch. 13. For Ferrer, Montserrat Galí Boadella, *Pedro García Ferrer, un artista aragonés del siglo XVII en la Nueva España* (Teruel, 1996); and above, p. 202.

126. For recent work on the transmission and diffusion of European influences in Spanish America, see, in addition to Pierce (ed.), *Painting a New World*, the catalogue of the important exhibition held in 1999–2000 in the Museo de América in Madrid, *Los siglos de oro en los virreinatos de América, 1550–1700* (Sociedad Estatal, Madrid, 1999).

127. Ramón María Serrera, 'Las Indias Españolas entre 1550 y 1700', in *Los siglos de oro en los virreinatos*, p. 55.

128. See Serge Gruzinski, *La Pensée métisse* (Paris, 1999), for the development of hybrid cultural forms in sixteenth-century New Spain.

129. Alberro, *Les espagnols dans le Mexique colonial*, p. 119.

130. For Villalpando, see especially Pierce, *Painting a New World*. For the arquebusier angels, above, p. 195.

131. See Cristina Esteras Martín, 'Acculturation and Innovation in Peruvian Viceregal Silverwork', in Elena Phipps, Johanna Hecht and Cristina Esteras Martín (eds), *The Colonial Andes. Tapestries and Silverwork, 1530–1830* (Metropolitan Museum of Art, New York, 2004), pp. 59–71.

132. Paz, *Sor Juana Inés de la Cruz*, p. 364. Paz points out that the poems of Anne Bradstreet were similarly published as being by 'The Tenth Muse Lately Sprung Up in America . . .'

133. See Irving Leonard, *Don Carlos de Sigüenza y Góngora. A Mexican Savant of the Seventeenth Century* (Berkeley, 1929).

134. Luis Eduardo Wuffarden, 'La ciudad y sus emblemas: imagenes del criollismo en el virreinato del Perú', in *Los siglos de oro*, pp. 59–75; Bernand, *Negros esclavos y libres*, p. 13.

135. See Mayer, *Dos americanos*, for an extended comparison of Mather and Sigüenza y Góngora and their respective worlds.

136. The comparison of New England and Mexican book inventories is made by Irving Leonard in his *Baroque Times in Old Mexico* (Ann Arbor, 1959), ch. 11. Leonard's book remains a valuable and highly accessible introduction to the literary culture of colonial New Spain. For brief accounts of the theatre in Spanish and British America, see respectively Oscar Mazín, *L'Amérique espagnole, XVIe–XVIIIe siècles* (Paris, 2005), pp. 162–3 and 215–16, and Kenneth Silverman, *A Cultural History of the American Revolution* (New York, 1976), pp. 59–69.

137. Above, p. 205.

138. 'A Proposal for Promoting Useful Knowledge among the British Plantations in America'. Franklin's 'Proposal' led to the formation of the American Philosophical Society in the following year, and is reproduced in facsimile in the Society's annual Year Book (see the Year Book for 2002–3, pp. 321–2).

139. For Nicholson and 'Virginian baroque', see Kornwolf, *Architecture and Town Planning*, 2, pp. 567–8, 586, 632, 725–7, and Bushman, *Refinement of America*, pp. 151–4, who also discusses the balance between ceremonial and commercial considerations.

140. For the comparison, with illustrations, see Bailyn, *To Begin the World Anew*, pp. 9–17.

141. See the essays in Carson, Hoffman and Albert (eds), *Of Consuming Interests*, especially Kevin M. Sweeney, 'High Style Vernacular: Lifestyles of the Colonial Elite', pp. 1–58.

142. Margaretta M. Lovell, 'Painters and Their Customers: Aspects of Art and Money in Eighteenth-Century America', in Carson, Hoffman and Albert (eds), *Of Consuming Interests*, pp. 284–306; Silverman, *Cultural History of the American Revolution*, pp. 11–30.

143. Bailey, *Art of Colonial Latin America*, pp. 173–4.

Chapter 9

1. Jorge Juan and Antonio de Ulloa, *Las 'Notícias secretas de América' de Jorge Juan y Antonio de Ulloa, 1735–1745*, ed. Luis J. Ramos Gómez (2 vols, Madrid, 1985), 2, p. 29.

2. Above, pp. 227–8.

3. Fisher, *Economic Aspects of Spanish Imperialism*, p. 95.

4. *Ibid.*, pp. 187–8; Bakewell, *History of Latin America*, pp. 257–8.

5. D. H. Brading, *Miners and Merchants in Bourbon Mexico, 1763–1810* (Cambridge, 1971), ch. 2, for possible explanations of the rise in output, and Bakewell, 'Mining in Colonial Spanish America', *CHLA*, 2, ch. 4.

6. Anthony McFarlane, *Colombia Before Independence. Economy, Society and Politics under Bourbon Rule* (Cambridge, 1993), p. 73, with reference to gold mining in New Granada.

7. Guillermo Céspedes del Castillo, *Ensayos sobre los reinos castellanos de Indias* (Madrid, 1999), p. 210. Fisher, *Economic Aspects of Spanish Imperialism*, p. 64, suggests a figure of probably less than 75,000 out of a total population of 17 million directly involved in silver mining in the late eighteenth century.

8. Brading, *Haciendas and Ranchos*, p. 18. This work is the classic study on eighteenth-century developments in this region.

9. Anthony McFarlane, 'Hispanoamérica bajo el gobierno de los Borbones: desarrollo económico y crísis política', in José Manuel de Bernardo Ares (ed.), *El hispanismo anglonorteamericano* (Actas de la I Conferencia Internacional, *Hacia un nuevo humanismo*, 2 vols, Córdoba, 2001), 1, pp. 531–63, at pp. 562–3.

10. See Studnicki-Gizbert, 'From Agents to Consulado', pp. 52–3.

11. Garner, 'Long-Term Silver Mining Trends', p. 902.

12. Bakewell, *History of Latin America*, p. 198; *CHLA*, 2, p. 100.

13. Bakewell, *History of Latin America*, pp. 262–3; and above, p. 227.

14. Above, p. 217.

15. For the eighteenth-century population increase and its implications, see McCusker and Menard, *Economy of British America*, ch. 10; Richard B. Johnson, 'Growth and Mastery: British North America, 1690–1748', in *OHBE*, 2, ch. 13; Jack P. Greene, *Pursuits of Happiness* (Chapel Hill, NC and London, 1988), pp. 177–84, and *Negotiated Authorities*, pp. 100–9. Herbert S. Klein, *A Population History of the United States* (Cambridge, 2004), ch. 2, provides a succinct survey of population trends over the colonial period.

16. McCusker and Menard, *Economy of British America*, p. 217.

17. See table 8.1 in Greene, *Pursuits of Happiness*, pp. 178–9.

18. Johnson, in *OHBE*, 2, p. 279.

19. McCusker and Menard, *Economy of British America*, p. 217.

20. Johnson in *OHBE*, 2, p. 280; McCusker and Menard, *Economy of British America*, pp. 231–4.

21. See A. Roger Ekirch, *Bound for America. The Transportation of British Convicts to the Colonies, 1718–1775* (Oxford, 1987).

22. William Moraley, *The Infortunate* (1743), ed. Susan E. Klepp and Billy G. Smith (University Park, PA, 1992), p. 52.

23. James Horn, 'British Diaspora: Emigration from Britain, 1680–1815', in *OHBE*, 2, ch. 2, p. 31.

24. Bernard Bailyn, *Voyagers to the West* (New York, 1986), p. 25.

25. See the chapter by Marianne Wokeck on German-speaking immigrants in Altman and Horn, '*To Make America*', ch. 7, and above, p. 213.

26. Moraley, *The Infortunate*, p. 89. The same expression occurs in a letter written by Christopher Sauer in 1724 giving an early description of Pennsylvania. See Lemon, *The Best Poor Man's Country*, p. xiii.

27. The estimate, however, of just over 50,000 for the whole century, seems unrealistically small. See Magnus Mörner on 'Spanish Migration to the New World, Prior to 1800', in Chiappelli (ed.), *First Images of America*, 2, p. 742.

28. Chiappelli (ed.), *First Images of America*, 2, pp. 745–6; *CHLA*, 2, pp. 31–2; Rosario Márquez Macías, 'La emigración española en el siglo XVIII a América', *Rábida*, 10 (1991), pp. 68–79.

29. See Manuel Hernández González, *Los canarios en la Venezuela colonial, 1670–1810* (Tenerife, 1999).

30. Canny (ed.), *Europeans on the Move*, p. 34; Weber, *Spanish Frontier*, pp. 182 and 192–3.

31. Jordi Nadal, *La población española (Siglos XV a XX)* (2nd edn, Barcelona, 1984), table 12, p. 90.

32. *CHLA*, 2, pp. 32–3, citing Curtin. The figures for 1651–1750 given in table III of Eltis, 'Volume and Structure of the Transatlantic Slave Trade', are much smaller – 53,400 – but there are many gaps, and the figures are for the direct trade from Africa, and do not include the large numbers of Africans shipped to Spanish America from receiving-points in the Caribbean.

33. McFarlane, *Colombia Before Independence,* pp. 66–7.

34. Ferry, *Colonial Elite of Early Caracas*, p. 72.

35. Thomas, *Slave Trade*, pp. 272–3; Klein, *Slavery in the Americas*, p. 150.

36. See chapter 8 ('Artisans') by Lyman Johnson in Hoberman and Socolow (eds), *Cities and Society*, especially pp. 244–5.

37. Bakewell, *Latin America*, p. 256.

38. See the suggestive table of child mortality rates, although for the period after 1755, in Brading, *Haciendas and Ranchos*, p. 57.

39. *Ibid.*, p. 177; *CHLA*, 2, pp. 23–5.

40. Marcello Carmagnani, 'Colonial Latin American Demography: Growth of Chilean Population, 1700–1830', *Journal of Social History*, 1 (1967–8), pp. 179–91.

41. Above, p. 170.

42. McFarlane, *Colombia Before Independence*, p. 34; Carmagnani, 'Colonial Latin American Demography', p. 187; Bakewell, *Latin America*, pp. 277–8.

43. McFarlane, *Colombia Before Independence*, pp. 34–8.

44. Figures for North America are taken from Bridenbaugh, *Cities in the Wilderness*, p. 303. Those for Spanish America from the table on p. 5 of Hoberman and Socolow (eds), *Cities and Society*. The figure for Quito, which does not appear on this table, comes from Martin Minchom, *The People of Quito, 1690–1810* (Boulder, CO, 1994), p. 135. I owe this reference to the kindness of Professor Anthony McFarlane. For an acute analysis of variations in the rate of growth in leading North American cities in the eighteenth century, and in particular of the stagnation of Boston after 1740, see Jacob M. Price, 'Economic Function and the Growth of American Port Towns in the Eighteenth Century', *Perspectives in American History*, 8 (1974), pp. 123–86.

45. McCusker and Menard, *Economy of British America*, p. 250.

46. Romano, *Conjonctures opposées*, p. 39–40 and table 3; *CHLA*, 2, p. 99, table 2.

47. Bridenbaugh, *Cities in the Wilderness*, p. 232.

48. Nash, *Urban Crucible*, pp. 63–5; Richard Middleton, *Colonial America. A History, 1585–1776* (2nd edn, Oxford, 1996), p. 245.

49. Above, p. 173.

50. See ch. 10 ('The Underclass') by Gabriel Haslip-Vieira in Hoberman and Socolow (eds), *Cities and Society*, pp. 302–4.

51. Bridenbaugh, *Cities in the Wilderness*, p. 233; Fischer, *Albion's Seed*, p. 178; Richard Hofstadter, *America at 1750. A Social Portrait* (1971; repr., New York, 1973), pp. 26–7.

52. Rutman and Rutman, *A Place in Time*, pp. 195–203.

53. Bridenbaugh, *Cities in the Wilderness*, p. 238, and see also for poverty and poor relief in North America the essays in Billy G. Smith (ed.), *Down and Out in Early America* (University Park, PA, 2004).

54. *Cambridge Economic History of the United States*, 1, p. 152.

55. Manuel Carrera Stampa, *Los gremios mexicanos* (Mexico City, 1954); *CHLA*, 2, pp. 233–4; Hoberman and Socolow (eds), *Cities and Society*, pp. 236–9.

56. Emilio Harth-Terré and Alberto Márquez Abanto, 'Perspectiva social y económica del artesano virreinal en Lima', *Revista del Archivo Nacional del Perú*, 26 (1962), pp. 3–96, at p. 36; Hoberman and Socolow (eds), *Cities and Society*, pp. 240–1.

57. For examples of land dispute cases brought by the Indian communities of New Spain before the General Indian Court, see Borah, *Justice by Insurance*, pp. 128–42. See also, for a Mexican regional study, William B. Taylor, *Landlord and Peasant in Colonial Oaxaca* (Stanford, CA, 1972), ch. 3.

58. Since the days of Herbert Eugene Bolton and Frederick Jackson Turner the literature on the frontier in American society has become very large. See David J. Weber, 'Turner, the Boltonians and the Borderlands', *AHR*, 91 (1986), pp. 66–81. For a recent overview of some of the major issues in debate, affecting both British and Iberian America, see the recent

survey by Jeremy Adelman and Stephen Aron, 'From Borderlands to Borders: Empires, Nation States, and the Peoples in Between in North American History', *AHR*, 104 (1999), pp. 814–41.

59. Peter Sahlins, *Boundaries. The Making of France and Spain in the Pyrenees* (Berkeley, Los Angeles, Oxford, 1989), pp. 2–7.
60. See Donna J. Guy and Thomas E. Sheridan (eds), *Contested Ground. Comparative Frontiers on the Northern and Southern Edges of the Spanish Empire* (Tucson, AZ, 1998), ch. 1.
61. Gregory Nobles, *American Frontiers. Cultural Encounters and Continental Conquest* (New York, 1997), pp. 60–2.
62. For expansion into the Ohio Valley, see Eric Hinderaker, *Elusive Empires. Constructing Colonialism in the Ohio Valley, 1673–1800* (Cambridge, 1997).
63. Francis Jennings, *The Ambiguous Iroquois Empire* (New York and London, 1984), p. 367.
64. *OHBE*, 2, p. 362.
65. Lepore, *The Name of War*, p. xiii.
66. Fred Anderson, *Crucible of War. The Seven Years' War and the Fate of Empire in British North America, 1754–1766* (London, 2000), pp. 11–12.
67. Jennings, *Ambiguous Iroquois Empire*, pp. 210–12.
68. Kammen, *Colonial New York*, p. 179.
69. Anderson, *Crucible of War*, pp. 17–18.
70. Crane, *Southern Frontier*, p. 111. For the Yamasee War, see Crane, ch. 7.
71. For Iroquois diplomacy, see Jennings, *Ambiguous Iroquois Empire*, and the more positive assessment of its achievements in Richard Aquila, *The Iroquois Restoration. Iroquois Diplomacy on the Colonial Frontier, 1701–1754* (Lincoln, NE, London, 1983, repr. 1997).
72. Crane, *Southern Frontier*, p. 8.
73. J. Leitch Wright Jr., *Anglo-Spanish Rivalry in North America* (Athens, GA, 1971), pp. 69–70.
74. Guy and Sheridan (eds), *Contested Ground*, p. 3. For the 'horse revolution' among the nomadic Indian tribes, see Hennessy, *The Frontier*, p. 63.
75. Solano and Bernabeu (eds), *Estudios sobre la frontera*, pp. 210–11.
76. John Hemming, 'Indians and the Frontier in Colonial Brazil', *CHLA*, 2, ch. 13, at pp. 505–12. For the arming of the Indians, Solano and Bernabeu (eds), *Estudios sobre la frontera*, pp. 213–14; and above, p. 186 for the Jesuit missions.
77. Solano, *Ciudades hispanoamericanos*, p. 30.
78. Manuel Lucena Giraldo, *Laboratorio tropical. La expedición de límites al Orinoco, 1750–1767* (Caracas, 1993), pp. 48–58.
79. Jean Claude Roux, 'De los límites a la frontera: o los malentendidos de la geopolítica amazónica', *Revista de Indias*, 61 (2001), pp. 513–39; and, for a map of the moving frontiers of Brazil, see Chaunu, *L'Amérique et les Amériques*, map 6, p. 135.
80. Spicer, *Cycles of Conquest*, p. 282; Suárez Roca, *Lingüística misionera*, pp. 254–76.
81. Above, pp. 86–7.
82. The term 'frontier of inclusion' seems to have been coined by a geographer, Marvin Mikesell, in 1960. See Weber, 'Turner, the Boltonians and the Borderlands', n. 30.
83. For what follows, see the article on the Chilean frontier by Sergio Villalobos, reprinted in Solano and Bernabeu (eds), *Estudios sobre la frontera*, pp. 289–359; and above, p. 62.
84. Jennings, *Ambiguous Iroquois Empire*, pp. 242–8. The existence of treaties between Spaniards and Indians is often denied, but see the essay by David J. Weber, 'Bourbons and Bárbaros', in Christine Daniels and Michael N. Kennedy (eds), *Negotiated Empires. Centers and Peripheries in the Americas, 1500–1820* (London, 2002), pp. 79–103, which provides evidence of their growing use. Also Abelardo Levaggi, *Diplomacia hispano-indígena en las fronteras de América* (Madrid, 2002).
85. Peter T. Bradley, 'El Perú y el mundo exterior. Extranjeros, enemigos y herejes (siglos XVI–XVII)', *Revista de Indias*, 61 (2001), pp. 651–71, at p. 654.
86. David J. Weber, *The Spanish Frontier in North America* (New Haven and London, 1992), provides a comprehensive account of the history of the northern frontier of Spanish America throughout the colonial period.

87. Gutiérrez, *When Jesus Came*, p. 107.

88. *Ibid.*, p. 147.

89. Weber, *Spanish Frontier*, pp. 141–5; Paul E. Hoffman, *Florida's Frontiers* (Bloomington, IN, and Indianapolis, 2002), ch. 7.

90. Gutiérrez, *When Jesus Came*, pp. 46–94 for the Franciscan century in New Mexico, and pp. 130–40 for the Pueblo revolt.

91. Crane, *Southern Frontier*, p. 10.

92. Weber, *Spanish Frontier*, pp. 137–41.

93. Donald E. Chipman, *Spanish Texas, 1591–1821* (Austin, TX, 1992), p. 94.

94. *Ibid.*, chs. 6 and 7.

95. James Logan, cited by Maldwyn A. Jones, 'The Scotch-Irish in British America', in Bailyn and Morgan (eds), *Strangers Within the Realm*, p. 285.

96. Above, p. 80.

97. See John Jay TePaske, *The Governorship of Spanish Florida, 1700–1763* (Durham, NC, 1964). Also Wickman, 'The Spanish Colonial Floridas', in Jackson (ed.), *New Views of Borderland History*, ch. 7.

98. Wright, *Anglo-Spanish Rivalry*, pp. 78–80.

99. Anderson, *Crucible of War*, p. 17.

100. Shy, *A People Numerous*, ch. 2.

101. Gutiérrez, *When Jesus Came*, p. 148.

102. *Ibid.*, p. 92, table 2.1, and p. 172.

103. Bailyn and Morgan (eds), *Strangers Within the Realm*, pp. 122–4.

104. Weber, *Spanish Frontier*, p. 263.

105. Cited by James Merrell in Bailyn and Morgan (eds), *Strangers Within the Realm*, p. 124.

106. Gutiérrez, *When Jesus Came*, pp. 148–56, and, for the *genízaros*, James F. Brooks, *Captives and Cousins. Slavery, Kinship and Community in the Southwest Borderlands* (Chapel Hill, NC and London, 2002), pp. 123–38. The janissaries were the elite soldiers of non-Turkish origin in the Ottoman army, but Covarrubias's *Tesoro de la lengua castellana* of 1611 shows that by the early seventeenth century the word *genízaro* was being used in Spain to describe someone whose parents were of different nationalities, presumably on the assumption that janissaries were the offspring of mixed unions of Turks and Christians. By the eighteenth century the word was being used, at least in Andalusia, simply to describe foreigners living among Spaniards. It remains a mystery when and how *genízaro* came to be used of detribalized Indians in New Mexico – a usage that is apparently not to be found in other borderland regions of Spain's American empire. I am indebted to David Weber for this information.

107. Brooks, *Captives and Cousins*, pp. 103–4.

108. The now fashionable term 'middle ground' was introduced by Richard White, *The Middle Ground. Indians, Empires, and Republics in the Great Lakes Region, 1650–1815* (Cambridge, 1991), where it is defined on p. x as 'the place in between: in between cultures, peoples, and in between empires and the nonstate world of villages'. In so far as it connotes the desire for mutual accommodation and understanding, it is obviously more applicable to some areas of contact between Europeans and non-Europeans than others, and can easily lead to the ignoring or under-estimation of the degree of coercion involved in many such areas.

109. See Axtell, *Invasion Within*, ch. 13 ('The White Indians').

110. For Johnson's background and rise, see Francis Jennings, *Empire of Fortune. Crown, Colonies and Tribes in the Seven Years War in America* (New York and London, 1988), pp. 75–9. His activities are traced in White, *The Middle Ground*.

111. Bailyn and Morgan (ed.), *Strangers Within the Realm*, p. 299.

112. Cited by Merrell, *ibid.*, p. 118.

113. *Ibid.*, pp. 306–7.

114. Cited by John Demos, *The Unredeemed Captive* (1994; New York, 1995), p. 230.

115. Cited from the Journal of the Rev. Charles Woodmason by Nobles, *American Frontiers*, p. 104.

116. James Logan, cited by Jones in Bailyn and Morgan (ed.), *Strangers Within the Realm*, p. 297.

117. Nobles, *American Frontiers*, pp. 107–8.
118. Breen, *Marketplace of Revolution*, p. 118; and see above, pp. 243–4.
119. See the listing of narratives in Lepore, *The Name of War*, pp. 50–1.
120. Slotkin, *Regeneration through Violence*, p. 97.
121. Axtell, *Invasion Within*, ch. 13; and see also, for captivity in North America, Linda Colley, *Captives. Britain, Empire and the World, 1600–1850* (London, 2002), part 2.
122. Above, p. 235.
123. Slotkin, *Regeneration through Violence*, p. 121.
124. Reprinted in Jehlen and Warner (eds), *The English Literatures of America*, pp. 349–82; and see for Mary Rowlandson, Lepore, *The Name of War*, especially pp. 126–31.
125. See Demos, *The Unredeemed Captive*.
126. Francisco Núñez de Pineda y Bascuñán, *Cautiverio feliz* (Santiago de Chile, 1863); abridged edn. by Alejandro Lipschutz and Alvaro Jara (Santiago de Chile, 1973). Abridged English trans. by William C. Atkinson, *The Happy Captive* (Chatham, 1979). A suggestive comparison of the two captivity narratives is to be found in ch. 4 of Ralph Bauer, *The Cultural Geography of Colonial American Literatures* (Cambridge, 2003), in the context of the transatlantic dialogue between creoles and their critics at the centre of empire.
127. Ed. Jara, pp. 102, 183–4, 187.
128. Cited by Lepore, *The Name of War*, p. 130.
129. First published in Zaragoza in 1542, and included in Ramusio's *Delle navigationi et viaggi* (vol. 3, Venice, 1565). See the edn by Enrique Pupo-Walker: Alvar Núñez Cabeza de Vaca, *Los naufragios* (Madrid, 1992), and Alvar Núñez Cabeza de Vaca, *The Narrative of Cabeza de Vaca*, ed. and trans. by Rolena Adorno and Patrick Charles Pautz (Lincoln, NE, 2003).
130. S. M. Socolow, 'Spanish Captives in Indian Societies: Cultural Contacts Along the Argentine Frontier', *HAHR*, 72 (1992), pp. 73–99; and see Peter Stern, 'Marginals and Acculturation in Frontier Society', in Jackson (ed.), *New Views of Borderland History*, ch. 6. The question of the relative scarcity of captivity narratives in Spanish America is addressed in Fernando Operé, *Historias de la frontera. El cautiverio en la América hispánica* (Buenos Aires, 2001).
131. Gutiérrez, *When Jesus Came*, pp. 203–4 and 211–12.
132. See Slotkin, *Regeneration through Violence*, ch. 7.
133. Slotkin, *Regeneration through Violence*, pp. 199–200; David A. Lupher, *Romans in a New World. Classical Models in Sixteenth-Century Spanish America* (Ann Arbor, MI, 2003), pp. 302–3.
134. Arturo Warman, *La danza de moros y cristianos* (Mexico City, 1972), pp. 80 and 118–20.
135. Above, p. 240.
136. See Richard R. Beeman, *The Varieties of Political Experience in Eighteenth-Century America* (Philadelphia, 2004), pp. 157–9; and, for a brief survey of backcountry history, Eric Hinderaker and Peter C. Mancall, *At the Edge of Empire. The Backcountry in British North America* (Baltimore and London, 2003).
137. Butler, *Becoming America*, p. 10.
138. Cited by Richard Hofstadter, *America at 1750. A Portrait* (1971; edn, New York, 1973), p. 23.
139. Figures as given in McCusker and Menard, *Economy of British America*, p. 222.
140. Morgan, *Slave Counterpoint*, p. 81; Berlin, *Many Thousands Gone*, p. 126.
141. Alan Taylor, *American Colonies. The Settlement of North America to 1800* (London, 2001), pp. 241–3.
142. See above, pp. 105–6. For a general survey of the Atlantic plantation complex, see Philip D. Curtin, *The Rise and Fall of the Plantation Complex. Essays in Atlantic History* (Cambridge, 1990).
143. McCusker and Menard, *Economy of British America*, p. 222.
144. For a valuable attempt to classify the varieties of labour systems that developed in British America, see Richard S. Dunn, 'Servants and Slaves: the Recruitment and Employment of Labor', in Greene and Pole (eds), *Colonial British America*, ch. 6.
145. These differences are skilfully charted in Morgan's *Slave Counterpoint*. For the summary account of slave societies that follows, I have also drawn on Allan Kulikoff, *Tobacco and*

Slaves. The Development of Southern Cultures in the Chesapeake, 1680–1800 (Chapel Hill, NC and London, 1986), as well as Berlin, *Many Thousands Gone*.

146. For Maryland, up to 1720, see Main, *Tobacco Colony*; and, for the general characteristics of tobacco culture, T. H. Breen, *Tobacco Culture. The Mentality of the Great Tidewater Planters on the Eve of Revolution* (Princeton, 1985).

147. See for this, and what follows, Jane Landers, *Black Society in Spanish Florida* (Urbana, IL and Chicago, 1999), ch. 1. Also Berlin, *Many Thousands Gone*, pp. 72–4.

148. Berlin, *Many Thousands Gone*, p. 160. For Africans in Spanish American cities, see above, pp. 100–1.

149. Ben Vinson III, *Bearing Arms for His Majesty. The Free Colored Militia in Colonial Mexico* (Stanford, CA, 2001).

150. Brown, *Good Wives, Nasty Wenches*, p. 182.

151. John Shy, *Toward Lexington. The Role of the British Army in the Coming of the American Revolution* (Princeton, 1965), p. 12.

152. The relationship between the two is explored with great subtlety by Morgan, *American Slavery, American Freedom*.

153. For the construction of this world in Virginia, see Mechal Sobel, *The World They Made Together. Black and White Values in Eighteenth-Century Virginia* (Princeton, 1987), and Morgan, *Slave Counterpoint*, part 2.

154. Bernand and Gruzinski, *Les Métissages*, pp. 253–5.

155. Cited by Rhys Isaac, *Landon Carter's Uneasy Kingdom. Revolution and Rebellion on a Virginia Plantation* (Oxford, 2004), p. 117. This book brilliantly re-creates the physical environment and troubled mental world of a Virginia planter who left a copious record of his daily life.

156. For a horrifying account of Jamaican plantation life, based on the diaries of Thomas Thistlewood, appointed overseer of a sugar plantation shortly after his arrival on the island in 1750, see Trevor Burnard, *Mastery, Tyranny, and Desire. Thomas Thistlewood and his Slaves in the Anglo-Jamaican World* (Chapel Hill, NC, 2004). There were, however, significant differences between the Jamaican and Virginian environments, as also between their African populations and the nature of their plantations, and it would be a mistake to extrapolate from one plantation to the entire plantation complex of the Caribbean and the American South.

157. Isaac, *Landon Carter's Uneasy Kingdom*, p. 75 (1757).

158. Sobel, *The World They Made Together*, pp. 147–52; Berlin, *Many Thousands Gone*, p. 161.

159. Berlin, *Many Thousands Gone*, pp. 178–9.

160. Nash, *Urban Crucible*, p. 107; Berlin, *Many Thousands Gone*, p. 107.

161. Nash, *Urban Crucible*, p. 107.

162. See Richard S. Dunn, 'The Recruitment and Employment of Labour', in Greene and Pole (eds), *Colonial British America*, pp. 182–3.

163. See Salvucci, *Textiles and Capitalism*, pp. 101–3 (for numbers employed), and 110–111.

164. Bennett, *Africans in Colonial Mexico*, p. 27.

165. John Lynch, *The Spanish American Revolutions, 1808–1825* (2nd edn, New York and London, 1973), pp. 191 and 380–1; CHLA, 2, pp. 375–7.

166. A point well made by Bennett in *Africans in Colonial Mexico*.

167. Dunn, 'The Recruitment and Employment of Labour', p. 182.

168. See Marc Egnal, 'The Economic Development of the Thirteen Colonies, 1720 to 1775', *WMQ*, 3rd ser. (1975), pp. 191–222, for a valuable discussion of the relationship between population growth, immigration and increasing productivity.

169. Greenberg, 'The Middle Colonies in Recent American Historiography'.

170. McCusker and Menard, *Economy of British America*, pp. 101–11.

171. Nash, *Urban Crucible*, pp. 136–8, and 212–14; T. H. Breen and Timothy Hall, 'Structuring Provincial Imagination: the Rhetoric and Experience of Social Change in Eighteenth-Century New England', *AHR*, 103 (1998), pp. 1411–39.

172. For the Great Awakening, see Bonomi, *Under the Cope of Heaven*, ch. 5, Butler, *Awash in a Sea of Faith*, ch. 6, and Robert A. Ferguson, *American Enlightenment, 1750–1820* (Cambridge, Mass., and London, 1997), ch. 3. For its impact in New England, see Nash, *Urban Crucible*, pp. 204–19, and Breen and Hall, 'Structuring Provincial Imagination'.

173. Beeman, *Varieties of Political Experience*, ch. 3; Breen, *The Good Ruler*.
174. Beeman, *Varieties of Political Experience*, ch. 2.
175. *Ibid.*, ch. 5.
176. Tully, *Forming American Politics*, p. 126.
177. Cited by Randall H. Balmer, *A Perfect Babel of Confusion. Dutch Religion and English Culture in the Middle Colonies* (Oxford and New York, 1989), p. 87. This book provides a cogent account of the attempt to anglicize, and Anglicanize, the New York Dutch.
178. Above, pp. 180–1.
179. In addition to Balmer, see Beeman, *Varieties of Political Experience*, p. 104; Patricia U. Bonomi, *A Factious People. Politics and Society in Colonial New York* (New York and London, 1971), and Kammen, *Colonial New York*.
180. See in particular Nash, *Urban Crucible*, and Tully, *Forming American Politics*.
181. Kammen, *Colonial New York*, ch. 8.
182. Nash, *Urban Crucible*, pp. 140–8.
183. Tully, *Forming American Politics*, pp. 140–9.
184. Butler, *Becoming America*, p. 200.
185. Ruth H. Bloch, *Visionary Republic. Millennial Themes in American Thought, 1756–1800* (Cambridge, 1985).
186. Above, p. 154.
187. Above, p. 151.

Chapter 10. War and Reform

1. Anderson, *Crucible of War*, ch. 5.
2. Above, p. 265.
3. Cited by Isaac, *Landon Carter's Uneasy Kingdom*, p. 157.
4. Anderson, *Crucible of War*, p. 135.
5. See John Robert McNeill, *Atlantic Empires of France and Spain. Louisbourg and Havana, 1700–1763* (Chapel Hill, NC and London, 1985), for the role of Louisbourg in the French imperial system.
6. See Anderson, *Crucible of War*, parts IV to VI, for a vivid account of the course and outcome of the conflict.
7. *Ibid.*, pp. 484–5 and 489–90.
8. For the siege of Havana see Hugh Thomas, *Cuba, or the Pursuit of Freedom* (London, 1971), ch. 1, and McNeill, *Atlantic Empires*, pp. 103–4.
9. For the terms of the Peace of Paris, see Wright, *Anglo-Spanish Rivalry*, pp. 107–8, and Anderson, *Crucible of War*, pp. 504–6.
10. Cited by Céspedes de Castillo, *América hispánica*, p. 324.
11. Above, p. 274.
12. Above, p. 284.
13. For the deficiencies of the militia system and military reorganization in New Spain, see Lyle N. McAlister, 'The Reorganization of the Army of New Spain, 1763–1766', *HAHR*, 33 (1953), pp. 1–32, and his *The 'Fuero Militar' in New Spain, 1764–1800* (Gainesville, FL, 1957), p. 2.
14. Shy, *A People Numerous*, pp. 37–9.
15. John Shy, 'Armed Force in Colonial North America: New Spain, New France, and Anglo-America', in Kenneth J. Hagan and William R. Roberts (eds), *Against All Enemies. Interpretations of American Military History from Colonial Times to the Present* (Greenwood Press, *Contributions in Military Studies*, no. 51, New York, Westport, Conn., London, 1986), at p. 9.
16. Cited by Andrews, *Colonial Period*, vol. 4, p. 417.
17. Anderson, *Crucible of War*, ch. 7. For ambivalent attitudes in London to plans for colonial union, see Alison Olson, 'The British Government and Colonial Union, 1754', *WMQ*, 3rd ser., 17 (1960), pp. 22–34.
18. Anderson, *Crucible of War*, p. 85. For William Johnson, who was appointed superintendent of Northern Indian affairs, see above pp. 275–6.

19. Cited by Anderson, *Crucible of War*, p. 148.
20. Jack P. Greene, 'The Seven Years' War and the American Revolution: the Causal Relationship Reconsidered', in Peter Marshall and Glyn Williams (eds), *The British Atlantic Empire Before the American Revolution* (London, 1980), pp. 85–105, at p. 88. For the problem, and extent, of illicit trade in these years see Barrow, *Trade and Empire*, ch. 7.
21. Cited by Barrow, *Trade and Empire*, p. 152.
22. Shy, *Toward Lexington*, p. 35 for troop numbers; for relative tax burdens, Taylor, *American Colonies*, p. 438.
23. John L. Bullion, '"The Ten Thousand in America": More Light on the Decision on the American Army, 1762–1763', *WMQ*, 3rd ser., 43 (1986), pp. 646–57.
24. Lynch, *Bourbon Spain*, pp. 312–17.
25. A. S. Aiton, 'Spanish Colonial Reorganization Under the Family Compact', *HAHR*, 12 (1932), pp. 269–80; Stanley J. Stein and Barbara H. Stein, *Apogee of Empire. Spain and New Spain in the Age of Charles III, 1759–1789* (Baltimore and London, 2003), pp. 58–68.
26. For the military reforms, see McAlister, 'The Reorganization of the Army of New Spain'; Céspedes del Castillo, *Ensayos*, pp. 261–9; Archer, *The Army in Bourbon Mexico*, pp. 9–16.
27. Archer, *The Army*, p. 12; Greene, 'Seven Years' War', p. 89.
28. *CHLA*, 1, p. 400.
29. Céspedes del Castillo, *América hispánica*, p. 325.
30. McAlister, *The 'Fuero Militar'*, pp. 10–11.
31. See Juan Marchena Fernández, *Ejército y milicias en el mundo colonial americano* (Madrid, 1992), table, p. 62, and his 'The Social World of the Military in Peru and New Granada: the Colonial Oligarchies in Conflict', in John R. Fisher, Allan J. Kuethe and Anthony McFarlane (eds), *Reform and Insurrection in Bourbon New Granada and Peru* (Baton Rouge, LA and London, 1990), ch. 3.
32. Shy, *A People Numerous*, p. 40.
33. Anderson, *Crucible of War*, pp. 560–2.
34. Greene, 'Seven Years' War', p. 95.
35. P. D. Thomas, *British Politics and the Stamp Act Crisis. The First Phase of the American Revolution, 1763–1767* (Oxford, 1975), p. 38.
36. Above, pp. 228–9.
37. Burkholder and Chandler, *From Impotence to Authority*, part 1; Mark A. Burkholder, 'From Creole to *Peninsular*; the Transformation of the Audiencia of Lima', *HAHR*, 52 (1972), pp. 395–415; Jaime E. Rodríguez O., *The Independence of Spanish America* (Cambridge, 1998), pp. 21–2.
38. Cited by Labaree, *Royal Government in America*, p. 308.
39. Greene, *Quest for Power*, pp. 70 and 360–1.
40. Olson, *Anglo-American Politics*, pp. 147–8; Barrow, *Trade and Empire*, pp. 157–8.
41. For 'rational' and scientific preoccupations in the Spain of Charles III, and their impact on imperial government, see in particular the essays in the exhibition catalogue, *Carlos III y la Ilustración*, 2 vols (Madrid and Barcelona, 1989). For Britain, Drayton, *Nature's Government*, especially pp. 67–9, and Shy, *A People Numerous*, pp. 77–9.
42. See Allan J. Kuethe and G. Douglas Inglis, 'Absolutism and Enlightened Reform: Charles III, the Establishment of the *Alcabala*, and Commercial Reorganization in Cuba', *Past and Present*, 109 (1985), pp. 118–43.
43. For the overthrow of Esquilache and its consequences, see Stein and Stein, *Apogee of Empire*, ch. 4, and the exhaustive study by José Andrés-Gallego, *El motín de Esquilache, América y Europa* (Madrid, 2003).
44. Céspedes del Castillo, *Ensayos*, p. 308; MacLachlan, *Spain's Empire*, pp. 93–4.
45. The administrative career of Gálvez deserves a comprehensive study. The now anti-quated study by Herbert Ingram Priestley, *José de Gálvez, Visitor-General of New Spain, 1765–1771* (Berkeley, 1916), does not extend beyond his visitation of New Spain. For a recent brief survey, see Ismael Sánchez-Bella, 'Las reformas en Indias del Secretario de Estado José de Gálvez (1776–1787)', in Feliciano Barrios Pintado (ed.), *Derecho y administración pública en las Indias hispánicas* (2 vols, Cuenca, 2002), 2, pp. 1517–54.

46. Above, p. 260. By 1800 Spanish America would have some 13.5 million inhabitants to Spain's 10.5 million (*CHLA*, 2, p. 34).
47. See Table 4.1 in *OHBE*, 2, p. 100.
48. Cited by Thomas, *British Politics*, p. 34.
49. Anderson, *Crucible of War*, ch. 59.
50. Robert L. Gold, *Borderland Empires in Transition. The Triple Nation Transfer of Florida* (Carbondale, IL and Edwardsville, IL, 1969); Cecil Johnson, *British West Florida, 1763–1783* (New Haven, 1943), ch. 1; C. L. Mowat, *East Florida as a British Province, 1763–1784* (Berkeley and Los Angeles, 1943), ch. 1.
51. For seventeenth-century French Acadia and its replacement in 1713 by the British colony of Nova Scotia, see John G. Reid, *Acadia, Maine and New England. Marginal Colonies in the Seventeenth Century* (Toronto, Buffalo, NY, London, 1981).
52. For the background to the promulgation of the 1763 Proclamation, see Jack M. Sosin, *Whitehall and the Wilderness. The Middle West in British Colonial Policy, 1760–1775* (Lincoln, NE, 1961), ch. 3.
53. Barrow, *Trade and Empire*, pp. 187–8.
54. Anderson, *Crucible of War*, pp. 583–5.
55. Barrow, *Trade and Empire*, pp. 183–4.
56. Andrien, *Crisis and Decline*, pp. 154–5.
57. Cited by Thomas, *British Politics*, p. 53.
58. Lynch, *Bourbon Spain*, pp. 344–5; Guillermo Céspedes del Castillo, *El tabaco en Nueva España* (Madrid, 1992), ch. 3; José Jesús Hernández Palomo, *El aguardiente de caña en México* (Seville, 1974).
59. Thomas, *British Politics*, p. 112.
60. Sosin, *Whitehall and the Wilderness*, p. 130. The estimates would be vastly exceeded as a result of extraordinary expenses.
61. Shy, *Toward Lexington*, pp. 188–9; Anderson, *Crucible of War*, pp. 720–2.
62. Cited in Barrow, *Trade and Empire*, p. 225.
63. Céspedes del Castillo, *Ensayos*, pp. 234–6.
64. Above, p. 232.
65. Vicent Llombart, *Campomanes, economista y político de Carlos III* (Madrid, 1992). Campomanes served in the Council of Castile for three decades, from 1762 to 1791.
66. N. M. Farriss, *Crown and Clergy in Colonial Mexico, 1759–1821* (London, 1968), p. 92.
67. Cited by Laura Rodríguez, *Reforma e Ilustración en la España del siglo XVIII: Pedro R. Campomanes* (Madrid, 1975), p. 59.
68. Horst Pietschmann, *Las reformas borbónicas y el sistema de intendencias en Nueva España* (Mexico City, 1996), p. 302.
69. Cited by I. A. A. Thompson in Richard L. Kagan and Geoffrey Parker (eds), *Spain, Europe and the Atlantic World. Essays in Honour of John H. Elliott* (Cambridge, 1995), p. 158.
70. See Farriss, *Crown and Clergy*. For provincial councils, pp. 33–8.
71. Taylor, *Magistrates of the Sacred*, pp. 83–6.
72. Mazín, *Entre dos majestades*, pp. 138–40.
73. The alleged involvement of the Jesuits in the overthrow of Esquilache is examined in Stein and Stein, *Apogee of Empire*, pp. 98–107. Andrés-Gallego, *El motín de Esquilache*, pp. 655–63, leaves the problem unresolved, but provides (pp. 501–28) a useful summary of attitudes to the Jesuits and to their activities, including their activities in the Indies, in the period leading up to their expulsion.
74. D. A. Brading, *Church and State in Bourbon Mexico. The Diocese of Michoacán, 1749–1810* (Cambridge, 1994), ch. 1; Antonio Mestre, 'La actitud religiosa de los católicos ilustrados', in Austín Guimerá (ed.), *El reformismo borbónico. Una visión interdisciplinar* (Madrid, 1996), pp. 147–63; Teófanes Egido (ed.), *Los jesuitas en España y en el mundo hispánico* (Madrid, 2004), pp. 256–73.
75. Andrés-Gallego, *El motín de Esquilache*, p. 596; and see more generally pp. 595–645 for his assessment of the consequences of the expulsion on both sides of the Spanish Atlantic.
76. Martínez López-Cano (ed.), *Iglesia, estado y economía*, p. 18; *CHLA*, 2, p. 194.
77. Brading, *Church and State*, pp. 4–7.

78. Cited by McFarlane, 'The Rebellion of the *Barrios*: Urban Insurrection in Bourbon Quito', in Fisher, Kuethe and McFarlane (eds), *Reform and Insurrection*, p. 202.

79. The account that follows is based on McFarlane, 'The Rebellion of the *Barrios*', and Kenneth J. Andrien, 'Economic Crisis, Taxes and the Quito Insurrection of 1765', *Past and Present*, 129 (1990), pp. 104–31.

80. McFarlane, *Colombia Before Independence*, pp. 232–3; Fisher, Kuethe and McFarlane (eds), *Reform and Insurrection*, pp. 3–4.

81. Andrés-Gallego, *El motín de Esquilache*, p. 194.

82. *Ibid.*, p. 197.

83. Cited in Edmund S. and Helen M. Morgan, *The Stamp Act Crisis. Prologue to Revolution* (1953; repr. New York, 1962), p. 43.

84. Thomas M. Doerflinger, *A Vigorous Spirit of Enterprise. Merchants and Economic Development in Revolutionary Philadelaphia* (Chapel Hill, NC and London, 1986), pp. 175–6. For the relationship of the Stamp Act crisis to the impact of the post-war depression on the port towns, see especially Nash, *Urban Crucible*, ch. 11.

85. Cited in David McCullough, *John Adams* (New York and London, 2001), p. 43.

86. Greene, 'Seven Years' War', p. 97.

87. Morgan and Morgan, *Stamp Act Crisis*, pp. 121–32.

88. *Ibid.*, pp. 123–4.

89. Above, p. 262.

90. Nash, *Urban Crucible*, p. 247; Morgan and Morgan, *Stamp Act Crisis*, pp. 48–9.

91. For the Loyal Nine and their transformation into the inter-colonial 'Sons of Liberty', see, in addition to Morgan and Morgan, *Stamp Act Crisis*, Pauline Maier, *From Resistance to Revolution. Colonial Radicals and the Development of American Opposition to Britain, 1765–1776* (1971; repr. New York and London, 1992), ch. 4.

92. Cited in John L. Bullion, 'British Ministers and American Resistance to the Stamp Act, October–December 1765', *WMQ*, 3rd ser., 49 (1992), pp. 89–107, at p. 91.

93. Burke, *European Settlements*, 2, p. 172.

94. *Ibid.*, p. 167.

95. Morgan and Morgan, *Stamp Act Crisis*, p. 139. New Hampshire declined, but approved the proceedings after the congress was over.

96. Cited in Morgan and Morgan, *Stamp Act Crisis*, p. 146.

97. For the response in the West Indies, where there were riots in the Leeward Islands, see O'Shaughnessy, *An Empire Divided*, pp. 86–104.

98. Cited in Anderson, *Crucible of War*, p. 684.

99. See Breen, *Marketplace of Revolution*, pp. 222–34, for the early stages of the non-importation movement.

100. C. Knick Harley, 'Trade, Discovery, Mercantilism and Technology', in Roderick Floud and Paul Johnson (eds), *The Cambridge Economic History of Modern Britain* (Cambridge, 2004), 1, p. 184. See also his table 7.1 for official values of British trade, 1663–1774 (p. 177). Part 1 of Breen, *Marketplace of Revolution*, provides a vivid account of the huge variety of British imports on offer and the patterns of marketing and consumption in the colonies.

101. Jacob M. Price, 'Who Cared About the Colonies?', in Bailyn and Morgan (eds), *Strangers Within the Realm*, pp. 395–436, at p. 417.

102. Barlow Trecothick to Rockingham, 7 November 1765, cited by Bullion, 'British Ministers', p. 100.

103. Price, 'Who Cared About the Colonies?', p. 412.

104. Bullion, 'British Ministers'.

105. See H. G. Koenigsberger, 'Composite States, Representative Institutions and the American Revolution', *Historical Research. The Bulletin of the Institute of Historical Research*, 62 (1989), pp. 135–53. See also Miller, *Defining the Common Good*, chs 3 and 4.

106. Above, p. 230.

107. Greene, *Peripheries and Center*, pp. 61–2.

108. Cited by Anderson, *Crucible of War*, p. 700.

109. Miller, *Defining the Common Good*, pp. 192–4. The Greeks did in fact consider their colonies as dependent on the mother city. The Roman notion of *colonia*, on the other

hand, lacked this notion of dependency, which may have arisen in the minds of British politicians as a result of confusing Rome's 'colonies', originally settlements of veteran soldiers, with its 'provinces', which were indeed dependent on the metropolis. I am grateful to Professor Glen Bowersock for guidance on this point. 'Colony' and 'plantation' were interchangeable terms in the early phases of English overseas colonization, but the notion of dependency had obviously established itself by 1705, when Lord Cornbury wrote that in his opinion 'all these Colloneys, which are but twigs belonging to the Main Tree [England] ought to be Kept entirely dependent upon and subservient to England' (E. B. O'Callaghan, *The Documentary History of the State of New York*, 4 vols (Albany, NY, 1850–1), 1, p. 485). For an example of the distinction drawn by eighteenth-century British commentators between Greek and Roman colonies, see James Abercromby's *De Jure et Gubernatione Coloniarum* (1774), reprinted in Jack P. Greene, Charles F. Mullett and Edward C. Papenfuse (eds), *Magna Charta for America* (Philadelphia, 1986), p. 203.

110. Cited by Anderson, *Crucible of War*, p. 642.
111. Cited by Edmund S. Morgan, *Benjamin Franklin* (New Haven and London, 2002), pp. 154–5.
112. Greene, *Peripheries and Center*, pp. 80–4. 'A mere cob-web', Daniel Dulany, in his 'Considerations on the Propriety of Imposing Taxes in the British Colonies', as cited in Samuel Eliot Morison (ed.), *Sources and Documents Illustrating the American Revolution, 1764–1788* (2nd edn, London, Oxford, New York, 1965), p. 26.
113. Robert W. Tucker and David C. Hendrickson, *The Fall of the First British Empire. Origins of the War of American Independence* (Baltimore and London, 1982), p. 157. See also Richard R. Johnson, '"Parliamentary Egotisms": the Clash of Legislatures in the Making of the American Revolution', *The Journal of American History*, 74 (1987), pp. 338–62.
114. P. J. Marshall, 'Britain and the World in the Eighteenth Century: II, Britons and Americans', *TRHS*, 9 (1999), pp. 1–16, at p. 11.
115. Cited by Stephen Conway, 'From Fellow-Nationals to Foreigners: British Perceptions of the Americans, circa 1739–1783', *WMQ*, 3rd ser., 59 (2002), pp. 65–100, at p. 84.
116. Cited by Eliga H. Gould, *The Persistence of Empire. British Political Culture in the Age of the American Revolution* (Chapel Hill, NC and London, 2000), p. 125.
117. Eyzaguirre, *Idearioy ruta*, p. 44.
118. Richard Morris, Josefina Zoraida Vázquez and Elias Trabulse, *Las revoluciones de independencia en México y los Estados Unidos. Un ensayo comparativo*, 3 vols (Mexico City, 1976), 1, p. 165.
119. Brading, *Miners and Merchants*, pp. 44–51.
120. Richard Konetzke, 'La condición legal de los criollos y las causas de la independencia', *Estudios americanos*, 2 (1950), pp. 31–54; Eyzaguirre, *Ideario y ruta*, p. 53; Brading, *First America*, p. 477.
121. John H. Elliott, *The Count-Duke of Olivares. The Statesman in an Age of Decline* (New Haven and London, 1986), pp. 191–202.
122. *Ibid.*, p. 244.
123. Konetzke, 'La condición legal', pp. 45–6.
124. Cited by Farriss, *Crown and Clergy*, p. 130.
125. Table 2 in Brading, *Miners and Merchants*, p. 40.
126. 'Representación que hizo la ciudad de México al rey D. Carlos III en 1771 . . .', in Juan E. Hernández y Dávalos (ed.), *Colección de documentos para la historia de la guerra de independencia de México de 1808 a 1821*, 6 vols (Mexico City, 1877–82), 1, pp. 427–55. There is an abridged English translation in John Lynch (ed.), *Latin American Revolutions, 1808–1826* (Norman, OK, 1994), pp. 58–70, which I have used here. See also Brading, *First America*, pp. 479–83.
127. Above, p. 319.
128. Marshall, 'Britain and the World', pp. 9–10.
129. Konetzke, 'La condición legal', p. 48; Brading, *Miners and Merchants*, p. 37.

Chapter 11. Empires in Crisis

1. Above, p. 321.
2. Above, p. 149.
3. *The Political Works of James Harrington*, ed. J. G. A. Pocock (Cambridge, 1979), pp. 168–9. For the tracing of this and other ideas about colonial dependence, see J. M. Bumsted, '"Things in the Womb of Time": Ideas of American Independence, 1633 to 1763', *WMQ*, 3rd ser., 31 (1974), pp. 533–64.
4. Caroline Robbins, *The Eighteenth-Century Commonwealthmen* (Cambridge, Mass., 1959), pp. 112–13. For the influence in America of Trenchard and Gordon's *Cato's Letters*, see Bernard Bailyn, *The Ideological Origins of the American Revolution* (1967; enlarged edn, Cambridge, MA, 1992), pp. 35–6.
5. Cited in Barrow, *Trade and Empire*, p. 176.
6. Above, p. 235.
7. For these works and the debate they produced on both sides of the Atlantic, see Gerbi, *Dispute of the New World*, chs 3–6; Durand Echevarria, *Mirage in the West. A History of the French Image of American Society to 1815* (1957; 2nd edn, Princeton, 1968), ch. 1; Jorge Cañizares-Esguerra, *How to Write the History of the New World. Histories, Epistemologies, and Identities in the Eighteenth-Century Atlantic World* (Stanford, CA, 2001).
8. Francisco Javier Clavijero, *Historia antigua de México*, ed. Mariano Cuevas, 4 vols (2nd edn, Mexico City, 1958–9). For Pauw's 'monstrous portrait of America', vol. 4, pp. 7–10; and see Brading, *The First America*, ch. 20, for Clavijero and the 'Jesuit patriots'.
9. Thomas Jefferson, *Notes on the State of Virginia*, ed. William Peden (Chapel Hill, NC and London, 1982), p. 64.
10. See note 4, above.
11. Federica Morelli, 'La revolución en Quito: el camino hacia el gobierno mixto', *Revista de Indias*, 62 (2002), pp. 335–56, at p. 342; Antonio Annino, 'Some Reflections on Spanish American Constitutional and Political History', *Itinerario*, 19 (1995), pp. 26–47, at p. 40.
12. Manuel Giménez Fernández, *Las doctrinas populistas en la independencia de Hispano-América* (Seville, 1947), p. 57.
13. René Millar Corbacho, 'La inquisición de Lima y la circulación de libros prohibidos (1700–1800)', *Revista de Indias*, 44 (1984), pp. 415–44.
14. Richard L. Bushman, *King and People in Provincial Massachusetts* (Chapel Hill, NC and London, 1992), p. 42; Amory and Hall (eds), *The Colonial Book in the Atlantic World*, pp. 367–73. For juries in pre-revolutionary North American politics, see John M. Murrin, 'Magistrates, Sinners and a Precarious Liberty: Tried by Jury in Seventeenth-Century New England', in Hall, Murrin and Tate (eds) *Saints and Revolutionaries*, pp. 152–206; Reid, *In a Defiant Stance*, especially ch. 8; and Hoffer, *Law and People*, pp. 87–9.
15. For the contrasts, see in particular the observations on colonial American newspapers in Benedict Anderson, *Imagined Communities* (London and New York, 1983, repr. 1989), pp. 61–5.
16. François-Xavier Guerra, *Modernidad e independencias. Ensayos sobre las revoluciones hispánicas* (Madrid, 1992), p. 285; Haring, *Spanish Empire*, pp. 246–9.
17. Amory and Hall (eds), *The Colonial Book*, 1, pp. 154 and 354.
18. *Ibid.*, p. 358.
19. Louis B. Wright, *The Cultural Life of the British Colonies, 1607–1763* (New York, 1957), pp. 241–2; Kammen, *Colonial New York*, pp. 338–41.
20. Butler, *Becoming America*, pp. 170–4; Maier, *From Resistance to Revolution*, pp. 83–91; Beeman, *Varieties of Political Experience*, p. 259.
21. Figures in Anderson, *Imagined Communities*, p. 64, n. 50. I am grateful to Peter Bakewell for advice on this point.
22. John Lynch, *The Spanish American Revolutions* (2nd edn., New York and London, 1973), p. 26.
23. John Leddy Phelan, *The People and the King. The Comunero Revolution in Colombia, 1781* (Madison, WI, 1978), p. 85.
24. John Dunn, 'The Politics of Locke in England and America in the Eighteenth Century', in John W. Youlton (ed.), *John Locke: Problems and Perspectives* (Cambridge, 1969),

pp. 45–80. See, however, Jerome Huyler, *Locke in America. The Moral Philosophy of the Founding Era* (Lawrence, KS, 1995), especially pp. 207–8. Against recent tendencies to play down the influence of Locke in pre-revolutionary America, Huyler makes a cogent case for the permeation of American culture by Lockean ideals.

25. Wright, *Cultural Life*, pp. 119–20, 151–2; Isaac, *Landon Carter's Uneasy Kingdom*, pp. 88 and 359.
26. Wright, *Cultural Life*, p. 121; Henry F. May, *The Enlightenment in America* (Oxford, 1976), pp. 61–4; Bonomi, *Under the Cope of Heaven*, pp. 131–2; Ferguson, *American Enlightenment*, p. 57.
27. May, *Enlightenment*, pp. 33–4.
28. See J. M. López Piñero, *La introducción de la ciencia moderna en España* (Barcelona, 1969), for the arrival of the new science and medicine in later seventeenth-century Spain.
29. See Richard Herr, *The Eighteenth-Century Revolution in Spain* (Princeton, 1958).
30. See Cañizares-Esguerra, *How to Write the History of the New World*, for innovation in the writing of history.
31. John Tate Lanning, *Academic Culture in the Spanish Colonies* (Oxford, 1940; repr., Port Washington and London, 1971), p. 65; Arthur P. Whitaker (ed.), *Latin America and the Enlightenment* (2nd edn, Ithaca, NY, 1961), p. 35.
32. Colley, *Britons*, p. 132; T. H. Breen, 'Ideology and Nationalism on the Eve of the American Revolution: Revisions *Once More* in Need of Revising', *Journal of American History*, 84 (1997), pp. 13–39.
33. Breen, 'Ideology and Nationalism', pp. 30–1.
34. There is a massive literature on the ideological shifts on both sides of the Atlantic in the years following the accession of George III. See in particular Robbins, *Commonwealthmen*, ch. 9; Bailyn, *Ideological Origins*; J. G. A. Pocock, *Virtue, Commerce, and History* (Cambridge, 1985), and the relevant essays in J. G. A. Pocock (ed.), *Three British Revolutions: 1641, 1688, 1776* (Princeton, 1980). I have drawn on all these for the brief account that follows.
35. In addition to the literature cited above, see Jonathan Scott, 'What were Commonwealth Principles?', *Historical Journal*, 47 (2004), pp. 591–613.
36. See Bailyn, *Ideological Origins*, pp. 86–93.
37. Bushman, *King and People*, pp. 194–5.
38. Beeman, *Varieties of Political Experience*, pp. 111 and 244.
39. Townshend's project is examined in detail in Peter D. G. Thomas, *The Townshend Duties Crisis. The Second Phase of the American Revolution, 1767–1773* (Oxford, 1987). See also Barrow, *Trade and Empire*, pp. 216–24.
40. Maier, *From Resistance to Revolution*, pp. 114–38; Breen, *Marketplace of Revolution*, ch. 7.
41. Maier, *From Resistance to Revolution*, p. 118.
42. Breen, *Marketplace of Revolution*, pp. 230–4.
43. 'Philo Americanus', cited in *ibid.*, p. 265.
44. Theodore Draper, *A Struggle for Power. The American Revolution* (London, 1996), pp. 356–60; McCullough, *John Adams*, pp. 65–8. For succinct accounts of the pre-revolutionary period in the aftermath of the Boston Massacre see Edmund S. Morgan, *The Birth of the Republic, 1763–1789* (Chicago, 1956), ch. 4, and Gordon S. Wood, *The American Revolution. A History* (London, 2003), pp. 33–44.
45. Nash, *Urban Crucible*, pp. 355–6; Maier, *From Resistance to Revolution*, p. 129.
46. See Nash, *Urban Crucible*, pp. 351–82.
47. Beeman, *Varieties of Political Experience*, pp. 258–62. For evidence that Adams made up his mind in favour of independence as early as 1768, see John K. Alexander, *Samuel Adams. America's Revolutionary Politician* (Lanham, MD, 2002), p. 65.
48. Nash, *Urban Crucible*, p. 371.
49. See Gordon S. Wood, 'A Note on Mobs in the American Revolution', *WMQ*, 3rd ser., 23 (1966), pp. 635–42.
50. Alexander, *Samuel Adams*, pp. 82 and 91–2.
51. *Ibid.*, pp. 117 and 122.
52. Draper, *Struggle for Power*, pp. 415–19.

53. Cited in Maier, *From Resistance to Revolution*, pp. 224–5.
54. Bonomi, *Under the Cope of Heaven*, pp. 199–200; Isaac, *Transformation of Virginia*, pp. 187–9.
55. Morgan, *Birth of the Republic*, p. 61; Draper, *Struggle for Power*, pp. 434–5. For the role of conspiracy theory in eighteenth-century thought, see the fine article by Gordon S. Wood, 'Conspiracy and the Paranoid Style: Causality and Deceit in the Eighteenth Century', *WMQ*, 3rd ser., 39 (1982), pp. 401–41.
56. Edward Countryman, *The American Revolution* (Harmondsworth, 1985), pp. 75–97; Beeman, *Varieties of Political Experience*, pp. 169–77 (the Regulator Movement), and pp. 228–42 (the Paxton Boys).
57. Cited in Wyatt-Brown, *Southern Honor*, p. 70.
58. Gordon S. Wood, *The Radicalism of the American Revolution* (New York, 1993), pp. 123–4; and see also for the historiographical debate over the relationship between the colonial social structure and the American Revolution, Pauline Maier, 'The Transforming Impact of Independence Reaffirmed', in James A. Henretta, Michael Kammen and Stanley N. Katz (eds), *The Transformation of Early American Society* (New York, 1991), pp. 194–217.
59. Wyatt-Brown, *Southern Honor*, pp. 67–8; Isaac, *Transformation of Virginia*, pp. 290–1.
60. See Bushman, *Refinement of America*, pp. 38–41.
61. Above, p. 289.
62. See Tully, *Forming American Politics*, especially pp. 423–5.
63. Beeman, *Varieties of Political Experience*, pp. 131–4.
64. Above, pp. 168–9.
65. Draper, *Struggle for Power*, p. 420; Breen, *Tobacco Culture*, pp. 201–2.
66. Breen, *Tobacco Culture*, pp. 80–2.
67. Wright, *The First Gentlemen of Virginia*, pp. 349–50; and, for the special characteristics of tobacco culture and its impact on the mentality of the Tidewater planters, Breen, *Tobacco Culture*.
68. Cited in Morgan, *American Slavery, American Freedom*, p. 373.
69. Isaac, *Landon Carter's Uneasy Kingdom*, p. 251.
70. Eduardo Arcila Farias, *Comercio entre Venezuela y México en los siglos XVII y XVIII* (Mexico City, 1950), pp. 114–16.
71. Ferry, *Colonial Elite*, ch. 5, and Guillermo Morón, *A History of Venezuela* (London, 1964), pp. 77–9, for the 1749 rebellion.
72. Ferry, *Colonial Elite*, p. 216.
73. Cited in Julian P. Boyd, *Anglo-American Union. Joseph Galloway's Plans to Preserve the British Empire, 1774–1788* (Philadelphia, 1941), p. 34.
74. Jerrilyn Greene Marston, *King and Congress. The Transfer of Political Legitimacy, 1774–1776* (Princeton, 1987), pp. 91–3.
75. Garry Wills, *Inventing America. Jefferson's Declaration of Independence* (1978; London, 1980), pp. 57–61.
76. Marston, *King and Congress*, pp. 103–4, 122–3; Breen, *Marketplace of Revolution*, pp. 325–6; and see, for the spread of English associational life to the colonies, Peter Clark, *British Clubs and Societies, 1580–1800. The Origins of an Associated World* (Oxford, 2000), ch. 11.
77. Marston, *King and Congress*, pp. 122–30; Beeman, *Varieties of Political Experience*, pp. 270–1; Gordon S. Wood, *The American Revolution. A History* (London, 2003), pp. 45–50.
78. Cited in Morgan, *Benjamin Franklin*, p. 172.
79. Franklin to Galloway, 25 February 1775, cited in Morgan, *Benjamin Franklin*, p. 211.
80. Maier, *From Resistance to Revolution*, pp. 246–53.
81. Tucker and Hendrickson, *Fall of the First British Empire*, pp. 358 and 378.
82. Cited by Marston, *King and Congress*, p. 185.
83. *Ibid.*, p. 150.
84. *Ibid.*, p. 38.
85. *Ibid.*, p. 54.
86. Below, p. 388.
87. Cited by J. D. G. Clark, *The Language of Liberty, 1660–1832* (Cambridge, 1994), p. 121.
88. Maier, *From Resistance to Revolution*, p. 266.

89. Cited by Tucker and Hendrickson, *Fall of the First British Empire*, pp. 66–7.

90. Cited by McCullough, *John Adams*, pp. 100–1.

91. *The Writings of George Washington*, ed. John C. Fitzpatrick, vol. 5 (Washington, 1932), p. 92 (31 May 1776).

92. Thomas Paine, *Common Sense*, ed. Isaac Kramnick (Harmondsworth, 1986), p. 8. For *Common Sense* and its impact, see especially Eric Foner, *Tom Paine and Revolutionary America* (1976; updated edn, New York and Oxford, 2005), ch. 3, and the acute analysis by Robert A. Ferguson, 'The Commonalities of *Common Sense*', WMQ, 3rd ser., 57 (2000), pp. 465–504.

93. Paine, *Common Sense*, pp. 68, 97 and 108–9. It should be noted, however, that Paine claimed never to have read Locke.

94. *Ibid.*, p. 68.

95. Cited by McCullough, *John Adams*, p. 97.

96. Paine, *Common Sense*, p. 82.

97. *Ibid.*, p. 94.

98. *Ibid.*, p. 98.

99. Pauline Maier, *American Scripture. Making the Declaration of Independence* (New York, 1997), pp. 34–6.

100. For the marginality of republics in the eighteenth century, see Franco Venturi, *Utopia and Reform in the Enlightenment* (Cambridge, 1971), ch. 3.

101. cf. Ezra Stiles to Catharine Macaulay, 6 December 1773, as cited in Maier, *From Resistance to Revolution*, p. 289: 'My ideas of the Eng[lish] constitution have much diminished.'

102. Paine, *Common Sense*, p. 120.

103. Above, pp. 187–8.

104. Bloch, *Visionary Republic*, p. 47, and see part 2 in general for the relationship between millenarianism and the revolution. Also, Ferguson, *American Enlightenment*, pp. 52–3.

105. Maier, *American Scripture*, pp. 38–41.

106. Morison, *Sources and Documents*, p. 148.

107. *Ibid.*, p. 63.

108. Foner, *Tom Paine*, especially pp. 56–66.

109. *Ibid.*, pp. 127–34; Beeman, *Varieties of Political Experience*, pp. 270–5.

110. Marston, *King and Congress*, pp. 286–8 and 292–6; and see also Countryman, *The American Revolution*, ch. 4, for the differences in the balance of forces and the outcome of the struggle over independence in the various colonies.

111. Maier, *American Scripture*, pp. 51–8.

112. Wills, *Inventing America*, p. 325; and for the Declaration of Independence in the context of international relations and alliances, see David Armitage, 'The Declaration of Independence and International Law', WMQ, 3rd ser., 59 (2002), pp. 39–64.

113. McCullough, *John Adams*, p. 120; Maier, *American Scripture*, pp. 100–1.

114. The text of this paragraph, an indictment of George III, as a Christian king, for not suppressing the slave trade, is reproduced in Appendix C of Maier, *American Scripture*, p. 239.

115. For the editorial process and the approval of the Declaration, see Maier, *American Scripture*, ch. 3.

116. For analyses of the text, together with the context in which it was produced, see especially Wills, *Inventing America*, and Maier, *American Scripture*.

117. For the Dutch Act of Abjuration, see H. G. Koenigsberger, *Monarchies, States Generals and Parliaments. The Netherlands in the Fifteenth and Sixteenth Centuries* (Cambridge, 2001), pp. 296–7. For the conceptual ambiguities involved in the transition from 'United Colonies' to 'United States', see J. R. Pole, 'The Politics of the Word "State" and its Relation to American Sovereignty', *Parliaments, Estates and Representation*, 8 (1988), pp. 1–10.

118. See Morton White, *Philosophy, the Federalist, and the Constitution* (New York and Oxford, 1987), pp. 208–11.

119. Wills, *Inventing America*, ch. 12.

120. I follow here the argument developed at length in Huyler, *Locke in America*.

121. White, *Philosophy*, p. 181; Wills, *Inventing America*, ch. 18; and overviews in Darrin McMahon, 'From the Happiness of Virtue to the Virtue of Happiness: 400 B.C. – A.D. 1780', *Daedalus* (Spring, 2004), pp. 5–17, and Jack P. Greene and J. R. Pole (eds), *The Blackwell Encyclopaedia of the American Revolution* (Oxford, 1991), pp. 641–7 (Jan Lewis, 'Happiness').

122. *The Boston News-Letter*, no. 1412, 18 February 1731.

123. Bailyn, *To Begin the World Anew*, p. 134.

124. Luis Ángel García Melero, *La independencia de los Estados Unidos de Norteamérica a través de la prensa española* (Madrid, 1977), pp. 297–8.

125. Richter, *Facing East in Indian Country*, pp. 219–21; Colin C. Calloway, *The American Revolution in Indian Country* (Cambridge, 1995), ch. 1.

126. For a nuanced account of West Indian reactions to the American Revolution, see O'Shaughnessy, *An Empire Divided*.

127. William H. Nelson, *The American Tory* (Westport, Conn., 1961), p. 133.

128. Paul H. Smith, 'The American Loyalists: Notes on their Organization and Strength', *WMQ*, 3rd ser., 25 (1968), pp. 259–77; R. R. Palmer, *The Age of the Democratic Revolution*, vol. 1 (Princeton, 1959), p. 188.

129. Wood, *The American Revolution*, p. 82.

130. For Spain's intervention in the war, see Thomas E. Chávez, *Spain and the Independence of the United States. An Intrinsic Gift* (Albuquerque, NM, 2003).

131. To Arthur Lee, 4 April 1774, cited in Draper, *Struggle for Power*, p. 469.

132. Above, p. 304.

133. For Spanish expansion into California, see Weber, *Spanish Frontier*, ch. 9, and O. H. K. Spate, *Monopolists and Freebooters* (Minneapolis, 1983), ch. 13.

134. For a brief survey of these various expeditions, including a chronological listing, see the essay by José de la Sota Ríus, 'Spanish Science and Enlightenment Expeditions', in Chiyo Ishikawa (ed.), *Spain in the Age of Exploration* (Seattle Art Museum Exhibition Catalogue, 2004), pp. 159–87. For Malaspina, see Juan Pimentel, *La física de la Monarquía. Ciencia y política en el pensamiento colonial de Alejandro Malaspina, 1754–1810* (Aranjuez, 1998), and Manuel Lucena Giraldo and Juan Pimentel Igea, *Los 'Axiomas políticos sobre la América' de Alejandro Malaspina* (Madrid, 1991).

135. This figure is taken from Carlos Marichal, *La bancarrota del virreinato. Nueva España y las finanzas del imperio español, 1780–1810* (Mexico City, 1999), Appendix I, table 1.

136. Garner, 'Long-Term Silver Mining Trends', p. 903.

137. Weber, *Spanish Frontier*, p. 266; Chávez, *Spain and the Independence of the United States*, p. 216.

138. Alberto Flores Galindo, *Buscando un Inca* (Lima, 1988), p. 156.

139. Humboldt, *Ensayo político*, 2, p. 105 (lib. II, cap. 6).

140. Charles F. Walker, *Smouldering Ashes. Cuzco and the Creation of Republican Peru, 1780–1840* (Durham, NC, and London, 1999), p. 12; Lillian Estelle Fisher, *The Last Inca Revolt, 1780–1783* (Norman, OK, 1966), p. ix. See also for Túpac Amaru's revolt Scarlett O'Phelan Godoy, *Rebellion and Revolts in Eighteenth-Century Peru and Upper Peru* (Cologne, 1985); Flores Galindo, *Buscando un Inca*; and parts I and II of Steve J. Stern (ed.), *Resistance, Rebellion, and Consciousness in the Andean Peasant World. 18th to 20th Centuries* (Madison, WI, 1987). For a short survey of the history of later Bourbon Peru, see John R. Fisher, *Bourbon Peru, 1750–1824* (Liverpool, 2003).

141. McFarlane, *Colombia Before Independence*, p. 250.

142. O'Phelan Godoy, *Rebellion*, pp. 161–70.

143. Phelan, *The People and the King*, p. 29.

144. Taylor, *Drinking, Homicide and Rebellion* , pp. 113–14; Stern (ed.), *Resistance, Rebellion*, pp. 75–6.

145. Above p. 298, and see especially White, *Middle Ground*, ch. 7. Gregory Evans Dowd, *War under Heaven. Pontiac, the Indian Nations and the British Empire* (Baltimore and London, 2002), provides an illuminating account of Pontiac's rebellion.

146. Mörner, *The Andean Past*, p. 91.

147. O'Phelan Godoy, *Rebellion*, p. 118.

148. Spalding, *Huarochirí*, p. 300.

149. Sergio Serulnikov, *Subverting Colonial Authority. Challenges to Spanish Rule in the Eighteenth-Century Southern Andes* (Durham, NC, and London, 2003), pp. 12–14.
150. O'Phelan Godoy, *Rebellion*, p. 166; Walker, *Smouldering Ashes*, pp. 22–3; Alberto Flores Galindo, 'La revolución tupamarista y el imperio español', in Massimo Ganci and Ruggiero Romano (eds), *Governare il mondo. L'impero spagnolo dal XV al XIX secolo* (Palermo, 1991), pp. 387–9.
151. Boleslao Lewin, *La rebelión de Túpac Amaru y los orígenes de la independencia de Hispanoamérica* (3rd edn., Buenos Aires, 1967), pp. 283–4; Walker, *Smouldering Ashes*, pp. 25–7.
152. Flores Galindo, *Buscando un Inca*, p. 148; Stern (ed.), *Resistance, Rebellion*, chs 4 and 6.
153. White, *Middle Ground*, pp. 279–80; Dowd, *War under Heaven*, pp. 94–105. For extirpation of idolatry campaigns, see above, p. 190.
154. For the ambivalent position of Catholic priests in Bourbon Peru, see Serulnikov, *Subverting Colonial Authority*, pp. 95–106, and Thomas A. Abercrombie, *Pathways of Memory and Power. Ethnography and History Among an Andean People* (Madison, Wisconsin, 1998), pp. 294 and 300. I grateful to Professor Abercrombie for advice and suggestions on the Andean world.
155. Cited by Flores Galindo, *Buscando un Inca*, p. 150.
156. Lewin, *La rebelión*, pp. 414ff.; Walker, *Smouldering Ashes*, p. 19.
157. Cited in Lewin, *La rebelión*, p. 414.
158. Flores Galindo, *Buscando un Inca*, p. 150.
159. O'Phelan Godoy, *Rebellion*, pp. 213–19.
160. For an excellent analysis of the Inca nobility of Cuzco and their responses to the rebellion, see David T. Garrett, '"His Majesty's Most Loyal Vassals": the Indian Nobility and Túpac Amaru', *HAHR*, 84 (2004), pp. 575–617.
161. David Cahill, *From Rebellion to Independence in the Andes. Soundings from Southern Peru, 1750–1830* (CEDLA Latin American Studies, 89, Amsterdam, 2002), ch. 7.
162. These figures, which come from an account of the rebellion written in 1784, have been contested. See Cahill, *From Rebellion to Independence*, pp. 120–1.
163. *Ibid.*, p. 118.
164. O'Phelan Godoy, *Rebellion*, p. 272.
165. For the revolt of the Comuneros, see Phelan, *The People and the King*, and McFarlane, *Colombia Before Independence*, pp. 251–71. Also, Fisher, Kuethe and McFarlane (eds), *Reform and Insurrection*.
166. McFarlane, *Colombia Before Independence*, pp. 209–14.
167. Phelan, *The People and the King*, p. 99.
168. *Ibid.*, p. 87.
169. Fisher, Kuethe and McFarlane (eds), *Reform and Insurrection*, p. 3.
170. Phelan, *The People and the King*, p. 30; McFarlane, *Colombia Before Independence*, p. 215.
171. Phelan, *The People and the King*, ch. 13.
172. McFarlane, *Colombia Before Independence*, pp. 264 and 278–9.
173. See Phelan, *The People and the King*, pp. 34–5.
174. Piers Mackesy, *The War for America, 1775–1783* (London, 1964), appendix, pp. 524–5.
175. McFarlane, *Colombia Before Independence*, pp. 259–60.
176. Robert A. Gross, *The Minutemen and their World* (New York, 1981), pp. 151–3; Shy, *A People Numerous*, pp. 127–32.
177. Phelan, *The People and the King*, p. 98.
178. For indications of atrocities in the War of Independence, see Shy, *A People Numerous*, ch. 8 ('Armed Loyalism').
179. See the preface to Joseph Ellis, *Founding Brothers. The Revolutionary Generation* (London, 2002).
180. McFarlane, *Colombia Before Independence*, p. 256.
181. Phelan, *The People and the King*, pp. 239–40; McFarlane, *Colombia Before Independence*, p. 217.
182. Góngora, *Studies in Colonial History*, pp. 195–6.
183. Fisher, *The Last Inca Revolt*, pp. 386–9; Walker, *Smouldering Ashes*, p. 69.

184. Joseph Pérez, *Los movimientos precursores de la emancipación en Hispanoamérica* (Madrid, 1977), p. 131; and see McFarlane, *Colombia Before Independence*, pp. 205–6, for the proposals for educational reform.
185. Phelan, *The People and the King*, p. 244.
186. Cited in Mackesy, *The War for America*, p. 187.
187. See Gould, *Persistence of Empire*, ch. 5.
188. Cited in Lewin, *La rebelión de Túpac Amaru*, p. 413 from Manuel Godoy, *Memorias* (Madrid, 1836), vol. 3, pp. 285–6.
189. Joaquín Oltra and María Ángeles Pérez Samper, *El Conde de Aranda y los Estados Unidos* (Barcelona, 1987), pp. 234–8. For the full text of the memorandum, see Manuel Lucena Giraldo (ed.), *Premoniciones de la independencia de Iberoamérica* (Aranjuez and Madrid, 2003), pp. 75–85.
190. Cited in Gould, *Persistence of Empire*, p. 166.
191. Cited by Liss, *Atlantic Empires*, p. 142.

Chapter 12

1. See Merrill Jensen, *The Articles of Confederation. An Interpretation of the Social-Constitutional History of the American Revolution, 1774–1781* (Madison, WI, 1940; repr. 1948) for the divisions between conservatives and radicals.
2. Above, p. 346.
3. Clinton Rossiter, *1787. The Grand Convention* (1966; New York, 1987), p. 138. For valuable insights into the national debate of 1787 and beyond, see John M. Murrin, 'The Great Inversion, or Court versus Country: a Comparison of the Revolutionary Settlements in England (1688–1721) and America (1776–1816)', in Pocock (ed.), *Three British Revolutions*, pp. 368–453, and Isaac Kramnick, 'The "Great National Discussion": the Discourse of Politics in 1787', *WMQ*, 3rd ser., 45 (1988), pp. 3–32. Also, more generally, for the creation of the republic, Gordon S. Wood, *The Creation of the American Republic, 1776–1787* (Chapel Hill, NC, 1969; repr. 1998), and Stanley Elkins and Eric McKitrick, *The Age of Federalism* (Oxford, 1993).
4. Rossiter, *1787*, p. 145.
5. *Ibid.*, pp. 266–7.
6. Bernard Bailyn (ed.), *The Debate on the Constitution*, 2 vols (New York, 1993), 1, p. 310 (Jefferson to William Stephens Smith, 13 November 1787).
7. Alan Knight, *Mexico. The Colonial Era* (Cambridge, 2002), pp. 233–5 and 290.
8. For discussions of the very mixed impact of free trade, see Jacques Barbier and Allan J. Kuethe (eds), *The North American Role in the Spanish Imperial Economy, 1760–1819* (Manchester, 1984), ch. 1; Josep Fontana and Antonio Miguel Bernal (eds), *El comercio libre entre España y América Latina, 1765–1824* (Madrid, 1987); Fisher, *Economic Aspects*, chs 9 and 10.
9. Wright, *Anglo-Spanish Rivalry*, pp. 163–4; Weber, *Spanish Frontier*, pp. 290–1; Hoffman, *Florida's Frontiers*, ch. 10.
10. Lynch, *Bourbon Spain*, pp. 380–95; Fisher, *Economic Aspects*, pp. 201–6; Liss, *Atlantic Empires*, pp. 112–13.
11. Sánchez Bella, *Iglesia y estado*, pp. 302–15; Brading, *Church and State*, pp. 222–7; Marichal, *La bancarrota*, ch. 4.
12. Lynch, *Bourbon Spain*, p. 415. For annual statistics and percentages of the American contribution to the Spanish royal treasury, 1763–1811, see table 1 in Appendix 1 of Marichal, *La bancarrota*.
13. Bliss, *Revolution and Empire*, pp. 60–6.
14. For a succinct account of the background to the convocation of the Cortes, see Timothy E. Anna, *Spain and the Loss of America* (Lincoln, NE and London, 1983), ch. 2.
15. Cited in Giménez Fernández, *Las doctrinas populistas*, p. 61.
16. Rodríguez O., *Independence of Spanish America*, pp. 55–6.
17. Timothy E. Anna, *The Fall of the Royal Government in Peru* (Lincoln, NE and London, 1979), p. 40.

18. Above, p. 320.
19. See Breen, 'Ideology and Nationalism', and above, p. 334.
20. See the arguments advanced by Anthony McFarlane, 'Identity, Enlightenment and Political Dissent in Late Colonial Spanish America', *TRHS*, 6th ser., 8 (1998), pp. 309–35, especially pp. 323ff.
21. Anna, *Loss of America*, p. 29.
22. Anna, *Fall of Royal Government*, ch. 2.
23. Lynch, *Spanish American Revolutions*, pp. 304–6; Knight, *Colonial Era*, pp. 292–6.
24. Cited in Simon Collier, *Ideas and Politics of Chilean Independence, 1808–1833* (Cambridge, 1967), p. 52. William Burke, the author of *An Account of the European Settlements in America* (1757), died in 1797, and cannot therefore be the William Burke who made this observation. There has been much speculation about his identity. See Mario Rodríguez, *'William Burke' and Francisco de Miranda. The Word and the Deed in Spanish America's Emancipation* (Lanham, MD, New York and London, 1994), especially ch. 4, where 'Burke' is identified with James Mill.
25. Decree of 22 January 1809, in Manuel Chust, *La cuestión nacional americana en las Cortes de Cádiz* (Valencia, 1999), pp. 32–3, n. 5.
26. Rodríguez O., *Independence of Spanish America*, pp. 59–64.
27. Chust, *La cuestión nacional*, p. 46.
28. Cited in Draper, *Struggle for Power*, p. 397.
29. See above, p. 318.
30. Quoted from a comment in *El Observador*, two weeks before the opening of the Cortes, by Demetrio Ramos, 'Las Cortes de Cádiz y América', *Revista de Estudios Políticos*, 126 (1962), pp. 433–634, at p. 488.
31. James F. King, 'The Colored Castes and the American Representation in the Cortes of Cadiz', *HAHR*, 33 (1953), pp. 33–64.
32. Chust, *La cuestión nacional*, pp. 39 and 55–62.
33. Miguel Izard, *El miedo a la revolución. La lucha por la libertad en Venezuela, 1777–1830* (Madrid, 1979), p. 30; Rodríguez O., *Independence of Spanish America*, pp. 109–11.
34. Guillermo Céspedes del Castillo, *Lima y Buenos Aires. Repercusiones económicas y políticas de la creación del virreinato del Plata* (Seville, 1947), pp. 122–9.
35. Tulio Halperín Donghi, *Politics and Society in Argentina in the Revolutionary Period* (Cambridge, 1975), pp. 29–40. For the effects of the creation of the new viceroyalty and the economic and social impact of the Bourbon reforms on the region, see also Jeremy Adelman, *Republic of Capital. Buenos Aires and the Legal Transformation of the Atlantic World* (Stanford, CA, 1999), ch. 2.
36. Adelman, *Republic of Capital*, p. 77; Lynch, *Spanish American Revolutions*, ch. 2.
37. Lynch, *Spanish American Revolutions*, pp. 52–8 and 135.
38. Collier, *Ideas and Politics*, p. 69.
39. Izard, *El miedo*, pp. 139–43; Lynch, *Spanish American Revolutions*, ch. 6.
40. Knight, *Colonial Era*, pp. 298–304; Lynch, *Spanish American Revolutions*, pp. 306–13; Eric Van Young, 'Islands in the Storm: Quiet Cities and Violent Countrysides in the Mexican Independence Era', *Past and Present*, 118 (1988), pp. 130–55 (also in Spanish in Eric Van Young, *La crisis del orden colonial* (Madrid, 1992), ch. 8); Archer, *The Army in Bourbon Mexico*, p. 299.
41. Izard, *El miedo*, p. 30.
42. Lynch, *Spanish American Revolutions*, pp. 58–60, 89–93; Adelman, *Republic of Capital*, pp. 85–7.
43. See above, p. 352.
44. Izard, *El miedo*, pp. 133–4.
45. Nelson, *The American Tory*, pp. 86–8.
46. Izard, *El miedo*, pp. 55 and 129.
47. Marchena Fernández, *Ejército y milicias*, pp. 162 and 182.
48. John Lynch, 'Spain's Imperial Memory', *Debate y Perspectivas*, 2 (2002), pp. 47–73, at p. 72.
49. Anna, *Fall of Royal Government*, p. 184.
50. Cited in Raymond Carr, *Spain, 1808–1939* (Oxford, 1966), p. 104, n. 1.

51. See Anna, *Loss of America*, pp. 80–3, for the free trade question in the Cortes.
52. Chust, *La cuestión nacional*, p. 54; Rodríguez O., *Independence of Spanish America*, p. 84.
53. Céspedes del Castillo, *Ensayos*, pp. 375–83.
54. Josep M. Fradera, *Gobernar colonias* (Barcelona, 1999), pp. 54–5.
55. Chust, *La cuestión nacional*, p. 71.
56. For the position of the *castas pardas*, see Fradera, *Gobernar colonias*, pp. 57–67.
57. Nettie Lee Benson (ed.), *Mexico and the Spanish Cortes, 1810–1822* (Austin, TX and London, 1966), p. 31.
58. King, 'The Colored Castes'; Anna, *Loss of America*, pp. 68–79; Rodríguez O., *Independence of Spanish America*, p. 86.
59. Thomas, *Slave Trade*, pp. 498–502. For a recent treatment of the slavery question in the age of revolution, see Ellis, *Founding Brothers*, ch. 3.
60. Chust, *La cuestión nacional*, pp. 102–14; Thomas, *Slave Trade*, pp. 578–81; Rossiter, *1787*, pp. 215–18.
61. Wilcomb E. Washburn, *Red Man's Land/White Man's Law. A Study of the Past and Present Status of the American Indian* (New York, 1971), p. 164. From the early nineteenth century the United States began conferring citizenship on some Indians, particularly those who had been allocated parcels of tribal land, and the process was accelerated following the Dawes Act of 1887. Two-thirds of the Indian population of the United States had full citizenship by the time when the Citizenship Act of 1924 extended it to all. Even after 1924, however, Indians were denied the franchise in some states.
62. Borah, *Justice by Insurance*, pp. 396–401, 412.
63. Anna, *Loss of America*, pp. 94–5.
64. Collier, *Ideas and Politics*, p. 105.
65. Anna, *Fall of Royal Government*, pp. 54–5.
66. Jaime E. Rodríguez O., 'Las elecciones a las cortes constituyentes mexicanas', in Louis Cardaillac and Angélica Peregrina (eds), *Ensayos en homenaje a José María Muriá* (Zapopan, 2002), pp. 79–109. The text of the constitution of 1812, with a helpful introduction, has been made conveniently available in Antonio Fernández García (ed.), *La constitución de Cádiz (1812) y discurso preliminar a la constitución* (Madrid, 2002).
67. Figure cited in Jaime E. Rodríguez O., 'La naturaleza de la representación en Nueva España y México', *Secuencia*, 61 (2005), pp. 7–32, at p. 25.
68. King, 'Colored Castes', p. 64.
69. Rodríguez O., *Independence of Spanish America*, p. 98.
70. Chust, *La cuestión nacional*, ch. 5; Rodríguez O., *Independence of Spanish America*, pp. 94–103.
71. Gibson, *Aztecs Under Spanish Rule*, pp. 175–9.
72. Rodríguez O., 'La naturaleza de la representación', pp. 16–17.
73. For the later eighteenth-century extension of schooling, and attempts at linguistic unification, see Serge Gruzinski, 'La "segunda aculturación": el estado ilustrado y la religiosidad indígena en Nueva España', *Estudios de historia novohispana*, 8 (1985), pp. 175–201.
74. Guerra, *Modernidad e independencias*, pp. 278–81; Rodríguez O., *Independence of Spanish America*, pp. 93–4; Clarice Neal, 'Freedom of the Press in New Spain', in Benson (ed.), *Mexico and the Spanish Cortes*, ch. 4.
75. Chust, *La cuestión nacional*, p. 308.
76. Rodríguez O., *Independence of Spanish America*, p. 103.
77. Van Young, *La crisis*, pp. 419–20.
78. Anna, *Loss of America*, pp. 135–8.
79. *Ibid.*, pp. 143–7; and, for Ferdinand's American policy, see Michael P. Costeloe, *Response to Revolution. Imperial Spain and the Spanish American Revolutions, 1810–1840* (Cambridge, 1986), especially pp. 59–100.
80. Lynch, *Spanish American Revolutions*, chs 2 and 3.
81. Anna, *Fall of Royal Government*, chs 6 and 7.
82. Robert Harvey, *Liberators. Latin America's Struggle for Independence, 1810–1830* (London, 2000), provides a graphic account of the various military campaigns that won independence for Spain's empire in America.

83. For the financial and political collapse of the Spanish monarchy in these years, see especially Josep Fontana, *La quiebra de la monarquía absoluta, 1814–1820* (Barcelona, 1971).

84. Benson (ed.), *Mexico and the Spanish Cortes*, ch. 6; Knight, *Colonial Era*, pp. 329–30.

85. Anna, *Loss of America*, pp. 255–6.

86. Bakewell, *History of Latin America*, p. 380; Thomas, *Cuba*, chs 5 and 6.

87. George Canning to Viscount Granville, 19 August 1825, in C. K. Webster, *Britain and the Independence of Latin America, 1812–1830* (2 vols, London, New York, Toronto, 1938), 2, doc. 416, p. 193.

88. Cited in Shy, *A People Numerous*, p. 331, n. 21.

89. *Ibid.*, p. 250.

90. Lynch, *Spanish American Revolutions*, pp. 199–204; Shy, *A People Numerous*, ch. 8 ('Armed Loyalism'); Shy, 'Armed Force', in Hagan and Roberts (eds), *Against All Enemies*, p. 13.

91. Anna, *Fall of Royal Government*, pp. 16–17.

92. Lester D. Langley, *The Americas in the Age of Revolution, 1750–1850* (New Haven and London, 1996), p. 185; Anna, *Fall of Royal Government*, p. 196.

93. 'Speech on the Independence of Latin America, 28 March 1818', in *The Papers of Henry Clay*, ed. James F. Hopkins (11 vols, Lexington, KY, 1959–92), 2, p. 551.

94. Richter, *Facing East*, pp. 217–21 for Indians; Shy, *A People Numerous*, pp. 130–1 and 205 for slaves.

95. Anna, *Fall of Royal Government*, ch. 5.

96. See Shy, *A People Numerous*, ch. 11 ('The Legacy of the Revolutionary War'); McCusker and Menard, *Economy of British America*, p. 367, for levels of income and wealth.

97. The expression is that of Van Young, 'Islands in the Storm'.

98. See the Introduction to Webster, *Britain and the Independence of Latin America*, vol. 1. For the ideological background to British policy towards Spanish America in this period, see Gabriel Paquette, 'The Intellectual Context of British Diplomatic Recognition of the South American Republics, c. 1800–1830', *Journal of Transatlantic Studies*, 2 (2004), pp. 75–95.

99. See Bernstein, *Origins of Inter-American Interest*, pp. 83–7; and, for the debate over the creation of a hemispheric system, Arthur P. Whitaker, *The Western Hemisphere Idea. Its Rise and Decline* (Ithaca, NY, 1954), ch. 2.

100. Above, p. 300; John Lynch, *Caudillos in Spanish America, 1800–1850* (Oxford, 1992), pp. 30–4.

101. Gerhard Masur, *Simon Bolivar* (2nd edn, Albuquerque, NM, 1969), ch. 2; for Belgrano, Lynch (ed.), *Latin American Revolutions*, p. 258.

102. Manuel Belgrano, *Autobiografía y otras páginas* (Buenos Aires, 1966), p. 24. The translation is taken from Lynch, *Latin American Revolutions*, p. 259.

103. Masur, *Bolivar*, p. 329.

104. McCullough, *John Adams*, p. 593.

105. The sixth, John Witherspoon, born in Scotland in 1723, moved to America in 1768 to become president of the College of New Jersey at Princeton.

106. Information on the Signers is taken from the *Dictionary of American Biography*. For Carroll's European upbringing, see Hoffman, *Princes of Ireland*, ch. 4.

107. Rossiter, *1787*, p. 140.

108. For Bolívar's political vision, see Anthony Pagden, *Spanish Imperialism and the Political Imagination* (New Haven and London, 1990), ch. 6.

109. Cited by David Brading in David A. Brading *et al.*, *Cinco miradas británicas a la historia de México* (Mexico City, 2000), p. 102.

110. For the problems of nation-building in Hispanic America, see Lynch, *Caudillos*, ch. 4.

111. See Benson, *Mexico and the Spanish Cortes*, ch. 1 (Charles R. Berry, 'The Election of the Mexican Deputies to the Spanish Cortes, 1810–1820').

112. See Collier, *Ideas and Politics of Chilean Independence*.

113. Robert W. Tucker and David C. Hendrickson, *Empire of Liberty. The Statecraft of Thomas Jefferson* (Oxford, 1992), pp. 26–7 and 64–5.

114. *Cambridge Economic History of the United States*, 1, ch. 9; Tucker and Hendrickson, *Empire of Liberty*, p. 190.

115. Leandro Prados de la Escosura and Samuel Amaral (eds), *La independencia americana: consecuencias económicas* (Madrid, 1993), p. 264.
116. See David J. Weber, *The Mexican Frontier, 1821–1846* (Albuquerque, NM, 1982).
117. John H. Coatsworth, 'Obstacles to Economic Growth in Nineteenth-Century Mexico', *AHR*, 83 (1978), pp. 80–100. The Spanish version of this important article is printed in ch. 4 of John H. Coatsworth, *Los orígenes del atraso. Nueve ensayos de historia económica de México en los siglos XVIII y XIX* (Mexico City, 1990), with a short addendum responding to a critique by Enrique Cárdenas.
118. *Cambridge Economic History of the United States*, 1, p. 396.
119. See Joyce Appleby, *Inheriting the Revolution. The First Generation of Americans* (Cambridge, MA, 2000), for the attitudes and achievements of this generation.
120. *Ibid.*, p. 52; Steven Watts, *The Republic Reborn. War and the Making of Liberal America, 1790–1820* (Baltimore and London, 1987), pp. 283–9.
121. Appleby, *Inheriting the Revolution*, p. 28.
122. *Ibid.*, pp. 69–71.
123. See Wyatt Brown, *Southern Honor*; also Appleby, *Inheriting the Revolution*, ch. 8.

Epilogue

1. Dennis D. Moore (ed.), *More Letters from the American Farmer. An Edition of the Essays in English Left Unpublished by Crèvecoeur* (Athens, GA and London, 1995), pp. 82–9. I have modernized the punctuation and spelling.
2. For a set of valuable discussions of the colonial legacy of Iberian America, see the essays in Jeremy Adelman (ed.), *Colonial Legacies. The Problem of Persistence in Latin American History* (New York and London, 1999).
3. The Black Legend was first systematically examined by Julián Juderías in *La Leyenda Negra* (Madrid, 1914, and frequently reprinted), and has been the subject of numerous subsequent studies, among them Sverker Arnoldsson, *La Leyend Negra. Estudios sobre sus orígenes* (Göteborg, 1960); William S. Maltby, *The Black Legend in England. The Development of Anti-Spanish Sentiment, 1558–1660* (Durham, NC, 1971); Ricardo García Cárcel, *La Leyenda Negra. Historia y opinión* (Madrid, 1992); J. N. Hillgarth, *The Mirror of Spain, 1500–1700. The Formation of a Myth* (Ann Arbor, MI, 2000). Charles Gibson, *The Black Legend. Anti-Spanish Attitudes in the Old World and the New* (New York, 1971), is an anthology of relevant contemporary and later extracts.
4. See Adelman (ed.), *Colonial Legacies*, p. 5.
5. Thomas Pownall, *A Translation of the Memorial of the Sovereigns of Europe Upon the Present State of Affairs Between the Old and New World* (London, 1781), p. 11. For the evolution of Pownall's ideas, see Shy, *A People Numerous*, ch. 3.
6. Smith, *Wealth of Nations*, 2, p. 486 (book 5, ch. 3).
7. See Stanley L. Engerman, 'British Imperialism in a Mercantilist Age, 1492–1849: Conceptual Issues and Empirical Problems', *Revista de Historia Económica*, 16 (1998), pp. 195–231, and especially pp. 218–19. This special issue of the journal, containing papers delivered at the Twelfth International Economic History Congress, and edited by Patrick K. O'Brien and Leandro Prados de la Escosura under the title of *The Costs and Benefits of European Imperialism from the Conquest of Ceuta, 1415, to the Treaty of Lusaka, 1974*, acknowledges and illustrates the many problems involved in attempts at drawing up a cost-benefit analysis of empire, but provides a valuable comparative survey using case studies based on the current state of knowledge.
8. See John TePaske, 'The Fiscal Structure of Upper Peru and the Financing of Empire', in Karen Spalding (ed.), *Essays in the Political, Economic and Social History of Colonial Latin America* (Newark, DE, 1982), pp. 69–94.
9. See Bartolomé Yun-Casalilla, 'The American Empire and the Spanish Economy: an Institutional and Regional Perspective', *Revista de Historia Económica*, 16 (1996), pp. 123–56.
10. Marichal, *La bancarrota*, pp. 22–3.

11. A purely monetary explanation of sixteenth-century Castilian inflation is no longer acceptable. Other considerations, and in particular population growth, need to be taken into account. For a lucid survey of the current state of debate over the monetary and other consequences of Spain's acquisition of an American empire, see Bartolomé Yun-Casalilla, *Marte contra Minerva. El precio del imperio español, c. 1450–1600* (Barcelona, 2004), ch. 3.

12. James Campbell, *A Concise History of the Spanish America* (London, 1741; facsimile edn, Folkestone and London, 1972), p. 291.

13. See Patrick Karl O'Brien and Leandro Prados de la Escosura, 'The Costs and Benefits for Europeans from their Empires Overseas', *Revista de Historia Económica*, 16 (1998), pp. 29–89. Also Renate Pieper, 'The Volume of African and American Exports of Precious Metals and its Effects in Europe, 1500–1800', in Hans Pohl (ed.), *The European Discovery of the World and its Economic Effects on Pre-Industrial Society* (Papers of the Tenth International Economic History Congress, *Vierteljahrschrift für Sozial-Und Wirtschaftsgeschichte*, Beihefte, No. 89, Stuttgart, 1990), pp. 97–117.

14. Above, p. 131.

15. I have attempted a brief counterfactual history along these lines in Armitage and Braddick (eds), *The British Atlantic World*, pp. 241–3.

Bibliography

Abbot, W. W., *The Colonial Origins of the United States: 1607–1763* (New York, London, Sydney, Toronto, 1975)

Abercrombie, Thomas A., *Pathways of Memory and Power. Ethnography and History Among an Andean People* (Madison, WI, 1998)

Acosta, José de, *Historia natural y moral de las Indias*, ed. Edmundo O'Gorman (2nd edn, Mexico City and Buenos Aires, 1962)

Adair, Douglas, 'Rumbold's Dying Speech, 1685, and Jefferson's Last Words on Democracy, 1826', *WMQ*, 3rd ser., 9 (1952), pp. 521–31

Adelman, Jeremy, *Republic of Capital. Buenos Aires and the Legal Transformation of the Atlantic World* (Stanford, CA, 1999)

Adelman, Jeremy (ed.), *Colonial Legacies. The Problem of Persistence in Latin American History* (New York and London, 1999)

Adelman, Jeremy, and Aron, Stephen, 'From Borderlands to Borders: Empires, Nation States, and the Peoples in Between in North American History', *AHR*, 104 (1999), pp. 814–41

Aiton, A. S., 'Spanish Colonial Reorganization Under the Family Compact', *HAHR*, 12 (1932), pp. 269–80

Alberro, Solange, *Inquisition et société au Mexique* (Mexico City, 1988)

Alberro, Solange, *Les Espagnols dans le Mexique colonial. Histoire d'une acculturation* (Paris, 1992)

Alberro, Solange, *Del gachupín al criollo: O de cómo los españoles de México dejaron de serlo* (El Colegio de México, Jornadas, 122, 1992)

Albònico, Aldo, *Il mondo americano di Giovanni Botero* (Rome, 1990)

Alencastro, Luiz Felipe de, *O trato dos viventes. Formação de Brasil no Atlântico Sul. Séculos XVI e XVII* (São Paulo, 2000)

Alexander, John K., *Samuel Adams. America's Revolutionary Politician* (Lanham, MD, 2002)

Alexander, William, *An Encouragement to Colonies* (London, 1624)

Altman, Ida, *Emigrants and Society. Extremadura and Spanish America in the Sixteenth Century* (Berkeley, Los Angeles, London, 1989)

Altman, Ida, and Horn, James (eds), *'To Make America'. European Emigration in the Early Modern Period* (Berkeley, Los Angeles, Oxford, 1991)

Alvarez de Toledo, Cayetana, *Politics and Reform in Spain and Viceregal Mexico. The Life and Thought of Juan de Palafox, 1600–1659* (Oxford, 2004)

Amory, Hugh, and Hall, David D. (eds), *The Colonial Book in the Atlantic World* (Cambridge, 2000)

Anderson, Benedict, *Imagined Communities* (London and New York, 1983, repr. 1989)

Anderson, Fred, *Crucible of War. The Seven Years' War and the Fate of Empire in British North America, 1754–1766* (London, 2000)

Anderson, Virginia DeJohn, *New England's Generation* (Cambridge, 1991)

Andrés-Gallego, José, *El motín de Esquilache, América y Europa* (Madrid, 2003)

Andrews, Charles M., *The Colonial Period of American History* (4 vols, New Haven, 1934–8; repr. 1964)

Andrews, Kenneth R., 'Christopher Newport of Limehouse, Mariner', *WMQ*, 3rd ser., 11 (1954)

Andrews, Kenneth R., *Elizabethan Privateering* (Cambridge, 1964)

Andrews, Kenneth R., *The Spanish Caribbean. Trade and Plunder 1530–1630* (New Haven and London, 1978)

Andrews, Kenneth R., *Trade, Plunder and Settlement. Maritime Enterprise and the Genesis of the British Empire, 1480–1630* (Cambridge, 1984)

Andrews, K. R., Canny, N. P., and Hair, P. E. H. (eds), *The Westward Enterprise. English Activities in Ireland, the Atlantic and America 1480–1650* (Liverpool, 1978)

Andrien, Kenneth J., *Crisis and Decline. The Viceroyalty of Peru in the Seventeenth Century* (Albuquerque, NM, 1985)

Andrien, Kenneth J., 'Economic Crisis, Taxes and the Quito Insurrection of 1765', *Past and Present*, 129 (1990), pp. 104–31

Andrien, Kenneth J., and Adorno, Rolena (eds), *Transatlantic Encounters. Europeans and Andeans in the Sixteenth Century* (Berkeley, Los Angeles, Oxford, 1991)

Anna, Timothy E., *The Fall of the Royal Government in Peru* (Lincoln, NE and London, 1979)

Anna, Timothy E., *Spain and the Loss of America* (Lincoln, NE and London, 1983)

Annino, Antonio, 'Some Reflections on Spanish American Constitutional and Political History', *Itinerario*, 19 (1995), pp. 26–47

Appleby, Joyce Oldham, *Economic Thought and Ideology in Seventeenth-Century England* (Princeton, 1978)

Appleby, Joyce, *Inheriting the Revolution. The First Generation of Americans* (Cambridge, MA, 2000)

Aquila, Richard, *The Iroquois Restoration. Iroquois Diplomacy on the Colonial Frontier, 1701–1754* (Lincoln, NE and London, 1983; repr. 1997)

Archer, Christon I., *The Army in Bourbon Mexico, 1760–1810* (Albuquerque, NM, 1977)

Archer, Richard, 'A New England Mosaic: a Demographic Analysis for the Seventeenth Century', *WMQ*, 3rd ser., 47 (1990), pp. 477–502

Arcila Farias, Eduardo, *Comercio entre Venezuela y México en los siglos XVII y XVIII* (Mexico City, 1950)

Armani, Alberto, *Ciudad de Dios y Ciudad del Sol. El 'estado' jesuita de los guaraníes, 1609–1768* (Mexico City, 1982; repr. 1987)

Armas Medina, Fernando de, *Cristianización del Perú, 1532–1600* (Seville, 1953)

Armitage, David, *The Ideological Origins of the British Empire* (Cambridge, 2000)

Armitage, David, 'The Declaration of Independence and International Law', *WMQ*, 3rd ser., 59 (2002), pp. 39–64.

Armitage, David (ed.), *Theories of Empire, 1450–1800* (Aldershot, 1998)

Armitage, David, and Braddick, Michael J. (eds), *The British Atlantic World, 1500–1800* (New York, 2002)

Arnoldsson, Sverker, *La Leyend Negra. Estudios sobre sus orígenes* (Göteborg, 1960)

Axtell, James, *The Invasion Within. The Contest of Cultures in Colonial North America* (New York and Oxford, 1985)

Axtell, James, *After Columbus. Essays in the Ethnohistory of Colonial North America* (Oxford, 1988)

Axtell, James, *Natives and Newcomers. The Cultural Origins of North America* (Oxford, 2001)

Bacon, Francis, *The Works of Francis Bacon*, ed. J. Spedding (14 vols, London, 1857–74)

Bailey, Gauvin Alexander, *Art of Colonial Latin America* (London and New York, 2005)

Bailyn, Bernard, *The New England Merchants in the Seventeenth Century* (1955; New York, 1964)

Bailyn, Bernard, *Education in the Forming of American Society* (New York and London, 1960)

Bailyn, Bernard, *The Ideological Origins of the American Revolution* (1967; enlarged edn, Cambridge, MA, 1992)

Bailyn, Bernard, *The Origins of American Politics* (New York, 1970)

Bailyn, Bernard, 'Politics and Social Structure in Virginia', in Stanley N. Katz and John M. Murrin (eds), *Colonial America. Essays in Politics and Social Development* (New York, 1983)

Bailyn, Bernard, *The Peopling of British America. An Introduction* (New York, 1986)

Bailyn, Bernard, *Voyagers to the West* (New York, 1986)

Bailyn, Bernard, *To Begin the World Anew. The Genius and Ambiguities of the American Founders* (New York, 2003)

Bailyn, Bernard, *Atlantic History. Concept and Contours* (Cambridge, MA, and London, 2005)

Bailyn, Bernard (ed.), *Pamphlets of the American Revolution, 1750–1776*, vol. 1, *1750–1765* (Cambridge, MA, 1965)

Bailyn, Bernard (ed.), *The Debate on the Constitution* (2 vols, New York, 1993)

Bailyn, Bernard, and Morgan, Philip D. (eds), *Strangers Within the Realm. Cultural Margins of the First British Empire* (Chapel Hill, NC and London, 1991)

Baker, Emerson W. *et al.* (eds), *American Beginnings. Exploration, Culture and Cartography in the Land of Norumbega* (Lincoln, NE, and London, 1994)

Bakewell, Peter, *Silver Mining and Society in Colonial Mexico, Zacatecas 1546–1700* (Cambridge, 1971)

Bakewell, Peter, *Miners of the Red Mountain. Indian Labor in Potosí 1545–1650* (Albuquerque, NM, 1984)

Bakewell, Peter, *Silver and Entrepreneurship in Seventeenth-Century Potosí. The Life and Times of Antonio López de Quiroga* (Albuquerque, NM, 1988)

Bakewell, Peter, *A History of Latin America* (Oxford, 1997)

Balmer, Randall H., *A Perfect Babel of Confusion. Dutch Religion and English Culture in the Middle Colonies* (Oxford and New York, 1989)

Barbier, Jacques, and Kuethe, Allan J. (eds), *The North American Role in the Spanish Imperial Economy, 1760–1819* (Manchester, 1984)

Barbour, Philip L. (ed.), *The Jamestown Voyages under the First Charter, 1606–1609* (2 vols, Hakluyt Society, 2nd ser., 136–7, Cambridge, 1969)

Bargellini, Clara, 'El barroco en Latinoamérica', in John H. Elliott (ed.), *Europa/América* (El País, Madrid, 1992)

Barnes, Viola Florence, *The Dominion of New England* (New Haven, 1923)

Barrett, Ward, *The Sugar Hacienda of the Marqueses del Valle* (Minneapolis, 1970)

Barrett, Ward, 'World Bullion Flows, 1450–1800', in James D. Tracy (ed.), *The Rise of Merchant Empires. Long-Distance Trade in the Early Modern World, 1350–1750* (Cambridge, 1990)

Barrios Pintado, Feliciano (ed.), *Derecho y administración pública en las Indias hispánicas* (2 vols, Cuenca, 2002)

Barrow, Thomas C., *Trade and Empire. The British Customs Service in Colonial America, 1660–1775* (Cambridge, MA, 1967)

Bataillon, Marcel, *Études sur Bartolomé de Las Casas* (Paris, 1965)

Baudot, Georges, *Utopía e historia en México. Los primeros cronistas de la civilización mexicana (1520–1569)* (Madrid, 1983)

Bauer, Arnold J., 'Iglesia, economía y estado en la historia de América Latina', in Ma. del Pilar Martínez López-Cano (ed.), *Iglesia, estado y economía. Siglos XVI y XVII* (Mexico City, 1995)

Bauer, Arnold J., *Goods, Power, History. Latin America's Material Culture* (Cambridge, 2001)

Bauer, Ralph, *The Cultural Geography of Colonial American Literatures* (Cambridge, 2003)

Bédouelle, Guy, 'La Donation alexandrine et le traité de Tordesillas', in *1492. Le Choc des deux mondes* (Actes du Colloque international organisé par la Commission Nationale Suisse pour l'UNESCO, Geneva, 1992)

Beeman, Richard R., 'Labor Forces and Race Relations: A Comparative View of the Colonization of Brazil and Virginia', *Political Science Quarterly*, 86 (1971), pp. 609–36

Beeman, Richard R., *The Varieties of Political Experience in Eighteenth-Century America* (Philadelphia, 2004)

Beeman, Richard R., and Isaac, Rhys, 'Cultural Conflict and Social Change in the Revolutionary South: Lunenburg County, Virginia', *The Journal of Southern History*, 46 (1980), pp. 525–50

Belgrano, Manuel, *Autobiografía y otras páginas* (Buenos Aires, 1966)

Bennassar, Bartolomé, *Recherches sur les grandes épidémies dans le nord de l'Espagne à la fin du XVIe siècle* (Paris, 1969)

Bennett, Herman L., *Africans in Colonial Mexico. Absolutism, Christianity, and Afro-Creole Consciousness, 1570–1640* (Bloomington, IN and Indianapolis, 2003)

Benson, Nettie Lee (ed.), *Mexico and the Spanish Cortes, 1810–1822* (Austin, TX and London, 1966)

Benton, Lauren, *Law and Colonial Cultures. Legal Regimes in World History, 1400–1900* (Cambridge, 2002)

Bercovitch, Sacvan, *The Puritan Origins of the American Self* (New Haven and London, 1975)

Bercovitch, Sacvan, *The American Jeremiad* (Madison, WI, 1978)

Bercovitch, Sacvan, 'The Winthrop Variation: a Model of American Identity', *Proceedings of the British Academy*, 97 (1997), pp. 75–94

Berg, Maxine, *Luxury and Pleasure in Eighteenth-Century Britain* (Oxford, 2005)

Berlin, Ira, *Many Thousands Gone. The First Two Centuries of Slavery in North America* (Cambridge, Mass., 1998)

Bernal, Antonio-Miguel, *La financiación de la Carrera de Indias, 1492–1824* (Seville and Madrid, 1992)

Bernand, Carmen, *Negros esclavos y libres en las ciudades hispanoamericanas* (2nd edn, Madrid, 2001)

Bernand, Carmen and Gruzinski, Serge, *Histoire du nouveau monde* (2 vols, Paris, 1991–3), vol. 2 (*Les Métissages, 1550–1640*)

Bernardini, Paolo, and Fiering, Norman (eds), *The Jews and the Expansion of Europe to the West, 1450 to 1800* (New York and Oxford, 2001)

Bernardo Ares, José Manuel de (ed.), *El hispanismo anglonorteamericano* (Actas de la I Conferencia Internacional *Hacia un nuevo humanismo*, 2 vols, Córdoba, 2001)

Bernstein, Harry, *Origins of Inter-American Interest, 1700–1812* (Philadelphia, 1945)

Berry, Charles R., 'The Election of the Mexican Deputies to the Spanish Cortes, 1810–1820', in Nettie Lee Benson (ed.), *Mexico and the Spanish Cortes, 1810–1822* (Austin, TX and London, 1966)

Bethel, Slingsby, *The Interest of Princes and States* (London, 1680)

Beverley, Robert *The History and Present State of Virginia*, ed. Louis B. Wright (Chapel Hill, NC, 1947)

Biermann, Benno M., 'Bartolomé de las Casas and Verapaz', in Juan Friede and Benjamin Keen (eds), *Bartolomé de Las Casas in History* (DeKalb, IL, 1971)

Billings, Warren M., 'The Growth of Political Institutions in Virginia, 1634–1676', *WMQ*, 3rd ser., 31 (1974), pp. 225–42

Billings, Warren M., *The Old Dominion in the Seventeenth Century. A Documentary History of Virginia, 1606–1689* (Chapel Hill, NC, 1975)

Billings, Warren M., 'The Transfer of English Law to Virginia, 1606–1650', in K. R. Andrews, N. P. Canny, and P. E. H. Hair (eds), *The Westward Enterprise. English Activities in Ireland, the Atlantic and America 1480–1650* (Liverpool, 1978)

Billings, Warren M., *Sir William Berkeley and the Forging of Colonial Virginia* (Baton Rouge, LA, 2004)

Billington, Ray Allen, 'The American Frontier', in Paul Bohannen and Fred Plog (eds), *Beyond the Frontier. Social Process and Cultural Change* (Garden City, New York, 1967), pp. 3–24

Biraben, J. N., 'La Population de l'Amérique précolombienne. Essai sur les méthodes', *Conferencia Internationale. El poblamiento de las Américas*, Vera Cruz, 18–23 May 1992 (Institut National d'Études Démographiques, Paris, 1992)

Bishko, Charles Julian, 'The Peninsular Background of Latin American Cattle Ranching', *HAHR*, 32 (1952), pp. 491–515

Blackburn, Robin, *The Making of New World Slavery. From the Baroque to the Modern, 1492–1800* (London, 1997)

Bliss, Robert M., *Revolution and Empire. English Politics and the American Colonies in the Seventeenth Century* (Manchester and New York, 1990)

Bloch, Ruth H., *Visionary Republic. Millennial Themes in American Thought, 1756–1800* (Cambridge, 1985)

Boccara, Guillaume, and Galindo, Sylvia (eds), *Lógica mestiza en América* (Temuco, Chile, 1999)

Bodle, Wayne, 'Themes and Directions in Middle Colonies Historiography, 1980–1994', *WMQ*, 3rd ser., 51 (1994), pp. 355–88

Bolland, O. Nigel, 'Colonization and Slavery in Central America', in Paul E. Lovejoy and Nicholas Rogers (eds), *Unfree Labour in the Development of the Atlantic World* (Ilford, 1994)

Bolton, Herbert E., 'The Epic of Greater America', reprinted in Bolton, Herbert E., *Wider Horizons of American History* (New York, 1939; repr. Notre Dame, IL, 1967)

Bonomi, Patricia U., *A Factious People. Politics and Society in Colonial New York* (New York and London, 1971)

Bonomi, Patricia U., *Under the Cope of Heaven. Religion, Society and Politics in Colonial America* (New York, 1986)

Bonomi, Patricia U., *The Lord Cornbury Scandal. The Politics of Reputation in British America* (Chapel Hill, NC and London, 1988)

Borah, Woodrow, *New Spain's Century of Depression* (Berkeley and Los Angeles, 1951)

Borah, Woodrow, *Early Colonial Trade and Navigation between Mexico and Peru* (Berkeley and Los Angeles, 1954)

Borah, Woodrow, 'Representative Institutions in the Spanish Empire in the Sixteenth Century', *The Americas*, 12 (1956), pp. 246–57

Borah, Woodrow, *Justice by Insurance. The General Indian Court of Colonial Mexico and the Legal Aides of the Half-Real* (Berkeley, Los Angeles, London, 1983)

Bowser, Frederick P., *The African Slave in Colonial Peru, 1524–1650* (Stanford, CA, 1974)

Boyajian, James C., *Portuguese Bankers at the Court of Spain, 1626–1650* (New Brunswick, NJ, 1983)

Boyd, Julian P., *Anglo-American Union. Joseph Galloway's Plans to Preserve the British Empire, 1774–1788* (Philadelphia, 1941)

Boyd-Bowman, Peter, *Índice geobiográfico de cuarenta mil pobladores españoles de América en el siglo XVI* (2 vols, Bogotá, 1964; Mexico City, 1968)

Boyd-Bowman, Peter, *Léxico hispanoamericano del siglo XVI* (London, 1971)

Bradford, William, *Of Plymouth Plantation, 1620–1647*, ed. Samuel Eliot Morison (New York, 1952)

Brading, D.A. *Miners and Merchants in Bourbon Mexico, 1763–1810* (Cambridge, 1971)

Brading, D.A., *Haciendas and Ranchos in the Mexican Bajío: León 1700–1860* (Cambridge, 1978)

Brading, D.A., *The First America. The Spanish Monarchy and the Liberal State, 1492–1867* (Cambridge, 1991)

Brading, D.A., *Church and State in Bourbon Mexico. The Diocese of Michoacán, 1749–1810* (Cambridge, 1994)

Brading, D.A., *Mexican Phoenix. Our Lady of Guadalupe: Image and Tradition Across Five Centuries* (Cambridge, 2001)

Brading, D.A., *et al.*, *Cinco miradas británicas a la historia de México* (Mexico City, 2000)

Bradley, Peter T., *Society, Economy and Defence in Seventeenth-Century Peru. The Administration of the Count Alba de Liste, 1655–61* (Liverpool, 1992)

Bradley, Peter T., 'El Perú y el mundo exterior. Extranjeros, enemigos y herejes (siglos XVI–XVII)', *Revista de Indias*, 61 (2001), pp. 651–71

Bradley, Peter T., and Cahill, David, *Habsburg Peru. Images, Imagination and Memory* (Liverpool, 2000)

Bray, Warwick (ed.), *The Meeting of Two Worlds. Europe and the Americas 1492–1650* (Proceedings of the British Academy, 81, Oxford, 1993)

Breen, T.H., *The Character of the Good Ruler. Puritan Political Ideas in New England, 1630–1730* (New Haven, 1970)

Breen, T. H., 'English Origins and New World Development: the Case of the Covenanted Militia in Seventeenth-Century Massachusetts', *Past and Present*, 57 (1972), pp. 74–96

Breen, T. H., *Puritans and Adventurers. Change and Persistence in Early America* (New York and Oxford, 1980)

Breen, T. H., 'The Culture of Agriculture: the Symbolic World of the Tidewater Planter, 1760–1790', in David D. Hall, John M. Murrin, Thad W. Tate (eds), *Saints and Revolutionaries. Essays on Early American History* (New York and London, 1984)

Breen, T. H., *Tobacco Culture. The Mentality of the Great Tidewater Planters on the Eve of Revolution* (Princeton, 1985)

Breen, T. H. '"Baubles of Britain": The American and Consumer Revolutions of the Eighteenth Century', *Past and Present*, 119 (1988), pp. 73–104

Breen, T. H., *Imagining the Past. East Hampton Histories* (Reading, MA, 1989)

Breen, T. H., 'Ideology and Nationalism on the Eve of the American Revolution: Revisions Once More in Need of Revising', *Journal of American History*, 84 (1997), pp. 13–39

Breen, T. H., *The Marketplace of Revolution. How Consumer Politics Shaped American Independence* (Oxford and New York, 2004)

Breen, T. H., and Hall, Timothy, 'Structuring Provincial Imagination: the Rhetoric and Experience of Social Change in Eighteenth-Century New England', *AHR*, 103 (1998), pp. 1411–39

Bremer, Francis J., *John Winthrop. America's Forgotten Founding Father* (Oxford, 2003)

Breslaw, Elaine, *Tituba, Reluctant Witch of Salem* (New York and London, 1996)

Brewer, Holly, 'Entailing Aristocracy in Colonial Virginia: "Ancient Feudal Restraints" and Revolutionary Reform', *WMQ*, 3rd ser., 54 (1997), pp. 307–46

Brewer, John, and Porter, Roy, *Consumption and the World of Goods* (London, 1993)

Bridenbaugh, Carl, *Cities in the Wilderness. The First Century of Urban Life in America, 1625–1742* (1939; repr. Oxford, London, New York, 1971)

Bridenbaugh, Carl, *Jamestown, 1544–1699* (New York and Oxford, 1989)

Brigham, Clarence S. (ed.), *British Royal Proclamations Relating to America, 1603–1763* (American Antiquarian Society, *Transactions and Collections*, XII, Worcester, MA, 1911)

Brooks, James F., *Captives and Cousins. Slavery, Kinship and Community in the Southwest Borderlands* (Chapel Hill, NC and London, 2002)

Brown, Alexander, *The Genesis of the United States* (2 vols, London, 1890)

Brown, John Nicholas, *Urbanism in the American Colonies* (Providence, RI, 1976)

Brown, Kathleen M., *Good Wives, Nasty Wenches, and Anxious Patriarchs* (Chapel Hill, NC and London, 1996)

Bullion, John L., '"The Ten Thousand in America": More Light on the Decision on the American Army, 1762–1763', *WMQ*, 3rd ser., 43 (1986), pp. 646–57

Bullion, John L., 'British Ministers and American Resistance to the Stamp Act, October–December 1765', *WMQ*, 3rd ser., 49 (1992), pp. 89–107

Bumsted, J. M., '"Things in the Womb of Time": Ideas of American Independence, 1633 to 1763', *WMQ*, 3rd ser., 31 (1974), pp. 533–64

Bunes Ibarra, Miguel Angel de, *La imagen de los musulmanes y del norte de Africa en la España de los siglos XVI y XVII* (Madrid, 1989)

Burke, Peter, Harrison, Brian, and Slack, Paul (eds), *Civil Histories. Essays Presented to Sir Keith Thomas* (Oxford, 2000)

Burke, William, *An Account of the European Settlements in America* (1757; 6th edn, London, 1777)

Burkholder, Mark A., 'From Creole to *Peninsular*: the Transformation of the Audiencia of Lima', *HAHR*, 52 (1972), pp. 395–415

Burkholder, Mark A., 'Bureaucrats', in Louisa Schell Hoberman and Susan Migden Socolow (eds), *Cities and Society in Colonial Latin America* (Albuquerque, NM, 1986)

Burkholder, Mark A., and Chandler, D. S. , *From Impotence to Authority. The Spanish Crown and the American Audiencias, 1687–1808* (Columbia, MO, 1977)

Burnard, Trevor, *Mastery, Tyranny, and Desire. Thomas Thistlewood and his Slaves in the Anglo-Jamaican World* (Chapel Hill, NC, 2004)

Burns, Kathryn, *Colonial Habits. Convents and the Spiritual Economy of Cuzco, Peru* (Durham, NC and London, 1999)

Bushman, Richard L., *King and People in Provincial Massachusetts* (Chapel Hill, NC and London, 1985)

Bushman, Richard L., *The Refinement of America* (New York, 1992)

Butler, Jon, '"Gospel Order Improved": the Keithian Schism and the Exercise of Quaker Ministerial Authority in Pennsylvania', *WMQ*, 3rd ser., 31 (1974), pp. 431–52

Butler, Jon, *Awash in a Sea of Faith* (Cambridge, MA and London, 1990)

Butler, Jon, *Becoming America. The Revolution before 1776* (Cambridge, MA, and London, 2000)

Cabeza de Vaca, Alvar Núñez, *see under* Núñez Cabeza de Vaca, Alvar

Cahill, David, *From Rebellion to Independence in the Andes. Soundings from Southern Peru, 1750–1830* (CEDLA Latin American Studies, 89, Amsterdam, 2002)

Calloway, Colin G. *The American Revolution in Indian Country* (Cambridge, 1995)

Calloway, Colin G. and Salisbury, Neal (eds), *Reinterpreting New England Indians and the Colonial Experience* (Boston, 2003)

The Cambridge History of Latin America, ed. Leslie Bethell (11 vols, Cambridge, 1984–95)

Campbell, James, *A Concise History of the Spanish America* (London, 1741; facsimile edn, Folkestone and London, 1972)

Campillo y Cosío, Joseph del, *Nuevo sistema del gobierno económico para la América* (2nd edn, Mérida, Venezuela, 1971)

Cañeque, Alejandro, *The King's Living Image. The Culture and Politics of Viceregal Power in Colonial Mexico* (New York and London, 2004)

Cañizares-Esguerra, Jorge, 'New World, New Stars: Patriotic Astrology and the Invention of Indian and Creole Bodies in Colonial Spanish America, 1600–1650', *AHR*, 104 (1999), pp. 33–68

Cañizares-Esguerra, Jorge, *How to Write the History of the New World. Histories, Epistemologies, and Identities in the Eighteenth-Century Atlantic World* (Stanford, CA, 2001)

Canny, Nicholas, *The Elizabethan Conquest of Ireland. A Pattern Established* (New York, 1976)

Canny, Nicholas, *Kingdom and Colony. Ireland in the Atlantic World, 1560–1800* (Baltimore, 1988)

Canny, Nicholas (ed.), *Europeans on the Move. Studies on European Migration, 1500–1800* (Oxford, 1994)

Canny, Nicholas, and Pagden, Anthony (eds), *Colonial Identity in the Atlantic World, 1500–1800* (Princeton, NJ, 1987)

Canup, John, 'Cotton Mather and "Creolian Degeneracy"', *Early American Literature*, 24 (1989), pp. 20–34

Canup, John, *Out of the Wilderness. The Emergence of an American Identity in Colonial New England* (Middletown, CT, 1990)

Cardaillac, Louis, and Peregrina, Angélica (eds), *Ensayos en homenaje a José María Muriá* (Zapopan, 2002)

Cárdenas, Juan de, *Problemas y secretos maravillosos de las Indias* (1591; facsimile edn, Madrid, 1945)

Careri, Giovanni Francesco Gemelli, *Viaje a la Nueva España*, ed. Francisca Perujo (Mexico City, 1976)

Carlos III y la Ilustración (2 vols, Madrid and Barcelona, 1989)

Carmagnani, Marcello, 'Colonial Latin American Demography: Growth of Chilean Population, 1700–1830', *Journal of Social History*, 1 (1967–8), pp. 179–91

Carr, Lois Green, and Menard, Russell R., 'Immigration and Opportunity: the Freedman in Early Colonial Maryland', in Thad W. Tate and David L. Ammerman (eds), *The Chesapeake in the Seventeenth Century* (New York and London, 1979)

Carr, Raymond, *Spain, 1808–1939* (Oxford, 1966)

Carrera Stampa, Manuel, *Los gremios mexicanos* (Mexico City, 1954)

Carroll, Peter N., *Puritanism and the Wilderness* (New York and London, 1969)

Carson, Cary, Hoffman, Ronald, and Albert, Peter J. (eds), *Of Consuming Interests. The Style of Life in the Eighteenth Century* (Charlottesville, VA and London, 1994)

Carzolio, María Inés, 'En los orígenes de la ciudadanía en Castilla. La identidad política del vecino durante los siglos XVI y XVII', *Hispania*, 62 (2002), pp. 637–92

Casey, James, *Early Modern Spain. A Social History* (London and New York, 1999)

Castañeda, Carmen, *Círculos de poder en la Nueva España* (Mexico City, 1998)

Castillo Gómez, Antonio (ed.), *Libro y lectura en la península ibérica y América* (Junta de Castilla y León, Salamanca, 2003)

Cavillac, Michel, *Gueux et marchands dans le 'Guzmán de Alfarache', 1599–1604* (Bordeaux, 1993)

Cervantes, Fernando, 'The Devils of Querétaro: Scepticism and Credulity in Late Seventeenth-Century Mexico', *Past and Present*, 130 (1991), pp. 51–69

Cervantes, Fernando, *The Devil in the New World. The Impact of Diabolism in New Spain* (New Haven and London, 1994)

Cervantes de Salazar, Francisco, *México en 1554 y el túmulo imperial*, ed. Edmundo O'Gorman (Mexico City, 1963)

Céspedes del Castillo, Guillermo, *La avería en el comercio de Indias* (Seville, 1945)

Céspedes del Castillo, Guillermo, *Lima y Buenos Aires. Repercusiones económicas y políticas de la creación del virreinato del Plata* (Seville, 1947)

Céspedes del Castillo, Guillermo, *América hispánica, 1492–1898* (*Historia de España*, ed. Manuel Tuñón de Lara, vol. 6, Barcelona, 1983)

Céspedes del Castillo, Guillermo, *El tabaco en Nueva España* (Madrid, 1992)

Céspedes del Castillo, Guillermo, *Ensayos sobre los reinos castellanos de Indias* (Madrid, 1999)

Chamberlain, Robert S., *The Conquest and Colonization of Yucatán, 1517–1550* (Washington, 1948)

Chapin, Howard Millar, *Roger Williams and the King's Colors* (Providence, RI, 1928)

Chaplin, Joyce E., *Subject Matter. Technology, the Body, and Science on the Anglo-American Frontier, 1500–1676* (Cambridge, MA, and London, 2001)

Chaplin, Joyce E., 'Enslavement of Indians in Early America. Captivity Without the Narrative', in Elizabeth Mancke and Carole Shammas (eds), *The Creation of the Atlantic World* (Baltimore, 2005)

Chapman, George, *Eastward Ho* (1605; repr. in Thomas Marc Parrott (ed.), *The Plays and Poems of George Chapman. The Comedies*, London, 1914)

Chaunu, Pierre, *L'Amérique et les Amériques* (Paris, 1964)

Chaunu, Pierre, *Conquête et exploitation des nouveaux mondes* (Paris, 1969)

Chaunu, Huguette and Pierre, *Séville et l'Atlantique, 1504–1650* (8 vols, Paris, 1955–9)

Chávez, Thomas E., *Spain and the Independence of the United States. An Intrinsic Gift* (Albuquerque, NM, 2003)

Chevalier, François, *La Formation des grands domaines au Mexique* (Paris, 1952). Eng. trans., *Land and Society in Colonial Mexico. The Great Hacienda* (Berkeley and Los Angeles, 1966)

Chiappelli, Fredi (ed.), *First Images of America* (2 vols, Berkeley, Los Angeles, London, 1976)

Child, Sir Josiah, *A New Discourse of Trade* (London, 1693)

Chipman, Donald E., *Spanish Texas, 1591–1821* (Austin, TX, 1992)

Chrisman, Miriam Usher (ed.), *Social Groups and Religious Ideas in the Sixteenth Century* (Studies in Medieval Culture, XIII, The Medieval Institute, Western Michigan University, Kalamazoo, MI, 1978)

Christian, Jr., William A., *Local Religion in Sixteenth-Century Spain* (Princeton, 1981)

Chust, Manuel, *La cuestión nacional americana en las Cortes de Cádiz* (Valencia, 1999)

Clark, J .D. G., *The Language of Liberty, 1660–1832* (Cambridge, 1994)

Clark, Peter, *British Clubs and Societies, 1580–1800* (Oxford, 2000)

Clark, Stuart, *Thinking with Demons. The Idea of Witchcraft in Early Modern Europe* (Oxford, 1997)

Clay, Henry, *The Papers of Henry Clay*, 11 vols, ed. James F. Hopkins (Lexington, KY, 1959–92)

Clavero, Bartolomé, *Derecho de los reinos* (Seville, 1977)

Clavijero, Francisco Javier, *Historia antigua de México*, ed. Mariano Cuevas (4 vols, 2nd edn, Mexico City, 1958–9)

Clendinnen, Inga, *Ambivalent Conquests. Maya and Spaniard in Yucatan, 1517–1570* (Cambridge, 1987)

Clendinnen, Inga, 'Ways to the Sacred: Reconstructing "Religion" in Sixteenth-Century Mexico', *History and Anthropology*, 5 (1990), pp. 105–41

Cline, Howard F., 'The Relaciones Geográficas of the Spanish Indies, 1577–1586', *HAHR*, 44 (1964), pp. 341–74

Coatsworth, John H. , 'Obstacles to Economic Growth in Nineteenth-Century Mexico', *AHR*, 83 (1978), pp. 80–100

Coatsworth, John H., *Los orígenes del atraso. Nueve ensayos de historia económica de México en los siglos XVIII y XIX* (Mexico City, 1990)

Cobb, Gwendolin B., 'Supply and Transportation for the Potosí Mines, 1545–1640', *HAHR*, 29 (1949), pp. 25–45

Cogley, Richard W., *John Eliot's Mission to the Indians before King Philip's War* (Cambridge, MA and London, 1999)

Cohen, Charles L., 'The Post-Puritan Paradigm in Early American Religious History', *WMQ*, 3rd ser., 54 (1997), pp. 695–722

Coke, Roger, *A Discourse of Trade* (London, 1670)

Colley, Linda, *Britons. Forging the Nation 1707–1837* (New Haven and London, 1992)

Colley, Linda, *Captives. Britain, Empire and the World, 1600–1850* (London, 2002)

Collier, Simon, *Ideas and Politics of Chilean Independence, 1808–1833* (Cambridge, 1967)

Colón, Cristóbal, *Textos y documentos completos*, ed. Consuelo Varela (2nd edn, Madrid, 1992)

Columbus, Christopher, *Journal of the First Voyage*, ed. and trans. B.W. Ife (Warminster, 1990)

El Consejo de Indias en el siglo XVI (Valladolid, 1970)

Conway, Stephen, 'From Fellow-Nationals to Foreigners: British Perceptions of the Americans, circa 1739–1783', *WMQ,*, 3rd ser., 59 (2002), pp. 65–100

Cook, Alexandra Parma, and Cook, Noble David, *Good Faith and Truthful Ignorance. A Case of Transatlantic Bigamy* (Durham, NC and London, 1991)

Cook, Noble David, *Born to Die. Disease and New World Conquest, 1492–1650* (Cambridge, 1998)

Cope, R. Douglas, *The Limits of Racial Domination. Plebeian Society in Colonial Mexico City, 1660–1720* (Madison, WI, 1994)

Corominas, Pedro, *El sentimiento de la riqueza en Castilla* (Madrid, 1917)

Cortés, Hernán, *Cartas y documentos,* ed. Mario Sánchez-Barba (Mexico City, 1963)

Cortés, Hernán, *Letters from Mexico*, trans. and ed. Anthony Pagden (New Haven and London, 1986)

Cosgrove, A. (ed.), *Marriage in Ireland* (Dublin, 1985)

Costeloe, Michael P., *Response to Revolution. Imperial Spain and the Spanish American Revolutions, 1810–1840* (Cambridge, 1986)

Countryman, Edward, *The American Revolution* (Harmondsworth, 1985)

Covarrubias, Sebastián de, *Tesoro de la lengua castellana o española* (facsimile edn, ed. Martín de Riquer, Barcelona, 1987)

Crane, Verner W., *The Southern Frontier 1670–1732* (Durham, NC, 1928; repr. New York, 1978)

Craton, Michael, 'Reluctant Creoles. The Planters' World in the British West Indies', in Bernard Bailyn and Philip D. Morgan (eds), *Strangers Within the Realm. Cultural Margins of the First British Empire* (Chapel Hill, NC, 1991)

Craven, Wesley Frank, *Dissolution of the Virginia Company. The Failure of a Colonial Experiment* (New York, 1932)

Craven, Wesley Frank, 'Indian Policy in Early Virginia', *WMQ*, 3rd ser., 1 (1944), pp. 65–82

Craven, Wesley Frank, *The Southern Colonies in the Seventeenth Century* (Baton Rouge, LA, 1949)

Craven, Wesley Frank, *White, Red and Black. The Seventeenth-Century Virginian* (Charlottesville, VA, 1971)

Cressy, David, *Coming Over. Migration and Communication between England and New England in the Seventeenth Century* (Cambridge, 1987)

Cronon, William, *Changes in the Land. Indians, Colonists, and the Ecology of New England* (New York, 1983)

Crowley, John E., 'A Visual Empire. Seeing the Atlantic World from a Global British Perspective', in Elizabeth Mancke and Carole Shammas (eds), *The Creation of the Atlantic World* (Baltimore, 2005)

Curtin, Philip D., *The Atlantic Slave Trade. A Census* (Madison, WI, 1969)

Curtin, Philip D., *The Rise and Fall of the Plantation Complex. Essays in Atlantic History* (Cambridge, 1990)

Daniels, Christine, ' "Liberty to Complaine". Servant Petitions in Maryland, 1652–1797', in Christopher L. Tomlins and Bruce T. Mann (eds), *The Many Legalities of Early America* (Chapel Hill, NC and London, 2001)

Daniels, Christine, and Kennedy, Michael N. (eds), *Negotiated Empires. Centers and Peripheries in the Americas, 1500–1820* (London, 2002)

Daniels, John D., 'The Indian Population of North America in 1492', *WMQ*, 3rd ser., 49 (1992), pp. 298–320

Darwin, John, 'Civility and Empire', in Peter Burke, Brian Harrison and Paul Slack (eds), *Civil Histories. Essays Presented to Sir Keith Thomas* (Oxford, 2000)

Davies, C. S. L., 'Slavery and Protector Somerset: the Vagrancy Act of 1547', *Economic History Review*, 2nd ser., 19 (1966), pp. 533–49

Davies, R. R., *The First English Empire. Power and Identities in the British Isles, 1093–1343* (Oxford, 2000)

Davis, David Brion, *The Problem of Slavery in Western Culture* (London, 1970)

Dawes, Norman H., 'Titles as Symbols of Prestige in Seventeenth-Century New England', *WMQ*, 3rd ser., 6 (1949), pp. 69–83

Deagan, Kathleen and Cruxent, José María, *Columbus's Outpost among the Taínos. Spain and America at La Isabela, 1492–1498* (New Haven and London, 2002)

Deive, Carlos Esteban, *La Española en la esclavitud del indio* (Santo Domingo, 1995)

Demos, John, *A Little Commonwealth. Family Life in Plymouth Colony* (London, Oxford, New York, 1970)

Demos, John Putnam, *Entertaining Satan. Witchcraft and the Culture of Early New England* (New York and Oxford, 1982)

Demos, John, *The Unredeemed Captive* (1994; New York, 1995)

Díaz del Castillo, Bernal, *Historia verdadera de la conquista de la Nueva España*, ed. Joaquín Ramírez Cabañas (3 vols, Mexico City, 1944)

Diccionario de autoridades (Madrid, 1726; facsimile edn, 3 vols, Real Academia Española, Madrid, 1969)

Doerflinger, Thomas M., *A Vigorous Spirit of Enterprise. Merchants and Economic Development in Revolutionary Philadelphia* (Chapel Hill, NC and London, 1986)

Domínguez Ortiz, Antonio, *Los extranjeros en la vida española durante el siglo XVII y otros artículos* (Seville, 1996)

Domínguez Ortiz, Antonio, *La sociedad americana y la corona española en el siglo XVII* (Madrid, 1996)

Dorantes de Carranza, Baltasar de, *Sumaria relación de las cosas de la Nueva España* (1604; ed. Ernesto de la Torre Villar, Mexico City, 1987)

Dowd, Gregory Evans, *War under Heaven. Pontiac, the Indian Nations and the British Empire* (Baltimore and London, 2002)

Draper, Theodore, *A Struggle for Power. The American Revolution* (London, 1996)

Drayton, Richard, *Nature's Government. Science, Imperial Britain, and the 'Improvement' of the World* (New Haven and London, 2000)

Dunn, John, 'The Politics of Locke in England and America in the Eighteenth Century', in John W. Youlton (ed.), *John Locke. Problems and Perspectives* (Cambridge, 1969)

Dunn, Mary Maples, *William Penn, Politics and Conscience* (Princeton, 1967)

Dunn, Richard S., *Puritans and Yankees. The Winthrop Dynasty of New England, 1630–1717* (Princeton, 1962)

Dunn, Richard S., *Sugar and Slaves. The Rise of the Planter Class in the English West Indies, 1624–1713* (New York, 1972)

Dunn, Richard S. and Dunn, Mary Maples (eds), *The Papers of William Penn* (5 vols, Philadelphia, 1981–6)

Dunn, Richard S., 'Servants and Slaves: the Recruitment and Employment of Labor', in Jack P. Greene and J. R. Pole (eds), *Colonial British America. Essays in the History of the Early Modern Era* (Baltimore and London, 1984)

Dunn, Richard S. and Dunn, Mary Maples (eds), *The World of William Penn* (Philadelphia, 1986)

Dunn, Richard S., Savage, James, and Yeandle, Laetitia (eds), *The Journal of John Winthrop 1630–1649* (Cambridge, MA and London, 1996)

Durán, Fray Diego, *Book of the Gods and Rites, and the Ancient Calendar*, trans. and ed. by Fernando Horcasitas and Doris Heyden (Norman, OK, 1971)

Durand, José, *La transformación social del conquistador* (2 vols, Mexico City, 1953)

Dusenberry, William H., *The Mexican Mesta* (Urbana, IL, 1963)

Dussel, Enrique, *Les Évêques hispano-américains. Défenseurs et évangélisateurs de l'Indien, 1504–1620* (Wiesbaden, 1970)

Duviols, Pierre, *La Lutte contre les religions autochtones dans le Pérou colonial* (Lima, 1971)

Eburne, Richard, *A Plain Pathway to Plantations* (1624), ed. Louis B. Wright (Ithaca, NY, 1962)

Echevarria, Durand, *Mirage in the West. A History of the French Image of American Society to 1815* (1957; 2nd edn, Princeton, 1968)

Egido, Teófanes (ed.), *Los jesuitas en España y en el mundo hispánico* (Madrid, 2004)

Egnal, Marc, 'The Economic Development of the Thirteen Colonies, 1720 to 1775', *WMQ*, 3rd ser. (1975), pp. 191–222

Eiras Roel, Antonio (ed.), *La emigración española a Ultramar, 1492–1914* (Madrid, 1991)

Ekirch, A. Roger, *Bound for America. The Transportation of British Convicts to the Colonies, 1718–1775* (Oxford, 1987)

Elkins, Stanley J., and McKitrick, Eric, *The Age of Federalism* (Oxford, 1993)

Elliott, John H., *Imperial Spain, 1469–1716* (1963; repr. London, 2002)

Elliott, John H., *The Old World and the New, 1492–1650* (Cambridge, 1970; repr. 1992)

Elliott, John H., 'Cortés, Velázquez and Charles V', in Hernán Cortés, *Letters from Mexico*, trans. and ed. Anthony Pagden (New Haven and London, 1986)

Elliott, John H., *The Count-Duke of Olivares. The Statesman in an Age of Decline* (New Haven and London, 1986)

Elliott, John H., *Spain and its World, 1500–1700* (New Haven and London, 1989)

Elliott, John H., 'A Europe of Composite Monarchies', *Past and Present*, 137 (1992), pp. 48–71

Elliott, John H., *Illusion and Disillusionment. Spain and the Indies* (The Creighton Lecture for 1991, University of London, 1992)

Elliott, John H., 'Going Baroque', *New York Review of Books* (20 October 1994).

Elliott, John H., 'Comparative History', in Carlos Barra (ed.), *Historia a debate* (3 vols, Santiago de Compostela, 1995), vol. 3

Elliott, John H., *Do the Americas Have a Common History? An Address* (The John Carter Brown Library, Providence, RI, 1998)

Elliott, John H., 'Mundos parecidos, mundos distintos', *Mélanges de la Casa de Velázquez*, 34 (2004), pp. 293–311

Elliott, John H. (ed.), *Europa/América* (El País, Madrid, 1992)

Ellis, Joseph, *Founding Brothers. The Revolutionary Generation* (London, 2002)

Eltis, David, *The Rise of African Slavery in the Americas* (Cambridge, 2000)

Eltis, David, 'The Volume and Structure of the Transatlantic Slave Trade: a Reassessment', *WMQ*, 3rd ser., 58 (2001), pp. 17–46

Emerson, Everett (ed.), *Letters from New England. The Massachusetts Bay Colony, 1629–1638* (Amherst, MA, 1976)

Engerman, Stanley L., 'British Imperialism in a Mercantilist Age, 1492–1849: Conceptual Issues and Empirical Problems', *Revista de Historia Económica*, 16 (1998), pp. 195–231

Engerman, Stanley L., and Gallman, Robert E. (eds), *The Cambridge Economic History of the United States*, vol. 1, *The Colonial Era* (Cambridge, 1996)

Escandell Bonet, Bartolomé, 'La inquisición española en Indias y las condiciones americanas de su funcionamiento', in *La inquisición* (Ministerio de Cultura, Madrid, 1982)

Esteras Martín, Cristina, 'Acculturation and Innovation in Peruvian Viceregal Silverwork', in Elena Phipps, Johanna Hecht, and Cristina Esteras Martín (eds), *The Colonial Andes. Tapestries and Silverwork, 1530–1830* (Metropolitan Museum of Art, New York, 2004)

Eyzaguirre, Jaime, *Ideario y ruta de la emancipación chilena* (Santiago de Chile, 1957)

Farriss, Nancy M., *Crown and Clergy in Colonial Mexico, 1759–1821* (London, 1968)

Farriss, Nancy M., *Maya Society under Colonial Rule* (Princeton, 1984)

Ferguson, Robert A., *American Enlightenment, 1750–1820* (Cambridge, MA and London, 1997)

Ferguson, Robert A., 'The Commonalities of *Common Sense*', *WMQ*, 3rd ser., 57 (2000), pp. 465–504

Fernández de Oviedo, Gonzalo, *Sumario de la natural historia de las Indias*, ed. José Miranda (Mexico City and Buenos Aires, 1950)

Fernández de Oviedo, Gonzalo, *Historia general y natural de las Indias* (5 vols, BAE, 117–21, Madrid, 1959)

Fernández Durán, Reyes, *Gerónimo de Uztáriz (1670–1732). Una política económica para Felipe V* (Madrid, 1999)

Fernández García, Antonio (ed.), *La constitución de Cádiz (1812) y discurso preliminar a la constitución* (Madrid, 2002)

Fernández-Armesto, Felipe, *The Canary Islands after the Conquest* (Oxford, 1982)

Fernández-Armesto, Felipe, *Before Columbus. Exploration and Colonisation from the Mediterranean to the Atlantic, 1229–1492* (London, 1987)

Fernández-Armesto, Felipe, *The Americas. A Hemispheric History* (New York, 2003)

Fernández-Santamaría, J.A., *The State, War and Peace. Spanish Political Thought in the Renaissance, 1516–1559* (Cambridge, 1977)

Ferry, Robert J., *The Colonial Elite of Early Caracas. Formation and Crisis, 1567–1767* (Berkeley, Los Angeles, London, 1989)

Finley, M. I., 'Colonies – an Attempt at a Typology', *TRHS*, 5th ser., 26 (1976), pp. 167–88

Fischer, David Hackett, *Albion's Seed. Four British Folkways in America* (New York and Oxford, 1989)

Fisher, John R., *The Economic Aspects of Spanish Imperialism in America, 1492–1810* (Liverpool, 1997)

Fisher, John R., *Bourbon Peru, 1750–1824* (Liverpool, 2003)

Fisher, John R., Kuethe, Allan J. and McFarlane, Anthony (eds), *Reform and Insurrection in Bourbon New Granada and Peru* (Baton Rouge, LA and London, 1990)

Fisher, Lillian Estelle, *The Last Inca Revolt, 1780–1783* (Norman, OK, 1966)

Flint, Valerie I. J., *The Imaginative Landscape of Christopher Columbus* (Princeton, 1992)

Flor, Fernando R. de la, *La península metafísica. Arte, literatura y pensamiento en la España de la Contrarreforma* (Madrid, 1999)

Flores Galindo, Alberto, *Buscando un Inca* (Lima, 1988)

Flores Galindo, Alberto, 'La revolución tupamarista y el imperio español', in Massimo Ganci and Ruggiero Romano (eds), *Governare il mondo. L'impero spagnolo dal XV al XIX secolo* (Palermo, 1991)

Florescano, Enrique, *Memoria mexicana* (2nd edn, Mexico City, 1995)

Florescano, Enrique, *Etnia, estado y nación. Ensayo sobre las identidades colectivas en México* (Mexico City, 1997)

Florescano, Enrique, *La bandera mexicana. Breve historia de su formación y simbolismo* (Mexico City, 1998)

Floud, Roderick, and Johnson, Paul (eds), *The Cambridge Economic History of Modern Britain* (Cambridge, 2004)

Foner, Eric, *Tom Paine and Revolutionary America* (1976; updated edn, New York and Oxford, 2005)

Fontana, Josep, *La quiebra de la monarquía absoluta, 1814–1820* (Barcelona, 1971)

Fontana, Josep, and Bernal, Antonio Miguel (eds), *El comercio libre entre España y América Latina, 1765–1824* (Madrid, 1987)

Force, Peter, *Tracts and Other Papers Relating Principally to the Origin, Settlement and Progress of the Colonies in North America* (4 vols, Washington, 1836–46)

Foster, George M., *Culture and Conquest. America's Spanish Heritage* (Chicago, 1960)

Fradera, Josep M., *Gobernar colonias* (Barcelona, 1999)

Frankl, Víctor, 'Hernán Cortés y la tradición de las Siete Partidas', *Revista de historia de América*, 53–4 (1962), pp. 9–74

Fraser, Valerie, *The Architecture of Conquest. Building in the Viceroyalty of Peru 1535–1635* (Cambridge, 1990)

Frederickson, George M., 'Comparative History', in Michael Kammen (ed.), *The Past Before Us* (New York, 1980)

Friede, Juan, *Los Welser en la conquista de Venezuela* (Caracas, 1961)

Friede, Juan, and Keen, Benjamin (eds), *Bartolomé de Las Casas in History* (DeKalb, IL, 1971)

Gage, Thomas, *Thomas Gage's Travels in the New World*, ed. J. Eric S. Thompson (Norman, OK, 1958)

Galenson, David, *White Servitude in Colonial America* (Cambridge, 1981)

El galeón de Acapulco (exhibition catalogue, Museo Nacional de Historia, Mexico City, 1988)

Los galeones de la plata (exhibition catalogue, Consejo Nacional para la Cultura y las Artes, Mexico City, 1998)

Galí Boadella, Montserrat, *Pedro García Ferrer, un artista aragonés del siglo XVII en la Nueva España* (Teruel, 1996)

Galí Boadella, Montserrat (ed.), *La catedral de Puebla en el arte y en la historia* (Mexico City, 1999)

Gallay, Alan, *The Indian Slave Trade. The Rise of the English Empire in the American South, 1670–1717* (New Haven and London, 2002)

Games, Alison, *Migration and the Origins of the English Atlantic World* (Cambridge, MA and London, 1999)

Ganci, Massimo, and Romano, Ruggiero (eds), *Governare il mondo. L'impero spagnolo dal XV al XIX secolo* (Palermo, 1991)

García, Gregorio, *Orígen de los indios del nuevo mundo, e Yndias Occidentales* (Valencia, 1607)

García Cárcel, Ricardo, *La Leyenda Negra. Historia y opinión* (Madrid, 1992)

García Cárcel, Ricardo, *Felipe V y los españoles. Una visión periférica del problema de España* (Barcelona, 2002)

García Fuentes, Lutgardo, *El comercio español con América, 1650–1700* (Seville, 1980)

García Melero, Luis Ángel, *La independencia de los Estados Unidos de Norteamérica a través de la prensa española* (Madrid, 1977)

García-Baquero González, Antonio, *Cádiz y el Atlántico, 1717–1778* (2 vols, Seville, 1976)

García-Baquero González, Antonio, *Andalucía y la carrera de Indias, 1492–1824* (Seville, 1986)

García-Baquero González, Antonio, 'Las remesas de metales preciosos americanos en el siglo XVIII: una aritmética controvertida', *Hispania*, 192 (1996), pp. 203–66

García-Gallo, Alfonso, *Los orígenes españoles de las instituciones americanas* (Madrid, 1987)

Garcilaso de la Vega, El Inca, *Comentarios reales de los Incas*, ed. Angel Rosenblat (2 vols, Buenos Aires, 1943; English trans. by H.V. Livermore, 2 vols, Austin, TX, 1966)

Gardyner, George, *A Description of the New World* (London, 1651)

Garner, Richard L., 'Long-Term Silver Mining Trends in Spanish America. A Comparative Analysis of Peru and Mexico', *AHR*, 93 (1988), pp. 898–935

Garrett, David T., '"His Majesty's Most Loyal Vassals": the Indian Nobility and Túpac Amaru', *HAHR*, 84 (2004), pp. 575–617

Gerbi, Antonello, *The Dispute of the New World. The History of a Polemic, 1750–1900*, trans. Jeremy Moyle (Pittsburgh, 1973)

Gerbi, Antonello, *Il mito del Perù* (Milan, 1988)

Gerhard, Dietrich, *Old Europe. A Study of Continuity, 1000–1800* (New York, 1981)

Gibson, Charles, *The Aztecs under Spanish Rule* (Stanford, CA, 1964)

Gibson, Charles, *The Black Legend. Anti-Spanish Attitudes in the Old World and the New* (New York, 1971)

Gillespie, Susan D., *The Aztec Kings* (Tucson, AZ, 1989)

Giménez Fernández, Manuel, *Las doctrinas populistas en la independencia de Hispano-América* (Seville, 1947)

Giménez Fernández, Manuel, *Hernán Cortés y la revolución comunera en la Nueva España* (Seville, 1948)

Giménez Fernández, Manuel, *Bartolomé de Las Casas* (2 vols, Seville, 1953–60)

Gleach, Frederic W., *Powhatan's World and Colonial Virginia. A Conflict of Cultures* (Lincoln, NE and London, 1997)

Godber, Richard, *The Devil's Dominion. Magic and Religion in Early New England* (Cambridge, 1992)

Gold, Robert L., *Borderland Empires in Transition. The Triple Nation Transfer of Florida* (Carbondale, IL and Edwardsville, IL, 1969)

Gómara, Francisco López de, *see under* López de Gómara, Francisco

Gomez, Thomas, *L'Envers de l'Eldorado: Économie coloniale et travail indigène dans la Colombie du XVIème siècle* (Toulouse, 1984)

Góngora, Mario, 'Régimen señorial y rural en la Extremadura de la Orden de Santiago en el momento de la emigración a Indias', *Jahrbuch für Geschichte von Staat, Wirtschaft und Gesellschaft Lateinamerikas*, 2 (1965), pp. 1–29

Góngora, Mario, *Studies in the Colonial History of Spanish America* (Cambridge, 1975)

Gonzalbo Aizpuru, Pilar, *Historia de la educación en la época colonial. El mundo indígena* (Mexico City, 1990)

Gonzalbo Aizpuru, Pilar, *Historia de la educación en la época colonial. La educación de los criollos y la vida urbana* (Mexico City, 1990)

González de Cellorigo, Martín, *Memorial de la política necesaria y útil restauración a la república de España* (Valladolid, 1600)

González Sánchez, Carlos Alberto, *Los mundos del libro. Medios de difusión de la cultura occidental en las Indias de los siglos XVI y XVII* (Seville, 1999)

Gould, Eliga H., *The Persistence of Empire. British Political Culture in the Age of the American Revolution* (Chapel Hill, NC and London, 2000)

Gradie, Charlotte M., 'Spanish Jesuits in Virginia. The Mission that Failed', *The Virginia Magazine of History and Biography*, 96 (1988), pp. 131–56

Greenberg, Douglas, 'The Middle Colonies in Recent American Historiography', WMQ, 3rd ser., 36 (1979), pp. 396–427

Greenblatt, Stephen, *Marvelous Possessions. The Wonder of the New World* (Chicago, 1991)

Greene, Jack P., *The Quest for Power. The Lower Houses of Assembly in the Southern Royal Colonies, 1689–1776* (Chapel Hill, NC, 1963)

Greene, Jack P. , 'The Seven Years' War and the American Revolution: the Causal Relationship Reconsidered', in Peter Marshall and Glyn Williams (eds), *The British Atlantic Empire Before the American Revolution* (London, 1980)

Greene, Jack P., *Peripheries and Center. Constitutional Development in the Extended Polities of the British Empire and the United States, 1607–1788* (Athens, GA and London, 1986)

Greene, Jack P., 'Changing Identity in the British Caribbean: Barbados as a Case Study', in Nicholas Canny and Anthony Pagden (eds), *Colonial Identity in the Atlantic World* (Princeton, 1987)

Greene, Jack P., *Pursuits of Happiness. The Social Development of Early Modern British Colonies and the Formation of American Culture* (Chapel Hill, NC and London, 1988)

Greene, Jack P., *Imperatives, Behaviors and Identities. Essays in Early American Cultural History* (Charlottesville, VA and London, 1992)

Greene, Jack P., *Negotiated Authorities. Essays in Colonial Political and Constitutional History* (Charlottesville, VA and London, 1994)

Greene, Jack P., '"By Their Laws Shall Ye Know Them": Law and Identity in Colonial British America', *Journal of Interdisciplinary History*, 33 (2002), pp. 247–60

Greene, Jack P. and Pole, J.R. (eds), *Colonial British America. Essays in the New History of the Early Modern Era* (Baltimore and London, 1984)

Greene, Jack P. and Pole, J. R. (eds), *The Blackwell Encyclopaedia of the American Revolution* (Oxford, 1991)

Greene, Jack P., Mullett, Charles F., and Papenfuse, Edward C. (eds), *Magna Charta for America* (Philadelphia, 1986)

Greenfield, Amy Butler, *A Perfect Red. Empire, Espionage, and the Quest for the Color of Desire* (New York, 2005)

Greven, Philip J., *Four Generations. Population, Land and Family in Colonial Andover, Massachusetts* (Ithaca, NY and London, 1970)

Griffin, Clive, *The Crombergers of Seville. The History of a Printing and Merchant Dynasty* (Oxford, 1988)

Griffiths, Nicholas, *The Cross and the Serpent. Religious Repression and Resurgence in Colonial Peru* (Norman, OK, and London, 1995)

Gross, Robert A., *The Minutemen and their World* (New York, 1981)

Gruzinski, Serge, 'La "segunda aculturación": el estado ilustrado y la religiosidad indígena en Nueva España', *Estudios de historia novohispana*, 8 (1985), pp. 175–201

Gruzinski, Serge, *La Pensée métisse* (Paris, 1999)

Gruzinski, Serge, *Les Quatre Parties du monde. Histoire d'une mondialisation* (Paris, 2004)

Gruzinski, Serge, and Wachtel, Nathan (eds), *Le Nouveau Monde. Mondes nouveaux. L'Expérience américaine* (Paris, 1996)

Guerra, François-Xavier, *Modernidad e independencias. Ensayos sobre las revoluciones hispánicas* (Madrid, 1992)

Guilmartin, John F., 'The Cutting Edge: an Analysis of the Spanish Invasion and Overthrow of the Inca Empire, 1532–1539', in Kenneth J. Andrien and Rolena Adorno (eds), *Transatlantic Encounters. Europeans and Andeans in the Sixteenth Century* (Berkeley, Los Angeles, Oxford, 1991)

Gurrin, L. D. (trans.), 'Shipwrecked Spaniards 1639. Grievances against Bermudans', *The Bermuda Historical Quarterly*, 18 (1961), pp. 13–28

Gutiérrez, Ramón A. , *When Jesus Came, the Corn Mothers Went Away. Marriage, Sexuality, and Power in New Mexico, 1500–1800* (Stanford, CA, 1991)

Gutiérrez de Medina, Cristóbal, *Viaje del Virrey Marqués de Villena*, ed. Manuel Romero de Terreros (Mexico City, 1947)

Guy, Donna J., and Sheridan, Thomas E. (eds), *Contested Ground. Comparative Frontiers on the Northern and Southern Edges of the Spanish Empire* (Tucson, AZ, 1998)

Hagan, Kenneth J., and Roberts, William R. (eds), *Against All Enemies. Interpretations of American Military History from Colonial Times to the Present* (Greenwood Press, Contributions to Military Studies, no. 51, New York, Westport, CT and London, 1986)

Hakluyt, Richard, 'Discourse of Western Planting' (1584) in E. G. R. Taylor, *The Original Writings and Correspondence of the Two Richard Hakluyts* (2 vols, Hakluyt Society, 2nd ser., vols 76–7, London, 1935) vol. 2, pp. 211–326

Hakluyt, Richard, *The Principall Navigations Voiages and Discoveries of the English Nation*, facsimile edn (2 vols, Hakluyt Society, Cambridge, 1965)

Hall, David D., *The Faithful Shepherd. A History of the New England Ministry in the Seventeenth Century* (Chapel Hill, NC, 1972)

Hall, David D., *Worlds of Wonder, Days of Judgment. Popular Religious Beliefs in Early New England* (New York, 1989)

Hall, David D., Murrin, John M., and Tate, Thad W. (eds), *Saints and Revolutionaries. Essays on Early American History* (New York and London, 1984)

Hall, Michael Garibaldi, *Edward Randolph and the American Colonies, 1676–1703* (1960; New York, 1969)

Halperín Donghi, Tulio, *Politics and Society in Argentina in the Revolutionary Period* (Cambridge, 1975)

Hamilton, Earl J., *American Treasure and the Price Revolution in Spain, 1501–1650* (Cambridge, MA, 1934)

Hamilton, Earl J., *War and Prices in Spain, 1651–1800* (Cambridge, MA, 1947)

Hampe Martínez, Teodoro, *Don Pedro de la Gasca. Su obra política en España y América* (Lima, 1989)

Hampe Martínez, Teodoro, *Bibliotecas privadas en el mundo colonial* (Madrid, 1996)

Hancock, David, *Citizens of the World. London Merchants and the Integration of the British Atlantic Community, 1735–1785* (Cambridge, 1995)

Handlin, Oscar and Mary, 'Origins of the Southern Labor System', *WMQ*, 3rd ser., 7 (1950), pp. 199–222

Hanke, Lewis, *The Spanish Struggle for Justice in the Conquest of America* (Philadelphia, 1949)

Hanke, Lewis, *Aristotle and the American Indians* (London, 1959)

Hanke, Lewis, *All Mankind is One* (DeKalb, IL, 1974)

Hanke, Lewis (ed.), *Do the Americas Have a Common History?* (New York, 1964)

Hanke, Lewis (ed.), *Los virreyes españoles en América durante el gobierno de la Casa de Austria. México* (BAE, vols 233–7, Madrid, 1967–8)

Hanke, Lewis (ed.), *Los virreyes españoles en América durante el gobierno de la Casa de Austria. Perú* (BAE vols 280–5, Madrid, 1978–80)

Haring, C. H., *The Spanish Empire in America* (New York, 1947)

Harley, C. Knick, 'Trade, Discovery, Mercantilism and Technology', in Roderick Floud and Paul Johnson (eds), *The Cambridge Economic History of Modern Britain* (Cambridge, 2004)

Harris, F. R., *The Life of Edward Mountague, K.G., First Earl of Sandwich, 1625–1672* (2 vols, London, 1912)

Harth-Terré, Emilio, and Márquez Abanto, Alberto, 'Perspectiva social y económica del artesano virreinal en Lima', *Revista del Archivo Nacional del Perú, 26 (1962)*, pp. 3–96

Hartz, Louis, *The Founding of New Societies* (New York, 1964)

Harvey, Robert, *Liberators. Latin America's Struggle for Independence, 1810–1830* (London, 2000)

Hatfield, April Lee, *Atlantic Virginia. Intercolonial Relations in the Seventeenth Century* (Philadelphia, 2004)

Headley, John M., 'The Habsburg World Empire and the Revival of Ghibellinism', in David Armitage (ed.), *Theories of Empire, 1450–1800* (Aldershot, 1998)

Helgerson, Richard, *Forms of Nationhood. The Elizabethan Writing of England* (Chicago and London, 1992)

Hennessy, Alistair, *The Frontier in Latin American History* (Albuquerque, NM, 1978)

Henretta, James, *'Salutary Neglect'. Colonial Administration Under the Duke of Newcastle* (Princeton, 1972)

Henretta, James A., Kammen, Michael, and Katz, Stanley N. (eds), *The Transformation of Early American Society* (New York, 1991)

Hermes, Katherine, ' "Justice Will be Done Us". Algonquian Demands for Reciprocity in the Courts of European Settlers', in Christopher L. Tomlins and Bruce T. Mann (eds), *The Many Legalities of Early America* (Chapel Hill, NC and London, 2001)

Hernández González, Manuel, *Los canarios en la Venezuela colonial, 1670–1810* (Tenerife, 1999)

Hernández Palomo, José Jesús, *El aguardiente de caña en México* (Seville, 1974)

Hernández y Dávalos, Juan E. (ed.), *Colección de documentos para la independencia de México de 1808 a 1821*, 6 vols (Mexico City, 1877–82)

Herr, Richard, *The Eighteenth-Century Revolution in Spain* (Princeton, 1958)

Herzog, Tamar, *Defining Nations. Immigrants and Citizens in Early Modern Spain and Spanish America* (New Haven and London, 2003)

Hillgarth, J. N., *The Mirror of Spain, 1500–1700. The Formation of a Myth* (Ann Arbor, MI, 2000)

Himmerich y Valencia, Robert, *The Encomenderos of New Spain, 1521–1555* (Austin, TX, 1991)

Hinderaker, Eric, *Elusive Empires. Constructing Colonialism in the Ohio Valley, 1673–1800* (Cambridge, 1997)

Hinton, R.W., *The Eastland Trade and the Common Weal in the Seventeenth Century* (Cambridge, 1959)

Hirsch, Adam J., 'The Collision of Military Cultures in Seventeenth-Century New England', *The Journal of American History*, 74 (1988), pp. 1187–212

Hoberman, Louisa Schell, *Mexico's Merchant Elite, 1590–1660. Silver, State and Society* (Durham, NC and London, 1991)

Hoberman, Louisa Schell, and Socolow, Susan Migden (eds), *Cities and Society in Colonial Latin America* (Albuquerque, NM, 1986)

Hodgen, T., *Early Anthropology in the Sixteenth and Seventeenth Centuries* (Philadelphia, 1964; repr. 1971)

Hoffer, Peter Charles, *Law and People in Colonial America* (Baltimore and London, 1992)

Hoffman, Paul E., *A New Andalucia and a Way to the Orient. The American Southeast During the Sixteenth Century* (Baton Rouge, LA and London, 1990)

Hoffman, Paul E., *Florida's Frontiers* (Bloomington, IN and Indianapolis, 2002)

Hoffman, Ronald, *Princes of Ireland, Planters of Maryland. A Carroll Saga, 1500–1782* (Chapel Hill, NC and London, 2000)

Hofstadter, Richard, *America at 1750. A Social Portrait* (1971; repr. New York, 1973)

Honour, Hugh, *The New Golden Land. European Images of America from the Discoveries to the Present Time* (New York, 1975)

Horn, James, *Adapting to a New World* (Chapel Hill, NC and London, 1994)

Hubbard, William, *General History of New England* (1680)

Huddleston, Lee Eldridge, *Origins of the American Indians. European Concepts, 1492–1729* (Austin, TX and London, 1967)

Humboldt, Alejandro de, *Ensayo político sobre el Reino de la Nueva España*, ed. Vito Alessio Robles (4 vols, Mexico City, 1941)

Hume, David, *Essays. Moral, Political and Literary* (Oxford, 1963)

Huyler, Jerome, *Locke in America. The Moral Philosophy of the Founding Era* (Lawrence, KS, 1995)

Imbruglia, Girolamo, *L'invenzione del Paraguay* (Naples, 1983)

Ingersoll, Thomas N., 'The Fear of Levelling in New England', in Carla Gardina Pestana and Sharon V. Salinger (eds), *Inequality in Early America* (Hanover NH and London, 1999)

Ingram, Martin, *Church Courts, Sex and Marriage in England, 1570–1640* (Cambridge, 1987)

Innes, Stephen, *Labor in a New Land. Economy and Society in Seventeenth-Century Springfield* (Princeton, NJ, 1983)

Isaac, Rhys, *The Transformation of Virginia, 1740–1790* (Chapel Hill, NC, 1982)

Isaac, Rhys, *Landon Carter's Uneasy Kingdom. Revolution and Rebellion on a Virginia Plantation* (Oxford, 2004)

Ishikawa, Chiyo (ed.), *Spain in the Age of Exploration* (Seattle Art Museum exhibition catalogue, 2004)

Israel, Jonathan, *Race, Class and Politics in Colonial Mexico, 1610–1670* (Oxford, 1975)

Israel, Jonathan, *Diasporas within a Diaspora. Jews, Crypto-Jews and the World Maritime Empires, 1540–1740* (Leiden, Boston, Cologne, 2002)

Izard, Miguel, *El miedo a la revolución. La lucha por la libertad en Venezuela, 1777–1830* (Madrid, 1979)

Jackson, Robert H. (ed.), *New Views of Borderland History* (Albuquerque, NM, 1998)

Jacobs, Auke P., *Los movimientos entre Castilla e Hispanoamérica durante el reinado de Felipe III, 1598–1621* (Amsterdam, 1995)

Jara, Alvaro, *Guerre et société au Chili. Essai de sociologie coloniale* (Paris, 1961)

Jefferson, Thomas, *Notes on the State of Virginia*, ed. William Peden (Chapel Hill, NC and London, 1982)

Jehlen, Myra, and Warner, Michael (eds), *The English Literatures of America, 1500–1800* (New York and London, 1997)

Jennings, Francis, *The Invasion of America* (Chapel Hill, NC, 1975)

Jennings, Francis, *The Ambiguous Iroquois Empire* (New York and London, 1984)

Jennings, Francis, *Empire of Fortune. Crown, Colonies and Tribes in the Seven Years War in America* (New York and London, 1988)

Jensen, Merrill, *The Articles of Confederation. An Interpretation of the Social-Constitutional History of the American Revolution, 1774–1781* (Madison, WI, 1940; repr. 1948)

Johnson, Cecil, *British West Florida, 1763–1783* (New Haven, 1943)

Johnson, Richard F., *Adjustment to Empire. The New England Colonies, 1675–1715* (Leicester, 1981)

Johnson, Richard R., 'The Imperial Webb', *WMQ*, 3rd ser., 43 (1986), pp. 408–59

Johnson, Richard R., '"Parliamentary Egotisms": the Clash of Legislatures in the Making of the American Revolution', *The Journal of American History*, 74 (1987), pp. 338–62

Jones, Maldwyn A., 'The Scotch-Irish in British America', in Bernard Bailyn and Philip D. Morgan (eds), *Strangers Within the Realm. Cultural Margins of the First British Empire* (Chapel Hill, NC and London, 1991)

Jordan, Winthrop D., *White Over Black. American Attitudes toward the Negro 1550–1812* (1968; Baltimore, 1969)

Juan, Jorge, and Ulloa, Antonio de, *Las 'Notícias secretas de América' de Jorge Juan y Antonio de Ulloa, 1735–1745*, ed. Luis J. Ramos Gómez (2 vols, Madrid, 1985)

Juderías, Julián, *La Leyenda Negra* (1914; 15th edn, Madrid, 1967)

Kagan, Richard L., *Lawsuits and Litigants in Castile, 1500–1700* (Chapel Hill, NC, 1981)

Kagan, Richard L., *Urban Images of the Hispanic World, 1493–1793* (New Haven and London, 2000)

Kagan, Richard L., 'A World Without Walls: City and Town in Colonial Spanish America', in James D. Tracy (ed.), *City Walls. The Urban Enceinte in Global Perspective* (Cambridge, 2000)

Kagan, Richard L., and Parker, Geoffrey (eds), *Spain, Europe and the Atlantic World. Essays in Honour of John H. Elliott* (Cambridge, 1995)

Kammen, Michael, *Deputyes and Libertyes. The Origins of Representative Government in Colonial America* (New York, 1969)

Kammen, Michael, *Colonial New York. A History* (New York, 1975)

Kammen, Michael, 'The Problem of American Exceptionalism: a Reconsideration', *American Quarterly*, 45 (1993), pp. 1–43

Kammen, Michael (ed.), *The Past Before Us* (New York, 1980)

Kaplan, Y., Méchoulan, H., and Popkin, R.H. (eds), *Menasseh ben Israel and his World* (Leiden, 1989)

Katz, Stanley N., and Murrin, John M. (eds), *Colonial America. Essays in Politics and Social Development* (New York, 1983)

Katzew, Ilona, *Casta Painting. Images of Race in Eighteenth-Century Mexico* (New Haven and London, 2004)

Katzew, Ilona (ed.), *New World Orders. Casta Painting and Colonial Latin America* (Americas Society Art Gallery, New York, 1996)

Keith, Robert G., *Conquest and Agrarian Change. The Emergence of the Hacienda System on the Peruvian Coast* (Cambridge, MA and London, 1976)

Kelly, Kevin P., '"In dispers'd Country Plantations": Settlement Patterns in Seventeenth-Century Surry County, Virginia', in Thad W. Tate and David L. Ammerman (eds), *The Chesapeake in the Seventeenth Century* (New York and London, 1979)

Keniston, Hayward, *Francisco de Los Cobos. Secretary of the Emperor Charles V* (Pittsburgh, 1960)

King, James F., 'The Colored Castes and the American Representation in the Cortes of Cadiz', *HAHR*, 33 (1953), pp. 33–64

Kingsbury, Susan Myra (ed.), *The Records of the Virginia Company of London* (4 vols, Washington, 1906–35)

Klein, Herbert S., *Slavery in the Americas. A Comparative Study of Virginia and Cuba* (Chicago, 1967)

Klein, Herbert S., *The American Finances of the Spanish Empire. Royal Income and Expenditures in Colonial Mexico, Peru, and Bolivia, 1680–1809* (Albuquerque, NM, 1998)

Klein, Herbert S., *A Population History of the United States* (Cambridge, 2004)

Klor de Alva, J. Jorge de, Nicholson, H. B., and Keber, Elise Quiñones (eds), *The Work of Bernardino de Sahagún. Pioneer Ethnographer of Sixteenth-Century Mexico* (Institute for Mesoamerican Studies, Albany, NY, 1988)

Knight, Alan, *Mexico. The Colonial Era* (Cambridge, 2002)

Kobayashi, José María, *La educación como conquista (empresa franciscana en México)* (Mexico City, 1974)

Koenigsberger, H. G., 'Composite States, Representative Institutions and the American Revolution', *Historical Research. The Bulletin of the Institute of Historical Research*, 62 (1989), pp. 135–53

Koenigsberger, H. G., *Monarchies, States Generals and Parliaments. The Netherlands in the Fifteenth and Sixteenth Centuries* (Cambridge, 2001)

Konetzke, Richard, 'Hernán Cortés como poblador de la Nueva España', *Estudios Cortesianos* (Instituto Gonzalo Fernández de Oviedo, Madrid, 1948)

Konetzke, Richard, 'La condición legal de los criollos y las causas de la independencia', *Estudios Americanos*, 2 (1950), pp. 31–54

Konetzke, Richard, *Colección de documentos para la historia de la formación social de Hispanoamérica 1493–1810* (3 vols, Madrid, 1953–62)

Konetzke, Richard, 'La legislación sobre inmigración de extranjeros en América durante el reinado de Carlos V', in *Charles-Quint et son temps* (Colloques Internationaux du Centre National de la Recherche Scientifique, Paris, 1959)

Konetzke, Richard, *América Latina. II. La época colonial* (Madrid, 1971)

Kornwolf, James D., *Architecture and Town Planning in Colonial North America* (3 vols, Baltimore and London, 2002)

Kramnick, Isaac, 'The "Great National Discussion": the Discourse of Politics in 1787', *WMQ*, 3rd ser., 45 (1988), pp. 3–32

Kuethe, Allan J., and Inglis, G. Douglas, 'Absolutism and Enlightened Reform: Charles III, the Establishment of the *Alcabala*, and Commercial Reorganization in Cuba', *Past and Present*, 109 (1985), pp. 118–43

Kulikoff, Allan, *Tobacco and Slaves. The Development of Southern Cultures in the Chesapeake, 1680–1800* (Chapel Hill, NC and London, 1986)

Kupperman, Karen Ordahl, *Settling with the Indians. The Meeting of English and Indian Cultures in America, 1580–1640* (Totowa, NJ, 1980)

Kupperman, Karen Ordahl, 'The Puzzle of the American Climate in the Early Colonial Period', *AHR*, 87 (1982), pp. 1262–89

Kupperman, Karen Ordahl, *Providence Island, 1630–1641* (Cambridge, 1993)

Kupperman, Karen Ordahl, *Indians and English. Facing Off in Early America* (Ithaca, NY and London, 2000)

Labaree, Leonard Woods, *Royal Government in America* (New Haven, 1930)

Labaree, Leonard Woods (ed.), *Royal Instructions to British Colonial Governors, 1670–1776* (New York, 1935)

Lafaye, Jacques, *Quetzalcoatl and Guadalupe. The Formation of Mexican National Consciousness, 1531–1813* (Chicago, 1976)

Lamb, Ursula, *Frey Nicolás de Ovando. Gobernador de las Indias, 1501–1509* (Madrid, 1956)

Landers, Jane, *Black Society in Spanish Florida* (Urbana, IL and Chicago, 1999)

Lang, James, *Conquest and Commerce. Spain and England in the Americas* (New York, San Francisco, London, 1975)

Langdon, George D. Jr., 'The Franchise and Political Democracy in Plymouth Colony', *WMQ*, 3rd ser., 20 (1963), pp. 513–26

Langford, Paul, *A Polite and Commercial People. England, 1727–1783* (Oxford, 1989)

Langley, Lester D., *The Americas in the Age of Revolution, 1750–1850* (New Haven and London, 1996)

Lanning, John Tate, *Academic Culture in the Spanish Colonies* (Oxford, 1940; repr. Port Washington and London, 1971)

Las Casas, Fray Bartolomé de, *Apologética historia sumaria*, ed. Edmundo O'Gorman (2 vols, Mexico City, 1967)

Las Casas, Fray Bartolomé de, *Tears of the Indians* (repr. Williamstown, MA, 1970)

Las Casas, Fray Bartolomé de, *A Short Account of the Destruction of the Indies*, trans. and ed. Nigel Griffin (Harmondsworth, 1992)

Lavallé, Bernard, *Las promesas ambiguas. Ensayos sobre el criollismo colonial en los Andes* (Lima, 1993)

Lavrín, Asunción (ed.), *Sexuality and Marriage in Colonial Latin America* (Lincoln, NA, and London, 1989)

Lee, Richard L., 'American Cochineal in European Commerce, 1526–1635', *Journal of Modern History* 23 (1951), pp. 205–24

Lee, Wayne E., 'Early American Warfare: a New Reconnaissance, 1600–1815', *Historical Journal*, 44 (2001), pp. 269–89

Lemon, James T., *The Best Poor Man's Country. A Geographical Study of Early Southeastern Pennsylvania* (Baltimore and London, 1972)

León Pinelo, Antonio de, *El Gran Canciller de Indias*, ed. Guillermo Lohmann Villena (Seville, 1953)

León Pinelo, Antonio de, *Questión moral si el chocolate quebranta el ayuno eclesiástico* (Madrid, 1636; facsimile edn, Mexico City, 1994)

Leonard, Irving, *Don Carlos de Sigüenza y Góngora. A Mexican Savant of the Seventeenth Century* (Berkeley, 1929)

Leonard, Irving A., *Books of the Brave* (1949; repr. Berkeley, Los Angeles, Oxford, 1992)

Leonard, Irving, *Baroque Times in Old Mexico* (Ann Arbor, MI, 1959)

Lepore, Jill, *The Name of War. King Philip's War and the Origins of American Identity* (New York, 1998)

Leturia, Pedro de, *Relaciones entre la Santa Sede e Hispanoamérica. 1. Época del Real Patronato, 1493–1800* (Caracas, 1959)

Levaggi, Abelardo, *Diplomacia hispano-indígena en las fronteras de América* (Madrid, 2002)

Levy, Barry, *Quakers and the American Family* (New York and Oxford, 1988)

Lewin, Boleslao, *La rebelión de Túpac Amaru y los orígenes de la independencia de Hispanoamérica* (3rd edn, Buenos Aires, 1967)

Lewin, Boleslao (ed.), *Descripción del virreinato del Perú* (Rosario, 1958)

Lewis, Clifford M., and Loomie, Albert J. (eds), *The Spanish Jesuit Mission in Virginia, 1570–1572* (Chapel Hill, NC, 1953)

Liebman, Seymour B., *The Jews in New Spain* (Coral Gables, FL, 1970)

Ligon, Richard, *A True and Exact History of the Island of Barbadoes* (2nd edn, London, 1673)

Liss, Peggy K., *Atlantic Empires. The Network of Trade and Revolution, 1713–1826* (Baltimore and London, 1983)

Llombart, Vicent, *Campomanes, economista y político de Carlos III* (Madrid, 1992)

Lockhart, James, *Spanish Peru, 1532–1560. A Colonial Society* (Madison, WI, Milwaukee, WI and London, 1968)

Lockhart, James, *The Men of Cajamarca. A Social and Economic Study of the First Conquerors of Peru* (Austin, TX and London, 1972)

Lockhart, James, *The Nahuas After the Conquest* (Stanford, 1992)

Lockhart, James, *Of Things of the Indies. Essays Old and New in Early Latin American History* (Stanford, CA, 1999)

Lockhart, James (ed.), *We People Here. Nahuatl Accounts of the Conquest of Mexico* (Repertorium Columbianum, vol. 1, Berkeley, Los Angeles, London, 1993)

Lockhart, James, and Otte, Enrique (eds), *Letters and People of the Spanish Indies. The Sixteenth Century* (Cambridge, 1976)

Lockhart, James, and Schwartz, Stuart B., *Early Latin America. A History of Spanish Colonial America and Brazil* (Cambridge, 1983)

Lockridge, Kenneth A., *A New England Town. The First Hundred Years. Dedham, Massachusetts, 1636–1736* (New York, 1970)

Lockridge, Kenneth A., *Literacy in Colonial New England* (New York, 1974)

Lockridge, Kenneth A., *The Diary and Life of William Byrd II of Virginia, 1674–1744* (Chapel Hill, NC and London, 1987)

Lohmann Villena, Guillermo, 'Las Cortes en Indias', *Anuario de Historia del Derecho Español*, 17 (1947), pp. 655–62

Lohmann Villena, Guillermo, *Los americanos en las ordenes nobiliarias* (2 vols, Madrid, 1947)

Lohmann Villena, Guillermo, *Las minas de Huancavelica en los siglos XVI y XVII* (Seville, 1949)

Lomax, D. W. , *The Reconquest of Spain* (London and New York, 1978)

López de Gómara, Francisco, *The Pleasant Historie of the Conquest of the Weast India, now called New Spayne* (London, 1578)

López de Gómara, Francisco, *Primera parte de la historia general de las Indias* (BAE, vol. 22, Madrid, 1852)

López de Gómara, Francisco, *Cortés. The Life of the Conqueror by his Secretary*, trans. and ed. Lesley Byrd Simpson (Berkeley and Los Angeles, 1964)

López de Velasco, Juan, *Geografía y descripción universal de las Indias*, ed. Justo Zaragoza (Madrid, 1894)

López Piñero, J. M., *La introducción de la ciencia moderna en España* (Barcelona, 1969)

Losada, Angel, *Fray Bartolomé de Las Casas a la luz de la moderna crítica histórica* (Madrid, 1970)

Lovejoy, David S., *The Glorious Revolution in America* (New York, 1972)

Lovejoy, Paul E., and Rogers, Nicholas (eds), *Unfree Labour in the Development of the Atlantic World* (Ilford, 1994)

Lovell, Margaretta M., 'Painters and Their Customers: Aspects of Art and Money in Eighteenth-Century America', in Cary Carson, Ronald Hoffman and Peter J. Albert (eds), *Of Consuming Interests. The Style of Life in the Eighteenth Century* (Charlottesville, VA and London, 1994)

Lucas, Paul, *Valley of Discord. Church and Society along the Connecticut River, 1636–1725* (Hanover, NH, 1976)

Lucena Giraldo, Manuel, *Laboratorio tropical. La expedición de límites al Orinoco, 1750–1767* (Caracas, 1993)

Lucena Giraldo, Manuel (ed.), *Premoniciones de la independencia de Iberoamérica* (Aranjuez and Madrid, 2003)

Lucena Giraldo, Manuel, and Pimentel Igea, Juan, *Los 'Axiomas políticos sobre la América' de Alejandro Malaspina* (Madrid, 1991)

Lucena Salmoral, Manuel, *La esclavitud en la América española* (Centro de Estudios Latinoamericanos, University of Warsaw, *Estudios y materiales*, 22, Warsaw, 2002)

Lupher, David A., *Romans in a New World. Classical Models in Sixteenth-Century Spanish America* (Ann Arbor, MI, 2003)

Lustig, Mary Lou, *The Imperial Executive in America. Sir Edmund Andros, 1637–1714* (Madison, NJ, 2002)

Lydon, James (ed.), *The English in Medieval Ireland* (Dublin, 1984)

Lynch, John, *The Spanish American Revolutions, 1808–1825* (2nd edn, New York and London, 1973)

Lynch, John, *Bourbon Spain, 1700–1808* (Oxford, 1989)

Lynch, John, *Caudillos in Spanish America, 1800–1850* (Oxford, 1992)

Lynch, John, *The Hispanic World in Crisis and Change, 1598–1700* (Oxford, 1992)

Lynch, John, 'Spain's Imperial Memory', *Debate y Perspectivas. Cuadernos de Historia y Ciencias Sociales*, 2 (2002), pp. 47–73

Lynch, John (ed.), *Latin American Revolutions, 1808–1826* (Norman, OK, 1994)

McAlister, Lyle N., 'The Reorganization of the Army of New Spain, 1763–1766', *HAHR*, 33 (1953), pp. 1–32

McAlister, Lyle N., *The 'Fuero Militar' in New Spain, 1764–1800* (Gainesville, FA, 1957)

McAlister, Lyle N., 'Social Structure and Social Change in New Spain', *HAHR*, 43 (1963), pp. 349–70

MacCormack, Sabine, *Religion in the Andes. Vision and Imagination in Early Colonial Peru* (Princeton, 1991)

McCullough, David, *John Adams* (New York, London, 2001)

McCusker, John J., *Money and Exchange in Europe and America, 1600–1771. A Handbook* (London, 1978)

McCusker, John J., and Menard, Russell R., *The Economy of British America, 1607–1789* (Chapel Hill, NC and London, 1985)

McFarlane, Anthony, *Colombia Before Independence. Economy, Society and Politics under Bourbon Rule* (Cambridge, 1993)

McFarlane, Anthony, *The British in the Americas, 1480–1815* (London and New York, 1994)

McFarlane, Anthony, 'Identity, Enlightenment and Political Dissent in Late Colonial Spanish America', *TRHS*, 6th ser., 8 (1998), pp. 309–35

McFarlane, Anthony, 'Hispanoamérica bajo el gobierno de los Borbones: desarrollo económico y crísis política', in José Manuel de Bernardo Ares (ed.), *El hispanismo anglonorteameri-cano* (Actas de la I Conferencia Internacional *Hacia un nuevo humanismo*, 2 vols, Córdoba, 2001)

Macías Márquez, Rosario 'La emigración española en el siglo XVIII a América', *Rábida*, 10 (1991), pp. 68–79

McKendrick, Neil, Brewer, John, and Plumb, J. H., *The Birth of a Consumer Society. The Commercialization of Eighteenth-Century England* (Bloomington, 1982)

Mackesy, Piers, *The War for America, 1775–1783* (London, 1964)

MacLachlan, Colin M., *Spain's Empire in the New World. The Role of Ideas in Institutional and Social Change* (Berkeley, Los Angeles, London, 1988)

MacLeod, Murdo J., *Spanish Central America. A Socioeconomic History, 1520–1720* (Berkeley, 1973)

McMahon, Darrin, 'From the Happiness of Virtue to the Virtue of Happiness: 400 B.C.–A.D. 1780', *Daedalus* (Spring, 2004), pp. 5–17

McNeill, John Robert, *Atlantic Empires of France and Spain. Louisbourg and Havana, 1700–1763* (Chapel Hill, NC and London, 1985)

Madre de Dios, Efrén de la, and Steggink, O., *Tiempo y vida de Santa Teresa* (Madrid, 1968)

Maghalaes Godinho, Vitorino de, *A economia dos descobrimentos henriquinos* (Lisbon, 1962)

Maier, Pauline, *From Resistance to Revolution. Colonial Radicals and the Development of American Opposition to Britain, 1765–1776* (1971; repr. New York and London, 1992)

Maier, Pauline, 'The Transforming Impact of Independence Reaffirmed', in James A. Henretta, Michael Kammen and Stanley N. Katz (eds), *The Transformation of Early American Society* (New York, 1991)

Maier, Pauline, *American Scripture. Making the Declaration of Independence* (New York, 1997)

Main, Gloria L., *Tobacco Colony. Life in Early Maryland 1650–1720* (Princeton, 1982)

Malagón, Javier, and Ots Capdequi, José M., *Solórzano y la política indiana* (2nd edn, Mexico City, 1983)

Maltby, William S., *The Black Legend in England. The Development of Anti-Spanish Sentiment, 1558–1660* (Durham, NC, 1971)

Mancall, Peter C., *At the Edge of Empire. The Backcountry in British North America* (Baltimore and London, 2003)

Mancke, Elizabeth, and Shammas, Carole (eds), *The Creation of the British Atlantic World* (Baltimore, 2005)

Manzano, Juan, 'La visita de Ovando al Real Consejo de las Indias y el código ovandino', in *El Consejo de las Indias* (Valladolid, 1970)

Maravall, José Antonio, *Utopía y reformismo en la España de los Austrias* (Madrid, 1982)

Marchena Fernández, Juan, 'The Social World of the Military in Peru and New Granada: the Colonial Oligarchies in Conflict', in John R. Fisher, Allan J. Kuethe and Anthony McFarlane (eds), *Reform and Insurrection in Bourbon New Granada and Peru* (Baton Rouge, LA and London, 1990)

Marchena Fernández, Juan, *Ejército y milicias en el mundo colonial americano* (Madrid, 1992)

Marichal, Carlos, *La bancarrota del virreinato. Nueva España y las finanzas del imperio español, 1780–1810* (Mexico City, 1999)

Marshall, P. J., 'Britain and the World in the Eighteenth Century: II, Britons and Americans', *TRHS*, 9 (1999), pp. 1–16

Marshall, Peter and Williams, Glyn (eds), *The British Atlantic Empire Before the American Revolution* (London, 1980)

Marston, Jerrilyn Greene, *King and Congress. The Transfer of Political Legitimacy, 1774–1776* (Princeton, 1987)

Martin, John Frederick, *Profits in the Wilderness* (Chapel Hill, NC and London, 1991)

Martín, Luis, *Daughters of the Conquistadores. Women of the Viceroyalty of Peru* (Dallas, 1983)

Martinell Gifre, Emma, *La comunicación entre españoles e indios: Palabras y gestos* (Madrid, 1992)

Martínez, José Luis, *Hernán Cortés* (Mexico City, 1990)

Martínez, José Luis (ed.), *Documentos cortesianos* (4 vols, Mexico City, 1990–2)

Martínez, María Elena, 'The Black Blood of New Spain: Limpieza de Sangre, Racial Violence, and Gendered Power in Early Colonial Mexico', *WMQ*, 3rd ser., 61 (2004), pp. 479–520

Martínez López-Cano, Ma. del Pilar (ed.), *Iglesia, estado y economía. Siglos XVI y XVII* (Mexico City, 1995)

Martínez Shaw, Carlos, and Alfonso Mola, Marina, *Felipe V* (Madrid, 2001)

Martínez Shaw, Carlos (ed.), *Sevilla siglo XVI. El corazón de las riquezas del mundo* (Madrid, 1993)

Marzahl, Peter, *Town in the Empire. Government, Politics and Society in Seventeenth Century Popayán* (Austin, TX, 1978)

Masur, Gerhard, *Simon Bolivar* (2nd edn, Albuquerque, NM, 1969)

Mather, Cotton, *A Christian at his Calling* (Boston, 1701)

Mather, Cotton, *Magnalia Christi Americana* (1702) (2 vols, repr. Edinburgh, 1979)

Mather, Cotton, *The Diary of Cotton Mather* (2 vols, Boston, 1911–12)

Matienzo, Juan de, *Gobierno del Perú (1567)*, ed. Guillermo Lohmann Villena (Paris and Lima, 1967)

May, Henry F., *The Enlightenment in America* (Oxford, 1976)

Mayer, Alicia, *Dos americanos, dos pensamientos. Carlos de Sigüenza y Góngora y Cotton Mather* (Mexico City, 1998)

Maza, Francisco de la, *El guadalupanismo* (Mexico City, 1953)

Mazín, Oscar, *Entre dos majestades* (Zamora, Michoacán, 1987)

Mazín, Oscar, *L'Amérique espagnole, XVIe–XVIIIe siècles* (Paris, 2005)

Mazín Gómez, Oscar (ed.), *México en el mundo hispánico* (2 vols, Zamora, Michoacán, 2000)

Meek, Wilbur T., *The Exchange Media of Colonial Mexico* (New York, 1948)

Meinig, D. W., *The Shaping of America*, vol. 1, *Atlantic America, 1492–1800* (New Haven and London, 1986)

Melgar, José María, 'Puerto y puerta de las Indias', in Carlos Martínez Shaw (ed.), *Sevilla siglo XVI. El corazón de las riquezas del mundo* (Madrid, 1993)

Mena García, María del Carmen, *Pedrarias Dávila o 'la Ira de Dios'. Una historia olvidada* (Seville, 1992)

Merrell, James H., ' "The Customs of Our Country". Indians and Colonists in Early America', in Bernard Bailyn and Philip D. Morgan (eds), *Strangers Within the Realm. Cultural Margins of the First British Empire* (Chapel Hill, NC and London, 1991)

Mestre, Antonio, 'La actitud religiosa de los católicos ilustrados', in Agustín Guimerá (ed.), *El reformismo borbónico. Una visión interdisciplinar* (Madrid, 1996)

Middlekauff, Robert, *The Mathers. Three Generations of Puritan Intellectuals, 1596–1728* (London, Oxford, New York, 1971)

Middleton, Richard, *Colonial America. A History, 1585–1776* (2nd edn, Oxford, 1996)

Milhou, Alain, *Colón y su mentalidad mesiánica en el ambiente franciscanista español* (Valladolid, 1983)

Millar Corbacho, René, 'La inquisición de Lima y la circulación de libros prohibidos (1700–1800)', *Revista de Indias*, 44 (1984), pp. 415–44

Miller, Perry, *The New England Mind in the Seventeenth Century* (Cambridge, MA and London, 1939)

Miller, Perry, 'Errand into the Wilderness', *WMQ*, 3rd ser., 10 (1953), pp. 3–19. Repr. in *In Search of Early America. The William and Mary Quarterly 1943–1993* (Richmond, VA, 1993)

Miller, Perry, *Errand into the Wilderness* (Cambridge, MA, 1956)

Miller, Peter N., *Defining the Common Good. Empire, Religion and Philosophy in Eighteenth-Century Britain* (Cambridge, 1994)

Millones, Luis, *Una partecita del cielo* (Lima, 1993)

Millones, Luis, *Perú colonial. De Pizarro a Tupac Amaru II* (Lima, 1995)

Millones, Luis, *Dioses familiares* (Lima, 1999)

Mills, Kenneth, *Idolatry and its Enemies. Colonial Andean Religion and Extirpation, 1640–1750* (Princeton, 1997)

Minchom, Martin, *The People of Quito, 1690–1810* (Boulder, CO, 1994)

Mínguez Cornelles, Víctor, *Los reyes distantes. Imágenes del poder en el México virreinal* (Castelló de la Plana, 1995)

Molinié-Bertrand, Annie, *Au siècle d'or. L'Espagne et ses hommes* (Paris, 1985)

Moore, Dennis D. (ed.), *More Letters from the American Farmer. An Edition of the Essays in English Left Unpublished by Crèvecoeur* (Athens, GA, and London, 1995)

Morales Padrón, Francisco, 'Descubrimiento y toma de posesión', *Anuario de Estudios Americanos*, 12 (1955), pp. 321–80

Morales Padrón, Francisco, *Historia general de América* (*Manual de historia universal*, vol. VI, Madrid, 1975)

Moraley, William, *The Infortunate* (1743), ed. Susan E. Klepp and Billy G. Smith (University Park, PA, 1992)

Morelli, Federica, 'La revolución en Quito: el camino hacia el gobierno mixto', *Revista de Indias*, 62 (2002), pp. 335–56

Moret, Michèle, *Aspects de la société marchande de Séville au début du XVIIe siècle* (Paris, 1967)

Morgan, Edmund S., *The Birth of the Republic, 1763–1789* (Chicago, 1956)

Morgan, Edmund S., *Visible Saints. The History of a Puritan Idea* (1963; repr. Ithaca, NY, 1971)

Morgan, Edmund S., *Roger Williams. The Church and the State* (1967; repr. New York, 1987)

Morgan, Edmund S., *American Slavery, American Freedom* (New York, 1975)

Morgan, Edmund S., *Benjamin Franklin* (New Haven and London, 2002)

Morgan, Edmund S., *The Genuine Article. A Historian Looks at Early America* (New York and London, 2004)

Morgan, Edmund S. and Helen M., *The Stamp Act Crisis. Prologue to Revolution* (1953; repr. New York, 1962)

Morgan, Philip D., 'British Encounters with Africans and African-Americans circa 1600–1780', in Bernard Bailyn and Philip D. Morgan (eds), *Strangers Within the Realm. Cultural Margins of the First British Empire* (Chapel Hill, NC and London, 1991)

Morgan, Philip D., *Slave Counterpoint. Black Culture in the Eighteenth-Century Chesapeake and Low Country* (Chapel Hill, NC and London, 1998)

Morineau, Michel, *Incroyables gazettes et fabuleux métaux. Les retours des trésors américains d'après les gazettes hollandaises, XVIe–XVIIIe siècles* (Cambridge and Paris, 1985)

Morison, Samuel Eliot (ed.), *Sources and Documents Illustrating the American Revolution, 1764–1788* (2nd edn, London, Oxford, New York, 1965)

Mörner, Magnus, *The Political and Economic Activities of the Jesuits in the La Plata Region. The Hapsburg Era* (Stockholm, 1953)

Mörner, Magnus, *Race Mixture in the History of Latin America* (Boston, 1967)

Mörner, Magnus, *La corona española y los foraneos en los pueblos de indios de América* (Stockholm, 1979)

Mörner, Magnus, 'Economic Factors and Stratification in Colonial Spanish America with Special Regard to Elites', *HAHR*, 63 (1983), pp. 335–69

Mörner, Magnus, *The Andean Past. Land, Societies and Conflicts* (New York, 1985)

Mörner, Magnus, 'Labour Systems and Patterns of Social Stratification', in Wolfgang Reinhard and Peter Waldmann (eds), *Nord und Süd in Amerika. Gegensätze – Gemeinsamkeiten – Europäischer Hintergrund* (Freiburg, 1992)

Morón, Guillermo *A History of Venezuela* (London, 1964)

Morris, Richard, Zoraida Vázquez, Josefina, and Trabulse, Elias, *Las revoluciones de independencia en México y los Estados Unidos. Un ensayo comparativo* (3 vols, Mexico City, 1976)

Morse, Richard, 'Toward a Theory of Spanish American Government', *Journal of the History of Ideas*, 15 (1954), pp. 71–93

Morse, Richard M., 'The Heritage of Latin America', in Louis Hartz, *The Founding of New Societies* (New York, 1964)

Morse, Richard M., 'A Prologomenon to Latin American Urban History', *HAHR*, 52 (1972), pp. 359–94

Morse, Richard M., *El espejo de Próspero. Un estudio de la dialéctica del Nuevo Mundo* (Mexico City, 1982)

Morton, Richard L., *Colonial Virginia* (2 vols, Chapel Hill, NC, 1960)

Morton, Thomas, *New English Canaan* (1632), in Peter Force, *Tracts and Other Papers Relating Principally to the Origin, Settlement and Progress of the Colonies in North America* (4 vols, Washington, 1836–46), vol. 2

Motolinía, Fray Toribio de Benavente, *Memoriales o libro de las cosas de la Nueva España y de los naturales de ella*, ed. Edmundo O'Gorman (Mexico City, 1971)

Moutoukias, Zacarias, *Contrabando y control colonial en el siglo XVII. Buenos Aires, el Atlántico y el espacio peruano* (Buenos Aires, 1988)

Mowat, C. L., *East Florida as a British Province, 1763–1784* (Berkeley and Los Angeles, 1943)

Moya Pons, Frank, *La Española en el siglo XVI, 1493–1520* (Santiago, Dominican Republic, 1978)

Mujica Pinilla, Ramón, *Ángeles apócrifos en la América virreinal* (2nd edn, Lima, 1996)

Mujica Pinilla, Ramón, 'Santa Rosa de Lima y la política de la santidad americana', in *Perú indígena y virreinal* (Sociedad Estatal para la Acción Cultural Exterior, Madrid, 2004)

Muldoon, James, 'The Indian as Irishman', *Essex Institute Historical Collections*, 111 (1975), pp. 267–89

Muldoon, James, *The Americas in the Spanish World Order. The Justification for Conquest in the Seventeenth Century* (Philadelphia, 1994)

Mundy, Barbara E., *The Mapping of New Spain* (Chicago and London, 1996)

Murra, John V., *Formaciones económicas y políticas del mundo andino* (Lima, 1975)

Murrin, John M., 'The Great Inversion, or Court Versus Country: a Comparison of the Revolutionary Settlements in England (1688–1721) and America (1776–1816)', in J. G. A. Pocock (ed.), *Three British Revolutions: 1641, 1688, 1776* (Princeton, 1980)

Murrin, John M., 'Magistrates, Sinners and a Precarious Liberty: Trial by Jury in Seventeenth-Century New England', in David D. Hall, John M. Murrin and Thad W. Tate, *Saints and Revolutionaries. Essays on Early American History* (New York and London, 1984)

Murrin, John M. 'English Rights as Ethnic Aggression: the English Conquest, the Charter of Liberties of 1683, and Leisler's Rebellion', in William Pencak and Conrad Edick Wright (eds), *Authority and Resistance in Early New York* (New York, 1988)

Nadal, Jordi, *La población española (Siglos XV a XX)* (2nd edn, Barcelona, 1984)

Nader, Helen (trans. and ed.), *The Book of Privileges Issued to Christopher Columbus by King Fernando and Queen Isabel 1492–1502* (Repertorium Columbianum, vol. 3, Berkeley, Los Angeles, Oxford, 1996)

Nash, Gary, *Quakers and Politics in Pennsylvania, 1681–1726* (Princeton, 1968)

Nash, Gary B., *The Urban Crucible. Social Change, Political Consciousness and the Origins of the American Revolution* (Cambridge, MA and London, 1979)

Nash, Gary B., *Race, Class and Politics. Essays on American Colonial and Revolutionary Society* (Urbana, IL and Chicago, 1986)

Nash, Gary B., 'The Hidden History of Mestizo America', *The Journal of American History*, 82 (1995), pp. 941–62

Nelson, William H., *The American Tory* (Westport, CT, 1961)

Nettels, Curtis Putnam, *The Money Supply of the American Colonies before 1720* (University of Wisconsin Studies in the Social Sciences and History, no. 20, Madison, WI, 1934)

Newell, Margaret Ellen, 'The Changing Nature of Indian Slavery in New England, 1670–1720', in Colin G. Calloway and Neal Salisbury (eds), *Reinterpreting New England Indians and the Colonial Experience* (Boston, 2003)

Newson, Linda A., 'The Demographic Collapse of Native Peoples of the Americas, 1492–1650', in Warwick Bray (ed.), *The Meeting of Two Worlds. Europe and the Americas 1492–1650* (Proceedings of the British Academy, 81, Oxford, 1993)

Newton, A. P. ,*The European Nations in the West Indies, 1493–1688* (London, 1933; repr. 1966)

Nobles, Gregory, *American Frontiers. Cultural Encounters and Continental Conquest* (New York, 1997)

Norton, Mary Beth, *Founding Mothers and Fathers. Gendered Power and the Forming of American Society* (New York, 1997)

Norton, Mary Beth, *In the Devil's Snare. The Salem Witchcraft Crisis of 1692* (New York, 2002)

Núñez Cabeza de Vaca, Alvar, *Los naufragios*, ed. Enrique Pupo-Walker (Madrid, 1992)

Núñez Cabeza de Vaca, Alvar, *The Narrative of Cabeza de Vaca*, ed. and trans. Rolena Adorno and Patrick Charles Pautz (Lincoln, NE, 2003)

Núñez de Pineda y Bascuñán, Francisco, *Cautiverio feliz* (Santiago de Chile, 1863); abridged edn by Alejandro Lipschutz and Alvaro Jara (Santiago de Chile, 1973). Abridged English trans. by William C. Atkinson, *The Happy Captive* (Chatham, 1979)

O'Brien, Patrick K., and Prados de la Escosura, Leandro (eds), *The Costs and Benefits of European Imperialism from the Conquest of Ceuta, 1415, to the Treaty of Lusaka, 1974,* Twelfth International Economic History Congress, *Revista de Historia Económica*, 16 (1998)

O'Brien, Patrick Karl, and Prados de la Escosura, Leandro, 'The Costs and Benefits for Europeans from their Empires Overseas', *Revista de Historia Económica*, 16 (1998), pp. 29–89

O'Callaghan, E. B., *The Documentary History of the State of New York* (4 vols, Albany, NY, 1850–1)

Offutt, William M., 'The Atlantic Rules: the Legalistic Turn in Colonial British America', in Elizabeth Mancke and Carole Shammas, *The Creation of the British Atlantic World* (Baltimore, 2005)

Olson, Alison, 'The British Government and Colonial Union, 1754', *WMQ*, 3rd ser., 17 (1960), pp. 22–34

Olson, Alison Gilbert, *Anglo-American Politics, 1660–1775* (New York and Oxford, 1973)

Olson, Alison Gilbert, *Making the Empire Work. London and American Interest Groups, 1690–1790* (Cambridge, MA, 1992)

Oltra, Joaquín, and Pérez Samper, María Ángeles, *El Conde de Aranda y los Estados Unidos* (Barcelona, 1987)

Operé, Fernando, *Historias de la frontera. El cautiverio en la América hispánica* (Buenos Aires, 2001)

O'Phelan Godoy, Scarlett, *Rebellion and Revolts in Eighteenth-Century Peru and Upper Peru* (Cologne, 1985)

O'Shaughnessy, Andrew J., *An Empire Divided. The American Revolution and the British Caribbean* (Philadelphia, 2000)

Otis, James, 'The Rights of the British Colonies Asserted and Proved', in Bernard Bailyn (ed.), *Pamphlets of the American Revolution, 1750–1776*, vol. 1, *1750–1765* (Cambridge, MA, 1965)

Ots Capdequi, J. M., *El estado español en las Indias* (3rd edn, Mexico City, 1957)

Otte, Enrique, *Las perlas del Caribe. Nueva Cádiz de Cubagua* (Caracas, 1977)

Otte, Enrique, *Cartas privadas de emigrantes a Indias, 1540–1616* (Seville, 1988)

The Oxford History of the British Empire, ed. Wm. Roger Louis (5 vols, Oxford, 1998)

Padrón, Ricardo, *The Spacious World. Cartography, Literature, and Empire* (Chicago, 2004)

Pagden, Anthony, *The Fall of Natural Man* (revised edn, Cambridge, 1986)

Pagden, Anthony, *Spanish Imperialism and the Political Imagination* (New Haven and London, 1990)

Pagden, Anthony, *The Uncertainties of Empire* (Aldershot, 1994)

Pagden, Anthony, *Lords of All the World. Ideologies of Empire in Spain, Britain and France c. 1500–c. 1800* (New Haven and London, 1995)

Paine, Thomas, *Common Sense*, ed. Isaac Kramnick (Harmondsworth, 1986)

Palacios Rubios, Juan López de, *De las islas del mar océano*, ed. S. Zavala and A. Millares Carlo (México and Buenos Aires, 1954)

Palm, Erwin Walter, *Los monumentos arquitectónicos de la Española* (2 vols, Ciudad Trujillo, 1955)

Palmer, Colin A., *Slaves of the White God. Blacks in Mexico, 1570–1650* (Cambridge, MA and London, 1976)

Palmer, R. R., *The Age of the Democratic Revolution*, 2 vols (Princeton, 1959–64)

Pané, Fray Ramón, *'Relación acerca de las Antigüedades de los Indios': El primer tratado escrito en América*, ed. José Juan Arrom (Mexico City, 1974). Eng. trans. by Susan C. Griswold, *An Account of the Antiquities of the Indians* (Durham, NC, 1999)

Paquette, Gabriel, 'The Intellectual Context of British Diplomatic Recognition of the South American Republics, c. 1800–1830', *Journal of Transatlantic Studies*, 2 (2004), pp. 75–95

Parker, Geoffrey, *The Military Revolution* (Cambridge, 1988)

Parker, Geoffrey, *Empire, War and Faith in Early Modern Europe* (London, 2002)

Parker, John, *Books to Build an Empire* (Amsterdam, 1965)

Parry, J. H., *The Sale of Public Office in the Spanish Indies under the Hapsburgs* (Berkeley and Los Angeles, 1953)

Paz, Octavio, *Sor Juana Inés de la Cruz* (3rd edn, Mexico City, 1985)

Pedro, Valentín de, *América en las letras españolas del siglo de oro* (Buenos Aires, 1954)

Peña, José F. de la, *Oligarquía y propiedad en Nueva España 1550–1624* (Mexico City, 1983)

Pencak, William, and Wright, Conrad Edick (eds), *Authority and Resistance in Early New York* (New York, 1988)

Pereña Vicente, Luciano, *La Universidad de Salamanca, forja del pensamiento político español en el siglo XVI* (Salamanca, 1954)

Pérez, Joseph, *Los movimientos precursores de la emancipación en Hispanoamérica* (Madrid, 1977)

Pérez, Joseph, *Histoire de l'Espagne* (Paris, 1996)

Pérez de Tudela, Juan, *Las armadas de Indias y los orígenes de la política de colonización, 1492–1505* (Madrid, 1956)

Pérez Prendes, José Manuel, *La monarquía indiana y el estado de derecho* (Valencia, 1989)

Pérez-Mallaína, Pablo E., *Spain's Men of the Sea. Daily Life on the Indies Fleets in the Sixteenth Century*, trans. Carla Rahn Phillips (Baltimore and London, 1998)

Perissat, Karine, 'Los incas representados (Lima – siglo XVIII):¿supervivencia o renacimiento?', *Revista de Indias*, 60 (2000), pp. 623–49

Perú indígena y virreinal (Sociedad Estatal para la Acción Cultural Exterior, Madrid, 2004)

Pestana, Carla Gardina, *The English Atlantic in an Age of Revolution, 1640–1661* (Cambridge, MA, 2004)

Pestana, Carla Gardina, and Salinger, Sharon V. (eds), *Inequality in Early America* (Hanover, NH, and London, 1999)

Peterson, Mark A., 'Puritanism and Refinement in Early New England: Reflections on Communion Silver', *WMQ*, 3rd ser., 58 (2001), p. 307–46

Phelan, John Leddy, *The Kingdom of Quito in the Seventeenth Century* (Madison, WI, Milwaukee, WI, London, 1967)

Phelan, John Leddy, *The Millennial Kingdom of the Franciscans in the New World* (2nd edn, Berkeley and Los Angeles, 1970)

Phelan, John Leddy, *The People and the King. The Comunero Revolution in Colombia, 1781* (Madison, WI, 1978)

Phillips, Carla Rahn, *Life at Sea in the Sixteenth Century. The Landlubber's Lament of Eugenio de Salazar* (The James Ford Bell Lectures, no. 24, University of Minnesota, 1987)

Phillips, J. R. S., *The Medieval Expansion of Europe* (Oxford, 1988)

Phipps, Elena, Hecht, Johanna, and Esteras Martín, Cristina (eds), *The Colonial Andes. Tapestries and Silverwork, 1530–1830* (Metropolitan Museum of Art, New York, 2004)

Pieper, Renate, 'The Volume of African and American Exports of Precious Metals and its Effects in Europe, 1500–1800', in Hans Pohl (ed.), *The European Discovery of the World and its Economic Effects on Pre-Industrial Society* (Papers of the Tenth International Economic History Congress, *Vierteljahrschrift für Sozial und Wirtschaftsgeschichte*, Beihefte, no. 89, Stuttgart, 1990), pp. 97–117

Pierce, Donna (ed.), *Painting a New World. Mexican Art and Life, 1521–1821* (Denver Art Museum, 2004)

Pietschmann, Horst, *El estado y su evolución al principio de la colonización española de América* (Mexico City, 1989)

Pietschmann, Horst, *Las reformas borbónicas y el sistema de intendencias en Nueva España* (Mexico City, 1996)

Pietschmann, Horst (ed.), *Atlantic History and the Atlantic System* (Göttingen, 2002)

Pike, Ruth, *Enterprise and Adventure. The Genoese in Seville and the Opening of the New World* (Ithaca, NY, 1966)

Pimentel, Juan, *La física de la Monarquía. Ciencia y política en el pensamiento colonial de Alejandro Malaspina, 1754–1810* (Aranjuez, 1998)

Pinya i Homs, Romà, *La debatuda exclusió catalano-aragonesa de la conquesta d'Amèrica* (Barcelona, 1992)

Plane, Ann Marie, *Colonial Intimacies. Indian Marriage in Early New England* (Ithaca, NY and London, 2000)

Plumstead, A. W. (ed.), *The Wall and the Garden. Selected Massachusetts Election Sermons, 1670–1775* (Minneapolis, 1968)

Pocock, J. G. A., *Virtue, Commerce, and History* (Cambridge, 1985)

Pocock, J. G. A. (ed.), *The Political Works of James Harrington* (Cambridge, 1979)

Pocock, J. G. A. (ed.), *Three British Revolutions: 1641, 1688, 1776* (Princeton, 1980)

Pohl, Hans (ed.), *The European Discovery of the World and its Economic Effects on Pre-Industrial Society* (Papers of the Tenth International Economic History Congress, *Vierteljahrschrift für Sozial und Wirtschaftsgeschichte*, Beihefte, no. 89, Stuttgart, 1990)

Pole, J. R., *Political Representation in England and the Origins of the American Republic* (1966; Berkeley, Los Angeles, London, 1971)

Pole, J. R., 'The Politics of the Word "State" and its Relation to American Sovereignty', *Parliaments, Estates and Representation*, 8 (1988), pp. 1–10

Ponce Leiva, Pilar, *Certezas ante la incertidumbre. Élite y cabildo de Quito en el siglo XVII* (Quito, 1998)

Poole, Stafford, *Juan de Ovando. Governing the Spanish Empire in the Reign of Philip II* (Norman, OK, 2004)

Popkin, Richard H., 'The Rise and Fall of the Jewish Indian Theory', in Y. Kaplan, H. Méchoulan and R. H. Popkin (eds), *Menasseh ben Israel and his World* (Leiden, 1989)

Porteous, John, *Coins in History* (London, 1969)

Porter, H. C., *The Inconstant Savage* (London, 1979)

Powell, Philip Wayne, *Soldiers, Indians and Silver. The Northwest Advance of New Spain, 1550–1600* (Berkeley, 1952)

Pownall, Thomas, *A Translation of the Memorial of the Sovereigns of Europe Upon the Present State of Affairs Between the Old and New World* (London, 1781)

Prados de la Escosura, Leandro, and Amaral, Samuel (eds), *La independencia americana. Consecuencias económicas* (Madrid, 1993)

Prestwich, Menna (ed.), *International Calvinism, 1541–1715* (Oxford, 1985)

Price, Jacob M., 'Economic Function and the Growth of American Port Towns in the Eighteenth Century', *Perspectives in American History*, 8 (1974), pp. 123–86

Price, Jacob M., 'Who Cared about the Colonies? The Impact of the Thirteen Colonies on British Society and Politics, circa 1714–1775', in Bernard Bailyn and Philip D. Morgan (eds), *Strangers Within the Realm. Cultural Margins of the First British Empire* (Chapel Hill, NC and London, 1991)

Priestley, Herbert Ingram, *José de Gálvez, Visitor-General of New Spain, 1765–1771* (Berkeley, 1916)

Puente Brunke, José de la, *Encomienda y encomenderos en el Perú* (Seville, 1992)

Quinn, David Beers, *The Elizabethans and the Irish* (Ithaca, NY, 1966)

Quinn, David Beers, *England and the Discovery of America, 1481–1620* (London, 1974)

Quinn, David Beers, *Set Fair for Roanoke. Voyages and Colonies, 1584–1606* (Chapel Hill, NC and London, 1985)

Quinn, David Beers (ed.), *The Voyages and Colonizing Enterprises of Sir Humphrey Gilbert* (Hakluyt Society, 2nd ser., vols 83–4, London, 1940)

Quinn, David Beers (ed.), *The Roanoke Voyages* (2 vols, Hakluyt Society, 2nd ser., vols 104–5, London, 1955)

Quinn, David Beers and Alison M. (eds), *The New England Voyages 1602–1608* (Hakluyt Society, 2nd ser., vol. 161, London, 1983)

Quitt, Martin H., 'Trade and Acculturation at Jamestown, 1607–1609: the Limits of Understanding', *WMQ*, 3rd ser., 52 (1995), pp. 227–58

Rabb, Theodore K., *Enterprise and Empire* (Cambridge, MA, 1967)

Ramos, Demetrio, 'Las Cortes de Cádiz y América', *Revista de Estudios Políticos*, 126 (1962), pp. 433–634

Ramos, Demetrio, 'El problema de la fundación del Real Consejo de las Indias y la fecha de su creación', in *El Consejo de las Indias en el siglo XVI* (Valladolid, 1970)

Recopilación de leyes de los reynos de las Indias (facsimile of 1791 edn, 3 vols, Madrid, 1998)

Reeves, Marjorie, *The Influence of Prophecy in the Later Middle Ages. A Study in Joachimism* (Oxford, 1969)

Reid, John G., *Acadia, Maine and New England. Marginal Colonies in the Seventeenth Century* (Toronto, Buffalo, NY and London, 1981)

Reid, John Phillip, *In a Defiant Stance* (University Park, Pennsylvania, and London, 1977)

Reinhard, Wolfgang, and Waldmann, Peter (eds), *Nord und Süd in Amerika: Gegensätze – Gemeinsamkeiten – Europäischer Hintergrund* (Freiburg, 1992)

Reps, John W., *Tidewater Towns. City Planning in Colonial Virginia and Maryland* (Williamsburg, VA, 1972)

Ricard, Robert, *La 'Conquête spirituelle' du Mexique* (Paris, 1933)

Richter, Daniel K., *Facing East from Indian Country. A Native History of Early America* (Cambridge, MA, and London, 2001)

Rink, Oliver A., *Holland on the Hudson. An Economic and Social History of Dutch New York* (Ithaca, NY and London, 1986)

Ritchie, Robert C., *The Duke's Province. A Study of New York Politics and Society, 1664–1691* (Chapel Hill, NC, 1977)

Robbins, Caroline, *The Eighteenth-Century Commonwealthmen* (Cambridge, MA, 1959)

Robertson, John, 'Union, State and Empire: the Union of 1707 in its European Setting', in Lawrence Stone (ed.), *An Imperial State at War. Britain from 1689 to 1815* (London, 1994)

Robertson, John, 'Empire and Union', in David Armitage (ed.), *Theories of Empire, 1450–1800* (Aldershot, 1998)

Rodríguez, Laura, *Reforma e Ilustración en la España del siglo XVIII: Pedro R. Campomanes* (Madrid, 1975)

Rodríguez, Mario, *'William Burke' and Francisco de Miranda. The Word and the Deed in Spanish America's Emancipation* (Lanham, MD, New York and London, 1994)

Rodríguez Cruz, Águeda Ma., *La universidad en la América hispánica* (Madrid, 1992)

Rodríguez Moya, Inmaculada, *La mirada del virrey. Iconografía del poder en la Nueva España* (Castelló de la Plana, 2003)

Rodríguez O., Jaime E., *The Independence of Spanish America* (Cambridge, 1998)

Rodríguez O., Jaime E., 'Las elecciones a las cortes constituyentes mexicanas', in Louis Cardaillac and Angélica Peregrina (eds), *Ensayos en homenaje a José María Muriá* (Zapopan, 2002)

Rodríguez O., Jaime E., 'La naturaleza de la representación en Nueva España y México', *Secuencia*, 61 (2005), pp. 7–32

Rodríguez Salgado, María José, 'Patriotismo y política exterior en la España de Carlos V y Felipe II', in Felipe Ruiz Martín (ed.), *La proyección europea de la monarquía española* (Madrid, 1996)

Romano, Ruggiero, *Conjonctures opposées. La 'Crise' du XVIIe siècle en Europe et en Amérique ibérique* (Geneva, 1992)

Rosenblat, Angel, *La población indígena y el mestizaje en América* (2 vols, Buenos Aires, 1954)

Rossiter, Clinton, *1787. The Grand Convention* (1966; New York, 1987)

Rountree, Helen C., *Pocahontas's People. The Powhatan Indians of Virginia Through Four Centuries* (Norman, OK, and London, 1990)

Roux, Jean Claude, 'De los límites a la frontera: o los malentendidos de la geopolítica amazónica', *Revista de Indias*, 61 (2001), pp. 513–39

Rowlandson, Mary, *The Sovereignty and Goodness of God* (1682)

Roys, Ralph, *The Indian Background of Colonial Yucatán* (1943; repr. Norman, OK, 1972)

Rubio Mañé, José Ignacio, *Introducción al estudio de los virreyes de la Nueva España, 1535–1746* (3 vols, Mexico City, 1955)

Ruiz Martín, Felipe (ed.), *La proyección europea de la monarquía española* (Madrid, 1996)

Russell, Peter, *Prince Henry 'the Navigator'. A Life* (New Haven and London, 2000)

Rutman, Darrett B., *Winthrop's Boston. Portrait of a Puritan Town, 1630–1649* (Chapel Hill, NC, 1965)

Rutman, Darrett B. and Anita H., *A Place in Time. Middlesex County, Virginia 1650–1750* (New York and London, 1984)

Sahagún, Fray Bernardino de, *Historia general de las cosas de Nueva España*, ed. Angel María Garibay K. (2nd edn, 4 vols, Mexico City, 1969)

Sahlins, Peter, *Boundaries. The Making of France and Spain in the Pyrenees* (Berkeley, Los Angeles, Oxford, 1989)

St George, Robert Blair (ed.), *Possible Pasts. Becoming Colonial in Early America* (Ithaca, NY and London, 2000)

Salas, Alberto Mario, *Las armas de la conquista* (Buenos Aires, 1950)

Salas, Alberto Mario, *Crónica florida del mestizaje de las Indias* (Buenos Aires, 1960)

Salinas y Córdova, Fray Bonaventura de, *Memorial de las historias del nuevo mundo Piru* (1630; ed. Luis E. Valcárcel, Lima, 1957)

Salvucci, Richard J., *Textiles and Capitalism in Mexico. An Economic History of the Obrajes, 1539–1840* (Princeton, 1987)

Sánchez Rubio, Rocío, and Testón Núñez, Isabel, *El hilo que une: Las relaciones epistolares en el viejo y el nuevo mundo, siglos XVI–XVIII* (Mérida, 1999)

Sánchez-Agesta, Luis, 'El "poderío real absoluto" en el testamento de 1554', in *Carlos V. Homenaje de la Universidad de Granada* (Granada, 1958)

Sánchez-Bella, Ismael, *La organización financiera de las Indias. Siglo XVI* (Seville, 1968)

Sánchez Bella, Ismael, *Iglesia y estado en la América española* (Pamplona, 1990)

Sánchez-Bella, Ismael, 'Las reformas en Indias del Secretario de Estado José de Gálvez (1776–1787)', in Feliciano Barrios Pintado (ed.), *Derecho y administración pública en las Indias hispánicas* (2 vols, Cuenca, 2002)

Sandoval, Alonso de, *Un tratado sobre la esclavitud,* ed. Enriqueta Vila Vilar (Madrid, 1987)

Sarabia Viejo, Ma. Justina, *Don Luis de Velasco, virrey de Nueva España, 1550–1564* (Seville, 1978)

Sauer, Carl Ortwin, *The Early Spanish Main* (Cambridge, 1966)

Schäfer, Ernesto, *El Consejo real y supremo de las Indias* (2 vols, Seville, 1935–47)

Schmidt, Benjamin, 'Mapping an Empire: Cartographic and Colonial Rivalry in Seventeenth-Century Dutch and English North America', *WMQ*, 3rd ser., 54 (1997), pp. 549–78

Scholes, France V., 'The Spanish Conqueror as a Business Man: a Chapter in the History of Fernando Cortés', *New Mexico Quarterly*, 28 (1958), pp. 5–29

Schumpeter, Joseph A., *History of Economic Analysis* (1954; 6th printing, London, 1967)

Schurz, William Lytle, *The Manila Galleon* (1939; repr. New York, 1959)

Schwartz, Stuart B., 'New World Nobility: Social Aspirations and Mobility in the Conquest and Colonization of Spanish America', in Miriam Usher Chrisman (ed.), *Social Groups and Religious Ideas in the Sixteenth Century* (Studies in Medieval Culture, XIII, The Medieval Institute, Western Michigan University, Kalamazoo, MI, 1978)

Schwartz, Stuart B., *Sugar Plantations in the Formation of Brazilian Society. Bahia, 1550–1835* (Cambridge, 1985)

Scott, Jonathan, 'What Were Commonwealth Principles?', *Historical Journal*, 47 (2004), pp. 591–613

Seed, Patricia, *To Love, Honor, and Obey in Colonial Mexico* (Stanford, 1988)

Seed, Patricia, 'Taking Possession and Reading Texts: Establishing the Authority of Overseas Empires', *WMQ*, 3rd ser., 49 (1992), pp. 183–209

Seed, Patricia, 'American Law, Hispanic Traces: Some Contemporary Entanglements of Community Property', *WMQ*, 3rd ser., 52 (1995), pp. 157–62

Seed, Patricia, *Ceremonies of Possession in Europe's Conquest of the New World, 1492–1640* (Cambridge, 1995)

Seed, Patricia, *American Pentimento. The Invention of Indians and the Pursuit of Riches* (Minneapolis and London, 2001)

Seiler, William H., 'The Anglican Parish in Virginia', in James Morton Smith (ed.), *Seventeenth-Century America. Essays in Colonial History* (Chapel Hill, NC, 1959)

Sepúlveda, Juan Ginés de, *Democrates segundo o de las justas causas de la guerra contra los indios,* ed. Angel Losada (Madrid, 1951)

Serrano y Sanz, Manuel, *Orígenes de la dominación española en América* (Madrid, 1918)

Serulnikov, Sergio, *Subverting Colonial Authority. Challenges to Spanish Rule in the Eighteenth-Century Southern Andes* (Durham, NC and London, 2003)

Service, Elman R., *Spanish-Guaraní Relations in Early Colonial Paraguay* (1954; repr. Westport, CT, 1971)

Sewall, Samuel, *The Diary of Samuel Sewall, 1674–1729,* ed. M. Halsey (2 vols, New York, 1973)

Shammas, Carole, 'English Commercial Development and American Colonization 1560–1620', in K. R. Andrews, N. P. Canny and P. E. H. Hair (eds), *The Westward Enterprise* (Liverpool, 1978)

Shammas, Carole, 'English-Born and Creole Elites in Turn-of-the-Century Virginia', in Thad W. Tate and David L. Ammerman (eds), *The Chesapeake in the Seventeenth Century* (New York and London, 1979)

Shammas, Carole, 'Anglo-American Household Government in Comparative Perspective', *WMQ*, 3rd ser., 52 (1995), pp. 104–44

Shammas, Carole, *A History of Household Government in America* (Charlottesville, VA and London, 2002)

Sheridan, Richard B., 'The Domestic Economy', in Jack P. Greene and J. R. Pole (eds), *Colonial British America. Essays in the New History of the Early Modern Era* (Baltimore and London, 1984)

Shy, John, *Toward Lexington. The Role of the British Army in the Coming of the American Revolution* (Princeton, 1965)

Shy, John, 'Armed Force in Colonial North America: New Spain, New France, and Anglo-America', in Kenneth J. Hagan and William R. Roberts (eds), *Against All Enemies. Interpretations of American Military History from Colonial Times to the Present* (Greenwood Press, *Contributions in Military Studies*, no. 51, New York, Westport, CT and London, 1986)

Shy, John, *A People Numerous and Armed* (revised edn, Ann Arbor, MI, 1990)

Las Siete Partidas del Sabio Rey Don Alonso el nono (Salamanca, 1555, facsimile edn, 3 vols, Madrid, 1985)

Los siglos de oro en los virreinatos de América, 1550–1700 (Sociedad Estatal, Madrid, 1999)

Sigüenza y Góngora, Carlos de, *Theatro de virtudes políticas* (1680; repr. in his *Obras históricas*, ed. José Rojas Garcidueñas, Mexico City, 1983)

Sigüenza y Góngora, Carlos de, *Relaciones históricas* (4th edn, Mexico City, 1987)

Silva Prada, Natalia, 'Estrategias culturales en el tumulto de 1692 en la ciudad de México: aportes para la reconstrucción de la historia de la cultura política antigua', *Historia Mexicana*, 209 (2003), pp. 5–63

Silverblatt, Irene, 'The Inca's Witches: Gender and the Cultural Work of Colonization in Seventeenth-Century Peru', in St George, Robert Blair (ed.), *Possible Pasts. Becoming Colonial in Early America* (Ithaca, NY and London, 2000)

Silverman, David J., 'Indians, Missionaries, and Religious Translation: Creating Wampanoag Christianity in Seventeenth-Century Martha's Vineyard', *WMQ*, 3rd ser., 62 (2005), pp. 141–74

Silverman, Kenneth, *A Cultural History of the American Revolution* (New York, 1976)

Simpson, Lesley Byrd, *The Encomienda in New Spain* (Berkeley and Los Angeles, 1950)

Simpson, Lesley Byrd (trans. and ed.), *The Laws of Burgos of 1512–1513* (San Francisco, 1960)

Skinner, Quentin, *The Foundations of Modern Political Thought* (2 vols, Cambridge, 1978)

Slotkin, Richard, *Regeneration through Violence. The Mythology of the American Frontier, 1600–1860* (Middletown, CT, 1973)

Smith, Adam, *The Wealth of Nations*, ed. Edwin Cannan (2 vols, 6th edn, London, 1950)

Smith, Billy G., *Down and Out in Early America* (University Park, PA, 2004)

Smith, James Morton (ed.), *Seventeenth-Century America. Essays in Colonial History* (Chapel Hill, NC, 1959)

Smith, Captain John, *The Complete Works of Captain John Smith*, ed. Philip L. Barbour (3 vols, Chapel Hill, NC and London, 1986)

Smith, Mark M., 'Culture, Commerce and Calendar Reform in Colonial America', *WMQ*, 3rd ser., 55 (1998), pp. 557–84

Smith, Paul H., 'The American Loyalists: Notes on their Organization and Strength', *WMQ*, 3rd ser., 25 (1968), pp. 259–77

Smith, Robert Sidney, *The Spanish Guild Merchant* (Durham, NC, 1940)

Smith, Robert Sidney, 'Sales Taxes in New Spain, 1575–1770', *HAHR*, 28 (1948), pp. 2–37

Smits, David D., '"Abominable Mixture": Toward the Repudiation of Anglo-Indian Intermarriage in Seventeenth-Century Virginia', *The Virginia Magazine of History and Biography*, 95 (1987), pp. 157–92

Smits, David D., '"We are not to Grow Wild": Seventeenth-Century New England's Repudiation of Anglo-Indian Intermarriage', *American Indian Culture and Research Journal*, 11 (1987), pp. 1–32

Sobel, Mechal, *The World They Made Together. Black and White Values in Eighteenth-Century Virginia* (Princeton, NJ, 1987)

Socolow, S. M., 'Spanish Captives in Indian Societies: Cultural Contacts Along the Argentine Frontier', *HAHR*, 72 (1992), pp. 73–99

Solano, Francisco de (ed.), *Cuestionarios para la formación de las relaciones geográficas de Indias, siglos XVI/XIX* (Madrid, 1988)

Solano, Francisco de, *Ciudades hispanoamericanas y pueblos de indios* (Madrid, 1990)

Solano, Francisco de, and Bernabeu, Salvador (eds), *Estudios (nuevos y viejos) sobre la frontera* (Madrid, 1991)

Solórzano Pereira [y Pereyra], Juan de, *Obras varias posthumas* (Madrid, 1776)

Solórzano y Pereyra, Juan de, *Política Indiana* (5 vols, BAE, 252–6, Madrid, 1959–72)

Solow, Barbara L. (ed.), *Slavery and the Rise of the Atlantic System* (Cambridge, 1991)

Sosin, Jack M., *Whitehall and the Wilderness. The Middle West in British Colonial Policy, 1760–1775* (Lincoln, NE, 1961)

Sosin, J. M., *English America and the Restoration Monarchy of Charles II* (Lincoln, NE and London, 1980)

Sosin, J. M, *English America and the Revolution of 1688* (Lincoln, NA and London, 1982)

Sota Ríus, José de la, 'Spanish Science and Enlightenment Expeditions', in Chiyo Ishikawa (ed.), *Spain in the Age of Exploration* (Seattle Art Museum, 2004)

Spalding, Karen, *Huarochirí. An Andean Society under Inca and Spanish Rule* (Stanford, CA, 1984)

Spalding, Karen (ed.), *Essays in the Political, Economic and Social History of Colonial Latin America* (Newark, DE, 1982)

Spate, O. H. K., *Monopolists and Freebooters* (Minneapolis, 1983)

Speck, W. A. 'The International and Imperial Context', in Jack P. Greene and J. R. Pole (eds) *Colonial British America. Essays in the New History of the Colonial Era* (Baltimore and London, 1984)

Spicer, Edward H., *Cycles of Conquest* (Tucson, AZ, 1962)

Steele, Colin, *English Interpreters of the Iberian New World from Purchas to Stevens, 1603–1726* (Oxford, 1975)

Steele, Ian K., *Politics of Colonial Policy. The Board of Trade in Colonial Administration, 1696–1720* (Oxford, 1968)

Steele, Ian K., *The English Atlantic, 1675–1740* (Oxford, 1986)

Steele, Ian K., *Warpaths. Invasions of North America* (Oxford, 1994)

Stein, Stanley J., and Stein, Barbara H., *Silver, Trade and War. Spain and America in the Making of Early Modern Europe* (Baltimore and London, 2000)

Stein, Stanley J. and Stein, Barbara H., *Apogee of Empire. Spain and New Spain in the Age of Charles III, 1759–1789* (Baltimore and London, 2003)

Stella, Aldo, *La rivoluzione contadina del 1525 e l'Utopia di Michael Gaismayr* (Padua, 1975)

Stern, Steve J. (ed.), *Resistance, Rebellion, and Consciousness in the Andean Peasant World. 18th to 20th Centuries* (Madison, WI, 1987)

Stewart, George R., *Names on the Land. A Historical Account of Place-Naming in the United States* (New York, 1945; repr. 1954)

Stone, Lawrence (ed.), *An Imperial State at War. Britain from 1689 to 1815* (London, 1994)

Strachey, William, *The Historie of Travell into Virginia Britania* (1612), ed. Louis B. Wright and Virginia Freund (Hakluyt Society, 2nd ser., vol. 103, London, 1953)

Strong, Roy, *Gloriana. The Portraits of Queen Elizabeth I* (London, 1987)

Studnicki-Gizbert, Daviken, 'From Agents to Consulado: Commercial Networks in Colonial Mexico, 1520–1590 and Beyond', *Anuario de Estudios Americanos*, 57 (2000), pp. 41–68

Suárez, Margarita, *Comercio y fraude en el Perú colonial. Las estrategias mercantiles de un banquero* (Lima, 1995)

Suárez, Margarita, *Desafíos transatlánticos. Mercaderes, banqueros y el estado en el Perú virreinal, 1600–1700* (Lima, 2001)

Suárez Roca, José Luis, *Lingüística misionera española* (Oviedo, 1992)

Super, John C., *Food, Conquest, and Colonization in Sixteenth-Century Spanish America* (Albuquerque, NM, 1988)

Sweeney, Kevin M., 'High-Style Vernacular. Lifestyles of the Colonial Elite', in Cary Carson, Ronald Hoffman and Peter J. Albert (eds), *Of Consuming Interests. The Style of Life in the Eighteenth Century* (Charlottesville, VA and London, 1994)

Sweet, David G., and Nash, Gary B. (eds), *Struggle and Survival in Colonial America* (Berkeley, Los Angeles and London, 1981)

Syme, Ronald, *Colonial Elites. Rome, Spain and the Americas* (Oxford, 1958)

Tannenbaum, Frank, *Slave and Citizen. The Negro in the Americas* (New York, 1964)

Tate, Thad W., and Ammerman, David L. (eds), *The Chesapeake in the Seventeenth Century* (New York and London, 1979)

Taylor, Alan, *American Colonies. The Settlement of North America to 1800* (London, 2001)

Taylor, E. G. R., *The Original Writings and Correspondence of the Two Richard Hakluyts* (2 vols, Hakluyt Society, 2nd ser., vols 76–7, London, 1935)

Taylor, William B., *Landlord and Peasant in Colonial Oaxaca* (Stanford, CA, 1972)

Taylor, William B., *Drinking, Homicide and Rebellion in Colonial Mexican Villages* (Stanford, CA, 1979)

Taylor, William B., *Magistrates of the Sacred. Priests and Parishioners in Eighteenth-Century Mexico* (Stanford, CA, 1996)

TePaske, John J., *The Governorship of Spanish Florida, 1700–1763* (Durham, NC, 1964)

TePaske, John J. and Herbert S. Klein, 'The Seventeenth-Century Crisis in New Spain: Myth or Reality?', *Past and Present*, 90 (1981), pp. 116–35

TePaske, John J., 'The Fiscal Structure of Upper Peru and the Financing of Empire', in Karen Spalding (ed.), *Essays in the Political, Economic and Social History of Colonial Latin America* (Newark, DE, 1982)

Thomas, Sir Dalby, *An Historical Account of the Rise and Growth of the West-India Collonies* (London, 1690)

Thomas, Hugh, *Cuba, or the Pursuit of Freedom* (London, 1971)

Thomas, Hugh, *The Conquest of Mexico* (London, 1993)

Thomas, Hugh, *The Slave Trade. The History of the Atlantic Slave Trade 1440–1870* (New York and London, 1997)

Thomas, Hugh, *Rivers of Gold. The Rise of the Spanish Empire* (London, 2003)

Thomas, P. D., *British Politics and the Stamp Act Crisis. The First Phase of the American Revolution, 1763–1767* (Oxford, 1975)

Thomas, P. D., *The Townshend Duties Crisis. The Second Phase of the American Revolution, 1767–1773* (Oxford, 1987)

Tibesar, Antonine, 'The Alternative: a Study in Spanish-Creole Relations in Seventeenth-Century Peru', *The Americas*, 11 (1955), pp. 229–83

Tomlins, Christopher L., and Mann, Bruce T., *The Many Legalities of Early America* (Chapel Hill, NC and London, 2001)

Tooley, Marian J., 'Bodin and the Medieval Theory of Climate', *Speculum*, 28 (1983), pp. 64–83

Tracy, James D. (ed.), *The Rise of Merchant Empires. Long-Distance Trade in the Early Modern World, 1350–1750* (Cambridge, 1990)

Tracy, James D. (ed.), *City Walls. The Urban Enceinte in Global Perspective* (Cambridge, 2000)

Tucker, Robert W., and Hendrickson, David C., *The Fall of the First British Empire. Origins of the War of American Independence* (Baltimore and London, 1982)

Tucker, Robert W., and Hendrickson, David C., *Empire of Liberty. The Statecraft of Thomas Jefferson* (Oxford, 1992)

Tully, Alan , *Forming American Politics. Ideals, Interests and Institutions in Colonial New York and Pennsylvania* (Baltimore and London, 1994)

Turner, Frederick Jackson, 'The Significance of the Frontier in American History' (1893 lecture to the American Historical Association), reprinted in *Frontier and Section: Selected Essays of Frederick Jackson Turner* (Englewood Cliffs, NJ, 1961)

Twinam, Ann, 'Honor, Sexuality and Illegitimacy in Colonial Spanish America', in Asunción Lavrín (ed.), *Sexuality and Marriage in Colonial Latin America* (Lincoln, NE and London, 1989)

Twinam, Ann, *Public Lives, Private Secrets. Gender, Honor, Sexuality and Illegitimacy in Colonial Spanish America* (Stanford, CA, 1999)

Uztáriz, Gerónimo de, *Theorica y práctica de comercio y de marina* (Madrid, 1724)

Val Julián, Carmen, 'La toponomía conquistadora', *Relaciones* (El Colegio de Michoacán), 70 (1997), pp. 41–61

Val Julián, Carmen, 'Entre la realidad y el deseo. La toponomía del descubrimiento en Colón y Cortés', in Oscar Mazín Gómez (ed.), *México y el mundo hispánico* (2 vols, Zamora, Michoacán, 2000)

Valcárcel, Carlos Daniel, 'Concepto de la historia en los "Comentarios reales" y en la "Historia general del Perú"', in *Nuevos estudios sobre el Inca Garcilaso de la Vega* (Lima, 1955)

Valenzuela Márquez, Jaime, 'La recepción pública de una autoridad colonial: modelo peninsular, referente virreinal y reproducción periférica (Santiago de Chile, siglo XVII)', in Oscar Mazín Gómez (ed.), *México y el mundo hispánico* (2 vols, Zamora, Michoacán, 2000)

Van Young, Eric, 'Islands in the Storm: Quiet Cities and Violent Countrysides in the Mexican Independence Era', *Past and Present*, 118 (1988), pp. 130–55

Van Young, Eric, *La crisis del orden colonial* (Madrid, 1992)

Vargas Machuca, Bernardo, *Refutación de Las Casas* (ed., Paris, 1913)

Varón Gabai, Rafael, *Francisco Pizarro and his Brothers* (Norman, OK, and London, 1997)

Vas Mingo, Milagros del, *Las capitulaciones de Indias en el siglo XVI* (Madrid, 1986)

Vaughan, Alden T., 'Blacks in Virginia: a Note on the First Decade', *WMQ*, 3rd ser., 29 (1972), pp. 469–78.

Vaughan, Alden, *American Genesis. Captain John Smith and the Founding of Virginia* (Boston and Toronto, 1975)

Vaughan, Alden T., *New England Frontier. Puritans and Indians 1620–1675* (1965; 3rd edn, Norman, OK and London, 1995)

Vázquez de Espinosa, Antonio, *Compendio y descripción de las Indias Occidentales*, transcribed by Charles Upson Clark (Washington, 1948)

Véliz, Claudio, *The New World of the Gothic Fox. Culture and Economy in British and Spanish America* (Berkeley, Los Angeles and London, 1994)

Venturi, Franco, *Utopia and Reform in the Enlightenment* (Cambridge, 1971)

Verlinden, Charles, *The Beginnings of Modern Colonization* (Ithaca, NY and London, 1970)

Vickers, Daniel, 'Competency and Competition: Economic Culture in Early America', *WMQ*, 3rd ser., 47 (1990), pp. 3–29.

Vila Vilar, Enriqueta, *Hispano-America y el comercio de esclavos* (Seville, 1977)

Vila Vilar, Enriqueta, *Los Corzo y los Mañara. Tipos y arquetipos del mercader con América* (Seville, 1991)

Vila Vilar, Enriqueta, 'El poder del Consulado y los hombres del comercio en el siglo XVII', in Enriqueta Vila Vilar and Allan J. Kuethe (eds), *Relaciones del poder y comercio colonial. Nuevas perspectivas* (Seville, 1999)

Vila Vilar, Enriqueta, and Kuethe, Allan J. (eds), *Relaciones del poder y comercio colonial. Nuevas perspectivas* (Seville, 1999)

Vila Vilar, Enriqueta, and Lohmann Villena, Guillermo, *Familia, linajes y negocios entre Sevilla y las Indias. Los Almonte* (Madrid, 2003)

Villalobos R., Sergio, 'Tres siglos y medio de vida fronteriza chilena', in Francisco de Solano and Salvador Bernabeu (eds), *Estudios (nuevos y viejos) sobre la frontera* (Madrid, 1991)

Villamarín, Juan A. and Judith E., *Indian Labor in Mainland Colonial Spanish America* (Newark, DE, 1975)

Villamarín, Juan A. and Judith E., 'The Concept of Nobility in Colonial Santa Fe de Bogotá', in Karen Spalding (ed.), *Essays in the Political, Economic and Social History of Colonial Latin America* (Newark, DE, 1982)

Vinson III, Ben, *Bearing Arms for His Majesty. The Free Colored Militia in Colonial Mexico* (Stanford, CA, 2001)

Vitoria, Francisco de, *Political Writings*, ed. Anthony Pagden and Jeremy Lawrance (Cambridge, 1991)

Vorhees, David William, 'The "Fervent Zeale" of Jacob Leisler', *WMQ*, 3rd ser., 51 (1994), pp. 447–72

Wagner, Henry R., *The Rise of Fernando Cortés* (Los Angeles, 1944)

Walker, Charles F., *Smouldering Ashes. Cuzco and the Creation of Republican Peru, 1780–1840* (Durham, NC and London, 1999)

Walker, Geoffrey J., *Spanish Politics and Imperial Trade, 1700–1789* (London, 1979)

Walsh, James P., 'Holy Time and Sacred Space in Puritan New England', *American Quarterly*, 32 (1980), pp. 79–95

Walsh, Lorena S., '"Till Death Us Do Part": Marriage and Family in Seventeenth-Century Maryland', in Thad W. Tate and David L. Ammerman (eds), *The Chesapeake in the Seventeenth Century* (New York and London, 1979)

Ward, Ned, *A Trip to New England* (1699), repr. in Myra Jehlen and Michael Warner (eds), *The English Literatures of America, 1500–1800* (New York and London, 1997)

Warman, Arturo, *La danza de moros y cristianos* (Mexico City, 1972)

Warman, Arturo, *La historia de un bastardo: maíz y capitalismo* (Mexico City, 1988)

Warren, Fintan B., *Vasco de Quiroga and his Pueblo-Hospitals of Santa Fe* (Washington, 1963)

Washburn, Wilcomb E., *The Governor and the Rebel. A History of Bacon's Rebellion in Virginia* (Chapel Hill, NC, 1957)

Washburn, Wilcomb E., *Red Man's Land/White Man's Law. A Study of the Past and Present Status of the American Indian* (New York, 1971)

Washburn, Wilcomb E., *The Indian in America* (New York, 1975)

Washington, George, *The Writings of George Washington*, ed. John C. Fitzpatrick, vol 5 (Washington, 1932)

Watts, David, *The West Indies. Patterns of Development, Culture and Environmental Change since 1492* (Cambridge, 1987)

Watts, Steven, *The Republic Reborn. War and the Making of Liberal America, 1790–1820* (Baltimore and London, 1987)

Webb, Stephen Saunders, *The Governors-General. The English Army and the Definition of the Empire, 1569–1681* (Chapel Hill, NC, 1979)

Webb, Stephen Saunders, *1676. The End of American Independence* (New York, 1984)

Weber, David J., *The Mexican Frontier, 1821–1846* (Albuquerque, NM, 1982)

Weber, David J., 'Turner, the Boltonians and the Borderlands', *AHR*, 91 (1986), pp. 66–81

Weber, David J., *The Spanish Frontier in North America* (New Haven and London, 1992)

Weber, David J., 'Bourbons and Bárbaros', in Christine Daniels and Michael N. Kennedy (eds), *Negotiated Empires. Centers and Peripheries in the Americas, 1500–1820* (London, 2002)

Webster, C. K., *Britain and the Independence of Latin America, 1812–1830* (2 vols, London, New York, Toronto, 1938)

Wertenbaker, Thomas J., *Torchbearer of the Revolution. The Story of Bacon's Rebellion and its Leader* (Princeton, NJ, 1940)

Whitaker, Arthur P., *The Western Hemisphere Idea. Its Rise and Decline* (Ithaca, NY, 1954)

Whitaker, Arthur P. (ed.), *Latin America and the Enlightenment* (2nd edn, Ithaca, NY, 1961)

White, Morton, *Philosophy, the Federalist, and the Constitution* (New York and Oxford, 1987)

White, Richard, *The Middle Ground. Indians, Empires, and Republics in the Great Lakes Region, 1650–1815* (Cambridge, 1991)

Wickman, Patricia R, 'The Spanish Colonial Floridas', in Robert H. Jackson (ed.), *New Views of Borderland History* (Albuquerque, NM, 1998)

Williams, G.H., *The Radical Reformation* (London, 1962)

Williams, Roger, *The Complete Writings of Roger Williams* (Providence, RI, 1866)

Wills, Garry, *Inventing America. Jefferson's Declaration of Independence* (1978; London, 1980)

Wilson, Charles, *Profit and Power* (London, 1957)

Wilson, Kathleen, *The Sense of the People. Politics, Culture and Imperialism in England, 1715–1785* (Cambridge, 1995)

Wilson, Samuel M., 'The Cultural Mosaic of the Indigenous Caribbean', in Warwick Bray (ed.), *The Meeting of Two Worlds. Europe and the Americas 1492–1650* (Proceedings of the British Academy, 81, Oxford, 1993)

Wood, Gordon S., 'A Note on Mobs in the American Revolution', *WMQ*, 3rd ser., 23 (1966), pp. 635–42

Wood, Gordon S., 'Conspiracy and the Paranoid Style: Causality and Deceit in the Eighteenth Century', *WMQ*, 3rd ser., 39 (1982), pp. 401–41

Wood, Gordon S., *The Creation of the American Republic, 1776–1787* (Chapel Hill, NC, 1969; repr. 1998)

Wood, Gordon S., *The Radicalism of the American Revolution* (New York, 1992; repr. 1993)

Wood, Gordon S., *The American Revolution. A History* (London, 2003)

Wood, William, *New England's Prospect*, ed. Alden T. Vaughan (Amherst, MA, 1977)

Worden, Blair, *The Sound of Virtue* (New Haven and London, 1996)

Wright, J. Leitch Jr., *Anglo-Spanish Rivalry in North America* (Athens, GA, 1971)

Wright, Louis B., *The First Gentlemen of Virginia. Intellectual Qualities of the Early Colonial Ruling Class* (San Marino, CA, 1940)

Wright, Louis B., *The Cultural Life of the British Colonies, 1607–1763* (New York, 1957)

Wrigley, E. A., *People, Cities and Wealth* (Oxford, 1987)

Wuffarden, Luis Eduardo, 'La ciudad y sus emblemas: imagenes del criollismo en el virreinato del Perú', in *Los siglos de oro en los virreinatos de América, 1550–1700* (Sociedad Estatal, Madrid, 1999)

Wyatt-Brown, Bertram, *Southern Honor. Ethics and Behavior in the Old South* (New York, 1982)

Youings, Joyce, 'Raleigh's Country and the Sea', *Proceedings of the British Academy*, 75 (1989), pp. 267–90

Youlton, John W. (ed.), *John Locke. Problems and Perspectives* (Cambridge, 1969)

Yun-Casalilla, Bartolomé, 'The American Empire and the Spanish Economy: an Institutional and Regional Perspective', *Revista de Historia Económica*, 16 (1996), pp. 123–56

Yun-Casalilla, Bartolomé, *Marte contra Minerva: El precio del imperio español, c. 1450–1600* (Barcelona, 2004)

Zahadieh, Nuala, 'The Merchants of Port Royal, Jamaica, and the Spanish Contraband Trade, 1655–1692', *WMQ*, 3rd ser., 43 (1986), pp. 570–93

Zakai, Avihu, *Exile and Kingdom. History and Apocalypse in the Puritan Migration to America* (Cambridge, 1992)

Zaldumbide, Gonzalo, *Fray Gaspar de Villarroel. Siglo XVII* (Puebla, 1960)

Zárate, Agustín de, *The Discovery and Conquest of Peru*, trans. and ed. J. M. Cohen (Harmondsworth, 1968)

Zavala, Silvio, *Ensayos sobre la colonización española en América* (Buenos Aires, 1944)

Zavala, Silvio, *Estudios indianos* (Mexico City, 1948)

Zavala, Silvio, *La encomienda mexicana* (1935; 2nd edn, Mexico City, 1973)

Zavala, Silvio, *Sir Thomas More in New Spain. A Utopian Adventure of the Renaissance* (*Diamante* III, The Hispanic and Luso-Brazilian Councils, London, 1955)

Zorita, Alonso de, *The Lords of New Spain*, trans. and ed. Benjamin Keen (London, 1963)

Zuckerman, Michael, 'Identity in British America: Unease in Eden', in Nicholas Canny and Anthony Pagden (eds), *Colonial Identity in the Atlantic World, 1500–1800* (Princeton, 1987)

Zúñiga, Jean-Paul, *Espagnols d'outre-mer. Émigration, métissage et reproduction sociale à Santiago du Chili, au 17e siècle* (Paris, 2002)

Index

Page references in **bold type** indicate maps.